Peter Norton's®
Complete Guide to
Windows® 95

Peter Norton
John Paul Mueller

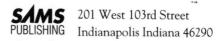

SAMS 201 West 103rd Street
PUBLISHING Indianapolis Indiana 46290

For Lisa—someone who not only understands, but actually appreciates, uniqueness.

Copyright © 1998 by Peter Norton

THIRD EDITION

International Standard Book Number: 0-672-31255-7

Library of Congress Catalog Card Number: 97-80755

01 00 99 98   4 3 2

Interpretation of the printing code: the rightmost double-digit number is the year of the book's printing; the rightmost single-digit, the number of the book's printing. For example, a printing code of 98-1 shows that the first printing of the book occurred in 1998.

Composed in Goudy and MCPdigital by Macmillan Computer Publishing

Printed in the United States of America

President:	Richard K. Swadley
Publisher	Don Fowley
Associate Publisher:	Dean Miller
Executive Editor:	Grace Buechlein
Managing Editor:	Sarah Kearns
Indexing Manager:	Ginny Bess

Acquisitions Editor
Sunthar Visuvalingam

Development Editors
Sunthar Visuvalingam
Kate Shoup Welsh

Production Editor
Kate Shoup Welsh

Copy Editor
Kris Simmons

Indexer
Kevin Fulcher

Technical Reviewer
Ron Ellenbecker
Brad Lindaas

Editorial Coordinator
Mandie Rowell

Resource Coordinator
Deborah Frisby

Editorial Assistant
Jen Chisholm
Tracy Williams

Cover Designer
Karen Ruggles

Book Designer
Gary Adair

Copy Writer
David Reichwein

Production Team Supervisor
Andrew Stone

Production
Jeanne Clark
Christy M. Lemasters
Julie Searls
Sossity Smith
Heather Stephenson

Overview

Part VI Networking and Security with Windows 95

Contents

Acknowledgments

Thanks to my wife, Rebecca, for working with me to get this book completed. I really don't know what I would have done without her help in proofreading my rough draft. Both Rebecca and Maxine Mueller deserve thanks for helping to research, compile, and edit some of the information that appears in this book.

Ron Ellenbecker and Bradley Lindaas deserve thanks for their technical edit of this book. Both people greatly added to the accuracy of the material you see here.

I would like to thank Scott Clark, Michael Meadhra, Wallace Wang, and Michael Desmond for their help and direction. Their input was instrumental in helping this book achieve the depth of information it required.

Matt Wagner, my agent, deserves credit for helping me get the contract in the first place and for taking care of all the details that most authors don't really think about.

The technical support staff at Microsoft (especially those on the Internet beta newsgroups) deserve credit for answering the questions that helped fill in the blanks and made the Windows 95 learning experience go faster.

Finally, I would like to thank Sunthar Visuvalingam, Kate Welsh, and Kris Simmons for their assistance in bringing this book to print.

–John Paul Mueller

About the Authors

Peter Norton

Computer software entrepreneur and writer Peter Norton established his technical expertise and accessible style from the earliest days of the PC. His *Norton Utilities* was the first product of its kind, giving early computer owners control over their hardware and protection against a myriad of problems. His flagship titles, *Peter Norton's DOS Guide* and *Peter Norton's Inside the PC* (Sams Publishing), have provided the same insight and education to computer users worldwide for nearly two decades. Peter's books, like his many software products, are among the best selling and most respected in the history of personal computing.

Peter Norton's former column in *PC Week* was among the highest regarded in that magazine's history. His expanding series of computer books continues to bring superior education to users, always in Peter's trademark style, which is never condescending nor pedantic. From their earliest days, changing the "black box" into a "glass box," Peter's books, like his software, remain among the most powerful tools available to beginners and experienced users alike.

In 1990, Peter sold his software development business to Symantec Corporation, allowing him to devote more time to his family, civic affairs, philanthropy, and art collecting. He lives with his wife, Eileen, and two children in Santa Monica, California.

John Paul Mueller

John Mueller is a freelance author and technical editor. He has writing in his blood, having produced 36 books and almost 200 articles to date. The topics range from networking to artificial intelligence and from database management to heads-down programming. Some of his current books include an ActiveX/ISAPI programmers guide and a Windows NT Web Server handbook. His technical editing skills have helped over 22 authors refine the content of their manuscripts, some of which are certification related. In addition to book projects, John has provided technical editing services to both *Data Based Advisor* and *Coast Compute* magazines. A recognized authority on computer industry certifications, he's also contributed certification-related articles to magazines such as *Certified Professional Magazine*.

When John isn't working at the computer, you can find him in his workshop. He's an avid woodworker and candle maker. On any given afternoon you can find him working at a lathe or putting the finishing touches on a bookcase. One of his newest craft projects is glycerine soap making, which comes in pretty handy for gift baskets. You can reach John on the Internet at JMueller@mwt.net.

Tell Us What You Think!

As a reader, you are the most important critic on and commentator of our books. We value your opinion and want to know what we're doing right, what we could do better, what areas you'd like to see us publish in, and any other words of wisdom you're willing to pass our way. You can help us make strong books that meet your needs and give you the computer guidance you require.

Do you have access to the World Wide Web? Then check out our site at http://www.mcp.com.

Note: If you have a technical question about this book, call the technical support line at 317-581-3833 or e-mail support@mcp.com.

As the executive editor of the group that created this book, I welcome your comments. You can fax, e-mail, or write me directly to let me know what you did or didn't like about this book—as well as what we can do to make our books stronger. Here's the information:

Fax: 317-581-4663

E-mail: gbuechlein@mcp.com

Mail: Grace Buechlein
           Comments Department
           Sams Publishing
           201 W. 103rd Street
           Indianapolis, IN 46290

Introduction

No matter how you look at it, the main focus of Windows 95, especially when it's integrated with Internet Explorer 4, is the Internet. Sure, you'll find a lot of really nice operating system features—such as Plug and Play—in this version of Windows, but the main reason for installing Internet Explorer 4 is to improve your efficiency when working online. With this Internet emphasis in mind, I decided to cover the Internet as the first topic in this book. You'll learn the fastest, most efficient way to get online fast.

Don't worry that I've forsaken everything else for the Internet, though. You'll learn about all the new hardware support that Windows 95 provides. There are a lot of new features to cover, such as infrared data port support, which is available in the OSR2 version of Windows 95.

You'll also explore the wealth of new software support that you'll get, especially in the area of diagnostics. Anyone who has had trouble getting their software to fit without using disk compression will love using FAT32, which comes with OSR2.

Overall, you're going to find that there's a lot to love about Windows 95 from the user perspective. With its greater reliability and ease of use, you'll find that the latest version of Windows 95 is a quantum leap over previous versions.

Who Should Read This Book?

This book's intended audience is intermediate to advanced Windows 95 users who need to get the last ounce of computing power from their machines. I'll provide you with tips and techniques to make Windows 95 easier to use, enhance overall system performance, and improve system stability. Of course, every Windows 95 user can gain something from this book, even if only a better understanding of how Windows 95 works. You'll also spend some time looking at the internal workings of Windows 95. Not only will you learn about where Windows 95 is today, but I'll also help you understand how Windows 95 differs from its predecessor and how these differences will help you become more productive. If you want the most detailed description of Windows 95 available, this is the book for you.

What You Will Learn

Here are some of the more important topics I cover in this book:

- Getting the most from the Internet
- Installation tips that everyone can use
- Architectural details—how things work under the hood

- Exploiting the new utilities that Windows 95 provides
- Learning how to use Active Desktop for intranets as well as the Internet
- The purpose of the files in the SYSTEM folder
- Windows 95 fonts and ways to make them easier to use
- Performance tips to turn your machine into a speed demon
- Using Outlook Express for all your communication needs
- OLE architecture and how to use OLE in your applications
- Navigating the Explorer interface
- The object-oriented approach to using resources on your machine
- How Plug and Play makes it easier to install new devices
- How to gain enhanced battery life and reduced power costs using Advanced Power Management (APM) and Advanced Configuration and Power Interface (ACPI) features.
- Compatibility tips about what works and what doesn't under Windows 95
- The objects available on the context menu and how you can modify it to meet your needs
- Modifying your system setup to fully meet your needs
- Workarounds for potential Windows 95 problems
- A preview of upcoming Windows 98 features such as the TV Viewer, Update Manager, and additional diagnostic utilities

I spend a great deal of time talking about the Windows 95 architecture in various chapters. There are two reasons for this extensive exposure. First, you, as a user, really need to know how the operating system works—or at least get an overview—so that you can maximize the way you use its features. Second, you need to know what Windows 95 provides that older versions of Windows didn't. Exploring the architecture is one of the best ways to meet this goal.

What's New in This Book?

The Internet has become a central focus of the whole computer industry, and Windows 95 is no exception to the rule. Combined with Internet Explorer 4, Microsoft has added a distinct set of Internet-oriented features to enhance the capabilities of Windows 95. With this in mind, you'll find that the book has been organized in such a way as to make your journey to the Internet faster and much less error prone. Chapter 1, "Opening Windows to the Internet with Internet Explorer 4," will take you through the process of getting online and finding what you need.

Of course, Windows 95 provides a lot of other new features as well. A visit to Chapter 4, "Working with the Active Desktop," will help you understand the new Active Desktop feature of Windows 95 and Internet Explorer 4.

Gamers will also like this edition of the book. It not only looks at how you can get your games to run better under Windows, but it looks at some of the theory behind what makes games work in this environment. Of even greater importance, it looks at how to make those older game programs work (I even provide recommendations on when it's time to retire an old game).

In previous editions of the book, I spent a good deal of time taking care of reader requests. This book is no exception. You'll find that I've included more detailed information in many of the sections where you requested it. For example, I received several e-mails asking for better descriptions of Windows utility programs. This book emphasizes the Windows 95 diagnostic aids, but you'll find that utility coverage is generally better throughout the book.

Some of you commented on how much you liked the Web site information I included in the previous edition of the book. You'll find this edition of the book includes even more links to additional information on the Web, which will make your journey to the Internet even easier than before. Don't worry, though; I didn't add these new links at the expense of information that already appears in the book. For the most part, these links to Web sites only improve your access to Windows 95 information.

How This Book Is Organized

This book divides Windows 95 into functional and task-oriented areas. These parts of the book break each piece of Windows 95 apart to see how it ticks and what you can use it for. Of course, many chapters help you understand what's going on under the hood too. Without this information, it would be difficult to make full use of the new features that Windows 95 offers.

I'd like to offer one final piece of advice. Windows 95 is a very user- and data-oriented operating system. It's probably the most user-tuned product available right now for the PC. This doesn't mean that Windows 95 is perfect, nor does it mean that everything is as it seems. Sometimes you'll find something that's so difficult to use that you'll wonder why Microsoft did it that way. For example, I found the Registry really difficult to work with until I discovered all the tools that Microsoft provides to make the job easier. You should take the time to really explore this product and figure out which techniques work best for you. Windows 95 offers more than one way to do every task.

Part I: Getting Started With Windows 95 and Internet Explorer 4

As I mentioned earlier, one the major changes that you'll see in Windows 95 is its emphasis on the Internet. That's why the very first chapter of this book shows you how to get online quickly and easily. Of course, you'll want to eventually read the detailed information provided later in the book. The whole purpose of Chapter 1 is to get you online.

Those of you who are upgrading from an older version of Windows will want to pay particular attention to Chapter 2, "Introducing Windows 95: What Else Is New?". This chapter helps you understand the new features that Windows 95 provides.

Even though the Internet is a major player in the Windows 95 update, there are a lot of other features that you need to know about as well. Chapter 4 helps you understand the new Active Desktop. The Active Desktop is for those people who want the Internet at their fingertips.

Part II: Power Primers

This section of the book has four chapters. The first, "Performance Primer," deals with tuning tips. Getting the best performance and highest reliability is the concern of everyone who's just starting to use a new operating system. Windows 95 offers many ways to tune your system. It would seem that all these controls could help you get a tuned system with very minimal effort. Actually, the exact opposite is true. All these controls interact—and you have to take these interactions into account as you change settings. Optimizing one area usually means detuning another area by an equal amount.

This section of the book will help you determine what type of tuning you need to perform and how that tuning will affect your system. A turn here and a bump there can really make a big difference in how your system performs. The idea is to tune each area of Windows 95 in moderation. You also need to take your special needs into account. Even the type of network you use will affect the way you tune your system.

One thing is certain: Windows 95 offers more in the way of reliability and performance features than previous versions of Windows did. Your job now is to decide how to use those features to your benefit. Getting that high-performance system together is the first goal you'll want to achieve under Windows 95. After that, the data-centric approach to managing your system should make operating it a breeze.

The second and third chapters of this section include coverage on startup shortcuts (Chapter 6, "Startup Shortcuts"), using the new Web views (Chapter 7, "Customizing Folders with Web Views"), and using the optional Microsoft PowerToys and KernelToys (Chapter 8, "Customizing with Microsoft PowerToys and KernelToys"). There are a number of ways to set up Windows 95. The Microsoft documentation tells you most of the mechanical information you need, but provides very little in the way of trade-offs. What do you have to give up in order to use a Server setup? How does a floppy setup differ from a CD-ROM? These are some of the questions you'll look at in this section.

Of course, I'll also offer a few tips on actually getting the installation done based on real-world experience rather than what should theoretically happen. Sometimes you'll want to do the opposite of what the Microsoft documentation says to do, just to get a more efficient setup. This section of the book looks at some of the tips and techniques I've accumulated over months of beta testing Windows 95.

Part III: Windows 95 Anatomy

Learning to use an operating system often means learning a bit about how it works inside. For some people, a quick overview of Windows 95's internals will be enough, especially if you plan to use Windows 95 only in a single-user mode and really don't need to get every ounce of power from your machine.

If you have to manage a large number of machines or need to get inside and learn how things work from a programmer's point of view, you'll really appreciate this section of the book. I don't go into a bits-and-bytes blow-by-blow description, but this section blows the lid off all the architectural aspects of Windows 95. You'll examine every major component of Windows 95, from the file system to the API.

Part IV: Advanced Windows 95 Usage Techniques

Windows 95 provides any number of techniques that allow you to use it to the fullest; this section examines these techniques in detail. You'll learn about the Windows 95 applets, DDE, OLE, DCOM, ActiveX, and DirectX. You'll learn how to exploit your hardware and software, as well as how to use Windows 95's multimedia and games features. Then you'll examine some of the nuts and bolts of using your system, from fonts and printing to mice and keyboards. You'll see how to configure your monitor for maximum performance, as well as how to get the most from your system as a mobile user.

Part V: Making the Right Connections

Getting online doesn't have to be difficult. This section begins by looking at how Windows helps you get online in a variety of ways, not just the Internet. Of course, the first thing you'll need to know how to do is make a connection; that's what Chapter 20, "Hardware and Software Connections," is all about. You'll also learn some details about how Windows 95 implements various communication features such as Unimodem V support.

This section of the book also spends time explaining the new features of Internet Explorer 4, including Webcasting, Outlook Express, and FrontPage Express. Finally, for those of you who like to experiment, you'll look at how you can use Personal Web Server (PWS) to set up your own small intranet site. Theoretically, you could also use PWS with the Internet, but don't plan on servicing a lot of requests when using it.

Part VI: Networking and Security with Windows 95

Very few companies do without the benefits provided by networks these days. The smallest office usually has a network setup of some kind if for no other reason than for simple e-mail and file sharing. The surprising thing is how many home networks are popping up. Not only are these networks used for the obvious applications, such as allowing a child to access some of the files on her parent's machine, but new applications such as ones for game playing are popping up as well. It's surprising to see just how many new games allow two or more people to play using a simple network setup.

Suffice it to say that with all these new applications for home and small business networks, the need for network-specific information becomes greater every day. Although this section can't fully explore every networking solution available to you, it does fully explore the solutions supported by Windows 95.

Given the networking environments in which you'll use Windows 95, security doesn't seem like it would be that big of an issue. However, even a small company has to protect its data. Needless to say, you'll spend some time looking at security issues in this section of the book as well.

Troubleshooting Windows 95

Have you ever installed something and gotten it to work right the first time? No? That's what I thought. I usually have some problems too. Unlike the Macintosh, the PC consists of parts that come from a myriad of vendors. All these parts are supposed to work together, but sometimes they don't.

A lot of hardware- and software-installation–related problems have nothing to do with hidden agendas or vendor ineptitude. Some problems occur because of a poorly written specification. One vendor interprets a specification one way, and another uses a very different interpretation. The result is hardware and software that don't work together. Each one follows the "standard," and each one follows it differently.

Other times, a user will shoot himself in the foot. How many times have you thought you did something according to the instructions, only to find out you didn't? It happens to everyone. Even a bad keystroke can kill an installation. Take the Windows Registry: It's all too easy to misstep when editing it and end up with an operating system that won't boot.

Even if you manage to get a fully functional system the first time through, what are the chances that the installation will stay stable forever? It's pretty unlikely. Your system configuration changes on a daily basis as you optimize applications and perform various tasks.

As you can see, the typical computer has a lot of failure points, so it's no wonder that things fall apart from time to time. This section of the book will help you quickly diagnose and fix some of the major problems you'll run into with Windows 95. You'll even look at a few undocumented ways to determine what's going on and how to interpret the information you get.

Conventions Used in This Book

I've used the following conventions in this book:

File | Open
: Menus and the selections on them are separated by a vertical bar. "File | Open" means "Access the File menu and choose Open."

Program Files\ Plus!\Themes
: The names of folders are separated by backslashes.

monospace
: It's important to differentiate the text that you use in a macro, that appears in a system file, and so on, from the text that explains it. I've used monospace type to make this differentiation. Whenever you see something in monospace, you'll know that this information will appear in a macro, within a system file such as CONFIG.SYS or AUTOEXEC.BAT, or something similar. You'll even see the switches used with Windows commands in monospace.

bold monospace
: Bold monospace is used to designate any items that you type (for example, at the command line).

italic monospace
: Sometimes you need to supply a value for a Windows or DOS command. For example, when you use the DIR command, you might need to supply a filename. It's convenient to use a variable name—essentially a placeholder—to describe the kind of value you need to supply. The same holds true for any other kind of entry, from macro commands to dialog box fields, to filenames. Whenever you see a word in italic monospace, you know that the word is a placeholder that you'll need to replace with a value. The placeholder simply tells you what kind of value you need to provide.

[*Filename*]
: When you see square brackets around a value, switch, or command, it means that this is an optional component. You don't have to include it as part of the command line or dialog field unless you want the additional functionality that the value, switch, or command provides.

italic
: I use italic wherever the actual value of something is unknown where more than one value might be correct. For example, you might see Windows 3*x* in text. The italicized *x* indicates that any version of Windows 3 is applicable. Italic is also used to introduce new terms in text.

ALL CAPS   Commands use all capital letters. Some Registry entries also use all caps even though they aren't commands. Normally you'll type a command at the DOS prompt, within a PIF file field, or within the Run dialog field. If you see all caps somewhere else, it's safe to assume that the item is a case-sensitive Registry entry or some other value. Filenames also appear in all caps.

➥   The code-continuation character is used when one line of code is too long to fit on one line of the book. Here's an example:

```
{DDE-EXECUTE "[InsertObject .IconNumber = 0,
➥.FileName = ""D:\WIN95\LEAVES.BMP"",
➥.Link = 1, .DisplayIcon = 0,
➥.Tab = ""1"", .Class = ""Paint.Picture"",
➥.IconFilename = """", .Caption = ""LEAVES.BMP""]"}
```

When typing these lines, you would type them as one long line without the continuation character.

Icons

This book contains many icons that help you identify certain types of information. The following paragraphs describe the purpose of each icon.

Note: Notes tell you about interesting facts that don't necessarily affect your ability to use the other information in the book. I use note boxes to give you bits of information that I've picked up while using Windows 95.

Tip: Everyone likes tips, because they tell you new ways of doing things that you might not have thought about before. Tip boxes also provide an alternative way of doing something that you might like better than the first approach I provided.

Warning: This means watch out! Warnings almost always tell you about some kind of system or data damage that will occur if you perform a certain action (or fail to perform others). Make sure you understand a warning thoroughly before you follow any instructions that come after it.

Caution: This means you should take care when performing a task to avoid possible pitfalls.

Peter's Principle: What It Is

I usually include a Peter's Principle to tell you how to manage your Windows environment more efficiently. Boxes with this icon might also include ideas on where to find additional information or even telephone numbers that you can call. You'll also find the names of shareware and freeware utility programs here.

Looking Ahead: It's always good to know what you'll find along the road. Whenever you see a Looking Ahead box, I'm providing a road sign that tells you where you're headed. That way, you can follow the path of a particular subject as I provide more detailed information throughout the book.

Knowing how something works inside is important to some people but not so important to others. Whenever you see the Architecture icon, I'm talking about the internal workings of Windows 95. Knowing how Windows 95 performs its job can help you determine why things don't work as they should.

You can't survive in the modern business world without spending some time talking to other people. Whether you spend that time on the phone or with an online service such as CompuServe or Microsoft Network, the result is the same. It's the exchange of information that drives business—at least in part. Whenever you see the Communications icon, you know that I'm describing some way of using Windows 95 to better communicate with those around you.

Whenever you change something as important as your operating system, there will be problems with older devices and applications that were designed for the older version. The Compatibility icon clues you in to tips, techniques, and notes that will help you get over the compatibility hurdle.

MS-DOS is still with us and will continue to be for the foreseeable future. Microsoft at least provides better support for MS-DOS applications under Windows 95. Whenever you see the MS-DOS icon, I provide you with a tip, technique, or note about a way to make MS-DOS applications and Windows coexist.

Even home users need to worry about networking these days. It's no surprise, then, that this book provides a wealth of networking tips and techniques that everyone can use. Expect to find one of these tidbits of knowledge wherever you see the Networking icon.

Microsoft released an updated version of Windows 95 that includes new features such as FAT32 support. Whenever you see this icon, you know that you're reading about the latest update of the operating system (other than enhancements now added by IE4). Unfortunate as it may seem, this update was released only to original equipment manufacturers (OEMs). Unless you buy a new machine with the OSR2 version of Windows 95 loaded, you'll receive only limited support for new Windows 95 features. However, many OSR2 features are downloadable so this info is relevant to those who have Windows 95 with older hardware.

I use the Performance icon to designate a performance-related tip. There are many throughout this book, and they cover a variety of optimization techniques. You'll need to read them carefully and decide which ones suit your needs. Not every performance tip is for everyone. Most of them require a trade-off of some kind, which I'll mention.

Your printer is probably the most used, yet most frustrating, part of your computer. I include the Printer icon to tell you when a tip or technique will help you keep your printer under control and make it work more efficiently.

Square pegs that had to fit in round holes—that's what some products were in the past. Recent standards efforts have helped reduce the number of square pegs on the market. I think it's important to know what these standards are so that you can make the best buying decisions possible. Getting a square peg at a discount rate isn't such a good deal if you end up spending hours making it round. Every time you see the Standards icon, you know that I'm talking about some standard that defines a product that will fit into that round hole with relative ease.

Technical details can really help you localize a problem or decide precisely what you need in order to get a job done. They can also help improve your overall knowledge of a product. Sometimes they're just fun to learn. However, sometimes you just need an overview of how something works; learning the details would slow you down. I use the Technical Note icon to tell you when a piece of information is a detail. You can bypass this information if you need only an overview of a Windows 95 process or feature. This icon also gives you clues as to where you can look for additional information.

Everyone encounters problems from time to time. It doesn't matter if the problem is hardware- or software-related if it's keeping you from getting your work done. Every time you see the Trouble-shooting icon, I'm providing you with a tool you'll need to find a problem.

If you see the Windows 98 beta release preview icon, you know that the adjacent paragraph is discussing features likely to be found in the final version of Windows 98. While not all of these points relate directly to Windows 95, it's always helpful to see what direction Microsoft is headed with Windows.

It's helpful to compare the benefits of using one operating system over another. I already gave you some tips in this regard earlier. You'll find a lot of other notes throughout this book. Every time I provide some insight into a comparison of Windows NT versus Windows 95, I use the Windows NT icon.

Peter Norton®

I

Getting Started with Windows 95 and Internet Explorer 4

1

Opening Windows to the Internet with Internet Explorer 4

Peter Norton®

Originally the Internet began as a simple research tool so scientists could exchange information among their colleagues quickly and easily. Soon the benefits of the Internet spread beyond universities and government agencies to include other computer users. However, as far as personal computers were concerned, accessing the Internet was a separate, distinct activity. You might connect to the Internet, chat with a few people, download a few files, and then log off to use your word processor, play a game, or calculate your budget.

That system is about to change. Rather than treat the Internet as a separate afterthought, the combination of Windows 95 and the latest version of Microsoft Internet Explorer can integrate the Internet into your computer's user interface. By doing so, Windows 95 allows you to connect your computer to the rest of the world without requiring you to learn new commands or memorize complex procedures.

To quickly introduce you to the new Internet emphasis of Windows 95, the first part of this chapter covers the basics of the Internet and introduces the new Microsoft Internet Explorer, Version 4 (also known as IE4). First, because you might not have IE4, I provide a short explanation of how to find a copy of IE4 and how to install it on your computer. Then, I touch on choosing an Internet service provider (ISP) and setting up a connection to that ISP using Windows 95 Dial-Up Networking. By the time you complete this section, you'll be able to connect your computer to the Internet and start some exploring on your own. I show you various ways that the Internet is integrated into Windows 95 throughout this book. If you're looking for more details on browsing the Web with Internet Explorer, check out Chapter 22, "Browsing the Internet with Internet Explorer."

Although Windows 95 tries to simplify the Internet, you still need to know the specific terms and protocols used by the Internet. As a result, the next section of this chapter helps you understand these potentially confusing terms. More importantly, I discuss what they mean to you as a user.

Learning about the Internet isn't much good if you can't find what you need. The next section of the chapter helps you get started searching the Internet quickly and efficiently. Understanding just a few basic rules will help you get more out of the Internet with a whole lot less work.

Finally, I touch on one of the major new features of the marriage of Windows 95 and Internet Explorer 4—the Active Desktop. A later chapter fully discusses the Active Desktop, but I introduce the concept here so you can get used to the idea. The final portion of this chapter provides a look at three features of the Active Desktop that you need to know immediately. All three of these features help you get information in ways that you couldn't imagine in the past. For example, you can use "push" technology to tell the Internet to deliver content automatically to your desktop. In other words, you don't have to remember to look for updates anymore; the Internet tells you about them automatically.

The Internet—A Window to the World

Just how you view the Internet depends on how you've used it in the past (if you've used it at all). For the corporate user, the Internet might represent a research tool. Many corporate users see the Internet as a way to get the information they need without spending a lot of time at the library or digging through books, magazines, or newspapers. Considering the speed at which information changes, there are some times when getting information any place but the Internet might actually result in inaccurate and obsolete information.

Many corporations also use the Internet as a tool for keeping in contact with employees, suppliers, customers, and friends through e-mail. E-mail allows people to exchange messages at any time of the day, from anywhere in the world. Sales people can transfer sales reports to a home office, secretaries can send important messages to executives traveling on the road, and customers can order products from the convenience of their computer screen.

Home users might see the Internet as a way for reading the latest news, tracking the latest sports scores, and charting their stock and mutual fund portfolios. Home users can also share their own knowledge with others through Usenet newsgroups and IRC chat rooms. With such a wealth of information available at your fingertips, it's no surprise that many students are finding the Internet an indispensable tool for researching term papers as well.

You might also enjoy the explosive growth in the gaming industry on the Internet. Through the Internet, you can play games against one another whether the players live in the same neighborhood or in another country. Even if you don't want to play games against others, you can still use the Internet to find tips and tricks for helping you master your favorite computer, board, or card game.

Despite the publicity surrounding the Internet, most uses for the Internet are relatively new. By now you should have the idea that there's a lot more going on with the Internet than playing games or sending e-mail. The Internet can be a window to the world. You can explore everything from the latest crime statistics in your local neighborhood to the most current photographs of the universe by NASA space probes.

Using the latest features of Windows 95, you can make sure that your computer is able to take full advantage of all current and future uses of the Internet.

Installing Internet Explorer 4

Internet Explorer has been available as part of various Microsoft software bundles from the original Plus! pack. Most new computers come with Internet Explorer preinstalled. However, unless your Windows 95 computer is a recent acquisition, it probably came bundled with an earlier version of the Internet Explorer dubbed IE3 (for Version 3). To get Internet Explorer 4, you have several options:

- Download a copy free of charge directly from Microsoft's Web site (http://www.microsoft.com). This option is available if you already have Internet access. However, IE4 and its companion programs make for a big download; it can take a couple of hours or so to complete the installation over a modem connection.

- Buy a copy from a mail-order house, a local computer store, or direct from Microsoft. You have to pay a few bucks for a copy of the program on CD, but it might be worth it to cut the installation time down from a couple of hours to a few minutes.

- Get a free copy from your Internet service provider such as Prodigy, EarthLink, CompuServe, or Concentric.

No matter how you get a copy of IE4, the installation procedure is basically the same. Before installing IE4, close any programs that might be running.

1. Click the Start button on the Windows 95 Taskbar and choose the Run option. You should see the Run dialog box.

2. Click the Browse button. You should see a Browse dialog box.

3. Click the IE4SETUP.EXE file. Depending on how you got your copy of IE4, the IE4SETUP.EXE file might be stored on your CD or in the directory where you downloaded IE4. You should see the Run dialog box again.

4. Click OK. When the Internet Explorer 4.0 Active Setup dialog box appears, click Next. The Setup wizard displays a licensing agreement and asks you to accept its terms.

5. Signal your agreement to the licensing terms by selecting the "I accept the agreement" radio button and then clicking Next. Setup displays a dialog asking you what type of installation you want to choose: Browser Only, Standard, or Full. If you only want to use IE4 as a browser, choose Browser Only Installation. (Choosing Browser Only sacrifices the Active Desktop Web integration features of IE4.) If you want most of the major features of IE4 while saving disk space at the same time, choose Standard Installation. You get the browser plus the Web integration features and also the Outlook Express e-mail program. Choose Full Installation to get all the standard features plus FrontPage Express, NetMeeting, and NetShow.

Note: If you chose Browser Only or Standard Installation, you can always install the additional components of IE4 at a later time by running the Setup program again. If you chose Full Installation, you can always remove components that you don't need at a later time as well.

Looking Ahead: Look in Chapter 24, "Outlook Express News and Mail," and Chapter 25, "FrontPage Express, NetMeeting, and NetShow," to learn more about the additional features of IE4 such as Outlook Express, FrontPage Express, and NetMeeting.

6. Click Next. Setup displays a folder to store IE4. By default, Setup chooses the folder that contains a previous version of Internet Explorer. If you want to specify the folder to store IE4, click Browse, click a folder, and then click OK.

7. Click Next. Setup begins installing IE4 on your computer. Depending on the type of installation you chose and the speed of your computer, the installation can take anywhere from several minutes for an installation from a CD to a couple of hours over a modem connection to the Internet. When the installation is finished, a dialog box appears.

8. Click OK. You have to restart Windows 95 to complete the installation.

After you install Internet Explorer 4 on your computer and restart your computer, a Welcome dialog box appears that provides a guided tour of the latest features of IE4 (see Figure 1.1). If you install IE4 as an upgrade to a previous version of Internet Explorer, you probably have your Internet connection already set up and you're ready to go with the new and improved version of the Web browser and many of the Internet integration features that come with it. Otherwise, you need to set up an Internet connection before you do anything else related to the Internet.

Figure 1.1.
Internet Explorer 4
provides a guided tour
for helping you get
acquainted with the
new features of IE4.

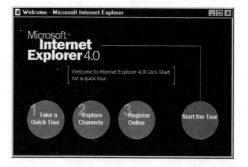

Note: To see the guided tour of IE4, you must have an Internet connection.

Using the Online Services Folder

Once you have IE4 installed properly on your computer, the next step is getting connected to the Internet. Unless you're fortunate enough to be on a local area network that is connected directly to the Internet, you need to go through an Internet service provider (ISP). Newer computers with

Windows 95 might include the Online Services folder, which contains icons that help you connect to one of several Internet service providers, including America Online, CompuServe, Prodigy, AT&T WorldNet, and the Microsoft Network. All these companies provide access to the Internet with varying prices and technical support. Should you use the ISPs offered in the Online Services folder? Maybe, but don't feel that you must use one of these ISPs. For example, although most of these major ISPs provide great service to large cities, they might not provide inexpensive access if you live in a smaller city or rural area.

Note: The Online Services folder is included only on new computers with Windows 95. If you have an older copy of Windows 95, you might not have the Online Services folder. Don't worry; you don't really need it because you can get the software you need to connect to the Internet directly from your ISP anyway.

After you select an ISP, the next step is establishing a connection to its network using your modem and phone line. For that, you need to set up a Dial-Up Networking connection, which is the topic of the next section. When that's done, you can launch IE4 and use its Internet Connection wizard to configure the software to use your new Internet connection. I explain that process in detail in Chapter 22. (Actually, the Internet Connection wizard walks you through the steps to set up a Dial-Up Networking connection if you haven't already set one up. However, I find that it's usually better to set up and test a Dial-Up Networking connection according to the ISP's instructions before attempting to run the Internet Connection wizard.)

Using Dial-Up Networking

Dial-Up Networking is the Windows 95 facility for making a modem connection to another computer or network. Under Windows 95, Dial-Up Networking is normally limited to calling into a server, such as for connecting to the Internet or an intranet.

Note: Before you can use Dial-Up Networking, you need to install it using the Add/Remove Programs applet in Control Panel. I cover that procedure in Chapter 11, "The Windows 95 Applets," so I don't discuss it here. The following paragraphs assume that you've already installed Dial-Up Networking.

Creating a Connection

In most cases, all you really want to do with Dial-Up Networking is create a simple connection. This section describes the minimum that you need to do to create a connection of any kind.

Dial-Up Networking has its own folder. You always see at least one component in that folder: the Make New Connection applet. Take a look at this part of the service first:

1. Double-click the My Computer icon on the Windows 95 desktop. The My Computer window appears.

2. Double-click the Dial-Up Networking folder. Double-click the Make New Connection applet. You should see the dialog box shown in Figure 1.2. No doubt, you want to enter a more descriptive name than the default name of My Connection. Notice that this dialog box also provides a Configure button. I describe this dialog in the faxes and modems section of Chapter 14, "Exploiting Your Hardware."

Figure 1.2.

The initial Make New Connection dialog box allows you to specify the name of the computer you're calling and the modem type.

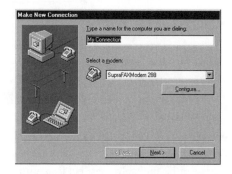

3. Once you select a connection name, choose a modem model, configure the connection, and click Next. (If you need help configuring the modem, see Chapter 14.) The next dialog box, shown in Figure 1.3, allows you to enter the area code and telephone number for your connection. Notice the Country code list box, which allows you to create connections even if you aren't currently in your home country.

Figure 1.3.

Here you can provide the area code and telephone number for the new connection.

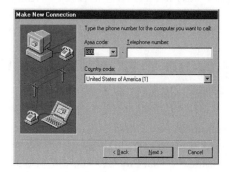

4. Click Next to see the final dialog box. The Make New Connection applet gives you one more chance to change the connection name before you click Finish to record the settings. Of course, you can always change the name later if you need to.

Using the Connection

Creating a connection is the first part of the equation. Using the connection after you create it is the second part. Just double-click the Connection icon in the Dial-Up Networking folder to see the dialog box shown in Figure 1.4. Notice that the telephone number you need to call is automatically added to the dialog box. The only thing you need to add is your user name and your password for the machine that you want to call.

Figure 1.4.
Using a connection after you define it is easy. Just a double-click and your user name and password are all you need.

If you use the same connection often, you might want to check the Save Password check box. Now all you need to do to use the connection is double-click to open it and then click the Connect button. Saving your password is probably a safe bet for an Internet connection, but you might want to refrain from saving passwords for a connection to the company network, where security is paramount.

Some people have had problems getting Windows 95 to remember their passwords. They check the Save Password check box, but the password is still missing the next time they use a connection. In many cases, the problem you're seeing is a corrupt password file. All you need to do is erase the PWL file that corresponds to your logon name in the main Windows 95 directory. Of course, you have to enter all your passwords from scratch again, but everything should work once you get this task accomplished.

Calling from Another Location

In most cases, you'll find that once you create a connection, you never need to look at it again. What happens, though, if you need to call from another location? You can select any predefined location from the Dialing from list box. Suppose that you're dialing from another location, perhaps outside the country. The following procedure shows you how to quickly add a new location to the Dialing from list box by using the Dial Properties button. (Double-click your connection to display the Connect To dialog box.)

1. Click the Dial Properties button shown in Figure 1.4. You see the dialog box shown in Figure 1.5. Notice that this dialog box contains everything you need to define a local connection.

Figure 1.5.
The Dialing Properties dialog box contains a complete description of your current location.

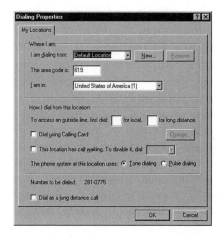

2. Click the New button. You see a dialog box containing a single text box.

3. Type a descriptive location name and click OK. You return to the Dialing Properties dialog box with the new location name in the I am dialing from: field. Notice that the dialog contains all the settings I described for the default location shown in Figure 1.5.

4. Change the area code and country fields to match your current location. Don't worry about any long-distance considerations. Windows 95 takes care of that for you automatically. All you need to know is your current location.

5. If you plan to use a calling card from this new location, click the Calling Card button. Windows 95 presents the dialog box shown in Figure 1.6. You need to work with your local calling-card company to fill this out completely. You need to supply a calling-card type and perhaps a calling-card number. In most cases, you also need to supply a PIN (personal identification number) for security reasons. Many calling cards also provide usage instructions that you can include with the dial-up connection.

Figure 1.6.
Setting your calling-card parameters correctly is very important.

6. Click OK to close the calling card dialogs once you've finished their setup.

7. Once you complete the Location dialog box, click OK to save it. Notice how the telephone number automatically changes to reflect your location. Windows 95 automatically includes all the required codes for you.

Of course, the last thing you need to do is click Connect to actually make the connection. When you do so, Windows 95 initializes your modem and dials the number. Then, when the other modem answers, Windows 95 sends the server your user name and password. It also takes care of details such as using your phone card if you supply that information. Configuring the connection the first time might take a little time, but once you get it done, everything is automatic from that point.

Modifying a Connection

You'll likely run into a situation where you want to modify an existing connection. For example, you might change ISPs, change your connection type or server type, troubleshoot a connection problem, or simply change your dialing country. It's important to remember that you can access the Dial-Up Networking folder in two ways: from Windows Explorer and by double-clicking the My Computer icon on the Windows 95 desktop. You can also find the Dial-Up Networking folder in the Accessories folder within the Start menu. Opening the Dial-Up Networking properties dialog box is easy. Just right-click the connection you want to modify, and select Properties from the context menu. You see a dialog box similar to the one shown in Figure 1.7.

Figure 1.7.
The Dial-Up Networking properties dialog box always contains the name of your connection in the title bar. In this case, it's SpryNet.

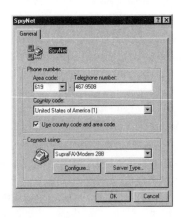

This dialog box contains most of the information you used to create the connection in the first place. You can use it to change the area code, telephone number, and country code, along with the modem you want to use. There isn't anything here that I haven't already discussed. To see some special settings, click the Server Types page.

Figure 1.8 shows some settings that you didn't get to change when you created the connection because Windows 95 assumes certain defaults. The first field contains a list of server types. Every Windows 95 installation supports at least five kinds of servers: NPN (Novell NetWare networks), PPP (Windows NT, Windows 95, or Internet connection), CSLIP (UNIX connection with IP header compression), SLIP (a standard UNIX connection), and a special connection for Windows for Workgroups (Windows 3.x).

Tip: If you're connecting to the Internet, disabling the Log On to Network option can significantly speed up connecting to the ISP.

Figure 1.8.
The Server Types dialog box allows you to configure your connection in a variety of ways.

Right below the Type of Dial-Up Server field, you find a group of check boxes that control the advanced options for your connection. In most cases, you never have to modify these options. The Log on to network check box tells Windows 95 that you want to log on to the server automatically. You can't use this option with callback systems; it only works with servers that allow automatic logon, such as the Internet. The second check box, Enable software compression, sets up software compression to reduce the transfer time for any data you want to send to or receive from the server. You'll find that this option works in most cases, but you'll want to disable it for UNIX connections or older mainframe connections that don't support encryption. You'll also want to disable this option if you're using hardware compression on a dedicated connection. The Require encrypted password option enables software encryption of your user name and password. Obviously, the server has to support this option before you can use it. Normally your user name and password are sent using plain ASCII.

The final section of this dialog box contains a list of allowed protocols. Normally you see every protocol installed on your machine checked. In some cases, this causes problems. For example, if you use Novell NetWare for your file server and use TCP/IP for a dial-up connection to the Internet, you'll want to disable the Novel NetWare protocol in the Dial-Up Networking connection. Otherwise, you'll find that your Internet connection might conflict with the NetWare connection. As a bonus, disabling the protocols you don't need also seems to speed up the connection because Windows 95 doesn't have to spend as much time monitoring it.

Figure 1.9.
You can configure the
TCP/IP settings used
on a connection-by-
connection basis,
using the TCP/IP
Settings dialog box.

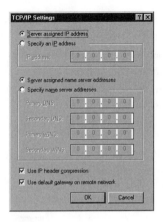

You'll notice that there's also a TCP/IP Settings button on this dialog box. It displays a TCP/IP Settings dialog box like the one shown in Figure 1.9. The section "Configuring TCP/IP—The Short Form" in Chapter 27, "Networks," discusses the ins and outs of TCP/IP.

Protocols and URLS

It's time to look at what you can expect to see when you log on to the Internet for the first time. There isn't any way that I can cover in two chapters all the specifics that some authors take an entire book to cover. What is covered is specific to what you, as the user, need to know.

I begin with a discussion of one important Internet topic—*uniform resource locators* (URLs). You can't get anywhere on the Internet without knowing something of this topic, yet few texts really tell you much about them. I give you an overview of URLs from the layman's point of view—how they're put together and what you need to know to use them. Another important topic is protocols. If you know anything about the history of the Internet, you see that the Internet was founded on several protocols such as TCP/IP and FTP.

Understanding Uniform Resource Locators (URLs)

The URL is the basis for movement on the Internet, so it's important to understand how it works. Begin by looking at the Microsoft home page address; that's where you check in before exploring the rest of the Internet:

```
http://www.microsoft.com/
```

At first, you might think that it's all gibberish, but there are some definite standards for putting these site locations together.

Actually, this is a typical URL that identifies a particular server and clues you in about its capabilities. Begin with the `http://` portion of the URL. This tells you what kind of data exchange protocol you use to access the server. In this case, you use the hypertext transfer protocol. I describe the two major data transfer protocols (HTTP and FTP) in the next section. There are other data transfer protocols as well, such as Gopher and Archie, but I leave them for you to explore at your leisure. Knowing the data transfer protocol tells you a lot about what to expect from the server.

The next section contains the *domain name system* (DNS) address for the site you want to visit, which could either be a numerical address, or more commonly a descriptive text address such as `www.microsoft.com/`. Typically, there are three subsections to a DNS address, each separated by a period. (Some DNS addresses have only two subsections and some have a fourth or even a fifth subsection that contains the computer or country name.) In this example, the first part of the DNS address tells you about the service (or, as some books call it, the subdomain). You're going to visit the World Wide Web (WWW) in this case. Nothing states you have to use WWW; for example, you can visit a site called `http://home.microsoft.com/` that takes you to the home page for Internet Explorer. Most sites use WWW as a convention because everyone expects to find their Web site on the World Wide Web.

The middle subsection of the DNS address contains the domain name itself. In this case, it's `microsoft` for Microsoft. If you want to visit the Microsoft Network, you use MSN as a domain name. You'll find that most domain names are either full names or acronyms for the organization—some of which can be quite convoluted. The Internet site must register the domain name with InterNIC. The domain name is the unique identifier you use in place of an IP address. Imagine having to remember 32-bit numbers for each site you want to visit in place of a convenient name.

The last part of a typical DNS address is the top-level domain identifier. Table 1.1 shows the basis for this part of the DNS address. InterNIC simply picks the one that fits the organization best. Note that this table doesn't contain every identifier that you'll ever see, but it does contain the more common identifiers.

Table 1.1. Common Internet domain identifiers.

Identifier	*Description*
`.com`	Any kind of commercial company such as Microsoft or CompuServe. Most online service Internet access providers have a `.com` domain identifier.
`.edu`	Educational institutions use this domain identifier. (Some recent refinements of the rules for assigning top-level domain names restrict this designation to four-year colleges and graduate schools. Elementary, secondary, and technical schools get a different designation.)
`.gov`	All U.S. government agencies use this domain identifier. If you see it, you know that you're dealing with someone from the United States government.

continues

Table 1.1. continued

Identifier	Description
.mil	The United States military uses this special domain identifier that keeps it separate from the rest of the government.
.net	Normally, this domain identifier is reserved for Internet access providers. Because many access providers are also commercial concerns, an ISP might use the .com domain identifier.
.org	This designation is usually the realm of non-profit organizations.

That's all there is to a basic URL. Some URLs are a lot longer than the one that I showed, however. What does the rest of the information mean? Look at another example. In this case, you look at a page for the National Science Teachers Association (NSTA):

```
http://www.gsh.org/NSTA_SSandC/nses_home.htm
```

Part of this address should already be familiar, so I won't cover it again. Look at the section after the domain name. In this case, you're looking at an organization that rented space on someone else's server. The NSTA SSC (Scope, Sequence, and Coordination Project)—/NSTA_SSandC—actually exists within a subdirectory on the gsh server. Think of those forward slashes in the same way you do subdirectories in a DOS path and you'll be right at home.

In this case, you're in a particular area of the NSTA SSC site—the /nses_home page that contains National Science Education Standards information. Notice the .HTM extension here. Some servers extend this to .HTML. HTML stands for *hypertext markup language*. I describe it more in the next section. For right now, all you need to know is that when you see these extensions, you're looking at a page that was formatted graphically for your browser.

There's one other form of the URL that I want to talk about, and it concerns e-mail addresses. Understanding how these addresses work is really easy if you understand a basic URL. You'll normally see something like this: JMueller@mwt.net. The first part of the address is the person you want to contact—in this case, JMueller. The @ (at) sign separates the receiver's name from the domain name.

A Quick View of Internet Standards

Because the Internet consists of diverse types of computers communicating with one another, the Internet has spawned several standards. You can use the Internet effectively without knowing much about the ins and outs of the various standards, but it helps to be able to recognize them when you see them. Table 1.2 shows some of the newer (and older) standards that you'll run into while you're surfing the Net.

Table 1.2. Common Internet standards.

Acronym	Full Name	Description
CGI	Common Gateway Interface	This is a special method for accessing an application from a Web page. When a vendor asks you to enter information on a form, for example, you're using CGI. The most common use for CGI is database applications. This is the only Web-server-to-background-application standard currently supported by the IETF. (I talk about them in a bit.) Two other proposed methods are ISAPI and NSAPI.
CORBA	Common Object Request Broker Architecture	You won't see this technology today (although it might be available by the time you read this). It might appear in a Java application that you see tomorrow, however. The purpose of this protocol is to describe data and application code in a way that a variety of computer types can use. It'll eventually allow you to go to a Web page and download a mini-application (applet) as part of that page. This is the Object Management Group's (OMG) alternative to Microsoft's ActiveX. CORBA was originally designed by IBM for inclusion with OS/2, but other companies such as Sun Microsystems now support this standard as well.
DCOM	Distributed Component Object Model	You might be more familiar with this term as ActiveX. (They aren't precisely the same thing, but that doesn't matter much for this discussion.) It's Microsoft's latest experiment in distributed mini-applications (applets). You'll be able to use OLE over the Internet in a new way. The applets provide all the features covered in Chapter 12, "DDE, OLE, DCOM, and ActiveX." The big difference is that you'll be able to use these features over the Internet. ActiveX applications require Internet Explorer 3.0 or greater.

continues

Table 1.2.   continued

Acronym	Full Name	Description
FTP	File Transfer Protocol	This represents one of the earliest forms of communication that the Internet recognized. There aren't any graphics to speak of at an FTP site—just files to download. This is the only file download protocol currently supported by the IETF. The limitations of this particular protocol have prompted other standards such as CORBA and DCOM.
HTTP	Hypertext Transfer Protocol	Whenever you go to a Web site that begins with http:, you're using this protocol. It's the technology that enables you to download an HTML (hypertext markup language) document—the kind that includes fancy graphics and buttons. Essentially, HTTP allows you to download an HTML script—a document containing commands rather than actual graphics. Your browser reads these script commands and displays buttons, text, graphics, or other objects accordingly. That's why the capabilities of your browser are so important (and also the reason you need a new browser if you want to use any of the new protocols I mentioned in this table). However, some vendors are already complaining that the IETF standard versions of both HTTP and HTML are old and less than optimal for tomorrow's needs. That's why there's such a proliferation of other protocol standards and associated HTML script commands on the Internet today; people are looking for better ways of making information accessible.
INFS	Internet Network File System	Think of this protocol as you do the file system on your own computer. Whether you use NTFS, HPFS, or VFAT, they all represent a way to organize the information on your drive and provide fast access to it. This file system does essentially the same thing for

Acronym	Full Name	Description
		Internet files. However, it has to have a connection to the data. That's done with TCP/IP—the networking standard I talk about elsewhere in this chapter.
ISAPI	Internet Server Application Programming Interface	This is another Microsoft protocol. I talked about other types of application programming interfaces elsewhere. ISAPI does the same thing for an Internet server; it allows you to access the features that the server has to offer. In this case, a programmer uses ISAPI to allow you to access a host application through an Internet server. You'll probably see ISAPI restricted to database and e-mail applications at first, but I already see other application types on the horizon. You might see it used as part of a turn-based game or even an online word processor, for example.
NSAPI	Netscape Application Programming Interface	Not to be outdone by Microsoft (see ISAPI), Netscape came up with its own API for connecting Web servers to background applications. As with ISAPI, NSAPI enables you to write a data entry or other application for the Internet by using advanced HTML scripting commands and allows it to interact with applications on your network. As with Microsoft's offering, the major application that I see for this API right now is some type of data entry or e-mail system.
ODSI	Open Directory Services Interface	The Microsoft Network (MSN) provides a somewhat better interface to the Internet than most of the other online services I've tried. At least it's faster than most, and ODSI is part of the reason. It provides a common naming convention API that will eventually enable you to treat an Internet Web site as you do any other folder in Explorer.

It's probably better to view Table 1.2 as a sampling of some of the more interesting technologies that you'll use. The problem with all these new technologies is that they aren't standardized. The

Internet has its own standards committee called the Internet Engineering Task Force (IETF), responsible for providing a standard set of HTML script commands. The problem with all these new protocols is that they introduce new scripting commands that could cause problems in the future. How can a browser handle a propriety script command? In most cases, it ignores it, but you can't be sure. Even if the browser does ignore the foreign command, you are stuck without access to some of the features on a given Web page. There are other problems with the current trend. What if a vendor simply modifies an existing script command? A browser doesn't know to ignore it in this case, and you can end up with a frozen machine as a result. I think you can start to see my point about the need for standards.

The problem is more severe than you might think. New Internet technologies are cropping up that don't have any old standards to follow. For example, just about every vendor out there has its own form of Virtual Reality Modeling Language (VRML), the format for defining 3D environments for games and such. Without a standard way to access this feature, you might find support for your browser to be spotty at best.

Finding What You're Looking For

There are so many Web sites available on the Internet that it's easy to get swamped with information. Many universities offer Web sites so you can see the courses they offer, such as the University of California San Diego (UCSD) at http://www.ucsd.edu/. These types of educational Web sites can help you gain access to the various kinds of research occurring at that particular university. Research was one of the main reasons for the early growth of the Internet and it continues to have a major impact on how the Internet is growing today.

What if you're not all that interested in attending college or finding out what they're doing with your tax dollars? You can always contact places such as NASA at http://www.nasa.gov/. You can view pictures of Mars or find out the current status of various space exploration projects.

If science doesn't interest you and you couldn't care less about NASA, how would you like to visit Malaysia? I was surprised by how much growth Malaysia has experienced as a nation and by how much we rely on it to create a variety of products. You'll probably use something made in Malaysia today. You can find out more about this country by looking at one of several Web sites. The government sponsored Web site is at http://www.mol.com/. Another good Web site to look at is http://www.pahang.com/. Needless to say, Malaysia isn't the only country you'll find on the Internet. I was able to find entries for even the smallest countries in the world.

If you spend any amount of time browsing the Internet, as I do, you'll realize the need for finding what you need quickly so you don't get overwhelmed with information.

Tip: There are probably more Internet sites to visit than you can imagine when it comes to finding great additions to the Windows 95 environment. One of these sites is the NoNags main page at `http://users.southeast.net/~itsvicki/nonags/main.html`. This site specializes in shareware utility-type programs, although you'll also find a variety of other offerings. As the home page title states, none of the software nags you to make a purchase. One of the more interesting aspects of this site is that you can find most of the software in both 16-bit (Windows 3.x) and 32-bit (Windows 95/NT) versions. If you want to choose from a broader range of Windows 95–specific software, take a look at Windows World on the Internet (`http://www.windows95.com/`). This site contains tutors on a variety of topics, an Internet hypertext glossary, an Internet TCP/IP connectivity guide, and even a full listing of Windows 95/NT–specific hardware drivers.

Fortunately, the Internet provides you with some handy tools to help you navigate. The most basic tool is a search engine. To use a search engine, you normally visit the search engine's Web site and then type a word or phrase (known as a keyword) that you want to find. The search engine displays a list of all Web sites that contain the keyword.

Of course, there are several search engines you can use. You might think that one search engine is enough to fulfill your needs, but that simply isn't true. The problem with coming up with a "best fit" answer for any of these search engines is that they work differently. A search engine that works fine for my needs might not work at all for you. I thought it important, therefore, to provide a list of some of the more common search engines and a quick overview of how they work. I encourage you to try them all to see what works best for you and in what situations. The following list discusses the search engines I use along with their URLs. The simplest way to access a search engine is to open a Web browser such as Internet Explorer, click in the Address box on the toolbar, and enter the URL. (Once you find a search engine you like, you might want to add it to your Favorites or Bookmark list so that you can find it easier the next time.) In Chapter 22, I show you some other ways to access search engines using IE4.

- Alta Vista (`http://www.altavista.digital.com/`): One of the benefits of using this search engine is a lack of information overload. It returns only the amount of information you want about each hit. The service tends to focus on Web pages containing articles, meaning that you get some pretty narrow hits when using it. Alta Vista uses excerpts from the articles or other sources of information that it accesses. This service uses a somewhat esoteric Boolean search engine, making it difficult to narrow your search criteria with any level of ease.

- AOL NetFind (`http://netfind.aol.com/`): Beneath the surface, this is really the Excite search engine and, predictably, the results of a keyword search are the essentially the same as you get using the Excite service directly. The reason for selecting AOL NetFind instead of Excite is for the Time Savers, such as Car Corner and Manage Your Investments, that provide quick access to pages of information and links related to those topics.

- Deja News (`http://www.dejanews.com/`): I've used this particular search engine when I needed to find a lot of information fast. You'll notice a Power Search button on the page when you arrive. Power search might be something of an understatement; you literally have to test it to see all that you can do. This is also one of the easier sites to use, despite its flexibility. It uses a lot of graphics, including radio buttons and other familiar controls. The only problem with this particular engine is that you might find yourself doing a search more than once to get everything it provides. There are so many search options that you'll find yourself thinking of new ways to search for a particularly tough-to-find bit of information. You can get two levels of detail—neither of which tell you much. All you can count on getting for each hit is an article title. This service doesn't provide either excerpts or summaries, but it does provide a broad base of information, meaning that you'll find just about anything you search for; you'll just spend some time weeding out the entries that really don't fit.

- Excite (`http://www.excite.com/`): This service tends to focus on Web sites rather than pages on a particular site. In other words, you get to a general area of interest, and then Excite leaves it to you to find the specific information you're looking for. I find that this is an advantage when I'm not really sure about the specifics of a search. A wide view, in this case, helps me see everything that's available and then make some refinements. Excite also provides a summary of what you'll find at a particular site. It tends to concentrate on discussion groups and vendor-specific information.

- HotBot (`http://www.hotbot.com/`): Many people consider this to be the premier search engine on the Web today and with good reason. The searches are fast and comprehensive, and HotBot gives you access to some power searching tools for customizing your searches that most of the other search engines reserve for advanced users only. On the other hand, you might need to take the time to learn about and use those extra searching tools to refine your HotBot searches or else the results you get may be overwhelming. For example, when I searched for ActiveX on HotBot, I got more than 130,000 hits.

- Infoseek (`http://www.infoseek.com/`): The strength of this particular service is that it provides just the facts. It uses excerpts from the articles or other sources of information from which it draws excerpts. The hits are a lot narrower than some search engines provide because Infoseek concentrates on Web pages rather than sites. The only problem with this particular service is that your ability to narrow the search criteria is severely limited.

- Lycos (`http://www.lycos.com/`): Of all the search engines I've used, Lycos tends to provide the most diverse information. It catalogs both Web sites and pages but concentrates on pages whenever possible. Lycos provides a combination of summaries and excerpts to describe the content of a particular hit. The ability to narrow your search is superior to most of the search engines available right now. One of the down sides to using this particular search engine is that there's almost too much detail. You'll quickly find yourself searching false leads and ending up with totally unusable information if you aren't sure what you're looking for.

- Magellan (`http://www.mckinley.com/`): You'll tend to find esoteric sources of information with this search engine. It doesn't appear to provide a broad base of information, but it usually provides interesting facts about what you're searching for. Magellan concentrates on Web sites rather than pages, so the view you get is rather broad. You'll also find that it provides few methods for narrowing the search criteria. This search engine relies on summaries rather than extracts to convey the content of a particular hit. One of the more interesting features is the method used to rate a particular site; clicking a Review button gives you a full-page summary of how the information relates to similar information on other sites.

- Open Text (`http://search.opentext.com/`): *Extremely comprehensive* and *flexible* are the words to describe this particular search engine. I find that this is one of the easier sites to use, and it provides a moderately broad base of information from which to choose. This particular search engine relies on extremely short excerpts, in most cases. It concentrates on Web pages rather than sites, meaning that you get a fairly narrow result.

- Yahoo! (`http://www.yahoo.com/`): This particular search engine provides the best organization of all those listed. It categorizes every hit in a variety of ways, making your chances of finding information contained in the search engine very high. However, this service doesn't provide the broad range of information that you'll find with other search engines. It also relies on short summaries to tell you the content of a particular hit. In most cases, I rely on Yahoo! as a first-look type of search engine—something that gives me the broad perspective of a single keyword.

- Web Crawler (`http://www.webcrawler.com/`): You'll find that this search engine requires a bit more work to use than most because it doesn't provide much in the way of excerpts or summaries. On the other hand, it provides a full Boolean search engine and an extremely broad base of information. The only search engine that provides a broader base in this list is Lycos.

- MetaCrawler (`http://www.metacrawler.com/`): Rather than use various search engines individually, the MetaCrawler search engine lets you query multiple search engines simultaneously. That way you won't have to check the same query with different search engines such as Yahoo! or Excite.

It's time to try a search. Visit the Lycos search engine as shown in Figure 1.10, type **ActiveX** in the blank, and then click Search. Depending on the security level you selected, you might see a Security dialog box before the browser does anything. (Use the View | Options command and then select the Security page of the Options dialog to change your security level with Internet Explorer.) Click Yes to clear it. You end up on a Web page like the one shown in Figure 1.11.

Figure 1.10.

A search Web page such as Lycos allows you to find specific information on the Internet.

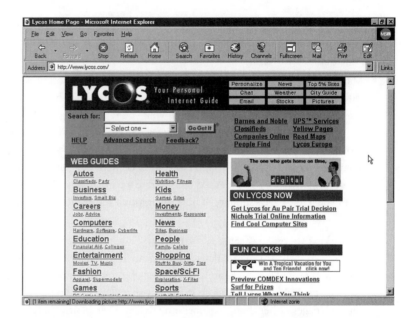

Figure 1.11.

The Lycos search engine displays a list of Web sites that match your query.

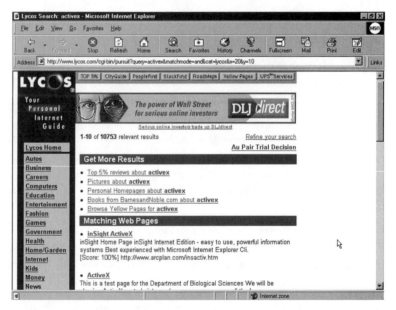

You should notice a few things about this page. The first feature is that you can refine your search. Maybe a single keyword really didn't refine the search enough and you need to find something more specific. I haven't found a single search Web page that doesn't provide this capability in some form. In fact, many of them provide very detailed search mechanisms.

There's something else you should notice. Each of the result entries (also called *hits*) contains a confidence level. This tells you how confident the search engine is about the results it found. Normally, the search engine uses a variety of criteria to determine this number—such as the number of times the keyword appears in an article or other source of information. Obviously, a Boolean search starts to make a confidence calculation more difficult. (A Boolean search uses terms such as "and" and "or" to allow you to look for phrases in a specific way. If you say, "help and context," then the search engine looks for articles with both help and context in them. On the other hand, if you told the search engine to look for "help or context," then either word satisfies the search criteria.) The method of determining a confidence factor is one of the things that determines which search engines you use. I use a variety of them for different purposes.

Web search pages normally don't list every site that the search engine finds. Notice that Lycos lists only ten of them. (Other services allow you to change the number of entries listed as part of the search criteria). You have to click the Next Documents button to see the next group of ten on the list. The confidence level assigned to the various hits usually determines which sites are listed first. Notice that Lycos defaults to listing the sites it finds by confidence level. This makes sense because you want to find the best sites first. If you want an alphabetical listing, click the Sort by Site button. Some search engines provide other sorting criteria. The Deja News site, for example, allows you to sort by author as well. I talk about that in a bit.

Special Active Desktop Features

I'm not going to go into detail on Active Desktop in this chapter; I spend a lot of time looking at it in Chapter 4, "Working with the Active Desktop." However, it's important to note that many of the Internet Explorer features that I talked about in this chapter can appear right on your desktop. All these features help you get information in ways that you couldn't imagine in the past. For example, you can use "push" technology to tell the Internet to deliver content automatically to your desktop. In other words, you don't have to remember to look for updates anymore; the Internet tells you about them automatically. That's right; you can set up links to any place on the Internet. Those links can be updated automatically. You can even create a link to your favorite search engine.

There are quite a few Active Desktop features that I haven't even begun to discuss in this chapter. For example, using the Channels feature of Windows 95 allows you to get connected to your favorite news or entertainment Web site quickly.

Getting connected to the Internet used to be an optional activity that some people did because they wanted to stay informed. With Windows 95, it makes little sense not to get connected. You literally have the entire world at your fingertips, and with the new features that Windows 95 provides, you don't have to spend a lot of time figuring out what you need and where to find it.

OEM Service Release 2—The Complete Story

To keep Windows 95 up to date, Microsoft has released a new version of Windows 95, dubbed OSR2. Unfortunately, this update to Windows 95 is available only to original equipment manufacturers (OEMs) and not to the public at large. Microsoft's reasoning is that most of the features provided by OSR2 (OEM Service Release 2) are really only useful if you have a new machine. If you have an older version of Windows 95, you can update it by downloading certain portions of OSR2. Table 1.2 lists the updated support that the OSR2 version of Windows 95 provides.

Table 1.2. OSR2 Update Information

Feature	Downloadable	Description
32-bit DLC	Yes	Data Link Control (DLC) support for SNA host connectivity.
ActiveMovie	Yes	See high-quality QuickTime and MPEG-1 format videos, even over an Internet connection.
Automatic Scandisk	No	Windows 95 now detects abnormal exits and automatically tests your hard drive before the next startup. This allows you to fix all errors on the hard drive, even if the files are normally used by Windows.
CDFS	No	The CD File System (CDFS) will now support ISO 9660 disks up to 4GB in size and CD-I (CD-Interactive) format CD-ROMs.
Desktop Management	Yes	Allows a desktop-management application to monitor devices on your PC. (This feature currently supports the Desktop Management Interface standard 1.1.)
Dial-Up Networking	Yes	The big news with this release is scripting capability. You also get a number of user-interface updates.
DirectX 2.0	Yes	Get high-performance 2D and 3D graphics. It also enhances your system's sound capabilities. Games are about the only applications that use this support right now, but expect other applications to use it in the future.

Feature	Downloadable	Description
Display	Yes	You can now dynamically change screen resolution and color depth (the resolution change was available in previous versions for certain displays). This update also allows you to change the refresh rate for most of the newer display adapter chip sets.
DriveSpace	No	This update allows DriveSpace to support drives up to 2GB in size. Unfortunately, you can't use this update and FAT32 at the same time.
FAT32	No	As hard disks increase in size, more and more users are complaining about lost disk space. FAT32 represents one way to get rid of this problem. It supports drives up to 2TB in size and uses a 4KB cluster size.
Fixes and Updates	Yes	You can download a variety of minor fixes and updates from this site. The most important updates are to the OLE components. You can also download an updated Windows Messaging client and fixes to Microsoft FAX.
Fonts	Yes	Updated support for the new Hewlett-Packard LaserJet 4 gray scale fonts.
Infrared Support	Yes	Need a nonwire connection for your laptop? This new infrared data support fits the bill. Your infrared port must support the Infrared Data Association (IrDA) 2.0 standard to use this support.
Intel MMX Support	No	Intel's multimedia extensions (MMX) support is available for applications that want to use it. Consider this future technology for the moment.
Internet Connection Wizard	Yes	A new utility that helps you configure a connection for your ISP. It can also help in the sign-up process.

continues

Table 1.2. continued

Feature	Downloadable	Description
Internet Explorer 4	Yes	This new version of Internet Explorer includes support for ActiveX, HTML style sheets, frames, Java, and a lot more.
Internet Mail and News	Yes	Unlike many browsers, the mail and news reader for Internet Explorer 3.0 comes as a separate product. I find this to be the most inconvenient feature of Internet Explorer. This product does support both SMTP and POP3 mail clients.
IRQ Routing	No	Along with enhanced PCI device support, this update includes support for PCI interrupt routers.
MSN 2.5	Yes	The biggest improvement here is speed.
NDIS 4.0	No	Supports NDIS 4.0 network interface card (NIC) drivers.
NetMeeting	Yes	You can use this handy utility to make phone calls over the Internet. It supports conference calling. You also get a whiteboard, chat, and file-transfer capabilities.
NetWare NDS Service	Yes	You'll get a better level of NDS support with this release, but the Novell version is still more capable.
Online Services Folder	No	Microsoft now provides client software for America Online, CompuServe, and AT&T Worldnet. Expect to see additional clients in the future. (Even though you can't download this support from a Microsoft site, you should be able to download it from the vendor-specific sites.)
OpenGL	Yes	This graphics API has been available to Windows NT users for quite some time—now Windows 95 users have it too. The OSR2 version of Windows 95 ships with screen savers that can use this support.

Feature	Downloadable	Description
PCI Docking/Bridging	No	You can now use PCI devices in PCI docking stations.
PCMCIA	No	This update adds support for PC Card 32 (Cardbus) bridges, PCMCIA cards that operate on 3.3 volts rather than 5 volts, multifunction PCMCIA network and modem cards, and PCMCIA Global Positioning Satellite (GPS) devices.
Personal Web Server	Yes	Although this product won't allow you to build a full-sized Internet site, you can use it for testing and for small-sized intranet purposes.
Power Management	No	Advanced Power Management (APM) features on computers get more complex all the time. This update adds support for APM BIOS 1.2, wake-on-ring modems, multibattery PCs, drive spin down, and powering down of inactive PCMCIA modems.
Storage Devices	No	New storage support includes IDE Bus Mastering, 120MB floptical drives, removable IDE media, ZIP drives, and CD changers. You'll also get better diagnostics through the use of the SMART predictive disk failure APIs.
Voice Modem	Yes	Voice modems are the wave of the future. With these API enhancements, you can use one device to accept faxes, transfer files, and record your voice mail.
Wang Imaging	Yes	This utility allows you to view graphics in the JPG, XIF, TIFF, BMP, and FAX formats. You can also scan and annotate images using the built-in TWAIN scanner support.

As you can see, OSR2 almost qualifies as a minor revision to the operating system rather than a patch. Some changes, such as FAT32, are so significant that they really affect the way you work with Windows as a whole. Throughout the book you'll look at how the OSR2 version of Windows 95 can benefit you as a user. You'll also look at some of the pitfalls of these new features. In the long run you'll develop a better understand of why Microsoft may have decided to make this a new machine update rather than release it to the general public.

On Your Own

Get connected to the Internet using one of the vendors in the Online Services folder.

Create a connection for the ISP if one wasn't created for you automatically. Some ISPs perform this step automatically when you install their software.

Try another browser, such as Netscape Communicator. How does it differ from Internet Explorer?

Study some of the URLs stored in your browser. What do these URLs tell you about the site that you've accessed? Spend some time on the Internet looking for various URL types.

Spend some time learning about the various institutions that manage the Internet. You can visit the InterNIC site at `ftp:\\ftp.internic.net` or `http:\\www.internic.net`, for example.

Install several browsers on your machine to see how they work on various Internet sites. At a minimum, try both Netscape Communicator and Internet Explorer. You can download a free trial copy of Netscape Navigator at `http://www.netscape.com/`. (You already have a copy of Internet Explorer.) Be sure to try some of the add-ons for both products, such as the sound-enhancing Real Audio Player (`http://www.realaudio.com/`). (If you do install a sound-related plug-in, be prepared for a few shocks. Some Web sites try to blast you out of your seat with high-volume sound effects. Needless to say, such sound effects at midnight aren't much of a treat to you or anyone else sleeping in your vicinity.) Although Communicator does make heavier use of plug-ins than Internet Explorer, both products benefit from third-party add-ons.

2

Introducing Windows 95: What Else Is New?

Peter Norton®

One of the biggest changes in combining Windows 95 with Internet Explorer 4.0 is the Active Desktop. The Active Desktop might look like the old Explorer interface, but it is as different from the Explorer interface in Windows 95 as Explorer was from the Program Manager in Windows 3.11.

What makes Active Desktop different from previous interfaces is its Internet orientation. You'll find that accessing the Internet is no longer a chore and can be a simple click away. In fact, with the addition of channels, you won't even have to click to see your favorite Web sites updated automatically.

Forget about working at getting to the company intranet as well. The new Active Desktop makes accessing a company intranet just as easy as accessing a local hard drive. You'll find that you can click your way around the company with an ease unheard of in previous releases of Windows.

Customization is also improved under the latest features of Windows 95. You'll find that your folders no longer have to maintain the same mundane appearance. Now you can customize the appearance of individual folders.

Because many people still use and prefer the older Explorer interface, this chapter also covers that interface. You might want to keep this older interface because you're familiar with it or because you actually find that the Explorer is more efficient for the way you work. Home users, especially, might not like having the Internet at their fingertips. Fortunately, Windows 95 and Internet Explorer 4.0 let you choose whether you use the new Active Desktop features.

The last section of this chapter covers the various accessory programs provided with Windows 95. I look at the applications that will make your life a little easier.

Keeping Windows 95 Up to Date

Since the introduction of Windows 95, Microsoft has been releasing a steady stream of accessories, add-ons, bug fixes, and updates to improve Windows 95 or fix problems that may occur when running Windows 95 under certain types of hardware. To keep your copy of Windows 95 as up to date as possible, you might need one or more of the following four types of Windows 95 upgrades:

- Microsoft Plus!
- OEM Service Release 2 (OSR2)
- System Updates
- Device Driver Updates

Installing Microsoft Plus!

Microsoft Plus! adds the following to Windows 95: Internet Explorer 3, System Agent, DriveSpace, Dial-Up Networking server, desktop themes, font smoothing, and full windows dragging capabilities, which lets you see the contents of a window as you're moving or resizing it. That way you can see how resizing a window affects the way the window displays its contents.

Because Microsoft Plus! was one of the first upgrades for Windows 95, it contains some features that are now obsolete or no longer needed if you already have OSR2. The most obvious feature you no longer need is the copy of Internet Explorer 3 that comes with Microsoft Plus! If you already have Internet Explorer 4, you won't need to install the older copy of Internet Explorer 3 that comes with Microsoft Plus!

Another feature of Microsoft Plus! that you might not need is DriveSpace, a disk compression utility that can increase the amount of space on your hard disk by shrinking the size of your files. Using DriveSpace can slow down your computer, but the savings in space might be worth it. Because OSR2 provides a more recent version of DriveSpace, you can skip the installation of DriveSpace from Microsoft Plus!

To install Microsoft Plus! from the CD, put the CD in your CD-ROM drive and follow the instructions displayed on the screen.

CD autolaunch doesn't work on some computers. In this case, simply run SETUP.EXE from the Plus! CD. For instance, if your CD-ROM drive is drive D:, you do the following:

1. Click the Taskbar's Start button and select Run from the Start menu.
2. Type **d:\setup** in the Run dialog box's Open text box.
3. Click the OK button.

Alternatively, you can double-click the My Computer icon on your Desktop and then double-click CD-ROM Drive, which should show up as a Plus! icon. Double-click the setup.exe icon to start the Plus! setup.

The Microsoft Plus! for Windows 95 Setup asks you to select the typical or custom installation. The typical installation, the choice for most people, simply installs all components. If you plan to install or have already installed OSR2 or other Windows updates, you should use the custom installation so that you can deselect items you don't need. In the Microsoft Plus! for Windows 95 Custom dialog box, shown in Figure 2.1, click the check box to the left of each option in the Options list that you want to deselect. If you're running low on disk space, you might need to do this so that you can load only the facilities that you need the most.

Figure 2.1.

All options in the
Options list are
selected by default.

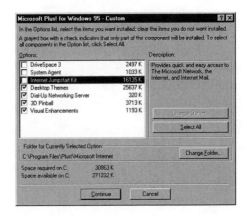

Table 2.1 lists all the Plus! options you can select or deselect during the Plus! custom installation.

Table 2.1. Microsoft Plus! options available during custom installation.

Option	Disk Space Required	Description
DriveSpace 3	2,497KB	Provides enhanced disk compression, including Compression Agent, to create more hard disk space. You do not need this feature if you have OSR2.
System Agent	1,033KB	Runs system maintenance tasks and other programs at regularly scheduled times. You do not need this feature if you have IE4 because IE4 comes with Task Scheduler, which replaces System Agent.
Internet Jumpstart Kit	16,135KB	Makes configuring access to the Microsoft Network, the Internet, and Internet Mail quick and easy. You do not need this feature if you have OSR2.
Desktop Themes	25,637KB	Customizes your Windows 95 Desktop around a central theme.
Dial-Up Networking Server	320KB	Configures your computer server so that you can dial into it from another location.
3D Pinball	3,713KB	The classic arcade game, including great graphics and sound.
Visual Enhancements	1,193KB	Enhancements for high-end systems to maximize graphics capabilities.

When you select the Desktop Themes or the Visual Enhancements options, you're given the opportunity to see additional options by clicking the Change Option button. When you click the Change Option button while Visual Enhancements is selected, the list of options shown in Figure 2.2 appears.

Figure 2.2.
The additional options for installing Visual Enhancements from Microsoft Plus!

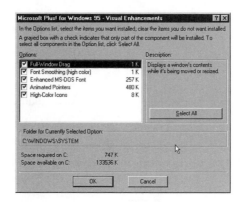

Upgrading to OSR2

New computers might already have OSR2 (OEM Service Release 2) installed. However, if your computer does not have OSR2, you can install the individual components that make up OSR2. Many of the features available in OSR2 are features that will eventually appear in Windows 98 as well.

The main features of OSR2 are hardware enhancements to make Windows 95 compatible with the latest hardware devices introduced since the original introduction of Windows 95. Table 2.2 lists all the OSR2 options that you can and cannot install to upgrade Windows 95. Don't worry, the later chapters of this book explain in more detail what these new features do. For now, just acquaint yourself with their existence and purpose.

Table 2.2. OSR2 options available for downloading and installing.

Option	Downloadable	Description
FAT32	No	Enhances the Windows 95 FAT file system to support large hard disk drives up to 2TB in size. Includes updates to FDISK, Format, ScanDisk, and Defrag utilities to support FAT32 partitions.
DriveSpace	No	Updated version of DriveSpace for compressing hard drives up to 2GB in size. Note that DriveSpace does not support FAT32 hard drives.

continues

Table 2.2. continued

Option	Downloadable	Description
Power Manager	No	Provides support for Advanced Power Management (APM) 1.2 BIOS, wake-on-ring for modems, multibattery PCs, drive spin down, and powering down of inactive PCMCIA modems.
Storage Enhancements	No	Support for IDE Bus Mastering, 120MB Floptical disk drives, removable IDE media, Zip drives, and CD changers. Also adds the SMART predictive disk failure APIs.
PCMCIA Enhancements	No	Adds support for PC Card 32 (Cardbus) bridges, PCMCIA cards that operate at 3.3 volts instead of 5 volts, multifunction PCMCIA network/modem cards, and PCMCIA Global Positioning Satellite (GPS) devices.
CDFS Enhancements	No	Support for ISO 9660 disks up to 4GB in size and CD-I format CED-ROM drives.
PCI Bridging/ Docking	No	Support for PCI devices for use in PCI docking stations.
IRQ Routing	No	Support for new PCI interrupt routers.
Internet Explorer 4	Yes	Internet browser with support for ActiveX, Java, frames, and style sheets.
Internet Connection Wizard	Yes	Wizard for simplifying the configuration and connection to an ISP.
Outlook Express	Yes	Send and receive e-mail and read Usenet newsgroups.
NetMeeting	Yes	Make telephone calls over the Internet and remotely view and control programs, chat, and transfer files online.
Personal Web Server	Yes	Allows you to publish and host HTML pages over the Internet or an intranet.
DirectX 5.0	Yes	Provides high-performance 2D and 3D graphics, sound, input, and communications, primarily for games.
ActiveMovie	Yes	Provides high quality playback for viewing video including QuickTime and MPEG-1 formats.
OpenGL	Yes	Support libraries for the OpenGL graphics standard.

Option	Downloadable	Description
Intel MMX Support	No	Provides support for building software that takes advantage of Intel Pentium Multimedia Extensions (MMX) for improved audio and video performance.
Dial-Up Networking	Yes	Adds user interface, scripting, and hands-free dial-up enhancements to dial-up networking.
Voice Modem Support	Yes	Support for VoiceView and AT+V modems to allow switched voice and data transmission and to allow modems to answer voice calls.
Directory Services for NetWare	Yes	Client support for Novell NetWare 4.*x*, including Directory Services.
32-Bit DLC	Yes	32-bit support for the Data Link Control protocol for SNA host connectivity.
Infrared Support	Yes	Support for Infrared Data Association (IrDA) 2.0 compliant devices including infrared LAN connectivity.
Desktop Management	Yes	Supports the Desktop Management Interface (DMI) 1.1 to allow desktop management application to monitor devices on the PC.
NDIS 4.0	No	Supports the new NDIS 4.0 network interface card drivers.
Display Enhancements	Yes	Supports dynamically changing screen resolution and color depth. Adapter refresh rate can also be set with the newer display driver chipsets.
Wang Imaging	Yes	Allows viewing of image data from various file formats including JPG, XIF, TIFF, BMP, and FAX. Scan and annotate images with built-in TWAIN scanner support and Imaging applet.
Fonts	Yes	Adds support for HP LaserJet 4 grayscale fonts.
MSN 1.3	Yes	The latest client program for MSN.
Fixes/Updates	Yes	Includes various Windows 95 updates such as updated OLE components, enhanced Windows Messaging client performance, and fixes to Microsoft Fax.

continues

Table 2.2. continued

Option	Downloadable	Description
Automatic ScanDisk on Boot	No	If the PC was not shut down normally, ScanDisk will automatically run at the next reboot to check for damaged or corrupted files.
Online Services Folder	No	Provides client software for various online services and ISPs including America Online, CompuServe, Prodigy, and AT&T WorldNet.

To get copies of the downloadable features of OSR2, visit the Microsoft Web site at `http://www.microsoft.com`.

Other Updates, Patches, and Bug Fixes

As Microsoft discovered problems or flaws with Windows 95, it released smaller bug fixes, updates, and patches to improve the performance. Fortunately, you can download these updates directly from the Microsoft Web site at `http://www.microsoft.com`. Table 2.3 lists the many updates and bug fixes available and what features they offer.

Table 2.3. Additional Windows 95 updates available for downloading and installation.

Option	Description
Internet Mail Service	Adds POP3 client mail services to the Microsoft Exchange client.
Kernel32 Update	Fixes a memory leak that occurs when opening and closing a socket using the Windows Sockets API.
OLE32 Update	Update OLE32 components to Windows 95.
MS Fax Cover Page fix	Fixes problems with MS Fax showing available cover pages.
Backup Update	Improves performance for the Windows 95 backup application.
Windows 95 Password Update	Fixes a bug that occurs when an application attempts to remove a cached password.
Exchange Update	Updates the Exchange components that shipped in Windows 95.
Disk Type Specific Update	Addresses a potential data-loss issue for users of large EIDE drives with multiple partitions that support LBA and extended INT13 functions.
Apple Printer Utility	Allows Windows 95 to run Apple Computer's Apple Printer Utility, which lets users manage Apple Color LaserWriter 12/660 PS and Apple Color LaserWriter 12/600 PS printers over the network using the IPX/SPX protocol.

Internet Explorer 4 Suite

Internet Explorer 4.0 is both a browser and a whole new interface to the Internet and your own personal computer. Some of the many features of Internet Explorer 4 include a browser, an e-mail and newsgroup reader, a Web page designer, and a program for conducting meetings over the Internet.

Looking Ahead: This section provides only an overview of Internet Explorer. Chapter 22, "Browsing the Internet with Internet Explorer," examines all the usage details for this product.

Internet Explorer 4

Internet Explorer 4 provides the capability to browse Web pages on the Internet or an intranet. Of course, one of the nicest features is that Internet Explorer can become part of the Windows 95 interface. You can put a Web page right on your desktop and use it as you do any other desktop element. I covered some of these new features in Chapter 1, "Opening Windows to the Internet with IE 4," and others at the beginning of this chapter. I spend plenty of time looking at all the features that this latest version of Internet Explorer provides as the book progresses.

Offline Browsing and Webcasting

The Internet Explorer 4.0 provides another way to view the Internet by automatically checking your favorite Web sites for new content, according to a schedule that you specify. For example, you can have Internet Explorer automatically download news from CNN overnight so you can read it the next morning. This automatic feature is called subscribing to a Web site and it doesn't cost you anything beyond your normal Internet account charges.

You can schedule Internet Explorer to automatically retrieve content on a daily, weekly, or monthly basis. After Internet Explorer downloads content from a Web site, you can view it at your leisure without connecting to the Internet again.

Besides automatically retrieving Web site content, Internet Explorer also lets you create channels. Channels are Web sites that automatically update your computer according to a schedule provided by the Web content provider.

Outlook Express

Internet Explorer 4 also includes Outlook Express, which provides access to newsgroups and e-mail. I examine Outlook Express in Chapter 24, "Outlook Express News and Mail."

Front Page Express

Internet Explorer 4.0 includes Front Page Express, which lets you design your own Web pages that can include ActiveX controls. ActiveX controls can greatly enhance the usability of a Web site by allowing the Webmaster to do things that HTML code normally wouldn't support. For example, you can use an ActiveX control to figure out the total owed on a purchase before sending the page to the Web server. A control can also change the appearance of the Web page on-the-fly and perform other tricks unavailable when using straight HTML.

In addition to the ActiveX control support, Front Page Express offers support for HTML-style sheets, frames, Java applets, JavaScript, and VBScript. HTML style sheets (also called cascading style sheets) let you create consistent Web pages with little effort. Instead of designing every page element, you can create an HTML style sheet that defines the use of icons and so forth. All that's left to the user is the placement of content. You can find out more about cascading style sheets at `http://www.w3.org/pub/WWW/Style/`. The actual specification is at `http://www.w3.org/pub/WWW/TR/WD-css1`.

Microsoft NetMeeting

NetMeeting is a new utility that provides you with the capability of holding meetings over the Internet. Immediately obvious are the voice capabilities of this product. There are separate controls for sending and receiving voice from other people. Because this is a duplex connection, you won't get the irritating "speaker phone" effect that's present in a conference call setup.

> **Looking Ahead:** Chapter 25, "FrontPage Express, NetMeeting, and NetShow," covers this utility in more detail. The chapter includes sections on setting up NetMeeting.

NetMeeting also allows you to perform all the standard functions that you normally associate with an Internet connection. For example, you can send a copy of a file to one or more meeting attendees or remotely control an application and perform other computer-related tasks.

One of the features I like best is the whiteboard. You can use it to give other people a visual representation of your idea. However, unlike the whiteboard in a meeting room, other people can draw on this one and help you expand your ideas. Overall, NetMeeting provides all the features of a physical meeting room without any of the inconvenience.

Task Scheduler

The Task Scheduler, which replaces the System Agent from the Microsoft Plus! upgrade, lets you schedule and run tasks each time you start Windows 95, such as running ScanDisk once a day or running an antivirus and backup program once a week. By using the Task Scheduler, you can automate many features of Windows 95 to make your computer easier and more helpful to use.

Active Desktop: A New Way to Approach Windows

The new Windows interface is the Active Desktop. Using the Active Desktop allows you to get work done more quickly and with a lot less effort. However, the place where I find that Active Desktop comes in the handiest is when it comes to handling information overload—too much information to wade through in too little time. Active Desktop can help you reduce the effects of information overload when used to its full potential.

This section looks at the Active Desktop approach to working with Windows. You'll learn what makes an Active Desktop unique when compared to the older Explorer interface. You'll also find out a few tips and techniques for making Active Desktop work for you.

What Is an Active Desktop?

All the desktops you've used to date are static: In other words, they don't change. An Active Desktop does change. The desktop you used today won't be the same desktop that you see tomorrow. When you arrive at work or start up your machine at home tomorrow, the contents of your desktop change to reflect the new day.

Here's a better idea of what I'm talking about. Think for a second about the newspaper. Your administrative assistant brings in a newspaper every day and places it on your desk. The one from yesterday gets thrown in the trash. Your desktop has changed; it contains new content that reflects what you're doing today. Likewise, Windows 95 and IE4 change the content of your desktop each day to reflect changing events. If you subscribe to a news channel and display it on your desktop, the display changes each day to reflect the changes in weather.

An Active Desktop is more than just changing weather. Consider, for a moment, what happens when you look for something on your local machine, the network, or the Internet. In the past, you had to think three different ways to get the data you need. Your local machine required one procedure, the network another, and the Internet something totally different. Windows 95 changes all that by allowing you to place all your resources in one place. You'll be able to find the data you need without really thinking about where it came from.

If you want to direct people's attention to a specific event, bit of data, or other company-related matter, you normally have to write a memo and distribute it to everyone. Wouldn't it be nicer if you could just place this information on the person's desktop along with all the required files and other materials? Windows 95 and IE 4 allow you to do this. A company intranet can easily supply everything needed to direct what an employee is doing. In addition, you can monitor an employee's progress without looking over his shoulder. All you need to do is look at the contents of his desktop on the company intranet.

By now you should have a pretty good idea of what the Active Desktop can mean to you and your company. The following sections help you get started using the Active Desktop. Once you know the principles, what you do is really a matter of how much imagination you have. An Active Desktop, unlike the static desktop of old, has few limitations.

HTML on Your Desktop: No Browser Need Apply

You might not notice much of a difference among the latest features of Internet Explorer when you first install Windows 95 on your machine. That's because it starts with some of the newer features turned off. You have to turn on some of the features before you actually see the Active Desktop features that Windows 95 provides.

The first step in turning on these new features is to right-click the desktop. Figure 2.3 shows the context menu you see. The item that you're interested in is Active Desktop. Notice that you can choose one of three options from a submenu. The following list tells you about the purpose of each option:

- View as Web Page: The Windows 95 Desktop can be viewed as a static desktop or as a Web page, which allows for active content. When you choose the View as Web Page option, any Web sites you've subscribed to appear on the desktop along with the Internet Explorer Channel Bar. I discuss these items in the section "Customizing Your Desktop Content" later in the chapter, so don't worry too much about them now.

- Customize my Desktop: Selecting this option displays the Display Properties dialog. I discuss the Web tab of the Display Properties dialog in the section "Customizing Your Desktop Content" later in this chapter. The Web tab is where you choose which subscribed items you want to display on the desktop and where. You also use it to choose between the standard desktop and the Active Desktop.

- Update Now: Once you have all these Web pages on your desktop, you need some way to keep them up to date. Windows 95 can update your desktop at scheduled times, but what happens if you need that last minute stock report or update on the latest technology? That's what this option covers. You can tell Windows 95 to update your content now, rather than wait for the automatic update time.

Tip: You can always view the Internet Explorer Channel Bar by clicking the View Channels entry on the Quick Launch Toolbar. This toolbar appears on the Taskbar; it contains three buttons, one of which is the View Channels icon.

Figure 2.3.
*Windows 95 provides
some new options on
the context menu for
the desktop that
enable the Active
Desktop features.*

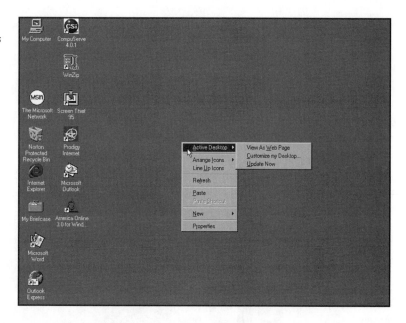

Start with something simple. Right-click the desktop, and then choose View as Web Page from the context menu. What you see is the Internet Explorer Channel Bar shown in Figure 2.4 because that's the only thing that you have an automatic subscription for during installation.

Figure 2.4.
*The Internet Explorer
Channel Bar is your
initial entry to the
Internet using Active
Desktop.*

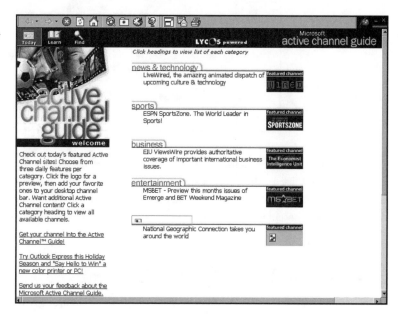

Note: To proceed beyond this point in this section, you need a connection to the Internet. Of course, you can always follow along in the text without actually performing the steps on your machine.

Using Channels

If you click one of the entries on the Internet Explorer Channel Bar, you start a copy of Internet Explorer and go to that site on the Web. Try it now with the Channel Guide. Click the Channel Guide entry. Once Internet Explorer makes a connection, you see a Web page similar to the one in Figure 2.5.

Figure 2.5.
Clicking an Internet Explorer Channel Bar icon opens a copy of Internet Explorer and then displays that Web site.

At this point, you can start roaming through the various channels and selecting one or more to place on your desktop. I discuss this process later in Chapter 22. What you should have learned in this section is that Internet access doesn't have to be complicated. You can optimize your Active Desktop to display the content you need with little or no work on your part. All you need to do is perform a little setup at the outset.

Customizing Your Desktop Content

To customize your Desktop content, begin with the Internet Explorer Channel Bar. Right-click an entry such as MSNBC News and you see a context menu like the one shown in Figure 2.6.

(Channels that you can't subscribe to, such as the Channel Guide, use a standard context menu; your only real option here is to open the Web site and view the list of channels it contains.) The following list describes the unique menu entries you need to know to customize your desktop:

- Open Channel: Selecting this option starts a copy of Explorer and opens the associated Web site so you can see if you actually want to subscribe to the channel. You can also use this option to better define your choice. For example, MSNBC News is a relatively large Web site; you might only want to subscribe to the weather portion, not the entire thing.

- Subscribe: Use this option to subscribe to your favorite channel. Of course, this option allows you to subscribe to the entire channel; you might want to refine your selection a bit by visiting the Web site first. For example, you might only want to know about the music (TuneDom) on the Warner Brothers Web site, not the movies (ScreenDom) as well.

- Refresh: You can count on Windows 95 to automatically check the Web sites you've selected for automatic update. This option allows you to refresh your display in case parts of it were erased or scrambled by another program.

- View Source: Sometimes you might want to view the actual HTML commands that create a particular channel. When you choose this option, the HTML commands appear in Notepad where you can modify them.

- Update Now: This option lets you immediately display a channel's content instead of waiting for the normally scheduled update time.

Figure 2.6.
The Internet Explorer Channel Bar context menu contains many entries that allow you to customize your desktop with a single selection.

Looking Ahead: Chapter 23, "Webcasting: Channel Surfing When You're Offline," explains different ways you can use channels and shows you how to automatically add new channels to your selection list. The section "Creating a Subscription" in that chapter shows you how to get your own channel subscription going. Make sure you check out the section "Using the Favorites Folder" in Chapter 23 to learn how to manage both subscriptions and channels.

What if you don't like where Windows 95 places the Internet Explorer Channel Bar or any other active context for that matter? Moving around these windows to the Internet is just as easy as moving any other window. There's a hidden title bar for each of the windows that you can use to move the window around. Place your mouse near the top of the window and the title bar appears. Grab the title bar to move the window where you want it onscreen. Resizing the window is just as easy. Just place the mouse cursor near one of the edges. When you see the double arrow, drag the mouse in the direction that you want to size the window.

The Internet Explorer Channel Bar and other Active Desktop items also have a drop-down menu on their title bars, as shown in Figure 2.7. As you can see, it contains two entries. The first shows the Display Properties dialog. Remember that this dialog contains the Web tab, which allows you to configure the Active Desktop. The second item allows you to close a particular Active Desktop item.

Figure 2.7.
Every Active Desktop item provides a drop-down menu on its title bar.

The final area I want to cover right now is the Web tab of the Display Properties dialog. You can display this dialog in several ways. One of the easiest methods is to right-click the desktop and choose the Active Desktop | Customize my Desktop option. What you should see is a dialog similar to the one shown in Figure 2.8. (You might have to actually select the Web tab.)

Figure 2.8.
Use the Web tab of
the Display Properties
dialog to configure
your Active Desktop
content.

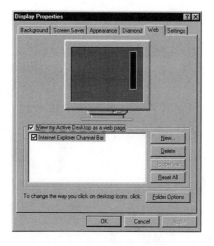

The first thing you should notice in Figure 2.8 is the monitor near the top. This monitor shows you the position of every Active Desktop item that you've chosen to display. The currently selected item is black, whereas the other items are displayed as outlines.

Right below the monitor is a list of Active Desktop items. You can have more items than you can actually display on the Desktop. Checking an item displays it, and unchecking it removes it from the Desktop. Windows 95 continues to update an item, even if you're not currently displaying it. The only item shown in Figure 2.8 is the Internet Explorer Channel Bar.

Tip: The View my Active Desktop as a Web page check box allows you to remove all Web content from your desktop. It performs the same function as the Active Desktop | View as Web Page option on the Desktop context menu.

Add a new item to the Items on the Active Desktop list. The following procedure shows you how to add a weather map to your desktop, but you can use it to add any other item as well:

1. Open the Display Properties dialog, and then choose the Web tab. You should see a display similar to the one shown in Figure 2.8.

2. Click the New button. You see the New Active Desktop Item dialog shown in Figure 2.9. If you click the Yes button on this dialog, Windows 95 closes the Display Properties dialog and takes you to the Active Desktop Gallery. Choosing No displays another dialog that allows you to enter your own URL. The No option is really designed for adding an intranet site to your Desktop.

3. Click Yes. The Display Properties dialog closes and Internet Explorer starts. Once Internet Explorer makes a connection and looks up the Active Desktop Gallery page on the

Internet, you see something similar to Figure 2.10. (The contents of this Web site change all the time, so your display will most likely differ from mine.)

Figure 2.9.

Click Yes to access the Active Desktop Gallery, which you can use to select Web sites that contain active content.

Figure 2.10.

The Active Desktop Gallery page allows you to add active content to your desktop.

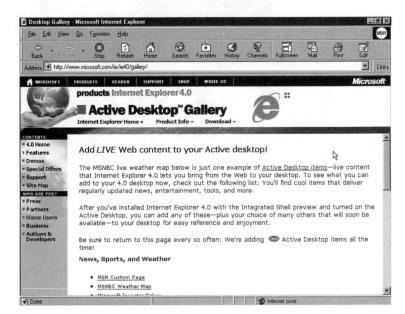

4. Click the MSNBC Weather Map link. Internet Explorer takes you to a page that features the weather map.

5. Click the Add to my Desktop button near the bottom of the page. Internet Explorer downloads a special file from the Internet. This file adds the MSNBC Weather Map to your desktop. Once the file is downloaded, you see a Subscribe dialog box. This dialog allows you to choose the method for updating your Active Desktop item. (I cover this procedure in the section "Creating and Managing Subscriptions" in Chapter 23.)

6. Click OK to accept the default update schedule and change notification method. At this point, you can click the Weather Map from MSNBC link to see another Web page where you can customize the weather map for your particular area of the country. Skip that part of the process for now; I want to show you the new content you added to your desktop.

7. Close Internet Explorer by clicking the Close button in the upper-right corner of the program. You should see the Active Desktop. Notice that nothing has changed.

8. Right-click the desktop, and then choose Refresh from the context menu. You see a weather map on the Active Desktop.

Changing the View of Your Folders

Windows 95 and IE 4 give you several ways to customize the appearance of your folders including Web views (which are covered in more detail in Chapter 7, "Customizing Folders with Web Views") and background images.

To switch to Web view, open the folder you want to change using the View | Folder Options command to display the Options dialog shown in Figure 2.11. Notice that this dialog contains three entries. The Web style option displays your folder as Internet Explorer displays a Web page. The only difference is that this page is local to your machine. The Classic style option sets your computer to display the folder using the same criteria (not the same precise display) as Windows 95. The third option, Custom, allows you to display the folder using a mixture of both Web and classic styles.

Figure 2.11.
Displaying a Web view of your folder means choosing the Web style option on the General tab of the Options dialog.

Choose the Web style option, and then click OK to close the Options dialog. The titles for all the files appear underlined and if you move the cursor to one of the file entries, you notice that it changes to a pointing finger, just as it does when you point to a link on the Internet. Instead of double-clicking to open a file, you point to it and single-click, just as you do to follow a link on the Internet.

Another interesting feature is the capability to display thumbnail views. Right-click within the folder (without touching any files) and choose Properties from the context menu. You notice a new Enable thumbnail view checkbox near the bottom of the dialog. Check this box, and then close the Properties dialog by clicking OK. Now you can view the thumbnails of files as shown in Figure 2.12.

Figure 2.12.
This Web style view of a folder uses thumbnails to display the contents of the graphics files it contains.

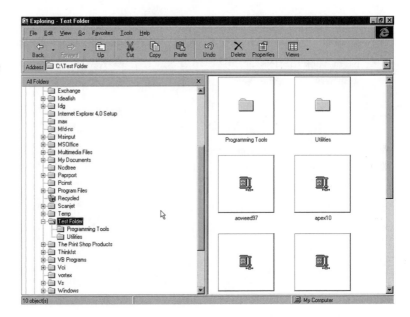

If this still isn't enough customization for you, one more new feature is sure to make your day. You can customize a folder using the View | Customize This Folder command. Figure 2.13 shows the three choices you have when you display the Customize this Folder dialog.

Figure 2.13.
It's easy to add either a background graphic or a Web page view to your folder using the Customize this Folder dialog.

Look at the Web page version of the customization process. Select the Create or edit an HTML document option, and then click Next. The next dialog details the procedure that Windows 95 follows in creating a new HTML document for your folder. Click Next. You see a window similar to the one shown in Figure 2.14. This is where you edit the HTML content for your folder. Save the document by clicking the File | Exit command. You return to the Customize this Folder dialog. Notice that it has the message, "Congratulations! You have chosen to make the following changes: -Folder.htt." This message tells you that you successfully installed the HTML support. Click Finish to close the Customize this Folder dialog. At this point, your folder should look similar to the one shown in Figure 2.15.

Figure 2.14.
You can use the
Notepad utility to edit
HTML code for your
folder.

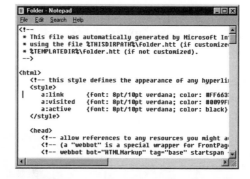

Figure 2.15.
An example of what
you might see if you
use HTML content
to customize your
folder.

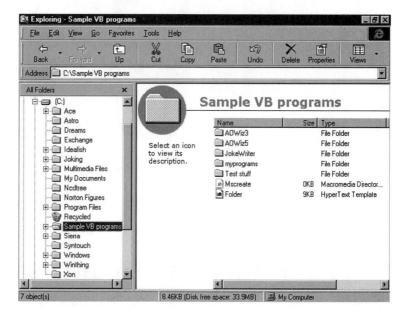

How do you reverse the change you just made? Use the View | Customize This Folder command to display the Customize this Folder dialog again. This time, choose the Remove Customization option, and then click Next. The next dialog warns you that you're about to remove the customization from your folder. Clicking Next displays a success message similar to the one you saw when adding the HTML content to the folder, but this one shows you what Windows 95 will remove. Click Finish and you are back to your original display.

Warning: Removing HTML customization from your folder means that the HTML file gets erased. In other words, this is a one-way process. If you remove the file without first creating a backup, you have to create the HTML page from scratch if you decide to reinstall the HTML customization.

What if you don't want to go through a lot of effort to customize your folder? You can always add some background graphic to give it some pizzazz. Take a look at that process. Use the View | Customize This Folder command to display the Customize this Folder dialog again. This time, select the Choose a background picture option, and then click Next. You see a Customize this Folder dialog, as shown in Figure 2.16.

Figure 2.16.
Graphic backgrounds are an easy way to add pizzazz to your folder.

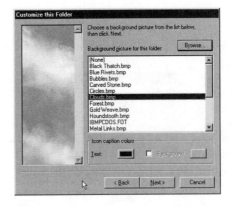

Choose one of the graphics from the list or use the Browse button to search for a particular graphic image. Notice that you can also customize the color text used for your folder. Once you choose an image and modify the color text you want to use, click Next. You see a success message. Click Finish to complete the process.

Explorer: the Familiar Interface

The familiar interface of Explorer shows a two-pane configuration. On the left side of the display is the directory tree. You need to make note of several features of this directory tree for future reference. The first thing you notice is that the tree doesn't represent a single drive or even the contents of all the drives; it's more of a "machine tree" than anything else. This "machine tree" is divided into three elements:

- The drive section: This is the area where the contents of all your data drives are displayed. This includes any network drives that you're connected to.

- The configuration section: This area contains four icons in our sample display. (You might also see other icons here.) Control Panel provides access to every machine configuration component that Windows 95 has to offer. It includes both hardware and software configuration. Windows 95 also provides a Printers icon. You could access this icon from Control Panel, but putting it here makes access a lot more convenient. The Dial-Up Networking folder contains your connections and a special icon for creating new connections. The Scheduled Tasks folder contains a list of tasks that you've asked Windows 95 to perform automatically.

- The ancillary section: The ancillary section could contain any number of icons such as the Recycle Bin icon. The Recycle Bin is where any documents end up that you erase in Explorer and performs the same function as the Recycle Bin on your desktop. The My Documents folder is where applications such as Microsoft Word normally place your data files. The Network Neighborhood icon appears when you have a network installed on your machine. It allows you to attach to network resources and view network data. You also find icons here for accessing the Internet, your Briefcase, and the Online Services folder.

Looking Ahead: Future chapters look at other aspects of Explorer. Read Chapter 7 if you want some additional tips on optimizing your work environment using Explorer.

Now that you have some idea of what the left pane contains, look at the right pane. Clicking any of the objects in the left pane displays its contents in the right pane. If you click a drive icon, you see the folders and files that the drive contains in the right pane. Click Network Neighborhood and you get a view of all the machines attached to the network. You can also use the icons in the right pane to open a file or folder. Double-click a folder and you see what it contains. Double-click a file and you perform the default action associated with that file.

Every object you use in Windows 95 provides a context menu. If you have a doubt about what something is, how to configure it, or just about anything else you can do with that object, a simple right-click will answer your question.

Every context menu for a file or folder contains five or six major sections where each section tells you something about the object associated with that menu. The following paragraphs outline each section and its purpose:

- Actions: The first section of the context menu tells you what kinds of actions you can perform with the object. The default action—normally Open—appears in bold print. In addition to the Open action, you see a Print data file action. Folders normally include an Explore and a Find action. You see one other type of entry in the context menu. If the file extension doesn't appear in the Registry, Windows 95 won't know what to do with it. In this case, you see an Open With entry in place of the usual ones.

- Network: This is an optional section that normally contains a single entry—Sharing. Some objects support sharing and others don't. It all depends on how you have your network set up. Normally, peer-to-peer networks enable this option only for folders. Larger networks— such as those from Novell—provide this entry for both files and folders.

- Send To: Use this special entry if you want to send the object to another location. Windows 95 supports the Briefcase, the desktop, a mail recipient, removable drives, and any floppies connected to your system as destinations.

Tip: It's often handy to create additional destinations for the Send To menu such as project folders and network drives. Always make these destinations practical. In other words, don't add another directory listing to this rather important list. All you need to do is add destinations that you use on a daily basis.

- Editing: Believe it or not, you can edit an object as you do everything else under Windows 95. This section contains entries for Cut, Copy, and Paste. You can place a copy of the object on the Clipboard and then paste as many copies as you need onto other objects. These are full-fledged copies, not the shortcuts (object links) that I examine in the next section. If you cut an object, Windows 95 doesn't remove the icon from the display. It grays the icon and waits until you paste the object somewhere else before removing it permanently. This prevents you from accidentally erasing objects. Cutting a new object before you paste the first one leaves the first object in its original location.

- Manipulation: This section usually contains three entries, but it can contain more. The Create Shortcut option allows you to place a link to a file or folder somewhere else. Chapter 6, "Startup Shortcuts," shows how you can use this feature to make your desktop a friendlier place. The Delete option sends the file to the Recycle Bin. You can still recover it later, if necessary. The Rename option allows you to change the long filename associated with the file.

Tip: You don't have to send objects to the Recycle Bin if you don't want. Simply select the object you want to delete, and then press Shift+Delete to erase it permanently.

- Properties: Every object contains a Properties entry on its context menu. Clicking this entry always displays a dialog box that allows you to view and configure the properties of that particular object. The Properties dialog box for a file shows the full filename, any attributes associated with the file, and some statistical information. Folders usually contain about the same information as files but provide some additional statistics as well. Disks, on the other hand, contain a wealth of information about the drive as a whole. This Properties dialog box even provides access to the three maintenance tools that Windows 95 provides to manage disk drives. You find that the Properties dialog box for other objects, such as the desktop, contains a wealth of information too. For example, the Desktop Properties dialog box allows you to change the system colors and display resolution. You can even use it to change your wallpaper.

Some objects on your system include some specialized context menu entries. For example, if you right-click the Recycle Bin, you see an option to empty it. Right-clicking the desktop provides a New option that you can use to create new files. (You see the same menu option if you right-click a blank area of Explorer.)

IE 4 and Windows 95 also provides three toolbars that replace and augment the single toolbar that you saw in Windows 95. You can choose any or all of the toolbars that you want.

The Standard Buttons toolbar contains all of the buttons required to move around in Explorer. The first three buttons are Forward, Back, and Up. You use the first two buttons to move from one location that you've already visited to another. The Up button takes you up one level in the directory structure. The next three buttons, Cut, Copy, and Paste, allow you to move files or folders from one location to another. All you need to do is cut or copy the file or folder in one location and then paste it in another. The Undo button allows you to undo the previous action you performed in Explorer. For example, if you rename a file and then click the Undo button, the original name returns. The Delete button allows you to move a file or folder from its current location to the Recycle Bin. Use the Properties button to display a file's or folder's Property dialog. Finally, the Views button allows you to see another view in Explorer. The four standard views are Small Icons, Large Icons, Details, and List. They control how Explorer displays the objects you see in the right pane. A fifth view, Thumbnail, allows you to see a small version of a file instead of the standard icon.

The Address toolbar might look extremely simple, but it's a powerful feature. If you place the cursor here, you can type a path to a local or network directory or a location on the Internet. Once you type the location you want to see and press Enter, it appears in the right Explorer pane. You can also type the name of an application or file here. Explorer automatically opens the file or starts the application for you once it finds what you're looking for. Finally, you can use the drop-down list box to browse within the current context. If you're looking at local or network drives, you get a directory tree to examine. On the other hand, if you're looking at the Internet, you see a history listing of Web sites that you've recently visited.

You'll find that you use the Links toolbar quite often if you set it up the right way. A single click on any icon takes you to that location. The Links folder in your Favorites folder controls the contents of this toolbar. You get a choice of five Microsoft-specific Web sites to begin with. However, there's nothing to stop you from adding your ISP's home page, the location of your company's intranet site, or any other link.

You'll find another new feature in Internet Explorer 4 as well. The Explorer Bar feature displays Search, Favorites, History, and Channels. You use the Explorer Bar just as you do in Internet Explorer. The only difference is that now you don't need a browser to access these features.

This section gives you a quick overview of using Explorer. Now it's time to take a more detailed look. The following sections discuss various ways that you can use Explorer. Once you finish these sections, you'll start to see why I call Explorer the Swiss army knife that you need to use Windows 95 efficiently. Of course, once you know how to use that tool well, everything else falls into place. Suffice it to say that you'll probably find more things you can do with Explorer as you become more proficient in working with Windows 95.

An Information Center

The most common way to look at Explorer is as your information center to tell you everything you need to know about your computing environment. A typical Explorer display shows a list of folders on your computer in the left pane and the contents of one particular folder in the right pane.

Once you have all the pieces of Explorer and understand how to use them, you can put them together so that you can use Explorer as your information center. Each of the following sections describes a major element of your information center. Remember that each element is a drive, control, or ancillary unit.

Drives

Windows 95 provides three different tools that you can use to manage your drives. You can start them from the Start menu, or you can use the Windows 95 method of managing your drives.

Take a look at what the drive icons have to offer. Right-click any of your hard drives. (Floppy and CD-ROM drives provide the same type of properties, but the hard drives are easier to use for purposes of this description.) You should see a dialog box similar the one in Figure 2.17. This is the General page of the Drive Properties dialog box.

Figure 2.17.
The General page of the Drive Properties dialog box tells you quite a bit about the current status of an individual drive.

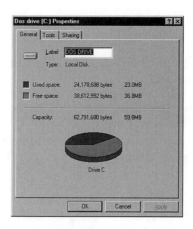

There are three noteworthy items on this page. First is the drive label. Labels aren't as important for hard drives, but I do use them on my floppy disks to identify projects that I'm working on. Second is the Free Space indicator (magenta). It tells the amount of drive space remaining. The corresponding Used Space indicator (blue) tells you how much space is used on the drive. The pie chart helps you to determine the current drive status at a glance. Third is the drive location. In this particular case, you can see that this is a local drive. You can pull up pages for network drives as well. However, you might not be able to do much because your access rights to that drive affect what Windows 95 will allow.

The Tools page of the Drive Properties dialog box, shown in Figure 2.18, can help you maintain your system. (You see a Tools page only for local drives.) I discuss how to use these tools in Chapter 9, "The Windows 95 Architecture." Notice that Windows 95 helps keeps track of the last time you used them. This can be a big help to folks who have trouble remembering the last time they maintained their machines.

Figure 2.18.
The Tools page of the Drive Properties dialog box allows you to keep your drive in peak condition.

Peter's Principle: Disk Maintenance: A Necessity, Not an Option

Windows 95 makes drive system diagnostics a lot easier to perform than any previous version of Windows and certainly easier than DOS. Drive system diagnostics are very important for maintaining data integrity. Even though the diagnostics are easier to access, a lot of people still don't use them because they really don't know how often they need to do so.

Chapter 10, "The Windows 95 File System," delves into the details of creating backups on your machine. However, simply backing up the data on your machine isn't enough. Your drives require more care than that if you plan to keep them in peak condition and your data error-free.

continues

Every day, I start my machine and perform a standard disk scan in the background. That way, I can catch major structural problems before they eat an important file. Once a week, I set aside some time to perform a thorough disk scan. I make sure that every other application is closed, including the screen saver, when I do this. ScanDisk can't really vouch for the status of any files you have open, so closing all your applications is a good idea.

Defragmenting your drive isn't a big deal from a data-security standpoint. If you don't defragment your drive, the worst thing that will happen is that the drive won't work as efficiently as it could. That said, do you really want to give up any performance due to a lack of maintenance? I usually defragment my drive once a week. In fact, I usually follow a routine of scanning the drive for errors, backing it up, and defragmenting. This is the same routine I recommend for you. The disk scan ensures that you get the best possible error-free backup. The backup itself ensures that your data is safe if a disk failure occurs while you defragment it, and the defragmenting program improves overall system efficiency.

The Check Now button opens ScanDisk, shown in Figure 2.19.

Figure 2.19.
ScanDisk allows you to check the current condition of your disk drive.

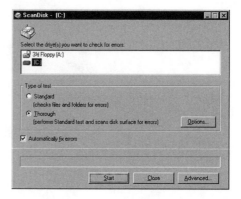

Tip: None of the three utility programs described in this section limits you to one drive. I usually check all the drives on my system at once instead of opening the Properties dialog box for each drive separately. Choosing to maintain your drives this way ensures that you don't miss any of them and also adds a certain level of automation to the process.

You can run two types of tests with this utility. The standard test simply checks the condition of your files and folders. All it does is check for major errors in the directory structure and the FAT. It also looks for cross-linked files and other structural problems. This test doesn't guarantee that the files are readable or that there isn't any damage to the drive media. Use the thorough test when you want to check for more than just structural integrity. The Automatically Fix Errors check box lets you tell ScanDisk to fix the problems without notifying you about each one in advance.

The Options button takes you to the dialog box shown in Figure 2.20, where you can modify the way that ScanDisk performs the thorough disk scan of your drive. The first group of options controls where ScanDisk looks for damaged media. Sometimes you might want to simply check the directory area for damage when troubleshooting your system. In most cases, you want to check both the system and data areas of your drive. The write test provides an added layer of testing integrity to your system. It actually tests to see whether the media is secure by writing to it and then reading back the results. This test helps you find certain types of drive failures that a read test won't find. The write test doesn't write to every data area on your drive; that would take an enormous amount of time. It simply checks a few unused areas of the drive. Some types of system and hidden file damage can't be repaired easily. You can check this option if you think that a section of your drive contains such damage and you don't want to risk making the problem worse by "fixing" it. In most cases, though, you leave this check box unchecked because ScanDisk can handle the vast majority of hard-drive errors.

Figure 2.20.
Use the Surface Scan Options dialog box to modify the way ScanDisk performs a thorough test of your hard drive.

Clicking the Advanced button at the bottom of the ScanDisk dialog box displays the ScanDisk Advanced Options dialog box shown in Figure 2.21. Most of these options are self-explanatory. I usually keep the Display Summary radio button set to Only If Errors Found so that I can check all my drives at once. If ScanDisk doesn't find any errors, it checks all the drives without disturbing me. Using this option means that I can run ScanDisk unattended in most cases.

Figure 2.21.
The ScanDisk Advanced Options dialog box contains some user interface and other automatic settings.

Clicking the Backup Now button of the Drive Properties dialog box opens the standard Backup utility described in Chapter 10. Because I discuss this utility in detail elsewhere, I won't describe it here. The Defragment Now button starts the Disk Defragmenter utility. I also describe this utility in detail in Chapter 10, so I don't discuss it here.

On to the third page of the Drive Properties dialog box—Sharing (see Figure 2.22). You normally see this page with systems that use a fully supported peer-to-peer network. This dialog box allows you to share resources with another machine. Turning on the Not Shared radio button prevents other people from looking at your drive. If you turn on the Shared As radio button, Windows 95 enables the other fields and buttons displayed here. The first field, Share Name, tells other machines what name to use when they access your drive. The second field, Comment, is a plain-language description of the drive that other users see.

Figure 2.22.

The Sharing page of the Drive Properties dialog box allows you to share resources with other machines.

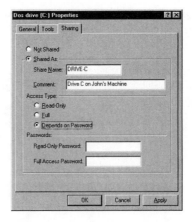

Note: Some people won't see the Sharing page because they don't have a network installed. This page appears only under specific conditions when you're using certain types of networks.

Tip: It's never a good idea to give someone more access to your machine than they need. Remember that you can provide access to individual files and folders. In most cases, you want to reserve drive-level access to common data drives on a server rather than the entire drive on a workstation. You can always give someone more access if he needs it. Taking back access after someone compromises your network is meaningless because the damage is already done.

After you decide on a name for your share, you need to determine what kind of access to it other people will have. In some cases, read-only access is all that the other person will need. This means that a person can see the file and read it but can't modify it in any way. (Of course, he can copy the file to his drive and modify it there.) You can use this option for drives with informational databases that you want the other person to use but not modify. Full access allows the other person to read from and write to your drive. This is the level of access most people require if you want to share data with them. A third possibility allows you to determine the level of access the other person gets to your system by the password he enters. This option provides the most secure access and flexibility. The two fields below these radio buttons are enabled if you select the appropriate access option. You can type any standard password to grant access to your machine to a select group of people.

Peter's Principle: Disk Access and Workgroup Activities

There are two schools of thought about the way a workgroup should use the Windows 95 security features to enforce a specific way of modifying files. I find that they're both good, but for different reasons and in different circumstances.

The first method is to allow the people in the group read-only access to the master files on the leader's disk. This allows them to copy the file and make any required changes on their local drive. It also preserves the integrity of the master copy. Once a person finishes his edit, he moves the file to a temporary directory on the leader's drive. You can also create a home directory for each person and have them place the modified files there. The leader can then choose which additions and comments to incorporate into the master document. If you use a common temporary directory, each person should change the file extension or some part of the filename to include a distinctive signature. This prevents their files from accidentally overwriting the modified files that other people submit.

The second method allows full access to the master document. Each member of the group uses the revision marks feature provided by the application to make changes to the document in his designated color. The advantage to this method is that everyone gets to discuss the document online in an interactive fashion. The group leader doesn't have to schedule a specific meeting to modify the document; changes are made on an ongoing basis. Of course, to implement this method, your application must support a revision marks feature that uses a different color of text for each member's modifications.

When you allow other people access to a drive on your machine, Windows 95 adds a hand to the drive icon. This visual signal appears wherever the drive icon appears but it doesn't tell you what level of access the drive provides. (For more information about sharing access across a network, see Chapter 27.)

Control Panel

I was surprised to see how many different ways that you can access the Control Panel or its components under Windows 95. Even Explorer provides a method of access, as shown in Figure 2.23.

Figure 2.23.
*You can access
Control Panel or its
components from
many places in
Windows 95,
including Explorer.*

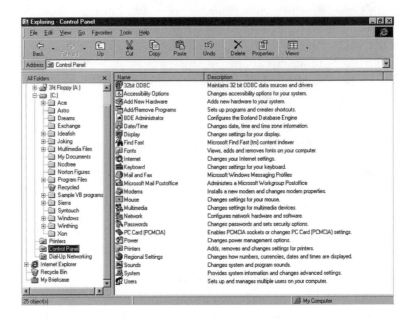

The number and types of icons (now called applets) you find here vary with the applications and
equipment you installed. Items such as the Printer folder always appear in your Control Panel. On
the other hand, you won't always see an ODBC folder or some of the other specialty items that Control
Panel provides.

Looking Ahead: I don't examine the individual Control Panel applets here. Chapter 11,
"The Windows 95 Applets," provides a full description of all the applets and what they
mean to you as a user and takes a look at some of the ways you can manipulate the
Windows 95 Control Panel.

Printers

As with just about everything else, you can control your printers from Explorer by accessing the
Printer folder. It usually appears right above the Control Panel folder in the system hierarchy. Chapter
16, "Fonts and Printing," explores the process of adding a new printer.

Looking Ahead: Chapter 16 covers all the details of managing your printers. It also discusses the process of adding a new printer to your system. The second half of the chapter explains the details of using fonts to dress up your output.

Dial-Up Networking

Dial-Up Networking allows you to connect to another machine. The Dial-Up Networking folder appears under the Control Panel folder if you installed the service. This folder, like the Printers folder, contains two types of icons. The first provides access to a wizard for creating new connections. The second type is the actual connections.

Looking Ahead: I take another look at Dial-Up Networking in several places. Chapter 19, "Mobile Computing: Notebooks, Telecommuting, and Remote Access," shows you how to use this feature of Windows 95.

Using the Dial-Up Networking client is easy. You double-click a connection to open it. The program dials the phone and tries to make a connection to the host for you. Right-clicking and selecting Properties displays the Properties dialog box, which allows you to change the connection information and other things.

Network Neighborhood

Think of Network Neighborhood as a dynamic extension of Explorer for a network. When you're connected to a network, the My Computer icon is replaced by the Entire Network icon. No longer are you looking at the local machine; you see all the resources that you can access on the network as a whole.

Note: Novell Client 32 handles Network Neighborhood entries differently from its Microsoft NDS client counterpart. I cover Novell Client 32 differences in the section "Using Novell Client 32" in Chapter 27, "Networks." Fortunately, the idea behind using the entries is the same, so you can still follow along in this section and learn what Network Neighborhood can do for you.

You might also see other entries at the same level as the Entire Network. These are machines that you can access on peer-to-peer networks. You can always access your own resources, so you always see your machine listed here.

You need to know a few interesting things about Network Neighborhood that make it different from the rest of Explorer. For one thing, you can't access the properties for the Entire Network. The Entire Network is simply a placeholder for Network Neighborhood; it doesn't exist as a concrete object.

Recycle Bin

The Recycle Bin works the same in Explorer as it does on the desktop. You can drop things into it, examine its contents, empty it, or restore a file that it holds to its original (or another) location. The Explorer copy of the Recycle Bin comes in handy if you see a file that you want to erase and the desktop copy is covered by another application.

> **Tip:** Files in the Recycle Bin continue to take up space on the drive. Windows 95 moves deleted files to the Recycle Bin—a special folder—until you erase them for good. (The short filenames or old DOS filenames are changed to allow multiple files of the same name in the Recycle Bin.) If you find that you're short on hard-drive space, you might want to see whether there's anything in the Recycle Bin you can get rid of.

In most cases, your bin won't contain anything. Files in the Recycle Bin look just like files anywhere else. You can move objects in the Recycle Bin to other areas of Explorer to "unerase" them. Until you do unerase them, the Properties dialog box won't tell you much except the file's name and the date you deleted it.

Briefcase

The Briefcase is one of the best Windows 95 features for mobile users. It allows you to pack everything you need for a project into one folder and then move that folder around, just like the briefcase you carry to and from work.

> **Looking Ahead:** Chapter 19 takes a look at how you can use Briefcase. You might want to read through this material even if you aren't a mobile computer user because I discuss a few techniques for using Briefcase that everyone will want to know.

Briefcase adds one option to the context menu of items it holds. The Update option allows you to update a file from its original copy on your hard drive. This is one of the steps you need to take before packing your briefcase to go on the road. I cover this topic in greater depth in Chapter 19.

The Startup Folder

Think of the Startup folder as a sort of AUTOEXEC.BAT file for your Windows applications. Windows automatically looks in this file during the boot process and launches anything it finds there. Chapter 6 covers start-up shortcuts in more detail.

Peter's Principle: Getting a Great Start in the Morning

A lot of people are under the impression that the Startup folder is only for loading applications. Other people feel that you should place only certain classes of applications there, such as screen savers. Although putting your screen saver in the Startup folder is a good idea, using the Startup folder for this purpose alone doesn't really make full use of this resource.

Placing a shortcut to the Startup folder on your desktop is a great idea because you can put things in there that you need the next morning. (Microsoft buried this folder so far in the directory tree that you'll quickly tire of using it if you don't take this step.) For example, if I'm working on a proposal over the course of a few days, I stick a shortcut to the master file in Startup. That way, it automatically opens when I start my machine the next day.

Adding objects to the Startup folder can really boost your productivity. Instead of spending the first 15 minutes of the morning getting set up, you can start your machine, get a cup of coffee, and be ready to work when you return. Making Windows 95 more efficient is largely up to the user now. Most of the tools are there; all you need to do is use them.

Standard Windows 95 Applications

Windows 95 has a lot more to offer than just Explorer. A whole new group of utility programs are available to make life a lot easier for the user. In the past, most of these applications were supplied by third parties, but today you get them as part of the operating system package.

The next few sections highlight these new utility programs. I take a close look at them in future chapters, but the information that follows should provide you with what you need to get started.

Looking Ahead: The following sections provide highlights of the utilities. Most appear in other, product-specific areas of this book. Visit Chapter 11 to find out more about all the Windows 95 applets.

Remote Access

There are two tools you can use for remote access. The first is Dial-Up Networking. Dial-Up Networking allows you to connect to another computer much as you do with any peer-to-peer connection. The second utility is Direct Cable Connection. It allows the client machine to access the host machine's drives and other resources. I find that I normally use it to move data from my notebook computer to the desktop machine. There are no controls to worry about with this application; just run the host and then connect to it using the client.

Tip: Always use a parallel connection if at all possible when using the Direct Cable Connection utility. Doing so greatly increases throughput. You can at least triple the amount of information moved per second by using a parallel cable. A machine-to-machine parallel cable might prove a little difficult to find. If so, you can modify a standard 25-pin serial cable by adding a gender changer to each end. Most electronics stores carry both serial cables and gender changers. The one advantage to this approach is that you can use the same cable for both serial and parallel connections.

Accessories

Windows 95 provides a lot of small utility programs that are grouped into the general category of accessories. Essentially, they dress up Windows 95 by adding some of the tools required to access common hardware. For example, the multimedia tools allow you to access your sound board. The multimedia offerings consist of a multimedia player (media player), (sound) recorder, mixer (volume control), and CD player.

ActiveMovie Control

The easiest way to look at the ActiveMovie Control is as a replacement for the Media Player utility, but that really doesn't cover the intended use for this utility program. There are three different applications that you can use to play multimedia files on your machine; each has a different strength. Chapter 15, "Exploiting Multimedia and Games," explains the ActiveMovie Control in more detail.

Tip: The ActiveMovie Control isn't limited to video files; you can also use it to play audio and filter graph files. Unfortunately, you have to either open the ActiveMovie control manually (using the Start menu entry) or pass the filenames on the command line to get it to play non-video file types. You could also change the file associations for audio files to use the ActiveMovie Control instead of the Sound Recorder for a more permanent setup. I show you how to do this in Chapter 15.

Tip: Tests on several machines and conversations with other users showed that most video files play fine in full-screen mode on a 200MHz Pentium machine with at least 16MB of RAM. If you've got a lower-speed machine, you want to use something other than full-screen mode in most cases.

Imaging

Imaging is a graphics manipulation program. You really can't draw with it (there's a set of tools designed to annotate images), but you can use it for a variety of other purposes such as scanning images. You can also use it for viewing existing graphics and preparing documents for fax or e-mail transmission.

Looking Ahead: The TV Viewer application lets you watch TV on your computer. In Chapter 18, "Video Configurations," I give more details about the TV Viewer.

Beta Release

On Your Own

You'll find that the latest version of Windows 95, when combined with the IE 4 features, provides more Internet access than ever before. In fact, saying that you'll have the Internet at your fingertips seems too pale when you consider the features Windows 95 provides. Try the various features discussed in this chapter to subscribe to an Internet site of your choice. Explore the channel feature as well. Make sure you understand how it can help you find things on the Internet quickly.

Explorer is one of the cornerstones of the Windows 95 interface. It allows you to move around your machine—and the network, for that matter. Spend some time getting used to the interface and trying the various display modes. Click the column headings in the Detail view to see how Explorer rearranges the filenames.

Taskbar toolbars are another feature that can make life easier for any Windows 95 user. Try creating at least one toolbar and using it for a week. If you're not happy with the way the toolbar turned out, tweak it to make it more efficient. You'll also want to try both toolbar types: folder-based and Web page.

Context menus are also an important part of Windows 95. Try right-clicking all the objects you see. See how the context menus vary from object to object. Don't forget that even the desktop is an object with a context menu. Make sure that you click the desktop to close its context menu without selecting anything.

3

Installing Windows 95: A Setup Primer

Peter Norton®

In today's world, software keeps gobbling up more hard drive space and memory. Because programs are getting more complicated, technical support problems can multiply if the user is bombarded by too many options during a program's installation.

Fortunately, Windows 95 simplified software installation. Unlike MS-DOS and even many of the previous versions of Windows, Windows 95 is fairly easy to install because it can detect most types of hardware automatically and decide what settings to use. Is Windows 95 perfect? No, you'll still find situations where you need to give it an assist, especially when using legacy or nonstandard hardware. To run Windows 95, you need the following equipment:

- Pentium processor: You can use one of the faster 80486 systems, but the performance you receive won't be all that useful, especially if you plan to use new Internet-related features of Windows 95. I wouldn't even consider using an 80386 machine, no matter what clock speed it is. Windows 95 requires too much processing power.

- 16MB memory minimum: I would really think about increasing your memory to 32MB to get the best performance, but a 16MB system will perform adequately.

- 100MB of free hard disk space: The Microsoft minimum of 50MB just isn't realistic unless you want to install a stripped version of Windows 95 with no room to run any applications.

- High-density 3 1/2-inch floppy drive: Everyone who installs Windows 95 should create an emergency boot disk. You need a high-density floppy to store the emergency files. Windows 95 can create this disk for you automatically during installation. You can also create or update the disk later from the Startup Disk page of the Add/Remove Programs Properties dialog box.

- SVGA (800×600) or higher display adapter: You can get by using a VGA display with Windows 95, but that doesn't really provide enough space to get any work done. If you have any plans to use the Internet features of Windows 95, you'll probably want to look at 1024×768 resolution as a minimum. Forget about using a 256-color display on the Internet as well. Some Web pages just don't render well using 256 colors. The minimum you should go for is 16-bit color (65,536 colors).

- Mouse (pointing device): Someone will tell you that you can work efficiently under Windows 95 using the keyboard. You can get around; there's no doubt about it. But a mouse makes Windows 95 so much more efficient that I can't understand why anyone would want to go without one.

- CD-ROM drive: Don't slow your system down by getting a slow CD-ROM drive. I'd suggest a 12X CD-ROM drive as a minimum. In fact, if you plan to use the CD-ROM a lot, make sure you get something a little faster such as one of the newer 24X drives on the market.

- Optional devices: You can also install any number of optional peripheral devices such as a modem, sound card, and graphics accelerator card to speed up your programs, especially games or other graphics-heavy applications such as computer-aided design.

The new installation used by Windows 95 is the best I've seen to date, but I still experienced a few problems during installation. Problems included hardware that was detected during one installation but not during another. Some of the worst failings of the installation routine in one way were the highlights in another. For example, during one installation I found it nearly impossible to get through the installation procedure and end up with the correct sound card installed in my machine.

Installing Windows 95

You might want to spend a little time preparing for your Windows 95 installation, especially if you want to maximize the capabilities you get to use or if you're planning on reversing the installation later. Of course, the first piece of preparation is to make a complete backup of each system before you start the installation. Backing out of a failed installation can prove to be quite a problem in some situations.

Peter's Principle: Boot Disks: The Cheap Form of Insurance

You just started an installation and it goes south for the winter. The machine is frozen and you can't get back to the DOS prompt. What do you do?

If you're like me, you stick your boot disk into the A drive and reboot the machine. I never start anything as involved as an operating system installation without making a boot disk first. (Chapter 10, "The Windows 95 File System," explains boot disks in more detail.) In fact, I usually make a boot disk for all my installations, even if I think the software will install without a hitch.

What does a boot disk contain? It has to contain the operating system; otherwise, you can't use it to boot the system. I usually include renamed copies of my CONFIG.SYS and AUTOEXEC.BAT files as well. You don't want to use the original files to boot the machine because they contain entries that you probably won't need. If I'm performing some type of Windows installation, I always include copies of my WIN.INI and SYSTEM.INI files as well. In fact, for shaky installations, I make a copy of all my .INI files on a separate disk. A copy of the Registry files USER.DAT and SYSTEM.DAT is handy too because an installation will usually cause problems with these files.

A boot disk really needs some utility programs. I usually include FDISK and FORMAT. DEBUG normally makes an appearance also. The disk has to include any files required to activate your disk compression, if the drive is compressed. A disk editor usually comes in handy, as does a small text editor. You'll probably want to include a disk-scanning program such as CHKDSK or its equivalent because a disk crash will require the services of such a diagnostic program.

Ideally you should also make a complete tape backup of your system. That way if it crashes, you can use your boot disk to start your machine and then restore the rest of the hard disk contents using your tape backup.

Tip: When you partition your hard drive, it's always a good idea to keep this principle in mind: Don't compress your boot drive. The reason is simple: You can't access a compressed drive easily in an emergency. Make sure your boot drive includes any files required to boot the machine in its normal configuration, a few utility programs, and some diagnostic aids. Compressing your boot drive is just another way to play Russian roulette. Somewhere along the line you'll shoot yourself, and it won't be in the foot.

Getting all the required equipment together to perform the installation is only the first step. You need to do other things before you perform the installation. The following sections give you the inside scoop on all the pre-installation steps you should take. Then you'll see several different installation methods.

Checking Your Hardware

Windows 95 automatically detects the vast majority of hardware out there including older hardware. However, the detection capabilities that Windows 95 currently provides are less than perfect, so you'll want to spend a little time checking your system hardware for potential problems.

Microsoft groups all Windows 95 auto-detection capabilities under Plug and Play. Even if your hardware isn't Plug and Play compatible, Windows 95 treats it as such for installation purposes. I look at Plug and Play from an installation perspective later in this chapter. Suffice it to say right now that Windows 95 won't do a perfect job of installing your hardware if you don't have a 100 percent Plug and Play–compatible machine.

Certain types of older hardware almost guarantee problems under Windows 95. It's pretty unlikely that you'll have any of this hardware on your machine, especially if you bought the machine within the last two years. If you have hardware with the following characteristics, you might want to take a second look at it before you install Windows 95. Of course, you can always try to install it, but I've run into more than my share of problems with these hardware types:

- Older disk controllers that don't provide their own BIOS: A lot of old MFM controllers fall into this category. Windows 95 depends on the contents of the peripheral BIOS as one of the means to detect it. Every vendor writes its company name (or at least someone else's name) into the BIOS. Looking for this company name is one way to determine who made the device.

- Machines that use a clone BIOS: Some older machines use what I call a "clone BIOS." These are the machines that boot with some strange logo from a company you've never heard of. A machine containing a BIOS from one of the mainstream companies, such as AMI or Phoenix, is almost always a better bet than a clone BIOS machine.

- Nonstandard peripheral devices: Standards evolve as users and companies gain knowledge about a particular area of technology. Unfortunate as it might seem, some of the hardware that appeared before the standard was introduced just isn't compatible with that standard.

- Peripherals that almost emulate something else: IBM and other vendors are to blame for this problem. They started placing their company name in the BIOS of some types of hardware. When someone used some piece of generic software developed by these companies, the first thing the software did is check the BIOS for the correct company name. Clone makers aren't stupid, so they started putting the IBM (or other) company name where needed in their BIOS chips too. That isn't a problem as long as the device in question completely emulates the hardware it replaces.

There's also some marginal hardware out there that you can fix after the initial installation is over. Sound boards are one big item that falls into this category. Windows 95 does a pretty good job of detecting them, considering that one sound board is designed to emulate the qualities of another. Just about every sound board claims some sort of SoundBlaster emulation mode. Trying to detect this hardware is a nightmare. In some cases, you must manually install the hardware later. You'll see the procedure for performing a manual installation later in this chapter.

A final potentially problematic hardware category is the older stuff that depends on a real-mode driver for support. I had an old Hitachi 1503S CD-ROM drive that fell into this category. Believe it or not, it worked just fine under Windows 95, even though I had to use real-mode drivers. The down side was that I couldn't seem to share it on the network and the stability and performance problems it introduced into the system weren't worth the effort of keeping it around. I finally replaced the drive with something a little less archaic and haven't looked back since.

Peter's Principle: Replacing Old Hardware to Save Money

Sometimes you'll actually save money right now by spending a little on new hardware. Whenever you choose to keep an old piece of hardware to save money but introduce some type of instability into your system as a result, you're actually wasting more money than you're saving.

Windows 95 provides an opportunity to rid your system of all the old hardware that makes it inefficient. Not only will you get your work done faster, but you'll also get it done with fewer problems. The hardware still works, so it's very difficult to give it up. However, doing so when you upgrade might mean you spend fewer hours trying to find those mysterious problems related to the real-mode drivers that the hardware requires to work.

Looking Ahead: Having a few pieces of older or incompatible hardware in your system is no reason to roll over and give up any idea of installing Windows 95. Chapter 30, "Hardware Problems," takes a detailed look at hardware-troubleshooting techniques—especially tough-to-install hardware. In some cases, you might find that Windows 95 even provides protected-mode drivers you can use with the old stuff.

To handle any potential problems with your hardware, make an inventory of what you have. Some hardware, such as sound boards, uses a real-mode driver that accepts configuration parameters as part of the device driver command line. If Windows supports the device, you can normally REM the driver out of CONFIG.SYS and AUTOEXEC.BAT before you start your Windows 95 installation. There are exceptions to this rule. You wouldn't want to get rid of any drivers needed for your CD-ROM drive or your hard drive controller. Any essential drivers should stay in place; any nonessential drivers should be REMed out.

Some hardware still uses jumpers for configuration purposes. The one big item that just about everyone will need to consider is NICs (network interface cards). NICs usually have one or more address settings and an IRQ setting. You need to write down the settings of any boards that use jumpers before you start your Windows 95 installation. This list will come in handy later as you resolve any IRQ or address conflicts that arise during installation.

When you get to this point, you have just about every piece of hardware information you need. There's one final piece of information that you should check for machines that use file compression. A few people say they had problems getting Windows 95 to work properly with their disk compression software. In most cases, it turned out to be some kind of interaction between the compression software, the drive controller, and Windows 95. Almost everyone will use their disk compression software without any problem under Windows 95. However, if you want to make absolutely certain that there aren't any problems, decompress the drive prior to installation and recompress it using Windows 95–specific disk compression software.

Getting Ready to Install

When you get to this point in the chapter, you should have created a boot disk and inventoried your hardware. You also should have removed many of the device drivers from CONFIG.SYS and AUTOEXEC.BAT. Before you begin the setup process, you might want to make a few additional changes to these two files. It might seem like a pain to preset your machine to provide the best possible environment for an operating system installation, but you really will get better results this way.

The first thing you'll want to do is REM out any unneeded TSRs from your AUTOEXEC.BAT. I even took out the little utility programs such as DOSKey. You'll also want to REM out ANSI.SYS (or a vendor-specific alternative) because you won't need it under Windows 95. If you use a real-mode network, disable it for the time being—at least as a server. Windows 95 has problems with some peer-to-peer real-mode network software when you install it with the server running. In addition, disable any drive mappings or Setup will run into problems while identifying your boot drive.

Tip: The Windows 95 Setup program will overwrite, delete, or replace some of the files in your DOS directory. If you have any intention of uninstalling Windows 95 later, it's a good idea to make a copy of this directory before you start the installation. That way, you can easily restore it later.

After you complete these final modifications, reboot your system. You should now have a completely clean environment in which to install Windows 95. One last check is a good idea: Use the MEM /C command to verify that memory is as clean as possible.

Take a look at some of the Setup command-line switches. They'll help you get around any problems you might experience while installing Windows 95. For example, some computers might freeze when Setup performs a disk scan, so you can use the /IQ or /IS switch to get around the problem. The following is a complete list of these switches. When you see something between angle brackets, it means that you have to supply a value of some kind. The description tells you what to provide. Don't type the angle brackets when you type the switch.

Warning: Using any of these command-line switches temporarily disables Setup from examining certain parts of your computer, such as available disk space. You might want to solve the problem first rather than rely on a command-line switch to get around the problem.

- /?: Use this switch to display a list of currently documented command-line switches.
- /D: The /D switch helps you get around situations in which one or more of your Windows 3.x or Windows for Workgroups 3.1x support files are missing or corrupted and Setup won't run properly. It tells Setup not to use the existing copy of Windows for the initial phase of the setup. As soon as the new Windows 95 support files get copied to your drive, Setup switches back to a Windows interface.
- /ID: Setup doesn't check for the required disk space when you use this switch. If your system is that short on hard disk space, you should consider clearing additional space before you try to install Windows 95.
- /IM: Sometimes Setup might freeze while checking your system's memory. This switch allows you to disable that check.
- /IN: You might not want the Setup program to set up your network immediately. If that's the case, then use this switch to start the installation without the network setup module.

- /IQ: Use this switch to bypass ScanDisk as the first step of the installation process when performing the installation from DOS. It's not a good idea to skip this step unless your system experiences some kind of problem running ScanDisk with Setup running. Be sure to do a separate scan of your drives if you use this switch.

- /IS: Use this switch to bypass ScanDisk as the first step of the installation process when performing the installation from Windows. It's not a good idea to skip this step unless your system experiences some kind of problem running ScanDisk with Setup running. Be sure to do a separate scan of your drives if you use this switch.

- /T:<Temporary Directory>: This switch allows you to tell Windows 95 which drive to use as a temporary directory. It usually tries to use the drive you're using for installation. However, if the drive you chose is a little short on space, you can use this switch to redirect installation-specific items to another drive.

Warning: Make absolutely certain that any temporary directory you select is empty. The Windows 95 Setup program erases the contents of any temporary directory that you select.

- <Batch>: This option allows you to use a MSBATCH.INF or other batch file that contains custom installation instructions.

Believe it or not, you're finally ready to install Windows 95. The very last thing you need to do before you start Setup is choose what type of installation you want. (My personal choice is the Custom Setup option because it gives you the most control over the final appearance of the installation.) You can perform four types of installations:

- Typical Setup: This is the default setup that Windows 95 provides. It allows you to install a standard set of options for your machine.

- Portable Setup: Use this setup if you're using a portable computer. It installs a minimal set of standard utility programs—the same set included with the Compact Setup option. This installation also includes all the special utilities that Windows 95 provides for portable computers, such as the Briefcase and Direct Cable Connection features.

- Compact Setup: This is the option to use if you're really tight on hard disk space. It installs only the bare essentials—perhaps a little too bare for many users. The nice thing about using this particular option is that you can get a minimal system started and then add other features as you need them.

- Custom Setup: The custom option provides the most flexibility of all the Setup options. It also requires the greatest amount of time to set up. This is the perfect option for those who already have a good idea of what they do and don't want out of Windows 95.

No matter which installation route you choose, you can always add or remove features later. A mistake right now doesn't mean that you have to start the installation from scratch later.

Installing Windows 95 from a CD-ROM

Installing Windows 95 from a CD-ROM is simple. All you need to do is start MS-DOS or Windows and run Setup. Microsoft suggests that you install Windows 95 over an existing copy of Windows 3.*x* so that you can retain your current program settings.

> **Note:** You need to retain any drivers and TSRs required to access your CD-ROM drive in the MS-DOS startup files to install Windows 95 from a CD. This usually includes a CD device driver in CONFIG.SYS and an MSCDEX entry in AUTOEXEC.BAT. Remember to REM out any unneeded drivers once the Windows 95 installation is complete.

Make sure you have your hard drive partitioned and formatted before you start this procedure. In most cases, your drive will come that way from the manufacturer. If you can boot off the drive, then it's ready to go. The following steps walk you through the installation procedure:

1. Type **Setup** at the Run (or MS-DOS) prompt and press Enter. You should see a display similar to the one in Figure 3.1.

Figure 3.1.
The initial Windows 95 screen starts as most Microsoft installation programs do.

2. Click Continue (or press Enter at the MS-DOS prompt). Setup displays a dialog saying that it's scanning your drive.
3. Click Continue. If Setup finds other applications running, a dialog box appears, telling you to exit them. When it gets past this point, Setup displays a message saying that it's installing the Windows 95 Setup wizard. When the Setup wizard installation is complete, Setup displays a licensing agreement and asks you to agree to the terms of the licensing agreement. If you decide that you don't like the terms, Setup exits.
4. Signal your agreement to the licensing terms by selecting the "I accept the agreement" radio button and then clicking Next. Setup displays a dialog asking you where you want to install Windows 95. It offers C:\WINDOWS as a default setting, which is what you should use unless you have a good reason to install Windows 95 elsewhere. If you install Windows 95 in a different directory, you will have to reinstall all your older Windows applications to run under Windows 95.

5. Click Next to accept the default location of `c:\WINDOWS`. The Setup wizard starts preparing the directory where you intend to install Windows. This means copying various files and performing a few setups. Once the installation files are copied to the hard drive, you see a Setup Options dialog.

6. Select one of the four installation types. These options are discussed in the preceding section. Most users should select either the Typical or Custom installation type.

7. After you select an installation type, click Next to get to the User Information dialog. This is where you enter your user information.

8. Type your name and company name (if applicable). Click Next. If you're using any of the setups other than Custom, you see the Windows Components dialog. This dialog gives you an opportunity to choose something other than the default components for a specific installation type. For example, you might want to use the Portable installation but add or remove a feature. (If you're using the Custom Setup option, skip to step 10.)

9. Choose whether you want to add or remove features. Click Next. If you want all the standard features, then skip to step 12.

10. At this point, you see the Select Components dialog. Choose one or more Windows 95 features from the list and then click Next.

11. At this point, the Setup wizard begins copying files to the hard drive. Once it completes the copying process, you may see the Identification dialog if your computer is connected to a network. This dialog contains a description of the computer (usually a location or the name of the person who normally uses it), your computer's network name, and the name of the workgroup you belong to. Each of the computers on the network must have a unique computer name, but all computers that belong to the same workgroup must have the same workgroup name.

12. Type your computer's name, workgroup name, and a description. Click Next and you see the Computer Settings dialog. This is where you define the common elements of your computer. For example, you tell Windows 95 what language you prefer to use and the type of keyboard you have. You won't tell it specifics such as the brand of display adapter you have; that part of the setup comes later.

13. Check through the list of computer settings and change any that don't match your computer. Be sure to check the User Interface setting. This is where you choose between the Windows 95 and Windows 3.x interface.

14. Once you verify that all the computer settings are correct, click Next. You see the Startup Disk dialog shown in Figure 3.2.

Figure 3.2.
Creating an emergency startup disk is an important part of the installation process.

Warning: Some people might not want to create an emergency startup disk because they don't have a floppy handy or they see it as a waste of time. Creating an emergency startup disk is essential because it represents the only way of recovering from some types of fatal system errors. Make absolutely certain that you don't skip this step.

15. Insert a floppy into your floppy drive, and then click Next. The Setup wizard begins the process of creating an emergency startup disk. After the Setup wizard gets all the information together, it displays an Insert Disk dialog.

16. Click OK to start copying the emergency startup disk data from your computer to the floppy. The Setup wizard initializes the floppy and then copies the emergency startup disk information to it. Once the Setup wizard completes the emergency startup disk, it displays a dialog telling you to remove the floppy from the drive.

17. Remove the emergency startup disk from the floppy drive and label it. Click OK to clear the message dialog. You should see a Start Copying Files dialog. Now you're finally ready to install Windows 95 to the hard drive.

18. Click Next. The Setup wizard copies all the required files to the hard drive. This might take quite a while, depending on what features you want to install. Once the files are copied, the Setup wizard reboots the machine. At this point, the Setup wizard goes through a hardware detection process. Once the hardware detection process is complete, the computer reboots again. (You may, in fact, go through several reboots.) The Setup wizard performs some system configuration and then displays the Date/Time Properties dialog. This is where you set up the time zone for your computer.

Note: Once all of the hardware setup is complete, the Setup wizard reboots one last time. At this point, you might get one or more network messages. You have to read the message and decide whether there is an actual problem. For example, you might get a message

continues

saying Windows 95 couldn't find a DHCP server. If your network doesn't have a DHCP server, then getting this message isn't a problem. Ask your network administrator for more information as needed.

19. Choose the time zone for your location. Windows 95 normally defaults to the Pacific time zone, but there are time zones for every area of the world. Click Close to complete the time setting process. The Setup wizard continues setting up various Windows 95 elements. It eventually displays the Inbox Setup Wizard dialog. I've already covered the procedure for working with the Inbox Setup Wizard dialog in the section "Using Dial-Up Networking" in Chapter 1, "Opening Windows to the Internet with Internet Explorer 4." Refer to that discussion if you want to configure your Inbox right now.

Tip: Now might be a good time to check your computer's time setting. Simply choose the Date & Time tab of the Date/Time Properties dialog. You see a clock that represents system time. Change the time to reflect the actual time.

20. Configure your Inbox using the procedures in Chapter 1 or click Cancel. You see the Add Printer Wizard dialog. I cover the procedure for adding a printer to your machine in the section "Installing a Printer" in Chapter 16, "Fonts and Printing."

21. Use the procedure in Chapter 16 to add a printer to your machine or click Cancel if you don't want to add one right now. At this point, you see a Restart Computer dialog. The Setup wizard reboots the computer. Windows 95 starts running once the computer reboots.

It's important to realize that while you have the operating system up and running, you still have more installation tasks to perform. For one thing, you might see the Add New Hardware wizard when you restart your machine. The section "Installing Hardware" in Chapter 14, "Exploiting Your Hardware," will help you through the process of using the Add New Hardware wizard.

Installing Windows 95 from a Server

A server installation can differ from the CD-ROM version in quite few ways. If the network administrator chooses to provide a lot of automation, the entire installation process might not require any interaction from you at all. On the other hand, if the network administrator chooses not to provide any automation at all, you see the same thing you did for the CD-ROM installation in the preceding section. Reality will probably fit somewhere between these two extremes. Make sure you contact your network administrator for details before attempting to install Windows 95 from a server.

Plug and Play Installation Tips

Windows 95 does a fairly good job of detecting non–Plug and Play hardware, even when it gets mixed with Plug and Play–compatible hardware. All the configuration information for the hardware that Windows 95 supports is stored on the hard disk. In fact, if you look in the `\WINDOWS\INF` directory, you see some of these files (they all have an `.INF` extension). Besides storing the required configuration information on disk, Windows 95 gives older hardware first choice of ports and interrupts. This allows older hardware to work most of the time.

Problems start to arise when the system doesn't or can't recognize one or more components in your system, causing some people to refer to Windows 95's hardware detection as "Plug and Pray." Usually, the unrecognized hardware refuses to work properly, if at all. The second this happens, Windows 95 has the unfortunate tendency of either going to pieces or ignoring the problem. Unrecognized hardware falls into two categories. The first consists of the difficult-to-recognize piece of hardware emulates something else so well that the computer has a hard time telling exactly what it is. The second category is older hardware that lacks Windows 95–specific drivers.

Now that you have some idea of what the problem is, take a quick look at ways you can fix it. This list isn't exhaustive, but it'll help you with the majority of the problems you're likely to encounter:

- Avoid interrupt and port address conflicts whenever possible. This is probably the number one reason that Windows 95 fails to recognize the board. If two devices use the same address, there's no way that Windows 95 can test for the presence of the second board.

- Plug all your older boards into the slots next to the power supply whenever possible. The BIOS checks the slots in order during POST. Placing these older boards first, followed by the Plug and Play boards, ensures that the BIOS sees the older ones first.

- Try different board configurations to see whether Windows 95 recognizes one of them. Sometimes the INF files that Windows 95 uses to check for the older boards contain only the default board settings. A good rule of thumb is to first try the best setting and then try the default setting if that doesn't work.

- Check the INF files to see whether they contain all the settings for your boards. There's an INF directory directly below the main Windows 95 directory. It contains ASCII text files that Windows 95 uses to search for these older boards. Modifying these files is a tricky proposition, but it could help Windows 95 find the peripherals in your machine.

Looking Ahead: If you didn't find a technique that helped you here, look at Chapter 30.

Installation with Real-Mode Drivers Intact

Some devices—especially those that rely on software configuration instead of jumpers—don't provide enough information for autodetection until you turn them on. Normally, this means that the user must install any required real-mode drivers in CONFIG.SYS. These drivers perform the setups required to make the device visible to Windows 95. The following procedure helps Windows 95 "discover" these hidden boards in most cases:

1. After you install these drivers, reboot the machine. When Windows 95 starts, use the Start | Settings | Control Panel command to open the Control Panel.

2. Double-click the Add New Hardware icon. You should see the dialog box shown in Figure 3.3.

Figure 3.3.
The Add New Hardware Wizard allows you to install new hardware with a minimum of effort.

3. Click the Next button. Don't worry if the screen blanks during this process; Windows has to check for display adapters too, which is the reason for the blank screen.

4. Wait until Windows completes the detection process. The detection dialog performs a check of your hardware using the INF files that I talked about previously. It takes a lot longer to check your hardware this way, but the check is a lot more thorough and your chances of finding what you need are greater.

5. Select Yes, and then click Next. Click Next a second time to start the detection process. Windows displays a indicator showing the detection progress. Once it completes the detection process, Windows tells you whether it actually detected any new hardware.

Note: The hardware detection phase can take quite a while—especially on older machines. But if disk activity stops for more than five minutes, it's a pretty safe bet that the machine is frozen. As long as you hear disk activity during this phase, you can assume that hardware detection is still taking place. (The hardware detection indicator doesn't move at a steady pace; it appears to take more time as it nears the end.)

6. Click the Details button to see if the hardware you were looking for actually was detected.

7. Click the Finish button to complete the installation process. Windows 95 might ask you to supply some setting information if this is a non–Plug and Play device. In most cases, it provides default settings that match your current real-mode setup. Windows 95 copies all the required drivers to disk. It also displays some messages about the new hardware it found and perhaps a "driver database building" message. In some cases, Windows 95 asks you to reboot when you complete this step. Even if it doesn't ask you to reboot, you must do so to make this procedure work properly. The real-mode drivers that you installed to aid in detection destabilize the system if you leave them in place.

8. Be sure to remove the real-mode drivers from CONFIG.SYS before you shut down and reboot the machine. If Windows 95 didn't detect the new hardware, remove the real-mode drivers from CONFIG.SYS, shut down and reboot the system, and then perform the manual installation procedure in the next section.

Manual Installation

It always seems to come down to the same old procedure. You finally get everything working using the automated procedures, except that old CD-ROM drive or an especially difficult sound card. Sometimes you have to help Windows 95 install an older device in your machine. Usually, something else you installed—probably a Plug and Play device—is using some resource that the older device needs. The following example shows how to install a CD-ROM drive; the same principles apply to any manual installation. However, let me warn you ahead of time that simply installing the device might not make it work. You might have to perform some troubleshooting to get this older device to work (see Chapter 30). At the very least, you may have to shuffle some IRQ and address settings around.

1. Use the Start | Settings | Control Panel command to open the Control Panel. Double-click the Add New Hardware icon. You should see the dialog box shown in Figure 3.3.

2. Click the Next button. You see a dialog saying that Windows is going to check for any Plug and Play hardware on your machine. Don't worry if the screen blanks during this process; Windows has to check for display adapters too, which is the reason for the blank screen.

3. Wait until Windows completes the detection process. The detection dialog performs a check of your hardware using the INF files that I talked about previously. At this point, I'm assuming that you tried the automatic installation procedure in the previous section and it didn't work.

4. Click the No radio button and then click Next. Highlight the CD-ROM Controllers entry of the Hardware Types field and then click the Next button. You should see the dialog box shown in Figure 3.4. The manufacturers and models lists in this dialog box allow you to scroll with ease through the list of devices supported by Windows 95. If the device installed on the current machine doesn't appear in the list, the dialog box also affords you the opportunity to use a third-party disk. This dialog box appears every time you select a device from the previous dialog box. The manufacturer list changes to match the selected device type.

Figure 3.4.

Use the lists in this dialog box to scroll through devices supported by Windows 95.

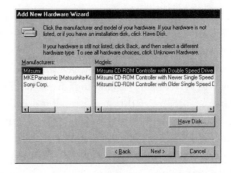

5. Normally, you select the device connected to your machine. In this case, however, select Sony Corp. in the Manufacturers field, leave the default device highlighted, and click the Next button. You see a dialog describing the process for installing your new hardware.

6. Click the Details button. Windows 95 displays a dialog box containing the interrupt and address settings for this particular device, as shown in Figure 3.5. Windows 95 chooses a device setting based on all available information; it chooses the best setting that won't interfere with other devices in the system (if possible).

Figure 3.5.

Windows 95 always tells the user what interrupts and addresses it uses for the devices it installs.

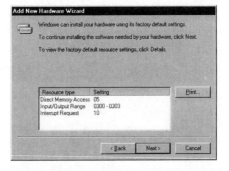

Tip: A special "Unknown hardware" device type allows you to view all the devices supported by Windows 95 on one screen. This comes in handy for two purposes. First, Microsoft doesn't always place devices in the category where you expect them to be. Searching through this list provides one final check if you don't find a device where you expect to see it. Second, you can use this list to choose a device that Windows 95 will definitely support. I'm not saying other products are incompatible—just that these products received a little more attention than some of the others you might find.

7. Clicking the Next button again installs the device drivers required for this device. Normally, you take this action. Windows 95 might prompt you for a disk if the driver didn't

appear on the hard drive and the appropriate disk didn't appear in the CD-ROM drive. It displays a dialog box showing the progress of the file copy process. However, because you don't want to install this particular device, click the Cancel button. Windows 95 exits the Hardware Installation wizard without installing the new device.

Adding Your Own Devices

Now that you have Windows 95 installed, take a look in your \WINDOWS\INF directory and you see a new type of file there. The INF file is part of the database of information that Windows 95 uses to recognize hardware that isn't Plug and Play compatible. These files contain a description of the hardware—the same type of information that the Plug and Play BIOS normally provides when Windows 95 scans it.

As good as these INF files are, there might be times when you want to modify them. For example, what if you have a piece of hardware that provides interrupt and port address settings in addition to those found in the INF file? Modifying the INF file to reflect these additional capabilities could help you install a piece of hardware in some cases.

Take a look at some of the general characteristics that every INF file shares. You might find all or only some of these sections in the file; it really depends on what kind of hardware the INF file is trying to define. An INF file needs to contain only the information required to fully define the characteristics of the hardware. For example, a display adapter needs to define the resolutions that it supports. A multiscanning monitor, such as the NEC MultiSync series, needs to define the precise frequency ranges that it supports. This includes the refresh rate, an important specification for the new ergonomic display adapters. Table 3.1 shows these generic sections and tells you what they mean. You might even want to open one of the INF files and see whether you can identify each section. (Just make certain that you don't save the file or change its contents in any way.)

Table 3.1. INF file generic sections.

Heading	Description
Version	This section provides version-specific information such as the operating system, vendor name, and the device class supported by the INF file. It also provides the name of the general setup file. The general setup file contains the definitions common to all the devices of that type. You might see some additional entries in this section. One special entry allows the vendor to link a new INF file into the list of files for a specific device type. Never change the contents of this section.

continues

Table 3.1. continued

Heading	Description
Manufacturer	The Manufacturer section contains a list of all the manufacturers for devices of this class. Not every INF file contains this section. For example, this section appears in the `MONITOR.INF` file but not in the `MSPORTS.INF` file. The only time you need to change this section is when you want to add a new vendor. The list might seem incomplete if there's more than one INF file required to describe a specific class of device. There are four monitor files, and each one contains only the vendors that appear in that particular file. You need to check all the INF files for a particular device class before you resort to adding a new vendor. Make sure that you add the new vendor in alphabetical order in the correct INF file (you see an example later in this chapter). There's a subsection after this one that provides specifics about each device supported by that vendor. If the vendor already appears in the manufacturer list, adding a new device consists of adding an entry here, in the Install section, and in the Strings section.
Install	This is the most important section of the file. It describes all the characteristics of the hardware and the device drivers needed to activate it. It also contains macro commands that perform the installation of support in the Registry. Follow the example of other entries in this section when adding a new device. When modifying an existing entry, change only physical characteristics such as port address and interrupt.
Miscellaneous Control	A vendor can use this section to describe how a device works with the Windows 95 interface. If you see this section, you need to use other entries as an example for creating your own entries. Most INF files don't contain this section.
Strings	Later in this chapter, you learn how to add a new device to Windows 95 by using the Add New Hardware dialog box. When you use this dialog box, you see some descriptive strings that tell you about the hardware. This is the section that contains those user-friendly strings. It identifies the device in human-readable form.

I won't go through the actual process of modifying an INF file here because it's unlikely that you'll ever need to do it. However, you should do a few things before you modify one:

- Always make a copy of the original INF file. This way you can copy it back to your hard disk if you need to.

- Use the other entries in the file as a guideline for your new entries. Windows 95 performs a strict interpretation of the contents of the INF file. Adding your own "enhancements" to what seems like an inadequate entry might make the INF file unusable. Remember, some of the INF file entries appear in one or more generic files that appear in the Version section of the file.

- Follow punctuation marks, spelling, and capitalization carefully when making a new entry. Windows 95 is extremely sensitive when it comes to how you format the entries in an INF file.

- Never change the Version section of the file. Yes, it's tempting to fiddle with what looks like an interesting file section, but don't do it in this case.

- Make your entries to an existing file. You might be tempted to create your own unique INF file. Don't do it! Always add new devices to existing files. That way you can be absolutely sure that your entries look like the other entries in the file.

Warning: Always make a backup before modifying the original copy of an INF file. Place the copy in a backup directory, using a different extension from the original file. Your modified version of the original file must appear in the INF directory for Windows 95 to recognize it. Keeping a copy of the original version in a temporary directory allows you to restore the file later.

Installing Windows 95 over an Existing Windows Installation

For the most part, installing Windows 95 over an existing Windows installation is the same as installing it on a new machine. There are two ways in which this type of installation differs. First, the installation program displays a dialog that allows you to back up your current installation before proceeding with the installation. Make sure you exercise this option. Sure, it takes quite a bit of hard drive space to do so, but you'll have an opportunity to uninstall the operating system later should you need to do so.

The second way in which it differs is that you see fewer configuration screens. The order in which the software gets installed is the same, but some of the screens I mention in the installation section of this chapter won't appear. The reason is simple: Windows 95 automatically detects which options you installed for the previous version of Windows. It assumes that you want to install the same options in this version as well.

> **Tip:** Some people have complained that the latest Windows installation program might actually be a little too automatic. You can always use the Add/Remove Programs applet in the Control Panel to customize your setup after installation. For the most part, the automation that Windows 95 provides is a welcome change from what we got in the past.

Uninstalling Windows 95

As of this writing, Microsoft hasn't decided to include an uninstall feature with Windows 95. You can install it on your system, but you won't get it back off very easily—that is, unless you took my advice earlier in this chapter.

It wasn't too difficult to figure out that there wasn't going to be an easy way to get rid of Windows 95 once I installed it if it overwrote all my system files and changed quite a few others. Even if I did manage to get my old operating system to boot, I'd have to spend a lot of time reinstalling applications.

There is an easier way. The following procedure assumes that you did three things. First, it assumes that you made a boot disk like the one I mentioned at the beginning of this chapter. Second, it assumes that you made a copy of your MS-DOS directory. Finally, it assumes that you installed Windows 95 in a new, unused directory. If you didn't follow one of those three steps, you won't have the resources to put your system back together:

1. The first step in this process is to get DOS to boot again. Use your boot disk to reboot your machine from the floppy. (Make sure you shut down Windows 95 properly first.)

2. Use the SYS command to restore the system files. Then, copy COMMAND.COM and an original copy of AUTOEXEC.BAT and CONFIG.SYS from your floppy to the hard drive.

3. Copy the contents of the DOS directory backup that you made to the DOS directory.

4. Take the floppy out of the drive and reboot your system. You should now get to a DOS prompt.

5. Carefully erase all the Windows 95–specific files. Make absolutely certain that you look for all the hidden files that Microsoft thoughtfully stored in your root directory. You can find them by using the DIR /AH /S command. The /AH switch displays every file with a hidden attribute. The /S command tells DIR to look in any subdirectories as well as the root directory. Don't erase any DOS-specific files such as IO.SYS and MSDOS.SYS. The date stamp on the file should give you a clue about which files belong to DOS and which ones belong to Windows 95. If in doubt, leave the file in place rather than remove it and make your system nonoperational. It's going to take a little effort to find all the entries. In fact, this is where a good disk editor comes into play.

6. Reboot your machine one more time to make sure everything works correctly.

That's it. This isn't the fanciest uninstall method in the world, but it works. You'll probably find bits and pieces of Windows 95 lying around on your system for a few weeks. If you were careful when you installed it, the pieces should appear in the root directory of all your drives. Of course, the first directory you erase is the \WINDOWS directory. Make sure you get all the Recycle Bin directories (one on each drive) and the program directory that contained Microsoft Network and other accessory applications.

On Your Own

Create your own boot disk that contains the items I mentioned earlier in this chapter. Be sure to test it before you install Windows 95. You'll also want to create a Windows 95–specific startup disk during installation. Label both disks and keep them until you're certain that your Windows 95 installation is stable. When it's stable, create a new startup disk, using the Startup Disk page of the Add/Remove Programs Properties dialog box.

Make a list of all the equipment you think you might have problems with. Include all the items for which Windows 95 doesn't provide entries in the existing INF files. Do you see any entries that you can fix by using the procedures provided in this chapter? Are there any ways to eliminate some of the real-mode drivers that you might need to use to keep older equipment running? Develop a comprehensive strategy for handling any problem areas before you begin the installation process.

4

Working with the Active Desktop

Peter Norton®

I predict that the Active Desktop will be the most misunderstood part of the Internet Explorer 4-enhanced Windows 95 interface. Just as people are learning to use the features provided by the regular Windows 95 interface, Microsoft decides to add yet more features and an Internet connection besides. Except for the Registry and networking (neither of which are interface elements), more people wrote messages concerning the desktop than anything else that I saw on various Internet newsgroups. Active Desktop questions headed the list of things where people really need help—especially when it comes to channels. Adding Internet Explorer 4 into the mix only complicates matters. (Refer to Chapter 1, "Opening Windows to the Internet with Internet Explorer 4," and Chapter 2, "Introducing Windows 95: What Else Is New?," for an overview of this new product.) Now you have two interfaces to choose from: Explorer (Windows 95) and Internet Explorer 4. Even with all this complexity, one fact is still clear: It's up to you to dress up the desktop of the evolving Windows 95 interface.

Note: You aren't even limited to the standard interface selections. Microsoft provides an updated version of Program Manager for die-hard Windows 3.1 fans. In addition, there are any number of Windows 95 shells available on the market. For that matter, you can choose to run a specific application instead of using Explorer by changing the `Shell=` statement in `SYSTEM.INI`. There are limits to what you can choose to use in place of Explorer because any limitations in the shell you choose translate into lost capability within the Windows 95 environment.

I cover some aspects of the new Internet Explorer interface in this chapter. Refer to Chapters 1 and 2 for an overview of Internet Explorer 4. Chapter 22, "Browsing the Internet with Internet Explorer," fills you in on the details specific to Internet Explorer. This chapter also covers the standard Windows 95 Explorer interface.

Once you figure out how Explorer can help you, giving your desktop a face you can really use becomes a much simpler matter.

The following sections help you see how to use the new Internet Explorer interface features. You'll also see how you can make the Windows 95 desktop and Explorer work together to create an environment that truly reflects the way that you work. It might take a little time for you to adjust to this new level of freedom, but once you do, you'll find that you work more efficiently, and you'll never view Windows the same way again.

Tip: A fully optimized Explorer interface contains all the objects you normally work with, including such things as backup files. Unless Windows 95 knows how to work with a particular object, you might find yourself fighting against Windows 95 instead of working with it. Optimizing Explorer is your first real step in optimizing Windows 95 from the user perspective.

Using the Active Desktop

So far you've taken a quick look at what you can do with Active Desktop, but I really haven't shown you how to use this new feature to your benefit. What happens now that you can also fill the desktop with additional information from the Internet? I can see that some people will have a real problem dealing with the temptation to clutter the desktop to the point that it's unusable. The following points should help you keep the clutter to a minimum.

- Avoid excess. When using Active Desktop, it's important to decide what you need and don't need. I find that determining the contents of my desktop by frequency of access keeps things uncluttered and makes me more efficient. If you find yourself visiting the same Web site each day, then it really does pay to place it on your desktop. Likewise, that folder containing all the data for your current project really does belong on the desktop, where you can access it with ease.

- Consolidate as necessary. There are some people who work on so many different projects at the same time and need access to so many sources of information that trying to keep their desktop uncluttered might seem like a losing proposition. There is a way to avoid part of the problem. Simply consolidate what you need into folders. For example, you might have four or five folders sitting on your desktop right now containing the information required for one project. Consolidating all of that information into one master folder will make life easier.

- Use a Taskbar toolbar. You can save a great deal of space on your Desktop and make it easier to access your projects in the process. All you need to do is create a toolbar for the Taskbar and point it to a local or network directory. Here's an added bonus for people in a workgroup. I cover the process for creating toolbars in the section "Creating Your Own Toolbars" later in this chapter. If the Taskbar becomes crowded, add a shortcut to the project folder to your Start menu. It's not quite as efficient as a Taskbar toolbar or a folder on your desktop, but it's space efficient and much faster than browsing through Explorer windows to access the folder.

- Decide on an efficient configuration. There are a few ways to make your desktop more efficient without giving up the convenience of having your work lying all over the place. One way to do it is reduce the size of the icons. Open the Display Properties dialog by right-clicking the desktop and choosing Properties from the context menu. Select the Appearance tab and then Icon in the Item field. Notice that you can change the icon size from the default of 32 to something as small as 16. Needless to say, this makes the icon a tad more difficult to see, but you can fit roughly twice as many on your desktop.

- Choose Web or Standard view. The Web view is extremely efficient from one perspective; it takes only one click to do just about anything. You can get from point A to point B with about half the clicks, which translates into more efficient time use. However, I find the

Web view slightly inefficient at using desktop space wisely. The icons take up more space and the underlined text requires more space as well. In the long run, you need to decide between efficient use of space and efficient methods of getting to where you need to go.

- Create channels that make sense. Windows 95 comes configured with some really nice channels if you have a wide variety of interests. Unfortunately, I don't know of anyone who has interests in all the areas that the default channel setup provides. You definitely want to optimize your channel setup so that you can quickly find things that interest you. One of the benefits of doing this is that you might be able to reduce the amount of space currently required by the Internet Explorer Channel bar on the Active Desktop.

- Minimize your Web pages. In most cases, you don't need to see the entire Web page you frequent. A small view is normally sufficient until you actually need the information that the Web page contains. I reduce the size of the Web page so that it takes up the minimum Active Desktop space available, but I can still see any changes that might occur as Windows 95 automatically updates the page content for me. You can always resize the Web page later to get a full view of the content it provides.

Once you look at these Active Desktop–specific ways of tuning your machine, it's time to look at the more generic Explorer methods in the sections that follow. You want to balance these Explorer tips with the ones I just covered. After all, you don't want to get rid of the bonuses the Active Desktop provides. The Internet is in everyone's future; make sure you integrate the Internet into your work environment now so that you really know how to get the most out of it.

Customizing Your Desktop

Windows 95 doesn't force you to do things its way as previous versions of Windows did. Someone at Microsoft must have followed Burger King's lead by allowing people to have it their way. The Explorer interface is so flexible that I doubt any two people will ever have the same desktop under Windows again. The desktop is one place where anything goes. The Windows 95 desktop is an object just like everything else in Windows 95.

The Windows 95 desktop has some features that you might not think about right away. For example, you can right-click the desktop. It has a context menu, just like everything else in Windows 95. I won't go into detail about the contents of the context menu right now; all that information appears in the section "Working with Desktop Objects" later in this chapter. Suffice it to say that there are plenty of nice surprises when it comes to arranging things under Windows 95.

Two entries I want to briefly mention are Arrange Icons and Line up Icons. Arrange Icons allows you to rearrange your desktop in a specific order. It works just like the same entry under Explorer. (Do you see how everything seems to have a bit of Explorer in it?) You can rearrange your icons by name, type, size, or date. Personally, I find the type and name orders the most convenient.

Some people detest all the standard arrangements so they just stick the icons in the order they want them. If you're one of these people, you might find that the Line up Icons option is custom tailored for you. It allows you to keep the icons in the order you want them but rearranges them into neat rows and columns. This option provides a grid effect that allows you to keep your desktop neat yet arranged in the order that you want to see it.

The following sections look at the desktop as a whole. They are meant as a guide to things you can do to make your desktop more usable, but I probably won't stop there. Think of this section as the most common tricks that people use to optimize their Windows 95 environment. This is the "must do" check list you should follow when getting the most out of your setup.

Taskbar

A major part of the Windows 95 interface is the Taskbar. This is the horizontal bar at the bottom of display. The Taskbar is the central control area for most of the things you do under Windows 95. It contains three major elements: a Start Menu, a Task List, and a Settings Area. You might also see one or more toolbars.

Before giving you a full description of each of the major elements, I want to show you a few ways you can configure the Taskbar itself. The Taskbar starts out at the bottom of the display, but you don't have to leave it there. With Windows 95, you can always change your desktop to suit your needs. For example, you can grab the Taskbar with the mouse pointer and drag it to the right side of the display. Windows 95 lets you place the Taskbar on any of the four sides.

Like the other objects under Windows 95, the Taskbar also provides a Properties dialog box. (Simply right-click the Taskbar and select the Properties option to display it.) This dialog box has two pages. One controls the Start menu setup, and the other controls the Taskbar itself. The four settings on the Taskbar tab enable you to change how it reacts. For example, you can remove the Taskbar from view by removing the check mark from the Always on Top field. The Show Clock field enables you to clear more space for applications on the Taskbar by removing the clock from view. My personal favorite is the Auto Hide field. When you select this option, the Taskbar appears as a thin gray line at the bottom of the display. As soon as the tip of the mouse cursor touches it, the Taskbar resumes its normal size. This enables you to minimize the Taskbar to clear space for application windows yet keep it handy for when you need it.

Right-clicking the Taskbar displays a few other object-specific options. All of them affect the way Windows 95 organizes the applications that currently display on the Taskbar.

- Toolbars: If you have Internet Explorer 4 installed, you see this option, which enables you to add and remove toolbars on the Taskbar. Toolbars are sets of buttons like the ones you find under the menu bar in Explorer and Internet Explorer. The buttons in a toolbar let you launch programs and open folders. Toolbars on the Taskbar are a new feature that arrived with the advent of Internet Explorer 4. I cover how to use toolbars in a moment.

- Cascade Windows: When you select this option, all the application windows are resized to the same size. Windows 95 arranges them diagonally, much like the display you normally see in a spreadsheet when opening more than one file. You can select any application out of the entire list by clicking its title bar (the area at the top of the application window that contains the application's name).

- Tile Windows Horizontally or Tile Windows Vertically: Use either of these options if you want to see the window areas of all your applications at once. Windows 95 uses every available inch of desktop space to place the applications side by side. Each application receives about the same amount of space.

- Minimize All Windows: If you ever arrive at the point where your screen is so cluttered that you can't tell what's opened and what's not, use this option to clean up the mess. The Minimize All Windows option minimizes every application you have running on the Desktop.

The Start Menu

The Start menu normally appears on the far-left side of the Taskbar. It contains a complete listing of all your applications, access to some system settings, and a few other things thrown in for good measure. Figure 4.1 shows how the Start menu looks. Notice that it has nine main entries. The following list describes each entry in detail.

Figure 4.1.
The Start menu replaces Program Manager as the means to start applications installed on your machine.

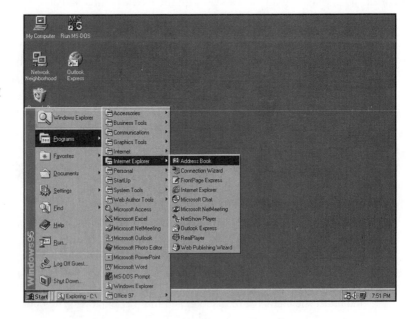

- Programs: This is the list of applications installed on your machine. Unlike Windows 3.*x*, the Explorer interface enables you to place folders within folders (programmers call this *nesting*). As Figure 4.1 shows, you can place applications several levels deep within the menu tree.

- Favorites: Here's where the Internet orientation of Windows 95 with Internet Explorer 4 is coming into play again. The original Windows 95 didn't include this entry. The Favorites entry allows you to access your favorite Web sites by using a couple of clicks rather than by opening a browser first. You use it just as you do the Favorites folder in Internet Explorer.

- Documents: Use this option to select a document you previously opened using Explorer. This list doesn't store the names of documents you open using your application's File | Open command. The list can contain up to 15 document names.

- Settings: Windows 95 provides you with a number of ways to change your environment. The Settings menu is just one centralized location for this information. It provides access to Control Panel, the Printers configuration dialog box, and the Taskbar configuration dialog box, among others.

- Find: This option opens the same dialog box you see when you use the Tools | Find command within Explorer. It enables you to find any file on your hard drive or on a network drive using a variety of search criteria. You can select a file by name, location, or modification date. The Advanced tab of this dialog box even enables you to look for a file based on its contents or size.

- Help: The Help option opens the main Windows 95 help file. You can use this file to search for information you need to run Windows 95.

- Run: Remember the File | Run command under Program Manager? You can still use it under Windows 95. The Run menu option opens a dialog box that enables you to start an application by typing its path and name, and you can also include any appropriate parameters.

- Log Off *User Name*: Sometimes you might be sharing a machine between two or more people. It hardly pays to shut down the machine just to switch users. The Log Off option allows one user to log off and another to log on.

- Suspend: This option isn't shown in Figure 4.1. In fact, the only time you normally see it is on a laptop computer that supports this feature. (A few desktop computers have similar power-saving features and include the Suspend option as well.) The Suspend option allows you to shut down the computer without actually leaving Windows. It's a productivity option that allows you to stop and start your work quickly without wasting power. The next time you power up your computer, you return to Windows exactly the way you left it. There are two potential problems with this particular feature. First, it circumvents the security provided by the initial logon screen. Anyone who starts the machine is logged in under your name and has the same access rights that you do. The second potential problem is that any applications or files that are open when you suspend Windows remain that way.

The potential for data damage is greatly increased when you suspend rather than shut down the machine.

- Shut Down: This option enables you to perform an orderly shutdown of Windows 95. This includes things such as making sure that all the data writes to disk and that the Registry information gets saved. You can use this option to power off at the end of a work session or to reboot the computer into either Windows or MS-DOS modes.

The Taskbar Buttons

The Taskbar proper contains one icon for each application currently running on the machine. This group of buttons replaces the Task Manager found in Windows 3.x. Instead of using the Alt+Tab key combination to switch from application to application, you can now choose an application much as you select a television station using a remote control. All you need to do is click the appropriate button.

> **Tip:** The convenience of the Windows 95 Taskbar buttons for switching between applications means you won't use it as much as you used to, but the Alt+Tab key combination is still around. Just press Alt+Tab to switch from the current application to the next most recently used application. You can also press and hold Alt while you tap the Tab key to open a dialog box displaying icons for each of the running applications. Just tap the Tab key until the application you want is highlighted and then release the Alt key to close the dialog box and bring the selected application window to the foreground.

You should be aware of a few features. For one thing, the buttons shrink in size as needed to accommodate all the running applications. You can increase the size of the Taskbar to hold two, three, or even more rows of buttons if you so desire. Placing the mouse cursor near the edge of the Taskbar produces the same double arrow that you use to resize other objects under Windows 95. Of course, there's a limit to the size the buttons can attain.

Another feature is the capability to obtain more information about the application by simply placing the mouse cursor over its button. After a few seconds, Windows 95 displays a long title for the application and the foreground data file (provided the application is "made for Windows 95" and supplies that information). The same principle holds true for other items on the Taskbar. For example, holding the mouse cursor over the time indicator shows today's date. In some cases, the information you receive is minimal; for example, the Volume icon displays a single word—Volume.

The Settings Area

The Settings area (also called the system tray) of the Taskbar usually contains two or more icons. Normally these icons are hardware related, but there isn't any reason that they couldn't be an application or a utility program. Each icon can serve multiple purposes depending on what piece of hardware it's supposed to control. The two most common entries in this area are the Clock and Volume icons. In the preceding section, I explained how each of them reacts when you position the mouse cursor over their respective icons.

The Volume icon does a couple things depending on the action you take. A single-click produces a master volume slider. You can use this to adjust the volume of all sounds produced by the soundboard. Double-clicking the same icon displays the Volume Control dialog box, which provides detailed control of each input to your sound board. It also includes a master volume slider. Right-clicking the icon displays the context menu. In this case, it displays only two entries. The first takes you to the Volume Control dialog box; the second displays the Audio Properties dialog box.

A double-click on the Clock icon displays the Date/Time Properties dialog box. A right-click shows the context menu. Detailed information about the clock appears later in this chapter.

Note: Several other interesting icons can appear in the Settings area. One of them enables international users to adjust their settings with ease. A special icon for PCMCIA-equipped machines displays the current bus status and the type of card plugged into the bus. Portable users will appreciate the battery indicator that appears in this area. With a quick click of the mouse, you can check your battery status before it becomes critical. If you see a plug in place of the normal battery indicator, you know that the laptop is plugged into the wall socket.

Using the Standard Toolbars

Installing Internet Explorer 4 causes numerous changes to the Windows 95 interface. Some are big changes, such as the capability to view your desktop as a Web page. Other changes, such as adding toolbars to the Taskbar, appear more subtle. However, appearances can be deceiving. Adding toolbars—sets of buttons that can open folders or launch applications—to the Taskbar's complement of Start menu, regular program buttons, and System Area is not a subtle change at all. Because toolbars give you a whole new way to launch programs and open folders, this new feature's effect on how you work can be anything but subtle.

The normal Internet Explorer 4 installation automatically adds the Quick Launch toolbar to your Taskbar. In Figure 4.2, the Quick Launch toolbar appears near the left end of the Taskbar, between the Start button and the program buttons.

If you look carefully, you notice a small vertical gray bar at the left end of the toolbar. This is a handle that allows you to rearrange the size and position of the toolbars on the Taskbar. If you let the mouse pointer rest on the handle for a few seconds, the pointer changes to a double-headed arrow and you can drag the toolbar to make it larger or smaller or to change its position on the Taskbar. The Start button and the system area anchor the two ends of Taskbar, but you can rearrange the order and size of the toolbars that appear in between (including the program buttons, which now occupy a toolbar of their own).

Figure 4.2.

The Quick Launch toolbar appears near the left end of the Taskbar, between the Start button and the program buttons.

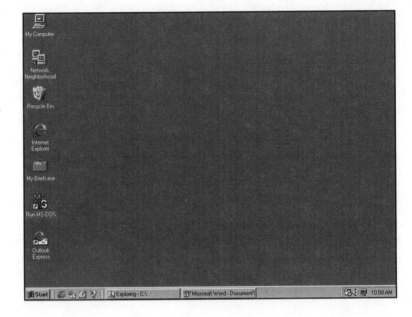

If there's not enough room on the Taskbar for all the buttons of a toolbar, small arrowheads appear at the ends of the toolbar to enable you to scroll through the toolbar's buttons.

> **Tip:** Toolbars are great additions to the Taskbar, but they can quickly overwhelm the limited screen real estate occupied by the Taskbar. Enlarging the Taskbar to display two rows of buttons helps, but even that expanded space gets crowded when you use too many toolbars at once. I usually stick with one, or at most two, toolbars in addition to the program buttons.

Adding a Standard Toolbar to the Taskbar

Once the toolbar feature is active, you always have at least one toolbar installed on your Taskbar. The toolbar containing the program buttons is a permanent fixture of the Taskbar. You can't remove it, but you can resize and rearrange it like other toolbars. In addition to the program button toolbar, you can choose to display any combination of four standard toolbars plus new toolbars you create yourself.

Adding one of the standard toolbars to your Taskbar is simplicity itself. You just right-click the Taskbar (not on a program button) to open the Taskbar's context menu, choose Toolbars, and then choose one of the four standard toolbars from the cascading menu that appears. A check mark beside a toolbar name in the menu indicates a toolbar that is already active. Choosing one of the unchecked toolbar names causes Windows to add that toolbar to your Taskbar immediately. You can choose from the following standard toolbars:

- Address: This toolbar places an Address box, like the one typically found in Web browsers for entering URLs, on your Taskbar. The Address toolbar serves the same purpose as the Address box in Internet Explorer or Windows Explorer. You type in an address—a filename, a folder, or a URL—and Windows launches the appropriate program and opens the address. If you type a local or network folder, Windows opens a standard Explorer window displaying its contents. If you type a Web address, Windows opens an Internet Explorer window and attempts to load the address. If you type a filename, Windows opens the document in the appropriate application. In addition, the Address toolbar is a drop-down-list box giving you easy access to previously used addresses.

- Links: You're probably familiar with the Quick Links toolbar in Internet Explorer with its list of buttons that provide quick one-click access to a handful of Web sites. Well, you can have the same toolbar of links on your Taskbar as well. I find this toolbar to be the least useful of the bunch, but you might want to use it if you visit the same Web sites daily. You can customize the links that appear on the Links toolbar by changing their counterparts in Internet Explorer. I'll show you how to do that in Chapter 22.

- Desktop: The Desktop toolbar consists of a button for each object (My Computer, Recycle Bin, shortcuts, and so on) on your desktop. This can be a handy way to get access to desktop objects that are hidden behind several open application windows.

- Quick Launch: The four buttons of the Quick Launch toolbar enable you to launch Internet Explorer, launch Outlook Express, show your desktop (minimize all open windows), or view channels (assuming that you enabled Active Desktop).

Tip: You can add buttons to the Quick Launch toolbar by simply dragging shortcut icons from the desktop or an Explorer window and dropping them on the toolbar.

Windows adds the toolbar to your Taskbar and resizes any existing toolbars to make room. After adding a toolbar to your Taskbar, you'll probably want to adjust the size and position of all the toolbars because Windows doesn't do a very good job on its own.

Creating Your Own Toolbars

If none of the standard toolbars meets your needs, you can create your own custom toolbar. Just as you can use the desktop toolbar to display the contents of your desktop folder as buttons in a toolbar, you can add any folder to your Taskbar as a custom toolbar. Windows displays the contents of the folder as buttons in a toolbar and clicking those buttons has the same effect as selecting and opening the objects in the folder.

You can use any folder or Internet address to create a custom toolbar. For example, you might want to create a toolbar from a project folder you're working in. That way, the documents in the folder are available from the Taskbar, without your searching through Explorer windows.

Tip: The only problem with creating a toolbar from a project folder is that there are likely to be files and documents in the folder that you don't need or want to appear as buttons in the toolbar. Scrolling through a lot of superfluous buttons to find the one you need can offset much of the speed advantage of having the buttons available on the Taskbar in the first place. As a result, when I need a custom toolbar, I usually create a special folder to use for the toolbar and populate it with selected shortcut icons. This gives me more control over the buttons that are in the toolbar than using the contents of one of my project folders as a toolbar.

Once you identify a folder that you want to use as a toolbar, adding the toolbar to your Taskbar is easy. Just right-click the Taskbar and choose Toolbars | New Toolbar to open the New Toolbar dialog box, as shown in Figure 4.3. Select a folder from the list or type an Internet address into the text box and then click OK. Windows creates a toolbar with buttons for each object in the folder and adds it to your Taskbar.

Figure 4.3.
Just select a folder and Windows makes a toolbar out of it.

Tip: A quick way to create a custom toolbar and add it to your Taskbar is to just drag a folder icon from an Explorer window and drop it on the Taskbar.

Getting Rid of a Toolbar You Don't Need

Sooner or later, you'll need to get rid of a toolbar that you no longer need on your Taskbar. Although you can't delete the program buttons from your Taskbar, you can remove any of the standard toolbars and any custom toolbars that you have added. Perhaps the most obvious technique for removing toolbars is to repeat the same process you used to add standard toolbars: Right-click the Taskbar, choose Toolbars from the context menu, and then click the toolbar you want to remove from the list of toolbars on the flyout menu. The technique I prefer is to right-click the toolbar I want to remove and choose Close from the context menu. The first time you use this technique, you have to confirm the action in the Confirm Toolbar Close dialog box, but a check box in the dialog box lets you elect to skip the confirmation dialog box in the future, which makes the Close command a little faster.

Your Password to Multiple Desktop Settings

What can you do if more than one person uses the same Windows 95 computer and each one wants to customize the system to his own taste and preferences? Never fear, Windows 95 has a solution. You can instruct Windows 95 to ask users to identify themselves at system startup using a simple logon dialog box that prompts for a user name and password. Then, Windows can display the desktop and other user interface components using the settings—called a User Profile—recorded for the user who logs on.

Oddly enough, you enable this feature by using the Password applet from Control Panel. Choose Start | Settings | Control Panel and then double-click the Passwords applet to open the Passwords dialog box. Click the User Profiles tab to display the options shown in Figure 4.4. Windows 95 allows you to select from two different desktop configuration methods. You can either force every user of a single machine to use the same desktop, or you can allow multiple desktop configurations. A single desktop is a lot easier to maintain, reduces training costs, and enhances security. However, multiple desktops provide much more flexibility and could make users happier and more efficient.

Figure 4.4.
A single desktop is easy to maintain, but multiple desktops are more flexible.

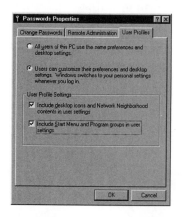

Once you decide to use multiple desktops, Windows 95 gives you two additional options that determine the level of flexibility this feature offers. The first check box in the User Profile Settings group allows the user to configure Desktop icons and Network Neighborhood. These user-specific settings are saved in that user's profile folder. The second check box allows the user to create a specialized Start menu and program groups. These settings also appear in that user's profile folder.

After you enable User Profiles, Windows 95 prompts you for a user name and password each time you start Windows. The first time you log on, you can create a new user name and password for yourself. Then you can customize your desktop while logged on under that user name. Other users can do the same using different user names. When you log on under your previously established user name, Windows displays your desktop using the settings linked to your user name.

Desktop Settings

Everyone looks at desktop settings in one way—as improving the appearance of their computer. A new piece of wallpaper or a change of colors can greatly affect the way you view your machine. Any positive change in attitude usually translates into improved efficiency. I find that changing my wallpaper and my display colors from time to time gives my computer that "new" feel that everyone needs occasionally.

Other reasons call for a change of configuration. For example, wallpaper, although attractive to the eye, chews up valuable memory. You might run into a situation where memory is at a premium. Giving up your wallpaper is one way to increase memory in order to complete a specific task.

Eyestrain is also a common problem among computer users. Somewhere along the way, you'll want to make your icons and text bigger to reduce eye fatigue. Changing your desktop settings to improve readability is a practical use of this feature.

Wallpaper

Wallpaper is one of those personal items that every computer user wants to customize. Windows 95 makes changing your wallpaper even easier than it was under Windows 3.1. Right-click the desktop and choose Properties. You should see the dialog box shown in Figure 4.5.

Figure 4.5.
*The Background page
of the Display
Properties dialog box
allows you to change
your wallpaper.*

This dialog box has two major sections. The first contains a monitor. Changing any of the wallpaper or pattern settings immediately affects the contents of this display. The monitor gives you a thumbnail sketch of how your background will appear.

The second section contains a listing of available patterns, bitmaps, and Web pages. The capability to display a Web page as your wallpaper is a new feature for Windows 95 with Internet Explorer 4 installed. Microsoft also reorganized the dialog so that one list contains everything you can display on the desktop. Previous versions of Windows provided one list for patterns and another for bitmaps.

As with previous versions of Windows, you can choose one of the existing patterns or create your own. To change a pattern, click the Pattern button to display a bitmap editor similar in function to those used by most paint programs.

> **Tip:** Patterns are a memory-efficient way to dress up a system. Because a pattern uses only two colors, it's a lot faster to draw and doesn't consume many system resources. If your system is short on memory but you want an interesting background, consider using patterns instead of wallpaper.

The Wallpaper listing defaults to the files found in your main Windows folder. Of course, you don't have to use these files. Click the Browse button if you want to look in other folders on your drive. To display wallpaper, center it on the background, the best choice for pictures, or tile it, the best choice for patterns.

Screen Saver

There's a healthy third-party market for screen savers. Some Windows users buy screen savers in bulk. You can find them in stores and on just about every BBS in existence. Unless you own an older monitor, using a screen saver probably isn't necessary, but it's fun. I own a *Star Trek* screen saver just for the "fun" element. A good Web site for all kinds of screen savers is `http://www.sirius.com/~ratloaf/` by Screensavers A to Z.

Windows 95 also provides a built-in screen saver feature, complete with an assortment of screen saver effects. Windows's own screen savers might not be as much fun as some of the screen savers on the market, but they do the job. You'll find them on the Screen Saver page of the Display Properties dialog box, shown in Figure 4.6.

Figure 4.6.
The Screen Saver page of the Desktop Properties dialog box allows you to change your screen saver and its settings.

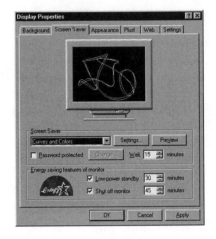

As with the Wallpaper selection, this dialog box contains a miniature view of your monitor. You can use it as a thumbnail sketch of what the display will look like when you configure the screen saver. The Screen Saver field allows you to choose one of the screen savers in the SYSTEM folder. If you decide to use a third-party screen saver that uses the Windows format, you need to place the file in the same directory as the others or Windows won't see it.

Once you select a screen saver, you can use the Settings button to change its settings. In most cases, the settings affect how Windows 95 displays the screen saver. For example, it might change the number of lines or the number of colors you see.

The Wait field allows you to change the number of minutes Windows 95 waits before it activates the screen saver. To turn off the screen saver, move the mouse cursor or press a key.

You can also password-protect your screen saver. This allows you to leave the room without any fear that someone will use your machine while you're gone because a password is required to turn off the screen saver once it comes on. I like the third-party screen savers that automatically restore their current condition even if you turn the machine off and reboot. Unfortunately, the Windows 95 screen saver doesn't provide this feature, so you can circumvent password protection by rebooting the machine. This does have the advantage of resetting the display so that no one knows what you were working on before he rebooted the machine. Some people might be thwarted if you also enable passwords on the opening Windows screen.

The final option, Preview, allows you to see what the display will look like when Windows 95 turns on the screen saver. I've used this as a quick way to hide my display when someone walks into my office and I don't want them to see what's on my display. It's a quick solution to a potential problem. Of course, you want to be careful around the mouse and keyboard if you use this method. Unless you enable the password option, your display clears if you bump the mouse or tap a key on the keyboard.

You'll notice that this page of the dialog box also contains an area where you can set up the energy-saving features of your monitor. The options in this area are available only if you have a monitor that supports energy-saving features.

How do you use the energy-efficient features? You might run the screen saver after 15 minutes of inactivity. You might set your monitor to go into low-power standby mode after 30 minutes. The screen goes blank and even the screen saver disappears, but the image returns immediately if you move the mouse or press a key on your keyboard. After 45 minutes of inactivity, you might want to turn your monitor off. That way, it won't waste power while you're at lunch or a long meeting. In fact, turning off the monitor will save the company a lot of money if you go to several meetings in a week. Even if you do shut off your monitor, you'll have the satisfaction of not needing to set up everything again when you return. Move the mouse, wait for the monitor to warm up again, and you're back to work. It's a lot faster than turning your machine completely off and starting everything from scratch.

Palette

The Appearance page of the Display Properties dialog box, shown in Figure 4.7, allows you to change the actual appearance of your windows, menus, and other desktop elements, not just the desktop background itself. All you need to do is click the picture of the display to select an item. (You can also select items from the Item drop-down list. In fact, there are a few items, such as Application Background, that you must manually select from the list because they don't appear in the picture.)

Figure 4.7.
You can change the colors and fonts used by your display with the settings on the Appearance page.

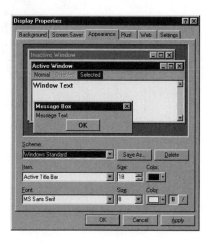

Windows 95 does provide a feature unavailable in Windows 3.x. The older versions of Windows enabled you to change the font used to display text only with a great amount of fiddling with the WIN.INI file. Windows 95 moves all this information into this dialog box and also gives you more flexibility. I have several configurations with "tired eye"–sized text settings. You can individually change the size of the menu and title bar text. Everything that has text also has a setting here for the font and type size.

Changing an entry consists of making list box selections. This dialog box has six of them. The first three affect the contents of the item itself and include the item name, size, and color. The size in this case is the size of the window or another display element. For example, you can change the width of a menu bar using this option. The second three control the text used within that display element. These settings include font style, size, and color. You can select any installed font as your display font, but most people find that the MS Serif or MS Sans Serif fonts work best on displays. They were specially designed for this purpose. I occasionally use Arial and find that it works quite well.

This dialog box also contains a list box for selecting from existing color schemes, a Delete button for removing the schemes you no longer want, and a Save As button for adding new schemes.

Resolution

The Settings page of the Display Properties dialog box, shown in Figure 4.8, allows you to change your display resolution, the number of colors, and the standard font with ease. Except for the system font setting, you can usually change the settings without rebooting your machine if you have a Plug and Play display adapter.

Figure 4.8.
You can change your display resolution using the controls on the Settings page.

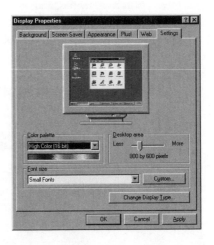

Windows 95 provides another feature you should check if the fonts provided by Microsoft don't quite fit the bill. You can click the Custom button beside the Font Size list box to display the dialog box shown in Figure 4.9. This dialog box enables you to create a custom-size system font. This is a very handy feature if you need a font that's either very large or very small. Normally, you want to use the standard sizes that come with Windows.

Figure 4.9.
Windows 95 enables
you to use custom
font sizes to optimize
your display's
appearance.

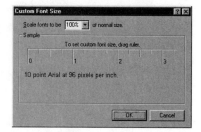

You can click another button, Change Display Type, to check the results of adding a new monitor to the system. I don't outline this particular part of this display settings here; I discuss the procedure for adding a new monitor or display adapter in Chapter 18, "Video Configurations."

System Setup

You can quickly access the System Properties dialog box from the Desktop by right-clicking My Computer and selecting the Properties option. I discuss this particular dialog box in detail in Chapter 5, "Performance Primer," so I won't go into its features now. You'll learn some ways to use this particular dialog box to assist in fixing software- and hardware-related problems in Chapter 29, "Software Problems," and Chapter 30, "Hardware Problems."

Clock

I took a quick look at the clock earlier when talking about the Taskbar. This clock affects the way the system reacts. You can actually use it to affect the CMOS setting and, therefore, the time stamp on all your files. Of course, it also affects any events you might schedule and anything else that relies on the clock.

The Clock properties consist of a single check box on the Taskbar Properties dialog box named Show Clock. The only thing this entry does is either display or not display the clock on the Taskbar. In most cases, you want to display the clock because there's nothing to be gained from shutting it off.

> **Tip:** When you display the clock, it shows only the current time. You can use the mouse cursor to also display the date. Move the mouse cursor over the Clock icon for a few seconds and the clock displays the current date.

Double-clicking the Clock icon displays the dialog box shown in Figure 4.10. This is the same dialog box you used during the installation process to set the clock. It contains a calendar and a clock. You use them to change the system settings.

Figure 4.10.
The Date/Time Properties dialog allows you to change the date and time displayed on your system.

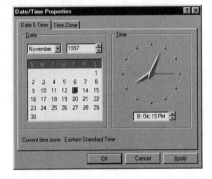

The second page of this dialog box, Time Zone, allows you to set your time zone (Eastern, Mountain, Pacific, and so on). Setting this dialog box is self-explanatory. The Daylight savings time check box allows the computer to automatically adjust the time for you.

Working with Desktop Objects

Making your desktop efficient is easy under Windows 95. The first thing you need to do is throw away those outdated application-centered ideas that Windows 3.x encouraged. The following sections provide some ideas on how to arrange your desktop to make maximum use of the new Windows data-centric approach. This is not the only way to pursue the problem, but it's the way that many people are starting to work with this new product. Try this approach and then modify it to meet your needs.

I start by looking at the methods of moving data around. Remember that Windows 95 uses objects. Everything is an object of some sort, and objects are easy to copy, cut, and paste. You can move them around just like any object in the physical world. Once I'm finished looking at data movement techniques, I review some methods to organize that data on your desktop.

Making Copies

Many people use cutting and pasting to move data around. You cut the data from the place where you no longer need it and then paste it to a new location. Windows 95 also supports cut and paste for objects. To move a file from one location to another, cut and then paste it. The beauty of this approach is that the copy of the file is now on the clipboard. This means that you can make as many copies of it as you want. Of course, anything you can cut, you can copy. Copying the object means that you leave the original in place and create copies where needed. One of the handy features of Windows 95 is that the copy, cut, and paste commands are conveniently located on the context menu for just about every imaginable object.

Obviously you can't paste a file on top of another file. You can, however, paste a copy of a file on the desktop or within a folder. If you take a logical, real-world approach to moving objects under Windows 95, you never run into problems getting objects to work.

Creating New Objects

Everywhere you can paste an existing object, you can also create a new object. The desktop, Explorer, and most Windows 95 folders have a New option on the context menu. This menu option displays a list of file types that Windows 95 can produce automatically.

Notice that one of the entries is a folder. You can always place a folder within another object normally used for storage (even another folder). Using folders helps you organize your data into more efficient units. You'll see later how you can combine these elements to make your desktop an efficient place to work.

Using a Template

One of the problems with the New submenu of the context menu is that it always creates objects of a default type. Take Word for Windows. If you create a new Word for Windows object using the selection on the context menu, that new object uses the Normal style sheet. What you really want is the Accounts style sheet, but there isn't a fast way to create a document using the current system.

I got around this problem by placing a folder named Templates on my desktop. Inside are copies of each of the sample files that I use to create new documents. For example, if you write a lot of letters that use the same format, you might want to use your word processor to create a document that contains everything that normally appears in a letter. You then place a copy of the letter template in your Templates folder, and every time you need to write another letter, right-click the template in your Templates folder and drag the template to a new destination such as a project folder. When the context menu appears, select Copy to create a copy of your template. This template approach to creating new documents can greatly reduce the time you need to start a task. You can create enough copies of a template to satisfy project needs in a few seconds. Using the template also means that all your settings are correct when you enter the document for the first time.

There are several ways you can use a template document. You can right-click, select Copy, right-click your project folder, and select Paste from the context menu. Another method is to drag the template with the mouse key depressed. When Windows asks what you want to do, select Copy from the menu.

Creating Work Areas

Now that you have some idea of how to move and copy data, look at a more efficient way to work with it. I've started using a new method of organizing information because of the way that Windows 95 works. You can follow several easy steps to start a project:

1. Create a main project folder on the desktop.

2. Open the folder and place one folder inside for each type of data that you plan to work with. For example, when writing this chapter, I created one folder for the word-processed document, another for the electronic research information, and a third for the graphics files.

3. Open the first data folder, create a copy of your template, and then make as many copies as you need of that template within the data folder.

4. Rename the data files to match what they will contain.

5. Close this data folder and repeat steps 3 and 4 for each of your other data folders.

6. Complete your project by filling each data folder.

Tip: Using a particular method of creating new data files for all your data might not work because of the way the application is designed. In other cases, as with the screen shots in this book, the data file creates in a different way. My screen shots are all captured from a display buffer. I don't need to create a blank file to hold them because the screen capture program does this for me. Always use the data creation technique that works best with the applications you use.

Figure 4.11 shows one way to arrange your projects. It contains a main folder, a few data folders, and some notes about the project. This is still only one approach to managing your data. The trick is to find the method that works best for you—one that reflects the way in which you work.

Figure 4.11.
One way to arrange your data for easy access. Windows 95 provides almost unlimited possibilities.

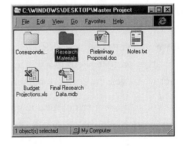

By now, you're wondering why you should go this route. After all, the old method of managing your data seemed to provide just about the same results as the method I've outlined. This new technique offers several advantages that you just can't obtain by using the application-centered approach:

- Data transmittal: Giving someone else access to a group project means sending him a folder, not a bunch of individual files. How often have you thought you had all the files for a project together, only to find you didn't send an important file? This method of organizing data prevents such problems.

- Application independence: It doesn't matter which application you need to use to modify a file. If everyone in your office uses the same applications, modifying a file means double-clicking it and nothing else. You no longer need to worry about which application to open or where that application is located. All that matters is the data.

- Location: Where is your data? Do you ever find yourself searching for hours to find that small file you thought you lost somewhere? This method enables you to place all the data relating to a project in one place. Its physical location no longer matters once the pieces are together. You still need to know, of course, where the data is when you organize the project folder. However, would you rather look for a file once or a hundred times? Using desktop folders means that you find the data once and never worry about it again.

- Ease of storage: When I finish a project under Windows 95, I don't worry about putting all the bits and pieces together. I send one folder to storage. When I need to work on the project again, I know I only need to load that one folder back onto my local drive.

Displaying Channels on the Desktop

I've already covered the fact that the collaboration between Windows 95 and Internet Explorer 4 enables you to display your desktop as a Web page and interact with desktop objects just as you do with elements on a Web page. Now, Web addresses and other Internet objects are just as much at home on your desktop as shortcuts to documents and folders on your local hard drive. It's not surprising that Microsoft decided to extend the desktop-as-window-to-the-Internet concept to encompass channels as well. I cover channels in detail in Chapter 23, "Webcasting: Channel Surfing When You're Offline." In the meantime, suffice it to say that when you choose Active Desktop, you are able to view channels on your desktop, just as you can in the Internet Explorer window. In fact, because channels normally appear full screen, they look and act the same whether you start from the desktop or from Internet Explorer 4.

To use channels from the desktop, you must first have Active Desktop active. Then, you need to display the channel selection bar so you can access the channels, just as you do from its counterpart in Internet Explorer. You enable both these options in the Display Properties dialog box. Right-click the desktop, choose Properties from the context menu to open the Display Properties dialog box, and then click the Web tab (see Figure 4.12). Make sure the View my Active Desktop as a

Web page option is checked. Then check the Internet Explorer Channel Bar option in the list box. Windows adds a box to the thumbnail representation of your display to represent the Channel bar. When you click the OK button, Windows adds the real thing to your desktop as shown in Figure 4.13.

Figure 4.12.
You can enable both Active Desktop and Internet Explorer Channel Bar in the Display Properties dialog box.

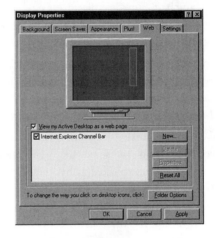

Figure 4.13.
The Channel Bar on the desktop works just like its counterpart in Internet Explorer.

Sprucing Up the Desktop with Microsoft Plus!

Microsoft Plus! is a collection of utility programs, games, and enhancements for the Windows 95 environment. Microsoft sells Plus! as a companion or add-on for Windows 95 because the components of the Plus! package require more processing power than the regular Windows 95 operating system. (Plus! requires a 486 or Pentium processor.) Originally, the centerpiece components of Plus! included Internet Explorer and utilities for disk compression and task scheduling. Those components have now been superseded by Internet Explorer 4 and OSR2, but Microsoft Plus! still enjoys the distinction of being the source of a great selection of wallpaper, sounds, desktop color schemes, and mouse pointers that you can use to customize your Windows 95 environment.

Desktop Themes

Desktop themes are complete, prepackaged desktop environments designed with a particular theme, or subject, in mind. Plus! gives you 12 desktop themes in addition to a Windows default. Six of the themes require a graphics card capable of high color (16-bit color). A graphics card capable of 256 colors (8-bit color) enables you to run the six 256-color themes and the Windows default.

A theme changes the entire look and sound of your desktop. (Yes, even sound, if you have a sound card.) Each theme has its own desktop wallpaper and icons, but it goes much further than that. Each theme also has a custom screen saver, sound events, mouse pointers, colors, font names and styles, and font and window sizes. Many of the pointers are animated, and all the screen savers have animation and sound.

If you feel that your creativity is stifled by prepackaged themes, never fear. You can mix and match elements from various themes. It takes a bit of work, but you can design and save your very own desktop theme.

Selecting a Theme

When you install Plus!, the setup routine asks you to select a desktop theme. If you want to change your desktop theme, select the Taskbar's Start menu, select Settings, select Control Panel, and then double-click the Desktop Themes icon. The Desktop Themes dialog box opens and shows what the current theme looks like.

You can select from the themes listed in the Theme drop-down list at the upper-left of the Desktop Themes dialog box. When you select a new theme, it's loaded into the preview window, as shown in Figure 4.14. The Sports theme is selected.

If you like what you see in the preview, click the OK button to apply this theme to your desktop and to close the Desktop Themes dialog box. If you prefer to keep the Desktop Themes dialog box open after you apply the theme, click the Apply button. Otherwise, try another theme, or if you decide that you don't want to change your desktop theme, click the Cancel button.

Figure 4.14.

Sports is selected in the Theme drop-down list. A preview of this theme is shown in the area below the Theme drop-down list.

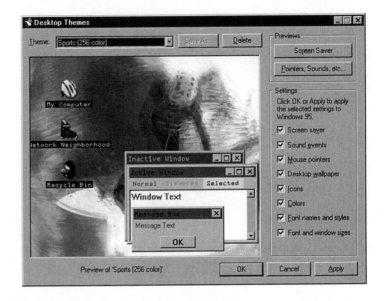

Customizing Desktop Themes

There are two ways you can create your own customized desktop theme. You can perform relatively minor adjustments to existing themes inside the Desktop Themes dialog box. For more ambitious customization jobs, you'll want to work with most of the tabs in the Display Properties dialog box and perhaps use the Desktop Themes dialog box to give your new desktop theme a name. Using either method, you can customize virtually every aspect of your desktop environment.

Note: To open the Display Properties dialog box, right-click the desktop and select Properties from the context menu.

Using the Desktop Themes Dialog Box

The desktop's current settings are always listed in the Desktop Themes dialog box as current Windows settings in the Theme drop-down list. After you select and apply a theme such as Dangerous Creatures to your desktop, all your settings reflect those specified by the Dangerous Creatures theme and are saved as the current Windows settings. You'll see in a moment why this is an important step.

Suppose that you like the Dangerous Creatures theme that you've applied to your desktop, but the colors are just too dark for your laptop computer. You prefer the color scheme in the Leonardo da Vinci theme.

You can remedy this problem easily. Assuming that your current desktop theme is Dangerous Creatures, open the Desktop Themes dialog box. Notice that the Theme drop-down list says Current Windows settings (see Figure 4.15). Notice also that the preview window shows the desktop configuration of the Dangerous Creatures theme.

Figure 4.15.
The Current Windows settings are now the same as if you had selected the Dangerous Creatures theme.

To change the color scheme in your Current Windows settings to the color scheme in the Leonardo da Vinci theme, select the Leonardo da Vinci theme in the list box, as shown in Figure 4.16.

Figure 4.16.
The Leonardo da Vinci theme.

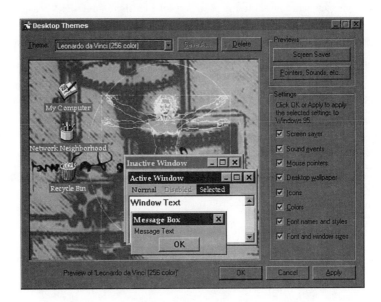

Notice that the preview window shows the full Leonardo da Vinci theme. Your Current Windows settings would change to reflect all the settings in the Leonardo da Vinci theme if you click the Apply button or the OK button now. Notice the Settings check boxes on the right side of the dialog box. Only the settings with check marks next to them are applied to your Current Windows settings. Because you want to change only the color scheme, remove the check marks next to all of the settings except Colors, as shown in Figure 4.17.

Figure 4.17.
The Leonardo da Vinci theme with every setting deselected except Colors.

The preview window should now look a lot like the Dangerous Creatures theme, except that the colors are from the Leonardo da Vinci theme. Click the Apply button, and your current Windows settings include the new, lighter colors.

If you like the desktop you've created, you can save it as your own custom theme. To save the current Windows settings as a desktop theme, click the Save As button. The Save Theme dialog box appears. Give the theme a name—Dangerous Creatures Light (256 color), for instance—and click the Save button.

Using the Display Properties Dialog Box

Windows 95 allows nearly complete customization of its Desktop environment without Plus! However, there is no way to save multiple Desktop environment configurations under the same user profile, and there is no way to customize the standard desktop icons without Plus!

Plus! adds a Plus! tab to the Display Properties dialog box, shown in Figure 4.18. This tab lets you change the standard desktop icons to anything you want.

Figure 4.18.
*The Display
Properties dialog box
lets you change the
standard desktop
icons and other visual
enhancement options.*

There's one major drawback to using the Background tab: You can't select from the different Plus! desktop theme wallpapers. Selecting Plus! from the Background tab's Wallpaper list displays the wallpaper from the last desktop theme you selected.

The reason for this is that Microsoft set up the Plus! desktop themes in a way that saves disk space. Wallpaper for all of the themes is stored in the `Program Files\Plus!\Themes` folder as JPEG (`.JPG`) files. You find wallpaper listed as the theme name followed by the word "wallpaper." For instance, the Dangerous Creatures theme wallpaper is listed as "Dangerous Creatures wallpaper." When you select a desktop theme, the theme's JPEG wallpaper file is converted to a bitmap (`.BMP`) file in the Windows folder. You can find a bitmap of the last desktop themes wallpaper you used as the Plus! bitmap file in your Windows folder.

Bitmap files are larger than JPEG files, but you can only work with bitmap files from the Background tab of the Display Properties dialog box. You either need to use the Desktop Themes dialog box to change between different desktop theme wallpapers or convert the desktop theme wallpaper JPEG files to bitmap files using an image conversion program.

Animated Mouse Pointers

Plus! gives you several animated mouse pointers. As I noted earlier, it provides several animated pointers with its desktop themes that are stored in the `\Program Files\Plus!\Themes\` folder. Plus! also places several other animated pointers in the `\Windows\Cursors\` folder along with the usual assortment of Windows 95 cursors. You can access animated mouse pointers by doing the following (and you don't need Plus! installed to do it). Open Control Panel and double-click the Mouse applet to open the Mouse Properties dialog box. Select the Pointers tab, as shown in Figure 4.19. Select the type of mouse pointer you want to change. The Busy pointer is selected in Figure 4.19.

Figure 4.19.
Select the Pointers tab
in the Mouse
Properties dialog box
to customize your
mouse cursor.

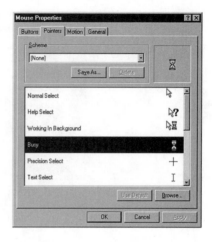

Click the Browse button to open the Browse dialog box. Navigate to the folder where the desired cursor is stored and select a cursor. When you select a cursor, it is displayed in the Preview area at the lower-left corner of the Browse dialog box. If it's an animated cursor, it is animated in the Preview area. Click the Open button. You should be back in the Mouse Properties dialog box with the new cursor added to the cursor type you selected earlier. Click the Apply button to add the cursor to your current list of cursors and to leave the dialog box open so that you can modify other cursor types. Otherwise, click the OK button to add the cursor to your list and exit the dialog box.

Full-Window Drag

With Plus! installed, you can set your desktop environment so that it shows a window's contents rather than just an outline when you drag or resize it. You can find the Show window contents while dragging option on the Plus! tab of the Display Properties dialog box inside the Visual Setting frame.

Font Smoothing

Font smoothing gets rid of any jagged edges that large fonts sometimes display. You must be running your video at 16-bit color (high color) or better to take advantage of font smoothing. You can find the Smooth edges of screen fonts option on the Plus! tab of the Display Properties dialog box inside the Visual Setting frame.

Wallpaper Stretching

Have you ever found an ideal wallpaper image, only to discover that it's either too small or too large for your desktop? Plus! gives you the ability to stretch the image to fit your desktop. This setting also shrinks images to fit your desktop. You can find the Stretch desktop wallpaper to fit the screen option on the Plus! tab of the Display Properties dialog box inside the Visual Setting frame.

Kids Plus!

Microsoft Plus! for Kids is a more recent companion product for Windows 95. Like the original Microsoft Plus!, Plus! for Kids includes an assortment of desktop themes—ten colorful themes designed to appeal to the younger set. You use the Plus! for Kids themes just like the desktop themes from the Plus! package I described previously.

In addition to desktop themes, Microsoft Plus! for Kids includes a parental control program that allows you to set up profiles for family members and control their access to the hard drive and Internet resources. I cover that in Chapter 28, "Setting Up Security." The final components of Plus! for Kids are Talk It!, a text-to-speech application that uses funny voices to speak the words that kids type in; Play It!, an onscreen music synthesizer keyboard; and Paint It!, a version of the Paint utility upgraded with special effects.

On Your Own

Use the new Active Desktop features to enhance your productivity. For example, place your favorite Web page on the desktop for a week or so to see how this new feature works. You might also want to create one or more toolbars in an effort to consolidate some of the icons currently on your desktop. Set up the channels as well to see if you can create one-click access to the Internet.

Open Explorer and check out each of the special sections I talked about in this chapter. Identify each section and its purpose without referring back to the discussion. Also look at some of the unique capabilities provided by your machine. For example, see if there are any special applets in Control Panel. You also want to check out your machine's network capabilities.

Spend some time customizing your desktop for optimum efficiency. See which wallpapers or other aesthetics you can change. Remove any features that might slow performance if you're using a memory-constrained system and try the screen saver and password options.

II

Power
Primers

5

Performance Primer

Peter Norton®

Tuning or optimizing a machine for maximum performance is one of the first things that many people think about when they install a new operating system. Although there's no way I can provide step-by-step tuning instructions for every computer, I can provide some guidelines and tips you can use to create your own solution.

Take a look at some of the things you should consider before you start tuning your machine. Of course, the time and effort you expend here is directly proportional to the amount of performance you can expect to receive:

- Memory: The amount of real memory your system contains is a big factor in how well Windows 95 operates. Although you can run Windows 95 with 8MB of RAM, you shouldn't consider starting to tune until you have a minimum of 16MB of real RAM. You need to tailor this number to meet the demands of the applications you plan to run. For example, a spreadsheet requires a lot of memory—a database even more—but a word processor is relatively light when it comes to memory consumption. You might find that a graphics application requires a moderate amount of memory but takes a heavy toll on both the processor and graphics adapter. The number of simultaneous applications you plan to run also affects the point at which you should start to tune your system. I equipped my system with 64MB of RAM because I often run a word processor, spreadsheet, and communications program simultaneously. Virtual memory helps take up the slack between real memory and what you need, but you can't count on it to assume the full burden.

- Hard disk size: Windows 95 runs best when you give it a large swap area to work with. In addition, you need space for the application itself and some space for data files. The one factor many people underestimate is the size of their data files. I was quite surprised the other day when I translated a small Word for Windows file from 1.0 format to 7.0. The file consumed almost twice as much space even though the amount of data hadn't changed one iota. Of course, the extra space used by the 7.0 format bought me added functionality—an important tradeoff to consider. The general rule of thumb I use for figuring out the amount of hard disk space I need is to add up the space required for installed configurations of my applications and triple it. This is a coarse calculation, but it works for me.

- Hard disk speed: Older operating systems were a lot less disk-intensive than Windows 95 is. Not only do you have the swap file that Windows 95 creates, but applications also make greater use of the hard drive today for temporary storage. To see what I mean, open just about any application and check for the number of TMP files on your drive. You might be surprised by what you see. All this disk access means just one thing: You need a fast drive to make Windows 95 jump through the hoops that you want it to.

Peter's Principle: Stretching Your Hard Drive

Originally, one of the best ways to make a hard drive hold more data was to use disk compression. Unfortunately, disk compression can cause problems with certain applications—most notably hard disk utilities such as disk defragmenters and file repair programs.

As a safer alternative, use FAT32 instead. Under FAT32, a 6MB file (such as a word processor document) requires 6MB of storage and a 2KB file only needs 2KB. Under FAT16, the file uses 64KB of disk space. That's because FAT16 uses a cluster size of 64KB on a 1GB or larger partition so the actual disk usage of a file is always rounded up to the cluster size.

Another disk space saver is to use compressed file formats whenever possible. This is especially true in the multimedia and graphics areas. For example, a CorelDRAW! file that consumes a mere 60KB in its native format can consume 1MB or more in AI (Adobe Illustrator) format. Another example is the PCX format. Storing a 1024×768 16-color image requires 90KB. That same image requires 200KB if you increase the number of colors to 256. Storing the same 256-color image in TIF format (using LZW compression) uses 136KB and only 124KB in GIF format. As you can see, something as simple as a file format can make a big impact on the amount of space available on your hard drive.

- Processor speed: Your processor speed affects the way your computer runs. Many people opt for a high-speed processor and then choke it with limited memory and hard drive space. Remember that the processor makes a big impact on system throughput only after you meet the basic storage requirements. A thrashing hard drive can eat up every bit of extra speed you might add to a system.

- Motherboard features: Items such as the size of the motherboard's SRAM cache might seem a bit on the technical side, but these features aren't just for technicians. An optimized system starts with an optimized motherboard. Get a motherboard that offers plenty of room to grow and the capability to tune.

- Peripheral devices: I/O has always been a bottleneck in the PC. The two peripherals you need to concentrate on the most are your disk controller and display adapter. Windows is a GUI; it consumes huge amounts of time simply drawing all those pretty images you see on the display. A display adapter that uses processor cycles efficiently (or even unloads some processing tasks) can greatly affect the perceived speed of your system. The less time Windows spends drawing icons and other graphics, the more time it has to service your application. Likewise, a slow controller makes even a fast hard disk look slow. It's the controller that becomes a bottleneck with many systems today. The short take on peripherals? Always get 32-bit (or better) peripherals whenever possible and make certain that they are fully compatible with Windows 95.

- Bus speed: You might not think much about the little connectors that you stick cards into, but the system does. The system bus has been a source of major concern for a great number of years, and I don't see this changing anytime soon. What good is a fast peripheral if you can't access it at full speed? The fastest (and most common) bus is the PCI bus. If you have an older motherboard that uses an older bus such as VL, MCA, or EISA, you should really consider buying a new motherboard, which might also mean buying a faster processor as well.

- Network interface card (NIC): If you spend a lot of time working on the network, you'll most certainly want a high-capacity NIC. The minimum you should settle for is a 16-bit Ethernet card. Anything less is a waste of perfectly good network bandwidth. People who share graphics or other large files across the system should consider getting 32-bit NICs for their machines. Some NICs also come equipped with an expandable cache. Using a larger cache can buy some additional network speed in some cases, especially under Windows 95.

Once you get your hardware configuration out of the way, it's time to consider your software configuration. Windows 95 does a much better job of managing resources than Windows 3.x did, but it's by no means perfect.

Under Windows 3.x, I started to run out of resources after loading my word processor, spreadsheet, communications program, and one or two small utility programs such as a screen saver or Notepad. I usually consider closing an application or two when I get to the 35 percent system resources level, which is about where I was with this configuration. Windows 95 still has 75 percent of its resources free when using the same configuration. This means that I can usually open two or three more applications on top of my usual configuration.

Of course, system resources are only one memory factor. There's also the actual level of RAM to take into consideration. Under Windows 3.x, you started to notice a fairly large performance penalty when you got to the point where the swap file was as large as real memory. Under Windows 95, this doesn't seem to be as much of a problem, but it's still noticeable. The bottom line is that if your swap file starts approaching the size of your installed memory, it's time for an upgrade.

You need to take into consideration the combination of system resources and system memory when thinking about your software situation. A memory-constrained system always lacks enough memory to perform the job you need it to do. It's a subjective type of measurement based on how you actually use your system. You should load the Resource Monitor (discussed in Chapter 2, "Introducing Windows 95: What Else Is New?") and, over a few days, track both the size of your swap file and the number of resources you have available. If you start to see a pattern of low memory, read the next section. You might even find that the problem isn't the amount of installed memory on your machine, but the way you use that memory.

Top Performance Tips for Memory-Constrained Systems

Although memory isn't free, it certainly isn't the most expensive upgrade you can make to your system. Few new items can provide as much potential for a noticeable increase in system performance as memory.

The minimum recommended RAM for running Windows 95 is 8MB, and that's if you intend to run only one application at a time. A more reasonable system contains 16MB or even 32MB of RAM. Even with 64MB of RAM, I find my system a tad constraining at times. Of course, the opposite extreme exists as well.

Suppose you're stuck at that 8MB level. How can you stretch 8MB of RAM enough to make your single-tasking system (from a memory perspective) work as a multitasking system?

Tip: The generic optimization techniques in this section work equally well with Windows NT, Windows for Workgroups 3.x, and Windows 3.x workstations. If you're using Windows 95 in a peer-to-peer LAN environment, it's very likely that you'll use Windows NT on your file server. You also might have some older machines that still use Windows for Workgroups 3.x connected to the network. Whatever your setup, these generic tips can help just about any workstation make better use of the memory it contains.

General Tuning Tips for Windows

There are a few methods that I recommend you start with. Anyone can use these methods, but using them always involves some level of compromise that you might or might not be willing to make. The following list shows my quick fixes to memory problems:

- Wallpaper: Did you know it costs you a little memory and some processing time to keep wallpaper on your system? If you have a memory-constrained system and can do without some bells and whistles, here's one item to get rid of. Don't think you save much by using smaller wallpaper or restricting yourself to patterns. Both items chew up some memory.

- Colors: The number of colors you use for your display directly affects the amount of memory it uses. A 16-color display uses roughly half the memory of a 256-color display. Although a 16-color display doesn't look as appealing as its 256-color or 32KB color counterpart, using 16 colors does help you save memory. You probably won't notice that much of a difference in appearance if the programs on your machine are word processors and spreadsheets.

- Screen resolution: The resolution at which you set your display affects processing speed and, to a much smaller degree, memory. Of course, the problem with changing your display resolution is fairly simple to figure out. You can probably get by with fewer colors, but fewer pixels are a different matter. You'll probably want to save changing the screen resolution as a last-ditch effort to get that last bit of needed performance.

- Doodads: I put a whole realm of utility programs into the "doodad" category. For example, if you run one of the fancier screen savers rather than the built-in Windows counterpart, you're wasting memory. Some people also keep a small game program such as Solitaire running. These small applications might provide a few seconds of pleasure here and there, but you really don't need to keep them active all the time. If you insist on using that screen saver, run it right before you leave the room for a while and then exit it when you return. The same holds true with a game program; keep it open when you play it, and then close it before you get back to work. To determine whether you have extra programs running, look for program icons on the System Tray (which appears on the Taskbar).

- Icons and other graphics: Every icon displayed on your desktop consumes memory. The same holds true for any other form of graphic image or window. At least Windows 95 doesn't penalize you for opening a folder as Windows 3.x does. You can actually recover the memory by closing the folder. The simple way of looking at this is to organize your data into folders and open only the folders that you need at any given time.

- Leaky applications: Some programs leak when it comes to memory. They allocate memory from Windows but never give it back, even after they terminate. After a while you might find that you don't have enough memory to run programs, even though you should. This problem is severe under Windows 3.x. It's less so under Windows 95 and Windows NT. However, the Windows 95 data-centric interface tends to accelerate the rate at which memory dissipates if you open and close an application for each data file. You can alleviate this situation by keeping leaky applications open until you know that you won't need them again. You can find a leaky application by checking system resources and memory before you open it, opening and closing the application a few times (make sure you also open some documents while inside), and then checking the amount of memory again after the last time you close it. If you find you have less memory—I mean a measurable amount, not a few bytes—the application is leaky.

- Extra drivers: Windows 95 and Windows NT do a fairly good job of cleaning old drivers out of the Registry. Even so, you want to take the time to see whether all the drivers got removed from the system after you remove an application. This isn't such a big deal for newer applications that are specifically designed for Windows 95 or Windows NT. Both of these newer operating systems provide a special installation utility that removes newer applications from the system—including the files they stick in the SYSTEM directory and any references to them in the system files. Unfortunately, in most cases, old Windows 3.x applications don't remove anything.

- DOS applications: Nothing grabs memory and holds it like an MS-DOS application under Windows. Unlike other applications, Windows normally can't move the memory used by an MS-DOS application around to free space. This means that you might have a lot of memory on your system, but Windows isn't able to use it because it's all too fragmented. If your system is so constricted on memory that it can't tolerate even the smallest amount of memory fragmentation, avoid using MS-DOS applications.

Windows 95–Specific Tuning Tips

Now that I'm past the generic tips, look at a few Windows 95–specific ways to enhance overall system performance and the amount of memory you have available:

- 486 versus Pentium processors: Windows 3.x doesn't care about the processor you use, only the processing speed. The facts are plain: Windows 3.x uses 16-bit code that runs equally well on any processor 386 or above. However, there's a big difference in performance when using different processor types under Windows 95 because it uses 32-bit code. A 486 processor is better optimized to take advantage of 32-bit code. The Pentium or Pentium II with MMX is better still. Theoretically, you should notice a fairly substantial improvement in processing capability between a machine equipped with a Pentium II versus a Pentium machine of the same processor speed. In reality, the difference is noticeable, but not that noticeable. You want the extra performance if possible, but don't worry about it until you take care of other problems, such as upgrading your memory.

- CONFIG.SYS and AUTOEXEC.BAT: In most cases, you're better off without any form of AUTOEXEC.BAT or CONFIG.SYS. If all you have in your CONFIG.SYS is a memory manager, get rid of it because Windows 95 supplies its own. Adding a memory manager to CONFIG.SYS reduces the amount of flexibility Windows 95 has in configuring your system. The only time you should keep CONFIG.SYS around is if you have to load real-mode drivers. It's also a good idea to get rid of AUTOEXEC.BAT in most circumstances, but it isn't always possible. There's a problem with old 16-bit Windows applications under Windows 95; they need some of the entries in AUTOEXEC.BAT. The most common requirement is the addition of entries to the PATH statement. You can open an MS-DOS window and add a PATH statement to a batch file to set the path. However, you don't have the same privilege for Windows applications. You have to set the path before you enter Windows for the application to work right.

- Real-mode drivers: As far as optimizing your system is concerned, real-mode drivers cost you in both performance and system reliability. The short explanation is that real-mode drivers force Windows 95 to make a transition between protected mode and real mode every time an application requires access to the device. Not only does this transition waste precious processor time, but it also makes it possible for an ill-behaved application to cause system failure.

- 16-bit drivers and DLLs: Windows 95 is essentially a 32-bit operating system with some 16-bit compatibility components and a few items left over from Windows 3.x. It runs every 32-bit application in a separate session. Doing this allows Windows 95 to perform some intense memory management on the resources needed by that application. 16-bit applications all share one session. The amount of management Windows 95 can perform on this one session is a lot less than what it can do for the individual 32-bit sessions because it can't make certain assumptions about how that memory is used. In addition, the 32-bit memory space is flat, reducing the number of clock cycles required to make a function call or look at something in memory. On the other hand, the segmented address space used by 16-bit components requires two to three times the number of clock cycles to process.

- Using Explorer in place of folders: Folders are more efficient to use than Explorer. This might seem like a contradiction in terms because folders use the Explorer interface, but it's not. Opening a copy of Explorer eats a lot more system resources than opening a folder. Actually, you might think this is a foregone conclusion: Opening any application eats system resources. Here's the memory saver for you. Place all your data in folders, and then place a shortcut to those folders on the desktop. You can still get to all your important files without opening a copy of Explorer. The cost in memory is a lot less than keeping Explorer running all the time.

- Use context menus in place of Control Panel: I find I occasionally need to adjust the properties of various system elements during a session. Windows 3.x always forced me to open Control Panel to make these adjustments. Old habits die hard. It took me a while to adjust to the new Windows 95 way of dealing with this situation. Chapter 2 talked a lot about the context menu attached to every object. Using that context menu is not only more efficient from a keystroke perspective, but it also uses less memory. This is something to consider if you need to keep a Properties dialog box open for any length of time.

- Reset your printer for RAW printing: Windows 95 automatically installs support for Enhanced Metafile Format (EMF) printing on systems it thinks will support it. This feature allows Windows 95 to print faster by translating the output to generic commands in the foreground and then creating printer-specific output in the background. Creating generic commands requires a lot less processing time than writing printer-specific output. Changing the setting of the Spool Data Format field of the Spool Settings dialog box to RAW forces Windows 95 to create a printer-specific output in the first pass. (You can access this dialog box by opening the Details tab of the Printer Properties dialog box and clicking the Spool Settings button.) Using the RAW setting means that less operating system code is maintained in memory during the print process. Some memory-constrained systems receive a large benefit by using this print mode. Of course, the tradeoff is longer foreground print times.

- Keep your disk defragmented: Older versions of Windows allowed you to create a permanent swap file. Using a permanent swap file improved performance by reducing hard disk head movement to read swap file data. It didn't matter how fragmented your drive got after you set up the swap file because the swap file always resided in the same contiguous disk sectors. Windows 95 doesn't provide the permanent swap file option, although it does let you specify a swap file size to emulate a permanent swap file. Of course, the system doesn't work perfectly. You can still get a highly fragmented drive that reduces system performance as Windows moves from area to area in an attempt to read the swap file. Defragmenting your drive reduces the possibility that the swap file will become too fragmented. Most people find that a weekly maintenance session takes care of this requirement.

- Place your swap file on the fastest drive: Windows 95 usually chooses the drive with the largest amount of available memory for the swap file. In most cases, the drive it chooses doesn't make that big of a difference. However, if you have a system with one large, slow drive and a second small, fast drive, you'll probably want to change the virtual memory settings. See the section "Using Windows 95 Automatic Tuning Features" later in this chapter for details.

- Get rid of nonessentials: You'll find that some parts of Windows 95 make you slightly more efficient, but at a fairly large cost in memory. For example, enabling the International Settings feature (described in Chapter 2) makes you more efficient if you work with several languages, but that enhancement costs you some memory. Unfortunately, once you activate this feature, you can't get rid of it until you reboot the machine; the memory is gone for good. The same holds true for many of the other icons that appear in the Taskbar tray with the clock. All these features are nice to have, but not essential.

Peter's Principle: Efficiency of Actions Versus Memory Usage

Using features such as a context menu might not seem like a very big deal—you save only two or three mouse clicks in most cases—but they also result in memory savings. Windows 95 provides other speed-enhancing features that save memory. For example, using the automatic settings for most of the system parameters such as virtual memory improves performance and enhances memory usage.

Some Windows 95 features aren't only extremely efficient, but also save you a considerable amount of time. For example, you'll find that using Explorer costs you a lot less memory compared to using Program Manager. (A comparison on my machine shows system resources at 94 percent when using Explorer but only 89 percent when using Program Manager in the same configuration.) You can check this out on your machine by changing the shell=Explorer.exe line in SYSTEM.INI to shell=Progman.exe and then shutting down and rebooting your system. Using the Explorer interface is so much more efficient that I would think twice about going back to Program Manager.

Using Windows 95 Automatic Tuning Features

Besides user-related activities, Windows 95 provides some additional features for making automated changes to your configuration. In most cases, you can determine at a glance whether all these automated features are in effect. All you need to do is display the Performance tab of the System Properties dialog box. Simply right-click the My Computer icon and select Properties from the context menu to display it. You should see a display similar to the one in Figure 5.1 if your system is completely tuned. Windows 95 provides some suggestions on things you can do to improve system performance. In most cases, this means enabling an automatic feature to provide additional memory, reducing the system's reliance on out-of-date drivers, or allowing some additional flexibility. If your system isn't completely tuned, Windows 95 provides tips on what you can do to make the automatic tuning features work properly.

Figure 5.1.
The Performance tab of the System Properties dialog box.

Notice the three buttons near the bottom. Clicking the first one displays a dialog box similar to the one shown in Figure 5.2.

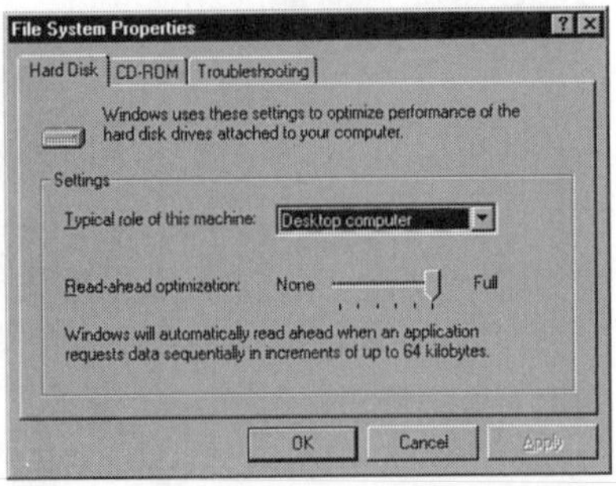

Figure 5.2.
The File System Properties dialog box.

The Hard Disk and CD-ROM tabs of the File System Properties dialog box allow you to change the way Windows 95 reacts to certain requests for information and allocates memory for the file system without really changing its overall management strategy. The following list describes each field in this dialog box:

- Typical role of this machine: This field appears on the Hard Disk tab and has three settings. The way you should use this field is pretty self-explanatory: Select the role that best describes your computer. In most cases, you select either Desktop computer or Mobile or docking system. If your machine acts as a file server on a peer-to-peer network, select the Network server setting. There's one way in which you can use this setting to improve performance. I found that the Network server setting actually seems to speed some tasks that perform small data reads, such as database managers.

- Supplemental cache size: This appears on the CD-ROM tab and is one field where you can save about 1MB on a memory-starved system. Of course, you trade performance for that savings. Because this setting affects only the CD-ROM cache, you might not notice much of a difference. Don't shortchange this area if you regularly use your CD-ROM to run applications because the loss in cache size becomes noticeable after a while. Using a large cache means that you set aside 1238KB of RAM for a cache. The small cache uses a mere 214KB.

- Optimize access pattern for: This appears on the CD-ROM tab. Set this field to reflect the speed of your CD-ROM drive. Windows 95 uses a different timing formula for each drive type. You can play with this field to see whether there's any performance benefit to changing it from the default. I actually found one double-speed Toshiba CD-ROM drive that worked better at the triple-speed setting. It's rare to get any kind of increase by doing this, but you never know.

The Troubleshooting tab (see Figure 5.3) is where you can really help or really damage your system's memory management strategy. Microsoft originally included this tab for the sole purpose of troubleshooting. However, on certain rare occasions, you can use these items as part of your tuning strategy. Each of the check boxes allows you to change a part of the Windows 95 file system management strategy. Be careful when changing these settings or you might find yourself troubleshooting a nonfunctional system.

Figure 5.3.
The Troubleshooting tab of the File System Properties dialog box.

The following list describes each of these options in detail:

- Disable new file sharing and locking semantics: Windows 95 uses new drivers to maintain file locks for networks. The new setup uses a 32-bit protected-mode driver. The old setup uses a 16-bit driver similar to the VSHARE.386 driver provided by Windows for Workgroups 3.x. The only reason to check this box is if you experience network-related file-locking problems. In some cases, file locking works either way, but checking this box reduces the number of failed attempts. The time differential is quite noticeable with applications such as database managers that require many locks during any given session.

- Disable long name preservation for old programs: Checking this box helps you maintain compatibility with existing MS-DOS machines. It forces Windows 95 to use the 8.3 file-naming scheme everyone has used from the earliest days of MS-DOS. Of course, you lose the benefits of long filenames, and you won't garner even one byte of additional RAM for your system. Companies that use a mixed group of workstations on the network, however, gain a benefit from consistent file naming. In most cases, you want to leave this box unchecked.

- Disable protect-mode hard disk interrupt handling: Some applications don't work properly using the new Windows 95 interrupt handlers. You can check this box to install the old real-mode handlers. One note of caution: Make sure that you don't use non–Windows 95 disk defragmenters or other low-level file management utility programs because they don't support long filenames and other Windows 95 features.

- Disable synchronous buffer commits: You can check this box to allow commits to the buffer without waiting for the previous commit to be acknowledged. Although this increases speed, it also increases the danger of losing data.

- Disable all 32 bit protected-mode disk drivers: A few hard drives and controllers don't work properly with the Windows 32-bit drivers. Although these drivers might not cause a total drive failure, they might cause the drive to slow down. If you notice that your drive's performance isn't what it used to be, you might want to see whether disabling 32-bit support brings it back to normal.

- Disable write-behind caching for all drives: Data loss on network drives is a major headache for most administrators at one time or another. Windows 95 uses a write-behind caching scheme to improve workstation performance. This same feature can actually cause data loss, especially with networked database managers. If you find you have records that don't get written or other forms of data loss, you might want to check this box. Even though checking this box most certainly reduces local workstation performance, it might improve overall network performance by forcing the workstation to write shared data faster. This is especially true in situations where many people share relatively few records in the database—for example, a reservation or scheduling system.

The Advanced Graphics Settings dialog box, shown in Figure 5.4, provides a single slider control. The new protected-mode drivers provided with Windows 95 accelerate writes to the display adapter.

The slider controls the amount of acceleration you receive. Most adapters work fine at the highest setting. However, if you find that your adapter performs only partial screen writes, or if you see other types of corruption, you might need to use a lower setting.

Figure 5.4.
The Advanced Graphics Settings dialog box.

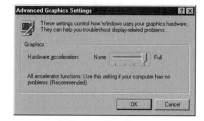

Figure 5.5 shows the Virtual Memory dialog box, which provides one way to enhance system performance when the automatic method selects the wrong drive for your swap file. In most cases, it pays to let Windows manage the virtual memory settings. However, there are a few cases where you want to manually adjust the virtual memory settings. Windows 95 normally selects the drive with the largest amount of free disk space as the virtual memory drive; this might not be the fastest drive on your system. In this case, it makes sense to manually adjust the virtual memory drive to be the fastest one on your machine.

Figure 5.5.
The Virtual Memory dialog box.

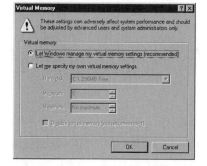

Warning: Never disable virtual memory. The Virtual Memory dialog box provides this setting for troubleshooting purposes only. Disabling virtual memory can (and probably will) result in some type of system failure. Such a failure can prevent Windows 95 from writing everything in disk cache to the drive. This can corrupt the Registry or other system files and prevent you from rebooting the operating system. If your computer doesn't have enough memory, disabling virtual memory can even keep Windows 95 from booting.

There are other ways to configure the swap file. For example, what if the fastest drive on your machine doesn't contain enough space for the size of swap file you need? Windows 95 allows you to individually configure the swap file for each drive on your system. If you don't want a swap file on a particular drive, set its minimum and maximum sizes to 0.

Finding Unneeded Hidden Drivers

Sometimes Windows 95 does a less-than-perfect job of setting up your machine. Earlier I mentioned that you should remove any unneeded drivers. What happens if you have some "hidden" drivers that you don't need installed on your system? Figure 5.6 shows a dialog box that illustrates this point. I installed Windows on a machine in a peer-to-peer networking environment. The installation program even asked about the level of support I wanted. However, it assumes that not everyone knows what they're talking about, so it installed both Microsoft and Novell support. The Novell support goes to waste because this is a peer-to-peer network that doesn't connect to a NetWare file server.

Figure 5.6.
*Sometimes Windows
95 installs too much
support. You can
reduce your memory
footprint and improve
performance by
getting rid of this
additional support.*

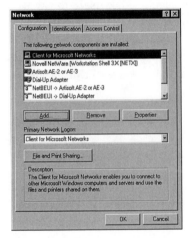

You need to look at three things in this particular situation. First, eliminate additional network support. You need to install support for only one network if you're using a peer-to-peer setup. In most cases, this means that you retain the Microsoft network and discard NetWare support. Likewise, if you don't plan to set up a peer-to-peer network, remove the Microsoft network support in a NetWare environment.

You also want to reduce the number of protocols you have installed. I typically maintain NetBEUI support for a peer-to-peer setup if at all possible. Of course, the protocol you choose must reflect the capabilities of the network you install.

Tip: If you remove one of the protocols from your workstation and find that you can't connect to the other workstations, make sure that all the workstations are using the same protocol. Many people find that working networks suddenly fail when they optimize their setup. This simple fix repairs the vast majority of "broken" installations.

Installing the fewest possible network services is the third step I take. For example, installing sharing support for a floppy drive is a waste of memory because it's unlikely that someone will need it. If someone does need it, you can always add the support later. Start out with the lowest level of support possible. You also want to think about which workstation printers you really want to share. If a workstation has an older printer attached, you probably won't want to install print sharing support for it.

Top Performance Tips for MS-DOS Applications

I'd love to say that Windows 95 will run every MS-DOS application you ever owned without any major configuration problems, but that isn't accurate. You'll encounter problems when running certain MS-DOS applications, and you need to tune your system to avoid them.

The good news is that you can make all the required changes using the application's Properties dialog box. You'll find that Windows 95 provides support for MS-DOS applications that's far superior even to Windows NT. Microsoft made some design decisions to make this support possible; I explore them in Chapter 13, "Exploiting Your Software: DOS, 16-Bit, and 32-Bit Windows Applications." This means that you can make the required changes by right-clicking the object and selecting Properties from the context menu. Suppose you want to change some of the settings for the DISKCOPY.EXE file. You just right-click the DISKCOPY icon in Explorer and then select Properties from the context menu. The first thing you see is a Diskcopy Properties dialog box similar to the one shown in Figure 5.7. (The Properties dialog always includes the application filename on the title bar; I use the Diskcopy Properties dialog throughout this section for explanation purposes.) Everything you need to run MS-DOS applications efficiently under Windows 95 appears in this dialog box.

Tip: Some Windows 95 users will find it easy to set all their MS-DOS applications to run in MS-DOS mode because this mode provides the most familiar configuration options. However, running your applications in this mode means that you have to forego any DOS-to-Windows interaction. It also means that you won't be able to use any Windows 95 features. Finally, because running an application in MS-DOS mode unloads all the Windows 95 drivers, you lose the benefits of 32-bit driver support along with the benefits of multitasking.

Figure 5.7.
The Diskcopy
Properties dialog box.

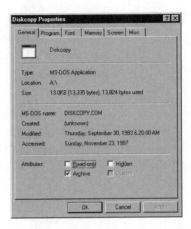

Looking Ahead: This chapter looks at the Properties dialog box settings that affect DOS application performance. I cover the rest of the settings in Chapter 13.

Several tabs directly affect the way an MS-DOS application behaves under Windows 95. The first one I examine appears in Figure 5.8. The visible part of the Program tab contains some fields that tell Windows 95 what application to run and where to run it. This includes the application name and its working directory. The area of concern for this chapter is the Advanced button near the bottom of the dialog box. Clicking that button displays the Advanced Program Settings dialog box, shown in Figure 5.9, which contains some of the DOS-specific settings that affect how Windows 95 reacts.

Figure 5.8.
The Program tab of
the Diskcopy
Properties dialog box.

Figure 5.9.
*The Advanced
Program Settings
dialog box.*

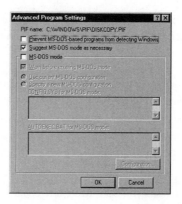

The check box I like the most in this dialog box is Prevent MS-DOS-based programs from detecting Windows. I had several applications that wouldn't work because the application looked for the Windows signature before it ran. Even if the application could run, it wouldn't. This check box allows you to fool those applications into thinking that they're all alone on the machine. In many cases, this is all you need to do to get an application to cooperate with Windows.

Many applications still experience problems when running under Windows 95. The next check box provides a diagnostic mode of sorts. The Suggest MS-DOS mode as necessary option is another automatic tuning aid that you can turn on. If you use an application that really has to be run in MS-DOS mode, Windows 95 displays a dialog box that suggests you do so. Unfortunately, Windows doesn't check this box for you automatically, so you need to check it yourself.

The final check box is a real performance-buster in every situation, according to Microsoft. The fact is that using MS-DOS mode slows the majority of your applications at least a little. However, there are at least two categories of applications in which you'll probably experience a performance gain, not a loss. The first one is games. Many MS-DOS games run correctly under Windows 95; many more don't. Your only choice in this case is to run the program in MS-DOS mode.

The other category—strangely enough—is older graphics applications. For some reason, they actually perform better in MS-DOS mode. For example, the old copy of Harvard Graphics I had lying around performed almost twice as fast in MS-DOS mode as it did under Windows 95. After a bit of research, I concluded that it was a combination of factors such as direct-screen writing and other rule-breaking behaviors that make these applications run faster in MS-DOS mode. In most cases, you want to replace it with a Windows 95–specific product if at all possible.

After you place a check in the MS-DOS mode check box, you get several more options. The first check box asks whether you want Windows 95 to warn you before it enters MS-DOS mode. Keep this one checked as a precaution. You wouldn't want to accidentally leave some other application in an uncertain state.

The two radio buttons allow you to choose between the default MS-DOS setup and a custom setup for this particular application. Because Windows 95 gives you the choice, I recommend a custom configuration whenever possible. If the application you want to run is having problems with Windows 95, it will probably also have special needs when running in MS-DOS mode.

> **Tip:** An easy way to take care of the various configuration needs you might have for MS-DOS mode applications is to specify the `CONFIG.DOS` and `AUTOEXEC.DOS` files as special configuration files. If the application worked with your old DOS setup, there's no reason why the same configuration won't work under Windows 95.

The Memory tab, shown in Figure 5.10, can also help you to obtain the best possible setup for your application. In most cases, you want to stick to the Auto setting. However, I have several applications that require more environment space than the Auto setting provides. All you need to do is adjust the setting in the list box as required. The same thing holds true for any other memory settings you might need to adjust.

Figure 5.10.
The Memory tab allows you to customize the DOS application's memory settings.

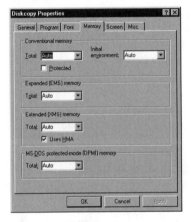

There's one thing you should always keep in mind with this tab. Setting any memory entries you don't need to None saves system memory and allows Windows 95 to provide better services to the rest of the applications on your machine. Windows 95 always assumes a worst-case scenario with MS-DOS applications; setting the various memory options gives it a little more information to work with.

The Protected check box in the Conventional memory group is a two-edged sword. Setting it allows some applications to run; it also prevents Windows 95 from moving applications around in memory. Some applications that access memory directly need this kind of protection. The down side of checking this box is that a fixed session in memory always increases memory fragmentation and the chance that you'll artificially run out of memory.

The last tab I look at from a performance perspective is the Screen tab, shown in Figure 5.11. I discuss only two of these check boxes in this chapter. Not surprisingly, both appear in the Performance group near the bottom of the dialog box.

Figure 5.11.
*The Screen tab
provides two
performance settings.*

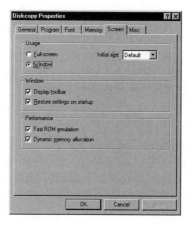

The Dynamic memory allocation check box is the important one here. As with the Protected check box in the Memory tab, this check box determines whether Windows 95 can move memory around. Here's the problem: Many graphics applications resort to using direct screen writes to get the performance they need. Those same graphics applications don't work under Windows 95 if you keep this box checked because Windows might move the "virtual" screen that the application is actually writing to somewhere else. The warning sign you need to look for on a graphics application is some type of distortion. Most applications display vertical bars or some type of striation. You might see part of the display shift or what appear to be cursor trails onscreen. All these types of distortion tell you that you need to uncheck the Dynamic memory allocation check box.

Another group of applications needs to directly access the ROM routines. The Fast ROM emulation check box tells Windows 95 to emulate the display ROM in fast protected-mode RAM. However, if your application is looking for the system ROM in conventional memory, it won't find the emulated version. One way to tell that your application needs to have this box unchecked is that you get unexplainable system crashes that you can't pinpoint to another cause. These crashes could be caused when the application looks for ROM code at a certain address and doesn't find it.

Top Performance Tips for Multitasking Systems

Getting more than one application to run on a system at the same time usually involves making some compromises. You can tune a single-tasking system to provide the best performance for that one application. For example, you can tune your system in such a way that a disk-intensive application gets everything it needs to get the job done quickly. What happens if you run one application that's disk-intensive and another that's CPU-intensive? Do you starve the resources of one to get better performance from the other?

Running more than one application at once always consumes a lot of memory. What you might not realize is that your performance levels might become artificially low because of the way Windows 95 handles memory management.

Disk swapping, the same feature that provides so much virtual memory for your applications, can wreak havoc in a multitasking environment. Two big clues tell you that disk swapping has become a problem and not a cure. First, you notice a dramatic increase in your system's disk activity. This isn't always a bad thing under Windows 95, but it is an indicator. Second, look at the size of your swap file. If your swap file is about the same size as your real memory, your system is memory-starved, and you really can't run the number of applications you're trying to run. These two clues provide you with a quick idea of what your system performance is like right this minute without wasting a lot of your time trying to define it completely. Of course, using System Monitor to display your actual system performance for your boss might get you the memory upgrade you've been wanting.

You also want to take into account the needs of the LAN as a whole if your system doubles as a file server. A peer-to-peer network depends on the resources of one or more workstations to act as file and print servers. This doubling of tasks is really another form of multitasking. You might run only one or two tasks on your machine, but it runs slowly if you don't take into account the needs of other people who use your system. In this case, however, a simple look at the swap file and disk activity probably won't provide you with enough information. You have to monitor the network statistics, using the System Monitor program.

Windows 95 also provides another utility that comes in handy here. The NetWatcher utility (described in Chapter 27, "Networks") provides information about who is logged in and what type of resources they're using. You can combine this information with that obtained from System Monitor to create a clear picture of how your machine is used in the network environment. Figure 5.12 shows a typical example of the type of information you can expect. Making a correlation between who is using which resource and what the level of activity is might seem like a difficult task, but after a while, you'll notice certain patterns emerging. You can use those patterns as a basis for tuning your system.

You can get better performance out of your system if you balance the types of tasks it performs. Scheduling all your disk-intensive tasks to run at the same time is one sure way to bring your system to its knees. If you're working on a spreadsheet in the foreground, that might be a good time to compile an application or perform some database-related task in the background. Of course, the opposite is true as well. You can always perform that intensive spreadsheet recalculation in the background while performing data entry in the foreground.

Tip: Unlike previous versions of Windows, Windows 95 actually does a reasonable job of downloading files and performing other forms of online communication in the background. I recently spent almost eight hours downloading a new copy of Internet Information Server from the Internet at 33.6Kbps while working on articles and my spreadsheet in the foreground. I never did miss a file or experience any form of corruption. Under Windows 3.x, I would've had to give up my system for the day in similar circumstances.

Figure 5.12.
NetWatcher allows you to monitor who is sharing your computer and which resources they're using.

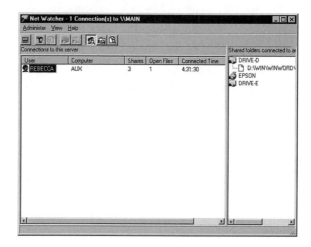

There's one final consideration you need to make when you want to get the most out of your multitasking environment. Using 16-bit applications under Windows 95 means that you must suffer the consequences of cooperative multitasking. In essence, a program can be a bad sport and grab the system for however long it wants. 32-bit applications don't get this kind of treatment. Ready or not, they have to return control of the system to Windows 95 at specific intervals. If you want to use multitasking, use only 32-bit applications.

Memory Tuning and Optimization

I've gone through most of the following material in other chapters. However, this is a good place to summarize the various tips and techniques that I present in Chapter 13. Here are my top ten tips and techniques for tuning your system to make the best use of memory:

1. Always use the built-in memory manager if possible.

2. Use your fastest drive for the swap file, but don't starve Windows in the process. Make sure the drive is large enough to hold the entire swap file.

3. Manage your system, but don't micromanage it. Tell Windows what you need to do, but don't worry too much about how it gets the job done.

4. Never load real-mode device drivers or TSRs you don't need. The old approach of loading everything before you start Windows is a dead end under Windows 95.

5. Use the automatic memory settings whenever possible. However, sometimes you have to step in and adjust them manually if you have an application that starts by grabbing everything available.

6. Avoid MS-DOS mode, but use it if you must. Windows 95 has come a long way in providing optimal support for MS-DOS applications.

7. Enhance your memory usage by getting rid of the frills. Wallpaper, excess icons, screen savers, and other doodads consume memory without giving you much in return.

8. Increase your level of physical RAM as needed. Windows 95 can literally make as much RAM as you need from your hard drive, but there's a limit to how much performance you can get by doing this.

9. Get a faster hard drive. Swap files are a fact of life under Windows 95, and that means you're at least partially dependent on its speed for overall system performance—even when it comes to memory.

10. Kill those old applications. If you're still using a lot of MS-DOS applications, it's time to upgrade. Of course, 16-bit Windows applications aren't much better, for the most part. Upgrading to the newer 32-bit applications helps you use memory efficiently and usually provides a speed benefit as well.

Disk Compression with DriveSpace 3

Unlike with some previous versions of Windows, disk compression in Windows 95 is reliable and is an excellent option to use when you need more disk space—and who doesn't? I especially like to use disk compression on my laptop computer. My 0.5GB drive gives me nearly 1.5GB of space when I use the compression facilities that come with Windows 95 and OSR2. Windows 95 comes with the disk compression program DriveSpace. OSR2 upgrades the standard DriveSpace to DriveSpace 3.

There are several advantages to using DriveSpace 3 disk compression instead of the standard DriveSpace. Perhaps the most important advantage is that you can create compressed drives larger than 512MB. DriveSpace 3 supports compressed drives of up to 2GB. With the ever-growing size of programs, this is a welcome capability. DriveSpace 3 uses all the free space on your drive, even if it's fragmented. The standard DriveSpace can use only contiguous, unfragmented disk space to compress files. DriveSpace 3 allows you to achieve maximum compression, called UltraPack compression, on files you don't use often, further increasing storage efficiency. Finally, DriveSpace 3 is built to work together with Compression Agent to maximize your storage efficiency and performance.

Choosing Between FAT32 and Disk Compression

As great as DriveSpace 3 might be, it does have one problem: It won't support hard disks that use FAT32 partitions. Of course, FAT32 is only available on new computers that had Windows 95 OSR2 originally installed. As a general rule, if your new computer already has OSR2 installed with Windows 95, you cannot use DriveSpace 3. In this case, you have to buy a third-party disk-compression program that supports FAT32 volumes. If you had to upgrade your copy of Windows 95 with OSR2, then DriveSpace 3 is a valid option.

What are the main differences between FAT32 and disk compression? Basically, FAT32 improves the foundation of the file system used to organize data stored on your hard disk. Microsoft created the original FAT file system to store data on floppy disks, which was later modified for managing data on both removable and fixed media.

Unfortunately, FAT can only support a single disk volume up to 2GB in size. FAT32 simply enhances the FAT file system to support hard drives up to 2TB in size.

In addition, FAT32 uses smaller clusters, resulting in 10 to 15 percent better efficiency in using disk space compared to large FAT drives. FAT32 also tends to be more reliable because FAT32 includes a backup of critical data structures. Unlike the older FAT system, FAT32 drives are less likely to fail than existing FAT volumes.

Although FAT32 improves the performance and reliability of your hard drive, DriveSpace 3 increases the amount of data you can store on your hard drive. Look for a future version of DriveSpace to compress FAT32 hard disks, but for now, you have to choose either FAT32 or DriveSpace 3; you cannot have both.

Compressing a Drive with DriveSpace 3

Compressing a drive with DriveSpace 3 is essentially the same as compressing it with the standard DriveSpace, except that you get the advantages of the extra features just discussed. If you want to create a compressed drive larger than 512MB, you must use DriveSpace 3. This substantial increase in capacity is welcome, but, sadly, there is still a limit—2GB. This means that you can compress up to between half a gigabyte and one gigabyte of uncompressed drive space. This number is sure to be closer to half a gigabyte because, in my experience, DriveSpace 3 really gives you about three times your original disk space.

Upgrading a Compressed Drive with DriveSpace 3

Like compressing an uncompressed drive with DriveSpace 3, upgrading a compressed drive using DriveSpace 3 is essentially the same as upgrading it with the standard DriveSpace. The exception is that you must also upgrade drives compressed with the standard DriveSpace to get the added features of DriveSpace 3.

Balancing Disk Space and Speed with DriveSpace 3

DriveSpace 3 allows you to fine-tune how your drive is compressed, giving you control over tradeoffs between disk space and operation speed. Three compression types used by DriveSpace 3 form the basis of these adjustments: Standard compression, HiPack compression, and no compression at all.

Standard Compression

With Standard compression, DriveSpace 3 typically compresses files to just over half of their uncompressed size. A special Plus! feature of Standard compression is that more of the disk drive is searched for repetitive data. This results in better compression ratios and relatively fast disk reads and writes.

HiPack Compression

With HiPack compression, files are typically compressed to just under half their uncompressed size. Reading data from HiPack compressed files is relatively fast. However, writing data to HiPack compressed files is relatively slow.

> **Tip:** You get the highest compression ratios from something called UltraPack compression. Only Compression Agent can pack your files using UltraPack. See the section "Compression Agent" later in this chapter.

Balancing Optimization and Compression Using DriveSpace 3

Nearly everyone will want to optimize his or her compressed drive for a balance between speed and drive space. Nevertheless, it's possible to fully optimize your compressed drive for either speed or space. I consider these extreme optimizations first because they're easy to understand and they demonstrate the principles behind disk compression optimization well.

Compression Optimized for Speed

If you want your machine to run at the maximum speed possible, you want your programs to load files from disk as rapidly as they can, and you want to optimize your compressed drive for speed. That's silly, you say. Everyone wants that! Right you are. The "gotcha" is that, in this extreme example, you don't care at all about disk space. Presumably, you have plenty of it. To maximize speed, configure DriveSpace 3 to save files uncompressed. That's right; compress your drives with DriveSpace 3 set so that it doesn't compress your files! Naturally, this is the fastest compression option. It also seems a bit silly. However, you'll see later that there are times when this setting can be useful.

To compress a drive for maximum speed, open DriveSpace 3. Select Advanced | Settings to open the Disk Compression Settings dialog box, shown in Figure 5.13. Select the No Compression (fastest) radio button. Click the OK button and compress the drive in the usual way.

Figure 5.13.
Select DriveSpace 3 compression features in the Disk Compression Settings dialog box.

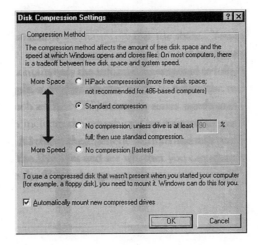

Compression Optimized for Space

If you're trying to squeeze a lot of program and data bytes onto a small disk drive, you want to maximize your disk compression with drive space. You can set DriveSpace 3 to maximize drive space while, for the most part, ignoring performance considerations. Of course, you take a performance hit if you do this, but it might be worth it if you need the space. Actually, the default DriveSpace 3 compression method compresses every file. However, it compresses them using Standard compression, which shows a small, if even noticeable, performance hit. You can squeeze even more space onto your drive if you select the HiPack compression method. You should compress your entire drive with HiPack compression only if you desperately need the space because this setting causes a substantial slowdown in writing data to the drive. You might find HiPack tolerable if your machine has a Pentium or faster central processing unit.

To compress a drive for maximum space with little degradation in performance, open DriveSpace 3. Select Advanced | Settings to open the Disk Compression Settings dialog box, shown in Figure 5.13. Select the Standard compression radio button. Click the OK button and compress the drive in the usual way.

To compress a drive for maximum space while throwing performance concerns to the wind, select the HiPack compression radio button instead.

Compression Optimized for a Balance Between Speed and Drive Space

DriveSpace 3 lets you have a balance between speed and drive space that best suits you and your computer hardware. It works like this: You tell DriveSpace 3 to use the uncompressed method on files until a specified percentage of the drive, predefined by you, fills up. Then DriveSpace 3 begins compressing files using Standard compression. The default is set so that when 90 percent of the compressed drive is filled, DriveSpace 3 begins compressing files. However, you can designate your own percentage. At the 90 percent setting, DriveSpace 3 is optimized to favor speed over space until it's absolutely necessary to have more room. In contrast, if you set it to 10 percent, you'd be optimizing DriveSpace 3 in favor of drive space over speed.

To compress a drive for a balance between space and performance, open DriveSpace 3. Select Advanced | Settings. In the Disk Compression Settings dialog box, shown in Figure 5.13, select the No compression unless drive is at least 90% full radio button. Modify the percentage if you want. Click the OK button and compress the drive in the usual way.

Compression Agent

Using Compression Agent can significantly increase the storage efficiency and performance of your drive compressed by DriveSpace 3. As you've seen, DriveSpace 3 compresses uncompressed drives, upgrades drives previously compressed using DoubleSpace or DriveSpace, and sets the compression method of saving new files to disk, allowing you to specify some optimizations for drive space and performance. Compression Agent picks up where DriveSpace 3 leaves off and works with DriveSpace 3 to optimize drive space and performance better than DriveSpace 3 can do on its own.

In particular, Compression Agent scans your compressed drive and looks at each file for the time it was last accessed and how it is compressed. If the file is seldom accessed, Compression Agent compresses it at the highest compression ratio—UltraPack compression. Only Compression Agent can compress files using UltraPack. If the file is used often but has been compressed, Compression Agent will probably uncompress it to increase system performance.

DriveSpace 3 sets the standard compression method, as discussed earlier. Compression Agent optimizes the compression method set through DriveSpace 3 by checking individual file usage against compression type.

The Compression Tab

The Compression tab contains different information, depending on whether the drive is compressed. If your drive isn't compressed, the Compression tab shows you the amount of used and free space currently on your drive and how much you would have of each if you compressed the drive. (See Figure 5.14.)

Figure 5.14.
The Compression tab in the disk drive Properties dialog box of an uncompressed drive.

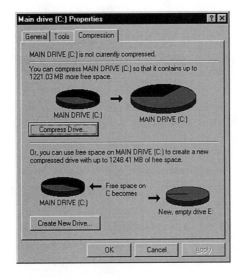

It also tells you the approximate size of a new drive that could be built by compressing your drive's remaining free space. This is the perfect option if you want to compress files on your boot drive but don't want to risk having your whole boot drive compressed. Buttons on this tab allow you to compress the drive or make a new compressed drive. If your drive is compressed, the Compression tab is filled with statistics on the percentage of files compressed, with various compression types and the amount of disk space you've gained.

When you select the Compression tab from the Properties dialog box of a compressed disk drive, all sorts of drive statistics are calculated, as shown in Figure 5.15. Beware that this can take a while. You can, however, cancel the operation if you want.

The Compression tab tells you how many megabytes of files are taken up by each compression type on your drive, the compression ratio achieved for each compression type, and the number of megabytes you gained by compressing the files.

Figure 5.15.
You can obtain
information about
your compressed drive
on the Compression
tab of the Properties
dialog box.

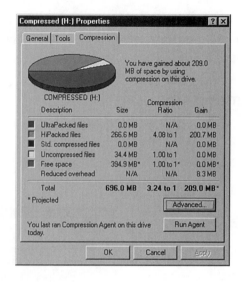

In the disk drive Properties dialog box, you have the option of clicking the Run Agent button to run Compression Agent to optimize disk compression. You can also click the Advanced button to open the Advanced Properties dialog box, shown in Figure 5.16, where you can elect to hide the host drive or click the Run DriveSpace button to reset various parameters inside DriveSpace 3.

Figure 5.16.
You can hide the host
drive using the
Advanced Properties
dialog box.

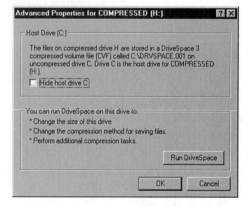

Defragmenting Your Hard Drive

Sometimes you might notice that loading an application takes an abnormally long time with the hard disk drive light flashing on and off. When this happens, you might need to defragment your hard drive.

If you do not defragment your hard disk, the operating system might have to access several different physical locations on the disk to retrieve the files you need to load. This process causes your hard drive light to flash on and off, making file access slower. Disk defragmenting simply places the files on your hard disk in contiguous clusters, making file access faster.

Using the Disk Defragmenter Optimization Wizard

Beta Release

To help you defragment your hard disk, Windows 98 offers the next step in drive defragmentation. If keeping all the clusters for a file together improves performance a little, then keeping all the files together for a particular application improves performance even more. That's precisely what the Disk Defragmenter Optimization wizard does for you. It helps keep track of the applications you use most often and then keeps all the files required for that application in one place. This technology relies on the same process as standard disk defragmentation for improved performance: reduced disk head movement.

Automating Tune-Ups with Task Scheduler

The Task Scheduler allows you to perform automated tasks using different criteria. For example, you can have the computer run ScanDisk at 7:00 P.M. every Sunday, your disk defragmenter at 5:00 P.M. every Friday, and your anti-virus program at 9:00 A.M. on the first Monday of every month.

> **Tip:** You can use the Task Scheduler to run a variety of applications, not just disk utility programs. For example, you can use the Task Scheduler to send out a fax in the middle of the night when phone rates are lower or print a database report after hours so it doesn't tie up your computer during the day.

The Task Scheduler can execute a variety of tasks, including applications designed for Windows 95/ NT, Windows 3.x, OS/2, MS-DOS, batch files (.BAT), command files (.CMD), or any properly registered file type. A task has one or more triggers that determine when the task should be executed.

A trigger is a set of criteria that, when met, activates and causes a task to be executed. There are two types of triggers: time-based and event-based. A time-based trigger activates at a specified time. Not only can you set the time that they become active, but you can also have them activate once, daily, weekly, monthly, on a specified day of the month (for example, the third day of the month), or on a specified day of the week of a month (for example, the second Tuesday of the month).

An event-based trigger activates in response to certain system events. Some event-based triggers become active when the system starts up, when a user logs on to the local computer, or when the system becomes idle. The last of these are known as idle triggers.

When no keyboard or mouse input occurs, the computer is considered to be in an idle state. An idle trigger is an event-based trigger that becomes active a specified amount of time after the computer becomes idle. When you set the idle-related flags for a task, you create an idle trigger.

Starting Task Scheduler

You can start the Task Scheduler by clicking the Start button, clicking Programs, clicking Accessories, clicking System Tools, and choosing Scheduled Tasks. This displays the Scheduled Tasks window, as shown in Figure 5.17.

Figure 5.17.
The Scheduled Task window lets you add, modify, or delete tasks.

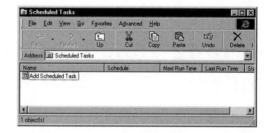

Scheduling a New Task

Before you can use the Task Scheduler, you have to schedule specific tasks that you want done:

1. Creating a new task is as simple as double-clicking the Add Scheduled Task icon that appears in Figure 5.17. As soon as you double-click this icon, the Add Scheduled Task wizard appears.

2. Click the Next button. Another Scheduled Task wizard window appears, letting you choose the application you want to run, as shown in Figure 5.18.

3. Click the application (such as ScanDisk) that you want to run. If you can't find the specific application you want to run, click the Browse button to look for the application file.

4. Click the Next button. The Scheduled Task wizard asks for a specific time to run the task—daily, weekly, monthly, one time only, at boot up, or when you log on, as shown in Figure 5.19. Click the option you want to use.

5. Click the Next button. Depending on the time you choose (daily, weekly, monthly, and so on), you see another list of options asking you to specify the exact time and date to run your chosen task. Figure 5.20 shows the options available for a weekly task.

Figure 5.18.
The Scheduled Task Wizard needs to know the application you want to run.

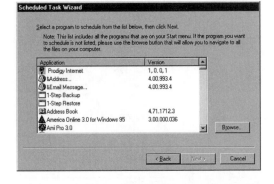

Figure 5.19.
You can choose from a variety of times to run your chosen application through the Scheduled Task Wizard.

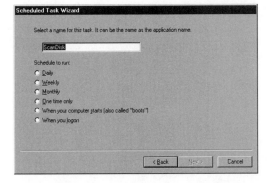

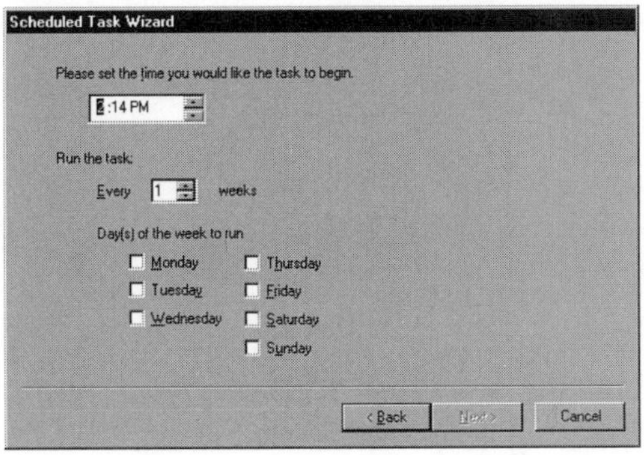

Figure 5.20.
You need to define additional options for running a weekly task.

6. Choose a time and date and then click the Next button. The Add Scheduled Task Wizard lists the application you chose to run and the time, as shown in Figure 5.21. Click the Finish button if you are ready to schedule the task. If you made a mistake, click the Back button to correct your scheduling of the task. Once you finish scheduling a task, the task appears in the Scheduled Tasks window, as shown in Figure 5.22.

Figure 5.21.
The Add Scheduled Task wizard is ready to schedule a task for you with the Task Scheduler.

Figure 5.22.
The Scheduled Tasks window lists all your scheduled tasks.

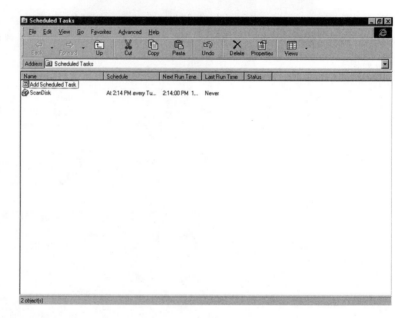

Tip: After scheduling a task, right-click that task and choose Run. This gives you a chance to see how your scheduled task actually runs. That way you can see whether your task hangs or needs additional input before running.

Customizing a Scheduled Task

After you create a task, the Task Scheduler continues running your task daily, weekly, monthly, at boot up, or when you log on until you either delete the scheduled task or specify a time to stop running a particular task.

Besides specifying a date to stop running a task, there's another reason to customize your tasks. You might want the Task Scheduler to automatically delete a scheduled task when you no longer need it after a certain date. If you're running the Task Scheduler on a laptop computer, you might not want to run tasks automatically, especially if your batteries are running low. Finally, you might only want to run a task when the computer is idle. After all, you might not want to have the Task Scheduler suddenly interfere with your work at the computer.

Customizing a scheduled task involves changing a task's properties. To view a task's properties, right-click the task and choose Properties. The task's properties dialog appears as shown in Figure 5.23. If you move an application to a different folder, you might need to type the new directory where the application file name is located.

Figure 5.23.
The Task tab specifies the location and file name of the application to run.

The Schedule tab lets you define the date and time to run a task, as shown in Figure 5.24. Clicking the Advanced button displays an Advanced Schedule Options dialog, as shown in Figure 5.25. This is where you can specify an ending date to stop running your task as well as the capability to repeat a task.

The Settings tab, as shown in Figure 5.26, lets you specify whether to delete a task after it's done, when to stop a task in case it's still running after a certain period of time, whether to run on a laptop using its battery power, and whether to run when the computer is idle.

If you ever need to delete a task, just click it and then click the Delete icon in the Task Scheduler toolbar.

Running Batch Files Automatically

Besides letting you choose to run an application, the Task Scheduler can also run old-fashioned batch files. Why would you want to run a batch file? The answer is easy. A batch file lets you specify command-line parameters for your applications as well as create a list of two or more applications to run one after another.

Figure 5.24.
The Schedule tab is where you can change or modify the date and time to run a task.

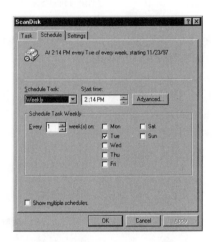

Figure 5.25.
The Advanced Schedule Options dialog lets you pick an ending date to stop running a task or provides the capability to run the same task repeatedly.

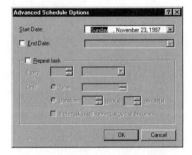

Figure 5.26.
The Settings tab lets you modify how the task runs when running on a laptop computer or when the computer is idle.

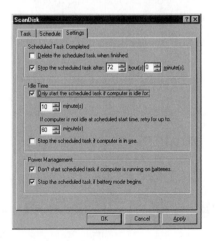

By running a single batch file, you can run two or more programs without scheduling each one individually within the Task Scheduler. For example, your batch file might contain the following two lines:

```
C:\WINDOWS\SCANDSKW.EXE
C:\WORD\WORD.EXE
```

The first line tells your computer to run the ScanDisk application (SCANDSKW.EXE), and the second line tells your computer to load Word for Windows.

In case you've forgotten how to create a batch file, they are simply ASCII files that end with the .BAT file extension. You can create batch files using any editor such as Notepad. Just remember to save your file with the .BAT file extension.

Suspending Task Scheduler

Sometimes you might want to temporarily halt the Task Scheduler from running scheduled tasks. Rather than suspend each scheduled task individually (and then worry about reactivating each task all over again), you can temporarily keep the Task Scheduler from running any of its scheduled tasks.

To suspend Task Scheduler temporarily, load Task Scheduler and choose Advanced | Pause Task Scheduler, as shown in Figure 5.27. When you want to reactivate Task Scheduler, choose Advanced | Continue Task Scheduler.

Figure 5.27.
The Pause Task Scheduler command temporarily stops all tasks stored in Task Scheduler.

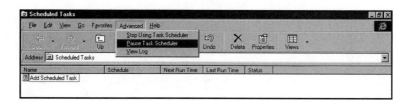

Disabling Task Scheduler

Rather than temporarily suspend the Task Scheduler, you might find it more convenient to turn it off altogether. To turn off the Task Scheduler, load Task Scheduler and choose Advanced | Stop Using Task Scheduler. To turn Task Scheduler back on again, choose Advanced | Start Using Task Scheduler.

Monitoring the Results of Performance Enhancements

System Monitor is an optional utility that you can install—and it's a worthwhile tool. It allows you to track a variety of system statistics, including CPU usage and actual memory allocation. Monitoring these statistics tells you whether a certain optimization strategy was successful. System Monitor also provides a means of detecting performance-robbing hardware and software errors on the system. Figure 5.28 shows a typical System Monitor display.

Figure 5.28.
System Monitor.

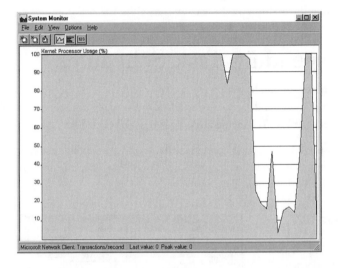

When you start System Monitor for the first time, it always displays the current Kernel Processor Usage. Figure 5.29 shows one way to display this information. You can use the View | Bar Chart or the View | Numeric Chart command to change the presentation. I find that the bar chart presentation (see Figure 5.29) is the most helpful when I want to monitor current system performance, and the numeric chart (see Figure 5.30) is handy when I need to troubleshoot a particular problem area. Notice the line displayed somewhere along the length of the bar. This line tells you the maximum usage level for that particular statistic. Of course, the bar itself shows the current usage level. You can also select any of the three chart types by clicking the correct toolbar icon.

Although System Monitor uses a default monitoring period, this default setting might not be fast enough in certain situations. If you're troubleshooting a bad NIC or you want instant feedback on a configuration change, change this setting to a lower value. Likewise, if you're performing long-term monitoring, you might want to set it high. (Just remember that increasing this interval adds a bit of processor overhead, which could slightly skew the monitoring results.) Use the Options | Chart command to change this setting. Figure 5.31 shows the dialog box that changes the interval.

Figure 5.29.
The bar graph presentation allows you to easily monitor current events.

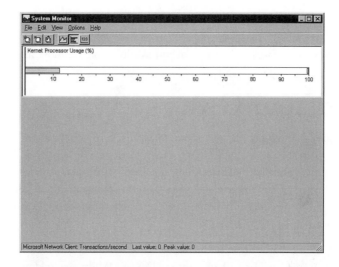

Figure 5.30.
You can use the numeric chart presentation to get a quick look at the current machine statistics.

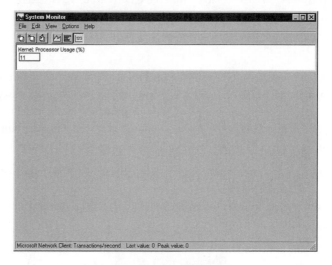

Figure 5.31.
Short intervals aid troubleshooting efforts; long intervals help you monitor your machine's performance more accurately.

The first three toolbar buttons allow you to change the items that System Monitor displays. Use the Add button to add new items to the list. Use the Edit button to change the way System Monitor displays a particular value. For example, you might want to display something in green rather than blue. You can also change the upper limit of some values to provide a consistent range of values for particular items. Finally, the Remove button allows you to remove an item from the monitoring list.

On Your Own

Practice creating long filenames that an MS-DOS or Windows 3.x user can understand. Use Explorer to create a new file in a temporary folder, and give it a long filename. Then open the MS-DOS prompt and view that same filename. Does the name make sense in both contexts? If not, you need to spend a little more time working on this. Remember that you're effectively reduced to six characters for the filename because of the way that Windows 95 differentiates between different files with similar long filenames.

Survey your hardware to see if there are any components that might be holding back your system performance. Consider replacing that old CD-ROM drive or adding more memory if necessary to enhance system throughput. A whole new machine might be in your future if the current one is completely out of date; don't waste a lot of money replacing all the components in your machine one at a time.

Check out the section "General Tuning Tips for Windows" earlier in the chapter to see if you can get rid of any memory- or performance-wasting features. For example, you might want to consider spending a week without wallpaper. The performance improvement you get might be worth the sacrifice. Look at some of the doodads you loaded as well. I'm often surprised at how many of these little utility programs get loaded on my machine and then never get used.

Look at the Performance tab of the System Properties dialog (refer to Figure 5.1) to see if your system is using all the automatic tuning features that Windows provides. Make sure that all the automatic tuning features are working for you, rather than against you. For example, you might want to change the drive used for the virtual memory swap file to a faster drive on your machine.

Hunt for any unneeded drivers on your machine (if you suspect there are any—new machines usually don't have unneeded drivers lurking around). Make sure you look for some of the non-obvious sources of wasted device drivers, such as network protocols that you don't use.

Start monitoring your machine once you get it optimized. Make sure that all the changes you made actually improved system performance rather than hindered it. If you do find that some change reduced system performance, figure out why. A good knowledge of how changes affect your machine makes it easier to tune in the future.

6

Startup
Shortcuts

Peter Norton®

This chapter looks at some of the ways you can make yourself a little more efficient so that you can get the full benefits of using Windows 95 as an operating system. This means everything from the way you start your applications to the way you arrange your desktop. Windows 95 provides many new tools that you can use to make each step a little faster.

Windows 95 Shortcuts and OLE

Every shortcut you create is a form of OLE, linking to another object on your machine. Windows 95 provides some special handling for these objects. (Chapter 12, "DDE, OLE, DCOM, and ActiveX," spends a lot of time discussing OLE from a user perspective.)

Unlike an application that can create compound documents to hold all the linking information, Windows 95 has to store that information someplace on the drive. The LNK file is the Windows 95 answer to this problem. It contains all the linking information needed to keep the shortcuts on your desktop current with the real object.

You can easily test this by creating a shortcut of a folder on your desktop. Every change you make to the real folder will appear in the linked copy. Likewise, every change you make in the linked copy will appear in the real thing.

Faster Startups

Windows 95 provides several ways to start your applications so you can choose the one you like best:

- Right-click the application's icon while in Explorer, and then click Open in the context menu.
- Double-click the application's icon while in Explorer or File Manager.
- Double-click a data file associated with the application while in Explorer. (This requires that you create a file association or that the application create it for you. To change file associations, open Windows Explorer, select View | Folder Options, click the File Types tab, and click the Edit button to define which application should open which type of file.)
- Choose Start | Run and then type the application's path and filename. Click OK to start the application.
- Choose Start | Run and then drag-and-drop the application's icon into the Run dialog box. Click OK to start the application.
- Select the application's entry from the Start menu.
- Create a shortcut icon on the desktop. You can start the application by right-clicking or double-clicking the icon.

- Assign a shortcut key to the application, and then start it by using the keyboard shortcut. (You must create a LNK file to do this. I look at the process for doing this later.)

- Use the Windows 3.*x* Program Manager (provided in the \WINDOWS directory) to run the application.

- Place the application's icon or associated data file in the Startup folder in the Start menu to run it automatically the next time you start Windows. Placing a data file in the Startup folder automatically opens it for you.

- Use the Find dialog to find your application, and then right-click or double-click it.

- Embed or link the application's data in an OLE compound document. The user can start the application by double-clicking the object embedded in the document. (The application must support OLE for this to work.)

Windows 95 provides a lot of neat ways to use the keyboard and mouse with your applications. You'll find that you can do a lot of things you couldn't do before with a simple mouse click.

Startups from the Keyboard

Some shortcut keys come installed with Windows 95. I find that many of them are attached to the Accessibility options, but you can change all that with a just a little effort. (I look at this later in this section.) Table 6.1 provides a list of keystrokes and the actions they perform. You're probably familiar with most of them, but others are new to Windows 95.

Table 6.1. Windows 95 shortcut keys.

Key or Key Combination	Purpose
Alt+F4	Exits the current application. You can also use this key combination to exit Windows if you're at the desktop.
Alt+Shift+Tab	Switches to the previous window.
Alt+Spacebar	Displays the Control menu of the currently active window.
Alt+Tab	Switches to the next window.
Ctrl+Esc	Opens the Start menu on the Taskbar. You can then use the arrow keys to select an application. Pressing Enter starts the application you selected.
Esc	Cancels the last action in most cases. However, you can't back out of some actions.
F1	Displays online help. In most cases, this help is general in nature but is application-specific.

continues

Table 6.1. continued

Key or Key Combination	Purpose
F2	Pressing this while an icon is highlighted allows you to change the object name.
F3	Unless your application uses this key for something else, you can press it to access the Find dialog. In most cases, you'll get better results if you press F3 while at the desktop. You can also use this key at the Taskbar and the Start menu.
Left Alt+Left Shift+ Num Lock	Holding these three keys down turns on the MouseKeys feature of the Accessibility options.
Left Alt+Left Shift+ Print Screen	Holding these three keys down turns on the High Contrast feature of the Accessibility options.
Num Lock	Holding the Num Lock key down for five seconds turns on the ToggleKeys feature of the Accessibility options.
Right Shift	Holding the right Shift key down for eight seconds turns on the FilterKeys feature of the Accessibility options.
Shift five times	Pressing the Shift key five times turns on the StickyKeys feature of the Accessibility options.
Shift+F1	Displays context-sensitive help when the application supports it. The Windows 95 desktop doesn't appear to support this option.
Shift+F10	You must select an object before you use this key combination. It displays the context menu. Considering the number of options on the context menu, this key combination allows you to do almost anything with the object.
Tab	Use this key while at the desktop to switch between the desktop, Taskbar, and Start menu. You also can use Ctrl+Esc to bring up the Start menu and then press Tab to switch between applications.

Tip: Combining the various keystrokes makes them much more powerful. For example, what if you have a lot of applications open and need to get to the desktop quickly? Use Ctrl+Esc to display the Start menu, Esc to close the menu itself, Tab to get to the Taskbar, and Shift+F10 to display the context menu. All you need to do now is select Minimize All Windows and press Enter. Pressing Tab one more time takes you to the desktop.

Windows 95 provides two additional methods of using the keyboard to start applications. You can use the Windows 3.*x* method of assigning a shortcut key to the application. There are also automated methods of starting some applications.

> **Tip:** Some keyboards, like the Microsoft Natural Keyboard, come with a Windows key. Pressing this key opens the Start menu when using Windows 95. In addition to the Windows key, a few keyboards also come equipped with a Menu key. (It actually has what appears to be a menu printed right on the key.) You can use this key to open a context menu, just as if you clicked the right mouse key.

Undocumented Parameters

The first program you need to learn to use this section of the book is START. It's a program that you'll find in your \WINDOWS\COMMAND directory. Take a look at some documented parameters that START provides:

- /MAX: Use this to run a maximized application in the background.
- /M: This switch allows you to run the application minimized in the background.
- /R: The default setting for START is to run the program in the foreground. You can still switch back to the DOS prompt, but you'll take a quick trip to Windows first.
- /W: Use this switch if you want to start a Windows application, work with it for a while, and return to the DOS prompt when you're done.
- *<program name>*: This is the name of the program you want to run and any parameters it needs in order to execute.

All this is fine if you want to run a Windows application from MS-DOS. However, this information doesn't really become useful until you can get some work done in Windows without leaving the MS-DOS prompt. What would happen if you wanted to gain the advantage of Windows background printing while performing other work at the MS-DOS prompt? You could switch back to Windows, start Notepad or some other appropriate application, load your file, and print, but that would disrupt what you were doing. The following line shows an easier, faster, and much better method:

```
START /M NOTEPAD /P SOMEFILE.TXT
```

There are a few things here you really need to notice. The first is the /P parameter right after NOTEPAD. Where did I get it? It isn't documented anywhere. All you have to do is look in Explorer.

Take a look at this now. Open Explorer. It doesn't matter what directory you're viewing or how it's configured. Use the View | Options command to display the Options dialog box. Click the File Types tab. Scroll through the file types until you come across an entry for Text Document. Highlight it and click Edit. Click Print and then Edit. You should see a display similar to the one in Figure 6.1.

Figure 6.1.
Windows 95 hides a wealth of information. Explorer is just one of the gold mines.

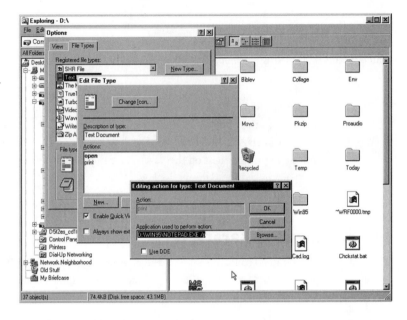

Now you can see where I came up with the /P parameter. Press Cancel three times to get back to the main Explorer display. Every other registered application will provide the same types of information. Some of them will be a little too complex to use from the MS-DOS prompt, but you could use them if you wanted to do so. The whole idea of this shortcut is that you get to stay at the MS-DOS prompt and still use the new features that Windows provides.

> **Tip:** Just about every Windows application provides undocumented command-line switches. Even though you can only guess at what those switches are in most cases, you can usually count on them supporting one or two switches. The /P parameter almost always allows you to print by using that application. Some applications also provide a /W parameter that suppresses the display of any opening screens. Looking through the Explorer file listings will provide you with additional ideas.

There are a few other caveats you need to consider. Notice how I formatted my command line. You have to place the START program command-line switches first and then the application name, the application switches, and any filenames. If you change this order, the application usually starts but reports some type of error in opening your file. I've even had some applications insist that the file isn't present on my drive.

Shortcut Keys

Remember the first section of this chapter, where I talked about the desktop and OLE? This is one of those times when that fact comes into play. To use the shortcuts Windows 95 provides, you have to create a shortcut. It doesn't matter where the shortcut is, but it does matter that it's a shortcut.

Tip: Every entry on the Start menu is a shortcut. If your application appears on the Start menu, you already have a shortcut to use. If it doesn't appear on the Start menu, you'll want to add it there or on the desktop.

Look at the Notepad shortcut on the Start menu. All you need to do is right-click the Start menu and choose Explorer. Use a combination of the arrow keys and Enter to get to the Notepad shortcut. Press Shift+F10 to display Notepad's context menu. Select Properties and press Enter. You need to select the Shortcut tab. You should see a display similar to the one in Figure 6.2.

Figure 6.2.
The Shortcut tab in the Properties dialog box allows you to add a shortcut key to an application or to another shortcut.

The Shortcut key field of this dialog box is where you enter the shortcut key combination you want to use. To save the setting, just close the dialog box as normal. The next time you press that key combination, Windows 95 opens the application for you.

Startups from the Desktop

Windows 95 may come installed with several applications already on the desktop, such as Internet Explorer and the Microsoft Network icon. As with the Start menu, none of these icons represents the actual application. You create a shortcut to the application, just as you do for the Start menu.

Adding shortcuts directly to the desktop lets you access an application without burrowing through several layers of menu to find it. Of course, your desktop has only so much space, so placing all your applications here would quickly lead to a cluttered environment. In addition, remember from Chapter 5, "Performance Primer," that each icon uses memory, so you need to consider whether the efficiency you'll gain is worth the memory you'll use by adding an icon.

However, placing on the desktop the one or two applications that you use regularly could mean an increase in efficiency. Just think how nice it would be if your word processor and communications program were just a double-click away. You could open them as needed and close them immediately after you finished using them. This would mean that the applications you used most would still be handy, but they'd be out of the way and wouldn't use up precious memory.

> **Tip:** Keyboard users will probably get the same response time by using shortcut keys instead of placing their applications on the desktop. Not only does this give you a neater-looking desktop, but it reduces the number of redundant links your computer has to maintain.

Placing a shortcut to your application on the desktop might provide an increase in efficiency, but double-clicking isn't the only way to open an application. The next few sections describe other ways you can access your applications faster by placing shortcuts to them on the desktop. The section "The Data-Oriented Approach to Applications" later in this chapter also looks at something new for Windows 95. You really owe it to yourself to get out of the application-centric mode and take the new data-centric approach.

Click Starts

Right-clicking displays a context menu for Windows 95 objects. Previous chapters took a quick look at the context menu. However, it's such an important concept that I felt you needed to take a special look at right-clicking for applications. To start an application this way, all you need to do is select the Open option from the context menu. This has the same effect as double-clicking, but it might be more convenient if you have slower fingers. Some people really do have a hard time getting the double-click to work. This new method of starting an application has the advantage of requiring only a single click.

I was kind of curious about the Quick View option on the context menu. If you select it for an executable object such as `Dialer.EXE`, you see a dialog box similar to the one in Figure 6.3. The majority of the information here is stuff that only a programmer could love. At first glance, you do see some useful information, such as the name of the program and the version of Windows that it expects to find on your machine. You might even be able to use some of the information here to determine the amount of memory that your application needs to run.

Figure 6.3.
The View option for executable files provides some interesting information that you can use to learn more about how the application works.

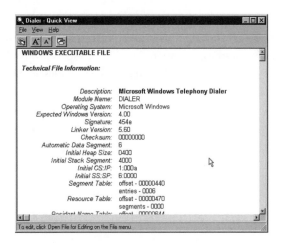

In reality, this isn't the information you want to see because you can determine most of it by using other methods. However, this view provides some special information that makes it easier for you to figure out which files to remove the next time you need to get rid of an old application. If you scroll down a bit, you'll notice a heading that says Imported-Name Table (Link-Time Imports).

> **Note:** Unfortunately, there are a number of ways to defeat the Quick View utility, and programmers use them all. The most common method is to mangle the names of the files used by the program in such a way that you can't read them but Windows can. The safest method for ensuring that you can remove a program you no longer need is to get those that are specially designed for Windows 95 and that include the requisite uninstall capabilities. That way, you can simply remove the program by using the Add/Remove Programs applet in the Control Panel. Chapter 13, "Exploiting Your Software: DOS, 16-Bit, and 32-Bit Windows Applications," covers the standard program-removal procedure.

Look at the list of files underneath this heading. All of them are somewhere on your drive—usually in the application folder or the `\WINDOWS\SYSTEM` folder. Unlike Windows 3.1, where it took some major tinkering to discover the files you needed to run an application, Windows 95 makes this information easy to find.

Use this information when the time comes to remove an application from your system. This view will help you come up with a list of files you need to delete. Of course, you don't want to delete any files that another application needs. Prune this list carefully so that it reflects only the files that are unique to a particular application. There's another problem with this list as well: It provides only one level of import file support. If one of the support files calls yet another group of files, you don't see that file here. Fortunately, you can also get to this view using other types of Windows executables. Be sure to look through the entire hierarchy before you consider your list of files complete.

There's another way to use this information to your advantage. Have you ever had an application that refused to start? Windows may have displayed a message about not finding one of the components needed to run the application. The Quick View dialog box can help you get past this situation. Coming up with a list of DLLs and other support files needed by the application is the first step in getting it to run. Next, check the application and the \WINDOWS\SYSTEM directory. As soon as you find which one of the files is missing, replace it and, voila, no more mystery message.

Auto Starts

Windows 95 provides a Startup folder to run specific applications every time you start your machine. All you need to do is add an application to the Startup folder to allow it to run automatically. I always start a copy of Explorer this way so that my machine is ready for use the instant Windows completes the boot process.

The Startup folder comes in handy for other tasks as well. I usually drag the data files I'm going to be working on for the next few days into my Startup folder. The reason is simple: Not only do I automatically start the application associated with that data file but I also automatically load the file itself. This makes morning startups extremely efficient. When I get back to Windows after starting it, my machine is completely set up for use. Every application I need is already loaded with the files I want to edit.

Peter's Principle: Becoming Too Efficient for Your Own Good

Be careful putting too many items in the Startup folder. It is easy for people to load every document they think they'll use for the entire week in there so that the documents are ready when they boot the machine the next morning.

The best way to use this feature is to think about what you plan to do first thing the next morning or perhaps for the majority of the day. Don't open more than two or perhaps three documents unless they all use the same application. Someone who works on the same document, such as a writer, can really benefit from this feature. People who create presentations or work on other documents for long periods of time can also benefit. However, if you work a little bit on one document and then a little bit on another one, you might be better off starting the main application you use and letting it go at that.

How do you add entries to the Startup folder? Just as you do with any other folder. The following procedure shows you a quick way to do it, using some of the new features that Windows 95 provides:

1. Right-click the Taskbar to display the context menu. Select the Properties option. Click the Start Menu Programs tab. You should see the Taskbar Properties dialog box shown in Figure 6.4.

Figure 6.4.

The Taskbar Properties dialog box allows you to add new programs to the Start menu using a menu-driven interface.

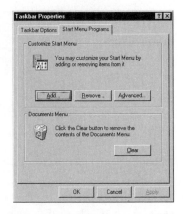

2. Click the Add button to open the Create Shortcut dialog box shown in Figure 6.5.

Figure 6.5.

The Create Shortcut dialog box is where you provide the name of the application or file that you want to add to the Startup folder (or another folder).

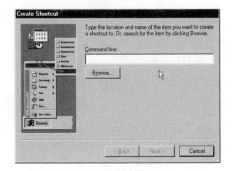

3. Click the Browse button to look for the file you want to add. As an alternative, you can type the full path and filename in the Command Line field of this dialog box. Click Next. You should see a Select Program Folder dialog. This dialog allows you to select the location of the shortcut in the Start menu. In this case, I selected the Startup folder, but you could just as easily select something else. Notice that you can add a new folder as well.

4. Scroll through the list of folders and highlight the Startup folder. Click Next. You should see the Select a Title for the Program dialog box, as shown in Figure 6.6. This is the final dialog box of the process. It allows you to change the name of the shortcut.

5. Type the name you want associated with this file. Using a name you can remember is the best idea. Changing the name here doesn't change the name of the file, only the shortcut; this is the entry as it will appear in the Startup folder.

6. Click Finish to complete the task, and then click OK to close the Taskbar Properties dialog box.

Figure 6.6.
The Select a Title for
the Program dialog.

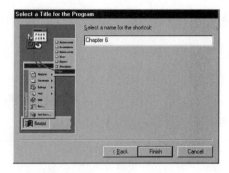

Once you complete this task, the application or data file you added to the Startup folder will load automatically each time you start Windows 95. Getting your system set up efficiently means that you can do a little extra reading or perform some other task while you wait for everything to load. Of course, adding a file to the load sequence won't make it load faster, but it'll give you a bigger block of time.

Controlled Starts

Windows 95 provides several ways to start an application by double-clicking:

- Explorer: You can double-click an application or its associated data file.
- Find: The Find dialog box comes in very handy. You can look for a data file and then double-click it to bring up the application associated with it. I've also used this dialog box as a quick method of finding the program I need.
- Desktop: Any data file or application sitting on the desktop follows the same rules as Explorer.
- Network Neighborhood: You can double-click any application or file sitting on someone else's machine.

The Data-Oriented Approach to Applications

The whole Windows 95 interface is oriented toward data-centric access. The next few sections discuss some of the tools that Windows 95 provides to make a data-oriented approach a lot easier.

Using Explorer to Get the Job Done

No longer are you tied to one specific action when it comes to data on your machine. If you've looked at the various context menus presented in this and other sections, you've noticed that there's always more than one thing you can do to a particular file. What you might not have realized is that the actions you saw are all under your control. You don't have to do things the Windows 95 way; you can do them any way that feels comfortable and allows you to get your work done faster.

> **Tip:** The first time you double-click a file that lacks a file association, Windows 95 asks which application you want to use to open it. You can choose an application that's already on the list or use the Browse feature to find a new one. Windows 95 defines only one action for this new association—open. Always take the time to modify that file association and add options for all the ways you plan to work with it. That way, the context menu associated with it is completely set up the next time you right-click the file or any others like it.

Take a look at how you can add a new file extension and then define a set of actions associated with that file:

1. Open a copy of Explorer.

2. Use the View | Options command to open the Options dialog box. Click the File Types tab. You should see a dialog box similar to the one shown in Figure 6.7.

Figure 6.7.
The File Types tab of the Options dialog box allows you to add, remove, and modify file associations.

3. Click New Type to display the Add New File Type dialog box.

4. Fill in the first two fields shown in Figure 6.8. The first field describes what kind of file it is. This is the text you'll see in various list boxes. The second field contains the exact file extension. If this were an Internet file association, you would also provide a Multipurpose Internet Mail Extensions (MIME) content type. This entry tells your browser which application to call when it runs into the associated file extension on the Internet. The last entry, Default Extension, allows you to assign an extension for Internet purposes. In some cases, this might be different from the extension used on your machine. For example, in this case, it would probably be ASC instead of ASCII.

Figure 6.8.
The Add New File Type dialog box contains several fields that you use to describe a file's association to an application.

Tip: One problem you might run into is thinking about file extensions in the DOS/ Windows 3.x format. Remember that Windows 95 supports long filenames, including long file extensions. You can define new file extensions that are more than three characters long. Windows 95 even allows some alternative characters in this format. For example, you could have a file extension of Word_Document if you wanted to. One character you need to avoid is the period (for obvious reasons).

5. Now you need to define some actions for this association. Click the New button. Fill out the information as shown in Figure 6.9. This is just one way to fill out this dialog box. WordPad uses a command-line interface, so all you need to do is fill out the Application used to perform action section of the dialog box. Click OK.

Figure 6.9.
This dialog box shows one type of file association entry. It uses command-line parameters.

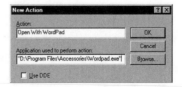

6. Create the same kind of entry for Notepad. Be sure to substitute NOTEPAD.EXE for the location and change the path as necessary. Also change the Action to read Open with Notepad.

7. Click the New button. Fill out the information as shown in Figure 6.10. This second type of association might look overly complicated, but it really isn't. It's the DDE format of a file association and an extremely powerful way to manage your data files. The DDE instructions form what equates to macros. They actually force the application to perform the same types of tasks that you accomplish by using a menu or the product's built-in macro capability. Chapter 11, "The Windows 95 Applets," discusses this topic at greater length. Right now, suffice it to say that if your application provides DDE support, you really owe it to yourself to use it.

Figure 6.10.
This dialog box shows the second type of association you can create. This DDE entry allows you to include macro-like instructions that control the way the application opens or works with the file.

8. Click OK. After you finish this entry, you should see three entries in the Add New File Type dialog. Notice the four check boxes near the bottom of the dialog box. Begin with the two check boxes on the left. Because this is an ASCII file, you probably should turn on the first check box, Enable Quick View. This allows you to use the Quick View utility provided with Windows 95. The second check box allows you to display the file extension at all times. Normally you leave this off to make it easier to rename files in Explorer without accidentally changing their extensions. The two check boxes on the right side of the dialog are Internet-specific. The first, Confirm open after download, tells Windows to display a dialog asking if you want to open the file after you download it from the Internet. The second check box, Browse in same window, allows you to view the file without opening a new copy of the browser.

9. Highlight Open with Notepad and click Set Default. This sets the double-click action for the file type. You can right-click to display the full context menu and use a different application to open the file, but this is the default action. You might also want to change the icon. I used the Notepad icon, but you can use any of those provided by the applications in this group or within an icon file. Click Close to complete the process. Click Close to close the Options dialog box.

10. Create a new file with an extension of .ASCII. I placed my copy on the desktop for sample purposes, but you can put your copy anywhere.

11. Right-click the file. You should see a list of opening options similar to the ones shown in Figure 6.11. Notice that Open with Notepad is highlighted, indicating that this entry is the default setting.

Figure 6.11.
The final result of the new file association is an extended context menu that allows any of three applications to open the file.

You can do a few additional things to really extend this new file association. Chapter 9, "The Windows 95 Architecture," tells about the Registry and the file association entries there. Because you just added a new text-file entry to the list of file associations, you can use the Registry to add a ShellX entry to it as well. That way, when you right-click the desktop or within Explorer, you see the new file extension as one of the files you can create by using the New option of the context menu. In most cases, there isn't a convenient method to add this support, but you should use it whenever possible.

This example also shows you something else. Productivity under Windows 95 is as much a matter of how you configure the desktop and the file associations as it is anything else. Being able to really use your machine's speed is what this data-centric approach to computing is all about.

Folders: A Real Organizational Tool

Folders aren't directories. They might look similar and provide about the same functionality when viewed from a certain perspective, but folders really do provide some features that directories don't. How do folders help you work efficiently? For one thing, folders support a context menu. As with most of the objects in Windows 95, you can open, explore, copy, and paste folders as you do any other object. Putting a group of files in a folder allows you to move an entire project from place to place or to make a copy of the data for someone else to use. It's actually faster to use folders than it is to type the required commands at the MS-DOS prompt—something I thought I would never see.

The Sharing option of the context menu allows you to share the folder with other folks on the network. Chapter 27, "Networks," covers this feature in greater detail.

You'll find the Send To option very useful. This option allows you to place the folder somewhere else. Default locations include the floppy drives and your Briefcase. You can even send the folder to

Microsoft Exchange. Imagine using e-mail to send the folder to a partner or co-worker who needs to see the information you've put together so far. Unlike past experiences in which I had to get all the files together and zip them up, this option is fairly convenient and makes the workflow smoother.

I use the Create Shortcut option to create a link to the existing file. Then I move the shortcut to my desktop or some other convenient place. Each shortcut uses 1KB of memory, a small price to pay for the convenience shortcuts provide.

Chapter 27 covers the Properties option in greater detail. For right now, suffice it to say that files and folders share many of the same characteristics. The Properties dialog box reflects this fact.

Desktop Tips and Techniques

I've moved to a totally data-centric approach on my desktop when it comes to projects. All I do is create a folder, give it a project name, and then gather shortcuts to everything I need for that project in that folder. It doesn't matter anymore where the data resides or what application I need to use to open the file. The only important factor is that I have a data file that needs editing, so I open the project folder and double-click its icon.

Of course, as with everything else under Windows 95, all is not perfect with the total data-centric approach. Even Microsoft agrees with me on this issue. They placed your Inbox, Recycle Bin, My Computer, and Network Neighborhood on the desktop for a reason. Sometimes you need to open an application instead of a piece of data.

I keep my communications program handy on the desktop. I can't really access any of its data from outside the application. My database manager sits on the desktop too, but that's for a different reason. I use Access to design databases more often than I use it for data entry, so, for me, it's really more important to work with the application.

You'll probably run into situations in which the application is more important than the data. The bottom line is that you should try to work with the data first. If this proves to be an inconvenient solution, the data-centric approach probably isn't correct for that situation. The following is a list of some of the types of data I work with, using the project folder approach I just described. You'll probably have some of these applications, too:

- Word processing: Every word processor is designed to work primarily with data, so it makes a perfect candidate for the data-centric approach. Microsoft Word even appears on the New submenu of the context menu, so there isn't any problem with creating new files without entering the word processor first. There's one minor inconvenience here: Word always creates a new document using the Normal template. This means that if I use the context menu to create a new file, I'll probably have to change the template after I open the file. It's a minor flaw, but an irritating one all the same.

- Spreadsheet: I seldom open just one spreadsheet. If I open one at all, I'm in there for hours. Therefore, I stick all my major files into a folder and place it on my desktop. That way, I can at least open a data file that will stay open throughout most of the editing session. I usually end up opening the other files I need in the usual way—using File | Open.

- Graphics: I work with quite a few different types of graphics, each of which requires its own application. Keeping the graphic files in a folder and opening them that way makes perfect sense. In fact, it's actually one of the application types that really made me see the value of a data-centric approach. By the way, this is one place where you really want to enable the Quick View option, if you haven't done so already. Most graphics files are time-consuming to load. Having Quick View handy for the files that it supports can really save time.

On Your Own

Add a shortcut to the Startup folder on your desktop. Tonight, place in that folder any work that you need to do tomorrow. Watch what happens when you start your machine tomorrow morning. You should get a desktop that has all the work you need to do loaded automatically.

Start separating your work into projects, if possible. Place each project in a separate folder on the desktop. Use separate folders, if necessary, to make it easier to find a particular kind of data. For example, you might need to place your graphics files in one subfolder to keep them from crowding the text files.

Look through your drives for data files that Windows 95 can't associate with a particular application. In Explorer, add any new file extensions that you might need, using the procedure discussed earlier. Check out each new association as you add it. Does the new addition work as anticipated? Evaluate the results you get after a few weeks to see if you need to add more options to the data file's context menu.

7

Customizing Folders with Web Views

Peter Norton®

The Windows Explorer program acts as your window to the contents of your hard disk by enabling you to see the organization of your hard disk divided into separate folders (directories). To help you locate specific files at a glance, Explorer can display your files as big or small icons with detailed information about each file such as its size and the date you last modified it.

The introduction of Internet Explorer 4.0 heralds another way for you to customize the appearance of your folders and files through the Windows Explorer program—Web views.

Why Use Web Views?

The main purpose of Web views is to provide a friendlier user interface for viewing the contents of folders stored on your hard disk. Figure 7.1 shows you the old-style of Explorer, and Figure 7.2 shows you the simpler Web view of the same folder.

Figure 7.1.
The old-style user interface of Explorer listing filenames.

There are two main differences between the old-style user interface and Web views. The first difference is that the Web view displays the folder name that you're currently viewing at the top of the right window pane. (In this case, the folder name is Dreams.) In this way, the Web view can help you better see at a glance which folder's contents you're viewing at any given time.

The second difference is that if you click a file or folder within the Web view, the Web view displays additional information on the left side of the window pane, such as listing the file type, the time stamp noting when it was last modified, and the file size. If you click a graphic or HTML file, the Web view also displays a thumbnail view of that file at the bottom-left corner of the pane.

Figure 7.2.

The Web-view–style user interface of Explorer can display file type, size, time stamp, and thumbnail view of graphics if you click a file.

Switching Web View On and Off

Turning on Web view within the Windows Explorer program is easy:

1. Load Windows Explorer.

2. Choose one of the following three ways to turn on Web view:

    • Select View | As Web Page.

    • Click the Views icon on the toolbar and choose the As Web Page option.

    • Right-click anywhere in the right window pane of Explorer to invoke a pop-up menu. Click View | As Web Page, as shown in Figure 7.3.

Figure 7.3.

You can turn on Web view by right-clicking the right window of Explorer and choosing As Web Page.

To disable Web view, simply choose whichever of the three methods listed previously that you used to enable Web view. When Web view is enabled, you see a check mark next to the As Web Page command. By choosing the As Web Page command a second time, you clear this check mark and disable Web view.

Viewing with Web Style

Although you might be happy with the old way Explorer displays your folders (before adding Internet Explorer 4), you might notice one inconsistency with the way Explorer works compared to the Internet. When you're using the Internet and want to choose an item from a Web page, you just have to point and click. When you want to choose an item within Explorer, you must double-click that item.

Trying to remember when to click and when to double-click might not be a problem for experienced computer users, but for novices, this inconsistency can be annoying at best and confusing at worst. Rather than force users to constantly switch between single-clicking when viewing Web pages on the Internet and double-clicking when viewing the contents of their own computers, you can use Web styles with or without Web views. The Web Style option simply lets you use the familiar one-click Web page interface every time you use the Windows Explorer program.

> **Note:** Single-clicking is much easier for novices to understand than double-clicking. For that reason, novices might prefer to use Web views exclusively.

To enable Web styles, follow these steps:

1. Choose View | Folder Options. The Folder Options dialog box, shown in Figure 7.4, appears.

Figure 7.4.
The Folder Options dialog box lets you choose how you want your folders to appear.

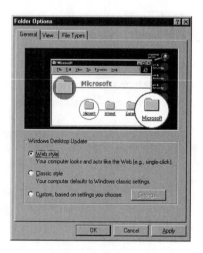

2. Choose the Web style option and click OK. The Web style option displays filenames with underlining, as shown in Figure 7.5. Web style also lets you single-click folders or files.

Figure 7.5.
Web style displays files and folders within Explorer as Web pages, including displaying the mouse pointer as a pointing hand.

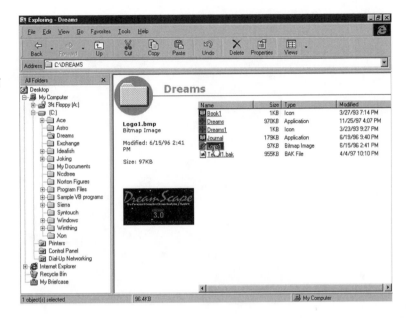

Enabling Web view and Web style changes the way Windows 95 appears on your computer. For example, the Control Panel appears as shown in Figure 7.6, and the Windows 95 desktop appears as shown in Figure 7.7.

Figure 7.6.
Enabling Web view and Web style changes the appearance of the Control Panel.

Figure 7.7.
*Enabling Web view
and Web style allows
one-click access to the
icons that appear on
the Windows 95
desktop.*

Creating Custom Web Views

If you choose to single-click items, you might notice that Windows 95 displays filenames and folders with an underline. However, staring at an entire screen of underlined filenames and folders can get tedious. To solve this problem, follow these steps:

1. Choose View | Folder Options. A Folder Options dialog box appears (see Figure 7.8).

Figure 7.8.
*The Folder Options
dialog box lets you
customize the
appearance of your
Web view.*

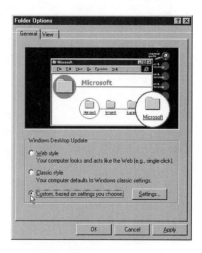

2. Click the Custom radio button and click the Settings button; this invokes the Custom Settings dialog box (see Figure 7.9). If you choose the Single click to open an item radio button in the Click items as follows section, you have two options:

- Underline icon titles consistent with my browser settings—Click this option to display filenames and folders with an underline at all times.

- Underline icon titles only when I point at them—Click this option to display the underline only when you move your mouse pointer over a filename or folder.

Figure 7.9.
The Custom Settings dialog box lists the ways you can alter the appearance of your Web views.

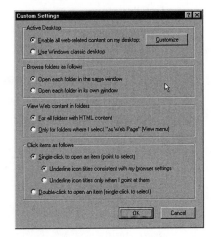

3. Click the radio button for the option you want and click OK. When the Folder Options dialog box appears, click OK to apply your settings.

For purely cosmetic reasons, you can also choose a background picture to appear within specific folders by following these steps:

1. Load Windows Explorer and click the folder you want to customize.

2. Select View | Customize This Folder to invoke the Customize this Folder dialog box, which is shown in Figure 7.10.

3. Click the Choose a background picture radio button, and then click the Next button. This invokes a dialog box that lists the available bitmap images that you can use for your background (see Figure 7.11).

4. Click a bitmap image that you want to use. At this point, you can also change the foreground and background colors of your icon captions. If you click the Text color button, you can choose a different foreground color. If you click the Background check box, you can choose a background color. Just make sure that the foreground and background icon colors don't clash with any bitmap images you choose; otherwise, you might have trouble seeing your icon captions. Click the Next button when you're done.

Figure 7.10.

The Customize this Folder dialog box lets you change the appearance of individual folders.

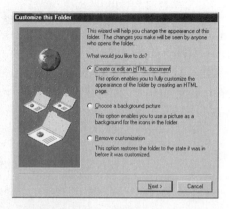

Figure 7.11.

You can choose a bitmap image for your background.

5. A final dialog box informs you of what you chose for your background bitmap image. If you made a mistake, click the Back button and choose again. Otherwise, click the Finish button to see the background image used for the folder you selected, as shown in Figure 7.12.

To remove any customization for a folder, follow these steps:

1. Click the folder you want to modify.

2. Select View | Folder Options. When the Customize this Folder dialog box (refer to Figure 7.10) appears, click the Remove customization radio button. This invokes another Customize this Folder dialog box, as shown in Figure 7.13. This dialog warns you that you are about to remove the folder's customization.

3. Click the Back button if you do not want to remove the customization. Otherwise, click the Next button.

4. Another dialog box appears, informing you of the changes you just made. Click the Back button if you want to keep your customized settings. Otherwise, click Finish.

Figure 7.12.
Changing a background bitmap image along with foreground and background icon caption colors can help you customize your folder's appearance.

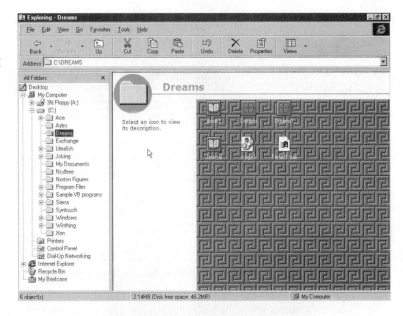

Figure 7.13.
The Customize this Folder dialog box warns you that you are about to modify the folder's appearance.

Customizing a Folder as a Web Page

Another way to customize your Web view is to run the Web View wizard:

1. Load Windows Explorer and click the folder you want to customize.

2. Select View | Customize This Folder; this invokes a Customize this Folder dialog box (refer to Figure 7.10).

3. Click the Create or edit an HTML document radio button, and then click the Next button. The dialog box informs you that your system will load an editor so you can edit your HTML folder document.

4. Click the Next button. An editor appears, displaying the HTML code used to customize your folder (see Figure 7.14).

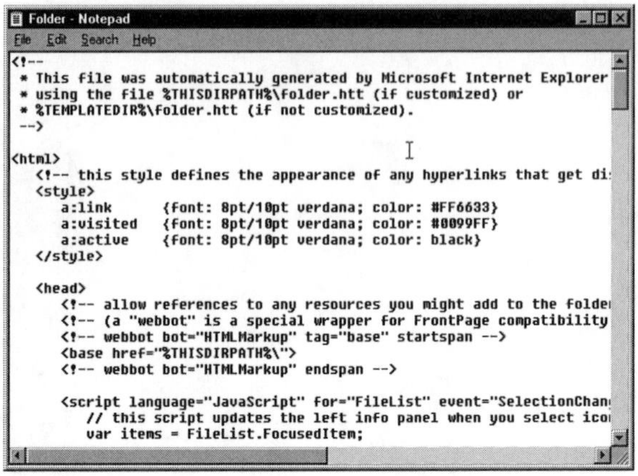


```
<!--
 * This file was automatically generated by Microsoft Internet Explorer
 * using the file %THISDIRPATH%\folder.htt (if customized) or
 * %TEMPLATEDIR%\folder.htt (if not customized).
 -->

<html>
   <!-- this style defines the appearance of any hyperlinks that get di:
   <style>
      a:link      {font: 8pt/10pt verdana; color: #FF6633}
      a:visited   {font: 8pt/10pt verdana; color: #0099FF}
      a:active    {font: 8pt/10pt verdana; color: black}
   </style>

   <head>
      <!-- allow references to any resources you might add to the folde
      <!-- (a "webbot" is a special wrapper for FrontPage compatibility
      <!-- webbot bot="HTMLMarkup" tag="base" startspan -->
      <base href="%THISDIRPATH%\">
      <!-- webbot bot="HTMLMarkup" endspan -->

      <script language="JavaScript" for="FileList" event="SelectionChan
         // this script updates the left info panel when you select ico
         var items = FileList.FocusedItem;
```

Figure 7.14.
The HTML code for customizing your folder appears in an editor.

5. Make any changes you want to the HTML code, save your file, and close the editor. When you close the editor, a final dialog box explains that you have just created a file called `folder.htt`. Click Finish.

`folder.htt` and `desktop.ini`

After you create the `folder.htt` file, you might not be able to see it within Explorer because it is a hidden file. To view hidden files, such as `folder.htt` and `desktop.ini` do the following:

1. Select View | Folder Options.
2. Click the View tab.
3. Click the Show all files radio button under the Hidden files folder, as shown in Figure 7.15.
4. Click OK.

`desktop.ini` contains the configuration settings for your folder, as shown in Figure 7.16. `folder.htt` contains the HTML code that defines the appearance of your folder. By editing `folder.htt`, you can customize the appearance of your folder.

Adding Links to Documents and Resources

One of the simplest ways to modify the `folder.htt` file is to add hyperlinks to different Web sites. Hyperlinks appear on the left side of the file and folder icons. By clicking a hyperlink, the user can open Internet Explorer and directly access the Web site.

Figure 7.15.
To see the
`folder.htt` *and*
`desktop.ini` *files,*
you must view hidden
files within Explorer.

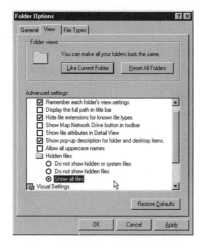

Figure 7.16.
The `desktop.ini`
folder contains the
configuration settings
for your folder.

Peter's Principle: Providing Helpful Hyperlinks Within a Folder

When I set up a computer for a friend, I like listing hyperlinks to Web sites that might come in handy for that particular folder. For example, if a folder contains Microsoft Office 97, I list Microsoft's Web site so that a user can click the hyperlink and retrieve the latest Microsoft Office 97 updates, bug fixes, or add-ons. Figure 7.17 shows a typical use for adding hyperlinks within a folder. For another example of adding relevant hyperlinks to a folder, open the Control Panel folder and you see two links to Microsoft's Web site.

To add hyperlinks to the Web view of a folder, you must do the following:

1. Make hidden files visible within Windows Explorer (refer to the section titled "`folder.htt` and `desktop.ini`").

Figure 7.17.

Adding hyperlinks, such as a link to program updates and bug fixes, can provide users with one-click access to a Web site that contains additional information.

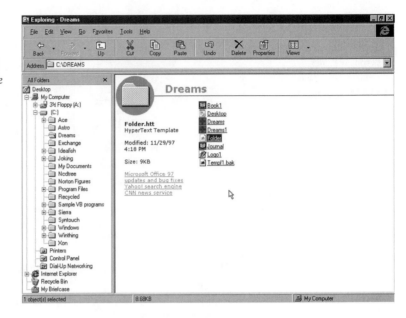

2. Open the `folder.htt` file using Notepad or a similar editor.

3. As shown in Figure 7.18, add your links between the following two lines:

```
<!-- start left info panel -->
<!-- end left info panel -->
```

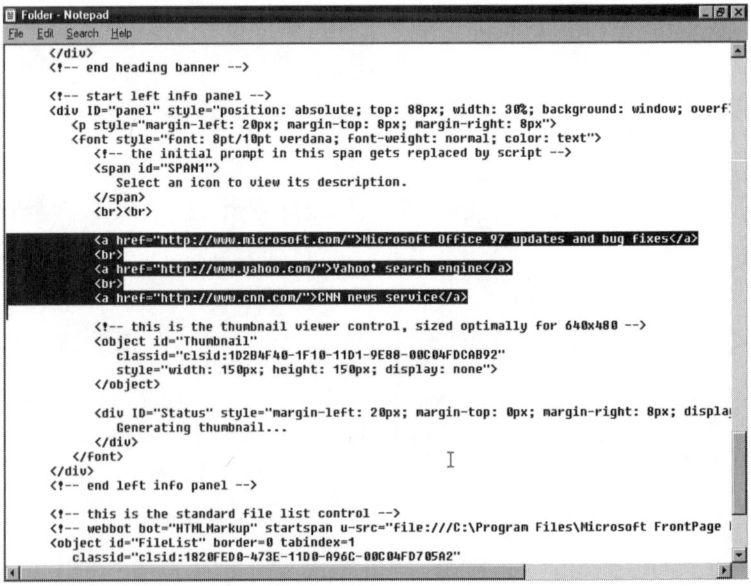

Figure 7.18.

Adding hyperlinks to the `folder.htt` file is as simple as typing the hyperlinks where they will appear within the left panel when you view the folder within Explorer.

Customizing the Heading of Web Views

A Web view normally displays the name of the folder at the top of the right window pane in the Explorer program. However, you can customize this heading by modifying the `folder.htt` file. That way, you can create your own personal folder heading (see Figure 7.19).

Figure 7.19.
A typical folder heading customized for display within Web view.

To customize the heading of the Web view of a folder, you must do the following:

1. Make hidden files visible within Windows Explorer (see the section titled "`folder.htt` and `desktop.ini`").

2. Open `folder.htt` using Notepad or a similar editor.

3. Modify your heading between the following two lines (see Figure 7.20):
   ```
   <!-- start heading banner -->
   <!-- end heading banner -->
   ```

Note: In the `folder.htt` file, the `%THISDIRNAME%` code displays the actual folder name. You can add any text before or after this code or even eliminate the `%THISDIRNAME%` code altogether if you don't want to display the folder name. (This isn't generally a good idea.)

Figure 7.20.

You can edit the `folder.htt` *file to customize the folder heading.*

```
Folder - Notepad
File  Edit  Search  Help
                    document.all.FileList.style.pixelLeft = document.all.panel.style.pixelWidth
              }
              document.all.FileList.style.pixelWidth = cw - document.all.FileList.style.pixelLeft
              document.all.FileList.style.pixelHeight = ch - document.all.FileList.style.pixelTop
              document.all.panel.style.pixelHeight = ch - document.all.panel.style.pixelTop
         }
    </script>
</head>

<body topmargin=0 leftmargin=0 rightmargin=0 bottommargin=0 scroll=no onload="FixSize()">

    <!-- start heading banner -->
    <div ID="heading" style="position: absolute; width: 100%; height: 88px; background: URL(res
        <p style="margin-left: 84px; padding-left: 20px; margin-top: 16px">
        <!-- using a table with nowrap to prevent undesirable word wrapping -->
        <table>
            <tr>
                <td nowrap>
                    <Font style="Font: 16pt/16pt verdana; Font-weight: bold; color: #0099FF">
                    <!--webbot bot="HTMLMarkup" startspan alt="&lt;B&gt;&lt;I&gt;Web View Folder
                    This is Joe's %THISDIRNAME% folder. Keep out!
                    <!--webbot bot="HTMLMarkup" endspan -->
                    </Font>
                </td>
            </tr>
        </table>
        <!-- this is more efficient than a long graphic, but we have to adjust it in FixSize() -
        <hr ID="rule" style="position: absolute; top: 44px; left: 84px" size=1px color=black>
    </div>
    <!-- end heading banner -->

    <!-- start left info panel -->
    <div ID="panel" style="position: absolute; top: 88px; width: 30%; background: window; overf.
        <p style="margin-left: 20px; margin-top: 8px; margin-right: 8px">
        <font style="Font: 8pt/10pt verdana; Font-weight: normal; color: text">
            <!-- the initial prompt in this span gets replaced by script -->
```

Customizing Text Fonts in Web Views

If you want to customize the Web views of your folders even further, you can change the appearance of the fonts used for hyperlinks, folder names, and descriptions of files that appear in the left info panel. As shown in Figure 7.21, you can change the size, font type, and color of your text.

Figure 7.21.

Changing the size and font type allows you to get creative in displaying your folders in Web view.

To change the fonts of your hyperlinks, open the `folder.htt` file and look for the following code near the beginning of the file:

```html
<html>
   <!-- this style defines the appearance of any hyperlinks that get displayed -->
   <style>
      a:link      {font: 8pt/10pt verdana; color: #FF6633}
      a:visited   {font: 8pt/10pt verdana; color: #0099FF}
      a:active    {font: 8pt/10pt verdana; color: black}
   </style>
```

This code defines four different font options:

- The type size to display text (8pt)
- The type size used to separate lines (10pt)
- The font type (verdana)
- The color of text (#FF6633, #0099FF, and black)

Note: You can define text colors with hexadecimal numbers or with textual descriptions.

To change the fonts of the heading banner of your folder, open the `folder.htt` file and look for the following code near the end of the file:

```html
<!-- start heading banner -->
<font style="font: 16pt/16pt verdana; font-weight: bold; color: #0099FF">
<!-- end heading banner -->
```

This code defines five different font options:

- The type size to display text (16pt)
- The type size used to separate lines (16pt)
- The font type (verdana)
- The font weight (bold)
- The color of text (#0099FF)

Note: The font weight can be either bold or normal.

To change the fonts of the descriptive text that appears in the left info panel of a Web view folder, open the `folder.htt` file and look for the following code near the end of the file:

```html
<!-- start left info panel -->
<font style="font: 8pt/10pt verdana; font-weight: normal; color: text">
<!-- end left info panel -->
```

This code defines five different font options:

- The type size to display text (8pt)
- The type size used to separate lines (10pt)
- The font type (verdana)
- The font weight (normal)
- The color of text (text, which is another name for black)

Tip: To see a list of different font types you can use, open the Fonts folder in the Control Panel (see Figure 7.22). This shows you the exact font names you can use to define the fonts displayed in your Web view folders.

Figure 7.22.
The Fonts folder in the Control Panel lists all the font names you can use to define fonts in your Web view folders.

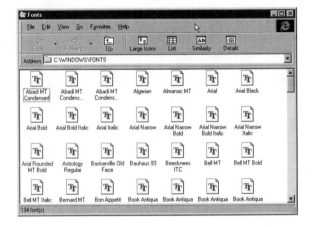

Removing Customization from a Folder

The good part about customizing the appearance of your folders is that you can personalize your folders however you like. The bad part about customizing your folders is that other users might find it confusing and disorienting to see colors and fonts that are different from the standard Windows 95 configuration. In the event that you need to remove customization from a folder, you can do so by following these steps:

1. Load Windows Explorer and click the folder whose customization you want to remove.

2. Select View | Customize This Folder; this invokes a Customize this Folder dialog box (refer to Figure 7.10).

3. Click the Remove customization radio button and click the Next button. As shown in Figure 7.23, the Customize this Folder dialog box warns that you are about to delete the `folder.htt` file and reset the configuration settings in the `desktop.ini` file.

Figure 7.23.
The Customize this Folder dialog box gives you one last warning that you are about to remove customization for a folder.

4. Click the Cancel button if you want to keep your customization for the folder. Otherwise, click the Next button. This invokes the final Customize this Folder dialog box, which informs you that `folder.htt` has been moved to the Recycle Bin and that the configuration of the `desktop.ini` file has been reset.

5. Click the Finish button. Windows 95 restores the default settings of your Web view folder.

On Your Own

Experiment with different fonts for your Web view folders. To see what each font looks like, load your word processor, type some text, and choose different fonts.

Open your My Documents folder and add different types of hyperlinks. For example, you might want to include hyperlinks to your own company's Web site, to the company that created your favorite application (such as Microsoft, Corel, or Lotus), or to your favorite news services (such as CNN).

Choose different bitmap images for a folder's background. If you have artistic skills, draw your own bitmap images and use them as your background picture. If you have a scanner, scan your favorite picture, save it as a bitmap file, and use it as a background picture in a folder.

8

Customizing with Microsoft PowerToys and KernelToys

Peter Norton®

Microsoft created PowerToys and KernelToys to provide special enhancements to Windows 95.
PowerToys focuses on adding user interface enhancements to make Windows 95 easier to use, and
KernelToys focuses on adding technical enhancements to make Windows 95 more reliable and stable.
OSR2 includes some features of PowerToys and KernelToys. Table 8.1 lists the features of PowerToys;
Table 8.2 lists the features of KernelToys.

Warning: PowerToys and KernelToys are not officially supported by Microsoft. Although
both have been extensively tested on a variety of machines, Microsoft offers no technical
support if you have questions or problems using PowerToys or KernelToys. As a result, you
should consider installing PowerToys and KernelToys only on machines used by experienced users.

Table 8.1. PowerToys components.

Component	Description
CAB File Viewer	This component lets you peek inside and manipulate CAB files, which contain one or more compressed files, stored on the Windows 95 CD-ROM and floppies.
DeskMenu	This component displays a pop-up menu for quick and easy access to all your desktop icons.
DOS Prompt Here	This component enables you to start an MS-DOS prompt by clicking a folder.
Explore From Here	This component lets you right-click a folder and choose the Explore From Here command. This makes your chosen folder appear as the root folder.
Fast Folder Contents	This component lets you right-click any folder to display a cascade menu that shows all the contents of that folder, one-level deep.
Find X	This component lets you add your own custom commands to the Find menu.
FlexiCD	This component provides a convenient, single-click play-and-pause control for playing audio CDs in your CD-ROM drive.
QuickRes	This component lets you change the screen resolution of your monitor via a pop-up menu.

Component	Description
Round Clock	This component displays a round or digital clock in a separate window.
Send to X	This component adds four new commands to your Send To menu: Send to Any Folder, Send to Clipboard as Contents, Send to Clipboard as Name, and Send to Command Line.
Shortcut Target Menu	This component displays the properties of a shortcut's target if you right-click that shortcut.
TapiTNA	This component provides quick access so you can change your TAPI location, display your dialing properties, and run the Phone Dialer application.
Tweak UI	This component lets you customize specific elements of the Windows 95 user interface, including mouse sensitivity, bou-parameters, window animation, and shortcut appearances.
XMouse	This component makes the focus follow the mouse without clicking, as with X Windows.

Table 8.2. KernelToys components.

Component	Description
Conventional Memory Tracking	This component deciphers all the memory that the mem command reports as belonging to vmm32.
MS-DOS Mode wizard	This component simplifies the process of configuring CONFIG.SYS and AUTOEXEC.BAT files to run MS-DOS games under Windows 95.
Windows Time Zone Editor	This component lets you change the way Windows 95 handles time-zone changes.
Windows 95 Keyboard Remap	This component lets you remap the way the keys on your keyboard act.
Windows 95 Program Monitor	This component monitors the memory and CPU usage of your computer.
Windows Logo Key Control	This component lets you configure your MS-DOS game so that Windows ignores the Windows logo key while the game is running.

Installing the PowerToys

PowerToys is a collection of free utilities for enhancing Windows 95. To install PowerToys on your computer, follow these steps:

1. Create a folder for the PowerToys. To do this, right-click the desktop and choose New | Folder from the pop-up menu. Name the folder Power.

2. Download a free copy of PowerToys from Microsoft's Web site at `www.microsoft.com` and save it in the Power folder you just created.

3. Double-click the file `PowerToy.exe`. This creates several new files in your Power folder.

4. Right-click the Install file and then click Install. This installs PowerToys in the default directory `C:\Program Files\PowerToys`.

Note: You might have to install some of the PowerToys components individually. This might involve dragging the program file into a folder on your hard disk or right-clicking an INF file and clicking Install.

Using TapiTNA (Telephony API Taskbar Notification Application)

If you use a laptop computer to connect to the Internet, you must change the telephone number each time you move to a different location. To make it easy to change phone numbers, use TapiTNA. To run TapiTNA, do the following:

1. Double-click the TapiTNA icon.

2. When the TapiTNA button appears on the Taskbar, right-click it.

3. Click the Open Dialing Properties option to access the Dialing Properties dialog box from a pop-up menu (see Figure 8.1). From this dialog box, you can specify your area code and location.

If you subsequently click the TapiTNA button on the Taskbar, a pop-up menu appears (see Figure 8.2). This menu lists the locations you defined using the Dialing Properties dialog box; simply click the location you want to use.

Figure 8.1.
The Dialing Properties dialog box appears when you right-click the TapiTNA icon on the Taskbar.

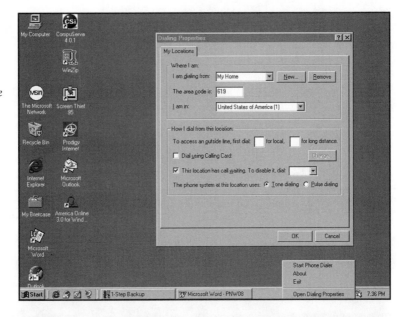

Figure 8.2.
Clicking the TapiTNA button on the Taskbar displays a list of different locations on a pop-up menu.

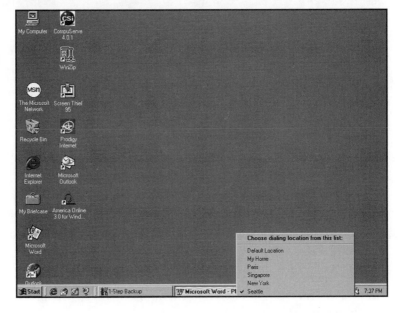

Modifying Your Environment with Tweak UI

Tweak UI is a special program that allows you to fine-tune (*tweak*) the Windows 95 User Interface (UI). Using Tweak UI, you can customize various Windows 95 settings, including mouse sensitivity, the speed that Windows 95 displays menus, and how Windows 95 boots up.

To run Tweak UI, do the following:

1. Open the Control Panel and double-click the Tweak UI icon. You should see the dialog box shown in Figure 8.3.

2. Click the tab corresponding to the feature you want to customize (such as Explorer or Mouse).

Figure 8.3.
The Tweak UI dialog box displays tabs for customizing different features of Windows 95.

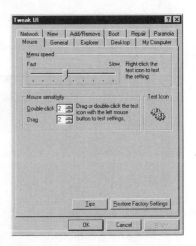

Mouse Settings

The Mouse tab in the Tweak UI dialog box (refer to Figure 8.3) enables you to customize the way your mouse works. You have five options:

*   The Menu speed slider enables you to adjust how quickly (or slowly) you want menus to pop up. The fast setting causes menus to appear immediately; the slow setting causes menus to appear extraordinarily slowly.

*   The Double-click box in the Mouse sensitivity section enables you to specify a number from 1 to 32. I found little difference between a double-click sensitivity of 1 and one of 32, but depending on your computer, you might notice more of a difference.

- The Drag box in the Mouse sensitivity section specifies how far (in pixels) you must move the mouse before Windows 95 decides that you actually want to drag an object. This value can range from 1 to 32.

Tip: If you find yourself accidentally dragging objects when you only meant to click them, increase the value in the Drag box in the Mouse Sensitivity section.

Note: To test changes you have made to the Double Click and Drag values, double-click or drag the test icon that appears as two gears. When you're happy with the way the test icon reacts, click OK to save your new mouse settings.

- If you need additional help, click the Tips button to display the Tweak UI help file.
- If you made some changes to the mouse that you want to erase, click the Restore Factory Settings button to return the Double Click and Drag values to 2 and to set the Menu Speed slider between Fast and Slow.

General Settings

If you click the General tab (see Figure 8.4), you see the following options:

Figure 8.4.
The General tab lets you modify window animation, scrolling, beeping, the location of special folders, and the search engine used by Internet Explorer.

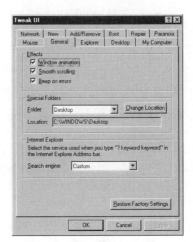

- Clicking the Window animation check box simply makes your windows look more interesting when you minimize or maximize them. If you disable window animation and minimize or maximize a window, the window simply pops up or disappears. If you enable window animation, Windows 95 displays simple animation to minimize or maximize that particular window.

- Clicking the Smooth scrolling check box enables animated window scrolling in Explorer and other programs.

- Clicking the Beep on errors check box enables your machine to beep when an error occurs.

- Components in the Special Folders section enable you to view and change the locations for the nine special Windows 95 folders:

    Desktop

    Document Templates

    Favorites

    My Documents

    Programs

    Recent Documents

    Send To

    Start Menu

    Startup

Windows 95 automatically assigns these folders to specific locations, but Tweak UI enables you to change the location of a different folder. To change the location of a special folder, select the folder from the Folder list box, click the Change Location button, and then click the folder you want to use.

Peter's Principle: Speeding Up Access to Your Important Files

When I load my word processor, it always looks for documents first in the My Documents folder, which is in the C:\My Documents directory. When I'm working on different projects, such as a book, I like to save my files in their own directories. By changing the location of the My Documents folder to my project directory, I can load my word processor and access the files I need without switching folders first.

- The Internet Explorer section lets you define what search engine to use if you type ? *keyword keyword* in the address box of Internet Explorer. If you type your query directly into the address box, you won't have to waste time visiting a search engine and then typing your query. Available search engines include Alta Vista, HotBot, InfoSeek, and Yahoo! You can even define your own search engine by choosing the Custom option.

- If you want to remove the changes you've made, click the Restore Factory Settings button to restore your original settings.

Explorer Settings

The Explorer tab, shown in Figure 8.5, enables you to modify the following:

Figure 8.5.
Use the Explorer tab to specify how Internet Explorer displays files on your screen.

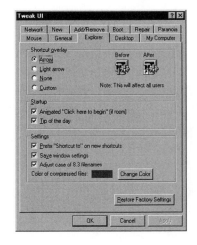

- The appearance of your shortcut icons—Use the Shortcut overlay section to specify whether shortcut icons appear with one of the following:
  - Arrow—This option is the default; if you select it, an arrow appears in the lower-left corner of an icon.
  - Light arrow—Selecting this option simply displays a smaller, less obtrusive arrow.
  - None—Select this option if you do not want to display an icon.
  - Custom—This option enables you to choose an entirely different graphic image.

> **Tip:** Generally speaking, it's best to have some sort of icon (such as an arrow) to help you distinguish between a shortcut icon and an application icon. If you delete a shortcut icon, you are still able to run the application; if you delete the application icon, you have to reinstall the application, which can be time-consuming and annoying.

- The startup of Windows 95—Use the Startup section to specify whether to the Tip of the Day dialog box is displayed and the Click Here to Begin animation is executed on the Taskbar when Windows 95 boots. If you're configuring a computer for a novice, the Tip of the Day dialog box and the Click Here to Begin animation make Windows 95 seem friendlier and more interesting to use. If you want to start loading applications right away, you should disable the Tip of the Day dialog box and the Click Here to Begin animation.

- The appearance of files—The Settings section enables you to define how Explorer displays your files. This section contains the following options:
  - Prefix "Shortcut to" on new shortcuts—Enable this check box if you want to include the Shortcut to prefix on all your shortcut icons (as in Shortcut to Microsoft Word).
  - Save window settings—Select this check box if you want Windows 95 to save the settings of a folder. When you shut down, Windows 95 remembers which folders were open; those folders are open the next time you view that folder.
  - Adjust case of 8.3 filenames—Enabling this check box can be useful when you view files created by Windows 3.x systems. The names of these files are limited to a maximum of eight characters with a three-character file extension and often appear in all uppercase. Instead of displaying an 8.3 filename in all uppercase, this option lets Explorer display the filename in mixed case to make it easier to read.
  - Color of compressed files—This option enables you to specify what color Explorer uses to display a compressed file (using this feature can make it easier to find compressed files). Unfortunately, this feature only works under Windows NT, not Windows 95.

If you click the Restore Factory Settings button, you can reverse any changes you made to the Explorer Settings.

Desktop Settings

The Desktop tab, shown in Figure 8.6, gives you the option of placing certain icons on the desktop. Alternatively, you can use the Desktop tab to create special files to represent applications. These special files act like desktop icons, but instead of appearing on the desktop, they can appear within folders. In either case, you can load an application simply by clicking its desktop icon or its special file.

To add an icon to the desktop, select the check box for that icon. (To remove an icon from the desktop, make sure a check mark does not appear for that icon.) Alternatively, you can right-click an icon and then click the Show on Desktop option. If an icon does not have a check box, the icon cannot be placed on the desktop.

Figure 8.6.

The Desktop tab lets you place icons on the desktop or create a special icon file that you can place anywhere.

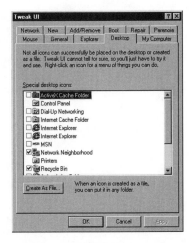

Note: If you remove a desktop icon, the application associated with it still remains on your hard disk. Removing a desktop icon merely deletes the icon representing an application. If you add or remove the Network Neighborhood, you must log off and log on for the changes to take effect.

The Desktop tab also enables you to create an icon as a special file that you can place in any folder rather than place an icon on the desktop. There are two ways to create a file for an icon: You can either click the Create As File button or right-click an icon and click the Create As File option.

Warning: Not all applications can be created as files. For example, the Microsoft Network icon is designed to exist only as a desktop icon. If you create a file for the Microsoft Network icon, the Microsoft Network might operate erratically.

My Computer Settings

The My Computer tab, shown in Figure 8.7, enables you to selectively hide or display drives within Explorer or when you double-click the My Computer desktop icon. The main reason to hide a drive is to prevent others from accessing the files on the drive.

Figure 8.7.
*The My Computer
tab displays all the
drives to hide or
display within
Explorer or the My
Computer desktop
icon.*

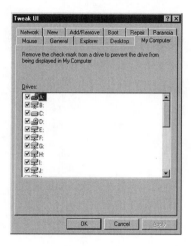

For example, suppose you store sensitive files on a separate hard disk. Rather than prevent other
people from using that computer, you can hide the drive containing your sensitive files, thereby
ensuring that others can't accidentally delete or move files on that drive. To hide or display a drive,
simply click its check box.

Network Settings

Click the Network tab, shown in Figure 8.8, to see a list of options that enable you to save your user
name and password so you can log on to a network as soon as Windows 95 loads.

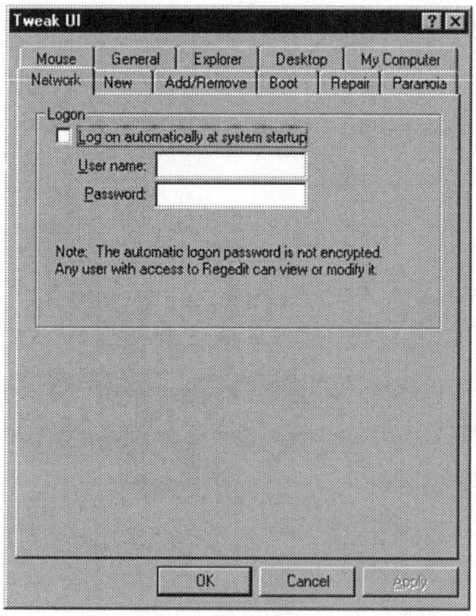

Figure 8.8.
*The Network tab lets
you save your user
name and password
so you can automati-
cally log on to a
network.*

Warning: If you use the Network tab to save your user name and password, be aware that your password is not safe. Anyone with RegEdit can view your password. Even worse, anyone with access to your computer can log on to the network using your saved user name and password—without even knowing your password. If security is crucial, don't use the Network tab.

New Settings

The New tab, shown in Figure 8.9, displays a list of document templates that you can create by dragging a file.

Figure 8.9.
You can use the New tab to create a new document template.

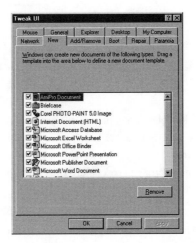

To create a new document template with the New tab, open Explorer and drag a file into the list of file types. After you've created a document template, you can create a new file by doing the following:

1. Open Explorer.
2. Right-click the right pane to invoke a pop-up menu.
3. Click New.
4. Click the type of file you want to create.

When you create a file this way, it is identical to the file you originally dragged on to the New tab. All you have to do is modify this new file.

Add/Remove Settings

The Add/Remove tab, shown in Figure 8.10, lists the programs that Windows 95 can uninstall. There are two reasons you might want to use the Add/Remove tab:

Figure 8.10.
The Add/Remove tab lists all the programs that Windows 95 can uninstall.

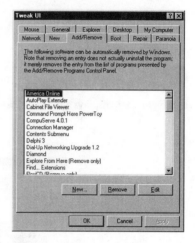

- If you manually delete an application from your hard disk instead of double-clicking the Add/Remove Programs icon within the Control Panel folder to delete it, Windows 95 still stores the name of the program in its list of applications that you can uninstall. By using the Add/Remove tab, you can delete the names of any programs that are no longer stored on the hard disk.

- By removing an application's name from the Windows 95 list of programs it can uninstall, you can prevent someone from uninstalling that particular application by mistake.

The Add/Remove tab displays three buttons:

- New—This button lets you add an application to the Windows 95 list of programs that can be uninstalled.

- Remove—This button lets you remove an application from the Windows 95 list of programs that can be uninstalled.

- Edit—This button lets you change the application's name and the directory where it is stored.

Note: The Remove button simply deletes the application name from the list of programs that Windows 95 can uninstall. The Remove button does not actually uninstall an application. Likewise, the New button simply adds an application name to the list, but does not guarantee that the added application can be uninstalled.

Boot Settings

The Boot tab, shown in Figure 8.11, enables you to modify how Windows 95 boots. The Boot tab contains a General section and a Boot Menu section.

Figure 8.11.

The Boot tab lets you define how Windows 95 boots.

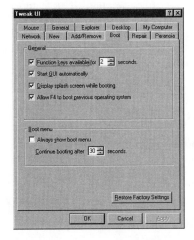

The General section contains four check boxes:

- Function keys available—This check box lets you disable the function keys that can modify the boot process (such as F5 and F8). If the select the Function Keys Available check box, you can specify how many seconds Windows 95 pauses after the Starting Windows 95 message to determine whether you are pressing a function key.

Tip: By disabling the Function Keys Available check box, you can provide a level of security to protect your computer from users who try to modify the boot process in order to bypass any Windows 95 security programs you have.

- Start GUI automatically—This check box gives you the choice of having Windows 95 stop the boot process after it reaches the MS-DOS command prompt or automatically continuing to the Windows 95 user interface. Most people want the Windows 95 user interface when they boot up their computer.

- Display splash screen while booting—This check box lets you display or suppress the Windows 95 splash screen that appears during the boot process. This option is used primarily for cosmetic purposes.

- Allow F4 to boot previous operating system—This check box lets you press the F4 key to load the operating system you were running before you installed Windows 95. This option works only if you didn't erase your previous operating system.

The Boot Menu section contains the following:

- Always show boot menu—This check box enables you to specify whether you want to see a boot menu every time you start Windows 95. Normally, Windows 95 shows a boot menu only if it detected a problem with the previous boot.

- Continue booting after *x* seconds—This feature defines how long the boot menu remains on the screen before the default action is taken.

If you want to revert to the original Windows 95 settings for all these options, click the Restore Factory Settings button.

Repair Settings

The Repair tab, shown in Figure 8.12, provides five buttons for fixing minor problems that occur under Windows 95:

Figure 8.12.
*The Repair tab
provides five different
ways to fix minor
problems with
Windows 95.*

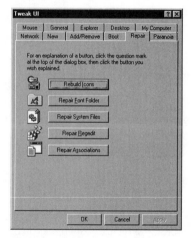

- Rebuild Icons—Click this button to ensure that Explorer displays the correct icon for your programs and shortcuts.

- Repair Font Folder—Click this button to fix any problems you are experiencing when you use different types of fonts.

- Repair System Files—Click this button to replace system files, commonly replaced by installation programs, that might be damaged or missing. This button can work only if the replacement system files are still located in the hidden SysBckup folder.

- Repair RegEdit—Click this button to reset the RegEdit view State Information when the RegEdit application doesn't show all columns.

- Repair Associations—Click this button to restore all icons to their original factory settings and to restore default associations for standard file types.

Paranoia Settings

If you're worried that someone might be spying on you or could determine what you've been doing with your computer, use the Paranoia tab (shown in Figure 8.13).

Figure 8.13.
The Paranoia tab helps you cover your tracks when using Windows 95.

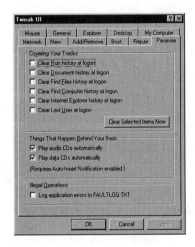

The Paranoia tab contains three sections: Covering Your Tracks, Things That Happen Behind Your Back, and Illegal Operations. The Covering Your Tracks section contains the following features:

- Clear Run history at logon—Clicking this check box erases the type and order of the applications the last user loaded. By choosing this option, you can ensure that no one knows which programs you've been using (such as games on an office computer).

- Clear Document history at logon—Clicking this check box erases the actual files the last user viewed or edited. If anyone is spying on you, it is often more important for him or her to know the actual files and data you accessed than to know the specific application you used.

- Clear Find Files history at logon—Clicking this check box removes the names of the files the last user searched for. This option does not affect the files themselves.

- Clear Find Computer history at logon—Clicking this check box erases the names of the computers the last user searched for, such as on a network.

- Clear Internet Explorer history at logon—Clicking this check box erases the URLs visited by the last user, preventing others from seeing which Web sites you visited using Internet Explorer. Note that this option does not erase the URL history from any other browsers.
- Clear Last User at logon—Clicking this check box erases the name of the last person who used the computer.
- Clear Selected Items Now—Click this button after you have clicked one or more check boxes to execute the associated actions.

The Things That Happen Behind Your Back section contains two check boxes, which control your CD-ROM drive:

- Play audio CDs automatically—Click this check box if you want to play audio CDs as soon as you insert them in the CD-ROM drive.
- Play data CDs automatically—Click this check box if you want to run data CDs as soon as you insert them in the CD-ROM drive.

The Illegal Operations section contains only one check box:

- Log application errors to FAULTLOG.TXT—Click this check box to save log application errors in a special FAULTLOG.TXT file.

Peter's Principle: Tracking Application Errors

I use the Log Application Errors to FAULTLOG.TXT check box to help track down buggy programs. For example, if my friend complains that his computer crashes all the time, I enable this option so I can determine exactly which applications seem to be crashing on a regular basis. Armed with this information, I can help determine the problem with the computer.

A Quick Look with Fast Folder Contents

If you want to see the contents of a folder, you normally have to click that folder. For a faster peek, PowerToys offers its Fast Folder Contents option. To quickly view the contents of a folder, simply right-click that folder from within Explorer and click Contents. This invokes a pop-up menu that lists the contents of that folder (see Figure 8.14).

Figure 8.14.
Fast Folder Contents provides a fast way to see inside a folder.

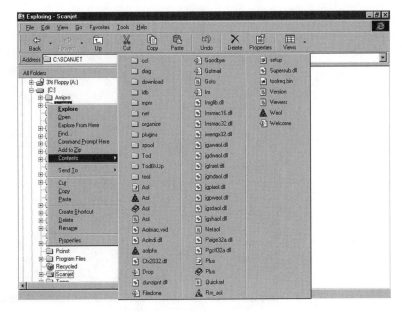

CD AutoPlay Extender

The AutoPlay Extender is designed to let you access a CD inserted in your CD-ROM drive. Simply right-click the CD-ROM drive icon from Explorer and click AutoPlay to start the installation of the CD application.

Controlling Audio CDs with FlexiCD

FlexiCD enables you to start, stop, eject, or switch tracks when you insert an audio CD in your CD-ROM drive. The FlexiCD icon appears on the Taskbar. Click the FlexiCD icon to pause or continue playing. If you right-click the FlexiCD icon, a pop-up menu appears (see Figure 8.15).

Seeing the Inside of CAB Files

CAB files are special, compressed files that come with the Windows 95 installation CD or floppy disks. Although you normally can't view the contents of a CAB file, PowerToys lets you do just that as well as selectively extract files from a CAB file. CAB files have names ranging from Win95_02 to Win95_28 and appear as a yellow folder icon with a piece of paper sticking out.

Figure 8.15.
The FlexiCD pop-up
menu enables you to
turn your computer
into an audio CD
player.

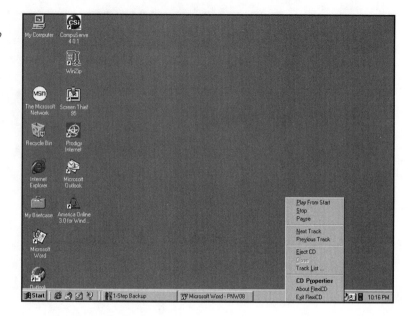

To view the inside of a CAB file, do the following:

1. Insert the Windows 95 CD or floppy disk in your computer.

2. Open Explorer.

3. Right-click a CAB file.

4. Choose View. A separate window appears, listing all the files stored within the CAB file
   you chose (see Figure 8.16).

Figure 8.16.
By viewing the inside
of a CAB file, you
can extract only the
files you need.

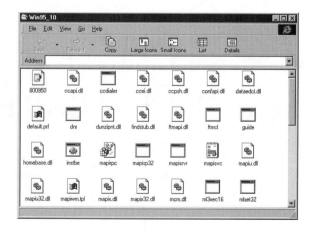

Peter's Principle: Extracting Files from a CAB File

Occasionally, Windows 95 accidentally deletes or corrupts a file. Rather than reinstall Windows 95 to copy only a single file, I use the CAB file viewer instead. With the CAB file viewer, I can pick the file I need, extract it, and copy it back onto my hard disk in just a few minutes.

Gaining Access to Your Desktop with DeskMenu

When I'm using my computer, I often need to temporarily load another application, such as a word processor to write a short note or Internet Explorer to check a particularly interesting Web site. Instead of using the Start button on the Taskbar to load an application, it's much easier to simply create a shortcut to an application and store it on the Windows 95 desktop.

Of course, one drawback is that if you're running an application and want to load another one right away, you must either use the Start button on the Taskbar or minimize your current application window so you can click the other application's shortcut on the Windows 95 desktop. This is not only clumsy, but it is also slow and annoying.

That's why Microsoft came up with the DeskMenu application. DeskMenu provides one-click access to all your Windows 95 desktop shortcuts in a simple pop-up menu. That way, you can simply click the name of the application you want to load without minimizing your current application. Using DeskMenu is simple, as you'll see in the following steps:

1. Click the DeskMenu icon on the Taskbar. You should see a pop-up menu similar to the one shown in Figure 8.17.
2. Click the application you want to load.

Note: DeskMenu also offers two other options: Minimize All Windows (which displays the desktop) and Undo Minimize All (which displays all loaded application windows).

Figure 8.17.
DeskMenu lists all
your desktop shortcuts
in a pop-up menu.

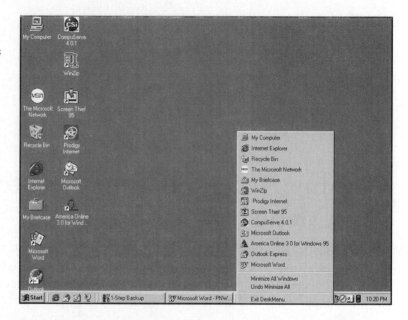

Peter's Principle: Using Desktop Shortcuts

Desktop shortcuts come in handy when you want to load an application quickly without going through the trouble of using the Start button on the Taskbar. If you're like me, you just want to load the application right away.

For all my favorite applications such as my word processor and spreadsheet, I always create a shortcut and put it on the desktop. By using DeskMenu, I can see all my desktop shortcuts in a simple pop-up menu without additional effort on my part.

Getting the Time with Round Clock

PowerToys comes with a simple clock application. You might be wondering why you want to install the PowerToys clock when Windows 95 comes with a clock that displays the time on the Taskbar. Good question. Unlike the Taskbar clock, which only displays the time in digital format (such as 10:35 AM), the PowerToys clock can display both the date and the time (in either digital or analog format).

Take some time to customize the way you want the PowerToys clock to display information. You can choose from the following options:

- Analog or Digital—Analog displays the time as a round clock with minute and hour hands. Digital displays time as numbers (such as 12:43 PM).

- Set Font—This option lets you choose a font and type size for displaying the time when displayed in digital format. The Set Font option appears dimmed if you choose to display time in analog format.

- No Title—This option hides the window and title bar of the clock. To redisplay the clock window and title bar, you must load the clock and press Esc. Figure 8.18 shows what the clock looks like in digital format with no title.

Figure 8.18.
The PowerToys clock can appear as a floating clock on the desktop.

- Seconds—This option hides or displays seconds. If the clock is in analog format, the Seconds option hides or displays a second hand. If the clock is in digital format, the Seconds option hides or displays seconds as numbers.

- Date—This option hides or displays the date. In analog format, the date appears in the title bar. In digital format, the date appears under the time within the window.

Creating a DOS Prompt Where You Need It

For some people, the MS-DOS prompt is a long-lost friend that Windows 95 buried beneath its glittery user interface. If you need to access the MS-DOS prompt right away, PowerToys provides a handy Command Prompt Here command. Simply right-click any folder within Explorer and click Command Prompt Here. A separate window appears, displaying the MS-DOS prompt. To close this window, type **EXIT** and press Enter at the MS-DOS prompt.

Exploring from Here

When using the Explorer to view your folders, there may be times when you want to examine only one folder and its contents. Unfortunately, Explorer by itself forces you to see the entire folder hierarchy of your computer. If you want to view only one folder and its contents, simply right-click the folder you want to examine and choose Explore From Here. A second Explorer window opens, displaying only your chosen folder and its contents (see Figure 8.19).

Figure 8.19.
The Explore From Here command lets you view only one folder and its contents in a separate window.

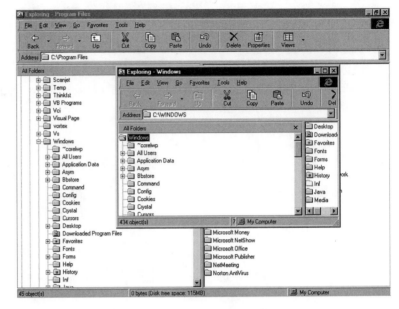

Getting Complete Application Details from Shortcuts

Shortcuts are additional icons that you can create so you can access a particular program quickly and easily. Unfortunately, if you want to view the properties of a shortcut's target, you must find the actual application that the shortcut represents. To avoid this problem, PowerToys lets you view the properties of a shortcut's target by simply right-clicking that particular shortcut.

Automatic Application Focus Using XMouse

If you often simultaneously display multiple windows on the screen, you already know what a nuisance it can be to click each window where you want to start working. To solve this problem, use XMouse, which is stored in the C:\Program Files\PowerToy folder. If you double-click the XMouse icon, you no longer have to click in a window to start working in it. Through the use of XMouse, Windows immediately switches the focus to a window the instant you move the mouse over that window.

Changing Your Desktop Resolution with QuickRes

To change the desktop resolution of your monitor, such as from 800×600 to 1024×768, you are usually required to follow several steps. For instance, you can open the Control Panel folder either by double-clicking the My Computer icon on the Windows 95 desktop or by clicking the Start button on the Taskbar and choosing Settings. Then you click the Control Panel folder and double-click Display.

Instead of following this convoluted series of steps, you can use QuickRes, which lets you modify your desktop resolution quickly and easily with just a few clicks of the mouse:

1. Click the QuickRes icon on the Taskbar. You should see a pop-up menu similar to the one shown in Figure 8.20.

Figure 8.20.
QuickRes provides a simple one-click access to changing your display resolution.

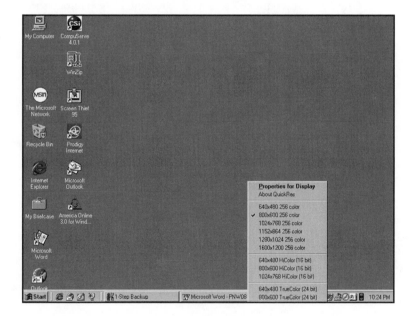

2. Click the resolution you want, such as 800×600. Windows 95 instantly changes your display resolution without displaying the confirmation dialog box that normally appears when you change the display resolution through the Control Panel.

Note: Instead of clicking a specific display resolution from the pop-up menu, you can click Properties for Display. This invokes the Display Properties dialog box, which enables you to customize your desktop by changing the number of colors, the display resolution, the screen saver, the desktop background, and the refresh rate.

Sending Anything Anywhere

Another feature of PowerToys is the Send to *x* feature, which adds the four new commands to the Send To menu:

- Send to Any Folder—This command lets you copy or move a file to another folder. You can either type the folder name or click the folder name displayed in a dialog box shown in Figure 8.21. If you use this command, you don't have to scroll your folders up and down within the left pane of the Explorer window.

Figure 8.21.
The Send to Any Folder command provides a convenient way to copy or move a file to another folder.

- Send to Clipboard as Contents—This command lets you copy the entire contents of a file to the clipboard. Then you can paste these contents within another file, such as a word-processor document.
- Send to Clipboard as Name—This command lets you copy the path of a file. For example, if you use this command on a file called HELP.TXT stored in the directory C:\Help Files, the Send to Clipboard as Name command copies the following text to the clipboard:

```
C:\Help Files\HELP.TXT
```

- Send to Command Line—This command lets you open the Run dialog box and copy the path of the file as the program to run. For example, if you use this command on a file called `GAME.EXE` stored in a directory called `C:\Toys`, the Send to Command Line command copies the following text to the Run dialog box:

`C:\Toys\GAME.EXE`

Finding What You Need Quickly

The Find Extensions PowerToy lets you modify the Find menu that appears when you click the Start button and then choose Find or when you select Tools | Find within Explorer. To configure your Find menu, do the following:

1. Open the Control Panel.
2. Double-click the Add/Remove Software icon.
3. Click the Install/Uninstall tab.
4. Double-click Find... Extensions.
5. Click the Add/Remove button. You see the dialog box shown in Figure 8.22.

Figure 8.22.
The Find Extensions Configuration dialog box lets you customize your Find menu.

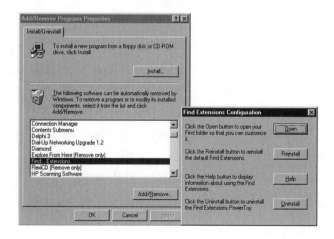

To customize your Find menu, click the Open button, which displays icons representing your Find command choices. You can delete, modify, or rename any of these icons.

KernelToys

KernelToys is a collection of free utilities for fine-tuning the performance of Windows 95. To install KernelToys on your computer, follow these steps:

1. Create a folder for the KernelToys by right-clicking the desktop and choosing New | Folder from the pop-up menu. Name the folder Krnltoys.

2. Download KernelToys from Microsoft's Web site at www.microsoft.com. Save the KernelToys file (called krnltoys.exe) in the Krnltoys folder.

3. Double-click the krnltoys.exe file. This creates several new files in your Krnltoys folder.

4. Install the KernelToys. You can install some of the KernelToys files by right-clicking the Setup Information file (INF file) that looks like a notepad with a little yellow gear and then clicking Install. You can run other KernelToys files directly from the Krnltoys folder or by copying them into another folder.

Convention Memory Tracking

The CONVMEM.VXD file tracks the amount of memory allocated by virtual device drivers (VxDs) in conventional memory and consists of a table that lists the following:

- The address at which the memory was allocated (hexadecimal)
- The size of the memory block (hexadecimal)
- The requested memory alignment
- The letter I if the block is instanced
- The virtual device driver that allocated the memory

By studying the CONVMEM.TXT file, you can determine exactly how your computer's memory is allocated among your different applications. To install CONVMEM.VXD, do the following:

1. Copy the file into your Windows\System directory.

2. Add the following line to the [386Enh] section of the system.ini file:

```
device=convmem.vxd
```

3. Restart Windows 95. You find a file called CONVMEM.TXT in your Windows directory.

To uninstall CONVMEM.VXD, delete the file CONVMEM.VXD and remove the above line from your system.ini file.

DOSWZCFG—MS-DOS Mode Configuration Wizard Customization Tool

DOSWZCFG lets you optimize MS-DOS programs running under Windows 95. To use DOSZCFG, do the following:

1. Right-click (or use a shortcut to) an MS-DOS application.

2. Click the Program page.

3. Click Advanced.

4. Click the Configure button to invoke the dialog box shown in Figure 8.23.

Figure 8.23.
DOSZCFG lets you customize an MS-DOS program to run under Windows 95.

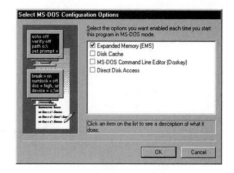

Keyboard Remap

The Keyboard Remap program lets you change the way the Ctrl, Alt, Window, and Menu keys work on your keyboard. This keyboard control panel extension lets you set up your keyboard the way you want it.

After installing the Keyboard Remap program, do the following:

1. Go to Control Panel.

2. Double-click the Keyboard icon.

3. Click the Remap tab.

4. Click the key you want to change (see Figure 8.24).

Figure 8.24.
The Keyboard Remap program lets you change the way certain keys work.

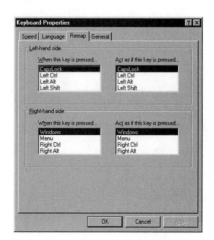

WinTop

WinTop lets you view the processes and threads currently running. To run WinTop, do the following:

1. Click the Start button on the Taskbar.

2. Select Run.

3. Type **WinTop**.

4. Click OK. The WinTop window appears as shown in Figure 8.25.

Figure 8.25.
WinTop lets you view the processes and threads currently running on your computer.

DOSWINKY—Windows Logo Key Control for MS-DOS Programs

DOSWINKY is a device driver that disables the Windows logo key while using an MS-DOS program. That way, if you press the Windows key by mistake, Windows 95 won't suddenly display the Start menu. To install DOSWINKY, do the following:

1. Right-click the DOSWINKY.INF file.

2. Click Install.

3. Restart the computer for the changes to take effect.

After you have installed DOSWINKY, do the following:

1. Right-click the MS-DOS program (or its shortcut).

2. Click Properties.

3. Click the Misc tab.

4. Clear the check mark from the Ctrl+Esc check box to disable the Ctrl+Esc key when running an MS-DOS program (see Figure 8.26).

Figure 8.26.
The DOSWINKY
program lets you turn
off the Windows logo
key.

On Your Own

Run the Tweak UI program and change various settings to see their effects on your computer. Find ways to simplify your favorite application such as a word processor or Internet browser.

Practice using the DeskMenu to switch back and forth between desktop icons. Now switch between the same desktop icons using the Windows 95 desktop to see which method you prefer.

Load the CONVMEM.VXD file and track the amount of memory allocated by your system's virtual device drivers. Look for any device drivers that gobble up too much memory that you could possibly delete.

Run your favorite MS-DOS game and see which PowerToys features can optimize the game for running under Windows 95. See if you notice any difference running an MS-DOS game under Windows 95 compared to running the same game under MS-DOS alone.

Put in your favorite audio CD and let the FlexiCD program play your favorite songs for you while you work at your computer.

III

Windows 95
Anatomy

9

The Windows 95 Architecture

Peter Norton®

Windows 95 uses an architecture that borrows from Windows 3.*x* and MS-DOS. That's the bad news. The good news is that the problems that plagued users in the past are a lot less noticeable under Windows 95. MS-DOS is used very little once you start Windows 95, and Windows 3.*x*'s 16-bit interface is augmented by new 32-bit underpinnings. All these new features make Windows 95 better than previous versions of Windows, but it's still far from the perfect operating system if reliability is your main concern.

Windows NT is a more stable operating system than Windows 95. Unfortunately, Windows NT isn't as compatible, especially with MS-DOS applications. The types of security required to make Windows NT or any other operating system stable also prevent it from running some types of ill-behaved applications. Windows 95 represents a halfway point; you get some added stability and a new 32-bit capability and still keep the compatibility that most people need to make Windows really work on a workstation.

The following sections examine the details of all these Windows 95 components. This chapter also provides a few additional glimpses of what Windows could become in the future. It's important to realize that, even with all its flaws, Windows 95 shows how workstation operating systems will evolve in the future.

A Quick Look Inside

Learning about a new operating system usually includes knowing a bit about the components that compose it. With this in mind, take a look at the Windows 95 architecture.

Architecture

Several elements make up the Windows 95 architecture, as shown in Figure 9.1. Each element takes care of one part of the Windows environment. For example, the Windows API (Application Programming Interface) layer lets applications communicate with Windows internals such as the file management system. You couldn't write a Windows application without the API layer.

The System Virtual Machine (VM) component of Windows 95 contains three main elements: 32-bit Windows applications, the shell, and 16-bit Windows applications. Essentially, the System VM component provides most of the Windows 95 user-specific functionality. Without it, you couldn't run any applications. Notice that I don't include MS-DOS applications here; Windows uses an entirely different set of capabilities to run MS-DOS applications.

Two Windows APIs are included with Windows 95. The first API is like the one supplied with Windows 3.*x* (although there are differences in the way low-level feature access to things such as drivers is implemented). It provides all the 16-bit services that the old Windows had to provide for applications. An older 16-bit application will use this API when it runs. The other API is the Win32 API, which is similar to the one used by Windows NT. It provides a subset of the features that all 32-bit applications running under Windows NT can access. The 32-bit API provides about the same feature set as the 16-bit API, but it's more robust. The next section explores both of these APIs as part of the system file discussion.

Figure 9.1.
Windows contains several major elements. Each element provides a different service to the user and to other applications running under Windows.

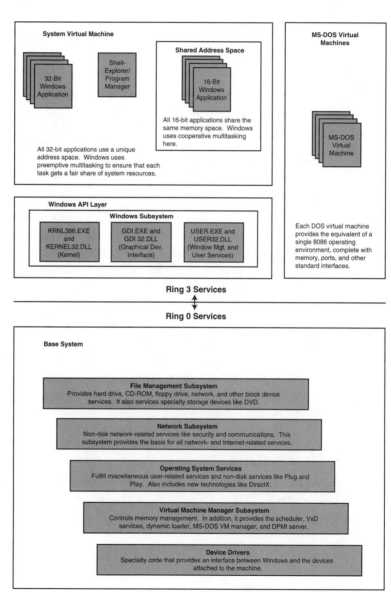

The Base System component of Windows 95 contains all the operating-system–specific services. This is the core of Windows 95, the part that has to be operating for Windows to perform its work. The following paragraphs describe each part of the Base System in detail:

- File Management Subsystem: Essentially, this part of the Base System provides an interface to all the block devices (such as hard drives and CD-ROM drives) connected to your machine. It doesn't matter how the connection is made—physically or through a network. All that matters is that your machine can access the device. The big thing to remember about the File Management Subsystem is that Windows 95 no longer relies on MS-DOS to manage files. This particular part of Windows 95 is examined in detail in Chapter 10, "The Windows 95 File System."

- Network Subsystem: Windows for Workgroups was the first version of Windows to address the networking needs of the workgroup. Windows 95 extends this capability. Not only can you run a Microsoft peer-to-peer network, but Windows 95 provides protected-mode clients for most major LAN products as well. In fact, you can keep more than one network active at a time. The modular nature of the Network Subsystem enables other vendors to add to Windows 95-inherent capabilities through the use of VxDs (virtual device drivers).

- Operating System Services: This is the part of the operating system that deals with features such as Plug and Play. Here you also find new Windows 95 capabilities such as DirectX (the new technology used by games and other programs requiring high-speed access to the hardware). The Operating System Services section also fulfills miscellaneous user and operating system requests. For example, every time the user asks Windows 95 for the time of day, he's requesting a service from this Windows 95 component.

- Virtual Machine Manager: The Virtual Machine Manager takes care of task scheduling, and it starts and stops every application on the system (including any MS-DOS applications that you might run). This operating system component manages virtual memory on your machine as well. Of course, your application uses the Windows API to make the request instead of talking directly with this part of the system. Because the Virtual Machine Manager handles all memory allocations, it also has to act as a DPMI (DOS Protected-Mode Interface) server for MS-DOS applications that run in protected mode. When an MS-DOS application makes a memory request, it's actually calling routines in this component of Windows. As with Windows applications, MS-DOS applications can't directly access this component of Windows. The MS-DOS application uses an MS-DOS extender API to make its call. Finally, the Virtual Machine Manager is responsible for intertask communication. All this means is that all DDE and OLE requests filter through this section of the operating system.

- Device Drivers/Win32 Driver Model (WDM): Windows would never know what to do with your system if not for the lowly device driver. This bit of specialty code acts as an interpreter. It takes Windows requests and provides them to the device in a format it can understand. Windows 95 supports two forms of device drivers. The first type is the real-mode device driver that you used with Windows 3.x. The problem with using this type of driver is that Windows has to keep switching between real and protected mode to use it. Windows 95 also provides support for VxD (virtual device driver), which lets Windows talk to the devices on your system without switching to real mode. There are three reasons to use VxDs over standard real-mode device drivers: Your system remains more stable, runs faster, and recovers from errors better.

Windows 95 deals with MS-DOS applications differently than it deals with the Windows-specific applications on your machine. Each MS-DOS application runs on what Intel terms a virtual machine. Essentially, the processor fools the application into thinking that it's the only application running on your machine at the moment. Each virtual machine has its own memory space and access to devices on the system. The amazing thing is that you can have many virtual machines running on your one physical machine at a time. I take a more detailed look at the DOS Virtual Machine later. Suffice it to say that Windows 95 has to literally perform backflips to make this whole concept work properly, especially when you consider Windows-hostile applications such as MS-DOS games.

This section gives you just a brief overview of the Windows 95 architecture. If you want a more in-depth view of the internal structure of Windows 95, look at the section "Windows 95 Internals" later in this chapter. It gives you a much more detailed look at how Windows 95 works as a whole.

The System Files

MS-DOS programmers know you're supposed to gain access to the operating system using an interrupt service routine. These interrupts ask the operating system to perform a specific task. All the code for the interrupt routines appears in the system files. This old method worked well in the MS-DOS single-tasking environment, where the application was in control. Under Windows, the user is in control, and the old system won't work properly. Every Windows application gains access to the operating system by using an API. Essentially, an API call does the same thing as an interrupt: It asks the operating system to perform a task. The code for the API appears in the system files, just as it does for MS-DOS. Of course, this is a simplified view of the API. An API is written using protected-mode code—unlike MS-DOS, which is written in real-mode code. In addition, API code is re-entrant; MS-DOS code isn't. A re-entrant piece of code allows Windows 95 to process more than one call at a time. Under MS-DOS, you couldn't re-enter a piece of code; you had to complete one call at a time. There are other differences, but the only people who really need to know about them are programmers. As discussed in the preceding section, Windows 95 actually uses two APIs—one 16-bit and one 32-bit.

DirectX—a Middle Road for Programmers

Anyone who plays games on the computer with any regularity understands the need for high-speed hardware. The entire gaming experience is built around fancy graphics and multimedia presentations. This kind of environment isn't forgiving when it comes to processor cycles and definitely doesn't allow much room for the programmer to work. It isn't any wonder then that Microsoft had a problem trying to convince game programmers to take Windows seriously. After all, direct hardware access provides a much faster interface than using the Windows API.

Unfortunately, direct hardware access is out of the question when using Windows. Unless the operating system knows exactly what's going on with all the hardware all the time, there isn't any way for it to provide access to more than applications. As far as game vendors were concerned, there wasn't any way for Windows to support games of any complexity under these conditions.

DirectX is a middle ground. It gives a game programmer (or anyone else, for that matter) a higher-speed interface than Windows normally provides, without taking Windows itself out of the loop. Windows still monitors the events taking place when using DirectX, but it provides a lot less in the way of support. DirectX technology provides the means for a programmer to access the hardware, without damaging the Windows multitasking environment.

DirectX does have a few problems. The biggest problem right now is that DirectX is evolving. That means that you might get a piece of software that doesn't work even if you have DirectX installed because the software is written to a newer standard. DirectX also causes compatibility problems on some machines when used in certain ways. In other words, there isn't any guarantee that a DirectX application will work all the time if the game vendor didn't follow the specifications to the letter (and even then, there isn't the best guarantee).

One of the fallouts of the new nature of DirectX is that some game vendors have decided to bypass it entirely and use an older technology instead. OpenGL, another graphics technology which is included with Windows 95 OSR2 and will also be used by Windows 98, is an older and more established technology. In fact, OpenGL originally appeared in Windows NT. The down side of using OpenGL is that it's not quite as fast for games as DirectX is. However, some vendors consider the enhanced stability of OpenGL a bigger plus than speed.

At best, DirectX represents a partial solution to a problem that people have had with Windows. It gives the programmer direct access to the hardware with a minimum of interference from Windows. Obviously, you need to carefully weigh the pros and cons of using DirectX before installing it on your machine. More importantly, you need to find out whether the software you're installing uses DirectX in the first place. When troubleshooting graphics problems with a particular piece of software, ask yourself whether DirectX might be the source of your problem.

The big news under Windows 95 is the 32-bit API. Not only are 32-bit system calls a lot more logical from a programmer's point of view (Windows 3.*x* was a programmer's nightmare; Windows 95 is merely an inconvenience), but they also provide many more features. In addition, a 32-bit application enjoys the benefits that this environment provides. Of course, the biggest benefit that you'll hear most programmers talk about is the flat memory address space. Every application running under Windows—until now—has had to spend time working with Intel's segmented address scheme. A 32-bit application doesn't need to worry about segmentation any more.

No matter which API you use, your application will address three basic components. The 16-bit versions of these files are GDI.EXE, USER.EXE, and KRNL386.EXE. The 32-bit versions of these files are GDI32.DLL, USER32.DLL, and KERNEL32.DLL. The following list describes these three components in detail:

- Windows Kernel (KRNL386.EXE or KERNEL32.DLL): This is the part of Windows 95 that provides support for the lower-level functions that an application needs to run. For example, every time your application needs memory, it runs to the Windows Kernel to get it. This component doesn't deal with either the interface or devices; it interacts only with Windows itself.

- Graphical Device Interface (GDI.EXE or GDI32.DLL): Every time an application writes to the screen, it's using a GDI service. This Windows component takes care of fonts, printer services, the display, color management, and every other artistic aspect of Windows that users can see as they use your application.

- User (USER.EXE or USER32.DLL): Windows is all about just that—windows. It needs a manager to keep track of all the windows that applications create to display various types of information. However, User only begins there. Every time your application displays an icon or button, it's using some type of User component function. It's easier to think of the User component of the Windows API as a work manager; it helps you organize things and keep them straight.

There's actually one more piece to the Windows API, but it's a small piece that your application will never use. Windows 95 still starts out as a 16-bit application so that it can implement Plug and Play. The Plug and Play BIOS contains separate sections for real-mode and 16-bit protected-mode calls. If Windows 95 started out in 32-bit mode, it couldn't call the Plug and Play BIOS to set up all your devices without a lot of overhead. (To understand why, see the section "Getting 16-Bit and 32-Bit Applications to Work Together" later in this chapter.) All device configuration has to occur before Windows actually starts the GUI.

The Plug and Play BIOS

Plug and Play (PnP) provides one of the easiest ways to configure the hardware on your machine. PnP is actually the work of three system components: hardware, BIOS, and the operating system. The BIOS queries all the system components during startup and activates essential system components such as the disk drive and display adapter. Everything else waits on the sidelines until the operating system boots. During the boot process, the operating system finishes the task of assigning interrupts and port addresses to every system component and asks the BIOS to provide a list of previous assignments so that it won't use them again.

In addition to cooperating with the operating system, PnP provides protected-mode routines. The current BIOS specification only requires vendors to provide 16-bit protected-mode routines. That's why Windows 95 still starts in 16-bit mode instead of 32-bit mode. In addition, that's one of the reasons why a real-mode MS-DOS stub (a functional subset of the MS-DOS that you're familiar with) is part of the picture. (The version of real-mode MS-DOS provided with Windows 95 also executes AUTOEXEC.BAT and CONFIG.SYS, but I look into that aspect later.) You can't use the protected-mode routines without first gathering the information that the BIOS needs in real mode. The real-mode MS-DOS stub performs this function for the BIOS.

Note: If your computer doesn't use a PnP BIOS, you might have trouble installing hardware. How can you avoid this problem?

There are several good places to get specifications for your PnP BIOS, but the best place is the Intel site at http://developer.intel.com/ial/plugplay/index.htm. You can also download a complete suite of tools for testing the compatibility of your Windows 95 machine at ftp://ftp.microsoft.com/services/whql/. This Microsoft site includes an HCL (hardware compatibility list) file that shows what hardware has already been tested for compatibility. All you need to do is download the file and extract the help file it contains to see if your hardware is compatible. Mobile computer users will also want to look at the special Intel PnP site at http://www.intel.com/mobile/tech/pnp.htm.

When looking at a PnP-compatible system, you should see a lot more than just three different entities cooperating to provide automatic system configuration. The following list outlines additional features that you get as part of a PnP system:

- Identify installed devices: Windows 95 automatically detects all the Plug and Play components attached to your system. This means that you need to provide a minimum of information during installation and nothing at all during subsequent reboots.

- Determine device resource needs: Every device on your computer needs resources in the form of processor cycles, input/output ports, DMA channels, memory, and interrupts. Windows 95 works with the BIOS and peripheral devices to meet these needs without any intervention.

- Automatic system configuration updates and resource conflict detection: All this communication between peripheral devices, the BIOS, and the operating system allows Windows 95 to create a system configuration without any user intervention. The Device Manager configuration blocks are grayed out because the user doesn't need to supply this information anymore. The enhanced level of communication also allows Windows 95 to poll the peripherals for alternative port and interrupt settings when a conflict with another device occurs.

- Device driver loading and unloading: CONFIG.SYS and AUTOEXEC.BAT used to contain line after line of device driver and TSR statements because the system had to bring these devices online before it loaded the command processor and Windows 3.*x*. Windows 95 can actually maintain or even enhance the performance of a Plug and Play–compatible system without using an AUTOEXEC.BAT or CONFIG.SYS. Plug and Play compatibility allows Windows 95 to dynamically load and unload any device drivers that your system needs.

- Configuration change notification: Plug and Play might make system configuration changes automatic, but that doesn't mean that Windows 95 leaves you in the dark. Every time the system configuration changes, Windows 95 notifies you by displaying a dialog box onscreen. Essentially, this dialog box tells you what changed. This capability provides an additional side benefit. Windows 95 also notifies you whenever your equipment experiences some kind of failure. When a piece of equipment fails, Windows 95 notices that it's no longer online. Plug and Play requires three-way communication, and a defective device usually fails to communicate. Instead of your finding out that you no longer have access to a drive or other device when you need it most, Windows 95 notifies you of the change immediately after it takes place.

An Overview of the Registry

When Microsoft started work on Windows NT, it looked for a better configuration tool than the INI file. Users were ending up with loads of these files in their Windows directory, not to mention the INI files floating around in application directories. Finding the right file to correct a problem when using Windows 3.*x* could be daunting, to say the least.

File bloat wasn't the only problem facing Microsoft. INI files also encouraged vendors to come up with distinct ways of configuring their software. No one could figure out one INI file from the other because they all used different formatting techniques. Obviously, this made life even more difficult for the user, not to mention the support staff at the various software companies.

To solve this problem, Microsoft created a special database called the Registry, which keeps track of all the applications stored on your computer. The Registry originally appeared in Windows NT, and Microsoft used the same idea for Windows 95.

Windows 95 can't boot without a clean Registry. Any corruption in this file causes a host of problems, even if Windows 95 does manage to boot. Although the Registry is a lot easier to maintain than the INI files of old and does provide a central repository of information, it also presents unique problems of its own.

> **Tip:** Windows 95 stores the previous copy of your Registry in the USER.DA0 and SYSTEM.DA0 files. If you make a mistake in editing the Registry, exit immediately, shut down Windows 95, and boot into MS-DOS mode. Change directories to your Windows 95 main directory. Use the ATTRIB utility to make the SYSTEM.DA0, SYSTEM.DAT, USER.DA0, and USER.DAT files visible by using the -R, -H, and -S switches. Now copy the backup of your Registry to the two original files (that is, SYSTEM.DA0 to SYSTEM.DAT and USER.DA0 to USER.DAT). This restores your Registry to its pre-edit state. Be sure to restore the previous file attribute state by using the +R, +H, and +S switches of the ATTRIB utility.

When you look at the Registry, you're seeing a complete definition of Windows 95 as it relates to your specific machine. Not only does the Registry contain hardware and application settings, but it also contains every other piece of information you can imagine about your machine. You can learn a lot about Windows simply by looking at the information presented by this database. For example, did you know that you can use multiple desktops in Windows 95? Of course, that leads to another problem: maintaining those separate desktops. The hierarchical format presented by the Registry editor helps the administrator compare the differences between the various desktops and allows the administrator to configure them with ease. Best of all, editing the Registry doesn't involve a session with a text editor. Windows provides a GUI editor that the administrator can use to change the settings in the Registry.

Knowing that the Registry contains a lot of information and is easy to edit still doesn't tell you what it can do for you. When was the last time you used Explorer to check out your hard drive? I use it a lot because it provides an easy way to find what I need. The Registry can help you make Explorer easier to use. One of my favorite ways to use it for Explorer modifications is to create multiple associations for the same file type. Suppose that you want to associate a graphics editor with .PCX and BMP files. This isn't difficult. However, what if each file type requires a different set of command-line switches? Now you get into an area where using the Registry can really help. Using the Registry to edit these entries can help you customize file access.

> **Note:** Before proceeding, you should add the Registry editor, RegEdit, to your Start menu. It helps to look at the Registry entries as you read about them. I also present some exercises that will help you better understand the inner workings of the Registry.

To start the Registry editor, simply open RegEdit as you do any other application on the Start menu. You'll probably get a lot more out of the detailed discussion that follows if you actually open the Registry editor now. Using the Registry editor to see how Windows 95 arranges the various entries can make using it in an emergency a lot easier.

The first thing you need to know about RegEdit is what you'll see. There are two panes in RegEdit, as in Explorer. The entries in the left pane are keys. Look at a key as you do the headings in a book; they divide the Registry into easily understood pieces. Using keys also makes finding a specific piece of configuration information fast. The entries in the right pane are values. A value is Registry content, just like the paragraphs in a book. There are three kinds of values: String, binary, and DWORD. The string type is the only one you can read directly. Binary and DWORD values contain computer readable data using two different sized variables. In most cases, you don't have to worry about what these kinds of values contain because your applications and Windows 95 take care of them automatically.

Be careful when using the Registry. You might want to follow the same procedure I use to back up the Registry before you go much further. The big advantage to this method is that it produces a text file that you can view with any text editor. (The file is huge, so Notepad won't handle it, but WordPad will.) You can use this backup file to restore the Registry later if you run into difficulty. Unfortunately, this method won't help much if you permanently destroy the Registry and reboot the machine. Windows 95 needs a clean Registry to boot. To preserve a clean, bootable copy of the Registry, you need to copy the USER.DAT and SYSTEM.DAT files to a safe location. (Later I cover a technique for importing a text copy of the Registry by using RegEdit at the MS-DOS prompt, but this technique isn't guaranteed by anyone to work. The bottom line is that a good backup is always worth the effort.)

Warning: RegEdit is an application designed to assist experienced users in changing Windows 95 and associated application behavior. Although it allows you to enhance system performance and make applications easier to use, it can cause unexpected results when misused. Never edit an entry unless you know what that entry is for. Failure to observe this precaution can result in data loss and even prevent your system from booting the next time you start Windows 95.

1. Highlight the My Computer entry of the Registry. Select Registry | Export Registry File to display the Export Registry File dialog box shown in Figure 9.2. Notice that the File name field already contains a name. You can use any name you want. I selected OLDENTRY to designate a pre-edited Registry. Notice that the All radio button is selected in the Export Range group.

2. Click the Save button to place a copy of the Registry on disk. The OLDENTRY.REG file in your main Windows 95 directory now contains a complete copy of your original Registry.

Figure 9.2.
The Export Registry File dialog box allows you to save your current Registry settings.

Now that you have a copy of the Registry, let's take that brief overview that I talked about previously. The next few sections acquaint you with the contents of the Registry as a whole. I don't go into much detail, but at least you'll know the general location for specific types of information.

HKEY_CLASSES_ROOT

There are two major types of keys under the HKEY_CLASSES_ROOT key. The first key type is a file extension. Think of all the three-letter extensions you've used such as .DOC and .TXT. Windows 95 still uses them to differentiate one file type from another. (Because Windows 95 also provides long filename support, you can use the Registry to create associations for extensions longer than three letters.) The Registry also uses extensions to associate that file type with a specific action. For example, even though you can't do anything with a file that uses the .DLL extension, it appears in this list because Windows 95 needs to associate DLLs with an executable file type. The second entry type is the association itself. The file extension entries normally associate a data file with an application or an executable file with a specific Windows 95 function. Below the association key are entries for the menus that you see when you right-click an entry in the Explorer. The association also contains keys that determine what type of icon to display and other parameters associated with a particular file type. Figure 9.3 shows the typical HKEY_CLASSES_ROOT organization.

HKEY_CURRENT_USER

The HKEY_CURRENT_USER key contains a lot of "soft" settings for your machine. These soft settings tell how to configure the desktop and the keyboard. It also contains color settings and the configuration of the Start menu. All user-specific settings appear under this key.

The HKEY_CURRENT_USER key is slaved to the settings for the current user, the one who is logged onto the machine at this time. This is differentiated from all the user configuration entries in other parts of the Registry. This is a dynamic setting category; the other user-related categories contain static information. The Registry copies the contents of one of the user entries in the HKEY_USERS category into this category and updates HKEY_USERS when you shut down.

This is the area where Windows 95 obtains new setting information and places any changes you make. As you can see from Figure 9.4, the keys within the HKEY_CURRENT_USER category are pretty self-explanatory in most cases. All the entries adjust some type of user-specific setting—nothing that affects a global element such as a device driver.

Figure 9.3.

A typical HKEY_CLASSES_ROOT *display. Notice the distinct difference between file extension and file association keys.*

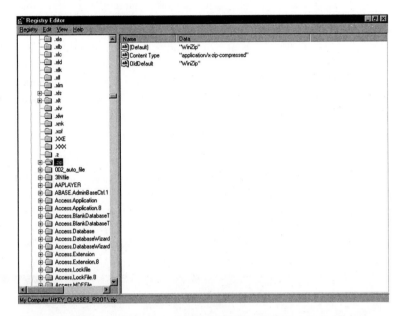

Figure 9.4.

HKEY_CURRENT_USER *contains all user-specific settings.*

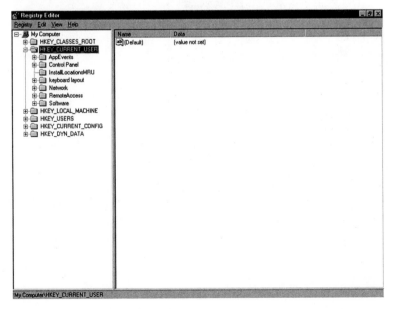

HKEY_LOCAL_MACHINE

The HKEY_LOCAL_MACHINE key centers its attention on the machine hardware. This includes the drivers and configuration information required to use the hardware. Every piece of hardware appears somewhere in this section of the Registry, even if that hardware uses real-mode drivers. If a piece of hardware doesn't appear here, Windows 95 can't use it.

A lot of subtle information about your hardware is stored under this key. For example, this key contains all the Plug and Play information about your machine. It also provides a complete listing of the device drivers and their revision levels. This section might even contain the revision information for the hardware itself. For example, there's a distinct difference between a Pro Audio Spectrum 16+ Revision C sound board and a Revision D version of that same board. Windows 95 stores that difference in the Registry.

This key does contain some software-specific information of a global nature. For example, a 32-bit application stores the location of its Setup and Format Table (SFT) here. This is a file that the application uses during installation. Some applications also use it during a setup modification. Applications such as Word for Windows store all their setup information in SFT tables. The only application information that appears here is global configuration specific such as the SFT. Figure 9.5 shows a typical HKEY_LOCAL_MACHINE category setup.

Figure 9.5.

HKEY_LOCAL_MACHINE *contains all the hardware and device-driver–specific information about your machine. It also contains the global-application–setup information.*

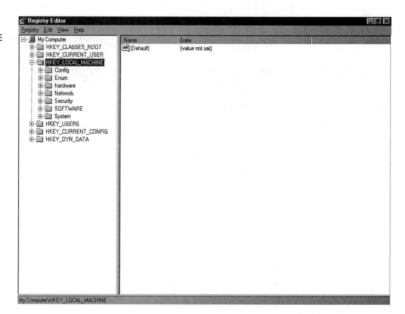

HKEY_USERS

The HKEY_USERS key contains a static listing of all the users of this particular Registry file. It never pays to edit any of the information you find under this key. However, you can use this key for reference purposes. The reason for this hands-off policy is simple: None of the entries here takes effect until the next time the user logs on to Windows 95, so you really don't know what effect they'll have until you reboot the machine. In addition, changing the settings for the current user is a waste of time because Windows 95 overwrites the new data with the data contained in HKEY_CURRENT_USER during logoff or shutdown.

There's one other problem associated with using this key as your sole source of information. Windows 95 actually maintains multiple Registries in a multiuser configuration—in some cases, one for each user who logs on to the system. Because of this, you never quite know where you'll find the information for a particular user. Windows 95 tracks this information, but it's really a pain for the administrator to have to track it as well. Besides, Microsoft thoughtfully provided a utility that helps the network administrator maintain the various Registries. The Policy Editor utility enables the network administrator to maintain static user information with ease. Using the Policy Editor lets the network administrator bridge the various Registry files on the system when each user provides his or her own desktop configuration.

Figure 9.6 shows a setup that includes the default key. If this system were set up for multiple desktops, each user would have a separate entry in this section. Each entry would contain precisely the same keys, but the values might differ from user to user. When a user logs on to the network, Windows 95 copies all the information in his profile to the HKEY_CURRENT_USER area of the Registry. When he logs off or shuts down, Windows 95 updates the information in his specific section from the HKEY_CURRENT_USER category.

Figure 9.6.

Windows 95 creates one entry in the HKEY_USERS *category for each user who logs on to the machine.*

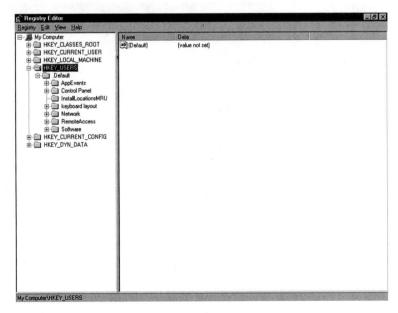

HKEY_CURRENT_CONFIG

The HKEY_CURRENT_CONFIG key is the simplest part of the Registry. It contains two major keys: Display and System. Essentially, these entries are used by the GDI API to configure the display and printer.

The Display key provides two subkeys: Fonts and Settings. The Fonts subkey determines which fonts Windows 95 uses for general display purposes. These are the raster (non-TrueType) fonts that it displays when you get a choice of which font to use for icons or other purposes. Raster fonts are essentially bitmaps or pictures of the characters. Chapter 16, "Fonts and Printing," takes a more detailed look at fonts.

The Settings subkey contains the current display resolution and number of bits per pixel. The bits per pixel value determines the number of colors available. For example, 4 bits per pixel provides 16 colors, and 8 bits per pixel provides 256 colors. The three fonts listed as values under this key are the default fonts used for icons and application menus. You can change all the settings under this key by using the Settings tab of the Display Properties dialog box.

The System key looks like a convoluted mess. Only one of the subkeys under this key has any meaning for the user. The Printers subkey contains a list of the printers attached to the machine. It doesn't include printers accessed through a network connection. Figure 9.7 shows the major keys in this category.

Figure 9.7.
HKEY_CURRENT_CONFIG *echoes the settings under the* CONFIG *key of the* HKEY LOCAL_MACHINE *category.*

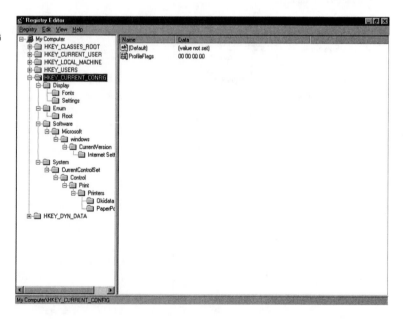

HKEY_DYN_DATA

The final key, HKEY_DYN_DATA, contains two subkeys: Config Manager and PerfStats. You can monitor the status of the Config Manager key by using the Device Manager. The PerfStats key values
appear as statistics in the System Monitor utility display. Figure 9.8 shows these two main keys and
their subkeys.

Figure 9.8.

HKEY_DYN_DATA
*contains Registry
entries for current
events. The values in
these keys reflect the
current (dynamic)
state of the computer.*

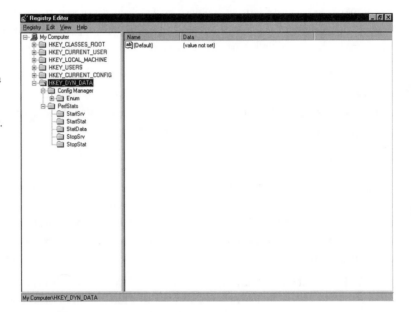

Windows 95 Compatibility Configuration Files

There's no doubt about it: Windows 95 starts by booting MS-DOS. Microsoft had to provide the
four compatibility files that older applications need to run. Some of these files are easy to bypass;
others don't go away until you get rid of all those applications. Part of the reason MS-DOS is still
hanging around is because of these compatibility files. Windows 95 has to boot using real mode so
that it can read and process both CONFIG.SYS and AUTOEXEC.BAT. The other reasons that Windows 95
boots into real mode are examined later in this chapter.

The following sections take an in-depth look at the four compatibility files: AUTOEXEC.BAT, CONFIG.SYS,
SYSTEM.INI, and WIN.INI. Fortunately, you really only need this one compatibility file—SYSTEM.INI—
to run Windows 95. The other files are there for compatibility purposes only.

AUTOEXEC.BAT

AUTOEXEC.BAT is the one file you could get rid of if you didn't have any 16-bit Windows applications that required a PATH statement. Windows 95 provides the means for defining a path and a prompt and loading any TSRs that an MS-DOS application might require to run. The most efficient way to use Windows 95 is not to load anything a DOS application would need here.

Use AUTOEXEC.BAT only for settings you need on a global basis or as part of the requirement for running an older Windows application. Some 16-bit Windows applications require SET and PATH entries to run. This is especially true of compilers and advanced applications.

Looking Ahead: I look at how you can replace both CONFIG.SYS and AUTOEXEC.BAT for MS-DOS applications in Chapter 13, "Exploiting Your Software: DOS, 16-Bit, and 32-Bit Windows Applications." If your only reason for keeping these two files around is so you can run MS-DOS applications, consider the faster alternative presented here.

The following list contains a few things you should never run from AUTOEXEC.BAT. Most of these items consume memory before you load Windows—memory you can't retrieve later. Using this technique might cost you a little conventional memory for your MS-DOS applications, but you'll still have about the same or perhaps even more than you had available under Windows 3.*x*. The reason for this is simple: You don't have to load a bunch of drivers in CONFIG.SYS to make Windows 95 run.

- TSRs: Avoid running any TSRs from AUTOEXEC.BAT. A small utility such as DOSKey might not appear to consume much memory, but why run it from AUTOEXEC.BAT at all? You can easily customize the settings for your MS-DOS applications. Those that will never use DOSKey don't need to give up the memory required to install it. In essence, loading a TSR in AUTOEXEC.BAT penalizes the applications that can't use it.

- MS-DOS application environment variables: If you have an MS-DOS application that requires a PATH entry or other environmental variables, load the variables as part of the application's special configuration rather than as part of AUTOEXEC.BAT. You can individually adjust the size of the environment for each MS-DOS application you run.

- MS-DOS applications with Windows counterparts: I used to run CHKDSK as part of every startup cycle. A lot of other people do the same thing. Running some MS-DOS applications before you enter Windows doesn't harm the amount of available memory you have one iota. Running other applications can consume memory. For example, if you run MODE to change your screen size to 43 lines before you enter Windows, every DOS program you load consumes 43 lines worth of memory (more if you ask for a larger screen in the custom settings). You can reduce the memory required for each MS-DOS session by using the application's custom screen settings.

- Disk- or printer-caching software: You'll find that the Windows 95 disk- and print-caching services are far superior to those provided with Windows 3.*x*. The memory allocated to these services is dynamic—Windows 95 can increase and decrease the amount of memory used as needed—as long as you use the Windows 95–specific capability. When you load disk- or print-caching software in AUTOEXEC.BAT, you lose the ability to control the size of that cache within Windows (in most cases). Even if you could change the size of the cache, it's unlikely that Windows 95 could use it, unless the caching program is specially designed to communicate with Windows.

CONFIG.SYS

Unless you're still playing Russian roulette with those real-mode drivers on your system, you can get rid of CONFIG.SYS. Windows 95 provides its own extended memory manager (EMM), so it doesn't need one loaded as Windows 3.*x* did. Windows 95 also takes care of the BUFFERS, LASTDRIVE, and STACKS entries for you. In other words, CONFIG.SYS is out of a job unless you give it one.

I recently threw caution to the wind and tried booting my system for several days with a pared down AUTOEXEC.BAT and no CONFIG.SYS. Not only did I notice a speed increase when loading Windows, but I also had far greater control over the settings for each individual DOS setting. Windows also could provide much better memory control than before. (I used the System Monitor utility described in Chapter 11, "The Windows 95 Applets," to check all this out.)

I had to deal with a few negatives, however. Getting rid of CONFIG.SYS lost me about 5KB of conventional memory. I still had 600KB of RAM available in an MS-DOS window, however, so the memory loss was pretty minimal. I could probably get even more available memory by decreasing the environment size and not loading DOSKey as part of my custom settings. It also cost me some time to set up each of my MS-DOS applications. The greater flexibility and better memory management came at the cost of increased complexity. Even though there were negative elements, I'd still say it was worth the effort.

Tip: In the past, users with large hard drives usually resorted to using special drivers such as those from OnTrack Systems to access their entire drive, using one partition. You can still do this under Windows 95 with relatively good success. However, such an action destabilizes your system. The reason is clear: Every time Windows needs to access the drive, it has to switch to real mode to access the real-mode driver. It's probably a better idea to partition your drive into more manageable partition sizes and get rid of the real-mode drivers if at all possible.

WIN.INI

Windows 95 can get along just fine without WIN.INI. However, before you get rid of your file, you might want to check it out first. A few applications, especially screen savers, load themselves by using the LOAD= or RUN= lines of this file. You can get around this limitation by adding the filenames to your Startup folder and changing the application settings as needed.

Many applications also store their file association information here. Windows 95 applications don't need these entries because they already appear in the Registry. Any new 32-bit applications know to look in the Registry for file association information, but some older 16-bit applications don't. You might want to check for problems by saving a copy of WIN.INI under a different name and then editing out the Extensions section. If all your applications seem to work properly, you might be able to remove this section for good.

> **Note:** Windows 95 always checks for new entries in both WIN.INI and SYSTEM.INI. It automatically adds any new entries that it finds to the appropriate section of the Registry. This is why you can get rid of these two files if you have a stable system and none of the 16-bit applications that you use relies on them. Of course, that's a big if, and you still have the mysterious Windows 95 problem with SYSTEM.INI to deal with. In reality, you probably need to wait until you've gotten rid of all your 16-bit applications before you can get rid of these two files.

If you look through the Windows 95 version of WIN.INI, you'll notice that it's a lot slimmer than that of Windows 3.x. Microsoft moved all the Windows-specific information that this file contained into the Registry. Windows 95 doesn't use it at all. In fact, if you compare the contents of the Registry to a Windows 3.x version of WIN.INI, you'll find every entry that the old file contained.

SYSTEM.INI

Getting rid of SYSTEM.INI will take a major miracle. Just about every application on my machine sticks something in there. Even Microsoft still uses this file—although Microsoft swears otherwise. Most of these settings have become so standard that other applications read the file in anticipation of finding out about the environment.

Of course, this is one source of the problem. Getting rid of SYSTEM.INI or even excluding some of the settings would break a lot of applications out there. Part of the goal of Windows 95 is to provide the compatibility people need out of a workstation. Windows NT is the place to go if you need reliability and stability. Microsoft probably made the right call by keeping SYSTEM.INI in place and up-to-date.

Note: Microsoft is spending a great deal of time telling programmers not to place anything in SYSTEM.INI anymore. The Registry is the new way to store all these settings. A quick look at SYSTEM.INI, however, shows some Windows 95–specific information there. For example, near the bottom of the file you'll see entries for passwords and VCache. These two entries don't appear in Windows 3.x–specific versions of the file.

A Look at the Windows 95 Boot Sequence

Getting your machine up and running after you turn on the power is called the boot process. It includes everything from the time that the Power On Startup Test (POST) routines begin until the time you can start to use the machine. Under MS-DOS, this boot process was relatively straightforward. Windows 95 requires something a bit more exotic because we expect it to do more.

The next few sections look at the boot process from a user's perspective. This means that you won't get a blow-by-blow "this bit does this and that byte does that" explanation. I just look at the highlights of the boot process.

Tip: If you ever want to see a blow-by-blow description of the entire boot process, look at BOOTLOG.TXT in the root directory of your boot drive. This file records every action that Windows 95 performs during the boot process. However, it doesn't include a few of the initial actions such as loading IO.SYS. At most, three or four actions take place before the log starts, however, so your chances of missing anything important are almost nonexistent.

Starting at the MS-DOS Prompt

Windows 95 doesn't (as some people think) start the boot process in protected mode. It actually starts up a copy of MS-DOS. The difference is that the copy of MS-DOS it uses isn't the same as the one you used in the past. Even the system files are different.

The whole reason for starting MS-DOS (at least the one that Microsoft sort of admits to) is compatibility purposes. All those machines with older hardware still need to run device drivers and the like from CONFIG.SYS and AUTOEXEC.BAT. Something has to read those files and act on their contents in a way that the drivers can understand.

Your system starts just as it always has. Installing Windows 95 doesn't stop the system from performing the POST. Once the ROM BIOS determines that your machine is working correctly, it takes care of any required hardware initialization and builds a vector table in lower memory. The vector table contains pointers to all the BIOS routines so that MS-DOS can use them later as part of its boot process. Once this initialization phase is over, the BIOS looks for a bootable drive. A bootable drive contains an operating system loader. In the case of both MS-DOS and Windows 95, that loader will look for a file called IO.SYS.

Up to this point, the workings of MS-DOS and Windows 95 are precisely the same. However, unlike the old version of MS-DOS, everything that the new version needs in the way of code appears in the IO.SYS file. The old MSDOS.SYS file is no longer required. Microsoft combined the contents of the two files that used to appear in your root directory into one.

By now you're looking at your drive and noticing that there's still an MSDOS.SYS file. The MSDOS.SYS file now contains important boot configuration information. You can include a lot of different configuration switches here. Most of them aren't essential, but some are. Fortunately, you don't have to worry too much about editing these entries by hand. Microsoft includes the TweakUI utility with Windows 95, which makes editing the MSDOS.SYS file by hand a thing of the past. I talk about the TweakUI utility in Chapter 8, "Customizing with Microsoft PowerToys and KernelToys."

IO.SYS reads the contents of MSDOS.SYS as part of the pre-booting cycle. Think of MSDOS.SYS as a configuration file for the boot process because that's exactly what it is. After IO.SYS configures itself, using the contents of MSDOS.SYS, it reads the contents of CONFIG.SYS (if there is one). There's no longer a need for CONFIG.SYS because IO.SYS has several features added to it. The following list tells you everything you need to know about these new settings:

- DOS=HIGH,UMB: IO.SYS always loads MS-DOS high unless you override this setting in CONFIG.SYS.

- HIMEM.SYS: IO.SYS always loads a copy of the real-mode memory manager. It doesn't load EMM386.EXE. You need to load this from CONFIG.SYS if you plan to run an application that requires expanded memory without going into Windows first.

- IFSHLP.SYS (installable file system helper): Loading this device driver also loads several others. It gives you full access to the file system.

- SETVER.EXE: Some of your older applications might require a specific version of MS-DOS. This program fools them into thinking that the version of MS-DOS provided with Windows 95 is the one they need.

- FILES=60: Windows 95 doesn't require this setting. It's provided for any MS-DOS applications that you might run. Some older applications require more than 60 file handles, but this setting should work for the majority of installations.

- LASTDRIVE=Z: This sets the last drive letter you can use for your MS-DOS applications. As with the FILES setting, Windows 95 doesn't require a LASTDRIVE setting.

- BUFFERS=30: The BUFFERS setting affects the number of file buffers that IO.SYS provides. Windows 95 uses its own file management system and is unaffected by this setting.

- `STACKS=9,256`: `IO.SYS` sets up a specific number of stack frames using this entry. Each stack frame is the same size.

- `SHELL=COMMAND.COM /P`: If you don't specify another command processor in `CONFIG.SYS`, `IO.SYS` defaults to using `COMMAND.COM`, just as it always has. The `/P` parameter makes the command processor permanent.

- `FCBS=4`: Ancient programs used file control blocks. These programs are so old that I really can't believe anyone still has them lying around. You can provide additional FCBs by overriding this setting in `CONFIG.SYS`.

As you can see, `IO.SYS` comes with a fairly complete `CONFIG.SYS` built in. Once `IO.SYS` loads the command processor, its job is finished for the time being. The command processor takes over and reads the contents of `AUTOEXEC.BAT`. At this point, you're running MS-DOS. You might not see a DOS prompt, but that's because Microsoft hides it behind a logo.

Loading the 16-Bit Core

After the command processor completes its work, a new phase in the boot process begins. You might wonder why Windows 95, a 32-bit operating system, would even think about starting in 16-bit mode. There are several interesting reasons.

One reason has to do with the way the Plug and Play BIOS specification is written. The current specification requires a vendor to provide a 16-bit protected-mode interface. This allows an operating system vendor such as Microsoft to check the Plug and Play hardware without switching to real mode. The result is a more stable operating system that (supposedly) always runs in protected mode.

The first thing Windows has to do once you start it is to check the status of all the hardware. It calls on the Plug and Play BIOS to provide it with a list of all the installed equipment. Windows uses this information to configure the system. Of course, it also has to take any non–Plug and Play peripherals into account as well. Once it comes up with a configuration list, Windows 95 starts to load all the 16-bit VxDs required to support that hardware.

What precisely is a VxD? It's a virtual device driver, the protected-mode version of the device drivers you used under MS-DOS. However, it's more than that because a device can be a lot more than just a piece of hardware under Windows 95. To avoid getting into the bits and bytes of device management, I'll just say that Windows uses virtual device drivers to manage all its low-level functions.

Once it completes this step, Windows initializes all those drivers. It starts with the system drivers—all the drivers required to make the low-level functions in Windows work (such as the file system drivers). The device drivers come next.

At this point, Windows 95 loads the three 16-bit shell components: `USER.EXE`, `GDI.EXE`, and `KRNL386.EXE`. It also loads some additional drivers and a few other components, such as fonts. Now Windows 95 is completely up and running in 16-bit mode. It doesn't have an interface yet, but every other component is present.

Loading the 32-Bit Core

The preceding section ended with a copy of Windows running in 16-bit mode without any form of user interface. The user shell, Explorer, is a 32-bit application. As soon as the 16-bit kernel sees the call for the shell, it loads an application called WWIN32.386. This little program loads the three 32-bit DLLs that form the Win32 API: USER32.DLL, GDI32.DLL, and KERNEL32.DLL. Once it completes this task, WWIN32.386 returns control to the 16-bit kernel, which in turn calls the 32-bit kernel.

Windows 95 then loads and initializes all the 32-bit drivers. This is the same process that the 16-bit part of the operating system performed, so I don't discuss it again here.

Somewhere in all of this, Windows 95 asks the user to provide some input in the form of a name and password (if you've enabled this feature). It checks this against the contents of the appropriate PWL file. If the password checks out, Windows 95 completes the boot process.

Finally, Windows gets the Explorer interface up and running. (It was loaded before but wasn't running.) It displays all the required objects on the desktop and initializes the Taskbar. This is the point where it also looks at your Startup folder to see which applications you want to start automatically. You're set up and ready to compute.

Cooperative Versus Preemptive Multitasking

A task is essentially an application that's running. When you start Windows, you might think that nothing is running, but there are already several applications getting work done on your machine. For example, Explorer (or Program Manager) is considered a task. Any network connections or print spoolers are considered tasks. A screen saver is yet another task. There are numerous system-related tasks as well. The Windows kernel is considered a task. The industry uses two terms to refer to a running application or thread: process and task. I prefer task because it's a little less nebulous than process. However, you'll probably see a mixture of both in the documentation you read.

When talking about Windows 3.x, you can associate every task with a single application. The definition of task doesn't really stop here for Windows 95 and Windows NT. Some 32-bit applications use a technique called multithreading, which enables them to perform more than one task at a time. For example, you can recalculate your spreadsheet and print at the same time if the application supports multithreading. What happens is that the spreadsheet starts a task (called a thread) to take care of printing. It might even start a second thread to do the recalculation so that you can continue to enter data. One way to look at threads is as a subtask under the application that's running.

Now that you understand what a task is, it's time to look at the definition of multitasking. Everyone assumes that multitasking is just that—several tasks (or processes) running simultaneously on one machine. This is a good start for a definition, but it doesn't end there. An important consideration is how the operating system allocates time between tasks. When talking about Windows, it becomes important to define the method used to manage tasks and to differentiate between different kinds of multitasking. Windows 95 supports two kinds of multitasking: cooperative and preemptive.

Windows 3.0 introduced a feature called cooperative multitasking. This is how it was supposed to work: Application A would run for a little while, just long enough to get one component of a task finished. It would then turn control of the system back over to Windows so that Windows could take care of any housekeeping chores and allow application B to run for a while. This cycle continued in a round-robin fashion between all the tasks running at any given time.

What really happened is that some applications followed the rules but others didn't. Under cooperative multitasking, the operating system gave up too much control; an application could hog all the system resources if it wanted to do so. Some applications do just that. The result is that cooperative multitasking doesn't really work all that well. Most of the time that the user spends looking at the hourglass is really time in which Windows has temporarily lost control of the system to an application that doesn't want to share with anyone else.

All the legacy applications that run under Windows 95—the 16-bit applications that you moved from Windows 3.x—still have to run in a cooperative multitasking mode. However, Windows 95 minimizes the impact of these applications by running them in one shared address space. All the 16-bit applications have to cooperate with each other, but they (theoretically) don't affect any 32-bit applications running on your machine. This includes Explorer and any other Windows 95–specific tools. (Of course, you'll upgrade most of your commonly used 16-bit applications, such as your word processor and spreadsheet, to Windows 95 versions. Right?)

In designing Windows 95, Microsoft wanted something better than cooperative multitasking and designed an operating system that uses preemptive multitasking. Windows 95 supports preemptive multitasking for any 32-bit application you run. Think of it this way: Preemptive multitasking works as a traffic light does. Traffic goes one way for a while, but then the light changes and traffic goes the other way. The amount of time each task gets is weighed by the user and the operating system to meet some criteria, but this access is supposed to be fair. Every application is supposed to get its fair share of processor time, and preemptive multitasking enforces this principle. Windows 95 monitors each application and interrupts it when its time is up. It doesn't matter whether the application wants to give up control over the system. Windows 95 doesn't give it a choice.

There's another, more important difference in the way the system reacts under preemptive multitasking. Under Windows 3.x, an hourglass means that the system is tied up. You can't do anything else until the hourglass goes away. On the other hand, an hourglass under Windows 95 means only that the current task is tied up. You can always start another task or switch to an existing task. If that task isn't busy, you can perform some work with it while you wait for the initial task to complete its work. You know when the original application has finished because the hourglass goes away when you place your cursor over the task's window. The bottom line? Preemptive multitasking means that the user doesn't have to wait for the system.

Finally, cooperative multitasking has a serious flaw. Because Windows lost control when some applications took over, there was no way to clear that application if the machine froze. Because Windows 95 maintains constant control of the machine, you (theoretically) no longer need to worry about the machine freezing in the middle of a task. (In reality, Windows 95 can still freeze up completely.) As with Windows 3.x, pressing Ctrl+Alt+Delete doesn't automatically reboot the machine. However, unlike Windows 3.x, Windows 95 displays a list of applications, and you get to choose which one to terminate. (See Figure 9.9.)

Figure 9.9.
Preemptive multitasking means that Windows 95 never loses control of the machine. It also means that you can recover from an application error with ease.

You might wonder why Microsoft (or any other vendor) would use cooperative multitasking if preemptive multitasking is so much better. There are a few good reasons. First, MS-DOS is nonreentrant. This means that you have to allow MS-DOS to complete one task before you give it another one. If you disturb MS-DOS in the middle of a task, the entire system could (and will) freeze. Because Windows 3.x runs on top of MS-DOS, it can't use preemptive multitasking for any services that interact with MS-DOS. Unfortunately, one of those services is the disk subsystem.

The second problem with preemptive multitasking is really a two-part scenario. Both relate to ease of designing the operating system. When an operating system provides preemptive multitasking, it also has to include some kind of method for monitoring devices. What if two applications decided that they need to use the COM port at the same time? With cooperative multitasking, the application that started to use the COM port would gain control of it and lock out the other application. In a preemptive multitasking situation, the first application could get halfway through the allocation process and get stopped, and then the second application could start the allocation process. What happens if the first application is reactivated by the system? You have two applications that think they have access to one device. In reality, both applications have access, and you have a mess. Windows 95 handles this problem by using a programming construct called a critical section. (I discuss this feature more in a moment.)

Preemptive multitasking also needs some type of priority system to ensure that critical tasks get a larger share of the processor's time than noncritical tasks. Remember, a task can no longer dictate how long it needs system resources; that's all in the hands of the operating system. Theoretically, you should be able to rely on the users to tell the operating system how they want their applications prioritized and then allow the operating system to take care of the rest. What really happens is that a low-priority task can run into a fault situation and need system resources immediately to resolve it.

A static priority system can't handle that situation. In addition, that low-priority task can end up getting little or no system resources when a group of high-priority tasks starts to run. The priority system Windows 95 uses provides a dynamic means of changing a task's priority. When a high-priority task runs, Windows 95 lowers its priority. When a low-priority task gets passed over in favor of a high-priority task, Windows 95 increases its priority. As you can see, the dynamic priority system enforces the idea that some tasks should get more system resources than others yet ensures that every task gets at least some system resources.

There's a final consideration when looking at preemptive multitasking. Even if you use the best dynamic priority system in the world and every piece of the operating system works just the way it should, you'll run into situations where a task has to complete a sequence of events without being disturbed. For example, the application might need to make certain that a database transaction is written to disk before it hands control of the system back to the operating system. If another task tried to do something related to that transaction before the first task completed, you could end up with invalid or damaged data in the database. Programmers call a piece of code that performs this task a critical section. Normally, a critical section occurs with system-related tasks such as memory allocation, but it also can happen with application-related tasks such as writing information to a file. Cooperative multitasking systems don't have to worry as much about critical sections because the task decides when the operating system regains control of the system. On the other hand, a preemptive multitasking system needs some way for a task to communicate the need to complete a critical section of code. Under Windows 95, a task tells the operating system that it needs to perform a critical section of code using a semaphore (a flag). If a hardware interrupt or some other application were to ask to perform a task that didn't interfere with any part of the critical section, Windows 95 could allow it to proceed. All that a critical section guarantees is that the task and its environment will remain undisturbed until the task completes its work.

Windows 95 Internals

The section titled "Architecture" earlier in this chapter provides an overview of Windows 95's internal architecture. This section of the chapter assumes that you've read that overview and are ready to move on to bigger and better things. The following paragraphs start where that discussion leaves off and show you some of the deeper and darker secrets of Windows 95.

Before I begin a discussion of individual Windows architectural components, I'd like to direct your attention to the "rings" of protection provided by the 80386 (and above) processor. There are four security rings within the Intel protection scheme, but most operating systems use only two of them (or sometimes three). The inner security ring is Ring 0. This is where the operating system proper is. The outermost ring is 3. That's where the applications reside. Sometimes an operating system gives device drivers better access to some operating system features than an application gets by running them at Ring 1 or 2. Windows doesn't make any concessions; device drivers run at Ring 0 or 3, depending on their purpose.

Windows uses these protection rings to make certain that only operating system components can access the inner workings of Windows—that an application can't change settings that might cause the entire system to crash. For example, Windows reserves the right to allocate memory from the global pool; therefore, the capabilities needed to perform this task rest at Ring 0. On the other hand, applications need to access memory assigned to them. That's why Windows assigns local memory a protection value of 3.

Think of each ring as a security perimeter. Before you can enter that perimeter, you have to know the secret password. Windows gives the password only to applications that it knows it can trust; everyone else has to stay out. Whenever an application tries to circumvent security, the processor raises an exception. Think of an exception as a security alarm. The exception sends the Windows police (better known as an exception handler) after the offending application. After its arrest and trial, Windows calmly terminates the offending application. Of course, it notifies the user before performing this task, but the user usually doesn't have much of a choice in the matter.

Figure 9.1 gives you a pretty good idea of exactly whom Windows trusts. Applications and device drivers running at Ring 3 have few capabilities outside their own resources. In fact, Windows even curtails these capabilities somewhat. Some of the activities that a MS-DOS application could get by with, such as directly manipulating video memory, aren't allowed here. The reason is simple: Video memory is a shared resource. Whenever another application needs to share something, you can be certain that your application isn't able to access it directly.

Now, on to the various components that actually make up Windows. The following sections break the Windows components into main areas. Each of these general groups contains descriptions of the individual components and what tasks they perform. Remember that this is only a general discussion. Windows is more complex than it might first appear. The deeper you get as a programmer, the more you'll see the actual complexity of this operating system.

System Virtual Machine

The System Virtual Machine (VM) component of Windows 95 contains three main elements: 32-bit Windows applications, the shell, and 16-bit Windows applications. Essentially, the System VM component provides most of the Windows 95 user-specific functionality. Without it, you couldn't run any applications. Notice that I don't include MS-DOS applications here. This is because Windows uses an entirely different set of capabilities to run MS-DOS applications. It even runs them in a different processor mode.

Theoretically, the System VM also provides support for the various Windows API layer components. However, because these components provide a different sort of service, I chose to discuss them in a separate area. Even though applications use the API and users interact with applications, you really don't think about the API until the time comes to write an application. Therefore, I always think of the API as a programmer-specific service rather than something that the user really needs to worry about. The following list describes the System VM components in detail:

- 32-bit Windows applications: These are the new Win32-specific applications that use a subset of the Windows NT API. In fact, many Windows NT applications, such as Word for Windows NT, run just fine under Windows 95. A 32-bit application usually provides better multitasking capabilities than its 16-bit counterpart. In addition, many 32-bit applications support new Windows features such as long filenames, whereas most 16-bit applications don't. 32-bit applications provide two additional features. The more important one is the use of preemptive versus cooperative multitasking. This makes your work flow more smoothly and forces the system to wait for you as necessary, rather than the other way around. The second one is the use of a flat memory address space. This feature really makes a difference in how much memory an application gets and how well it uses it. In addition, an application that uses a flat address space should run slightly faster because it no longer has to spend time working with Intel's memory segmentation scheme. Programs that have the "Designed for Windows NT and 95" logos fit into this category.

- The shell: Three shells are supplied with Windows 95, and you can choose any of them. The standard shell, Explorer, provides full 32-bit capabilities. Explorer combines all the features you used to find in Program Manager, Print Manager, and File Manager. You can also use the older Program Manager interface with Windows 95. It doesn't provide all the bells and whistles that Explorer does, but it'll certainly ease the transition for some users who learned the Program Manager interface. The third interface is the result of using Internet Explorer 4.0. It allows you to maintain your local and remote resources in one place. Obviously you have to purchase or download this shell before you can use it; Microsoft doesn't provide Internet Explorer 4.0 as part of the Windows 95 package. (This interface will become standard with Windows 98.) Switching between shells is easy. All you need to do is change the `Shell=` entry in the Boot section of `SYSTEM.INI`.

- 16-bit Windows applications: All your older applications are 16-bit applications, unless you bought them for use with Windows 95 or Windows NT. Windows 95 runs all these applications in one shared address space. Essentially, Windows 95 groups all these 16-bit applications into one area and treats them as if they were one task. You really don't notice any performance hit as a result, but it does make it easier for Windows 95 to recover from application errors. With it, Windows 95 can mix 16-bit and 32-bit applications on one system.

The Windows API Layer

Two Windows APIs are included with Windows 95. The first is exactly like the one supplied with Windows 3.x. It provides all the 16-bit services that the old Windows had to provide for applications. This is the API that an older application will use when it runs.

The other API is the new Win32 API used by Windows NT. It provides a subset of the features that all 32-bit applications running under Windows NT can access. The 32-bit API provides about the same feature set as the 16-bit API, but it's more robust. In addition, a 32-bit application enjoys the benefits that this environment provides. Check out the section "The System Files" earlier in this chapter for more details about the system files and the Windows 95 API.

Getting 16-Bit and 32-Bit Applications to Work Together

Windows 95 consists of a combination of 16-bit and 32-bit applications. All those older applications and device drivers you use now have to work within the same environment as the new 32-bit drivers and applications that Windows 95 provides. You already know how Windows takes care of separating the two by using different memory schemes. The 16-bit applications work within their own virtual machine area. It would be nice if things ended there, but they can't.

There are times when 16-bit and 32-bit applications have to talk to each other. This doesn't just apply to programs that the user uses to perform work, but it applies to device drivers and other types of Windows applications as well. Most Windows applications use a memory structure called the stack to transfer information from one application to another. Think of the stack as a database of variables. Each record in this database is a fixed length so that every application knows how to grab information from it. Here's where the problems start. The stack for 32-bit applications is 32 bits wide. That makes sense. It makes equal sense that the stack for 16-bit applications should be 16 bits wide. See the problem?

Of course, the problems are only beginning. Remember that 16-bit applications use a segmented address space. An address consists of a selector and an offset. A 16-bit application combines these two pieces to form a complete address. On the other hand, 32-bit applications use a flat address space. They wouldn't know what to do with a selector if you gave them one. All they want is the actual address within the total realm of available memory. How do you send the address of a string from a 16-bit to a 32-bit application?

By now you're probably wondering how Windows keeps 16-bit and 32-bit applications working together. After all, there are a number of inconsistencies and incompatibilities to deal with. The stack is only the tip of the incompatibility iceberg. It's easy to envision a method of converting 16-bit data to a 32-bit format. All you really need to do is pad the front end of the variable with zeros. But how does a 32-bit application send data to a 16-bit application? If the 32-bit application just dumps a wide variable onto the stack, the 16-bit application will never know what to do with the information it receives. Clearly, the data needs to go through some type of conversion. Windows uses something called the thunk layer to allow 16-bit and 32-bit applications to communicate. Figure 9.10 shows the interaction of 16-bit and 32-bit applications through the thunk layer.

Figure 9.10.
The thunk layer makes it possible for 16-bit and 32-bit applications to coexist peacefully under Windows.

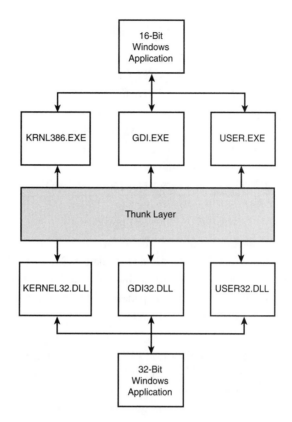

As you can see, the three components of the API layer provide translation services in addition to the other services they perform. Each API component translates the data and addresses within its area of expertise. For example, the two GDI components translate all graphics data between 16-bit and 32-bit applications.

Most thunking is pretty straightforward. For example, Windows simply moves register data to the appropriate register. The thunk layer builds a new stack to meet the needs of the application receiving it. Address translation takes a little more work. In addition, address translation is expensive, time-wise. Every time Windows has to translate an address, it must perform several selector loads. The processor has to verify every selector load, so these translations can get cumbersome. Fortunately, you, as an application programmer, don't have to worry too much about the actual thunk process. What you do need to worry about is making certain that the process actually takes place when calling a piece of code that needs it.

Windows and DLLs

Under MS-DOS, an application must contain every component it needs to execute. The programmer links library support for graphics, low-level utilities, and a variety of other needs. Of course, this whole scenario is based on the fact that the application is the only thing running under MS-DOS.

Windows is a different kind of environment. There's always more than one task running under Windows. Somewhere along the way, someone figured out that if you have multiple applications running, there might be some duplicate code out there as well. For example, the display routines used by one application are probably the same as the display routines used by another application at some particular level. The same person probably figured out that you could reduce the overall memory requirements of a system if you allowed all the applications to share these redundant pieces of code instead of loading them from scratch for each application.

The DLL (dynamic link library) is the culmination of just such an idea. There are two forms of linking under Windows (or OS/2 or UNIX, for that matter). The first link combines all the object modules required to create a unique application. That link cycle happens right after the programmer finishes compiling the code. The second link cycle happens when the user goes to load the application. This is where the DLL comes in.

Every Windows application has unresolved references to functions. Microsoft calls them import library calls. What these calls do is load a DLL containing the code required to satisfy that function call. If the DLL happens to be in memory when Windows calls it, Windows increments the DLL's usage level to indicate that more than one application is using the DLL. When an application stops using a DLL, Windows decrements its usage level. When the DLL's usage count goes to 0, Windows can unload it from memory. In effect, using DLLs can save quite a bit of memory when you're loading multiple applications.

What does this have to do with the API? The Windows API starts with three files, as just described. However, these three files call other files—DLLs, to be exact. Rather than create three huge files, Microsoft chose to reduce the size of the Windows kernel by using DLLs.

This capability also makes Windows more flexible. Consider printer support. All you need to do to add printer support for a new printer is copy some files to disk. At least one of those files is a DLL. Every printer DLL contains the same entry points (function names), so Windows doesn't need to learn anything new to support the printer. The only thing it has to do is install a new DLL. Your application performs the same task when you tell it to print. It looks at the DLLs currently installed for the system. The application doesn't have to care whether the printer is a dot matrix or a laser. All it needs to know how to do is tell the printer to print; the DLL takes care of the rest.

The Base System

Windows 95 uses the Base System component to take care of any system-specific services. The section "Architecture" earlier in this chapter covers this particular component in detail. Refer to that discussion if you want to know the details of the Base System.

The DOS Virtual Machine

The word *virtual* gets severely overused in the Windows environment. We have virtual memory, virtual system machines, and every other kind of virtual device you can think of. I want to make sure that you understand that the DOS virtual machine is a different kind of virtual than all these other virtuals on the system. A DOS virtual machine runs in the virtual 8086 mode of the processor. All the other virtual machines in Windows run in protected mode. Virtual 8086 mode creates multiple 1MB 8086 machines in protected memory. Each machine has its own copy of MS-DOS, device drivers, I/O space, and everything else that an 8086 would have. About the only thing missing is the hardware itself, and that's why this machine is known as a virtual machine. You can't touch it, but it does exist. As far as the application is concerned, there's no difference between this machine and any real machine it could run on.

Except for a few new features designed to enhance the performance of applications running under the Windows virtual machine, this aspect of Windows hasn't really changed much from Version 3.1. However, there's one exception to this rule. Some MS-DOS applications use DPMI-compatible extenders that allow them to run in protected mode. Under Windows 3.x, these applications would still run under the processor's virtual 8086 mode. Windows 95 improves system performance by allowing these applications to run in protected mode.

On Your Own

Spend some time looking through the SYSTEM directory on your machine. Can you identify the various operating system files discussed in this chapter? Go through the architecture overview again to make sure that you fully understand it before going on to the subsystem-specific sections in the rest of the book.

Check out any Windows 95 games you have. Which ones use DirectX and which use OpenGL? Can you see a performance difference between the two? Which games seem to be more stable? Knowing how various multimedia technologies affect you can make a big difference in how you'll actually use them in the future.

Download the appropriate hardware compatibility list file from `ftp://ftp.microsoft.com/services/whql/`. Find out which of your hardware is tested for Plug and Play compatibility and which isn't. Remember, even if the outside of the box says Plug and Play (PnP) compatible, it doesn't necessarily mean you'll get full PnP functionality.

10

The
Windows 95
File System

Peter Norton®

One of the newest features of OSR2 is FAT32 support, which reduces the cluster size of large hard disks—improving storage efficiency and also providing a small increase in speed.

Of course, every time you change the file system, you must change the utilities to manage that file system. Windows 95 comes with wealth of revised utilities that you can use to manage your hard drive. I'm sure that most disk utility vendors will be on hand with new FAT32-compatible disk utilities as well.

Warning: Watch for two potential problems with your FAT32-formatted Windows 95 disk drive. Using an old MS-DOS disk management utility with Windows 95 might mean a loss of your long filenames because these old utilities don't know to move everything needed to support them. A loss of long-filename support might seem like only an inconvenience until you realize that loss of the long filenames will also mean a loss of the Start menu and other Windows 95-specific long filenames. Windows 95 might not even restart in certain cases if you lose the long filenames it requires.

You also need to be careful of using Windows 95 disk utilities that don't know how to work with FAT32-formatted drives. You could potentially damage the partition in information using one of these old utilities and lose your data in the process. Make certain that any disk utility you use on a FAT32 drive is designed for that purpose.

This chapter takes you on a tour of the Windows 95 file system from a user perspective. I even take a brief look at the architecture and put on the programmer's hat for a while. The Windows 95 VFAT (virtual file allocation table) file system might look and act like an enhanced version of the old system, but I think you'll be surprised by all the new features under the hood.

Note: From this point on, unless I specifically mention the FAT32 file system, assume all conversation about the FAT file system refers to the older FAT16 file system. The new file system presents many issues that I discuss in the section "What Is 32-Bit VFAT?" later in this chapter. Any discussion of VFAT-specific issues refers to the FAT32 and FAT16 file systems equally.

File Structures

Windows 3.*x*, Windows 95, Windows NT, and OS/2 support the FAT file system, although all but Windows 3.*x* also support their own file systems. Of the three, only the VFAT file system used by Windows 95 is based on the old FAT standard. The following paragraphs take a look at a few of the remaining problems with VFAT.

With so many competing file systems, if you stick with the FAT file system, you'll maintain compat-ibility with almost any operating system.

If you stick with the FAT file system, you'll have compatibility, but you'll also miss out on the spe-cial features each of the other file systems has to offer. Both NTFS (Windows NT file system) and HPFS (high-performance file system) offer improved reliability over the old FAT file system.

Peter's Principle: A Method of Dealing with Multiple File Systems

After a lot of thought, I finally came up with a middle-ground solution to the problem of dealing with multiple file systems on one computer. It offers the maximum in compatibility yet lets me make the most out of what the other file systems have to offer.

The first thing I did was partition my drives. I set aside one partition for each of the operating systems installed on my machine. I had to do that anyway to have everything boot correctly. Each operating system's specific partition uses the special file format it provides. This way, the operating system and its utility programs can benefit from the improved performance and reliability that the new file system has to offer. I also stick any operating-system–specific applications in these partitions.

Once I figured out where each operating system would go, I installed them. Each installa-tion required a bit of time and patience, but I got through it. It's important to test the ability to boot each operating system after you install a new one. Both Windows NT and Windows 95 like to overwrite the bootable partition marker. This means that whatever boot manager you have installed won't boot until you use a disk editor to set the active partition back to its original position.

After I installed the operating systems and tested the boot sequence, I had one large partition left. I labeled the partition on this drive COMMON and placed all my data and common applications there. It uses the FAT file system so everyone can access it. In some cases, I had to install each application once for each operating system.

FAT Versus VFAT

The main reason Windows 95 changed its file system to VFAT is that people weren't satisfied with the old 8.3 filenames. They wanted long filenames, and the FAT file system can't provide this fea-ture. The VFAT file system represents an effort on the part of Microsoft to give people what they want and still maintain a level of compatibility with previous versions of MS-DOS (and more im-portantly, the applications that ran over it).

The Windows 95 Alternative

Windows 95 incorporates all operating system functions into a 32-bit architecture named the VFAT interface. Its full name is the Protected-Mode FAT File System. Using protected-mode drivers means that there's less chance that a random application will cause a system failure because Windows 95 always runs in protected mode. (The only exception to this rule is if you install real-mode drivers in CONFIG.SYS to support an antiquated device such as a CD-ROM drive. Windows 95 does switch to Virtual 86 mode when accessing a device that uses a real-mode driver.) Using protected mode means that the operating system constantly monitors every event taking place on the machine, reducing the chance of system crashes (due to disk-related problems) to nearly zero and greatly enhancing disk access speed.

There are 32 possible layers in the Windows 95 file system, starting at the I/O subsystem. (The current configuration doesn't use all 32 layers.) Layer 0 is closest to the I/O subsystem, whereas Layer 31 is closest to the hardware. The current version of Windows 95 requires only a few of these layers (normally 12) to do the job. The other layers are placeholders for future use. Each layer provides hooks for third-party software used to support custom file systems and devices. For example, adding a network driver to the file system layer enables you to access drives on other machines. Unlike previous versions of Windows, a vendor can retrofit the Windows 95 file system to provide additional capabilities with relative ease. Each of these components performs a different task:

- Installable File System (IFS) Manager: This is the highest layer in the file system. The IFS is a VxD that provides the interface to applications. It doesn't matter whether the application uses the Interrupt 21h interface or either the 16-or 32-bit Windows interface; this is the component that receives application requests. It's the responsibility of the IFS to transfer control to the appropriate file system driver (FSD).

- File System Driver (FSD) layer: The most common file system driver layer component is the VFAT FSD. This is the VxD that takes care of all local hard drive requests. It provides the long filename support and protected-mode stability that makes Windows 95 better than its predecessors. Your machine might have several other FSDs, depending on the type of equipment you've installed. For example, Windows 95 installs a network file system handler if you install any form of a LAN. All the FSDs talk with the IFS manager and send requests to the layers that directly communicate with the hardware.

- I/O Subsystem (IOS) layer: This is the highest level of the block device layer. A block device is any device that sends information in blocks. A hard drive usually uses some multiple of 512 bytes as its block size but other devices might use a different block size. Network devices, tape drives, and CD-ROM drives all fall into the block device category. The IOS provides general device services to the FSDs. For example, it routes requests from the FSDs to various device-specific drivers and sends status information from the device-specific drivers to the FSDs.

- Volume Tracking Driver (VTD) layer: Windows 95 may or may not install this driver. It handles any removable devices attached to your system. For example, if you have a floppy or CD-ROM drive, Windows 95 installs this component. On the other hand, if you use a diskless workstation or rely on local and network hard drives alone, Windows 95 doesn't need to install this component. The VTD monitors the status of all removable media drives and reports any change in media. This is the component that will complain if you remove a floppy prematurely (usually in the middle of a write), or that plays an audio CD that you insert into your CD-ROM drive.

- Type-Specific Driver (TSD) layer: Every type of device needs a driver that understands its peculiar needs. For example, the hard disk drive driver wouldn't understand the needs of a floppy drive very well. This layer deals with logical device types rather than specific devices. For example, one TSD handles all the hard drives on your system, another TSD handles all the floppy drives, and a third TSD handles all network drives.

- Vendor-Supplied Driver (VSD) layer: This is where a vendor would install support for a proprietary bus CD-ROM or a removable media device, such as a floptical drive. Every specific device type needs a driver that can translate its requests for Windows. This is the layer that performs those services. The VSD knows such things as the number of heads a disk has or the amount of time it needs to wait for a floppy to get up to speed.

- Port Driver (PD) layer: The PD performs the actual task of communicating with the device through an adapter. It's the last stage before a message leaves Windows and the first stage when a message arrives from the device. The PD is usually adapter specific. For example, you have one VSD for each hard drive and one PD for each hard drive adapter. If your system uses an IDE hard drive, Windows loads the IDE PD to talk to the IDE adapter.

- SCSIzer: Don't let the strange-looking name for this layer fool you. It deals with SCSI command language. Think of the command language as the method the computer uses to tell a SCSI device to perform a task. It isn't the data the SCSI device handles; rather, it's the act the SCSI device will perform. Windows 95 has one SCSIzer for each SCSI device.

- SCSI Manager: Windows NT introduced something called the miniport driver. With Windows 95, you can use the Windows NT miniport binaries. However, before you can actually do this, Windows 95 must translate its commands to a format that the miniport driver understands. The SCSI Manager performs this service.

- Miniport Driver: This is a device driver that provides support for a specific SCSI device. No other device uses the miniport driver. The miniport driver works with the SCSI manager to perform the same task as a PD. Both Windows NT and Windows 95 use the same miniport drivers.

- Protected-Mode Mapper: This layer performs a special task. It enables you to use your MS-DOS drivers under Windows 95. Without the support of this VxD, Windows 95 couldn't support devices that lack Windows 95–specific drivers. Essentially, the protected-mode mapper disguises a real-mode driver to look like a Windows 95 protected-mode driver.

- Real-Mode Driver: It's almost certain that some vendors don't supply drivers for every device they ever made, and in reality, they have no reason to do so. The older device that still does the job for you is probably so far out of date that you're the only one still using it. Still, as with a comfortable pair of shoes, you hate to give up that old device. One of the goals of the Windows 95 development team was to allow you to keep that old device hanging around until you're ready to give it up. It's going to cost some system speed to keep it, but that real-mode driver will work just fine under Windows 95.

Windows 95 Updates to the I/O Subsystem (IOS)

The previous section discussed the purpose of the IOS as part of the Windows 95 file system. OSR2 provides some updates to the Windows 95 version of this part of the operating system, and these updates are in addition to the FAT32 support that I talk about later. The following list provides a brief description of each feature:

- Drive Spin-Down Support Enabled: This new feature will power down your hard disk drives after a period of inactivity.

- 120MB Floptical Support: As with everything else, the amount of data you can store on a floptical (a hybrid floppy/hard disk) is on the rise. Windows 95 enables you to use 120MB flopticals natively.

- IDE (Integrated Development Environment) Busmaster Support: A busmaster setup can greatly improve system performance by reducing or completely eliminating the need for processor calls when servicing a hard disk drive. Obviously, this calls for some level of support by the operating system. It needs to issue calls that make use of this special disk controller feature instead of using the old calls that use the processor instead.

- SMART Predictive Disk Failure API: RAID (redundant array of inexpensive disks) and other disk technologies take a reactive approach to disk failure. In other words, they help you recover after a problem has already occurred. Sometime in the future, drives will accurately predict when they're going to fail and send that information to the operating system. By having this information, you could back up your drive and replace it before it actually fails.

- Removable IDE Media Support: Removable media is an important element in data management strategies today. For example, a floptical or SyQuest drive can provide high-speed, intermediate storage for files that you don't use every day, but often enough, that tape storage proves inconvenient. Your vendor previously had to provide special support software to manage removable IDE media under Windows 95. Windows 95 corrects that oversight by providing removable IDE media support within the IOS.

VCache

The VCache VxD found in Windows 95 is a 32-bit protected-mode replacement for SmartDRV. It supports local hard drives, network drives, and CD-ROM drives. VCache creates a separate cache for each type of drive. It also balances the total cache size with the memory requirements of your system. The result is a dynamically sized cache that's optimized to meet the needs of the particular kind of access you're performing most often. If you're loading a lot of data from the network, VCache increases the size of your network cache. Loading a new application from the CD-ROM drive allocates more space for the CD-ROM cache. Likewise, local drive access will change the size of that cache.

VCache works with the CDFS (compact disk file system) to support CD-ROM drives and CDI (CD-ROM Interactive). CDFS cooperates with VCache to create a part of the drive cache picture. Likewise, the network redirector (depending on which network you install) works with VCache. Windows 95 automatically changes the configuration of both drivers as the configuration of your system changes. For example, it doesn't add network redirector support on systems that don't have access to a network. The same holds true for CD-ROM drive support on non-CD–equipped systems.

Peter's Principle: Real-Mode and 16-Bit Windows Drivers: Just Say No

Everything that VCache provides works as I described if you use 32-bit drivers for all your drives. However, if you use an older CD-ROM that needs a real-mode or 16-bit driver, you lose part of the dynamic caching that VCache provides. MSCDEX uses a static cache that VCache won't override and it needs the cooperation of CDFS to provide support for CD-ROM drives.

Likewise, if your network uses real-mode drivers, VCache can't provide network drive cache support. The network runs just as sluggishly as it did before. You don't see any of the anticipated speed boost because Windows 95 can't override those real-mode drivers. It has to have a 32-bit substitute before it can remove the old drivers.

The entire Windows 95 drive system relies on the new 32-bit drivers to provide a complete package. If you replace an element with a real-mode or 16-bit Windows driver, you remove a piece of the picture. Getting the most out of VCache means that your network and CD-ROM has to use the 32-bit drivers.

What's the bottom line? If you want maximum reliability and performance, don't use old drivers. A piece of equipment that requires a real-mode or 16-bit Windows driver is a disaster waiting to happen. Replace your old equipment whenever possible.

VCache also supports a feature you might not want to use. Lazy writes enables Windows 95 to write data to the cache and then write the data from the cache to your hard drive during idle time. Lazy writes is an industry term for a cache—especially a hard drive cache—that delays writing data from the cache to the drive until a time of low disk activity. Because writing to the cache is faster, you get a speed boost by using this feature. I keep it enabled on my system because I haven't experienced too many lockups or GPFs since I installed Windows 95. However, if you fall into the select group that does experience problems, turning off lazy writes may save your database.

Here's the way to disable lazy writes. Right-click the My Computer icon and select Properties. Click the Performance page and then the File System button. Select the Troubleshooting page. You should see a display similar to the one shown in Figure 10.1. This dialog box enables you to disable lazy writes for all drives by checking the Disable write-behind caching for all drives option. All you need to do now is click OK twice to save your changes. Windows then tells you to reboot your machine (in most cases) to allow the change to take effect.

Figure 10.1.
The Troubleshooting page of the File System Properties dialog box enables you to disable lazy writes for all drives.

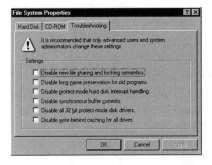

The positive side of this change is that all writes go directly to the drive instead of the cache. This might actually help you resolve some database problems where the program displays old or incorrect data on another user's display after the first user changes it. The negative aspect is that you lose a lot of performance by going this route. In other words, lazy writes offer a big plus in the way of a speed boost for your system, especially for network drive access.

The main reason to disable lazy writes is to avoid losing data due to a system crash. If Windows 95 writes some data to the cache, the machine freezes before Windows has a chance to write that data to disk and you experience a data loss. It's unlikely that you'll recover the data if Windows can't move it to disk. Fortunately, this is a rare event under Windows 95, barring any major problems with drivers, MS-DOS applications, or older 16-bit Windows applications. Many applications provide an autosave feature that you might want to set to a shorter interval on systems that experience many problems with machine freezes.

> **Tip:** Occasionally, Windows 95 may freeze to the point where pressing Ctrl+Alt+Delete won't allow you to regain control of the system. You can usually reduce data loss under Windows 95 if you allow the system to go idle before performing a reboot after a system freeze. Wait for all data to be written to disk before you reboot the system. When the disk access light goes out and stays out for at least 30 seconds, you can reboot the system with a minimum of data loss.

What Is 32-Bit VFAT?

FAT32, or more precisely 32-bit VFAT, is a new file system supported by Windows 95. At a very basic level, FAT32 is a file allocation table method of storing data that uses 32 bits instead of 16 bits.

Why use FAT32? Storage efficiency is the big plus. In fact, you can boil the whole thing down to one disk parameter—cluster size. A 1GB or larger drive that uses the FAT16 file storage system requires 32KB clusters. This means that even a 1 byte file requires 32KB of disk storage space. If you have a lot of small files on your drive, the waste of storage space begins to mount quickly. FAT32 allows a cluster size of 4KB. That's still a lot of wasted space for a 1 byte file, but a lot less than FAT16 would waste. The range of space savings can be anywhere between 20 percent and 50 percent disk storage without compressing the drive. On my computer that included Windows 95, Microsoft Office, CorelDRAW, and a couple of game programs, disk space requirements went from a whopping 870MB to 650MB for a savings of 220MB.

FAT32 is also more reliable than FAT16. Unlike FAT16, the root directory of a FAT32 volume can be located anywhere on the drive. Drive utility software is able to relocate root directory information as needed to repair drive problems. The relocatable root directory also means that FAT32 doesn't suffer from the old root directory limitations, such as the number of files you can store there. FAT32 uses the copy and the default copy of the FAT. This means that FAT problems that used to stop your machine cold don't even appear to the user. (Even though FAT16 maintains two copies of the FAT, it can only use the default copy.) The ability to use more than one FAT also allows dynamic partition resizing. Another feature is that FAT32 keeps a copy of critical drive structures in the boot record. Unlike FAT16, there aren't any single point of failure errors that can kill your hard drive.

> **Warning:** If you choose to use FAT32 on your machine, it's an all-or-nothing decision for the drive you use it on. FAT32 is incompatible with FAT16. This means that any old disk utilities (including disk compression) have to go out the door; you can't use them on a FAT32 drive.

Any software that writes directly to the disk is suspect when it comes to using FAT32. Most of us know not to use disk utilities that would allow you to edit the disk directly, but this problem could also affect other kinds of utility programs. For example, many utility programs check the format of your drive before they do anything to it, just to make sure you don't lose data. One user of a FAT32 drive reported that his CD-ROM writing software wouldn't work with FAT32 installed. That's because the CD-ROM writing software checked the drive configuration before doing anything— even on the drives that it wasn't writing to. FAT32 confused the utility program. The user finally ended up reinstalling Windows 95 without FAT32 support just to get the CD-ROM drive writing software to work.

Despite the growing pains that some people experience when using FAT32 support, there are some other file-system–related benefits to look at. I talked about one of them already—CDI support. Another benefit is a little difficult to see at first, but I think you'll find it very helpful along the way. Open a Drive Properties dialog box by right-clicking the drive and selecting Properties from the context menu. Notice that instead of simply telling you that the drive is local or remote, Windows 95 now tells you what file system it's using in the Type field. In most cases, the Type field is right on the money. For example, when you open a Windows NT drive, it tells you that it uses NTFS. Likewise, a FAT32 drive actually says FAT32. The only problem area is NetWare drives with long filename support enabled; they show up as HPFS drives because of the driver that Novell uses to enable long filename support.

> **Note:** A lot of applications don't report the correct size of your drive if it's over 2GB. The reason is pretty simple: Microsoft artificially limited drive size reported by the `GetDiskFreeSpace()` function to 2GB for compatibility reasons. If a programmer wants to find out the true size of large drives, he must use the `GetDiskFreeSpaceEx()` function. When in doubt, always check the space remaining on your drive using Explorer.

You can still boot a FAT32 machine into MS-DOS mode and use it to play games. However, you absolutely can't use a boot disk formatted using previous versions of MS-DOS or Windows 95. You must format any boot disks with FAT32 to access a FAT32 drive on your machine. (There isn't any actual difference in the formatting process; you just have to format the disk from a machine running FAT32.)

Beta Release

Windows 98 provides a new FAT32 conversion utility so you can upgrade your hard drive from FAT16 to FAT32. (Just remember that once you convert from FAT16 to FAT32, you can't reverse the process at a later date.)

Using LNK Files

LNK files act as pointers to an object, such as a file or a folder. That way, instead of storing multiple copies of a file or folder for different people to access, you just provide them with a LNK file. When users double-click the LNK file, the LNK file looks for the file or folder to open.

Your Start Menu folder contains a ton of LNK files. If you erase a Start menu entry, you only erase a LNK file, not the application itself.

Right-click the Start Menu icon on the Taskbar and select the Explore option. What you should see now is a dual-pane Explorer view of your Start menu entries. You can easily recognize the LNK files because they look like shortcuts (the icons with the arrow in the lower-left corner). Right-click any of the LNK files, click Properties, click the General tab, and you see a display similar to the one in Figure 10.2.

Figure 10.2.
A LNK file's Properties dialog box provides a General page similar to that provided by other file types.

As with the General page of any file Properties dialog box, you can set the file attributes: Hidden, Archive, and Read-only. This page also tells you the short and long filename and other statistics, such as when someone last modified the file. This is all interesting information, but you'll probably bypass this page, in most cases, to get to the Shortcut page by clicking the Shortcut tab. Figure 10.3 shows what this page looks like.

The four major fields on this page are listed in the following bullets, along with the function of each entry. The two you'll use most often are the Target and Run fields. I never use the Start in field, but you're likely to need it sometime.

Figure 10.3.
The Shortcut page contains all the LNK file setup information.

- Target: This is the name of the program you want to run. Notice that this dialog box doesn't provide any way to change the settings for that file. You must change the original file instead of the link. This makes sense when you think about it because each file could have multiple links pointing to it.

- Start in: Windows 95 always assumes that everything the file needs appears in its target directory. This is probably true for data files. However, you might find that some applications need to use a different "working directory" than the one they start in. It's the directory that Windows tells the application to look in for data files.

- Shortcut key: It enables you to assign a shortcut key combination to this particular LNK file. Using a shortcut key can dramatically speed access to your favorite applications or data files.

- Run: Windows provides three run modes for applications. You can run them in a window, minimized or maximized. I find the default setting of the window mode works for most of my applications. (In most cases, this is a normal window.) I start data files maximized for certain jobs. This is especially true of my word processing files because I like to see a full screen of them. How you set this field is solely determined by the way you work.

That's all there is to LNK files. You'll want to read about the various methods you can use to create shortcuts to your data files and applications. The desktop is where you can really benefit from using these productivity enhancers.

VxDs and DLLs

There are a lot of reasons why Windows uses VxDs (virtual anything drivers) and DLLs (dynamic link libraries), but you can sum it all up in two words: modular programming. Here's how modular programming works. A program calls a DLL or VxD to perform specific tasks. Essentially, both files contain executable code—similar to a mini application. When Windows sees the request, it loads the program (DLL or VxD) into memory. Of course, this sounds similar to what DOS does with external files called overlays. In theory, DLLs and VxDs do act somewhat as overlays from a code use point of view, but that's where the similarities end.

Like overlays, both file types contain entry points. Unlike overlays, any number of applications can simultaneously access the program file and use whatever parts are needed. For example, you might have noticed that the File | Open command in most applications produces the same dialog box. That dialog box is actually part of the COMMDLG.DLL file located in your SYSTEM directory. An application makes a call to the COMMDLG.DLL to display a File Open dialog box. Windows loads the DLL, looks for a specific function number, and then lets the DLL do its work. (You can always view the functions in a DLL using the Quick View utility; just right-click the DLL and choose Quick View from the context menu.)

Tip: Learning what the DLLs do for you can help when something doesn't work the way it should. For example, what do you do if the File Open dialog box suddenly stops working? It might seem to be an unlikely prospect, but data corruption can affect any file on your system. Knowing the File Open dialog box appears in the COMMDLG.DLL file can help you fix the system with just a few minutes of work. All you need to do is restore a good copy of this file from your backup. (I cover backups later in this chapter.)

What DLLs do for software, VxDs do for hardware. When part of your system needs to access a piece of hardware, it normally calls a VxD. Of course, drivers can also work with software components, but from a different perspective than DLLs. Drivers always provide some type of interface to a system component. For example, some types of memory allocation are performed with a VxD. This isn't a function most users worry about, but one that's important to the proper functioning of your system.

Tip: If you right-click a VxD file, you notice that it offers no Quick View option. To view the file, make a copy and give it a .DLL extension. You can now use Quick View to see the header of this file. This same technique also works with other executable file types. Unfortunately, about the only things the file header tells you are the amount of memory that the VxD requires to load and some programmer-specific information, such as the size of the stack that the VxD creates. In most cases, it isn't worth your while to look at the file heading unless you're low on memory and are looking for a peripheral to unload from your system. Unloading a peripheral device can free memory that you can use for applications. (Be sure to make a backup of any drivers that you unload using the procedures near the end of this chapter.)

Formatting Disks

Formatting floppy disks is one of those tasks that everyone must perform from time to time. To start the formatting process under Windows 95, do the following:

1. Right-click the drive you want to format within Explorer, as shown in Figure 10.4.

Figure 10.4.
Windows 95 always displays a Format option for any drive that supports formatting.

2. Select the Format option and you see the dialog box shown in Figure 10.5.

Figure 10.5.
The Windows 95 Format dialog box is an enhanced version of the File Manager dialog box used with Windows 3.x.

> **Tip:** Always use the Quick (erase) option to format floppies that you know are good. This option formats the floppy in a little over a tenth of the time that a full format takes.

3. Select the options you want and click OK.

Backup

Backing up your data is like buying insurance: No one ever sees a good reason to do it until disaster strikes, and then it's too late to do anything if you didn't prepare in advance.

Windows 95 comes with Microsoft Backup. Before backing up your data, Backup gives you the opportunity to create an Emergency Recovery Disk. This is the same disk that you created during installation, but you always want to be sure to have the latest setup for your computer, so it's usually a good idea to update your Emergency Recovery Disk before you start the backup. Go ahead and start Backup if it's installed so you can take a look at this utility with me.

Backup might take a few seconds to complete the hardware detection process. You can always tell whether the detection was successful by the status of the Tools menu. If you see that all the tools are available, Backup successfully detected your drive. Make sure you perform the detection with a tape installed. Backup can't detect some tapes correctly if the tape isn't in place. Of course, the first thing you see is the Microsoft Backup dialog, which allows you to create a new backup job, back up files using an existing job, or restore files. Now you're ready to perform any of the three actions outlined in the following sections: back up, restore, or compare.

Creating a Backup

The first activity you perform with Backup is creating your first backup tape. Figure 10.6 shows the initial Backup window. As you can see, there are boxes next to each drive and folder on the left side of the display and next to each folder and file on the right side of the page. (The interface works much like Explorer, in which the right pane shows a detailed view of whatever you select in the left pane.) You select the items you want to back up by clicking the boxes. An empty box means that Backup doesn't send that item to tape. A gray box with a check mark appears next to a folder or drive that you intend to partially back up. A check mark appears next to a file, folder, or drive that you intend to completely back up.

Figure 10.6.

*The initial Backup
window allows you to
select the files you
want to store on tape.*

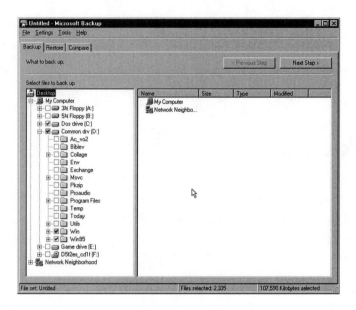

You'll probably see a dialog during the file selection process. Windows 95 continues to peel blank pages from a stack and adds check marks to them as long as it is selecting files. You can usually detect a problem if the pages continue to peel after the disk activity stops. Make sure you check the client machines, as well as the local machine, when backing up more than one machine on a peer-to-peer network.

> **Tip:** The first time you back up your system, Backup might find some files that it can't verify. Always check the ERROR.LOG file in the \PROGRAM FILES\ACCESSORIES\LOG folder. This file tells you which files Backup couldn't verify. In most cases, you want to exclude these files unless you have a good reason to keep them in the backup set. I've found most of these files end up being system-specific files I normally need to install manually before a restore.

Once you complete the selection process, it's time to select a target for the backup. Figure 10.7 shows a typical selection window. As you can see, Backup allows you to select any drive or the tape as a storage location. Now is the time to save your backup set. If you try to save it before this point in the process, Backup displays an error message. Notice that a target is part of the set file information. You need this information to conduct automatic backups by double-clicking a file set icon in Explorer.

Figure 10.7.
This is the window where you select the backup target. You also use it to save the backup set.

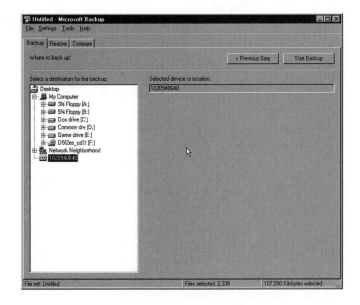

After you save the file set, click Start Backup to begin the actual backup process. Backup asks you to provide a set label for this particular session because a tape can contain more than one session. This dialog also allows you to password-protect the backup. Adding a password isn't required for on-site storage. However, if you plan to use off-site storage, a password will protect your valuable data.

Click OK on the Backup Set Label dialog and you see Backup start storing the data on your machine to tape. I did skip past a few of Microsoft Backup's features during this quick look. Take a look at some of them now. All the feature dialogs appear under the Settings menu. They include File Filtering, Drag and Drop, and Options.

The File Filtering dialog appears in Figure 10.8. This dialog looks complicated but contains only two settings. The first allows you to exclude files by date range. Suppose you want to back up only files from this week. Using this entry allows you to do that. The second allows you to select files by type. Here's another quirk of Microsoft Backup: You can exclude only registered file types. Most people don't register the file types they don't plan to use. For example, the .BAK extension rarely appears in the Registry naturally. If you want to exclude that file type from your backups, you need to register it. All the file types you can select for exclusion appear in the upper list box. The file types that get excluded from this backup appear in the lower list box.

You control the exclusion and inclusion of file types by using four pushbuttons. Select All highlights all the files in the File Types list box. Exclude places any highlighted file types in the Exclude File Types list box. You can remove a file type from the Exclude File Types list box using Delete. Finally, the Restore Default pushbutton removes all the file types from the Exclude File Types list box.

Figure 10.8.
The File Filtering dialog allows you to select which files appear in the backup set.

The Drag and Drop dialog appears in Figure 10.9. Notice that this dialog contains only three entries. The first automatically keeps Microsoft Backup minimized when it starts. The second forces it to display a dialog asking your permission to start the backup. The third automatically ends the application once it completes the backup. Microsoft Backup defaults to checking all three entries. It's a good idea to leave them this way unless you have a reason for changing one or more of them. (I usually uncheck the second check box—Confirm operation before beginning—if I plan to be away from my desk when the backup starts.)

Figure 10.9.
The Drag and Drop dialog allows you to set the automatic settings for Microsoft Backup.

I look at two pages of the Options dialog in this section. The first page, General, contains two check boxes, as shown in Figure 10.10. The first check box tells Backup to prompt you with a beep at the end of an operation. For example, if it completely fills one tape, Backup beeps and asks you to supply another. The Overwrite old status log files option, the second check box, prevents Backup from saving old information. This keeps your drive relatively free from extra clutter and still allows you to retain the status of the previous backup.

The second page I look at is the Backup page, shown in Figure 10.11, which has three main sections. The first entry, a check box, tells Backup to exit as soon as the backup is completed. The second section of the Backup page contains two radio buttons. Select the first radio button if you want Backup to perform a full backup of the selected files on the drive. The second option allows you to perform a differential backup. The only files that Backup selects from the backup set are those with the archive bit set. Backup resets this bit each time it backs up your files. Whenever you change the file, Windows sets the archive bit. The status of this bit tells Backup whether you changed the file since the last time you archived it to disk. (You can see whether the archive attribute of a file is set by right-clicking it in Explorer and selecting the Properties option. The file attributes appear on the General page of the file Properties dialog. A check in the Archive checkbox tells you that the file will get backed up.)

Figure 10.10.

The General page of the Options dialog allows you to select the notification and log settings.

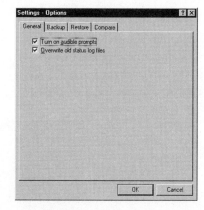

Figure 10.11.

The Backup page of the Options dialog contains all the parameters that affect how Microsoft performs the backup.

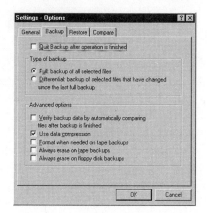

The third section of this dialog contains some special settings. I always check the first check box. Making a backup without performing a compare afterward is one sure way to end up with something unusable. If you don't perform a compare, you don't know if the backup is any good. The other options in this group are fairly self-explanatory. You can usually count on a 2:1 ratio for a normal backup if you turn on data compression. I've gotten as high as 15:1 for graphic and sound file backups. An all-data backup usually nets a 4:1 ratio with compression turned on. You probably want to use the 2:1 figure for your first few backups. Once you figure out the compression ratio, use it to determine how many tapes you need to complete a backup.

Restoring a Backup

Restoring a backup follows a process that reverses the one you used for creating the backup in the first place. You start by specifying the original target device and the backup set that you want to use. In most cases, this is a hard drive or a tape drive. Then select the files from that backup set you want to restore. Finally you start the restore process.

Just as with the backup process, you can also access settings for the restore process using the Settings | Options command. Figure 10.12 shows an example of this dialog. As you can see, it has three groups of controls, similar to the Backup dialog. The first control tells Backup to automatically exit when it completes the restore, if checked.

Figure 10.12.
The Restore page of the Options dialog allows you to set all the restore options.

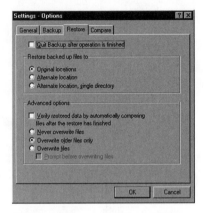

The second group of controls is fairly straightforward. These options allow you to select a restore location. Normally you choose the same directory Backup originally copied the files from. However, you can choose the second option to restore the file to an alternate location. This particular option retains any directory structure. If you want to place all the files in a single directory, no matter where they originally appeared in the directory tree, select the third option.

The final group of controls allows you to change the way Backup restores the files. As with the Backup page, I always select the compare option here as well. If you don't compare the restored file with what appears on tape, you can't be sure you got a good restore. I also use the Overwrite files option so I can replace corrupted files with good ones. Checking the Prompt before overwriting files option still gives you the option to keep the original file. Of course, using these two options together means you have to sit in front of the machine during the restore to answer any questions it might have about overwriting files. Select one of the other two overwrite options if you want to perform an automatic restore.

Performing a Compare

The compare feature of Backup works much like restore. You begin by selecting the backup device. In most cases, this is the tape drive. As usual, you select the files, folders, and directories you want to compare. Once you make your selections, Backup compares the contents of the selected files with the files that exist on the hard drive in the same location. I find that a compare is useful when I want to check the status of a master backup. It lets me know how out-of-date the material really is. Figure 10.13 shows the Compare page of the Options dialog. Notice that it contains the same first and second group of controls that the Restore page did.

Figure 10.13.
The Compare page of the Options dialog box looks very similar to the Restore page. The options let you compare the contents of the original file to your backup.

The main features that Windows 98 provides in its Backup program is greater tape drive support and disaster recovery for restoring a hard drive after a hard disk crash.

Beta Release

Using the LFNBACK Utility

Whenever you use a disk utility to perform some kind of task on your drive—whether it's a file recovery, a disk optimization, or a backup—that utility could destroy the long filenames that Windows 95 needs in order to operate correctly. You don't have to let it happen, of course. Windows 95 comes with a utility called LFNBACK that can save your long filenames to a file and restore them later. You can find it in the `\WIN95\OTHER\LFNBACK` folder of the Windows 95 installation CD-ROM.

This isn't a fancy utility and it doesn't even sport a GUI. You need to use it from the MS-DOS prompt without having Windows 95 loaded. I just boot into MS-DOS mode, perform it from the MS-DOS prompt, and type exit, and I go right back into Windows 95.

Warning: Never use LFNBACK within Windows because you don't know which files are open. If Windows has a file with a long filename opened, that filename won't appear in the LFNBK.DAT file. This means that you lose the filename if you perform a restore on the drive. Always use LFNBACK from the MS-DOS prompt. Using MS-DOS mode is fine, but using the Windows 95 DOS prompt is probably even safer. (To go to the MS-DOS prompt, press F8 at the boot message and select that mode from the menu.)

I use LNFBACK about once a week to create a backup of the long filenames on each hard drive. It's easy to do—just type **LFNBACK /B DRIVE** at the MS-DOS prompt. You need to do this once for each drive on your machine. The result is a file called LFNBK.DAT that contains all the long filename information for that particular drive.

Peter's Principle: LFNBACK as a Maintenance Tool

Backing up your long filenames should be a regular part of your maintenance cycle. I usually back them up right before I perform a full backup of the machine. That way, the long filename backup ends up on the tape that I'm using. This double backup provides an extra measure of security when it comes to your long filenames. Remember, you could have a perfectly functional machine that won't boot because the long filenames on your drive got corrupted. Restoring them using LFNBACK could make a bad situation right again in a matter of minutes.

To restore a drive, follow the reverse procedure. Make sure you run LFNBACK on a drive that has the LFNBK.DAT file on it. To perform the restoration, type **LFNBACK /R DRIVE** at the DOS prompt.

On Your Own

Spend some time looking at the file-system–related files in the Windows SYSTEM folder. Look especially at the exported functions for DLLs such as COMMDLG.DLL. What do these entries tell you about the DLL and its purpose?

If you have a CD-ROM drive, spend some time optimizing the VCache now that you know a little more about how it works. What size of CD-ROM cache seems to use memory the most efficiently? How much of a speed difference do you notice between a large and a small cache when using applications directly from the CD-ROM drive?

Determine if you have FAT32 installed on your machine using the various clues I talked about in this chapter. Make certain you also know what kind of installation you're getting on a new machine so that you don't inadvertently corrupt your hard drive using old utilities on a FAT32-formatted drive.

Use the LFNBACK utility to create a backup of the long filenames on your drive. Make sure you don't erase the `LFNBK.DAT` file; it contains all the long filename information. Keep this file handy, just in case one of your older applications removes the long filename information from your drive. Update the `LFNBK.DAT` file on a weekly basis to keep it current.

Determine what kind of an effect disabling lazy writes has on your system from a performance perspective. Use the following procedure to disable it. (If the performance penalty is too great, you can always use this same procedure to enable lazy writes again later.)

1. Right-click the My Computer icon and select Properties.
2. Click the Performance page and then the File System button.
3. Select the Troubleshooting page. Click the option Disable write-behind caching for all drives.

Click OK twice to save your changes. Windows tells you to reboot your machine in most cases to allow the change to take effect.

Peter Norton®

IV

Advanced
Windows 95
Usage
Techniques

11

The
Windows 95
Applets

Peter Norton®

Windows 95 includes several applets that help you configure your machine. This chapter covers these utility applets so you'll know when you need to use them, but most of these applets are a one-shot deal: You generally use them when you install the operating system or change a piece of hardware.

Configuring Windows 95 Applets

When you install an applet, you should configure it at the same time. For example, when you install Dial-Up Networking, Windows 95 automatically asks you for information regarding your computer setup. You can't dial up without a telephone number, so it makes sense that Windows 95 asks about this information before it completes the installation process.

Tip: Every applet that appears in the Control Panel has a corresponding file with a .CPL extension in the SYSTEM folder. Sometimes a user might think that a particular applet has disappeared. In most cases you'll find that the CPL file was corrupted or deleted. An administrator can simply move to another directory the CPL files that he doesn't want the user to access. No CPL file means that the user cannot access a particular Windows 95 configuration feature. Finally, you can double-click most CPL files to open them. This allows you to determine the exact identity of any CPL files on your system.

The following sections outline four different methods of installing applets on your system. The standard method allows you to install or remove standard Windows 95 features. The "Special Utility Installation" section tells you how to install some of the extra utilities that Windows 95 provides. For example, you use this procedure to install the Policy Editor and other utilities that the standard user probably shouldn't know about. Make sure you read any text files provided with the utilities because it's unlikely that you'll find sufficient documentation elsewhere. Windows 95 also provides printer utilities that help you manage this resource better when using certain types of printers. I tell you how to install them in the "Special Printer Installation" section. Finally, you'll find that Windows 95 provides a wealth of network management tools. You'll read about the installation procedure for them in the "Special Network Installation" section. A few of the applets you can install are so specialized that Microsoft provides a special installation method for them. Although I can understand Microsoft's willingness to hide a nonstandard utility from a user who might not know how to use it properly, it seems to me that there's got to be a better way. Of course, part of the reasoning behind this four-layered approach to installation is the nature of the applets themselves. They aren't all necessarily applets in the full sense of the word. You can't execute them and expect something useful to happen. Some of them are halfway between a driver and an applet. Other types of applets work almost as TSRs, helping Windows 95 to monitor specific items of information in the background.

Make sure you scan the Windows 95 CD-ROM when you get it. All the floppy disk utilities install using the first method I cover. The special programs appear on the CD-ROM version of Windows in a variety of folders that don't appear on the floppy version. If you want to get these utilities, you need the CD-ROM version of Windows or you need to download them from the Internet site at `http://www.microsoft.com/windows95/default.asp`. Most of these specialized programs appear in the ADMIN folder. Beneath this folder are three subfolders that categorize the type of applet. This makes it easy to tell which of the following methods you should use to install a specific applet.

> **Tip:** Keeping average users on your network away from some of the utilities that might damage the system could prove difficult if you give them the CD-ROM version of Windows and users decide to experiment on their own. If you really want to keep those utilities away from prying eyes, get the floppy disk version of Windows 95 for your network users or use the network-based installation I covered in Chapter 3, "Installing Windows 95: A Setup Primer," instead. Using a script file keeps the installation easy, but floppies keep the installation from getting corrupted—at least by a stray applet.

Standard Installation and Removal

You start the standard installation in Control Panel. Simply double-click the Add/Remove Programs applet and select the Windows Setup page, as shown in Figure 11.1. Looking through the list of applications you can install using this dialog, you see all the familiar utility programs Windows provides. You'll notice one thing: This list has no network administration tools. You take care of that deficiency a little later.

Figure 11.1.
*The Add/Remove
Programs applet
allows you to install
the standard
Windows user
applications.*

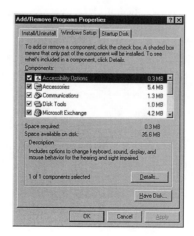

Completing this particular installation process is easy. Simply check the items you want to install and click OK. The Add/Remove Programs applet takes care of the rest. You might need to supply a disk or two if you aren't using the CD-ROM installation. Otherwise, the rest of the process should be fairly automated.

Note: Make sure you don't accidentally uncheck any item you want to keep. The Add/Remove Programs applet automatically uninstalls any applet you uncheck. Accidentally removing something can cause problems as you frantically try to figure out what went wrong with your system.

Most of the Windows 95 applets wait until you run them the first time to either automatically detect the required configuration information or ask you to supply it. Some of them, however, ask for this information immediately if they provide a system service. For example, installing modem support requires an immediate answer because the system never knows when it will need that information.

Special Utility Installation

The CD-ROM contains some utilities that don't appear on the Add/Remove Programs dialog box. You either need to know they exist, read about them in one of the files located on the CD-ROM, or do a little exploring as I did. It's kind of surprising to see just how many different utilities the CD-ROM contains. To check your CD-ROM, just use Explorer's Find tool to look for INF files. You won't find any of the Windows system installation INF files because they're in compressed format. It's usually safe to assume that any INF files you see on the CD-ROM have something to do with an applet's installation routine. Figure 11.2 shows the results of my search.

Tip: Many of these applets appear in the Windows 95 Resource Kit provided in the \ADMIN\RESKIT\HELPFILE folder on your CD-ROM. Searching for the utility name using the Explorer Find tool and the Containing text field of the Advanced page helps you find the needed information quickly. Don't be surprised if you don't see the applet listed in the online help. Some of these applets are for network administrators only, so you need to look at the documentation provided in the applet folder instead. Using the Resource Kit and applet documentation together should help reduce any confusion over the applet's intended use.

As you can see from Figure 11.2, my list extends for quite a way. The CD-ROM has lots of INF files, and it's pretty difficult to tell which ones you want installed on your machine. However, knowing that the file exists provides some information. A lot of INF files contain notes about the application they're supposed to work with. The folder that holds the INF file and the application might provide a README file as well.

Figure 11.2.

INF files on your CD-ROM usually provide support for some type of applet installation routine.

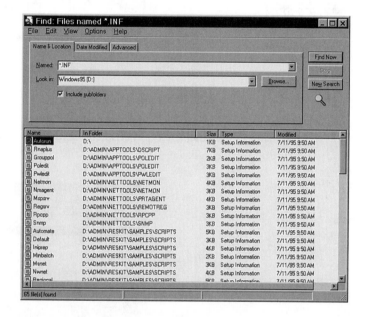

Note: I hope that Microsoft will provide better documentation for these utilities in the future. At the time I wrote this, the documentation hadn't changed. Some of these utilities get only a single line of description in the Resource Kit (provided as part of the CD-ROM). You might need to do a little detective work before using any of these other utility programs.

After you decide that an applet meets your need, you need to decide what type of installation to perform. Use the procedure described in the following paragraph to install them. Other applets require special installation. Use the section "Special Printer Installation" later in this chapter to install printer-specific applets. Likewise, use the "Special Network Installation" section for any network-related applets. Using the correct installation procedure ensures that you get a useable utility when you finish. When in doubt, use this general-purpose installation and test the application to see if it works:

1. To perform a special utility installation, open Control Panel and double-click the Add/Remove Programs applet as you did before. Select the Windows Setup tab.

2. Instead of choosing an applet from the list, click the Have Disk pushbutton. You should see a dialog similar to the one in Figure 11.3.

Figure 11.3.
*The Install From
Disk dialog allows
you to install an
applet that normally
doesn't appear in the
Add/Remove
Program Properties
dialog.*

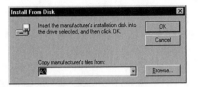

3. Click the Browse pushbutton and use the Open dialog to find the applet's INF file. Double-
click this file to add its name to the Copy manufacturer's files from field of the Install From
Disk dialog. Click OK to complete the selection process. Windows 95 displays a dialog
similar to the one shown in Figure 11.4.

Figure 11.4.
*The Have Disk dialog
displays a list of any
special applets that the
INF file contains.*

4. Use the Have Disk dialog to select the applets you want to install. Notice that, as usual,
you make the selections using a check box.

Tip: If you find an INF file that doesn't contain a list of applets, cancel the installation
process immediately. Some INF files on the CD-ROM don't contain applet-specific
information. Fortunately, the installation doesn't proceed unless you have some boxes to
check in the Have Disk dialog.

5. Click the Install pushbutton to complete the installation. Windows 95 copies the required
files from the CD-ROM and returns to the Add/Remove Programs Properties dialog.
Scrolling through the list of installed components should reveal the new applets you
installed. Figure 11.5 shows an example of the applets I installed using this procedure.
Unchecking a box next to one of these utilities uninstalls it. This process works exactly the
same as for the standard applets. Notice that these special applets use a diamond-shaped

icon to differentiate them from the standard applets in the list. You can depend on this indicator for any special applets that appear in the list.

Figure 11.5.
Any new applets you install appear in the Add/Remove Programs Properties dialog.

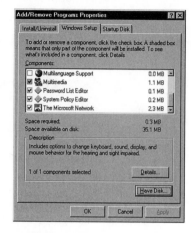

Special Printer Installation

Windows 95 provides some special printer support. It would seem that you should use the standard installation methods to install these applets, but Microsoft decided to take a different path. The printer applet installation looks almost the same as a printer installation, with a few important differences:

1. To begin the installation process, open the Printers folder and double-click the Add Printer icon. You should see the Print wizard opening display. Click Next to get to the next screen.

2. Select Local Printer and click Next to get to the next screen. You should see the Add Printer Wizard dialog box, shown in Figure 11.6.

Figure 11.6.
The Add Printer Wizard dialog allows you to add a new printer or applet.

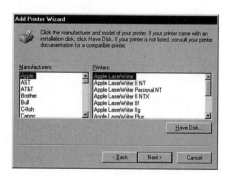

3. Click the Have Disk pushbutton. You should see a dialog similar to the one shown in Figure 11.3.

4. Click the Browse pushbutton and use the Open dialog to tell Windows where to find the applet's INF file (located on the disk or CD provided by the printer manufacturer or in the folder where you saved the files after downloading them from the manufacturer's Web site). Double-click this file to add its name to the Copy manufacturer's files from field of the Install From Disk dialog. Click OK to complete the selection process. Windows 95 displays a dialog similar to the one shown in Figure 11.7.

Figure 11.7.

Adding a printer resource using a disk is fairly easy under Windows 95.

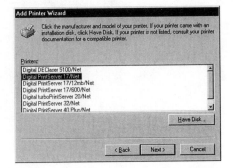

5. Use the Add Printer Wizard dialog to select the applets you want to install. Notice that the method of listing the potential resource has changed.

6. Windows 95 copies some files to disk and then asks some additional questions based on the type of resource you want to install. Following the prompts is fairly easy and should resemble the process of adding a printer.

Special Network Installation

Some special network administration tools appear on your CD-ROM as well. As with the printer-specific resources, you don't use the standard installation routine to add these applets to your system. The following procedure will help you perform a special network installation:

1. Open Control Panel and double-click the Network icon. Click the Add pushbutton, select Service, and click the Add pushbutton. You should see a dialog similar to the one in Figure 11.8.

2. Click the Have Disk pushbutton. You should see a dialog similar to the one shown in Figure 11.3.

3. Click the Browse pushbutton and use the Open dialog to tell Windows where to find the applet's INF file (located on the disk or CD provided by the printer manufacturer or in the folder where you saved the files after downloading them from the manufacturer's Web site). Double-click this file to add its name to the Copy manufacturer's files from field of the Install From Disk dialog. Click OK to complete the selection process. Windows 95 displays a dialog similar to the one shown in Figure 11.9.

Figure 11.8.
The Select Network Sevice dialog allows you to install a new network resource.

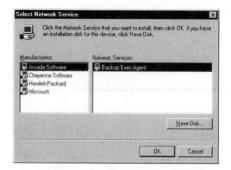

Figure 11.9.
Use this dialog to select a special network-related resource.

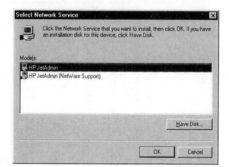

4. Use the Select Network Service dialog to select the applets you want to install. Notice that the method of listing the potential resource has changed.

5. Click OK. Windows 95 copies some files to disk and then displays the Network dialog with a new entry added. In this case, I added a HP LaserJet administration tool. Figure 11.10 shows the new addition.

Figure 11.10.
Adding this new applet helps an administrator manage an HP LaserJet on the network.

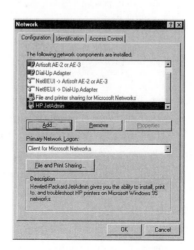

The Control Panel

Few people ever get comfortable with the Control Panel. You access it to change a major hardware or software configuration item and then leave. You don't come back to it until your system needs adjustment again. You don't visit the Control Panel on a daily basis.

Figure 11.11 shows a typical Control Panel setup. However, no two Control Panel setups are alike. The Control Panel usually contains a set of default icons and a bunch of icons related to your particular system configuration.

Figure 11.11.
The Control Panel is a deep, dark secret to some people and none too familiar to everyone else.

Now might be a good time to check out some of the applets in the Control Panel. Some of them will seem familiar because I've already discussed them elsewhere in the book. Others will be new because I haven't really covered them yet. The following list provides an overview of the Control Panel's contents:

- Accessibility Options: This allows you to change some Windows 95 features to make them easier to use. For example, this applet allows you to enable the StickyKeys option for the keyboard.

- Add New Hardware: This applet allows you to install new hardware on your system. You can choose one of two installation methods—manual or automatic. Microsoft recommends the automatic method in most cases because it's the least error-prone (assuming that the detection program works properly).

- Add/Remove Programs: Adding and removing applications is easy in Windows 95, but probably not as easy as it could be. I've looked at some of the difficulties of using this particular applet in this chapter.

- Date/Time: Keeping the date and time current on your machine becomes more important as your machine makes more connections to other resources. Older installations had to worry about the date and time only when it came to time-stamping files. New users rely on the clock to schedule automated tasks, keep track of appointments, and a host of other responsibilities.

- Display: I use this applet the most. Not only does it allow me to change my display resolution and colors with ease, but I can also use it to enlarge the display fonts and change the wallpaper on the desktop. All these features add up to an incredibly flexible and easy-to-modify display system. The big surprise is that you no longer have to reboot your machine to see the effect of a change.

- Fonts: This lets you manage your font libraries.

- Joystick: This provides full joystick support and includes both a calibration and a testing module.

- Keyboard: If you've ever had to do strange things such as write entire sentences using the Character Map utility under Windows 3.x, you'll really appreciate the keyboard support under Windows 95. Now you can have more than one language available as needed. A simple click on the International icon on the Taskbar allows you to choose between any of the installed keyboard layouts. This applet not only installs support for these languages, but it also provides other forms of keyboard support, such as repeat rate adjustment.

- Mail and Fax: If you have a network installed, you'll probably have some type of mail module in the Control Panel. This particular applet is Microsoft network-specific, but I'm sure you'll find similar applets for NetWare and Banyan. The Mail and Fax applet helps you configure your online connections and even the location of your address books. It's the configuration utility for Microsoft Exchange/Windows Messaging.

- Microsoft Mail Postoffice: The difference between this applet and the preceding one is that the Microsoft Mail Postoffice is specific to the local e-mail setup. Although the Mail and Fax applet helps you make the right connections, this applet deals with the intricacies of managing a post office. You can change security levels and add new users when using this applet.

- Modems: The Modems applet allows you to configure your modem settings for optimum performance under Windows 95 and includes a diagnostic so that you can troubleshoot any problems that the modem might experience.

- Mouse: The purpose of this applet is to help you configure the mouse. This doesn't mean just the double-click speed and other mouse-specific features; it also includes the actual pointers that the mouse uses and whether Windows 95 displays mouse trails. I find the addition of pointers to Windows 95 a welcome change. The animated icons might prove bothersome on some displays, but they show up well on the LCDs I've checked out.

- Multimedia: This applet controls everything relating to the new sound and video features supported by Windows 95. It not only controls the actual drivers and their settings, but it helps you configure the interface as well. One thing you won't find here is a way to control the system sounds. Other than that, this applet is the one you want to check out when you have a sound or video problem.

- Network: This lets you set your network's password policy and how the network controls access to your resources. TCP/IP users use this applet to configure the various addresses needed to make their networks functional. Overall, this is the one place you need to go to get the overall picture of your network's current setup.

- ODBC and ODBC32: Anyone who deals with database management systems for very long understands the importance of this applet. It allows you to create new table connections and modify old ones. You also can see which drivers your system has available. Each ODBC applet is separate. There's one applet to manage 16-bit applications and a second applet for 32-bit applications. Unfortunately, I see this as another source of confusion. Make sure you use the correct applet for your application when changing its setup. I was surprised to see some of the 32-bit drivers listed in my 16-bit applet and vice versa. If I hadn't looked carefully, I could have made the changes using the wrong applet. Whenever you start creating configuration errors, there's a chance of data loss.

- Passwords: This applet provides one of the ways you can control access to the network and its resources.

- Power: You may or may not see this applet. Most laptop users will be familiar with the version of this applet shown in Figure 11.12. In just about every case, you'll find a page for controlling battery usage and another for controlling the sound hardware. The battery usage page simply shows how much time you have left. It normally allows you to place a battery meter on the Taskbar as well. The other pages normally define a time limit for inactivity before a specific piece of hardware shuts down. Obviously, the contents of your applet will vary some from the one shown here depending on the kind of support your laptop provides. In many cases, the Power applet gets added to desktop machines as a result of installing OEM Service Release 2 (OSR2) enhancements to Windows 95. For example, OSR2 supports full hard disk shutdown after a period of activity. Figure 11.13 shows a typical example of this version of the Power applet. Notice that in the case of this desktop machine, hard disk shutdown is the only entry you see. It's also important to note that energy-saving monitors and display adapters are still controlled from the Display Properties dialog. (I discussed this dialog in the Screen Saver section of Chapter 4, "Working with the Active Desktop.")

Tip: Because OSR2 allows you to shut down both the display and the hard drive, it becomes feasible for you to leave your machine on all the time. A machine that's totally powered down uses around 20 watts—not much more power consumption than keeping a night light on all night. The positive side of this arrangement is that you reduce the amount of time it takes to get started in the morning. You also reduce wear and tear on your machine from turning it on and off. The negative side is that you create a security hole by using this feature. Because your machine is already on and set up for use, a hacker need only figure out your screen saver password (assuming you use one). Of course, another problem is that the disk shutdown feature might not work in some cases. For example, if you use a screen saver that accesses the hard drive, you may find that the drive won't shut down. The Power applet keeps the drive active because it thinks you're using it.

Figure 11.12.

Just about every laptop computer on the market sports some type of Power Properties dialog.

Figure 11.13.

Desktop computers recently added the Power applet to the repertoire as a result of OSR2 installation.

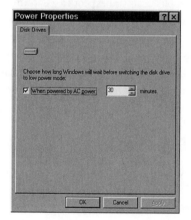

- Printers: A printer is the one item no one can do without. If you don't have a printer connected directly to your machine, there's a good chance you maintain a network connection to one. The Printers applet allows you to configure existing printers or add new ones and maintain control over any print jobs that the printer is processing.

- Regional Settings: This applet manages all the text-formatting information required to make the output of an application correct, including the actual time zone. You also use this applet to change the numeric, currency, time, date, and regional settings.

- Sounds: This allows you to add a sound to just about any Windows event. The list of events definitely changes as you install and remove applications from your system.

- System: This applet allows you to maintain your computer as a whole. It provides access to the Device Manager. Not only is this an invaluable tool for configuring your system, but it also acts as a troubleshooting aid. Even though you don't get specific feedback, Device Manager at least lets you know which card is bad. This applet also allows you to enhance system performance. It even displays a list of things you can do to enhance system performance.

Your setup might have more or fewer applets than mine did, but this list should give you a good idea of what the common applets do. If you have a few additional icons, the vendor documentation should tell you what types of configuration tasks you can use them for.

> **Warning:** Some applications insist on installing a custom applet in the Control Panel. In most cases, Windows 95 ignores any incompatible applets it doesn't need to work with the hardware or software you installed. If you do get into a situation where the old driver gets loaded and affects system stability, call the vendor and see if there's an easy way to remove the applet. In most cases, you can eliminate the problem by deleting a few lines of text from SYSTEM.INI.

What other kinds of applets can you expect to see in the Control Panel? This is limited only by the types of applications and hardware you install. A few examples include a digitizer pad, CAS-compliant fax, and data-capture boards. You'll probably see special applets for certain types of network connections. Most mail packages require an entry here. It's surprising to note that applications such as Lotus 1-2-3 might place an applet here to manage their data connections. (Most applications use ODBC now, so you'll see more options in the ODBC applet rather than more applets.)

On Your Own

Open the Control Panel and check its contents against the list of standard applets in this chapter. Does your Control Panel contain additional applets? Open any additional applets to see if you can figure out what purpose they serve. If there's a Help or About button, click it to see what kind of information it provides.

Use the START command to open Control Panel from the DOS prompt. Do you notice any differences in the Control Panel's contents? Exit the Control Panel and reopen the DOS session. Use the various switches that I discussed in Chapter 6, "Startup Shortcuts," to open the Control Panel. What effect do they have?

If you have OSR2 installed on your machine, see if you have a Drive Shutdown page in the Power applet. Set the drive shutdown time to match that for the Shut Off Monitor field on the Screen Saver page of the Display Properties dialog. Make sure you also disable any screen saver that requires access to the hard drive.

12

DDE, OLE, DCOM, and ActiveX

Peter Norton®

Dynamic data exchange (DDE) and object linking and embedding (OLE) are both methods for sharing data between documents. Of the two, DDE is older. There are actually two versions of OLE. Windows 95 supports the newer OLE 2 standard, but that doesn't mean that your applications do. The first thing you need to understand about OLE is that it's not just cut and paste. In most of the chapters in this book, I talk about the objects that Windows 95 uses to make life simpler for the user. Would it surprise you too much to learn that these objects are a form of OLE support?

A problem with OLE is that it's pretty much limited to documents that you can access from the local machine. In addition, you have to rely on the local hardware to perform any required object processing. That brings us to the last entry in the title of this chapter, ActiveX. It relies on a new kind of OLE technology called DCOM (distributed component object model). OLE 2 uses COM (component object model) as the basis for creating compound documents—ones that contain other objects. When you embed or link an object by using OLE, COM is the underlying technology that makes this possible. As the DCOM acronym implies, this is a form of object that resides not only on the local machine, but anywhere on the network. In other words, a compound document can consist of objects created in a variety of places.

Why is DCOM important? It's the basis for new Internet-based technologies such as the ActiveX controls used with Internet Explorer 4.0. It's also the technology that allows people to create Internet Information Server add-ons that execute only on the server. The most common use for DCOM today is on the Internet, where people want to share data over the World Wide Web. DCOM is also embedded into Windows 95 itself, although it may be a while before you see it used for things such as data sharing on your local network.

Objects (not object orientations) can really make your documents easier to use and maintain if you use them correctly. At first it'll seem as if there are a lot of rules to follow, but once you learn the rules of the road, you'll find that you can create complex documents in a lot less time and with far better results than before. (The actual benefits that you receive vary widely, so I cover those in the information-specific sections of the chapter.)

Compound Documents: the Microsoft Strategy

The following list defines some of the terms you'll see in this chapter (and those that follow):

- Client: This term refers to the application that holds the linked or embedded object. For example, if you place a spreadsheet object in your word-processed document, the word processor becomes the client. The differentiation between client and server used to be pretty easy to figure out. You see later on that ActiveX technology has created some subtle changes in the way that clients appear. With the advent of Active Document, the application you see as a client might actually be just a frame for another application beneath. The idea of a container within a container isn't new, but ActiveX makes it easier to see.

- Server: The server is the application that the client calls to manipulate an object. Embedded or linked objects are still in the native format of the application that created them. A client must call on the originating application to make any required changes to the object's content. What you really have are two applications working together to create a cohesive document. When using OLE, it's usually assumed that the server resides on the local machine. For example, when you embed an Excel spreadsheet into a Word document, you need to have both applications on your machine. When using ActiveX, the server need not exist on the local machine (although it does improve response time in some cases). For example, if a programmer develops an ActiveX extension for Internet Information Server, the actual processing occurs on the server, not your local machine. The server always returns data in a form that the local application can accept.

- Compound document: This is a document that contains one or more objects. Every OLE document is considered a compound document. I take a better look at what this means a little later in this chapter.

- Object: An object is a piece of data that you move from one application to another in its native format. You can create objects from any data if the originating application supports OLE. This is the big difference between an object and cutting and pasting. You can do a lot more with an object because it contains intelligence that a simple piece of text doesn't.

- Object menu: I take another look at how to use this particular OLE menu later. Suffice it to say that this is the menu you use to change the contents of an OLE document, convert it, or perform any other operations that the object allows.

- Container: This is an object that holds other objects. Visualizing a folder like the ones used by Explorer will give you a good idea of what a container represents. However, instead of simply holding files like a folder, an OLE container can hold any kind of object.

Now that you have some idea of what these OLE terms mean, you can take a look at some examples. I used Microsoft Paint and WordPad for my example so that you can follow along if you want.

The first thing I did was open a BMP file—Carved Stone—in the main Windows folder. Then I opened a copy of WordPad. There isn't anything particularly special about these two applications, but they do both support OLE 2.

Use the Edit | Select All command in Paint to select the entire image, and then right-click it. You should see the object menu shown in Figure 12.1. Notice that you can't drag and drop this image because Paint doesn't support that particular OLE 2 feature. If it did support drag and drop, you could simply right-click the object and drag it where you wanted it to go in WordPad. I need to take a somewhat longer route.

Figure 12.1.
*This object menu
contains options that
allow you to place the
object on the
clipboard.*

The object menu allows you to cut or copy the image. Notice the number of other editing options this menu contains. You might want to make note of what's available and compare it to the object menu after copying the image to WordPad. For right now, select the Copy option to place a copy of the object on the clipboard.

> **Note:** You can use the Edit | Paste Special command in place of the object menu when working with WordPad (or another application that provides this feature). In fact, some applications don't provide an object menu, so you have to resort to using the Edit menu. I demonstrate this method of linking or embedding an object later in this book.

Click WordPad to bring it forward. Right-click anywhere within the window. You should see an object menu similar to the one in Figure 12.2. Notice how this menu differs from the one in Paint. Each object menu has features that are unique to that application. A graphics application needs menu entries to help it manipulate graphic images. A word processor needs a different set of options to manipulate text.

Select the Paste option from WordPad's object menu. You should see a copy of the graphic image in WordPad. The first thing you should notice is the sizing handles around the image. These handles allow you to increase or shrink the object as needed. For example, when I need to draw a logo, I usually draw it very large. That way, I can get it done quickly without worrying too much about detail. When I paste the logo into a document, I shrink it to the size I really need it to be. As you shrink the graphic, it actually gains some amount of detail that you normally wouldn't get if you drew the image that size.

Now that the image is stored in WordPad, go ahead and close Paint. You can always open it back up if you need it later. If you right-click the graphic object, you see a menu similar to the WordPad object menu that you saw earlier. Notice the two bottom options, Bitmap Image Object and Object Properties. Highlight Bitmap Image Object to display a submenu.

Figure 12.2.
The WordPad object menu differs from the one found in Paint because it needs to perform different work.

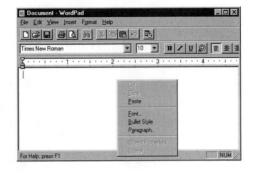

There are two options here: Edit and Open. The difference between them is distinct. You select Edit if you want to perform in-place editing. The Open option actually opens a copy of Paint with which you can edit the graphic. To see what I mean, select Edit now. You should see a display similar to the one in Figure 12.3. You should notice quite a few changes. For one thing, there's a hatched box around the object. This is an OLE 2 way of telling you which object you're currently editing. Also notice that the toolbar and menus changed to match those of Paint. This is what I mean by in-place editing. The window didn't change, but the tools did to meet the editing needs of the object.

Figure 12.3.
In-place editing is one of the new OLE 2 features.

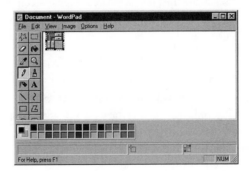

You can click anywhere outside the object to restore the original WordPad menu and toolbar. This time, select the Open option to see what happens. You should see a display similar to the one shown in Figure 12.4. This figure provides you with some visual cues. The most obvious is the fact that you're editing the graphic object outside WordPad, using the originating application. The method you use is largely dependent on personal taste because the end result of using either method is the same. The advantage of using the in-place method is that you remain in the same window all the time. The Open method has the advantage of returning you to the native editing environment. If I chose to edit one of my logos instead of opening it, I would have to perform in-place editing on a much smaller version of my original picture. Of course, I could always resize it to its original state, but that would be as inefficient as any other method—perhaps more so. Notice also that the object is hatched over in WordPad. This is another visual cue telling you which object you're editing externally.

Figure 12.4.

The Open option produces an entirely different result than Edit does.

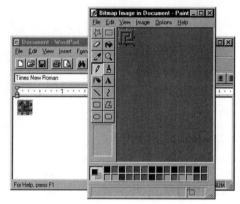

The Open method does require one extra step. You need to tell Paint to update the copy of the graphic that's still in WordPad. Use the File | Update Document command to get the job done. Notice how this option replaces Save. In essence, the update process does save the graphic. The only difference is where the graphic is saved.

Exit Paint and return to WordPad. Notice that the Exit entry on the File menu now says Return to Document. Now it's time to see what that other object menu entry contains. Right-click the graphics object and select the Object Properties option. You should see the Bitmap Image Properties dialog box shown in Figure 12.5. Clicking the Convert button displays another dialog box with a list of conversion options. In essence, this option allows you to convert the graphic object from one file type to another while also displaying the file size and type.

Figure 12.5.

The General page of the Bitmap Image Properties dialog box provides access to the Convert dialog box.

> **Note:** Each object type provides a unique set of pages in the object dialog box. It's important to remember that each dialog box reflects a combination of the capabilities of the server applications and the needs of the data file format. Some file formats can't support some application features. As a result, some options might appear grayed out.

Click the View tab. You see the View page of the Bitmap Image Properties dialog box, shown in Figure 12.6. This page has several interesting entries. The first is the radio button that determines whether the image is displayed as an editable object or as an icon. You can make your machine run faster and use less memory if you select the icon option. Using an icon means that Windows doesn't need to load the actual image or the application required to support it unless you decide to edit the image. Windows suggests a default icon, but you can use the Change Icon button to select another.

Figure 12.6.
The View page of the Bitmap Image Properties dialog box allows you to change the appearance of the object.

The bottom part of this dialog box is fairly interesting too, even if you can't select it at the moment. It allows you to select a precise scale to use when displaying your graphic. The BMP format and application used to display it don't support the scaling option in this particular case. Close WordPad; you don't need it anymore for now. You don't have to save the image unless you want to.

Data Exchange: a Static Solution

DDE still keeps popping up in Windows 95, and I think we'll continue to see it for some time to come. Even Explorer, an application designed for Windows 95, provides DDE capability. The fact is that every OLE application uses a little DDE to make it run. One of the most significant problems with using DDE is that it creates a static link, much like the one you get using cut and paste. The fact that it provides a stable macro language that you can use to open files and perform other fancy maneuvers from the command line doesn't change much.

DDE is a messaging protocol that sends a message from one application to another and asks it to do something. Originally, DDE was supposed to provide the means to open another application and copy some data to the clipboard. You could also get it to do other chores, such as printing files. A DDE macro contains part DDE and part application macro language. This is another problem with using it. Not only do you need to learn the native language of the application you're using and DDE itself, but you also have to learn the macro language for the server application. Needless to say, DDE didn't get the kind of reception that Microsoft originally hoped it would. DDE is simply too hard for the average user to consider using. In fact, even some programmers find it difficult to use (unless they use it on a regular basis).

The reason that DDE hangs around despite its difficult-to-learn nature is that it's pretty tough to create the same kind of link that the DDE procedure performs without performing it manually. OLE just doesn't provide all the features necessary to create every type of link you need, and it certainly doesn't allow you to create those links as part of a macro or program. OLE automation has changed that fact, but it's not in wide usage.

Linking Versus Embedding

You saw the object part of object linking and embedding earlier. There was no doubt that what you were working with was an object, not merely a cut-and-paste example of the graphic. Now it's time to take a look at the linking and embedding part of the picture.

Peter's Principle: A Time to Link and a Time to Embed

Some people get confused about when it's appropriate to use linking versus embedding. Embedding works best when you need to share a file with a lot of people. If the compound document is going to move around, you want to package it in such a way that nothing gets lost. An embedded object meets this criterion.

On the other hand, linking does work well in this instance. If you plan to use the same file in more than one place, linking is the route to go. I almost always use this technique instead of embedding when working with logos.

When you link a document, you are, in essence, creating a pointer to that file on disk. Think of a link as a road sign pointing to your house. As long as you don't move the house, everyone is able to find it because the road sign points them there. What happens if you do move the house? The sign still points to where it thinks your house is, but anyone who follows the sign finds nothing but an empty foundation.

The same principle holds true for links in compound documents. The link works fine as long as you don't move the document. The second you do move the document, you break the links. Of course, you can always reestablish the links, but that's a waste of time when not moving the file in the first place would require a lot less work.

OLE 1 had a significant problem in this regard because it noted the location of the linked file in precise terms. It is the same as using your complete address to tell someone how to get to your house. Again, if you move, the address information does them little good. OLE 2 takes a different approach. Instead of using a precise location, it uses a relative direction. For example, what if you told your friends that you live two blocks south of Joe? As long as you and Joe always lived two blocks apart, people can find your house. (Of course, they need to know the location of Joe's house.)

Embedding is a different process from linking. Instead of creating a pointer to your data, embedding actually places the data object within the compound document. This means that wherever the compound document goes, the data follows. This sounds like a great fix for the problems with linking. However, embedding comes with several price tags attached. First, you'll find it difficult to update multiple compound documents at once. For example, suppose that your company just decided to use a different logo and it wants all the letters updated to reflect that change. If you had linked the logo file to the letters, the change would be simple. You need to change only one file. The first person who opens each document after that sees the new logo. With embedding, you have to change each document on an individual basis.

You also use a lot more disk space to store an embedded file. A link takes only a few bytes to create a pointer. An embedded object is complete. If the object is 4KB, your compound document grows by 4KB to accommodate it. Unfortunately, you don't get off that easily. In addition to the size of the object, some "housekeeping" data is included as well. The server needs this information to help you maintain the object.

Now that you know the difference between linking and embedding, take a look at how you implement them. Begin by opening a copy of WordPad. You're going to explore another route you can take to link and embed objects in your documents. Use the Insert | Object command to display the dialog box shown in Figure 12.7. Notice that you can take two routes at this point. You can insert either a new object or an existing one.

Figure 12.7.
Use the Insert Object dialog box to embed or link a new or existing object into your document.

Click the Create from File radio button. The dialog box changes to the one shown in Figure 12.8. This allows you to embed or link an existing file. Click the Browse button and find any BMP file that you like. Double-click to select it. Select the Link check box. If you don't check this box, Windows automatically embeds the object instead of linking it. Notice the Display As Icon check box in Figure 12.8. Clicking this option displays the object as an icon rather than as a full image. Displaying the image as an icon significantly increases performance.

Figure 12.8.
The Insert Object dialog box allows you to embed or link an existing file into your document.

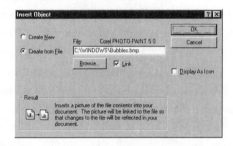

Click OK to place a link to the object in the current document. A quick glance at this object doesn't show anything different from the last time you created a compound document. However, when you right-click the object, you notice that the menu entries are slightly different, especially when you try to edit the file. Instead of the in-place editing you could do after embedding the object, linking always opens the server application. You must edit the object in a separate window when using linked objects rather than embedded ones. If you really dislike seeing the other application start, you might want to use embedded rather than linked objects.

Clients and Servers

Every application that supports OLE provides one or more services. You might have noticed in all the previous examples that I used Paint as the server and WordPad as the client. The reason is simple: Paint can't function as a client; it offers itself only as an OLE server.

This distinction is important because it affects the way you use an application. More than that, limitations of OLE support necessarily limit an application's value for creating a finished product. Consider what would happen if you tried to use a graphics program to create a poster, but it didn't support OLE as a client. Would you simply settle for cut and paste if you might need to modify the chart frequently? If Paint supported OLE as a client, you could create a chart for your poster in one application, the text in another, and the graphic elements in a third and then link them all together within Paint. The lack of client support would mean that you would have to copy the text to the clipboard. When you pasted it into Paint, the text would become a graphic element, part of the Paint graphic image. The text wouldn't be an OLE object that you could easily manipulate later using a word processor; it would be a graphic element that you would have to erase and redo from scratch. This makes changes as small as using a different type style or font size a lot more difficult than they need to be.

Any application that will serve as a central location for all the objects in a project must support OLE. In most cases, you want to use a word processor or presentation graphics program for this purpose. They provide the greatest amount of flexibility when it comes to formatting your data. Charts and graphs might need the services of a graphics program. Unfortunately, most low-end packages won't work as clients, so you need to invest in a high-end package such as CorelDRAW!. You definitely want a package of this sort to provide both client and server capabilities because you'll need to use both.

You can do quick-and-dirty edits with low-end packages. They usually have just enough features to get the job done and don't waste a lot of precious memory. Programs of this sort usually support OLE as a server but not as a client. No one would want the output from these programs; it just doesn't look professional. Microsoft Paint and other low-end graphics packages commonly fall into this category. You might also see some note-takers here too. In some cases, all you need is the text. A note-taker (such as the Notepad utility provided with Windows 95) works fine for this purpose.

Finally, you'll never use some packages as servers because they just don't generate enough data on their own to make it worth your while to use them in that capacity. Some presentation graphics programs fall into this category. Because their output looks nice, you can use them as OLE clients without worrying about their server capabilities.

Differences Between OLE 1 and OLE 2

Microsoft introduced OLE 1 as part of Windows 3.x. It provided a basic set of linking and embedding features that users soon outgrew. One of the biggest problems was the huge amount of memory that OLE required to create more than one or two links with other applications. The lack of speed was also a major concern.

OLE 2 remedies these problems and provides more functionality to boot. Unfortunately, both applications have to support OLE 2 before you get an actual benefit from these new features. The following list gives you an idea of all the improvements Microsoft made in OLE 2. Some of them are programmer-specific, but everyone benefits from something that makes a programmer's life even a little easier.

- Visual editing: One of the problems with OLE 1 was that the user's train of thought got disrupted every time he needed to make a change to an object because the object had to load in the originating application's window for editing. OLE 2 allows visual (in-place) editing. Instead of opening a new window, the host merely overlays its toolbar, menu structure, and controls with those of the client.

- Nested objects: OLE 1 allowed you to place one object at a time in the container document. An object couldn't become a container; all the objects existed as a single layer within the container. OLE 2 treats every potential container as just that—a container. It doesn't matter how many containers you place inside a container or how many ways you stack them.

- Drag and drop: You used to cut or copy an object in the server application and then place it in the client by using the Paste Special command. This option still works. However, OLE

2 provides a new method of creating links to other documents. You can simply grab the object and move it wherever you want.

- Storage-independent links: OLE 2 allows you to create links to other documents, even if they aren't physically located on the local drive.

- Adaptable links: If you moved any of the files required to create a compound document under OLE 1, all the links were destroyed, and you had to re-create them. OLE 2 stores only enough path information to maintain the link. If you create links between two files in the same directory, you can move these two files anywhere on the drive, and OLE 2 can maintain the link. The only criterion for maintaining a link under OLE 2 is that the relative path remain the same.

- OLE automation: OLE automation is part of Visual Basic for Applications (VBA). VBA defines a standard interface for talking with the server application. This allows the client application to send commands to the server that will change the contents of an object indirectly. OLE automation is the direct descendent of the DDE macro language that many applications still use. The big difference from the user's perspective is that DDE macros were difficult to write and prone to error. VBA is the native language of the application and is consistent across platforms.

- Version management: OLE 2 can store the application name and version number as part of the link. If an application developer implements this feature correctly, a server (or client, for that matter) will detect an old version of a file and ask whether you want to update it. This means that you never have an old file sitting around just waiting to make life difficult.

- Object conversion: Object conversion allows Excel to act as a server for a compound document containing a Lotus 1-2-3 object and vice versa. All you need to do is select the Convert option from the object menu in most cases.

- Optimized object storage: This feature allows the linked documents to stay on disk until needed. That way, Windows doesn't need to load every application and data file required to support the compound document, which reduces the amount of memory required to support OLE.

- Component object model: This is the programmer issue I mentioned. Essentially, it means that Microsoft simplified the application programming interface (API) for OLE 2. An API is a set of tools that programmers use to create applications. Simpler tools mean programs with fewer bugs. This also means that the programmer can write at least that part of the application faster.

Application Interoperability

Getting two applications to work together might not always be as easy as it seems. You've already seen a lot of different ways that two applications can differ in their implementation of OLE, and this barely scratches the surface. For the most part, you've looked at the standard ways that two applications can deviate. The following list gives you some ideas of what to look for when you can't get your objects to work properly:

- Neither application is a server; remember that you must have a server and a client to make OLE work.

- Data corruption has ruined one or more OLE files.

- One program provides 32-bit services and the other 16-bit.

- Corrupted entries in the Registry prevent the application from working correctly.

- Old entries in the Registry are confusing the application.

- Your network doesn't fully support OLE links.

This is just a sample of the types of problems you can encounter with a common setup. Add to these problems a vendor who doesn't fully support the OLE 1 or OLE 2 standard. I actually ran into one piece of software that ended up providing some strange cross of support between the two standards (and I don't think this vendor was alone). These support problems only make the situation worse. If every application supported OLE perfectly, you could probably get past the other problems I listed in this section. The combination of faulty support and less-than-adequate linking mechanisms paints a grim picture for the user. It is easy to point a finger and say that the vendor is totally at fault—yet anyone who has tried to read the OLE standards, much less follow them, will attest to the level of difficulty involved.

Before you get the idea that all is lost with OLE, let me inject a dose of reality. I want you to be aware of all the problems you might find. In most cases, it's unlikely that you'll experience any problems with using OLE at all. To ensure OLE compatibility, it's usually best to stick with programs from a single company, such as from Microsoft, Lotus, or Corel.

OLE Components

You'll probably see a whole group of files in your SYSTEM directory that provide support for OLE. The following list provides some details on the tasks each file performs. You can use this list if you ever run into a problem with corruption or if you simply want to know what level of support you can expect from a certain application. The presence or absence of these files might indicate problems with your installation as well. Missing OLE files means that you don't get the kind of support needed to make your system work efficiently.

- OLE2.DLL: If you see this file, you know that some part of the Windows installation on your machine supports the OLE 2 standard. Windows 95 always installs this file. This dynamic link library (DLL) provides some "foundation" functions. (A DLL is a special Windows program.)

- `OLECLI.DLL`: This file contains all the basic client code your application needs. Your application uses this file as a base for building its own client features.

- `OLESRV.DLL`: This file contains all the basic server code your application needs. Like the client code, this DLL doesn't provide everything. Your application uses it as a basis for building its own set of features.

- `OLE2CONV.DLL`: This file provides the generic routines a program needs to convert an object to the client program's native format.

- `OLE2DISP.DLL`: Every OLE client application uses this program to help it display the objects it contains.

- `OLE2NLS.DLL`: Most versions of Windows provide National Language Support (NLS). This program helps OLE keep pace with the rest of Windows in providing support for other languages.

- `OLE2.REG`: You can import this Registry file into your Registry to install OLE 2 support. In most cases, your application does this automatically, so you don't need to worry about it. The only time you need to use it is when you can't get OLE 2 to work and you discover that the Registry doesn't contain the correct entries.

- `MCIOLE.DLL`: Sounds require special handling under Windows. Unlike with most objects, you don't display a sound. This special DLL provides the support that an application needs to handle a sound object.

- `OLE32.DLL`: A whole group of OLE files in the SYSTEM directory has 32 somewhere in the names. These files provide the same services as their 16-bit counterparts to 32-bit applications.

- `MFCOLEUI.DLL`: C programmers need every bit of help they can get. They use something called *Microsoft Foundation Classes* to make their workload a little lighter. This file (and any with similar names) provides the C interface to OLE. If you see a file with MFC in its name, you know one of your applications uses the Microsoft Foundation Classes.

These are all the files you need for OLE 2. There is also a wealth of files required for ActiveX. Precisely what files you need to perform a specific activity depends on the needs of the ActiveX control itself. As a minimum, each ActiveX control requires the use of an OCX file, but there isn't any limitation on the number of files that a vendor could use. You'll normally find permanent ActiveX controls in the SYSTEM folder. Your Internet browser might place some ActiveX controls on your hard drive as well when you visit Web pages that use those controls. The precise location depends on your browser (to some extent). Internet Explorer places these files in the OCCACHE folder (normally located within the main Windows folder), unless the Web site specifies a different location. Because Netscape Navigator doesn't support ActiveX directly (at least not as of this writing), the default location for ActiveX controls is up to the plug-in that you use.

ActiveX controls are fairly easy to spot. They always have an extension of .ocx (OLE control extension). This file contains a combination of executable code and data. Where's the OLE connection?

The connection comes from the way that data is managed by the control. Think of an ActiveX control as a specialized form of OLE client or server and you have a pretty good idea of how things work. The next section of this chapter, "ActiveX—an Internet Strategy," gives you a pretty good idea of what the controls look like from the user perspective.

Unlike other kinds of files on your machine, simply erasing an ActiveX control to remove it isn't a good idea. ActiveX controls make their presence known to Windows by "registering" themselves. In fact, there's a special program in the SYSTEM folder, RegSvr32, that gets called to register the control within the Registry. You can register a control that Windows loses by typing **RegSvr32 OCX name** at the command line. Likewise, if your OCCACHE folder starts getting too full from visiting numerous Internet sites, you can unregister an ActiveX control by typing **RegSvr32 /U OCX name** at the command line. Always unregister the control before you erase it. How do you know whether you were successful? Windows always displays a dialog telling you that you successfully unregistered the ActiveX control. RegSvr32 displays a similar dialog box when you register an ActiveX control.

> **Warning:** Never remove ActiveX controls that appear in the SYSTEM folder (under your main Windows directory). Doing so might disable one or more of your applications. Most applications clean up any ActiveX controls they've installed when you remove them from your machine. In addition, use the greatest care when removing ActiveX controls that appear in other folders. An ActiveX control that appears in an application directory usually belongs to that application. Fortunately, you can always assume that the controls that appear in the OCCACHE folder are safe to remove.

ActiveX—an Internet Strategy

ActiveX has actually been around in one form or another for quite a while. The ActiveX technology is actually an extension of a technology that appears with the first 32-bit compilers from Microsoft. Originally, programmers called ActiveX controls OLE control extensions. The official name now is ActiveX—although you'll more than likely find the old name in more than a few places (even Microsoft's documentation).

OCXs (ActiveX controls) originally provided a component capability for products such as Visual Basic. You build an application by placing various components on a form and then setting their properties. The control doesn't actually exist within the application; it exists in a separate file. The application and the control talk to each other. A programmer monitors the communication by looking at the contents of the properties and by asking the application to react to certain events. Rather than get into bits and bytes here, however, take a look at ActiveX in action.

Figure 12.9 shows a Web page that contains some ActiveX controls. In this case, you're looking at a button and a set of radio buttons that control its properties. Any Webmaster will tell you that standard HTML (hypertext markup language) supports only three kinds of buttons: submit, reset, and cancel. The use of ActiveX in this case allows you to define any kind of button. The dialog box shows the result value of the button, which changes to reflect the kind of button you select by using the radio buttons.

Figure 12.9.
ActiveX works on Web pages as it does within an application; it allows a program- mer to build the page using components.

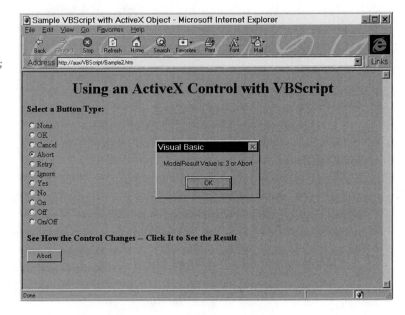

Okay, you're a little underwhelmed by a Web page containing some radio buttons and a command button. ActiveX has a lot more to offer than components. Take a look at Figure 12.10. What you're seeing is another kind of ActiveX application, called Active Document. In this case, you're looking at a Word for Windows document displayed within a browser window. Unlike other kinds of Web documents, you can edit this one and save the changes locally. If the Web server allows you to do it, you can also publish the changed document on the Web server.

There are a lot of ways to use Active Document, but the way that I see most people using it is as a method for exchanging information without resorting to groupware. Think about the advantage of allowing four people—one in New York, another in Delhi, another in London, and still another in Tokyo—to collaborate on a document located on the company's Web server in Los Angeles (all without a single long-distance phone call). That's the beauty of using Active Document. You can create connections through the Internet that were difficult or even impossible in the past.

Still not very impressed? ActiveX is used for a variety of other technologies as well. For example, ActiveMovie allows you to play multimedia over a Web connection. That's not so spectacular until you consider that a single player located on your machine allows you to play most multimedia file types. Figure 12.11 shows an example of ActiveMovie in action.

Figure 12.10.
Active Document, a special form of ActiveX, allows you to interact with a link on an Internet site.

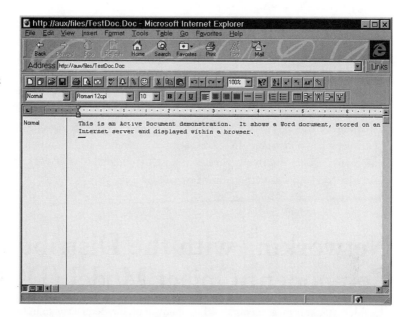

Figure 12.11.
ActiveMovie provides the means to work with multimedia over the Internet.

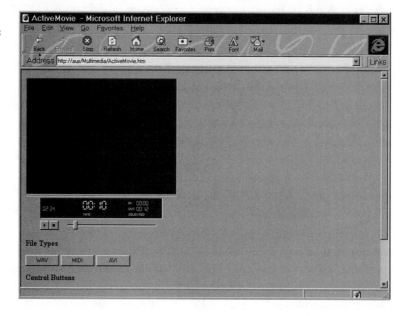

I really haven't covered everything there is to know about ActiveX, even from a user perspective. Suffice it to say that this is a vast new technology that you really need to know about. Don't think that you're limited to using Internet Explorer, either. There are several good plug-ins for Netscape Navigator that give you full access to everything that the Internet provides.

Tip: NCompass Labs produces a selection of plug-ins for Netscape Navigator that allow you to work with ActiveX-enabled Web pages. The first is ScriptActive. It allows you to download and use ActiveX controls. The second is called DocActive, which allows you to work with Active Document. The only problem with this solution is that the Webmaster at the Web site you want to visit has to cooperate. ScriptActive provides a conversion tool that implements every <OBJECT> tag that ActiveX normally uses as an <EMBED> tag that Navigator can understand. In some cases, you'll run into an Internet site that you still can't access with Navigator simply because it wasn't converted to work with a plug-in. You can contact NCompass at http://www.ncompasslabs.com.

Networking with the Distributed Component Object Model (DCOM)

DCOM, better known as network OLE to many of us, has been a gleam in Microsoft's eye for many years now. Although the original version of Windows 95 did not offer DCOM, Microsoft has provided DCOM that you can download from http://www.microsoft.com/com/dcom95/download-f.htm. Once you have access to DCOM, it's time to look at precisely what DCOM is and what it can do for you.

Just what DCOM is from the user perspective is all in the title. The *distributed* part is pretty easy to understand. Instead of working just locally, this new version of COM works on other machines as well. The *component* part is best described as Legos, those little blocks that you can build almost anything with. DCOM will allow programmers to take a bit of this and a bit of that and add something else to come up with complete applications. You've already studied the meaning of the word *object*. Simply put, DCOM objects work about the same as any other object in Windows. They all perform some task and have predefined rules on how you can interact with them. Finally, the term *model* tells you that this is a guideline for the real thing. DCOM is a specification that tells programmers how to create a specific kind of an object.

What will DCOM do for you? Well, for one thing, it'll eventually allow you to execute parts of your program on other machines. No longer will you need to worry just where the parts of an application are kept. DCOM will allow the application to find the parts that it needs and execute some or all of those parts on other machines as needed. Of course, DCOM also means that someone may borrow some of the capacity of your machine from time-to-time as well.

Tip: Curious about what objects might be lurking on your machine? Microsoft has provided a special OLE/COM Object Viewer at http://www.microsoft.com/oledev/olecom/

oleview.htm. This viewer allows you to see what's installed on your machine, including any new DCOM objects. You can even use the viewer to execute the various objects and see what they do. For the most part, however, you'll want to leave using DCOM objects to programmers who know what they're doing.

What makes DCOM different from COM or OLE? Both COM and OLE are architectures. They define how you put something together at a basic level. DCOM does this too, but it's not much different from COM in this regard. In fact, if you already know about COM, then you know just about everything about DCOM as well.

The thing that makes DCOM different is that it also acts as a network protocol; it defines a set of rules that allows a client and server to talk with each other. Normally COM objects talk with each other through local memory. DCOM extends that over network cabling. Instead of talking through local memory at high speed, the connection may be through a modem or ISDN line. DCOM is the world view of COM.

There are a few hurdles that Microsoft had to jump to make DCOM work properly. First of all, you can always depend on being able to talk with other areas of memory in your computer—that is, unless it's frozen (and then you have other things to worry about). DCOM has to work reliably over a network connection that may not be there five minutes from now. That means Microsoft had to develop some methods for ensuring an object could recover gracefully from a loss of communication.

Another problem is time. Communication takes place almost instantaneously on your computer. One object can talk to the other and you hardly notice the time it takes at all. Objects that talk over a network connection could take a noticeable amount of time to complete their conversation. What Microsoft has done to make this feasible is to allow the conversation to occur asynchronously. In other words, you can continue to work with your machine while the object-to-object conversation takes place in the background. Does this mean you won't notice the delay at all? No, if you're waiting for something to print, the conversation over network cabling will still be noticeable. All that asynchronous communication means is that you can do something else while you wait.

There's another element that you need to make DCOM work. How does another machine know what objects are installed on your machine right now? It can't know unless you publish that information in some way. That's just what the DCOM change does; it allows Windows 95 to publish a list of objects on your machine. This open Registry approach allows other machines to find objects on your machine and use them as needed.

What are the potential pitfalls of DCOM? Well, there are two big ones, although other problems may appear in the future. The first is security. It's important to keep your machine secure even if other people are allowed to use the objects that you've installed. The programmer who creates a DCOM object for your machine has to provide some type of security features. Unfortunately, there aren't any standard ways of doing that right now, making some people leery of placing DCOM objects on machines where security is a major concern (such as servers).

The other potential problem is network traffic. Remember that all those messages have to travel across the network cabling. If DCOM uses the same kind of communication as COM objects do, then the network could get very busy indeed. Fortunately, Microsoft has provided some tools to make it possible to combine several requests into one and reduce network traffic as a result. Of course, the programmer designing your DCOM object has to actually use the features that Microsoft provides. Because the requirement to combine several calls into one isn't enforced in any way, some network administrators are afraid that DCOM objects could bring a network to its knees. I hope that some standards will ensure that programmers will make DCOM objects as efficient as possible.

On Your Own

Test the OLE capabilities of the various applications on your machine. Which ones support OLE as a client? Which ones support it as a server? Do you see any difference between the applications that support OLE 1 and OLE 2?

Use the various techniques that I covered in this chapter for inserting an object into a container. Which methods do you find easiest to use? Why do you think that some applications support one technique and others another technique?

Make an OLE link in a large document using an OLE 1 application. Make the same link using an OLE 2 application such as WordPad. Do you see a difference in the load time of the two documents? What additional features does WordPad provide that the OLE 1 application doesn't?

Open a copy of Explorer and use it to search your SYSTEM folder. Can you find all the OLE-specific files installed on your system? What does the name of each of the various files tell you about that file's purpose?

Use an ActiveX-capable Internet browser to find one or more ActiveX-enabled Web sites. Microsoft provides a gallery that you can use for ideas at http://www.microsoft.com/gallery/. If you can't find one immediately, try the NCompass Labs ActiveX Showcase at http://www.ncompasslabs.com/framed/product.htm. It contains examples of the most common ActiveX technologies. Another good place to look is Stroud's CWSApps List—Windows 95/NT Apps—ActiveX Controls at http://cws.internet.com. This site features vendors that write ActiveX controls. Be sure to take the time to interact with the site and see how these technologies work. Think of ways that your company could use ActiveX to improve its Web site (if your company has a Web site).

13

Exploiting Your Software: DOS, 16-Bit, and 32-Bit Windows Applications

Peter Norton®

This chapter is about optimizing your software to make it run as efficiently as possible on your computer. That means making the software do the following:

- Produce results faster and easier. Your software should help you work faster and more accurately. Many programs include templates and wizards to make it faster to produce the first copy of a document, in addition to variations of that document later.

- Produce output that requires the least amount of system resources. Ideally, software should use a minimum of system resources such as memory and hard disk space. As shown in Chapter 12, "DDE, OLE, DCOM, and ActiveX," there are a number of ways to embed or link an object into your document. Other chapters in this book show various aspects of other forms of optimization.

- Produce the best results possible. The bottom line is the results you get from your software. It doesn't matter if your software is the best, fastest, or most expensive if it doesn't get the job done. Remember, software must accomplish only the tasks that you want done regardless of any awards, features, or positive reviews competing programs might get. If you aren't getting the result you want, you're using the wrong software.

Tip: Optimizing your software means optimizing your computer and operating system, too. Optimizing your software doesn't make sense if you don't spend time optimizing Windows 95 as described in Chapter 5, "Performance Primer."

Using the Add/Remove Programs Utility

To help you quickly install and uninstall software, Windows 95 includes a special Add/Remove Programs utility so you can add or delete your Windows 95 applications with ease.

Note: The Windows 95 Install/Uninstall capability doesn't extend to non–Windows 95 products. This includes both Windows 3.x and older Windows NT products. When you buy software, look for a logo or note on the package that says, "Designed for Windows 95 or Windows NT." Any software with this logo was designed to install and uninstall cleanly with the Add/Remove Program utility.

What's involved in removing an application? Every uninstall program must take into consideration the following items:

- Application directory: Removing an application and its directory isn't a problem; the problem is the application's data. Some uninstall programs leave it in place so that you can recover it later; others simply remove the entire directory and wipe out the data it contains. I prefer the first approach because it keeps me from shooting myself in the foot.

- Windows directory: Some applications place an INI file in the Windows directory so that they can find it easily. Some applications place two or more files there. Unfortunately, some uninstall programs don't take these files into account, so you need to delete them manually.

- Windows system-file modification: Windows 95 has some of the same problems that previous versions of Windows did when it comes to spurious entries in WIN.INI and SYSTEM.INI. Even though Windows provides only compatibility support for these files, it reads them when you boot. Suffice it to say that some of the same problems you had in the past will still crop up when you install 16-bit applications.

- Windows Registry: To keep track of all the applications stored on your hard disk, Windows 95 stores information about each program in a special database called the Registry. When you uninstall an application, the uninstall program should also remove the application's listing in the Registry.

- SYSTEM directory: Your SYSTEM directory contains a ton of files, and there's no way of knowing which ones belong to your application. Even if an uninstall program tracks these files, it has no way of knowing how many applications use a particular file. For example, multiple programs might share the same VBRUN300.DLL file. When you install another application that requires that same file, the second application might not add the file because it sees that the file is already present. If the uninstall program removes VBRUN300.DLL along with all the other files for the first application, the second application also ceases to work.

Tip: Chapter 10, "The Windows 95 File System," contains a procedure for viewing the contents of DLLs and other system files. You can use this procedure to view the files that you suspect an application uses and to decide whether to delete them. An alternative is to download the QFEcheck.EXE file from the Microsoft Web site. This program can help you keep track of your system files. Making a list of the DL_ and DLL files on the distribution disk is also very helpful. Compare this list to the contents of the SYSTEM directory to get clues on what you can remove. Be careful, however, not to remove any "common" files that your SYSTEM directory might contain.

- Common application directories: Many applications reduce the number of files on your hard drive by placing files that more than one application could use in a separate directory. The positive side of such directories is that they do reduce the load on your hard drive. The negative aspect is you really don't know which files to remove if you use multiple products from the same vendor and you want to remove only one product.

Removing a Windows application from your machine isn't easy because Windows applications can spread files all over the place and make entries in system files that you might need even if you remove the application. (Multiple applications might need the same entry to run.) As a result, it's not too surprising that older Windows uninstall programs normally do a partial rather than a complete job of removing old programs from your system. Fortunately, a Windows 95 application gives the operating system more information about what it installs in the form of Registry entries. That's why you can uninstall only Windows 95–specific applications with the Install/Uninstall feature.

> **Tip:** Windows won't let you remove a file that's in use. Even if you close an application, Windows might not unload all its associated DLLs right away. Whenever you want to remove an application from your drive, shut down everything, reboot, and perform the uninstall routine with all applications closed. This ensures that the uninstall program can actually remove all the files it identifies as part of the application.

Adding an Application

The following paragraphs tell you how to use the Install/Uninstall program. If you want to speed up the process and skip to step 6, double-click the SETUP.EXE on the floppy or CD-ROM that comes with the application you're installing.

1. Open the Control Panel by using the Start menu or Explorer.

2. Double-click Add/Remove Programs. You should see a dialog box like the one shown in Figure 13.1.

Figure 13.1.
The Install/Uninstall page of the Add/Remove Programs Properties dialog lets you install/uninstall Windows 95–specific programs.

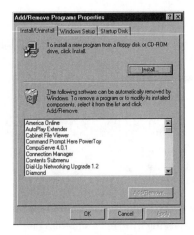

3. Click Install. You see an Install Program from Floppy Disk or CD-ROM dialog box. Notice that this dialog box tells you to place a floppy in one of the floppy drives or a CD-ROM in the CD-ROM drive.

4. Click Next. The Install wizard searches drives A and B and the CD-ROM drive for SETUP.EXE. If you're installing a program from the hard drive, or if the setup program uses a different name, the wizard won't find it. You need to enter the value or use the Browse dialog box.

5. If the Install wizard finds a setup program, it enters the name here for you. If not, you see a dialog box like the one shown in Figure 13.2. Type the name of the application you want to install or use the Browse dialog box to find it. To use the Browse dialog box, simply click the Browse button.

Figure 13.2.
The Run Installation Program dialog box is the last time you see the Install wizard.

6. As soon as you complete step 5, Windows 95 launches the setup application. Follow the vendor instructions for installing it. You don't come back to the Install wizard when you get done. However, you might want to open the Add/Remove Programs Properties dialog box again to make sure that the application name appears in the list of products you can remove. If the application name does not appear, then the application most likely hasn't been fully tested under Windows 95 or Windows NT. (If you install a compliant application by running its setup program from outside this dialog box, it still makes the Registry changes needed to appear in this Add/Remove list.)

Removing an Application

Uninstalling an application is as easy as installing it using the Install wizard. The following procedure shows you the steps you'll follow in most cases. Remember that you may also have the option of using the application's uninstall utility to get this done:

1. Open the Control Panel by using the Start menu or Explorer.

2. Double-click Add/Remove Programs. You should see a dialog box like the one shown earlier in Figure 13.1.

3. Select the application you want to uninstall and click Add/Remove. A warning box may appear to tell you that you are about to uninstall the application.

4. Click Yes one last time. Windows 95 attempts to remove all the application components. If successful, it displays a success message. Otherwise, it displays an error message with the components that you need to uninstall manually. You can use the contents of this dialog box to complete the uninstall process.

5. Click OK to exit the Install wizard.

Optimizing Windows Applications

Once you get a new application installed, you might want to optimize it for the application's speed and memory requirements.

Installation Options

The decisions you make when installing an application can affect the way the application performs. The following list should help you make some of the hard decisions that come up during installation:

- Hard disk space: If hard disk space is at a premium, you might need to limit the number of installation features you provide. For example, many applications come with a tutorial or sample files. If you don't need these files, don't install them and you can save your hard disk for more important files.

- Uninstall capability: Many applications now provide a partial install capability. That way you can choose only those features you absolutely need.

- Memory: Many applications might ask what types of filters and other "utility" elements you want to install. It might seem like a good idea to select them all because you might need them sometime. From a memory standpoint, this decision can be fatal. Some applications load all those fancy utilities and filters whenever you start the application. Each filter and other add-on may cost you memory that you could use for some other purpose.

- Interapplication communication: If you install a suite of products (such as Microsoft Office) instead of separate applications, there's a much better chance that they'll communicate seamlessly. Unless there's a good reason to install applications from different publishers, you probably want to go with a "one-stop shop" solution to fulfill the better part of your application needs.

- Other support options: Some applications provide features that don't relate directly to how that product works, but how it reacts in a given situation. I just installed a new utility that gives me a thumbnail-sketch view of several files on my system. One of the installation options was to add that utility to my Startup folder. I had the memory required, so I said yes. It seems like a straightforward decision, but you still need to make it. Some of the other decisions aren't quite so straightforward. For example, one application provided the capability to track my OLE links across the network. To do this, it had to load a rather large piece of code and allow it to remain resident. Because I seldom even think about using such a capability, I didn't install it. Another example is the ability to run the program from the CD, which makes the program run slower, but keeps your hard disk from getting loaded with too many programs.

The tips that I just mentioned will help you decide what to expect when installing software, but there are other problems to consider. For example, how do you balance workgroup and individual needs? For some products, such as Lotus Notes, this is a major concern. When working with workgroup-specific applications, you probably need to consider some additional problems:

- Installation location: Deciding where to put a workgroup application is a major decision. Placing all the installation files on the network makes it easier for the administrator to manage, reduces the chance that someone will pirate the application, and reduces overall application size because not every workstation needs a copy of the common files, such as DLLs. The negative aspects of using a server installation include handling a lot more network traffic as the application requests DLLs and other support files from the server. In many cases, users don't get as many configuration options as they do using a workstation installation.

- Local support for network features: Many network products secretly invade the user's system and steal workstation statistics on a regular basis. However, unless you're the sole administrator for a large network, you have to weigh the importance of such a feature against the memory it takes from each workstation.

Getting Application Settings Right

Few applications use the same settings. Similar applications (such as word processors) might share a few of the same settings, but here are some general principles for customizing your applications. Changing your settings is largely a matter of personal preference. However, even a small change can make a big difference in the way you use an application. For example, you can do something as small as customize a toolbar and reap a fairly large increase in efficiency. Not using an application's autocorrect feature might allow you to run background tasks more efficiently. It's not the major changes you'll notice the most, but the little extras that you add to your computing environment. The following tips can help you get the most out of your applications:

- Toolbars: A toolbar represents one way that you can greatly increase your efficiency for a small increase in memory usage. Remember, every icon you allocate uses some additional system resources, but the amount of memory an icon uses is very small—usually less than 1KB. When setting up my toolbar, I don't assume that the vendor provided anything close to optimal, so I track which commands I use the most. I keep the commands I use a lot on the toolbar because it takes less time to access a command from the toolbar than from a menu. Seven icons should appear on every toolbar: Open, Close, New, Print, Cut, Copy, and Paste. Be certain to remove any standard toolbar buttons that you don't use to save memory.

- Printer settings: Most applications allow me to set the printer configuration separately from the Windows general configuration. I usually set my printer configuration to match my use of that application. For example, I use my word processor for final output, in most cases, so I use the best letter-quality resolution available. On the other hand, I never use my graphics programs for final output, so I select draft quality there. A draft printout might not seem very acceptable, but it's a lot more efficient than letter quality when you just want a quick look at your document. (A minor benefit of using draft output whenever possible is that you use less toner, making those expensive toner cartridges last longer.) You can also vary the print resolution. A low-resolution letter-quality printout might work fine for workgroup presentations, but you'll want to use the highest available quality when making the same presentation to a larger audience. The resolution you use affects the amount of memory and time required to complete the printout.

- Macros: A macro lets you replay the keystrokes you normally make by hand by recording them in a separate area of memory. I almost always create macros for every repetitive task I perform with my main applications. For example, I always set up my word processing files using a macro. It makes more sense for the computer to do the work than for me to do it. In fact, I use this macro so often that I attached it to my toolbar as an icon. Other tasks don't work well as macros. For example, I always thought that changing the format of a document from one form to another would make a great macro, but implementing it proved frustrating. Sometimes it takes a human mind to perform some tasks.

- Style sheets and templates: One thing you can never have too many of are custom style sheets and templates. I always use a style sheet or template for my documents if the application supports them. The reason is simple: Style sheets and templates don't take more than a few minutes to create, but they can save a lot of time later. Templates and style sheets also provide one other benefit: They tend to enforce uniformity in the format of your document. This is important whether you're part of a group or working as an individual. I view consistent output as one of the marks of a professional, and most other people do, too.

- Autocorrect: The autocorrect features provided by many applications are a source of much consternation for me. On the one hand, they provide a valuable aid—automatically correcting misspelled words I might type. The problem is that the autocorrect feature can chew up valuable memory and processor cycles—resources that you could use to run a task in the background. I normally turn off my autocorrect features and rely on my spelling checker (or other tools) to find all those mistakes at one time.

Tip: There's another way to use autocorrect. You can use it to substitute short phrases for long ones. For example, suppose you have to type your company name a lot—Jackson Consolidated Freight Company. You can add an acronym such as JCFC to your autocorrect dictionary. Then, every time you need to type your company name, you type JCFC, and your application substitutes the long name in its place.

- Autoload: This goes back to those utility and filter programs mentioned earlier, in the "Installation Options" section. Some programs, such as Microsoft Access and Lotus 1-2-3, let you autoload some of your utilities or filters so you can access them faster. There's a tradeoff for the convenience of instant access. You have to give up some memory and perhaps a few processor cycles to do it.

Peter's Principle: My Settings Won't Work on Your Machine

We're all individuals. Nowhere is this more apparent than in the way we use software. I might think that the way you do something is absurd, but if it works for you, it's probably the right way to go (at least until you learn otherwise).

For example, I usually include the Insert Annotation command for Word for Windows on my toolbar because I use this feature a lot. I suggested the same thing to a colleague and he found it a waste of time because he used a different technique for making annotations.

For another example, I usually use three different user dictionaries: common, computer, and jargon. This allows me to keep some words separate so that they don't contaminate my general-purpose dictionary. In a workgroup situation, you might find that everyone needs to use the same dictionary to ensure consistent results for a project. A group project usually requires the individual to defer to the group's needs to enforce a certain level of consistency.

The point is that you need to work with an application long enough to build a rapport with it. Once you figure out how you want to work with the application, you can start changing some of those personal settings to meet your specific requirements. In fact, you might find that some of your settings end up working for the group as well. Experimentation is a prime ingredient in finding the settings that work best for you.

Setting up an application is a continual process. However, don't give up too much personal comfort for a perceived memory or speed benefit. You have to weigh the time that a specific feature saves against what it costs.

Tip: Everyone's first inclination is to get into the application and complete this part of the setup immediately. That is probably the worst mistake you could make. Software settings change as you learn how to use the application more efficiently. A little change here and there can make a big difference in how well the application works for you. Take the time required to go through the tutorial first, and then make any settings changes you think will help. I usually keep Notepad handy to record any ideas I come up with while running the tutorial.

Running 16-Bit Windows Applications

16-bit applications have special problems because all 16-bit applications share one address space. This means they have to share the system resources required to display windows, icons, and graphic elements of all sorts. A 16-bit application also faces other problems, such as cooperative multitasking. That particular problem only gets worse under Windows 95 because 32-bit applications run in their own session.

Tip: Some older Windows applications display an invalid dynalink call error message when you try to run them. This means that they're incompatible with a new Windows 95 version of a DLL. You have two choices. Upgrading the application is the best alternative because you replace that old product with something that will work better with Windows 95. If upgrading isn't an option, reinstall the application, reboot Windows 95, and try it again. You have to reboot to reload the DLL into memory. If you still get an invalid dynalink call message, there's some incompatibility between the application and a basic Windows 95 system file. You must upgrade in this case because you can't replace those common files to meet the needs of one program. Some Windows 95 applications might cease to function if you do (including the operating system itself). Windows 95 always maintains a copy of its system files in the SYSBCKUP folder under the main Windows folder. You can use this copy of the file to replace the old DLL if necessary.

The same types of optimization techniques you used under Windows 3.x will probably work here as well. You still need to keep in mind the cooperative multitasking aspect of 16-bit applications when running certain types of applications in the background. For example, you'll probably find it difficult to run your 16-bit database and your communications program at the same time at high speed. The cooperative nature of these applications means that the database will probably take control of the system for that one second longer than the communications program can hold data in the buffer. The result is lost data. Windows 95 is a lot better in this regard than Window 3.x was, but it still isn't perfect because the applications it runs aren't perfect.

Chapter 5 looks at many ways in which you can tune the Windows environment, by getting rid of excess icons and the like. These same tips apply to applications, for the most part. Be sure to spend some time reviewing that chapter for some additional hints.

> **Tip:** Some 16-bit applications give you a choice between storing DLL files locally or in the Windows SYSTEM directory. Choose the local option to make it easier to remove the application later. This also reduces the chance that the application's setup routine will accidentally overwrite a Windows 95 version of a file.

One Windows 3.x optimization technique you should ignore when using Windows 95 is the use of virtual memory. Virtual memory means using your hard disk to temporarily store information, thereby fooling your computer into thinking it has more memory than it really does. If your system contained enough memory under Windows 3.x, you could get a performance boost by disabling virtual memory. Of course, this meant that you were effectively limited in the amount of system memory you could expect, but the performance gain was worth it. Don't disable virtual memory under Windows 95 because it will likely slow down your computer.

Using the Print Manager was something else that a lot of people avoided when they needed to get their output fast. Windows 95 uses a much-improved form of Print Manager that you'll want to use for optimum performance. I'll stop short of saying that the output arrives at the same speed, however. If you have a heavy system load when you start the print job, you definitely see a decrease in print speed. However, you gain increased system performance and regain control of your application faster as a result. It's another tradeoff, but I think it's a good one in this case.

Running 32-Bit Windows Applications

32-bit applications are more efficient than their equivalent 16-bit counterparts because they can accomplish more tasks in the same amount of time. More importantly, 32-bit applications support true multitasking, which lets you run multiple tasks at the same time, such as repaginating a document while you're still editing it.

Multitasking also helps you to perform some tasks, such as printing, a lot faster than 16-bit applications. For one thing, Windows can make better use of idle time with a 32-bit application. However, this isn't the big feature that users notice. You'll notice that you regain control of the system faster. After a 32-bit application spawns a print task, it can return control of the computer immediately without checking on the status of the "background" print job, as a 16-bit application does.

The big performance-tuning tip for Windows 95 and 32-bit applications is to use as many automatic settings as possible. The more room you give Windows 95 to compensate for changing system conditions, the better. Chapter 5 contains quite a few tips that you can follow to optimize the environment. For example, it looks at the need to monitor the swap file size to ensure that you don't end up wasting processor cycles in thrashing. Once you optimize the environment for a 32-bit application, you've essentially optimized the application itself. All you need to do is check out the earlier section called "Getting Application Settings Right" to make the application as efficient as possible during use.

Optimizing DOS Applications

More people are using Windows 95, but many people still use Windows 3.*x* or MS-DOS. Few companies still make MS-DOS applications except in the game market. Game publishers like MS-DOS because they have access to more of the hardware to write a fast and visually stimulating program.

Game vendors are starting to produce more Windows 95 games that use DirectX technology for displaying speedy graphics. Just check with your video and audio card vendor to make sure you have the latest drivers from them; some vendors are coming out with DirectX-specific drivers. If for some reason your copy of Windows 95 doesn't have DirectX, you can download the current version of DirectX at http://www.microsoft.com/directx/default.asp. Make absolutely certain that you have a complete copy of your current video drivers. Some users have complained of severe compatibility problems when using DirectX with certain display adapters. You'll want a copy of your current drivers just in case you need to remove DirectX from your machine.

Custom applications are another area where people are still using DOS. This time it's for a different reason. A custom application can cost thousands of dollars. The consultant who writes the program has to charge that much because the chances of his selling more than a few hundred copies are slim. Because custom applications usually manipulate sensitive company data that's hard to move to another application, people are going to think twice before attempting to move that data somewhere else. Fortunately, I see this particular class of DOS application coming to an end as Windows tools become easier and faster to use. A consultant can be a lot more productive, so the cost is less for creating a new application, in some cases.

Also, old habits die hard. Some people are accustomed to using DOS utility programs, so that's what they'll continue to use. There are good substitutes for these applications in most cases—substitutes that are easier to use and that run faster—but some people just won't use them. This is the third group of people who make at least some use of DOS under Windows 95.

The following sections explore a variety of DOS options. In most cases, I show you the best methods first and later add a few marginal methods you can use in a pinch. Of course, my advice is to move to a 32-bit Windows application as soon as possible. DOS isn't dead yet, but eventually future versions of Windows (such as Windows NT) won't support MS-DOS applications, which means you have to stop using your old DOS applications eventually.

MS-DOS Emulation

You use MS-DOS under Windows 95 through MS-DOS emulation mode. What actually happens is that Windows makes a copy of the phantom DOS session stored in memory, spawns a new VM session, and places the copy it made in the new session. What you see is either a windowed or full-screen MS-DOS session. All you need to do to open a DOS session is select MS-DOS Prompt from the Start | Programs menu option. You also start an MS-DOS session whenever you select an MS-DOS application from either Explorer or the Start menu.

Windows 95 makes the MS-DOS window easy to use and configure. All the controls you need immediately are displayed as part of a toolbar on the window. There are also many hidden configuration options, which I discuss later. Here's the list of controls:

- Font Size: This list box allows you to choose the size of the font used to display information in the MS-DOS window by defining the number of horizontal and vertical pixels used for each character. You need to find a balance between readability and the capability to view the entire screen at once. An MS-DOS window normally defaults to the Auto setting. What this means is that Windows 95 attempts to find the proper font size based on the number of lines of text in the MS-DOS box and the resolution of your display.

- Mark: Use this control to select an area of the screen for copying. Windows 95 places the selected area on the clipboard when you select the Copy command so that you can use the selection in other applications. The selected area is highlighted, as shown in Figure 13.3. You can use either the cursor keys or the mouse to select the desired area.

Figure 13.3.
You can use the Mark button to copy part of the DOS screen to the Windows clipboard.

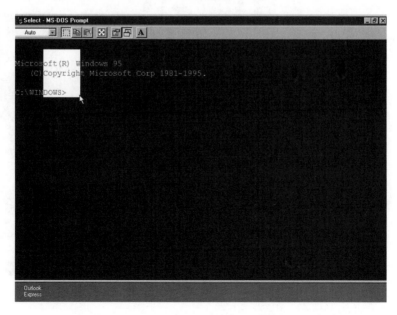

- Copy: The Copy button places in the clipboard the area you highlighted by using the Mark button.

- Paste: You can also paste information from a Windows application into the DOS box. Obviously, you can't paste anything other than text unless the display is in graphics mode. Even then, your ability might be limited by the MS-DOS application running at the time.

- Full screen: Clicking this button changes the windowed DOS prompt into a full-screen version.

- Properties: Every MS-DOS application has a number of properties that you can set (discussed later in this chapter). Clicking this button displays the Properties dialog box for the current application.

- Background: Click this button to run the current MS-DOS application in the background. This comes in handy when you want to monitor the application but don't really need to interact with it.

- Font: This button performs about the same task as the Font Size list box mentioned earlier. However, instead of merely displaying a list of font sizes, it displays the Font page of the program's Properties dialog box.

You'll see that MS-DOS doesn't really provide anything more than you had in the past. One feature that it does provide is long filename support. Use the DIR command if you want to see what I mean. Figure 13.4 shows the results of using it to display all the BMP files in the \WINDOWS directory.

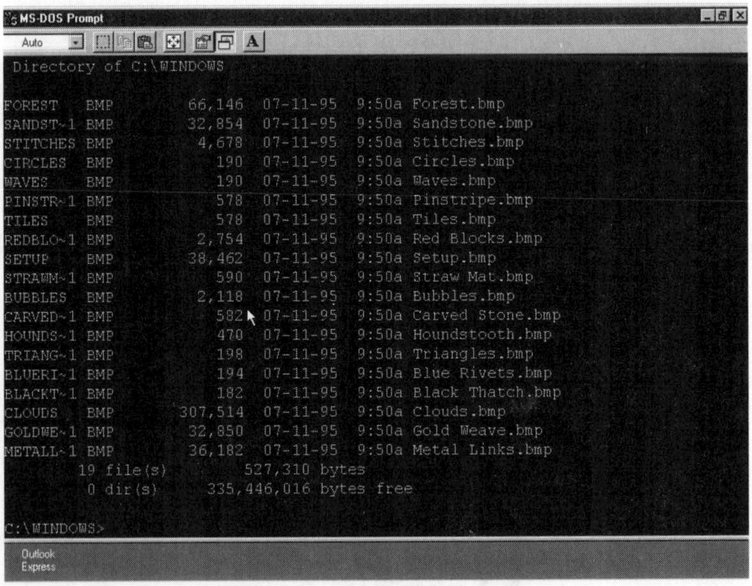

Figure 13.4.
DOS reacts differently when you use the DIR command under Windows 95.

Note: Long filename support is available only under Windows 95. Once you leave that environment to work in MS-DOS mode, the DIR command operates exactly as it did before. The MS-DOS mode of operation is also known as raw DOS mode. None of the Windows 95 drivers is loaded when you use this mode, including long filename support. Obviously, you must be careful about corrupting your long filenames when in this mode.

Tip: You can also use long filenames when typing commands. The only requirement is that you use quotes to enclose the long filename or directory, if the filename includes spaces such as DIR "Some Long Directory Name".

In addition to long filename support, there are a few new utility programs and changes to some old utilities. For example, you no longer need to run a copy of QBasic to use Edit. The next section covers the specific changes in MS-DOS utility support.

DOS Versus Windows 95 Commands

Microsoft must have expected people to use the MS-DOS prompt, or it wouldn't have improved some of the utilities that come with Windows 95. I really don't have room here to explore all the MS-DOS commands, so I'm going to give you the highlights. The following list shows the changes that MS-DOS (running under Windows 95) provides:

- All the disk-scanning utilities from previous versions of MS-DOS are upgraded to support long filenames and FAT32. Windows 95 also replaces many of these files with batch file substitutes, in case you decide to maintain a dual-boot capability. The renamed files include DBLSPACE.BAT, DRVSPACE.BAT, DEFRAG.BAT, and SCANDISK.BAT.

- EDIT is a standalone command now. It also provides the means for editing more than one file and larger files than before.

- Some applications, such as ScanDisk, start the Windows version of the program even when executed at the DOS prompt.

Along with the new features that the Windows 95 version of MS-DOS provides are a few features that you won't find. The Windows 95 version of MS-DOS doesn't include any of the following commands:

APPEND	INTERLINK	RAMDRIVE.SYS
ASSIGN	INTERSVR	RECOVER
BACKUP	JOIN	REPLACE
COMP	MEMCARD	RESTORE
DOSSHELL	MEMMAKER	ROMDRIVE.SYS

EDLIN	MIRROR	SHARE
EGA.SYS	MSAV	SMARTMON
FASTHELP	MSBACKUP	TREE
FASTOPEN	POWER	UNDELETE
GRAFTABL	PRINT	UNFORMAT
GRAPHICS	PRINTER.SYS	VSAFE
HELP	QBASIC	

Warning: Users who have Windows 95 installed on their machines can't use any of these old utility programs. Doing so causes problems with any long filenames on the drive. You also risk problems with a FAT32-formatted drive. As a minimum, you'll lose a few files—but you could lose everything on your drive. Use only Windows 95–specific utilities.

Creating a DOS Session

You can create an MS-DOS session by using a variety of methods. Double-clicking an MS-DOS application from Explorer creates an MS-DOS session. The session ends as soon as you end the application.

Like previous versions of Windows, Windows 95 includes an MS-DOS prompt. All you need to do is click the MS-DOS Prompt option found in the Programs section of the Start menu. You need to type **exit** and press Enter to end this session.

Another way to start an MS-DOS session is to select the Restart the Computer in MS-DOS Mode entry of the Shutdown dialog box. This takes you to a full-screen raw MS-DOS session. You can perform any required tasks and then type **exit** and press Enter to leave. Windows 95 automatically reloads itself.

DOS Objects

As with any other object under Windows 95, right-clicking an MS-DOS object displays a context menu. You can cut, copy, and paste a DOS object as you do any other object that Windows 95 supports. The Properties option takes you to the Properties dialog box, described in the next section. This is one major area where MS-DOS applications are treated differently from Windows applications.

Settings

An MS-DOS application's Properties dialog box contains a lot more than the same dialog box for a Windows application. In fact, in case you are looking for the PIF (program information file) Editor, here it is. The Properties dialog box shown in Figure 13.5 allows you to change every setting that the PIF Editor provided—and more. In fact, Windows 95 provides several new features for MS-DOS applications that make running them a snap. The following paragraphs describe each section of the Properties dialog box in detail.

Figure 13.5.
The Properties dialog box replaces the old PIF Editor that you used under Windows 3.x.

Program

The Program page allows you to change the way Windows executes the program. At the top of the page are an icon and a field containing the application's name. This is the name you see within Explorer.

The next three fields determine which application to run. The Cmd Line field contains the name of the application you want to run. It must end with an .EXE, .COM, or .BAT extension. In this case, I'm running a copy of the command processor. The Working field tells Windows 95 what directory to start the application from. In most cases, you start the application from either its home or its data directory. The choice depends on what kind of information the application requires to start. I run the command processor from the \WINDOWS directory. The third field, Batch File, allows you to designate a batch file that runs with the application. For example, you can include a batch file that sets up the path and prompts and loads any TSRs you might need when starting the command processor.

The Shortcut Key field allows you to assign a shortcut key to the program. Use the Run field to determine how Windows 95 runs the application. There are three choices: Normal Window, Minimized, and Maximized. The first two choices affect both windowed and full-screen sessions. The third choice starts windowed sessions maximized.

It's normally a good idea to close the MS-DOS session as soon as you get done. Checking the Close on Exit field does just that.

Clicking the Change Icon button displays the Change Icon dialog. It allows you to select the icon used to identify the application within Explorer and the Start menu. Windows 95 provides the same default choices as other versions of Windows. You can also choose from custom icon sets by clicking the Browse button.

MS-DOS Mode

There's one more button left on the Program page, and I wanted to give it special attention. If you click the Advanced button, you see the dialog box shown in Figure 13.6.

Figure 13.6.
The Advanced Program Settings dialog box is where you make the selections that enable MS-DOS mode for an application.

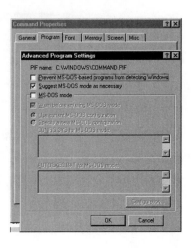

The first three check boxes control the actual implementation of MS-DOS mode. Some applications run fine under Windows 3.*x* but quit if they see Windows 95. Checking the first check box prevents an application from detecting Windows 95. The problem with using this particular feature is that the application has less conventional memory and runs more slowly as Windows works to keep itself hidden.

The second check box in this group keeps a detection program running with the MS-DOS application. You can use this as a diagnostic aid when the application won't run properly under Windows 95. However, keeping this box checked after you're reasonably sure that the application doesn't require MS-DOS mode just wastes processor cycles and memory. Unfortunately, Windows 95 automatically defaults to checking this box. This means that you must remember to uncheck it to gain optimum performance from your application.

The MS-DOS Mode check box is third in this dialog box. Checking it means that the application won't run under Windows 95. It also changes the opt Üs you have available by allowing you to add custom `CONFIG.SYS` and `AUTOEXEC.BAT` settings. If you double-click an application to start it, Windows 95 shuts down all running applications, shuts itself down and unloads from memory, and executes the application. You use this option as a last-ditch effort to get an application to run under Windows 95. Unfortunately, many game programs fall into this category.

I recommend that you always have Windows 95 warn you about entering MS-DOS mode by checking the first new check box in this dialog box, Warn Before Entering MS-DOS Mode. This action prevents you from entering the mode accidentally. It can prevent data loss in some rare cases, where an application doesn't react properly to the Windows shutdown message.

Windows 95 usually provides default CONFIG.SYS and AUTOEXEC.BAT files for your application. I recommend against using them for one very good reason: The whole purpose of MS-DOS mode is to get your application to run. Using a set of configuration files specifically designed for MS-DOS mode is a good first step in ensuring that you get the application to run and run efficiently. I usually check the second radio button to enable the configuration entries, as shown in Figure 13.7.

Figure 13.7.

Always use custom configuration files if your application requires MS-DOS mode to run.

There are a number of ways to create a configuration for your application. You can even use the automated configuration method that Microsoft provides, by clicking the Configuration button. However, I usually copy the appropriate sections of the CONFIG.DOS and AUTOEXEC.DOS files to these screens. (You can perform the paste by using Ctrl+V; Microsoft didn't add a Paste button to this dialog box.) These files contain the old configuration that ran the application. I usually modify the entries as appropriate for this particular situation, but you don't need to do too much tuning.

As you can see, setting up an application for MS-DOS mode doesn't have to be difficult. It's inconvenient, however, because you can't run any other applications while an MS-DOS-mode application runs. Your hard drive (and associated long filenames) are also susceptible to damage from an MS-DOS–mode application. Make certain that the application is relatively well behaved in regard to writing to disk before you trust it with your setup.

Font

The Font page allows you to change the appearance of the fonts used to display data in a windowed MS-DOS application. These settings don't affect a full-screen session. This dialog box contains four main sections. The first section controls the type of fonts you get to see in the Font Size list box. You'll normally want to use the fullest set of fonts available, by selecting Both Font Types. The only time you might want to switch to one font type or another is when your display has problems displaying one type of font.

The Font Size list box in the second section contains a list of the font sizes you have available for the DOS window. The numbers represent the number of pixels used for each character. A higher number of pixels make the display more readable. A smaller number of pixels make the window smaller.

The Window Preview section of this dialog box shows how big the window will appear on the display. The Font Preview section shows the size of the print. You should combine the output from these two displays to determine how large a font to use. It's important to reach a setting that balances the need to see what you're doing with the need to display the entire DOS box at once.

Memory

The Memory page, shown in Figure 13.8, is the most important page in the Properties dialog box, from a tuning perspective. Notice that there are only five list boxes and two check boxes, but the decisions you make here affect how the application runs. More importantly, they affect the way that Windows runs.

Figure 13.8.
The Memory page allows you to modify the way Windows allocates and manages memory for your DOS application.

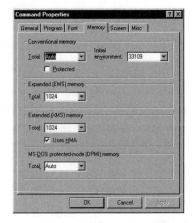

The first group of settings affects conventional memory. The Total field allows you to select any value up to 640KB. Windows normally allocates a 1024-byte environment for your MS-DOS application, which should be enough to handle most situations. However, I usually set mine to 4096 to provide space for all those environment strings required by real-mode compilers. The Protected check box is another diagnostic aid. Checking it tells Windows 95 to monitor the application for memory protection errors. The only problem is that you suffer a performance loss when using it. If your application tends to corrupt memory, then by all means check this box to keep your environment stable. Otherwise, consider leaving it unchecked for better performance.

The second group of settings contains a single list box that controls how much expanded memory Windows 95 allocates for your application. If you leave it on Auto, MEM reports expanded memory up to the amount of memory your machine has installed. Windows 95 makes only 16MB of it usable if you have more RAM than that installed. The only time you should change this setting is when the application grabs every bit of expanded memory it can find. Some older MS-DOS applications get a little greedy, so you need to provide some controls for that greed.

The third group of settings controls the amount of extended memory available to your application. The default setting allocates the full amount of RAM installed on your system. This isn't an unlimited amount of memory, but it could be fairly high—much higher than the automatic expanded memory setting. As with the expanded memory setting, I usually change this setting from Auto to some specific number if the application gets greedy or if it has problems coping with the full amount of extended memory available on my machine. I usually leave the Uses HMA check box blank, because I normally load MS-DOS in the high memory area. However, if you don't use the HMA, you can always choose to load all or part of an application there by checking this box.

The final group of settings allows you to determine the amount of DPMI memory available to applications. Windows 95 normally sets this to a value that reflects the current system conditions. There's little reason to change this setting from the default.

Screen

The Screen page, shown in Figure 13.9, allows you to configure the screen settings. The first group of settings, Usage, determines the screen mode and number of display lines. You should set the number of display lines here before you set the options on the Font page of this dialog box. Otherwise, a setting that worked well at 25 lines might not work at 50.

Figure 13.9.
The Screen page allows you to adjust the size and type of display, as well as the method that Windows uses to display it.

The second group of settings lets you change the window settings. It doesn't come into play if you use full-screen mode. I always turn on the toolbar, which allows you to modify the font size and perform many other tasks with your application without opening the Properties dialog box. The second check box tells Windows 95 to update the PIF to reflect any changes you made while using the toolbar. Normally the entries are good only for that session. I prefer that Windows remember my settings from session to session, so I check this box.

The third group of settings on this page affects your application's performance. The first setting, Fast ROM Emulation, acts as shadow RAM by allowing your application to use a RAM version of your display ROM. If an application had trouble with shadow RAM under DOS, it will also have trouble with this setting. Otherwise, you'll want to leave this option checked to get maximum performance from your application.

The second setting in the Performance group helps Windows more than it helps the application. This setting allows Windows to retrieve some of the memory that the MS-DOS application uses for graphics mode, when it goes into character mode. This modicum of memory isn't much, but it could add up if you run a lot of MS-DOS sessions. The only time you want to remove the check mark from this setting is when your application spends all or most of its time in graphics mode.

Misc

The Misc (miscellaneous) page mainly provides settings that determine how Windows interacts with your application from a functional point of view. Figure 13.10 shows the settings you find here.

Figure 13.10.
The Misc page allows you to control a variety of settings that don't fit into the other categories explored earlier.

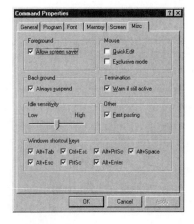

The Allow Screen Saver setting doesn't really have much of an effect when you're using windowed applications. It determines whether Windows can interrupt a full-screen session to run a screen saver. Some full-screen applications, such as graphics applications, really get confused if you allow the screen saver to operate.

The Mouse group contains two settings. The QuickEdit check box allows you to use a mouse within an MS-DOS window, just as you do with any Windows application. The Exclusive Mode check box gives a windowed application exclusive control over the mouse. This means that you can't use the mouse with your regular Windows applications as long as this application is active. It is probably a better idea to run this application in a full-screen session if it has this much trouble sharing the mouse.

Some of the settings on this page such as the Background and Idle Sensitivity controls provide subtle performance control over your application. Checking the Always Suspend check box frees resources for Windows 95 to use with other applications. If you're using an MS-DOS application for something like data entry that requires continuous input, it pays to check this box and use the resources for other applications. Idle Sensitivity also changes how Windows allocates resources. Normally, Windows tracks the amount of activity from an application to see if it is sitting there doing nothing while waiting for input from you. If so, Windows 95 reduces the application's CPU resources. This normally works fine, but sometimes Windows doesn't give the application enough resources to complete the task it's performing. If this is the case, lowering the Idle Sensitivity setting gives the application the resources it needs, at the expense of other applications running on the system at the time.

The Warn If Still Active check box in the Termination group displays a message if you terminate the DOS application window without ending the program first. Normally you want to keep this checked to prevent potential data loss from a premature application termination.

Another performance enhancement is the Fast Pasting check box. You normally keep this box checked so that Windows can use a high-speed method of pasting information into your MS-DOS application. The only time you change this is when data gets damaged during transition if you're using the fast-paste mode.

The final group on the page regulates the use of Ctrl-key combinations under Windows 95. Checking a box in the Windows Shortcut Keys group allows Windows to use that key combination. Unchecking it allows the application to use the key combination. The only time you need to change these settings is when the application needs them for some purpose and you can't change the application's settings.

Windows Scripting Host (WSH) in Windows 98

Beta Release

Windows 98 contains a new capability to write and execute scripts at a system level, which means that you no longer have to go through repetitive tasks to get the applications you need to work together. For example, you can have a script that scans your hard drive for errors, backs it up, and then optimizes it all without any work on your part (unless the script encounters an error).

Microsoft plans to ship Windows 98 with support for VBScript and JavaScript, but they hope to see other vendors add support for languages such as Perl, TCL, REXX, and Python. The level of support you could see is virtually unlimited.

There are actually two scripting engines provided with Windows 98; one operates at the command prompt (CScript.EXE) and the other in a window (WScript.EXE). The major difference between the two scripting engines is that the command-line version operates at the DOS prompt, whereas the window version operates within Windows itself.

On Your Own

Find a DLL for one of the smaller applications installed on your machine. Use the procedure described in Chapter 10 for viewing the contents of files to determine which DLLs and other system files this application needs in order to work. Once you make up the list, see whether other applications require the same files. You might be surprised by what you find. Windows 95 reuses a lot of files.

Use the procedures outlined in this chapter to create an MS-DOS-mode session for one of your ill-behaved applications. Does the application run any better in MS-DOS mode? Try this with an application that seems to work fine under Windows 95. Does the application run any faster in MS-DOS mode than under Windows 95? Can you see any difference in the way it runs?

Try some of the sample scripts in the \WINDOWS\SAMPLES\WSH folder. If you right-click on one of these scripts and then select Edit from the context menu, you can see how it uses WSH objects to accomplish a task. (Make sure you don't save any changes so that the script continues to run.)

14

Exploiting Your Hardware

Peter Norton®

Chapter 13, "Exploiting Your Software: DOS, 16-Bit, and 32-Bit Windows Applications," looked at some of the things you can do to optimize your software. This chapter provides information for optimizing your hardware.

Installing and Deleting Devices

Windows 95 normally detects all the hardware on your machine during setup and then loads the appropriate drivers. However, what happens if you install a new piece of hardware after installing Windows 95? What do you do with old devices that are no longer installed? These are the topics I cover in this section of the chapter along with troubleshooting procedures that you can follow if Windows doesn't act as expected.

Installing Hardware

Windows 95 normally conducts a check of your system during startup and installs and loads the appropriate drivers. If Windows 95 finds a new device, it performs the same kind of INF file search that it did during initial installation to detect the kind of new device. Unfortunately, this doesn't always work and you have to give Windows 95 a little help to find your new device. The following sections provide some techniques you can use to get the job done.

Automatic Installation

Now that you understand the problems, what do you do to get around them? I usually get Windows 95 to detect the device automatically, using the following procedure. Always try this method first:

1. Open Control Panel and double-click the Add New Hardware applet. You should see the Add New Hardware wizard.

2. Click Next twice.

3. Windows 95 actually begins the search for new Plug and Play hardware. Don't worry if your screen blanks during this process because Windows 95 needs to check for new display adapters as well as other hardware. When Windows 95 gets done, you might see a dialog like the one shown in Figure 14.1.

4. Click the Details button to determine whether Windows 95 successfully detected the new hardware (see Figure 14.2).

Figure 14.1.
Use this dialog box to determine whether Windows 95 detected your hardware correctly.

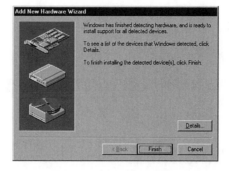

Note: The hardware-detection phase can take quite a while, especially on older machines. If disk activity stops for more than five minutes, it's a pretty safe bet that the machine is frozen. As long as you hear disk activity during this phase, you're fairly safe in assuming that hardware detection is still taking place. (The hardware detection indicator doesn't move at a steady pace. It appears to take more time as it nears the end.)

Note: If Windows 95 doesn't detect any new hardware, it displays a dialog box telling you so. You then have the opportunity to perform the manual installation that I outline next. All you need to do is click Next to start the process.

Figure 14.2.
The Add New Hardware Wizard tells you exactly what hardware it detected.

5. If Windows 95 successfully detected the new hardware, click the Finish button to complete the installation process. Windows 95 might ask you to supply some setting information if this is a non–Plug and Play device. In some cases, Windows 95 asks you to reboot after you complete this step. If it doesn't ask you to reboot, you should do so anyway to make certain that all new drivers are loaded properly.

> **Note:** If the Add New Hardware wizard didn't correctly detect your device, click Cancel. Check your hardware's settings to make sure that they don't conflict with any other devices, using the initial steps of the manual process outlined next. If the hardware settings do conflict with something else, change them to an unused setting and try the automatic installation procedure again. Otherwise, proceed with the manual installation.

Manual Installation

Windows 95 might not detect some of your hardware when using the Add New Hardware wizard's automatic-detection method. There are usually two causes for this problem. Either your hardware didn't get turned on because it needs real-mode devices to do so, or there's a device conflict that prevents Windows 95 from seeing the device.

The following procedure starts by showing you where to look for the settings that your machine is currently using. Determining this information in advance allows you to set the jumpers correctly the first time. If you're using this section to continue from an automatic installation, go to the section "Manual Installation" in Chapter 3, "Installing Windows 95: A Setup Primer." You can also proceed to Chapter 3 if you've already installed your adapter and don't need to find a set of nonconflicting IRQ and I/O settings. Otherwise, be sure to check your hardware settings before you start the manual installation.

1. Right-click the My Computer icon and select the Properties option.
2. Select the Device Manager page. You should see a dialog box similar to the one shown in Figure 14.3. (The dialog box for your machine will look slightly different from mine because your machine probably contains different equipment.) Notice that this dialog box displays a complete list of each category of equipment installed on your machine.

Figure 14.3.
The Device Manager shows you a list of all the equipment installed on your system.

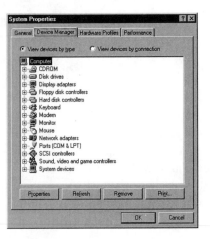

3. Select the Computer entry, as shown in Figure 14.3, and click the Properties button. Click the View Resources tab and the Interrupt Request (IRQ) radio button on that page. You should see a dialog box similar to the one shown in Figure 14.4. This is a complete list of all the interrupts that are in use on your machine. What you need to do is select an interrupt for your new device that doesn't conflict with any of these current settings. If all 16 interrupts are in use and your new device requires one, you must remove an old device before you can install the new one.

Figure 14.4.
The IRQ section of the Computer Properties dialog box shows you all the interrupts that are in use on your machine.

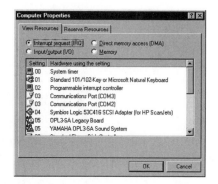

4. Click the Input/Output (I/O) radio button. You see the list of port addresses that I mentioned earlier. You need to select an unused port address range for your new card. Some adapters don't let you select a port address, which means that you might have to change the settings for another card to make this one fit. Fortunately, this is pretty rare.

5. You need to follow the same steps to find a DMA setting if your card uses one. Once you get all the required settings, close the dialog box by clicking Cancel twice. Shut down the machine and install your adapter according to manufacturer instructions. Restart Windows.

6. Proceed to the section "Manual Installation" in Chapter 3. This section tells you how to manually install a piece of hardware on your machine.

Removing Hardware

Removing hardware—at least the driver—is usually easier than installing it. In most cases, you want to remove the drivers for a device first and then remove the device. Reversing the process can prevent Windows 95 from booting properly. Fortunately, Windows 95 at least boots in Safe mode even if you leave the device in place. However, I always like to take the safest route possible when it comes to my machine's configuration. Removing the driver first is the safest route. The following procedure shows you the method for removing a driver from your machine:

1. Right-click My Computer and select the Properties option. Click the Device Manager tab. Select the device category you want to remove and click the plus sign next to it. You should see a dialog box similar to the one shown in Figure 14.5.

Figure 14.5.
*Clicking a device
category shows you a
list of installed
devices.*

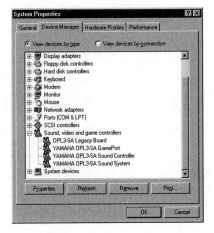

2. Click the device you want to remove. Click the Properties button and select the Drivers tab. Click the Driver File Details button (if present). You should see a list of device drivers. Make a copy of the driver list so that you can later verify that Windows 95 removed them. Otherwise, you end up with a lot of additional disk clutter after installing and removing a few devices.

Note: Some adapters contain more than one real device. For example, the Pro Audio Spectrum adapter in my machine contains a sound board, a joystick controller, and a SCSI adapter. Each device requires a separate entry in the Device Manager. To remove the device, you must find the main entry and remove it. Windows 95 automatically removes all of the supporting entries. Make sure that you record the drivers used by each entry because the main entry doesn't provide you with a master list.

3. Once you finish recording the driver names, click Cancel to clear the device Properties dialog. (You might have to click Cancel twice.)

4. With the device that you want to remove highlighted, click the Remove button. Windows 95 removes the device and all supporting entries.

5. Shut down Windows and reboot your machine to allow the changes to take effect.

Configuring Ports

Ports provide the means for the processor and other devices to communicate with the peripheral hardware on your machine. Any data that a device requires to work goes through the port. Think of the port as a mailbox and the data as the mail. If everyone had the same address, the mail carrier would cram all the mail in the same mailbox. The same idea holds true in your computer. If two devices were to use the same address, the computer would cram all the data to the same address.

A port conflict does more than just annoy the user; it can cause system instability or a malfunction of some type. Fortunately, there's an easy way to get rid of port conflicts. Windows 95 provides three port configuration methods, depending on the type of hardware you want to configure. Most hardware uses the first method, which I present in the next section. The second and third methods apply to your parallel and serial ports.

Standard Port Configuration

For communication to occur in your computer, there must be some way to exchange information. In the PC, the physical part of the communication path is called an I/O (input/output) port. If you want to send data from one area of the machine to another, your application must first tell the computer what I/O port (or address) to send it to. I discussed part of this process earlier in this chapter when I examined hardware installation. The Computer Properties dialog box tells you the address of every port on your machine. The following procedure takes you through the process of changing an I/O port on your machine:

1. Right-click My Computer, click the Properties option, and click the Device Manager tab.
2. Select one of the device classes—such as Sound, Video, and Game Controllers—and click the plus sign to display the list of devices it contains.
3. Select one of the devices and click the Properties button. Click the Resources tab. You should see a dialog box similar to the one shown in Figure 14.6. Notice that this dialog box has a Use automatic settings check box. Letting Windows 95 manage the settings for your equipment is always a good idea.
4. Uncheck the Use automatic settings check box. This should enable the Change Setting button and the Setting based on list box.
5. Click the Setting based on list box. You see a list of basic configurations.
6. Try each setting in turn to see whether one of the other settings allows you to resolve the port conflict. Windows 95 alerts you to any conflicts with registered devices, as shown in Figure 14.7. Notice that the error message tells you exactly which device you're conflicting with. This allows you to change that device's settings, if necessary, to resolve the conflict. Obviously, you want to keep the number of changes to an absolute minimum. The more you change the Windows 95 setup, the greater your chances of introducing unforeseen conflicts.

Figure 14.6.
The Resources tab of the Device Properties dialog box makes it easy to see what settings each peripheral uses.

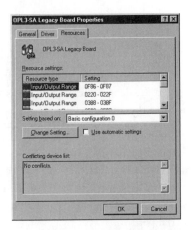

Figure 14.7.
Windows 95 instantly alerts you to any problems in the settings you choose.

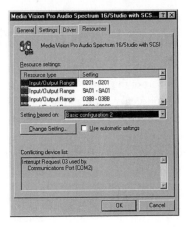

7. If you try all the basic configurations offered and none of them work, reset the Settings based on list box to its original setting. Otherwise, click OK twice to save the setting and then shut down and reboot the machine to make the setting active.

8. To change a single port address, highlight it and click the Change Setting button. You should see the dialog box shown in Figure 14.8.

Tip: Some revisions of a specific piece of hardware provide more settings than Windows 95 recognizes. Modifying the INF file using the procedure in Chapter 3 often resolves this problem. All you need to do is add the settings that Windows 95 doesn't recognize and then shut down and reboot the machine.

Figure 14.8.
This dialog box allows you to change the setting of a single port.

9. Scroll through the list of acceptable settings. As before, Windows 95 tells you if you selected a conflicting setting by displaying a message in the Conflict Information field.

10. Once you select a new port address, make it permanent by clicking OK three times. Shut down your machine and reboot.

Serial Port Configuration

The serial port offers a variety of configuration options that go beyond address conflict resolution. Several options control both the speed of the port and its compatibility with software. Figure 14.9 shows the Port Settings page, where you make changes of this nature. You access it through the System Properties dialog box. Just select the serial port you want to change, and then click the Properties button. Notice that this page controls the actual port parameters such as communication speed and number of data bits. Normally, you set a port's parameters to match those of your modem and any online service you want to access.

Figure 14.9.
The Port Settings page of the Communications Port Properties dialog box allows you to change some of the port's speed-enhancing features.

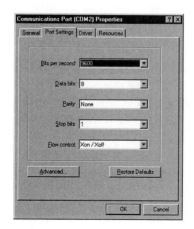

The one area where Windows 95 rises above its predecessors is in the way that it handles advanced UART (universal asynchronous receiver transmitter) chips. A UART contains the intelligence of the serial port, and some of the newer models contain features that provide better performance in a multitasking environment. It's this support that lets Windows 95 provide a higher level of support for background communications than you might expect.

Clicking the Advanced button displays the dialog box shown in Figure 14.10. Notice that it contains only one check box and two sliders. Windows 95 automatically checks the Use FIFO buffers check box if it detects the proper port. This option is available only on the 16550 UART. Attempting to use it with an older 8250 UART results in lost data.

Figure 14.10.
The Advanced Port Settings dialog box is one place where you can tweak the performance of your communications program.

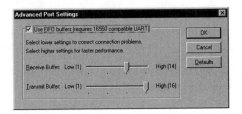

Once you select the Use FIFO buffers option in the Advanced Port Settings dialog box, Windows 95 enables the two sliders, which control the FIFO buffer. There are actually two buffers: one for data you want to send and another for data you receive. The setting affects the number of buffer slots that the CPU can use. Setting a high number allows a longer time between CPU checks, making your system more efficient. However, using a large number also increases the margin of error. You might find that your application no longer transmits or receives data accurately. The way to fix this is to reduce the number of buffers, giving the CPU a smaller margin of error. Tuning your buffer for maximum performance involves some experimentation, but it's well worth the effort.

Parallel Port Configuration

The parallel port offers fewer, yet more customized, opportunities for tuning than does the serial port. You need to consider a few things when making changes to the printer port settings that you don't need to consider with the serial port. The most important is that a device attaches to the serial port. In other words, the device must abide by the settings that the serial port provides. This is why you have one centralized dialog box for tuning a serial port. On the other hand, the parallel port attaches to the device. You can hand-tune the parallel port settings for each device that connects to it. When you think about it, this arrangement makes a lot of sense. Seldom do you see more than one device attached to a serial port, yet AB switches for parallel ports abound. People are always attaching multiple devices to their parallel ports.

With this first difference in mind, you'll probably figure out that you don't change the printer port settings in Device Manager. You use a simple four-step approach to open the dialog box shown in Figure 14.11: Open Control Panel, double-click the Printers folder, right-click the printer, and select Properties from the context menu. All the port settings appear on the Details page of the Properties dialog box, as shown in Figure 14.11.

Figure 14.11.
A parallel port's configuration settings are attached to a particular printer.

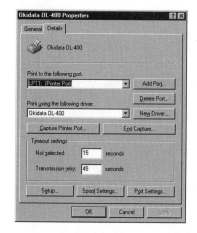

Two different settings affect the efficiency of your printer connection to varying degrees: port and spool. Clicking the Port Settings button displays the Configure LPT Port dialog. The first check box, Spool MS-DOS Print Jobs, tells Windows 95 to place a copy of any MS-DOS print jobs in the spooler so that they can print in the background. Using this setting returns control of the machine to you faster. The tradeoff is that you experience reduced machine efficiency until the print job completes. The Check Port State Before Printing option tells Windows to check the printer's status before it starts the print job. If the printer is offline or otherwise unable to print, Windows displays an error message. You get a chance to fix the problem and then retry the print job.

Clicking the Spool Settings button opens the dialog box shown in Figure 14.12. Of all the radio groups shown, only the first is always available. Spooling print jobs is a requirement if you use the printer as a network printer. Selecting the first suboption in this group tells the spooler to send data to the printer after it spools the last page of the print job, which returns machine control to you a lot faster. I normally use it for long print jobs because the machine is tied up printing for a while anyway. The second suboption, Start printing after first page is spooled, allows the spooler to start printing immediately. If you normally print short jobs, this option makes more sense because it completes the overall print job faster.

Figure 14.12.
Use this dialog box to change the way your printer handles spooling.

The Spool Settings dialog box also includes a list box with two entries: RAW and EMF. EMF (enhanced metafile) is a new way of sending information to the printer in Windows 95. It uses a data-independent method that's much smaller than the RAW option and frees up your program faster. The downside to this format is that it takes longer for the print job to complete in the background because Windows 95 still must convert the metafile format to something printer-specific. The RAW format sends the data to the printer in a format it already understands. It takes your application longer to produce this output, but this could save substantially on the amount of time the spooler spends working in the background. Combining the EMF spool data format with the Start printing after last page is spooled setting provides the fastest method of sending data to your printer.

If this isn't a shared printer, you can choose to print directly to the printer. The advantage of this method is that you don't waste time spooling the job and then sending it to the printer. When the machine returns control to you, it's at full efficiency because the print job is finished. This particular feature comes in handy when I have one or two pages and I don't want to wait long for them to print.

Peter's Principle: A Printer for Every Task

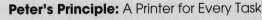

No law states that you can't create multiple copies of the same printer connected to the same port but configured in different ways. I do it to improve the flexibility of the Windows environment. I have one printer with spooling disabled, and I don't share it with anyone. It allows me to print small jobs quickly.

A second copy of the same printer is shared with everyone on the network. I enable spooling with it and allow it to start printing after the first page. This way, my machine doesn't get a lot of heavy jolts as someone else uses the printer attached to it. There's a constant but barely noticeable load. I also use this strategy for my medium-sized print jobs. It reduces the overall time that I wait for the print job to complete.

A third copy of the same printer isn't shared with anyone, but it does use spooling. I set up this one to wait until the last page of the print job appears in the spooler. This allows me to regain control of my machine in the minimum amount of time. I use this particular setting when I have a long print job that's going to reduce overall machine efficiency for a long time anyway.

There are numerous ways you can set a single printer on your machine to look like more special-purpose printers. Doing this might take a little time and thought, but it enhances your overall efficiency and improves printer throughput. You can also use this same idea for control. For example, what if you don't want a particular group to use the font cartridge attached to the machine? You can create a special setup for them that allows full printer access but doesn't provide access to the fonts. (All you have to do is choose "none" when asked for fonts on the Font page.)

Normally, you want to enable bidirectional printer support. This allows your printer to communicate with the computer when the printer needs maintenance. Bidirectional support also allows the computer to get better information about printer failures. However, bidirectional support also exacts a toll in speed. This isn't a problem with the printer or the computer, but with the amount of traffic flowing through the parallel port. The port must support a lot more traffic in bidirectional mode than it does regularly. As a result, you might notice slightly better printer performance when you turn off bidirectional support. The speed gain is minimal, however, so think twice before you actually take this step. The loss of information can make a big difference in the computer's ability to help you diagnose problems.

Fonts and Printers

Fonts can create problems in a number of efficiency-related ways. For example, every font you load consumes disk space. If you have a lot of disk space, this isn't a problem. However, at an average size of 60KB, each TrueType font you load can quickly start to consume space that your hard drive can't afford to provide. Windows 95 makes it easy to load and unload fonts as necessary. Chapter 16, "Fonts and Printing," covers this in more detail.

Miniport Driver Support

A miniport driver is a device-independent way of moving data. It doesn't matter what form that data takes; it can be graphics, sound, or text. Windows 95 uses the miniport driver concept for every subsystem on your machine. The benefit of using the miniport driver for your applications is improved speed. The application worries only about the data it wants to output, not the format that the data takes.

Not only does miniport driver support mean a better and easier-to-use interface for the user, but it also means a lot to software vendors. Under MS-DOS, you have to write code for every little function. If you want to provide a File menu, you have to write all the code that the File menu requires. The same thing holds true for every other function a program might perform.

Windows 95 simplifies things with the miniport driver support it provides. If you develop communications programs, you used to worry about the differences in control sequences for each modem type. Using Windows 95 Unimodem support (a miniport driver), the programmer opens each modem and writes to it as a file. The miniport driver takes care of details such as control codes.

There are other significant advantages to this approach. For one thing, you no longer need to worry as much about how well an application handles the details. Because each vendor is writing to the same interface, any changes to that interface come from Microsoft. Using a common interface also means that every application provides the same level of support for the various devices on your system. If one application supports a device, they all do and to the same level.

I outline the specifics of miniport driver support as I visit each subsystem. Chapter 10, "The Windows 95 File System," covers the miniport driver concept from the file-system point of view. Chapter 16 covers printer support in much more detail. Look in Chapter 17, "Mice and Keyboards," for information about mouse miniport driver support and in Chapter 18, "Video Configurations," for the same information on the video subsystem. Details on network miniport driver support appear in Chapter 27, "Networks." You get your last bit of miniport driver support information in Chapter 20, "Hardware and Software Connections," when I cover the mobile computing environment. In most cases, I've shortened "miniport driver" to "driver" in the rest of this book because a miniport driver is simply a special form of driver.

Faxes and Modems

Communication is a major part of the job these days. Online services are becoming a major source of information for many people. Sometimes I can actually get an answer to a networking or application-related question faster by getting online than I can by calling a vendor support line. The difference is the vast amount of knowledge that these online services represent.

Looking Ahead: Chapter 21, "Network Connections with an Internet Appeal," takes a closer look at using your fax and modem under Windows 95. Chapter 19, "Mobile Computing: Notebooks, Telecommuting, and Remote Access," looks at the mobile computer user's point of view.

Configuring your machine for optimum performance when using background communication isn't difficult; it just takes a little time. You need to try a setting, communicate a little to see its effect, and then tune a little more as necessary. Unlike other tuning tips I've presented in this chapter, there's no quick and easy way to tune your communications programs. The problem is that every machine is slightly different, as is every modem and every communications program that uses the modem.

Tuning Your Modem

To tune your modem settings, open Control Panel and double-click the Modem applet (which opens the Modem Properties dialog). Select your modem and click the Properties button. Select the Connection page. You see a modem device Properties dialog box similar to the one shown earlier in this chapter for the serial port.

> **Note:** These settings affect your communications program only if it uses the Windows 95 miniport driver setup. Older 16-bit communications programs maintain their own settings. Check the software vendor's manual for the procedure to tune these applications.

Click the Advanced button. You see a dialog box similar to the one in Figure 14.13. This is where you can modify your connection settings for added efficiency. If your modem supports error correction, it's normally a good idea to select it. The same holds true for data compression, which boosts your effective transfer rate by as many as four times.

Figure 14.13.
The Advanced Connection Settings dialog box allows you to configure your modem for maximum efficiency.

> **Tip:** Sometimes, using error correction and data compression can actually hurt the efficiency of your transmission. Certain types of Telnet connections fall into this category, as do some BBS calls in which the host modem doesn't quite support your modem's protocols. If you're having trouble maintaining the connection, or the data transfer rate isn't as high as you expected, try turning off data compression first, then error control, to see if there's any improvement.

I've found an interesting use for the Required to connect check box. Some BBSs have more than one connection. They use a switch to move you to the nearest unused connection when you call. If this is a local call, the fact that you can't use error correction and data compression might not be a big deal. On the other hand, the cost of using such a connection during a long-distance call can add up quickly. I use this check box when I don't want to make a connection that disables the advanced features of my modem—the ones that reduce my overall telephone bill.

The Modulation type list box allows you to select from the various forms of signal modulation that the modem provides. Using the standard modulation is usually more efficient than the alternatives. However, using the modulation that gives you the best connection is always the route to follow. I always try the standard connection first. If it proves reliable, I use that mode. I switch modes only when the connection doesn't work properly.

Some modems provide additional control sequences that you can use in specific situations for added speed. The Extra settings field allows you to enter these control sequences. Consult your modem manual for details.

Tuning Your Fax

The number of fax settings that Windows provides is fairly minimal. To access them, open the MS Exchange Settings Properties dialog box. I usually do this by double-clicking the Mail and Fax applet in Control Panel. After you open this dialog box, select Microsoft Fax, click the Properties button, and select the Modem tab. You see a Microsoft Fax Properties dialog box.

I cover the user-specific fields in this dialog box later. For now, select the modem you use to transmit faxes and then click the Properties button. Once you see the Fax Modem Properties dialog box, click the Advanced button. You see the dialog box shown in Figure 14.14.

Figure 14.14.
This dialog box allows you to select the advanced properties for your fax modem.

The settings in this dialog box allow you to change either the usability or efficiency of your modem. Checking the first setting, Disable high speed transmission, keeps you from transmitting or receiving faxes above 9600 baud. This can actually improve your machine's multitasking capability. Receiving high-speed faxes in the background might improve transmission speed, but it also costs you processor cycles. Microsoft also mentions that you can check this box if you can't receive faxes without error. Normally, errors occur when the serial port starts dropping characters due to high traffic. (Incidentally, this situation has much more to do with the other background and foreground tasks that you're running than with which UART you have. If your CPU is heavily bogged down with other tasks, the CPU itself—not the UART—becomes the bottleneck and you open yourself to the danger of degraded performance or lost data.)

The Disable error correction mode setting also affects efficiency. In one way, working without error correction is faster. The additional processing time required for error correction slows down transmission speeds. However, without error correction, you might find yourself resending faxes. You normally want to leave error correction turned on, unless the receiving modem uses a different protocol.

I can understand why Microsoft didn't default to checking the first two options. Using them does improve foreground fax transmission speeds. However, disabling data compression doesn't make a lot of sense unless you have a noisy line. In most cases, you want to enable data compression to gain the additional transmission speed that it offers.

The Enable MR compression option allows you to use one of two advanced fax data compression techniques: MR and MMR. The actual technique used depends on the capabilities of the fax you call. Each of these techniques provides data compression as follows:

- Modified Huffman (MH): This is the standard compression technique used by all fax machines today, which can nearly double the transmission speed of most fax machines.
- Modified read (MR): Some of the newer fax modems provide this option. The first line of fax data is compressed using the MH technique. The second line begins with only the changed data. In other words, if at a specific point in the data stream the first line contains a 0 and the second line contains a 1, the fax records the bit's location and difference. You see a 15 to 20 percent increase in data transmission rate using this method of compression.
- Minimized modified read (MMR): Using this option gives up some of the security of MR in exchange for speed. The fax transmits only the first line of the fax as a full line of data. All remaining lines are transmitted as change data only. Normally, you can expect a near doubling of transmission speed when using this method.

The next option, Use Class 2 if available, prevents you from receiving Class 1 faxes. The only time you want to check this box is if the software you're using won't let you receive Class 1 faxes. Class 2 faxes are the standard graphic type. Class 1 faxes are editable and therefore easier to manipulate.

Finally, the Reject pages received with errors list box and check box combination lets you do a couple of things. Removing the check from this box tells Windows that you don't want to receive any pages a second time, even if they're totally garbled. This usually isn't the best route to pursue. On the other hand, checking the box and selecting very low in the Tolerance list box virtually guarantees that you get at least one resend of each page. (Tolerance is the level of tolerance that Windows has for errors on a fax page.) I usually use the high setting unless I need better fax quality for some reason. For example, if I want to use the information in the fax for a presentation, I might select the low or medium setting. The only time I select very low is if I need to use the pages as is, without any changes at all, for some type of presentation or formal document.

TAPI and MAPI Support

Application programming interfaces (APIs) allow programmers to accomplish a lot of work with only a little effort. That's the first goal of every API. The second goal is to ensure a standardized form of access to specific system resources and capabilities. Using a standard interface allows the operating system vendor to change the implementation details without "breaking" too much code. Finally, an API also standardizes the results of using specific system resources and capabilities. For example, using the Windows API ensures that the user sees some of the standard types of interface components that we take for granted.

Windows 95 provides two new APIs. The Telephony API (TAPI) provides a standardized method of handling telephone services. The Messaging API (MAPI) provides a standardized method of handling online services and other forms of messaging. Both APIs provide standardized methods for utilizing your modem more efficiently to conduct business. I examine both APIs in depth later in this book. Right now, the important thing to remember is that both APIs exist under Windows 95 in the form of new utilities.

You see the effects of TAPI directly in the Modem applet in Control Panel. It allows you to configure your modem in one place. Any application that supports TAPI uses those settings. This includes Outlook Express and Microsoft Network as native Windows 95 applications but doesn't include older 16-bit Windows applications. If you want the benefits of TAPI, you must upgrade those applications as the vendors come out with new versions.

MAPI and TAPI aren't limited to Windows 95–specific applications. For example, Microsoft Word provides a Send option on the File menu. This option allows you to send all or part of a document using MAPI anywhere you can communicate. Using the native capabilities of Windows 95, this means you could send it as a fax or an e-mail or to an online service—all without leaving Word.

Windows 98 New Generation Hardware Support

Windows 98 provides a wealth of new hardware support features including support for a Universal Serial Bus (USB), Accelerated Graphics Port (AGP), Advanced Configuration and Power Interface (ACPI), and Digital Video Disk (DVD).

The Universal Serial Bus (USB) is a new method for connecting peripheral devices to your machine. It only uses one kind of connector, so you don't have to worry about attaching that peripheral to the wrong connector. The Accelerated Graphics Port (AGP) takes the connection for your display adapter off the PC bus and places it on the memory bus for the computer to move data faster. This simple move can provide as much as a fourfold speed increase over the speed that a display adapter can move data on the PCI bus.

Advanced Configuration and Power Interface (ACPI) allows you to control when your hard drive and monitor turn themselves off after a period of non-use.

Digital Video Disks (DVDs) are the latest high storage capacity drives.

On Your Own

Use the automatic installation technique in this chapter to determine whether your machine has any undetected devices. Normally, Windows 95 reports that it didn't find anything. If so, click Cancel to exit the detection routine.

Change the configuration settings of various devices listed on the Device page of the System Properties dialog box. Be sure to save the settings in case you can't get Windows 95 back to its original configuration. Use settings that conflict with another device to see how Windows reacts. Be sure to change the setting back so that you can use the device again.

15

Exploiting Multimedia and Games

Peter Norton®

Considering the multimedia orientation that the Internet is taking, everyone's use of multimedia is only going to increase in the future. Multimedia on the Internet won't include just visual effects; it'll include audio effects as well. For example, consider a Web site such as CD-Now (http://www.cdnow.com), which includes the capability to play sound samples from CDs before you buy.

Besides the Internet, the average user may use multimedia for training, for education, and (of course) for games. Many games provide intense graphic and sound presentations meant to thrill the user. It takes considerable hardware horsepower to play some of these games, and in fact, some of the more robust sales campaigns for multimedia hardware actually appear in gaming magazines.

Obviously, this isn't even the tip of the iceberg when it comes to multimedia. As voice-recognition technology improves, more people will use sound for feedback, for controlling their computer, and for storing and recording their own sounds. Because multimedia requires advanced hardware, I look at the hardware and software technologies you might need. By the time you finish this chapter, you'll have a better idea of what multimedia under Windows 95 entails and how you can make it easier to use.

Multimedia Hardware

Multimedia is a big area of improvement under Windows 95. The CD-ROM ships with several samples of multimedia presentations. They don't fully exploit the potential of multimedia, but they do give you an idea of what's possible. The sections that follow give you an overview of multimedia under Windows 95 and how it allows you to better exploit your hardware. Right now, it's hard to say who's ahead in the game—hardware or software. Neither is to the level where I'd say that it gives you the kind of presentation you're looking for, but I'll leave it for you to decide just how far it needs to go.

MPEG Support

Motion pictures revolutionized the world, and now they'll revolutionize your PC. MPEG (Motion Pictures Experts Group) is a method of compressing VHS video into a small format that will fit on a CD-ROM. The VHS used by Windows 95 is the same format that your VCR uses.

The technical term for the type of functionality that MPEG provides is a codec (coder/decoder). Think of a codec in the same way you think of a modem. It allows you to send and receive video data using a standard medium. Instead of a telephone wire, you're using a CD-ROM drive. In place of digital data, you're receiving video images.

Windows 95 currently provides the capability to display VHS-quality images in a 640×480 window at 30 frames per second. That's about the same rate that you see on television. You're supposed to get this level of performance from a double-speed CD-ROM drive, but I tested it with a quadruple-speed unit connected to my system and just barely got what I would call acceptable performance.

I'm sure part of Microsoft's assumption is that you won't be running anything else when using the multimedia capabilities, but that probably isn't valid. Most people will want to use this capability for training, which means that they'll probably have another application open. A 12X and 24X CD-ROM drive will probably provide the level of support you really need to use MPEG video.

Suffice it to say that if you want to fully exploit your machine's hardware capabilities, make sure that you get more than a minimal system. Otherwise, you'll probably be disappointed with the performance that low-end hardware will provide.

Note: The latest standard is now MPEG2, which is being used by digital video disc (DVD) drives. To learn more about MPEG, visit the official MPEG Web site at `http://drogo.cselt.stet.it/mpeg/about_mpeg.htm`.

Sound Boards

There are all kinds of sounds and all kinds of hardware to play it on. You don't have to settle for the mediocre level of sound that previous versions of Windows provided. Windows 95 provides the controls required to fully exploit the expanded capabilities that modern sound boards provide. All you need to do to start using these capabilities is adjust the settings found in the Audio Properties dialog box. To access this dialog box, right-click the Speaker icon on the Taskbar and select Adjust Audio Properties. You should see a dialog box similar to the one shown in Figure 15.1.

Figure 15.1.
The Audio Properties dialog box allows you to make full use of the audio capabilities your system provides.

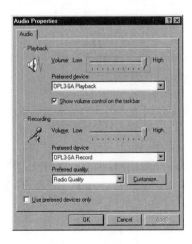

Windows 95 will always play back any audio using the full capability of the sound board you select. However, there's a lot of room to customize the recording of sound. Microsoft thoughtfully provided three default recording selections. Each selection reflects the kind of sound recording quality these settings will give you: CD, radio, or telephone.

The actual level of quality you get has to do with the frequency, or the number of samples of sound that Windows takes per second. The more samples it takes, the better the quality of your sample. Using stereo and 16-bit samples also improves the sound quality, as does the recording format. Before I go much further, let me define a few terms.

- Sample rate: The number of times per second that Windows samples the microphone input line. A higher setting means that you get more samples. More samples always provide a better playback.

- Sample size: Windows supports two sample sizes: 8-bit and 16-bit. A 16-bit sample allows you to record a broader range of values. This means that you can better differentiate between various sounds, resulting in a higher-quality recording.

- Format: There are many ways to store a sound, just as there are many ways to store graphics. Some formats take more space but preserve image quality better. Likewise, some audio formats are better than others at preserving sounds. You have to experiment to see which one sounds the best to you. Most recordings use the PCM (pulse-code modulation) format. Because this is the most common format, you'll probably want to use it when you need to exchange the recording with someone else, unless there's an overriding reason to do otherwise.

- Number of channels (mono or stereo): You probably already know the implication of this setting. A stereo recording uses two microphones to record the sound from different perspectives. During playback, a stereo recording has much greater depth than a mono recording of the same quality.

Now that you have some ideas of the ways you can customize sound under Windows 95, take a look at the dialog box you use to do it. Click the Customize button to see the Customize dialog box, shown in Figure 15.2.

Figure 15.2.
Use the Customize dialog box to change the way you record sound under Windows 95.

Notice that there are two list boxes. One determines the recording format and the other allows you to select from a variety of options, including the sample rate, sample size, and number of channels. Notice that this list box also tells you the storage requirements for the sample in kilobytes per second. This is the number of kilobytes that the sample consumes for each second you record. Obviously, some formats can eat a lot of storage space quickly.

You can save any custom settings that you create by using the Save As button. Windows stores the settings and presents them later in the Preferred Quality list box of the Audio Properties dialog box.

What's the best way to customize these settings? Remember that the better the quality, the higher the storage requirements. I tend to prefer stereo over mono recordings because the depth of sound can make up for a host of other problems. The trouble comes when you have only one microphone. In that case, selecting stereo is a waste of disk space because you can record only one channel of information. Selecting 16-bit sound improves quality a great deal for a small increase in storage size. You get a sample 2^{16} (65,536 possible combinations) versus 2^8 (256 possible combinations) for a mere doubling of disk space. Unless you're recording music, the highest sampling rate you need is 22,050Hz. In fact, using 11,025 for simple voice recordings usually proves sufficient.

Virtualizing Your Hardware

To make the best use of your hardware under Windows 95, you must be able to access it. There are three ways to do this, and I've mentioned them all before. If absolutely necessary, you can use a real-mode driver to access an older device. DLLs allow you to access devices that provide Windows 16-bit support but don't provide a Windows-95–specific driver. This is better than using a real-mode driver but shy of the real goal you want to achieve. The best driver to use is a Windows 95–specific virtual "anything" driver (VxD). The following sections cover all three types of support from an efficiency and ease-of-use standpoint.

Real-Mode Drivers for Older Devices

There are a lot of problems with using real-mode drivers under Windows 95. Other areas of this book cover just about every problem you can experience. Suffice it to say that a real-mode driver isn't the best choice you could make.

The first decision you need to make is whether the device is even needed all the time. You had to load a device you intended to use at bootup with MS-DOS and Windows 3.x because there was no way to load it later. If you need a device for a special purpose under Windows 95, you can always load it later in an MS-DOS mode session. Simply set up a copy of the command processor with the CONFIG.SYS and AUTOEXEC.BAT settings required to load the device in its optimum environment. Of course, you won't be able to load Windows 95 when using MS-DOS mode—or access other applications, for that matter. It's a problem of balancing convenience with overall system performance and stability.

You need to make a few decisions when using such a driver under Windows 95. The first choice is the amount of MS-DOS space you need in comparison to the flexibility you want to give Windows when it comes to managing your memory. Loading all your device drivers low affects the amount of conventional memory you need. However, this choice also means that you won't have to load a memory manager and that Windows will be able to provide the maximum flexibility possible.

If you find that you have to load the driver high, you also have to load something other than the Windows memory manager. Optimize both the driver and memory manager settings to reduce their impact on the Windows environment. For example, use the least amount of memory possible for buffers.

Using 16-Bit Drivers

Using an older 16-bit Windows driver is a little bit better than using a real-mode driver. At least Windows still controls the memory environment. Unfortunately, using these older drivers still has an effect on overall system efficiency. Remember that all 16-bit applications, including drivers, run in a single session. Using that session's resources for a driver doesn't seem like the best way to go.

The 32-bit drivers that come with Windows 95 also provide built-in safeguards to help protect your system environment. The older 16-bit drivers provide no such protection. They're more likely than a newer driver to crash or at least destabilize the system.

Finally, a 16-bit driver won't know how to interact with the miniport driver architecture used by Windows 95. This means that you lose all the user and programmer benefits of such an architecture for that specific device.

Default 32-Bit Drivers

Using 32-bit Windows 95 drivers is the best solution if you want to get the most out of your hardware. Windows 95 isn't a perfect operating system, but it does provide enough advanced features that updating your hardware to use the new drivers is the best way to go. Using old drivers is just another way to introduce inefficiencies and stability problems into your system.

Software for Games and Multimedia

MS-DOS and earlier versions of Windows provided little, if anything, in the way of multimedia support. If an application such as a game or presentation graphics program wanted to draw something onscreen, it had to provide all the processing instructions required to perform the task. Likewise, if you wanted to hear some sounds, then the software was responsible for providing the required drivers. There were times where you just couldn't get everything to work together, no matter what you tried. Because of the lack of operating system support, a dearth of multimedia standards, and poor documentation from vendors, those early games were an exercise in frustration for anyone unlucky enough to install them.

Windows 95 provides much more robust support than these early operating systems. You'll find that many of the features you need for playing a game or displaying a presentation are built right into the operating system. The fact that the operating system supports your hardware means that you have fewer problems getting single applications to work. Finally, there are more standards now, so it's easier to find drivers to get the job done.

There are some drawbacks to all this standardization and support from Windows 95. Placing the need for driver support at the operating level is a good idea because you reduce the number of places to look when it's time to figure out why your hardware isn't working. However, it still doesn't reduce the problems you'll have getting the hardware to work in the first place. Multimedia software support under Windows 95 is normally an all-or-nothing proposition. Getting standardized hardware and associated drivers is one sure way to make sure that you'll have the fewest problems possible getting Windows 95 to work with your software and recognize your hardware. The following sections explore some of the software solutions that Microsoft provides to getting your hardware and applications to talk with each other.

ActiveMovie

I've talked about ActiveMovie several times in the book so far. In essence, ActiveMovie is Microsoft's method for distributing multimedia in a relatively small package. The ActiveMovie player allows you to play various kinds of multimedia files, including both audio and video files. The section "ActiveMovie Control" in Chapter 2, "Introducing Windows 95: What Else Is New?," provides full details about this particular utility program.

WinG—Yesterday's Solution

There have been several attempts to get game developers to seriously consider Windows as a gaming platform. One of the earliest attempts was WinG. Fortunately, Microsoft acknowledged the shortcomings of WinG and produced the Windows Games SDK, which is more commonly referred to today as DirectX.

DirectX—the Solution for Today

The latest multimedia technology in the news is DirectX. If you want to find out the latest about Microsoft's DirectX technology, look at `http://www.microsoft.com/directx/default.asp`. Visit the Data Visualization site at `http://www.directx.com/` if you want to get the non-Microsoft point of view when it comes to various graphics technologies including OpenGL and DirectX. You'll also want to check out the page of links at `http://www.cs.montana.edu/~pv/programing_links.html`. This particular site covers a range of new technologies including DirectX. If you need help solving problems with DirectX, take a look at `http://www.microsoft.com/support/products/home/directx/default.htm`.

Understanding DirectX

DirectX is actually composed of several software layers. Each layer performs a specific purpose. The following list describes each layer and tells you what purpose it serves.

- Components: DirectX components represent the topmost layer of the DirectX hierarchy; most people would have simply called them applications. Obviously, any game or multimedia application that uses DirectX resides at this level. You'll also find that Windows 95 comes with four DirectX components: ActiveMovie, VRML 2.0, NetShow, and NetMeeting.

- DirectX Media: This is the layer that manages all your resources such as video memory and access to the sound board. It's the application service level. You'll find several pieces of DirectX here, including DirectShow, DirectModel, DirectPlay, DirectAnimation, Direct3DRetainedMode, and VRML.

- DirectX Foundation: All the system-level services appear at this level. When the operating system needs to know what's going cn, it talks to one of the pieces at this level. You'll find DirectDraw, DirectInput, DirectSound, DirectSound3D, and Direct3DImmediateMode at this level.

- Hardware and Network: None of this technology matters if you can't make your display present believable 3D graphics. DirectX is more than just software that helps you get the most from your games and multimedia applications; it also means getting hardware that you normally expect to find with your favorite stereo.

Tip: If you want to update an existing Windows installation to use DirectX 5, you can download it from `http://www.microsoft.com/directx/default.asp`. Look for the `IDX5RDST.EXE` file on the DirectX 5 SDK page. Downloading and installing this file gives your machine DirectX 5 capability. You might not notice an immediate difference, however. Most of the changes that DirectX 5 provides have to be programmed into the application software.

Now that you have a better idea of how DirectX is put together, I talk about three utilities you need to know when it comes time to diagnose problems. Look in your `Program Files\DirectX\Setup` folder and you see three new applications designed to make working with DirectX easier. Take a look at the first one: DXSetup.

DXSetup is the utility that you'll work with most often. Figure 15.3 shows a typical dialog, although there's more than one version. This is the dialog that you see during DirectX setup and when you need to update your DirectX drivers. The dialog shown in Figure 15.3 shows two grayed-out buttons. The first allows you to restore your video driver; the second allows you to restore your audio driver. Microsoft recognizes the fact that your machine is a complex environment and that not every DirectX update will work as anticipated. These two buttons allow you to return your video and audio drivers to their previous state. Even if those drivers didn't provide flawless operation, you'll still be able to use your applications as before.

Figure 15.3.
The DirectX Setup utility allows you to accomplish a number of tasks, including restoring your audio and video drivers when needed.

You should also notice two other features of the DirectX Setup dialog. The first is a list of drivers and their revision number. This information could help a support technician diagnose problems with your machine. You could also use it to ensure you have the latest driver installed when deciding whether to download the latest update from a Web site. The second feature is the Direct3D Hardware Acceleration Enabled check box. You may experience problems with certain games if you have this box checked and the game really isn't programmed to use the hardware you have installed on your machine. Unchecking the box might allow the application to run.

The second utility that you see is DXInfo. This utility allows you to collect every piece of available information about your DirectX installation and display it onscreen. In fact, the initial dialog that you see when you start this utility will tell you that DXInfo is gathering the required information. Once DXInfo has the information gathered, you see a dialog similar to the one shown in Figure 15.4. Notice that there are actually two panes, one for component-level information on the left and another for device-specific information on the right.

Notice the two buttons at the bottom of the DXInfo dialog. One allows you to exit the program. The other allows you to save the information displayed in the dialog to a text file on disk. A technical support person might ask you to save this information and send it to him. The text file contains a lot of useful DirectX setup information that he could use in helping you solve your problem.

The final DirectX utility is DXTool. In most cases, you never even look at this utility. Starting it shows you why. Figure 15.5 shows that the DXTool utility can provide some pretty detailed DirectX information in a hierarchical format that only a programmer might love. However, it's good to know that this utility exists, just in case you need to provide a technical support person with more information than the DXInfo utility can provide (or provide it in a different format).

Figure 15.4.
In many cases, you use the DXInfo utility to gather information for technical support personnel.

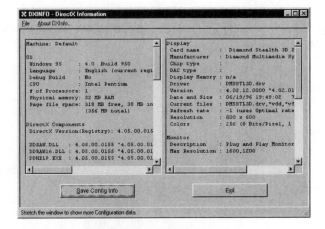

Figure 15.5.
Clicking on the plus signs in the DXTool utility can display extremely detailed information about your DirectX drivers.

The New Features of DirectX 5

You'll find a whole range of new features in DirectX 5. Most of them help fine-tune game software, but you'll find a few general multimedia features packed in as well. The following list explores the various DirectX 5 features:

- DirectX 5 provides better image quality and a longer list of features because Microsoft has spent a lot of time improving the Direct3D API (application programming interface).

- The DrawPrimitive services allow a developer to pass polygon information directly to the hardware now instead of going through a buffer, which results in better application execution speed.

- Animation capabilities have been improved.

- There are a lot of new technology features such as sort-independent anti-aliasing, range-based fog, anisotropic texture filtering, and bufferless hidden surface elimination. What does this all mean? Essentially, you get more realistic images that also include special effects.

- Accelerated Graphics Port (AGP) support for DirectDraw in low-resolution mode along with MMX optimizations means that you get all the speed that your hardware has to offer.

- DirectX now supports force-feedback devices such as joysticks through the DirectInput API. The game controller control panel has been improved as well.

- Games can support Internet and LAN play through the DirectPlay API. This API comes with Windows NT security, client/server support, and lobby client API.

- Audio is a lot easier to create because of the DirectSound Capture and Notify APIs. Essentially, a game is able to use audio streams to make sound more fluid.

- Hearing where a sound originates becomes a reality because of the DirectSound 3D support built into DirectX 5.

- Setup is going to be a lot easier, too. DirectX Setup can detect most of the hardware and automatically configure it for you. This means you spend a lot less time figuring out how to get your hardware to work and more time playing games.

Getting Your Games to Cooperate

With all the tweaking that game vendors do to get the ultimate level of efficiency from their products, it's not too difficult to understand that you'll run into some problems when using them. In most cases, these glitches represent something that the game vendor couldn't test during the product development cycle. Still, the root of the problem is the direct screen writes and hardware manipulation that game programs perform to give you those dramatic effects.

Getting your game to work with your hardware and software setup can be an exercise in frustration, especially if you purchase games that don't adhere to published standards. Unfortunately, it's pretty difficult to tell much about a game by looking at the outside. In many cases, you have to actually install the game and try it on your machine to see if it works.

The problem is severe enough that I've actually had a game install perfectly on one machine and not at all on another, even when the two machines used identical hardware and drivers. In some cases, the problem could be traced to a compatibility problem with DLLs installed by other software on the machine. This particular problem is actually worse under Windows because many DLLs are common to several pieces of software.

One of the best ways to protect yourself from potential problems when buying games is to buy the software from a store that has an exchange policy. Some stores actually refuse to accept a game back once you've opened it (and for good reason—some buyers don't return all the pieces, making it impossible for the store to sell the game to someone else). I usually make sure that the store at least offers store credit for a game that won't work on my machine. If at all possible, I buy the game at a place that offers a full cash refund especially if there aren't any other games I want at the time of purchase.

Another way to help protect yourself is to look at game reviews in magazines. In a lot of cases, a game review will tell you about potential problems that the author saw when installing the game. A buggy game will probably receive a poor review. Unfortunately, like many things in life, a game review is also subjective. You might find that your tastes are completely different from those of the reviewer. In other words, don't look for a review to tell you whether you'll like a game or not; just look at it for clues about whether the game will play as expected.

The following paragraphs discuss some of the things you can do to further reduce your risk when making a game purchase. I look at some of the more common problems that people run into. Of course, there's any number of other problems that you could run into such as simple hardware failure. In other words, make sure you look for every potential source of problem before you throw in the towel.

> **Tip:** You don't have to conquer your gaming problems alone. The Internet has a wealth of game-related newsgroups that you can use to resolve your problem. There are no fewer than ten newsgroups you can check out under `comp.sys.ibm.pc.games`. For example, `comp.sys.ibm.pc.games.strategic` will help you with strategy games. Make sure you check your game packaging for any vendor-related Web sites as well. Even though you might find help a little lacking on some of these Web sites, you'll be able to find out about patches and updates to your game.

Windows Games

Windows games do have certain advantages over their MS-DOS counterparts. In most cases, you'll find that a Windows game requires less setup and that the setup issues you do run into are easier to resolve. The reason is simple: The game is going to use the same drivers that your other Windows applications do, for the most part. Setting up Windows is enough to ensure the game has everything it needs to perform a semi-automatic installation. You won't have to worry about what interrupt your sound board uses or how much memory is installed on your display adapter. You might still have to worry about whether to install DirectX because many games use DirectX to speed things up.

You'll also find that most Windows games have fewer compatibility problems because there's at least a little standardization between them. The use of common drivers is a major plus in the Windows environment. Standards such as OpenGL and DirectX have also gone a long way toward making it easier for the game vendor to ensure that its product will run on your machine.

Another reason to use Windows games is that they normally provide a standard interface. Sure, there are going to be differences between games, much more so in fact than other application types. However, you'll see evidence of the Windows interface in small things such as saving your files. I won't go so far as to say you won't have any problems using Windows games, but you'll find them less difficult to use in most cases.

There are some problems with using Windows as a platform. The most notable problem is that Windows games tend to run slower than their MS-DOS counterparts. You'll also find that many Windows games require more hardware resources than the MS-DOS counterparts. There isn't any good rule of thumb in determining how much of a difference there is; you have to make that judgment for yourself when looking at the game package in the store.

Other problems I have run into often relate to color depth and resolution. This is unique to Windows because of the flexibility of the display configuration in Windows. I run 1024×768 in 16-bit color mode, but many games seem to want 640×480 and 256-color mode.

Looking for the Microsoft Seal of Approval

Most of us who use Windows applications on a regular basis wrongly assume that any game you pick up in the store is going to be on Microsoft's approval list. The one thing you should always look for is the Microsoft seal. This is your assurance that someone at Microsoft has at least looked at how the game is designed. There might be nothing wrong with a non-approved game, but you don't know that.

On the other hand, a Microsoft seal isn't necessarily a guarantee that you won't run into any problems at all. All that the seal tells you is that the game was programmed in accordance with Microsoft's guidelines. In other words, the game meets certain minimal requirements. Whether that's enough to get the game to run on your machine isn't assured.

You'll still want to make sure that you can return a game to the store even if it has a Microsoft seal on it. However, I always buy approved games because I've had far fewer problems with them. Not only that, but companies who take the time to go through the certification process usually provide a better level of customer support as well. Getting a game with Microsoft's seal almost always ensures that you'll be able to get help resolving compatibility problems.

What Windows 95–Compatible Means

The most Windows 95–compatible games have the "Designed for Windows 95" logo on the box. However, some game companies have been pulling a fast one on their customers by adding a Windows 95 compatible sticker to their products. In addition, many of these games do have a Microsoft seal on them. However, close examination shows that this is a Windows 3.x seal, not a Windows 95 seal.

What does this mean to you as a customer? It means that you have a game that was ported from the Windows 3.x environment. In many cases, all that means is that it was tested to run under Windows 95 and nothing more. You may actually be using a 16-bit application, not the 32-bit application you were expecting.

Getting one of the Windows 95–compatible games isn't necessarily a bad choice. The Windows 3.x seal is a lot less stringent than the requirements for either Windows 95, but at least the game has gone through some outside certification process. In addition, the 16-bit orientation of the game means you won't get the protection offered by the 32-bit Windows 95 environment.

The bottom line is that you have to determine whether you're willing to live with the limitations that these games have. I doubt many people run their word processor, or any other application, for that matter, while relaxing with a game, so it's unlikely that you'll run into data corruption problems. (If you're in the habit of playing games at work, you might want to reconsider this policy, at least with 16-bit games that could crash your system.)

Compatibility Issues

There are a few Windows compatibility problems that I haven't covered in other areas of the chapter, most of which you'll run into only under some very specific conditions. One of the most common problems that I run into involves old drivers. For example, some game installation programs won't bother to check which DirectX drivers you're using and overwrite your new files with the old ones on the CD. Other game installation programs will misread the drivers and assume that you have whatever it takes to run the game when in reality, you don't.

Another problem that I run into is laptop specific. For whatever reason (I've heard more than a few conflicting reasons), the flat screen display provided with laptop computers doesn't react as well to DirectX as the displays used with desktop machines. As a result, I've had more than my share of video problems when running games on laptop machines. The thing you should do if you run into this problem is check with the laptop vendor for updated drivers. In many cases, someone else has already run into the problem and the laptop vendor has the fix you require.

You'll also run into problems that I place into the strange category. For example, one game that I liked playing had a problem with IP addresses. You could contact another party on the Internet only if the first IP number was two digits or fewer. You couldn't enter a three-digit beginning IP number. Fortunately, the vendor came out with a patch in short order and the problem was fixed. However, a good number of people assumed there was some problem with their machine and went through all kinds of troubleshooting procedures before contacting the vendor. If you have a problem with a game, contact the vendor first (or at least a suitable newsgroup on the Internet) to see if it's a common problem.

> **Tip:** Use the WinIPCfg utility (found in the main Windows folder) to determine your Internet IP address. Simply select the PPP Adapter entry to see the current IP address for your Internet connection. Pass this information on to the person that you want to play a game with over the Internet. Make sure that you get this information every time because you'll get a different IP address every time you connect to the Internet.

Newer MS-DOS Games Using XMS

Most newer MS-DOS games use XMS, which means you don't have to do a lot to make them run under Windows 95. In fact, I've gotten most of these games to run just by double-clicking them in Explorer. (You can also add them to your Start menu or as a shortcut on the desktop.)

There are a few things that you want to be aware of when playing newer MS-DOS games under Windows. The first is to try them without any configuration changes at all. In some cases, game vendors have actually added code to make MS-DOS games Windows-friendly. If you change any of the settings in the PIF file associated with the MS-DOS game, you could disable this special code and prevent your game from running. (Some game vendors have also come to the conclusion that the only way you'll be able to play their games is using MS-DOS mode; in some cases, that conclusion is wrong, so you'll want to try running the program in Windows first.)

If you try the game by just double-clicking it and it doesn't work, then you may perform some additional configuration setup. I talk about the various PIF configuration issues in Chapter 13, "Exploiting Your Software: DOS, 16-Bit, and 32-Bit Windows Applications." In most cases, you'll want to work with the settings on the Memory, Screen, or Misc tabs of the program Properties dialog. Unfortunate as it seems, you might finally have to rely on MS-DOS mode to get your game to run. Check out the procedure for using MS-DOS mode in Chapter 13.

Older MS-DOS Games Relying on EMS

Most of the older games you'll work with won't run at all under Windows 95. The reason is simple: Even though Windows 95 tries to be as accommodating as possible, these older MS-DOS applications break too many rules such as accessing the display in a way that Windows 95 doesn't expect. When this happens, you have two choices. You can create a boot disk that allows you to boot MS-DOS without Windows 95, or you can use MS-DOS mode to at least automate the process. You'll find out about MS-DOS mode in Chapter 13.

When It's Time to Shelve That Game

You'll eventually get to the point where a game can no longer keep up with technology. For example, one game that I had wouldn't work with Pentium processors because of an assumption made by the original programmer. In this particular case, the game vendor released a patch to fix the Pentium problem, but this situation is the exception rather than the rule. When a game ages sufficiently, you'll find that the game vendor will provide a modicum of technical support and that's about it. Technology will eventually leave these games gathering dust on your shelf.

I use a simple rule of thumb when it comes to shelving a game. Playing games is supposed to be fun and relaxing. If you have a game that starts to take more time to set up and fix, you might want to put it on the shelf. Yes, it's hard giving up a game that feels as comfortable as an old pair of shoes, but even old shoes have to go by the wayside. The same can be said of many games.

Is there an exact measure of time that you can expect to get from a game? Probably not. I recently took out a copy of Zork III. Despite the old text interface, the game was still a lot of fun to play. It even runs under Windows 95. Was the thrill still there? Well, the game was showing its age. Having great graphics to look at is pretty addicting. The point is that I could have played it if I wanted to. Some games aren't quite that lucky. For example, I can't get M1 Tank Platoon to play under Windows 95, no matter what I do. This was one of the games I was able to get to work under Windows 95 with the Pentium patch, but I think it's seen its final playing day.

On Your Own

Go to the Microsoft site at `http://www.microsoft.com/directx/default.asp` to determine whether you have the latest version of DirectX. Making sure you have the latest operating system support is one way to reduce the number of problems you'll encounter. You'll also want to spend some time checking your hardware and associated drivers. Most vendors have Web sites where you can download updated drivers. Hardware that uses flash ROM technology can benefit from downloads as well.

Visit various Internet sites to see how they use multimedia. You might even want to make some suggestions to the Webmaster on what you like and what you don't. Make sure you get the whole experience by using both sight and sound.

Try to get a game running under Windows 95. Some older games are a special challenge because you have to use special settings to get them to run. Make sure you take a close look at the game to see if it's getting too old to run. As technology advances, it leaves some games behind, making it difficult to install or play them. You'll also want to check game vendor Web sites to see if there is a patch available for your game. In many cases, these patches fix compatibility problems.

Check your game packages to see if they all have the Microsoft seal. Which ones have a Windows 3.x seal and a Windows 95–compatible sticker? You might want to contact the vendor to see if it got the game through the Windows 95 certification process. If it has, see if there's a patch available to bring your game up to that standard. If not, you might want to ask why it hasn't bothered to certify its game in the Windows 95 environment.

16

Fonts and Printing

Windows 95 improves on the process of printing a great deal. Even the simple act of installing a printer is easier now. Removing one is easier still. Managing your fonts has also taken a turn for the better. For one thing, you no longer have to dig through your SYSTEM directory looking for them. Windows 95 places them in a separate directory and provides a utility that you can use to manage them.

The following sections take you on a tour of the complex world of printers. Windows 95 has taken some of the pain out of managing your printer; now there are more choices and more features than ever before. I show you how to use these features to your benefit and explain some of the more intriguing aspects of the new environment that Windows 95 provides.

Installing a Printer

Before you can use a printer, you have to install and configure it. I looked at the topics of installing and configuring your printer briefly in Chapter 11, "The Windows 95 Applets," and Chapter 14, "Exploiting Your Hardware." Chapter 11 told you how to perform a special file installation. Chapter 14 looked at a few of the most efficient ways to use your printer's capabilities. This section provides the details required to install a printer. It also includes some productivity tips.

The Printers Folder

Even if you don't have any printers installed on your system, you have a Printers folder in Control Panel. At a minimum, this folder contains an applet that allows you to install a new printer. This is the applet you use to add a new printer to your system. The following procedure takes you through a generic installation session. I take a look at some configuration details as well.

1. Use the Start | Settings | Printers command to open the Printers folder. You might see one or more printers already installed in the folder, along with the Add Printer applet.

2. Double-click the Add Printer applet. You see the first page of the Add Printer wizard.

3. Click Next. Assuming that your computer is connected to a network, the next page of the wizard lets you determine whether this is a network or local printer. Selecting the Network printer option allows you to connect to a shared printer located anywhere on your network. Selecting the Local printer option restricts your choices to printers connected to your local machine. If your computer isn't connected to a network, the Network/Local option page won't appear and you continue the wizard with step 4.

Tip: Windows doesn't restrict you from creating multiple installations for the same printer. In fact, doing so allows you to create multiple setups that are optimized for specific types of jobs. I covered this topic in detail in Chapter 14.

4. Click Next. The Add Printer wizard asks you to select a printer using the dialog shown in Figure 16.1. Notice that there are two lists. The one on the left contains a list of printer manufacturers. Selecting a vendor changes the list on the right to display printers manufactured by that vendor. Windows also allows you to install an unsupported printer by clicking the Have Disk pushbutton. I covered this procedure in Chapter 11, so I won't talk about it again here.

Figure 16.1.
Use the entries in this dialog to select a printer vendor and model.

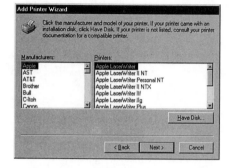

5. After you've selected a printer vendor and model, click Next. The next dialog (see Figure 16.2) asks you to select a printer port. In most cases, you see only the local ports if you haven't used a network printer port before. I show you how to add a network printer port in the section "Configuration." I also look at a problem with using network ports with Windows 95.

Figure 16.2.
The port selection list might not include any network connections if you haven't used them before.

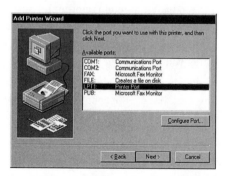

Tip: You can create multiple connections for one printer. I normally add a File connection as a minimum so that I can delay printing until later. A fax connection is also a good idea to support applications that don't provide a fax connection.

6. Select a port. You can configure the DOS options for the port by clicking the Configure Port pushbutton. I covered these options in Chapter 14. Click Next to continue. You see the dialog shown in Figure 16.3.

Figure 16.3.
This dialog allows you to select a printer name and whether it is the default printer.

7. You have two important decisions to make in this dialog. The first is what to name the printer. The Add Printer wizard suggests something appropriate, and you can accept this name if you intend to create only one copy of the printer. However, you might want to use a more descriptive name if you plan to install multiple configurations of the same printer. The second decision is whether to make this the default printer. Windows applications use the default printer unless you specifically select something else. You should make the default printer the one you use the most often.

8. Click Next to continue. The next page of the wizard gives you a simple yes-or-no choice on whether to send a test page to the printer. I always send a test page to a local printer connected to an actual port. It makes little sense to print a test page for a file connection. Unless you already have your network connections configured, you need to test them later. Choose whether you want to print a test page and click Next to complete the installation.

9. Windows 95 displays a status dialog as it copies all the needed files to your drive. Once it completes this task, you see the appropriate icon in the Printers folder. Double-clicking this icon allows you to view the current print jobs. Right-clicking allows you to see the context menu.

As you can see, installing a printer isn't difficult. You probably need to configure the printer for your specific needs. The next section takes you through the process of adding a port. Then I look at the overall configuration procedure.

Adding a Port

Adding a network port is easy under Windows 95. All you need to do is right-click the Printer icon, select Properties, and click the Details tab. You should see a dialog similar to the one shown in Figure 16.4. Windows 95 allows you to perform a variety of tasks in this dialog, including changing the printer by changing the driver you're using. The port-specific buttons allow you to add a new port or delete an existing one.

Figure 16.4.
The Details page of the Printer Properties dialog allows you to add, delete, and configure the ports your printer attaches to.

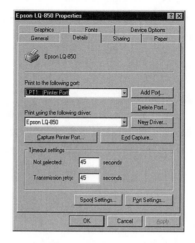

Clicking the Add Port pushbutton displays the dialog shown in Figure 16.5. You can choose from two different types of ports using the radio buttons: local and network. The local (Other) options vary according to the utilities you have installed. They include a local port as a minimum. The options could include fax and Microsoft Network if you have them installed. The network connections depend on the type of network you have installed and the devices that are shared on the network. You can use the Browse button to find a particular device.

Figure 16.5.
You can select from a variety of print connections in this dialog.

Note: If your network isn't directly supported by Windows 95, you won't be able to browse for its connections in Network Neighborhood. This means that you have to type the precise network connection information by hand. Don't use any mapped names. Always use the fully qualified network path in this dialog.

Clicking OK at this point stores the new connection name and returns you to the Details page. Windows 95 automatically selects the port as a destination. There's a problem with network connections, however: You can't configure them. You must capture the port first before you configure it. Capturing a port assigns it to a local connection. To capture a port, all you need to do is highlight it and click the Capture Printer Port button. You see a dialog that consists of three entries: a local port name, the network connection path, and a check box that asks if you want to reconnect to the port after each logon.

> **Tip:** If you don't plan to use the network connection on a daily basis, use the End Capture pushbutton to remove the connection. This saves system resources and reduces boot time. It also keeps Windows 95 from displaying an error message if the connection isn't available the next time you boot the machine.

There's a final configuration issue you need to address on the Details page of the printer's Properties dialog. You need to decide what timeout settings to use. The first field, Not selected, determines how long Windows 95 waits for a printer-ready signal. The only time that the printer provides this signal is when it's online and ready to go. The default value normally provides sufficient time. However, some specialty printers might require additional time if they perform some type of paper cycling or other maintenance procedure. The second setting, Transmission retry, determines how long Windows tries to send data to the printer. Normally the default value works fine here as well. However, you might need to increase the value for network printers, especially on networks with print servers such as NetWare. Sometimes the print server is slow to respond because it's servicing another request.

Now I come to one of the problem areas associated with Windows 95 and ports. What happens when the network connection that you just created becomes invalid? Logic dictates that you should be able to remove the network connection by using the Delete Port dialog. However, doing so only nets you an error message in some cases. Windows 95 refuses to delete the port.

There's a way around this problem. Simply open the Registry to the HKEY_CURRENT_USER\ Network\Persistent key. Notice that this key contains subkeys, each one a network connection. For example, LPT2 might be assigned to the \\AUX\LABELS connection. You can delete the LPT2 key to remove the old network connection from your system. Directly editing the Registry is risky, but it can provide more control for the savvy network administrator.

Configuration

Configuring your printer should be the next step after you assign it to a port. Most of the settings control the appearance of the output and the features that the printer provides to the user. In some cases, a configuration option also affects the speed of printing. I let you know what kind of choices you make as you go along.

Opening the Printer Properties dialog is as simple as right-clicking the Printer icon and selecting the Properties option from the context menu. The first page you always see is the General page, shown in Figure 16.6. All this page contains is the printer name, a comment that other users can use to identify the printer, and a separator page entry. The comment can contain any information you want it to, such as the days and times that the printer is available for use. You shouldn't make any temporary comments because this field gets copied only once to other machines that need to use the printer. In other words, the comment is permanent and won't change as you change the comment on your machine. The Separator page option is useful when more than one person uses the printer. It sends a page containing your name and other identifying information to the printer before it actually prints your document. Using a separator page wastes a piece of paper for each print job, but it does make sorting through the printouts a lot easier. There's also a Print Test Page pushbutton at the bottom of the screen. You can use this to test the capabilities of your printer at any time.

Figure 16.6.
The General page of the Printer Properties dialog allows you to change the basic identification of the printer.

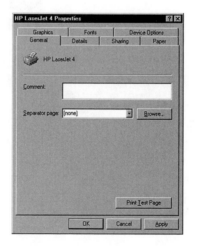

If you make a connection to a network printer (one attached to a file or print server), you see a Printer Settings page like the one shown in Figure 16.7. There are three main sections of this page: Output Settings, Banner Settings, and Other Settings. The Output Settings section defines how you want the print server to handle specific page elements such as form feeds and tabs. You can also tell the print server to always output a specific number of copies. For example, you could tell it that you always need three copies: one for you, another for your boss, and a third for the file. The banner settings are very important for home network users. You want to uncheck the Enable Banner check box as shown in the figure to avoid wasting a lot of paper. Business users, especially those in large offices, want to enable this feature to help keep print jobs separate. There are two banner-specific text boxes if you do enable the banner feature. Both are normally 12 characters long. The first text box tells what will appear in the upper half of the banner. The second text box tells what will appear in the lower half of the banner. A banner page is always one full page long. The final section, Other Settings, allows you to define three print characteristics. The Hold check box tells the print server to place this job in the print queue but not to print it until you tell it to do so. The Keep check box tells the print server to print the job as usual but to retain a copy of the job in the print queue afterward. Finally, the Notify check box tells the print server to notify you when the print job is complete—an especially handy feature on large networks when you're printing a large number of pages.

Figure 16.7.
The Printer Settings pageof the Printer Properties dialog box allows you to change the basic identification of the printer.

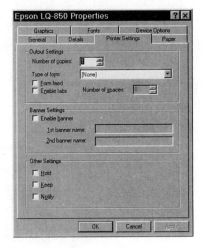

The Sharing page, shown in Figure 16.8, allows you to share the printer with other people. It contains two radio buttons. Selecting the Shared As button allows other people to use the printer. You must provide a share name. The comment and password are optional. I always recommend including a comment so that other people know whether this printer's the one they're actually looking for. Once you share a printer, Windows 95 adds a hand to its icon. This shows that the printer is shared and helps prevent any confusion over local and network resources.

Tip: Sharing reduces your spooling options. In addition, using a shared printer imposes other speed penalties on the local user. I always create a second printer for myself that isn't shared. This way, I get the best of both worlds: a shared printer for other people to use and a nonshared printer that's configured specifically for my needs.

Figure 16.8.
Use the Sharing page
to allow other people
to use your printer.

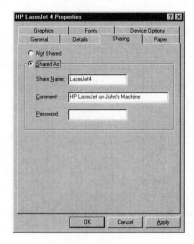

The Paper page, shown in Figure 16.9, allows you to select the paper you want to use. The Orientation section allows you to choose the direction of printing: landscape or portrait. The Paper source list box allows you to choose from the various paper bin options that the printer provides. The Copies field tells Windows how many copies of the printout to make. I usually find it easier to select the number of copies within the application than to specify it here.

Figure 16.9.
The Paper page
contains all the entries
required to select your
paper type and print
orientation.

Clicking the Unprintable Area pushbutton displays a dialog where you can fine-tune the unprintable margins or "dead zone" where the toner or ribbon can't reach. The default settings are usually adequate unless you run into a special printing situation.

Tip: Some applications, such as Netscape Navigator, rely on the settings in the Unprintable Area dialog to determine where to stop printing. If you have fan fold paper installed in a dot matrix printer and set the Top and Bottom fields to 0, these programs continue to print without observing any margins at all. (This happens despite any margins you set using the Printer Setup option of the program.) As a minimum, they place any headers or footers you create in strange places. If you run into a situation where an application doesn't seem to observe any margin settings that you request, change the settings in the Unprintable Area dialog.

The name of the Graphics page is somewhat misleading. It also determines the print quality of the text you output using TrueType or other nonresident fonts when using some types of printers. For example, the settings on this page affect a dot matrix or inkjet-type printer but not a laser printer. The laser printer downloads its fonts, so the printer determines their quality level within the limitations of the resolution you set for it. Figure 16.10 shows the Graphics page.

Figure 16.10.
The Graphics page might affect more than just graphics, depending on the type of printer you use.

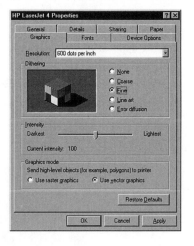

The Resolution field on this page has a significant effect on the output quality of your document. It also has an effect on print speed and could affect system memory. High-resolution printouts require more time, especially from a dot matrix printer, in which the output speed could drop to as little as one tenth the normal level. In addition, managing these printouts requires more system resources such as CPU cycles and memory. Finally, any high-resolution printout that uses the spooler needs more temporary disk storage as well. Always consider all the factors before choosing a particular course of action with your printer. A lower-resolution printout might not look as appealing, but it reduces the drain on system resources.

The various dithering options allow you to determine how Windows represents color on your printer output. It's especially important to use the correct settings for black-and-white printers because

Windows has fewer methods to provide aesthetically pleasing color differentiation. The following list describes the most common dithering options that you see:

- None: This option forces Windows to use the printer's built-in capabilities rather than dither the image. This usually doesn't work well with noncolor printers.

- Course: This option takes less time to process but produces less pleasing results. Coarse dithering normally provides one fourth the number of color combinations that the Fine option produces.

- Fine: I use the Fine option for final print output. It provides the best color differentiation your printer can support.

- Line Art: Use this option if you want to remove the colors and print only the lines used to create a graphic. It comes in handy when you need to print an outlined graphic and don't want the colors to interfere with the quality of the output.

- Error Diffusion: Windows 95 provides this option to take care of special color dithering problems. Have you ever seen a pattern in the dithering scheme used by some printers? This is called a moiré pattern. Most artists consider it a nuisance. The Error diffusion option trades a little additional processing time for a random dithering scheme. It reduces the chance that you see patterns in your printed output.

The Intensity slider allows you to change the darkness of your printout. It works like the slider on your toaster. The default value of 100 usually produces the crispest printout when you're using a new ribbon or cartridge.

Tip: The Intensity slider can actually save you money. Simply set it lower when you first install a ribbon or cartridge. This reduces the amount of ink or toner that you use per page. Of course, the quality of the printout suffers slightly. Increasing the darkness as you near the end of the ribbon or cartridge's life allows you to use it longer. Doing so might cause some graphics to look "muddy," but this setting won't adversely affect text.

Some printers include an additional setting like the one shown at the bottom of the page. In this case, the Printer Properties dialog is asking whether you want to output graphics in vector or raster mode. Using vector graphics might provide a little more flexibility. This also reduces the processing load on the machine at the expense of the printer. In addition, vector graphics require more printer memory because you need to store both a vector graphic and its raster counterpart. Using raster graphics means a slower printout, but this could allow you to print pages that wouldn't otherwise fit in printer memory.

The Fonts page,shown in Figure 16.11, allows you to control how the printer handles fonts. Because the font capability of a printer varies from machine to machine, it's likely that your Font page will look different from mine. However, there are some standard capabilities, and I cover them here.

Figure 16.11.
The contents of the Fonts page can vary greatly from machine to machine.

Most printers support cartridges these days. Even the lowliest dot matrix printer usually provides some type of cartridge support. The Cartridges list box in this dialog allows you to tell Windows which cartridges the printer contains.

Most laser printers provide the capability to manage TrueType fonts. There are three options in this case, but your printer might support only one or two of them. The first option allows you to download the fonts as an outline. This is the most flexible option and the one that I generally recommend. The advantage of this method is that the printer can create the full range of type sizes that TrueType allows. This method also saves memory because the TrueType font probably takes less room than the bitmap equivalents. The negative side to this selection is that it costs you some print time. The printer must render all the fonts that it needs for a print job rather than just use them. The second option allows you to download the fonts as bitmaps. You use this option if you intend to use only a few fonts for your print jobs and speed is a critical factor. This option probably uses more memory, but it really depends on how many bitmaps you download and their size. The third option is for people who don't have much printer memory to spare. It keeps the TrueType fonts loaded on the local machine. The advantage is greatly reduced printer memory requirements. The disadvantage is greatly increased print times. Sending output to a printer in graphics rather than text mode takes at least twice as long under the best circumstances. Think twice before committing to this particular option.

The HP LaserJet (and other printers) come with a special utility that allows you to download fonts. You access the download utility by clicking the Install Printer Fonts pushbutton near the bottom of the dialog. Essentially, you tell the utility which fonts you want to download to the printer, and it takes care of the rest. Because each download utility is different, I won't go into further detail here.

The final page of the printer configuration dialog is Device Options (see Figure 16.12). As in so many other cases, the laser printer provides more options than other types of printers you might use. Just about every printer you use includes a Print quality list box. This allows you to select from the various quality modes that the printer supplies. In most cases, the term is a little nebulous. A printer might provide a "letter quality" mode and a "draft" mode. Don't confuse this setting with resolution because the two settings are completely different. The best course of action is to check out your printer manual to find out exactly what this term means to a particular vendor. In general, letter quality is always better than draft.

Figure 16.12.
The Device Options page can contain just about anything.

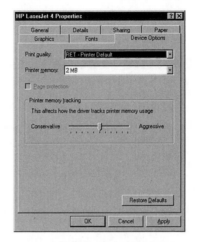

There are three other optional fields on this page. One that's common to most laser printers is the Printer memory field. The printer normally knows how much memory it has, but the Windows 95 driver doesn't. The LaserJet 4 also includes special features such as page protection and a printer memory manager. You want to spend some time reading your printer manual to determine precisely what these settings will do for you.

Point and Print

Point and print is a new Windows 95 feature. It allows you to do a few things you couldn't do with previous versions of Windows. The most significant thing it does is simplify remote printer installation. All you need to do to install a remote printer from a Windows 95, Windows NT, or NetWare network location is drag the icon from Network Neighborhood into the Printer folder. Windows 95 takes care of the rest. It might ask you to insert the CD-ROM so that it can load the proper drivers on your machine. Other than that, installation is as close to automatic as you can get.

Note: If you need access to a printer attached to a Windows for Workgroups workstation or a print server that doesn't support point and print, you can still load the printer driver using the standard technique I mentioned at the beginning of this chapter. Dragging any

continues

icon from Network Neighborhood to your Printer folder should at least start the installation utility. Double-clicking the Printer icon in Network Neighborhood accomplishes the same thing as Windows attempts to open the Printer Status dialog. (Whether it is successful or not depends on the limitations of your network, the printer driver, and whether the remote workstation responds.)

Quick Printing Techniques

Windows 95 takes a proactive approach when it comes to printing. There are a lot of different ways you can get a document to the printer. I usually use the Print command on the context menu because most of my documents go to the same place if I don't have them open. Of course, you still have the usual Windows defaults for sending a document to the printer, including your application's Print menu.

Tip: I viewed DDE in a variety of ways throughout this book. The most recent was in Chapter 12, "DDE, OLE, DCOM, and ActiveX," where I discussed some of the ways you can use DDE with a document. In Chapter 6, "Startup Shortcuts," I looked at the way Explorer uses DDE. Here's one additional way to use DDE: Use Explorer to add another menu option to the context menu of your documents if you normally use more than one printer. This allows you to select something other than the default printer with the context menu. Unfortunately, your application must support DDE for this option work. Use the current Print entry as a basis for creating your advanced Print option.

Another method that people use to send documents to the printer is to place a shortcut to the printer on their desktops. Then, all you need to do to print a document is drag its icon to the printer you want to use and drop it.

32-Bit Printing

Now that you have a printer configured and ready for use, it might be a good time to look at the way Windows 95 handles this task. An understanding of how printing works often helps you discover new optimization techniques or track down an equipment failure with ease. Figure 16.13 gives you an overview of the Windows 95 print architecture. I describe each component in the following list.

Figure 16.13.
Windows 95 uses an improved print architecture that depends on minidriver support.

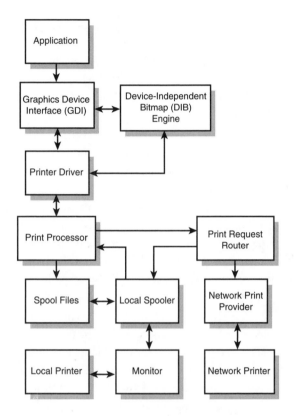

- Graphics device interface (GDI): I talked about this particular element of the printing picture in the past. The GDI is the API that an application uses to talk to the printer. An application doesn't directly access a printer as DOS did. It uses the Windows services. This allows for centralized scheduling and control of print jobs, a necessary requirement of a multitasking environment.

- Device-independent bitmap (DIB) engine: The DIB engine is normally associated with the display adapter. It works with the GDI to produce the bitmap you see onscreen. For example, when Windows displays wallpaper on the desktop, it's the DIB engine that actually produces the bitmap under the instruction of the GDI. I talk about this topic more in Chapter 17, "Mice and Keyboards." As far as a printer is concerned, the DIB engine provides a convenient method of manipulating graphics. For example, if you choose to print a file in graphics mode instead of text mode, the DIB engine helps prepare the print job for you.

- Printer driver: This is the third piece of the print page preparation. It interfaces with both the GDI and the DIB engine to produce printer-specific output in the form of journal records. Think of a journal record as the disassembled pieces of a puzzle. All the pieces are eventually put together, but for right now, each record is just a piece of that puzzle. As with puzzle pieces, you can look at them individually and recognize what they will eventually become.

- Print processor: The print processor accepts the printer-ready data from the printer driver. Its only function at this point is to de-spool the data to the print request router. In other words, it sends the journal records out single file in an orderly manner. Later, the print processor takes care of spooling the data to the local hard drive (spool files) if this is a local print job. This means that it takes all the puzzle pieces (journal records) and connects them into a single document.

- Print request router: This component routes the formatted data to the appropriate location. It determines whether the job is for a local or remote printer. If it's for a remote printer, the print request router sends the data to the network print provider. Otherwise, it sends the data to the local spooler.

- Network print provider: The network print provider is network-specific. It's the interface between your machine and the beginning of the network data stream. Its job is to accept the journal records, connect them into a single document, convert the document into a network-specific format (if required), and transmit the converted data to the next component in the network data stream. If all goes according to plan, this data eventually finds its way to a network printer.

- Local spooler: The first job of this particular component is to hand off print jobs to the print processor. The print processor converts the journal records it receives into a document. The local spooler reads the data files that the print processor stores on disk and sends them to the monitor. It also accepts messages from the monitor regarding the status of the printer. I discuss the types of information it receives when I discuss the monitor.

- Spool files: These are the physical files that the print processor stores in the Spool folder under the main Windows folder. Each printer type has its own storage location in this folder.

- Monitor: The monitor handles all communication with the printer. It accepts data from the spooler and transmits it to the printer. The monitor is also responsible for providing the spooler with Plug and Play information about the printer. Finally, the monitor provides the spooler with printer error information. Instead of giving you a "printer not ready" message, printers that support a bidirectional port can supply an "out of paper" or "toner low" message.

This might look like a lot of work just to get your document from an application to the printer that's connected to your machine. You're right. If that's all the tasks that Windows 95 could handle, this architecture would be very inflated indeed. However, there's much more here than meets the eye. Using this kind of interface provides the user with a lot more freedom in regard to printer usage. It ensures that everyone gets equal access to the printer. Programmers benefit as well because it's easier to write print drivers. The DIB engine improves the quality of your output. I could go on, but I think the point is made. The printing architecture might be complex, but it makes printing easier from a user perspective.

Managing Print Jobs

With so many new capabilities, it's no wonder that your ability to manage print jobs under Windows 95 is improved as well. Gaining access to the print jobs you have running is no problem. Whenever you print, Windows adds a Printer icon to the control area of the Taskbar. Resting your mouse pointer over the Printer icon tells you how many print jobs are pending. This provides a quick method of monitoring your printer status without opening any new windows.

If multiple printers are in use on your workstation at one time, right-clicking the Printer icon displays a menu of available printers. You can choose to open one or all of them. The top menu item opens all active printers—those with print jobs. It doesn't matter if the print job is paused or not.

The following sections describe the management tools that Windows provides for printers. I look at both local and remote printers.

Local Printers

The first type of printer I look at is the local printer. All you need to do to open a printer is right-click the Printer icon and select it from the list. As an alternative, double-clicking this icon displays the current print jobs for the default printer. The printer management display is shown in Figure 16.14.

Figure 16.14.
Getting to the dialog needed to manage your print jobs under Windows 95 is easily accomplished from the Taskbar.

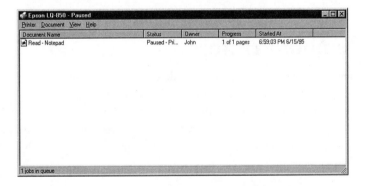

Document Name	Status	Owner	Progress	Started At
Read - Notepad	Paused - Pri...	John	1 of 1 pages	6:59:03 PM 6/15/95

Epson LQ-850 - Paused

Printer Document View Help

1 jobs in queue

Note: Windows 95 always defaults to a printer with an error. If you're having a printing problem, double-clicking the Printer icon displays the window for the problem printer. The Printer icon also changes in appearance to tell you there's a failure. This allows you to track the status of all your print jobs, even if the printer isn't in the same room as you.

Managing jobs is fairly simple. Once you open the printer management display, you can access all the print jobs on an individual basis. The Printer menu contains two options that allow you to control the printer itself: Pause Printing and Purge Print Jobs. The Pause Printing option allows you to stop the printer momentarily and restart it later. You can use this option to stop the printer for a quick toner change or to correct a paper jam. Purge Print Jobs clears all the print jobs from the spooler. Use this option with care because you might accidentally remove something you didn't want to.

This menu has several other options as well. The Save as Default option allows you to maintain any configuration changes you make as permanent settings. The Properties option opens the Printer Properties dialog I discussed earlier.

You can access the Document menu in one of two ways. The first method is to select a document and access the menu directly. The second method is faster: Just right-click the document you want to work with and select the option from the context menu. The Document menu has two options. You can pause print jobs using the Pause Printing option. The Cancel Printing option removes the print job from the spooler.

> **Tip:** One thing that isn't apparent when you look at this display is the fact that you can select a print job and drag it somewhere else in the list. This allows you to change the priority of print jobs by simply moving them around as needed. You can move groups of print jobs with equal ease.

Remote Printers

Managing a remote printer under Windows 95 is nearly as easy as managing a local one. The only caveat is that the print server must be a Windows 95, Windows NT, NetWare, or other network that supports point and print. Otherwise, remote print jobs don't show up on your display. Once you do establish a connection with the remote printer, you can exercise all the document management capabilities you have with a local printer. (All this assumes that you have the access rights required to perform the task.)

Remote printing does offer one opportunity that local printing doesn't. You can perform what is called an *offline* print. Essentially, this is a form of pause. The Printer menu contains a special option for remote printers called Work Offline. Checking the Work Offline selection pauses the printer and stores the print jobs on disk. When you uncheck this entry, all the print jobs get sent to the remote printer.

In the Printer folder display, the printer that's in Work Offline mode is grayed out. Windows 95 provides this visual indicator to tell you that you can use the printer but that none of the print jobs actually go anywhere. Another reminder is the Printer icon on the Taskbar. You see the Printer icon, but it includes the error indicator I mentioned earlier. Again, this tells you that one of the printers requires service. In this case, it isn't an unexpected error, but merely a feature that Windows 95 provides.

Installing Fonts

Under Windows 3.*x* it was fairly easy to install a font, but you were never quite sure what you were getting. In addition, you had to use a program that made the whole process seem a little more mysterious than it needed to be.

The standard method of installing a font in Windows 95 is pretty straightforward, but it does prevent you from really seeing the font before you install it. In this way, it shares some of the deficiencies of the older Windows 3.*x* method. On the other hand, it's safe because it's guaranteed to work every time. With that in mind, I show you the standard method of font installation. (Don't miss my favorite alternative in the tip at the end of this section.)

1. Open Control Panel and double-click the Fonts icon. You should see the display shown in Figure 16.15.

Figure 16.15.
This Explorer-style display allows you to view all the fonts installed on your machine.

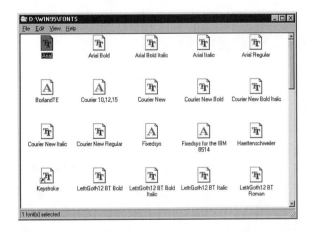

2. Use the File | Install New Fonts command to display the Add Fonts dialog, shown in Figure 16.16.
3. Browse your hard disk, floppy disk, or CD-ROM drive until you find the fonts that you want to install. Highlight the desired fonts and click OK. You will see the new fonts in your Font folder.

Figure 16.16.
The Add Fonts dialog
allows you to select
fonts to add to your
Windows installation.

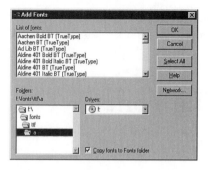

Tip: You can get a look at a sample of a TrueType font by simply double-clicking its icon in Explorer. Windows opens a dialog that displays information about the font, an alphabet, and several lines of text in different sizes. If you like what you see and want to install it, just arrange the Explorer window so that both the font file and the Fonts folder are visible and then drag the font file and drop it onto the Fonts folder. Windows installs the font automatically.

Removing Fonts

Removing fonts is easy under Windows 95. All you do is open the Fonts folder—either through Explorer or by double-clicking the Fonts applet in Control Panel—select the fonts you want to remove, and press the Delete key. It's that easy.

You need to observe a few precautions. First and foremost, don't erase any font that you're not sure of. Windows 95 requires several fonts for system use, and erasing them can cause problems. Second, if you do erase a font, make sure that you don't need it anymore or that you have a copy stored somewhere.

Tip: Instead of deleting a font that you no longer require, archive it. All you need to do is move it from the Fonts folder to a floppy disk or a network drive. You can even use the Send To option on the context menu to do it. This technique saves you heartache later when you look for the font you deleted and it's no longer available.

Viewing and Printing Fonts

The interface in the Fonts folder might be Explorer, but the options are different. The View menu contains some unique features that you want to use to really see your fonts. I'm not talking about the files themselves, but the fonts. Let me show you what I mean.

Open Control Panel and double-click the Fonts applet. (You can get to the same place using the Explorer technique that I talked about earlier.) Open the View menu. You notice that Explorer now sports some new View options. The List Fonts By Similarity option is the one I like. It allows you to see which fonts you can use as a substitute for something else. For example, what if you really like the font you're using for a particular purpose but want a slightly different effect? You can use this option to find the closest match in your directory or on a CD-ROM full of fonts. Figure 16.17 shows this display. Notice the field at the top of the display. This is where you select the name of the font you want to use for comparison purposes.

Figure 16.17.
You can quickly find font families on a disk full of fonts using the List Fonts By Similarity option.

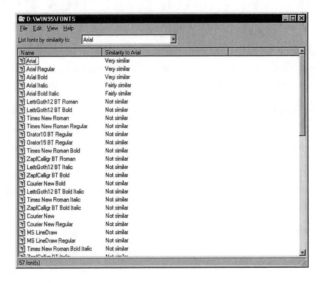

Another handy view selection is the Hide Variations option. You can use it with any of the display formats to hide the different files required to create a complete font family. For example, if you turn this option on, you see only one Arial font, even though there are files for regular, italic, bold, and bold italic variations in the folder.

Unlike with Windows 3.x, it is easy to print a sample of a font. All you need to do is right-click and select Print from the context menu. As an alternative, you can always click the Print pushbutton when viewing the font or use the File | Print command. The printout you get looks similar to the font sample that Windows displays when you double-click a font file (see Figure 16.18).

Figure 16.18.
*Double-clicking a font
allows you to see
what it looks like.*

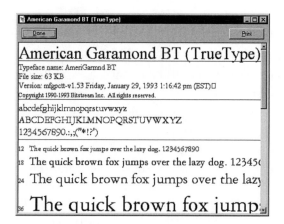

How Windows Matches Fonts

Windows uses a specific set of criteria to find a replacement font if the one you request isn't available. To get an idea of how this works, use the List Fonts By Similarity option in the Font folder. The results tell you a lot about how Windows 95 implements the rules in something called the font matching table.

The font matching table isn't actually a table; it's an algorithm that Windows 95 uses to match fonts. Windows uses the following criteria to find a matching font: the character set, variable versus fixed pitch, family, typeface name, height, width, weight, slant, underline, and strikethrough.

A TrueType font is always replaced with another TrueType font, even if a raster or vector font is a closer match. This enables your application to maintain the flexibility that TrueType provides. The negative aspect of this is that the output might not look even close to what you originally anticipated.

If the font you're trying to use is either a vector or raster font, Windows 95 uses some additional methods to obtain a good match. The following list shows, in order, the sources that Windows 95 tries to tap:

- Printer ROM font
- Printer cartridge slot font
- Downloadable soft font
- TrueType font

Note: Microsoft Plus! adds font smoothing to Windows 95 if you're running high-color video or better. Font smoothing gets rid of jagged edges you might see when the fonts are very large. To turn on font smoothing after installing Microsoft Plus!, right-click the

Desktop icon in Explorer and select Properties from the context menu. On the Plus! page of the Display Properties dialog box, check the Smooth edges of screen fonts check box.

On Your Own

This chapter showed you two different ways to install fonts. Try both methods to see which works best for you. Many graphics programs include additional fonts. You can also download them from CompuServe and many BBSes. Use this exercise to install the set of fonts that gets the job done for you.

Look in your Fonts folder to see if you can identify the various types of fonts that Windows 95 supports. How can you tell them apart? What purpose does each kind of font serve?

Install several versions of your printer, each with different settings. Try this new installation for several weeks and see if you notice the additional ease of use that several pseudo-printers can provide. Also try the various print settings to see if you notice the variations in print speed and output quality that I mentioned earlier.

Place a shortcut to your printer on the desktop and try the drag-and-drop method of printing. Simply drag a file with your mouse pointer to the Printer icon and drop it. This is the easy way of sending output to the printer using the default setup. You might want to experiment to see which printer settings work best as a default setup for you.

17

Mice and Keyboards

Peter Norton®

Even though the keyboard remains basically unchanged from the early days of personal computers, there are still a few changes to note. For example, the Microsoft Natural Keyboard (and others like it) attempt to solve the problems of repetitive stress injury by splitting the keyboard in half so there's less stress on the wrists.

A little less strange are the permutations of the mouse, which started out looking like a bar of soap. Today's versions are shaped to fit the palm of your hand. The fact that every vendor used a different human for measurement is reflected in various sizes and shapes available, along with a choice of two or three mouse buttons.

The following sections give you a tour of the great and not-so-great mouse and keyboard improvements that Windows 95 has made.

Multilingual Support

Windows comes with a variety of language options to provide multilingual support.

Installing a New Language

Installing a new keyboard language is as simple as a few clicks:

1. Open Control Panel. Double-click the Keyboard applet and select the Language tab. You should see a dialog box similar to the one shown in Figure 17.1. Notice that English is the only language listed in the Language field. This field also provides other information that you can use to determine the installed language type. In this case, it tells you the type of English (United States) and the keyboard layout (United States).

Figure 17.1.
The Language page of the Keyboard Properties dialog box allows you to select one or more languages for your computer.

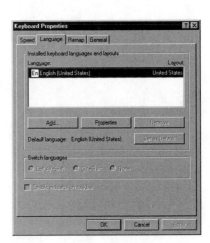

2. Click the Add button. You see the dialog box shown in Figure 17.2. It's important to consider which version of a language to choose. I currently have United States English installed. There's also a selection for other forms of English that might require a different keyboard layout. For example, pressing Shift+4 could produce a pound symbol instead of a dollar sign. The choice of language also affects the way Windows makes assumptions about other setup needs. For example, it affects the default selection for monetary and numeric formats.

Figure 17.2.
Make your choice of language carefully because there are several variations of some languages.

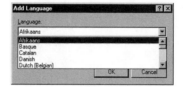

3. Click OK to complete the process. You should see a new language added to the Language field. Completing this process also enables several other fields. For example, you can now choose which Ctrl+*key* combination to use to switch between languages. You can also choose whether to display the International icon on the Taskbar. (I show you how to use this icon in a little while.)

4. Choose a default language by highlighting and then clicking the Set as Default button. You see the new default displayed in the Default Language field.

5. You'll probably want to check the layout for your new language. Highlight the new language and click the Properties button. You should see the dialog box shown in Figure 17.3. (This dialog box also displays the other changes you've made.) The dialog box is a little deceptive. At first, you might think that it's asking you to change the language again, but this isn't so. What it's asking you to change is your keyboard layout. Select a new layout to see for yourself.

Figure 17.3.
This dialog box changes your keyboard layout, not the language you're using.

6. Click OK to complete the process. In this case, I chose the DVORAK layout. Figure 17.4 shows the results. Notice that the language remains the same; only the keyboard layout has changed. I'll use the DVORAK layout whenever I choose the German language from my list.

Figure 17.4.
This dialog box shows
the results of choosing
another layout using
the Properties button.

7. Close the Keyboard Properties dialog box to complete the process. You can accomplish the same thing by using the Apply key if you don't want to close the Keyboard Properties dialog box.

8. Close Windows and reboot your computer to make the change permanent.

Changing your keyboard layout and language won't display prompts in the language you select. It affects only the way your keyboard reacts and, to some extent, helps Windows 95 provide better input in regard to other configuration selections.

Removing a Language

You'll probably run into a situation in which you no longer require a specific keyboard layout. Whatever your reason for wanting to remove the language, Windows 95 makes it easy. The following procedure shows you how.

> **Tip:** This is a good time to use the procedures shown in Chapter 9, "The Windows 95 Architecture," for checking the filenames of the drivers used to support the language you want to remove. Windows 95 won't remove these drivers, which means that they clutter your hard drive until you decide to install Windows from scratch—a long time from now, I hope.

1. Open Control Panel. Double-click the Keyboard applet and select the Language page. You should see a dialog box similar to the one shown in Figure 17.1.

2. Highlight the entry for the language support you want to remove from your machine—in this case, the German language support.

3. Click the Remove button.

4. Close the Keyboard Properties dialog box to complete the process. Windows might get confused and think that another application is using the keyboard layout if you activated it at any time during this session. All you need to do is click OK to accept the error message. Windows still removes the layout, but it won't do so until the next session.

5. Close Windows and reboot your computer to make the change permanent.

Accessing a Language from the Taskbar

Whenever you have more than one language installed on your machine, Windows gives you the opportunity to automatically add the International icon to your Taskbar. Figure 17.5 shows what this icon looks like.

Figure 17.5.
The International icon provides quick access to multiple language selections.

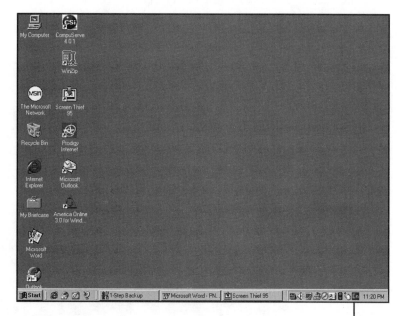

International icon

Peter's Principle: Easy Keyboard Access

Adding the International icon to your Taskbar is more than just a convenience that comes in handy when you need to change layouts. It provides a quick way to change all your keyboard settings whenever you need to do so. However, the icon doesn't normally appear

continues

unless you install more than one language on your machine. You can manually add this icon to your Taskbar by adding the International Settings application—INTERNAT.EXE—to your Startup folder. You'll find it in the SYSTEM folder under the main Windows folder for your machine. This gives you access to the keyboard settings, even if you have only one language installed.

There are several ways to use the icon. The first is to determine which language you're currently using. Each language has a two-character abbreviation. (Refer to the dialog box in Figure 17.4.) The Taskbar is where this two-digit abbreviation is used. For example, the icon shown in Figure 17.5 tells me that I have the United States English configuration installed.

Clicking the International icon displays a list of languages currently installed on the machine, as shown in Figure 17.6. Notice that each entry is preceded by its two-digit abbreviation. This is one way to determine which language you're using if you forget what the abbreviation on the icon means. All you need to do to select a new language is click it, just as you do with any other menu.

Figure 17.6.
Clicking the International icon allows you to switch quickly between installed languages.

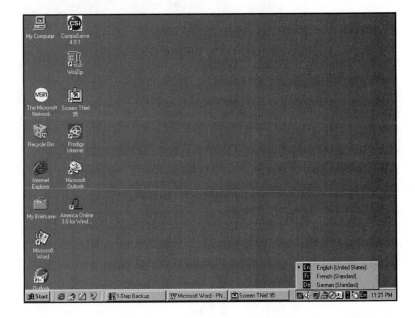

A right-click brings up the context menu that shows a What's This? entry. The associated help text could help someone who is learning how to use Windows 95.

The Properties option of the context menu acts as you would expect. It takes you to the Keyboard Properties dialog box that you looked at earlier. Even though it automatically displays the Language page, you can quickly switch to other pages as needed.

As with many of the other icons on the Taskbar, you can also momentarily hold your mouse cursor over the International icon to get more information. Doing so displays the full name of the language that you're currently using.

Configuring Your Keyboard

Languages aren't the only things you can change about your keyboard. There is one more page of selections that you can make regarding its setup. Figure 17.7 shows the page where you decide how the keyboard reacts to your key presses.

Figure 17.7.
The Speed page contains the settings required to adjust the keyboard to your typing habits.

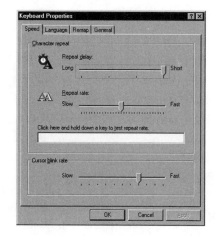

The Repeat delay setting adjusts how long the keyboard waits before it starts repeating keys. Setting this value too short could force you to undo a lot of excess keystrokes. The Repeat rate setting adjusts how fast the characters repeat across the screen. Setting a slightly lower rate enables you to control repeated keys better. Microsoft thoughtfully provided a test area that you can use to check the combination of settings. Make sure that you actually try the keyboard settings before changing them.

Use the Cursor blink rate setting to change how often the edit cursor blinks per second. Some people like a very fast rate, and other people like things a bit slower. You'll want to use a slower rate on portables because their displays take a little longer to react.

Configuring Your Mouse

A mouse is a necessity for using Windows 95. Some tasks are difficult or impossible to perform through the keyboard alone.

Standard Mouse Configuration

Just as you should configure your keyboard for optimum performance, you should configure your mouse as well. To do this, open the Mouse Properties dialog box by double-clicking the Mouse applet in Control Panel. If you have the Microsoft Intellimouse, you see a dialog box similar to Figure 17.8.

Figure 17.8.
The StepSavers page of the Mouse Properties dialog box allows you to change the way the mouse is configured and how it reacts.

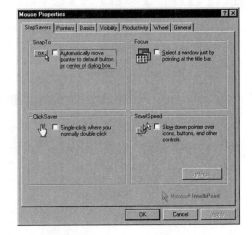

The StepSavers page provides four options: SnapTo, Focus, ClickSaver, and SmartSpeed. The SnapTo option automatically moves the mouse pointer to the default button of a dialog box. That way, you can just click the mouse to choose the default option. The Focus option is useful if you have two or more windows open at the same time. Rather than click inside a window to change the focus, you can just point at the window's title bar. The ClickSaver option lets you replace double-clicks with a single-click. If you find double-clicking awkward, you can just single-click items instead. The SmartSpeed option automatically slows down the mouse pointer when you move it over buttons, icons, or other items that you can click. Using SmartSpeed, you can better control the movement of the mouse pointer.

The Pointers page, shown in Figure 17.9, allows you to change the mouse pointers used to indicate specific events. In addition to the standard cursors that previous versions of Windows provided, Windows 95 provides a few fancy cursors, such as the reptiles version displayed in the figure. In addition to the static cursors, Windows 95 also provides some cursors that move.

The upper section of this page allows you to save and load various mouse schemes. Think of a mouse scheme in the same way that you do a color scheme under previous versions of Windows, and you have the right idea. Use the list box to select a previously saved scheme. Clicking the Save As button displays a dialog box that you can use to enter the name of a new scheme.

Figure 17.9.
The Pointers page of the Mouse Properties dialog box allows you to change the appearance of the mouse cursor.

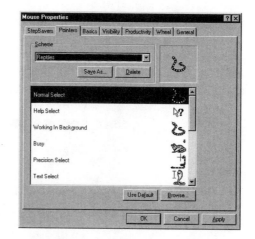

Tip: Windows 95 provides a wealth of mouse pointers, including some extra-large ones. The extra-large pointers are actually designed for use with some of the Accessibility options. However, they also come in handy on laptops, where seeing the cursor can be a real chore, and also in presentations, where a larger-than-normal cursor helps you make your point.

The lower section of the Pointers page contains the actual mouse pointers. The purpose of each pointer is self-explanatory. To change a cursor, highlight it and click the Browse button. Windows displays a list of cursors in the CURSOR folder (found within the main Windows folder), as shown in Figure 17.10. All you need to do is double-click the cursor you want. Windows replaces the current cursor with the one you selected. Notice that this dialog box also displays a preview of the cursor. Any animated cursors appear to move within the preview box so you can see how they'll look when you use them in an application. If you ever select a cursor by accident and want to return to the default setting, click the Use Default button at the bottom of the Pointers page.

Figure 17.10.
Use the Browse dialog box to select from the list of currently available cursors.

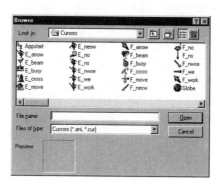

The Basics page, shown in Figure 17.11, affects the pointer speed, button selection, and double-click speed. The Pointer Speed option determines how the mouse cursor tracks your hand movements with the slider at the top of the page. Setting the speed too high can cause jerky cursor movement and make it difficult to control some operations, such as drawing. Set the speed too low and you need to make a large movement with the mouse to get a small movement onscreen.

Figure 17.11.
The Basics page defines how the mouse works.

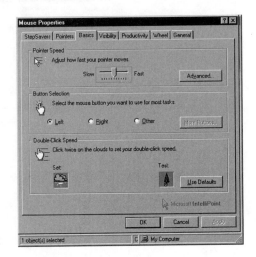

The Button Selection option lets you choose which mouse button to use as the primary button. The default button is the left mouse button, but you can switch it to the right button or the middle button if you have a three button mouse. The Double-Click Speed option lets you adjust how your mouse responds to double-clicks. You might want to adjust the double-click speed if you have trouble double-clicking an item.

The Visibility page, shown in Figure 17.12, provides four different options for keeping track of the mouse pointer. The Sonar option lets you press the Ctrl key to find the mouse pointer. The Vanish option makes the mouse pointer disappear while you're typing, which can be especially handy if you have a large mouse pointer that gets in the way of your typing. The Trails option displays multiple mouse pointers as you move the mouse, making it easier to find the mouse pointer. The PointerWrap option displays the mouse pointer on the opposite edge of the screen when you move the mouse pointer off the screen.

The Productivity page, shown in Figure 17.13, provides three options: an Odometer, an Orientation, and a ClickLock option. The Odometer option lets you track how far you've moved the mouse during the day. The Orientation option lets you calibrate the mouse for your personal style. For example, some people hold the mouse straight up and down, others hold it slightly cockeyed, and still others hold it sideways. By adjusting the orientation, you can make the mouse adapt to your particular style of holding and moving the mouse. The ClickLock option lets you click once to represent the same action as holding the mouse button down. When you click a second time, this action is the same as releasing the mouse button as if you held it down the whole time. The ClickLock option can especially be useful for people who find holding the mouse button cumbersome.

Figure 17.12.
The Visibility page gives you different options for tracking the mouse pointer on your screen.

Figure 17.13.
The Productivity page provides options for personalizing the mouse.

The Wheel page, shown in Figure 17.14, defines how the wheel of the Intellimouse works. If you turn on the Wheel option, click the Settings button to further define the direction and scrolling of the wheel as shown in Figure 17.15. The Wheel Button option defines how the wheel button works, such as a double-click to display the Start menu.

Figure 17.14.
The Wheel page lets you customize the third wheel button on the Intellimouse.

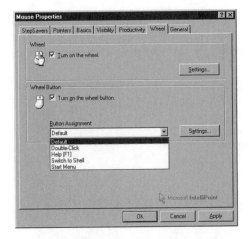

Figure 17.15.
The Settings for Wheel dialog defines the direction the wheel scrolls a window and how many lines it scrolls within a window.

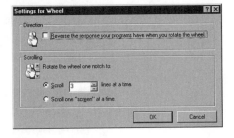

The General page, shown in Figure 17.16, defines the type of mouse attached to your computer. If you switch to a different mouse, you might have to use the General page to define your new mouse type.

Figure 17.16.
The General page defines the type of mouse attached to your computer.

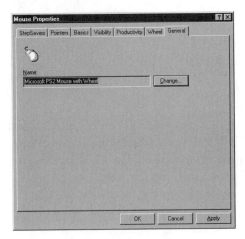

Special Laptop Configuration Considerations

Laptop computers normally have a special built-in pointing device or touchpad. Whatever type of mouse your laptop uses, it likely requires some special form of configuration. (The pages you actually see depend on the laptop vendor and the type of mouse you have installed.) As with a desktop machine, you access the Mouse Properties dialog box on a laptop by double-clicking the Mouse applet in the Control Panel. The first page you're likely to see is the Quick Setup page.

Unlike when using a desktop machine, you can't rely on your laptop's environment staying the same. You may prefer to use a standard mouse at the office, another type of standard mouse at home, and the built-in mouse on the road. Because each mouse configuration is different, you need to rely on vendor documentation to actually set it up.

Another problem with laptops is addressed by the Orientation page. For example, trackball users might need to place the trackball at the right side of the laptop for part of a trip but move it to the left side for another part of the trip because the seat is next to the window and there isn't any room to move. To use this feature, click the Set Orientation button. Windows 95 asks you to move the balloon toward the clouds at the top of the screen. Moving the trackball adjusts the orientation as needed to keep mouse movement the same as it normally is when you use a standard mouse. (In other words, moving the mouse up actually moves the cursor toward the top of the screen.) If you don't move the mouse cursor in a straight line, Windows displays an error message telling you so. Simply choose to try again and Windows 95 will set the orientation for you.

Unlike other hardware components, Windows 95 won't automatically register a mouse change—especially if your laptop has a built-in mouse. That's what makes the Devices page so important. It allows you to do two things: add a new mouse device to those that your laptop supports or select an existing one.

To select an existing device, choose it from the drop-down list, and then click Apply. Make sure that the mouse is plugged in before you do this or you may find yourself without a functional pointer device. (Most laptop software searches for the pointing device before switching over, but you can't be sure that it will.)

To add a new device, simply click the Add Device button. The first thing you see is a warning message. As stated by the message, you can normally plug in a serial mouse while the machine is running. If you plug in a PS/2 port mouse while the machine is running, there's a good chance that you'll damage it. Always shut down the machine first and then plug in the PS/2 mouse. Once you see this warning message, you can click OK to start the search for a new pointing device. If Windows 95 finds a new mouse, it takes you through the setup and configuration process.

Access for Users with Disabilities

Windows 95 provides special access features for people with disabilities. What I look at is the features themselves and how you can use them to enhance productivity. The first thing you need to do to examine these features is open Control Panel and double-click the Accessibility Options applet.

Special Keyboard Features

Windows provides three special keyboard features: StickyKeys, FilterKeys, and ToggleKeys. You'll find them on the Keyboard page of the Accessibility Properties dialog box, as shown in Figure 17.17. You can turn on any of them by using the special key combinations that Microsoft provides.

Figure 17.17.
You can turn on any of the keyboard accessibility functions from this page.

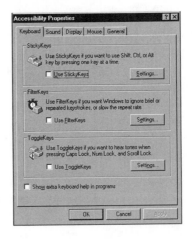

All these features have one thing in common: They change the way that the keyboard works, independently of the keyboard driver. You must install the Accessibility Options feature to make them work. The option that intrigued me was the Show extra keyboard help in programs check box at the bottom of the page. It adds help information to applications that support this feature.

Using StickyKeys

The StickyKeys feature comes in handy for a variety of purposes. It makes the Shift, Ctrl, and Alt keys act as a toggle switch. Press the key once and it becomes active. Press it a second time and it's turned off. One of the ways I use StickyKeys is in graphics programs that require you to hold down the Ctrl key to select a group of items. It's inconvenient to hold down the Ctrl key while you look around for objects to select. The StickyKeys feature alleviates this problem. To look at some of the options you can select, click the Settings button to open the Settings for StickyKeys dialog box shown in Figure 17.18.

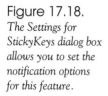

Figure 17.18.

The Settings for StickyKeys dialog box allows you to set the notification options for this feature.

There are several groups of settings for StickyKeys. The first option, Keyboard shortcut, allows you to enable StickyKeys using the shortcut key. There really isn't any good reason to turn this off because it's unlikely that any application would use the same control key sequence.

The Options group contains two settings. Normally, the StickyKeys option works as a toggle. Checking the first box tells Windows to wait until you press the same control key twice before making it active. The second check box is designed to allow two people to use the same keyboard. Pressing a control key and a non-control key at the same time turns StickyKeys off.

The Notification group also contains two settings. The first setting tells Windows to play a different sound for each unique control key that it makes active. This can keep you from activating a control key by accident. The second option displays an icon on the Taskbar so that you can control StickyKeys more easily. I normally select this option to make it easier for me to turn StickyKeys on and off.

Using FilterKeys

FilterKeys helps you get rid of extra keystrokes so that you don't get "tthis" instead of "this." As with StickyKeys, you can adjust the way FilterKeys works by clicking the Settings button. The Settings for FilterKeys dialog box is shown in Figure 17.19. Notice that the first option in this dialog box allows you to turn the shortcut key on and off. It works just like the same feature in StickyKeys. The Notification group at the bottom of the page should look familiar. The only difference is that instead of playing a sound, FilterKeys beeps when you activate it.

The Filter options group allows you to select between two ways of filtering keystrokes. The first option filters keys that get pressed in rapid succession. For example, this feature would filter the rapid typing of the extra "t" in the example I mentioned. The Settings button displays a dialog box that allows you to select how long an interval must pass between the first and second times you press the same key. The second option in this group filters accidental key presses. You might press a key without meaning to. As with the StickyKeys option, the Settings button takes you to a dialog box where you select how long you have to press a key before Windows will accept it.

Figure 17.19.
The Settings for
FilterKeys dialog box
offers you different
filter options.

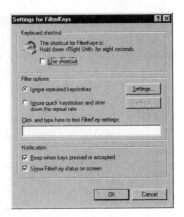

Using ToggleKeys

ToggleKeys alerts you each time you turn one of the Lock keys on or off. It emits a tone every time you turn the Caps Lock, Scroll Lock, or Num Lock keys on or off. Figure 17.20 shows the Settings for ToggleKeys dialog box. Notice that it has only a single option. This option allows you to turn the shortcut key on or off.

Figure 17.20.
The Settings for
ToggleKeys dialog box
allows you to use a
shortcut key to turn
this feature on and
off.

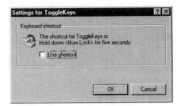

Special Mouse Settings

MouseKeys allows you to use the arrow keys as a mouse. Instead of moving the mouse cursor with the mouse, you can move it with the arrow keys. Of course, this doesn't disable your mouse; it merely augments it. Figure 17.22 shows the Mouse page of the Accessibility Properties dialog box.

MouseKeys has only one dialog box of settings. You access it by clicking the Settings button; the Settings for MouseKeys dialog box is shown in Figure 17.22. The first option, Keyboard shortcut, allows you to enable MouseKeys using a shortcut key. There really isn't any good reason to turn this off; it's unlikely that any program would use the same control key sequence.

Figure 17.21.
MouseKeys can put the control back into your mouse cursor.

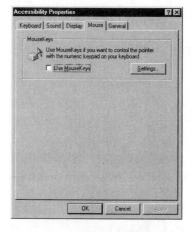

Figure 17.22.
The Settings for MouseKeys dialog box allows you to change the speed of the pointer.

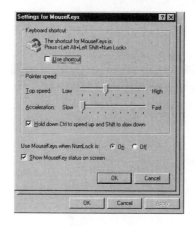

The second group, Pointer speed, is where you can optimize the performance of this particular feature. The first option allows you to set the fastest speed at which you can move the mouse cursor by using the arrow keys. The Acceleration setting determines how fast the cursor reaches full speed after you press it. Windows doesn't start the cursor at full speed; it brings it there gradually. The combination of these two settings determine just how much added control MouseKeys gives you over the cursor. Checking the check box in this group gives you another option. Pressing the Ctrl key speeds up the mouse cursor; pressing the Shift key slows it down.

The final group contains two settings. The radio button controls when MouseKeys is active. You must specify whether the Num Lock key should be on or off when you use MouseKeys. The second option determines whether the MouseKeys icon appears on the Taskbar.

New Accessibility Tools for Windows 98

Windows 98 will offer two new accessibility tools called the Accessibility Settings wizard and the Microsoft Magnifier. The Microsoft Magnifier can magnify a small portion of the screen so you can momentarily view something onscreen in a larger format.

The Accessibility Settings wizard asks you what type of problem you're having and helps you define a solution. For example, if you tell the Accessibility Settings wizard that items are too small in Windows, it displays a dialog containing a sample window with all the current font sizes and a slider.

On Your Own

Try all the different Accessibility options to see if any of them provide features you can use. I provided suggestions on how you could use each feature in this chapter.

Use the DVORAK keyboard layout, which lets you type faster with a lot less fatigue. Go back to earlier chapters—especially Chapter 6, "Startup Shortcuts,"—and practice using various shortcuts with the Accessibility options turned on. Does using this feature with your standard shortcuts make a difference? Try a variety of combinations to create the fastest keyboard interface possible.

18

Video
Configurations

Peter Norton®

Video is the underlying combination of hardware and software that allows you to see the graphics, dialog boxes, icons, and other elements that make Windows 95 worth using. Unfortunately, this combination isn't always flawless. The following list illustrates some of Windows 95's possible video problems:

- Application level: Three different kinds of applications use Windows 95. MS-DOS applications normally think that they're alone in the world, so they violate just about every imaginable rule for displaying information. Although 16-bit Windows applications are a bit more conscientious than their MS-DOS counterparts, they still use an older interface to draw to the display. Finally, newer 32-bit Windows might offer the ultimate in available features right now, but they're often hampered by other applications running on the machine.

- Device driver: If the display driver doesn't correctly interpret the commands issued by applications running under Windows, or if those applications use undocumented command features, there's a good chance of miscommunication. For example, if the adapter misinterprets some of the commands that an application uses, you get an unreadable screen.

- Adapter: In the beginning, IBM's leadership was responsible for the standard way in which the CGA and EGA display adapters worked. By the time VGA came around, IBM was starting to lose its leadership position. Then came SVGA (super VGA), and there was no IBM standard to follow. For a while, there was a lack of any kind of standardization for the extended modes that vendors built into their display adapters. The result was total chaos. A little later in this chapter, I look at how this problem was finally resolved.

- Operating system requirements: Normally, the operating system itself is the least of your worries with the display. However, sometimes it can actually be the source of your problems. Take icons, for example. We all take them for granted because they generally work without any difficulty. What happens if some file that the operating system needs gets changed by an application or gets corrupted somehow? In most cases, you need to replace this file before things will work again.

Now that you have a better idea of the video problems that Windows encounters, you might wonder why it works at all. Windows uses something known as an *event loop* to talk with applications. Think of an event loop as a bulletin board where Windows and applications post messages. A message can ask for a service such as opening a file or telling an application that it needs to perform some maintenance task. Windows notifies the application that it has a message waiting. The application picks up its messages and acts on them. The event loop allows Windows to send "paint" messages to any application that might require them. The combination of an event loop and constant redrawing allows Windows to keep your display up-to-date, even if small amounts of miscommunication do occur.

You can usually tell when Windows is going through a repaint cycle. You can actually see each application quickly flash as it redraws itself. Of course, the cycle becomes a lot more prominent if each application uses a conflicting palette because then you can also see the color changes.

This chapter discusses video under Windows 95. However, more than that, it discusses communication. Without the required level of communication between all the system elements, you'd never see anything when using Windows 95. I refer to this idea of communication whenever necessary. Look for the communication requirements, however, as I discuss each of the following topics.

Graphics Standards

Many standards organizations help keep things running smoothly on your computer. Several competing standards affect how your modem works. Other organizations define specifications for the various port connectors, serial and parallel, that attach your machine to the outside world and peripheral devices. The standards organization you want to watch for display adapters and monitors is the Video Electronics Standards Association (VESA).

> **Tip:** VESA can provide you with detailed specifications for a number of display adapter and monitor standards. You can contact VESA directly using the following information:
>
> Video Electronics Standards Association
> 2150 North First Street, Suite 440
> San Jose, CA 95131-2029
> Voice: (408) 435-0333
> Fax: (408) 435-8225
> Internet: http://www.vesa.org/

I first ran into VESA in 1989, but it was probably around a while before that. IBM dropped VGA in favor of its proprietary 8514/A display adapter. Without a leader in the field to dictate a standard, the entire display adapter arena fell into a state of disarray. VESA stepped in to make sense of all this chaos. The result of the initial efforts was several VESA standards and some additional software for each display adapter. The following list shows many of the common standards that VESA has produced:

- Super VGA protected-mode interface (VS911020): This document provides information on a standardized method of accessing the BIOS routines from a protected-mode program.

- Video cursor interface (VS911021): Use this standard to learn how to build an interface between a pointing device and the display adapter.

- Super VGA BIOS extension (VS911022): This is the document you need to learn about VESA standard display modes for the SVGA.

- XGA extensions standard (VXE 1.0): This document tells you about some of the standardization efforts underway for the XGA.

- Monitor timing standard for 1024×768 with 70Hz refresh rate (VS910810): This standard provides a consistent method of producing ergonomically correct displays with a 70Hz refresh rate, which greatly reduces eyestrain.

- Standard 8514/A register bit fields (VS900601): This standard provides the details of how an 8514/A register works.

- Standard VGA passthrough connector (VS890803): This standard defines the passthrough connector and allows you to use multiple adapters in one machine.

- Standard 8514/A registers (VS890804): This standard defines what registers an 8514/A contains.

Of course, this selection of standards is by no means complete. VESA works on a whole array of other standardization efforts, such as industrial guidelines for the manufacture of computer components. Its most famous non-display–related standard is probably the VESA Local (VL) bus. The VL bus has since been replaced by the general-purpose PCI bus.

Windows 95 supports several new standards, including DirectX 5 and OpenGL. These standards allow vendors to write high-speed graphics routines to write directly to the hardware. Windows still tracks everything that the program does, but without the overhead that a normal application encounters. The plus side of using DirectX or OpenGL is high speed and maximum flexibility. The minus side is that the vendor has to do more work to get an application up and running. In addition, many people run into compatibility problems when using DirectX or OpenGL with older or less popular display adapters.

Intel introduced its own standard for all kinds of multimedia, including video. The MMX (multimedia extension) Pentium and Pentium II processors greatly increase the speed at which applications can display multimedia onscreen. Unfortunately, the programs you're using must be written to take advantage of these new extensions.

The Windows 95 Graphics Architecture

Now that you have some idea of the problems that Microsoft (and any other vendor) faces in providing something for you to look at, it's time to discuss how it does it. Figure 18.1 provides an overview of the Windows 95 architecture.

Figure 18.1.
An overview of the Windows 95 graphics architecture.

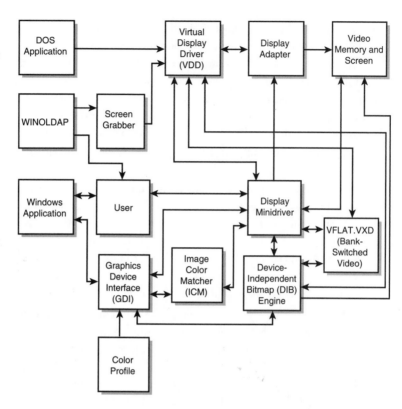

The following paragraphs tell you what task each of the components performs:

- **WINOLDAP:** This module senses when a MS-DOS application is about to take control of the display area. It notifies the User module and the screen grabber so that they can preserve the graphics system status information. You find this module listed as `WINOA386.MOD` in your SYSTEM directory.

- Screen grabber: The screen grabber preserves a picture of the screen. This allows Windows to restore the screen to its former appearance after you exit a DOS session. Any file with a `.2GR` or `.3GR` extension in your SYSTEM directory is a screen grabber.

- User: This module tracks the state of all the display elements, such as icons and dialog boxes, in addition to drawing them. That's why it needs to be informed before a MS-DOS session comes to the foreground—so that it can take a snapshot of the current state of these components. There are actually two User-related files on disk—a 16-bit and a 32-bit version.

- GDI: The GDI module works with the display driver and the DIB engine to produce the graphic components of a Windows display. Like the User module, there are two physical files—one for 16-bit and another for 32-bit needs.

- Display minidriver: Windows 95 can use a combination of the display minidriver and the DIB engine for adapters that can support them. Using this driver combination results in a speed increase from 32-bit code. The name of this file varies, depending on the type of display you're using. On my system, it's named SUPERVGA.DRV. Unlike the VDD, which performs all video processing, the display minidriver takes care of only device-specific details. The DIB engine takes care of graphics rendering. A minidriver contains a lot less code than a full-fledged VDD, reducing the amount of code that a vendor must write.

- Device-independent bitmap (DIB) engine: The DIB engine takes the graphics instructions provided by the GDI and renders them into an image. Unlike printing, the DIB engine actually draws the rendered image on the frame buffer. A *frame buffer* is a piece of system memory set aside to represent video memory. When the drawing on the buffer is complete, the entire buffer is sent to video memory at one time. Anything sent to video memory usually ends up on the display. This process is known as *virtualization*. The DIB engine itself is found in DIBENG.DLL. There's also a compatibility module for previous versions of Windows applications called DISPDIB.DLL, which was the predecessor to the DIB engine. The frame buffer management routines are found in FRAMEBUF.DRV.

- Color profile: This is a data file that contains the color capabilities for your output device. It doesn't matter whether the device is a printer or a display adapter; the type of information is the same. The purpose of a color profile is to provide the ICM with the information it needs to keep the display and other color devices in sync. That way, when you select dark red on the display, you get the same dark red on your printer. You find all the color profile files in the COLOR folder in the SYSTEM folder. All these files have an .ICM extension.

- Image color matcher (ICM): The ICM is the module that performs the work of subtly changing the output of your printer and display so that they match. The GDI, display minidriver, and ICM work together to compare the current color set and translate it into something that works on both devices. The files that contain the ICM include ICM32.DLL and ICMUI.DLL; both appear in the SYSTEM folder.

- VFLATD.VXD: This module is used only for bank-switched video adapters. Its main purpose is to manage the video memory window that these devices provide. The display adapter on your machine can contain a very large amount of memory. Unfortunately, there's only a 64KB window set aside to access that memory. Depending on your adapter's configuration, Windows might not be able to get around this limitation. VFLATD.VXD can manage up to a 1MB frame buffer. It reads this buffer into video memory as required, in 64KB chunks.

- Virtual display driver (VDD): Previous versions of Windows used this module as its sole source of communication with the display adapter. Windows 95 provides it for compatibility purposes and for DOS applications. In most cases, the name of this file contains some part of the name of the display adapter vendor. For example, the name of the VxD for my system is VIDEO7.VXD. You find it in the SYSTEM folder. This driver converts drawing commands into signals that the display adapter can use. It also manages the display adapter and performs a variety of other tasks related to the way that all the applications on your machine share the display adapter. In essence, it's a 16-bit version of the display minidriver and DIB engine combination.

- Display adapter: This is the physical piece of hardware in your machine.

- Video memory and screen: Video memory is where the electronic form of the image that you see onscreen is stored.

Keep in mind that this is a quick tour of the video subsystem. The actual inner workings of this part of Windows are a lot more complex than you might think.

Video Boards

While I have your attention focused on the complexities of the video subsystem, let's take a quick look at video boards. You may have missed a few performance clues tucked away in the discussion of architecture. Did you notice that VFLATD.VXD supports only a 1MB address space? What happens if your display adapter contains 2MB or more of memory? Don't worry. Windows 95 completely supports the entire range of memory provided by your display adapter.

First, more memory means more colors. A higher number of colors can result in a sharper appearance of fonts and other aesthetic qualities of your display. Second, more memory means higher resolution. A higher level of resolution can help you more accurately position graphic elements and can result in reduced eye fatigue.

No matter which way you look at it, more colors and high resolution spell decreased performance. Moving the video window around takes a little time; allowing the frame buffer to manage more than 1MB of video memory takes even more. Each layer of management you add to the video subsystem chews up processor cycles. How do you get around these problems?

- Dual-ported video RAM (VRAM): Many display adapters come with this feature. The reason that it's called dual-ported is that it actually contains two ports. A serial buffer allows the display to read the contents of video memory. A parallel buffer allows Windows to simultaneously write to video memory. Dual-ported memory allows an application to write to video memory at any time instead of only during part of the display cycle.

- Display coprocessor: Quite a few display adapters come with a coprocessor. Windows 95 offloads as much of the display processing as possible to the display coprocessor. Offloading part of the graphics processing responsibility frees processor cycles, improving overall system speed. In addition, the display processor is usually a special-purpose-state machine that processes graphics instructions faster than the DIB engine.

- 32/64/128-bit display adapter: To display an image, you have to move data, and that requires time. However, you can reduce the amount of time by using a wider data path. Some display adapters come with a 32-bit, 64-bit, or 128-bit path, which improves graphics performance.

- MMX Pentium processor: A lot of the processing required to display an image onscreen is done within the processor. In most cases, the display functions use generic processor calls to get the job done. The MMX version of the Pentium processor from Intel is designed to process graphics and audio much faster than its predecessors. Unfortunately, only newer software, specifically designed to use MMX, can take advantage of an MMX Pentium-enabled chip.

There are other things that you need to look for in a Windows 95 display adapter. One of the biggest convenience items is Plug and Play. Not only are Plug and Play devices self-configuring, but they also allow a greater level of flexibility. One of the ways that Windows 95 limits you with a non-Plug and Play device is color selection; you can change the resolution of your display adapter without rebooting, but you can't change the number of colors.

Installing Video Display Adapters

Chapter 14, "Exploiting Your Hardware," covers the physical process of installing your display adapter as part of the hardware installation process. The process for installing a new display adapter isn't all that much different. However, I want to show you an alternative to that process.

Installing a Display Adapter

Installing a new display adapter can be very easy, whether you're installing a display adapter for the first time or upgrading to a new display adapter. Because hardware vendors are constantly upgrading their drivers to provide bug fixes and new capabilities, it's quite likely that you'll need to upgrade a device driver on your machine at least once during the time you use it. The following procedure shows you how:

1. Right-click the desktop and choose the Properties option. You should see the Display Properties dialog box. This particular dialog box has nine tabs allowing you to customize your video display adapter and monitor. (Your dialog box may look slightly different than this one.) Click the Settings tab as shown in Figure 18.2. This tab displays the refresh rate. Setting a higher refresh rate usually results in less eye fatigue. Unfortunately, a high refresh rate also produces more heat. In addition, there are situations where one refresh rate interacts with the lighting in your office and another doesn't.

2. Click the Advanced Properties button to see the Advanced Display Properties dialog box shown in Figure 18.3. Notice that this dialog box tells you the current display adapter type and its version number. This can provide important information when you're troubleshooting.

3. Click the Change button on the Adapter tab. You see the Select Device dialog box shown in Figure 18.4. Notice that only one display adapter type is listed. If other display adapters were compatible with this one, this list box would contain those as well.

Figure 18.2.

The Display Properties dialog box allows you to reconfigure your display adapter or monitor.

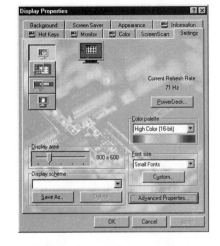

Figure 18.3.

The Advanced Display Properties dialog box displays information about your current display adapter.

Figure 18.4.

The Select Device dialog box lists all compatible display adapters.

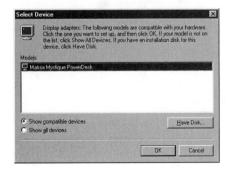

Note: If you have a vendor disk containing drivers for your display adapter, click the Have Disk button to look at it. The Have Disk dialog box works as any other browser does under Windows 95.

4. Click OK. Windows might ask you to insert disks as it installs the new adapter. To complete the process, click the Apply button.

Installing a Monitor

It might not seem like a very big deal to tell Windows 95 which monitor you're using, especially if that monitor doesn't provide any special capabilities. However, the monitor you use determines which display adapter features you can use. Selecting the right monitor type helps Windows 95 provide you with better information regarding your display choices.

1. Right-click the desktop and choose the Properties option. You should see the Display Properties dialog box. Click the Settings tab (refer to Figure 18.2).

2. Click the Advanced Properties button to see the Advanced Display Properties dialog box (refer to Figure 18.3). Click the Monitor tab. The Monitor Type group tells you which monitor you currently have installed.

3. Click the Change button in the Monitor tab. You see the Select Device dialog box, as shown in Figure 18.5.

Figure 18.5.
The Select Device dialog box lists all compatible monitors.

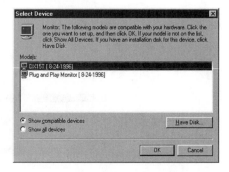

Note: If you have a vendor disk containing drivers for your monitor, click the Have Disk button to look at it. The Have Disk dialog box works as any other browser does under Windows 95.

4. After you select the correct manufacturer and monitor model from the list, click OK. Windows might ask you to insert disks as it installs the new monitor. To complete the process, click the Apply button.

Windows 98 Video Enhancements

Beta Release

Windows 95 might work well with a variety of display adapters and monitors, but that doesn't mean there isn't room for improvement. Windows 98 plans to expand its video features in three major ways:

- Displaying data on more than one monitor: This can be useful for viewing a chart in one monitor and a spreadsheet in a second monitor, allowing you to see more of your data without constantly scrolling or switching between windows.

- Creating faster graphics with the Accelerated Graphics Port (AGP): This is another attempt to speed up graphics displays, particularly for graphics-intensive programs such as computer-aided–design or virtual-reality applications.

- Allowing users to view television broadcasts on their monitors: This can be useful for video capturing or just watching TV while using your computer.

Using the Performance Page Provided by OSR2

The OSR2 version of Windows 95 provides an additional tab on the Advanced Display Properties dialog as shown in Figure 18.6. You can choose three options.

Figure 18.6.
The OSR2 version of Windows 95 allows you to set the performance features of your display adapter.

The first radio button tells Windows 95 to reboot any time you change the color settings for your machine. The second radio button lets you change color and resolution settings without rebooting. This can cause problems when running some applications, so I recommend the third option, which tells Windows to prompt you about rebooting the machine after a color (and in some cases, a resolution) change. This is the default option and I find it works just fine in most cases. If you make a color change without any problem, then you simply tell Windows that you don't want to reboot the machine.

On Your Own

Some people find that an underpowered machine might not provide all the speed they need to get their work done fast. Try a variety of display resolutions and color-level settings to find a compromise between system performance and the aesthetic value of the display. Also try the various font-size settings. Perhaps a custom setting will provide that perfect balance between readability and the number of icons you can fit on the desktop or within an Explorer pane.

Check your SYSTEM folder and see whether you can find all the files that make up the video subsystem. Use the video subsystem discussion in this chapter as the basis for your search.

19

Mobile Computing: Notebooks, Telecommuting, and Remote Access

Peter Norton®

Few people who travel can get by without their constant companion, the notebook computer. In this chapter, I use the term *notebook* to refer to every kind of mobile computer. Of course, mobile computers actually range in size from the smallest PDA (personal digital assistant) to some of the luggable dinosaurs I still see from time to time.

Before Windows 95 came along, many notebook computer users were still strapped to a desktop. For example, what happens when you need to change a modem card in your laptop to replace it with a NIC to access the network? Unless you have some special setup software, you actually have to turn off the machine and reconfigure it to make the switch. It's time-wasting events such as this that really frustrate people who use a notebook from time to time. Fortunately, Windows 95 addresses these problems and many more.

Of course, Windows 95 won't take your PDA and make it into a desktop equivalent. I'm looking at machines that are really capable of running Windows 95. This means that they have to meet all the installation criteria I discussed earlier. A notebook has to provide a PCMCIA (Personal Computer Memory Card International Association) slot or its equivalent to use some of the features that Windows 95 provides. You also want a computer that can use a docking station. In other words, I really don't care how heavy or large the computer is, but it has to provide enough features to take the place of a desktop.

Tip: The OEM Service Release 2 (OSR2) version of Windows 95 contains infrared port support. You must have an Infrared Data Association (IrDA) 2.0–compliant device to use this support. The current software also includes infrared LAN connectivity. Fortunately, you can download this update from http://www.microsoft.com/windows/software/irda.htm. This same site has several other interesting programs that you can download. For example, there's a file-transfer program for moving files from one computer to another using an infrared data port.

Looking Ahead: The OSR2 version of Windows 95 also provides voice modem support. Chapter 20, "Hardware and Software Connections," covers this in the section "Understanding Voice Communications."

I also revisit Plug and Play (PNP) in this chapter. There are some new capabilities that really make a difference for notebook computer users. If you're at all intrigued, read on.

PCMCIA Devices on Your Notebook Computer

The first topic on the agenda is the PCMCIA bus. This is a "little" bus that is specially designed to meet the needs of the notebook computer market, but it's found in a growing number of desktop machines as well. The PCMCIA bus uses credit-card–sized cards that connect to external slots on the machine. This is perfect for a notebook because notebooks are notorious for providing few, if any, expansion slots. A PCMCIA bus makes it easy for the user to change a machine's hardware configuration without opening it. For example, you could take out a memory card to make room for a modem card.

Note: The OSR2 version of Windows 95 provides additional levels of PCMCIA support. For example, it supports the new PC Card 32 (Cardbus) bridges. You can also use 3.3 volt cards in addition to the older 5 volt models. This latest version of Windows 95 also supports multifunction PCMCIA cards and specialty devices such as Global Positioning Satellite (GPS) cards. Unfortunately, you can't download the files required to update an existing system; you must get a new one with OSR2 installed.

This bus also supports solid-state disk drives in the form of flash ROM or SRAM boards. The flash ROM boards are especially interesting because they provide the same access speeds as regular memory with the permanence of other long-term storage media such as hard drives. Unlike SRAM boards, flash ROM boards don't require battery backup. Many people use solid-state drives to store applications or databases that change infrequently. This frees up precious space on the internal hard disk for data and applications that the user needs to access on a continuous basis.

Unfortunately, the PCMCIA bus also creates a problem for people who use it. Imagine the reaction of Windows 3.x to the user taking a card out of the system and replacing it with another. The user will definitely see the difference right after rebooting the machine. Every time you plug in a new card type, you need to reconfigure your system to accept it. (Of course, this doesn't necessarily apply to exchanging one hard disk, or another like card, for another.) Configuration programs make this really neat feature a real pain to implement under Windows 3.x. Of course, some vendors provide utility programs to make the change easier, but this still doesn't change the way Windows itself operates or make up for deficiencies in MS-DOS. The operating system must provide dynamic loading and unloading of device drivers to make the system as user-friendly as possible.

PNP changes all of this. No longer do PCMCIA bus users need to reconfigure their systems when a component changes. Windows 95 is designed to detect system changes and make the appropriate modifications to its setup. However, this flexibility comes at a price. Users must disable their

PCMCIA-specific utilities and allow Windows to manage the bus. The bus vendor must also provide the 32-bit drivers needed under Windows 95 (unless your bus already appears in the Windows 95 support list). Doing this enables the PCMCIA enhanced mode. Figure 19.1 shows a typical PC Card (PCMCIA) Properties dialog. (You access it by double-clicking the PC Card (PCMCIA) applet in the Control Panel.) The following list provides an overview of enhanced support features:

- Friendly device names: This feature provides users with device names they can recognize. Instead of the more familiar XYZ.VXD, the user will see something like Flash ROM Driver. It also helps the user determine which devices are actually present and which ones are disconnected.

- Automatic installation: This feature allows the user to hot-swap various devices in and out of the PCMCIA slot without worrying about reconfiguring the machine.

- Drive change detection: In some situations, the user will have to unmount and then mount a PCMCIA drive before Windows 95 will recognize the change if enhanced support is disabled.

- Other device-specific mode and configuration information: Each PCMCIA card vendor implements special features for its device. Check the documentation that comes with the device for further details.

Figure 19.1.
The PC Card
(PCMCIA)
Properties dialog
provides access to the
PCMCIA cards
installed on your
machine.

As Figure 19.1 shows, there are a few options you can use with PCMCIA cards. The first check box, Show control on Taskbar, displays an icon in the Taskbar tray. You can use it to get a list of currently installed cards, stop one that's installed, or (by right-clicking) display a context menu containing the Properties option. The second check box tells Windows to display a message if you try to remove a card before you stop it.

Normally, Windows 95 detects changes in your PCMCIA setup. However, you can help things along by stopping the card before you remove it. Stopping the card tells Windows 95 to remove support for that feature. All you need to do is highlight the card you want to stop and then click the Stop button shown in Figure 19.1 to stop a card.

Take a look at the Global Settings page of the PC Card (PCMCIA) Properties dialog shown in Figure 19.2. Notice that there are only a few options on this page. Normally, you want to keep the Automatic selection check box checked as shown in Figure 19.2. Unchecking this box allows you to manually set the card service memory area—a task that you normally need to perform for troubleshooting purposes only. The second check box, Disable PC card sound effects, tells Windows that you don't want to hear a sound effect every time the status of the PCMCIA bus changes. This is a handy feature in an office where you don't want to disturb other people with sound effects from your computer.

Figure 19.2.
The Global Settings page of the PC Card (PCMCIA) Properties dialog contains a handy check box for silencing your machine during card changes.

In most cases, Windows 95 automatically enables enhanced mode, but it won't do so if you have any real-mode PCMCIA drivers loaded. Fortunately, it's easy to see if Windows 95 enabled enhanced mode on your machine. Right-click My Computer and select the Properties option to open the System dialog. Click the Performance tab to display the dialog shown in Figure 19.3.

Figure 19.3.
The Performance tab helps you optimize system performance. It displays all performance bottlenecks, including PCMCIA status.

If your dialog box looks like the one in Figure 19.3, Windows 95 hasn't enabled enhanced support. The first method you should use to correct the problem is clicking the Details pushbutton. This displays the help dialog shown in Figure 19.4.

Figure 19.4.

This help dialog provides a button that enables PCMCIA 32-bit support.

Notice the button that enables 32-bit PCMCIA support. If you click it, you see PCMCIA wizard, shown in Figure 19.5. Windows 95 attempts to help you enable 32-bit support. All you need to do is follow the prompts to diagnose any problems that Windows can detect. However, sometimes this attempt will fail. The following list provides some troubleshooting tips.

Figure 19.5.

Use the PCMCIA wizard to help you diagnose problems with your installation or with the bus itself.

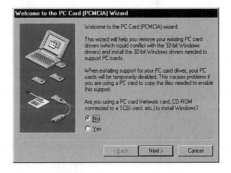

- The most common problem associated with enabling enhanced support is that there are PCMCIA device drivers in CONFIG.SYS or TSRs in AUTOEXEC.BAT. Removing these entries should fix the problem.

- Windows 95 normally tells you if there's an I/O port address or interrupt conflict, but you should check the settings under the Resources tab of the PCIC (peripheral connect interface card) or compatible PCMCIA controller Properties dialog, shown in Figure 19.6, to make sure. (To open this dialog, simply right-click My Computer, select the Properties option from the context menu, and select the Device Manager tab of the System Properties dialog.) Any conflicting devices appear in the Conflicting device list field near the bottom of the dialog.

Figure 19.6.

The Resources tab of the PCIC or compatible PCMCIA controller Properties dialog box alerts you to any conflicting devices.

- Always install a card in the slot while booting. Failure to do so could prevent Windows 95 from detecting the PCMCIA card slot.

- Make sure Windows 95 supports your card by checking it with the Hardware Installation wizard in Control Panel. (You can browse through the list of hardware presented on the second screen and then click Cancel to exit the utility without installing anything.)

Even if Windows 95 doesn't support your PCMCIA slot, you can still use it by installing real-mode drivers. Of course, using real-mode drivers means that you won't gain any benefit from the PNP features, so you should always contact the bus vendor to see if a 32-bit driver is available.

Hot Docking

A PNP feature called hot docking allows you to remove a portable computer from its docking station without turning it off. The portable automatically reconfigures itself to reflect the loss of docking station capability. Plug that portable back into the original docking station, or a new one somewhere else, and it automatically reconfigures itself to take advantage of the new capabilities that the docking station provides.

Tip: Try not to move your computer with the power on. Otherwise, a sudden jolt could crash your hard drive or you could create surges or other electrical interference that could shorten the life of your machine. For example, you could accidentally short something out when removing the notebook from its docking station. Moving your machine from place to place without turning it off is OK—it's a supported feature—but you need to consider the cost of exercising that option.

Hot Swapping

Another problem that I talked about at the beginning of this chapter was the capability to take one card out of the PCMCIA slot and plug another in its place. A PNP-compatible system reconfigures itself dynamically, a capability called hot swapping.

Hot swapping allows you to remove components from a machine without rebooting it (provided that the machine also supports hot swapping). For example, what if you had a modem card in your PCMCIA slot and needed to exchange it for a network card? Currently, you need to turn off the machine, exchange the cards, and reboot. Of course, you also need to remove any modem-specific device drivers or TSRs and add the network card software.

> **Warning:** Never touch the contacts of your PCMCIA cards when you remove them from the bus. Doing so could give the card a static electric shock that will damage it or shorten its life.

Hot swapping allows you to take the card out and put the new one in without turning off the machine. The PNP component of Windows 95 even installs the required drivers and configures them for you in the background. This means that users no longer need to worry about how a device works; they only need to think about what work they need the device to perform. (The only exception to this rule is when Windows 95 can't find the required drivers on your hard disk. It asks you to supply a disk containing the required drivers.)

Windows 95 Mobile Computing Services

Microsoft added several features to meet the needs of notebook computer users with the release of Windows 95. One of feature is the Briefcase, which lets you send files to other people across a network.

I also take a quick look at Dial-Up Networking in this section from a notebook computer user's point of view. I take a look at some of the ways you can get around potential problems using this new feature to communicate on the road. I cover all the usage basics in Chapter 20, so you can skip this section if you really don't foresee a need to use Dial-Up Networking on your next business trip.

Briefcase

Windows 95 includes a Briefcase. Like its physical counterpart, the Windows Briefcase can store files that you need to move from place to place. Of course, a physical briefcase uses paper as its storage media, whereas the Windows Briefcase uses electronic media. The Briefcase sits on the desktop along with the Recycle Bin and My Computer.

Setting up your Briefcase is easy. All you need to do is install the Windows software (it's optional), and a Briefcase icon appears on the desktop. Stuff the Briefcase with files that you plan to move from place to place. What you should get is a centralized storage location for all the files you work on, even if those files appear in different areas of your hard drive. (For that matter, they could appear on a network drive.)

Working with Briefcase files is no different from working with any other file. Windows 95 monitors the status of the files and presents a display of their status when you open the Briefcase icon, as shown in Figure 19.7. Notice that it tells you when your Briefcase requires an update to keep it up-to-date with the files on your machine. All you need to do is select Briefcase | Update All if the files are out of date. Once the files are up to date, you can move the briefcase from your machine to a network drive or floppy.

Figure 19.7.
Briefcase offers a fast and convenient method of centralizing your files. It also provides the means to move those files from work to home and back with a minimum of fuss.

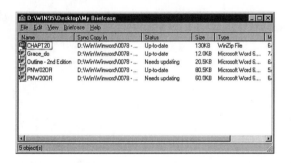

Briefcase also provides a context menu for each of its files, just like the context menus you're accustomed to seeing in Explorer. It also provides a Document Properties dialog, shown in Figure 19.8. The General, Summary, and Statistics pages all look like the ones you see in a standard document.

The one change you'll notice is the addition of an Update Status page (see Figure 19.9). This page provides you with quite a bit of information about the document in your Briefcase versus the one on your drive. It also provides some options that you wouldn't normally get from the menu. The middle of the page shows the current document status—which document has been updated and when you made the changes.

Figure 19.8.
A Briefcase file
provides a standard
Document Properties
dialog that looks
similar to the ones in
Explorer.

Figure 19.9.
The Update Status
page shows you the
current document
status and gives you
the capability to
update the file.

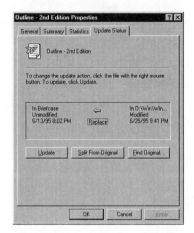

There's an interesting feature in the information box, which tells you that the original document has a newer date than the one in the Briefcase. However, if you click the Replace icon in the middle of these two entries, you see the context menu shown in Figure 19.10. The interesting thing about this menu is that you can choose to replace your updated document with the original in your Briefcase.

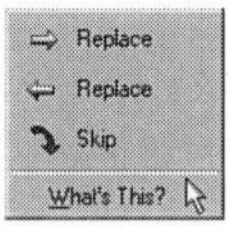

Figure 19.10.
The Replace context
menu item is a hidden
extra that Briefcase
provides.

How many times have you wished that you had a copy of your original file when the changes you made didn't quite fit? Wouldn't it be nice if you could restore the document to its original form without resorting to a backup tape? Using this feature will help. If you keep your Briefcase up-to-date, you can always restore an original copy of a document after you change it. This safety feature comes in handy when a few hours of editing just don't turn out as you anticipated. Notice that this list has a third entry. You can choose to skip an update. Just select the Skip option and close the dialog. This allows you to use automatic updating for all your other files and still retain the original version of this particular file.

> **Tip:** You can use Briefcase as a rudimentary version control system. Here's how it works. Create a new Briefcase as you reach each new milestone in a project. Change the name of the Briefcase to match the milestone's name or date. Place a copy of all the files in the Briefcase but never update it. What you should end up with is a bunch of Briefcases, each one representing a stage of your project. Even though this technique does consume a lot of hard drive space, it could also save you a lot of rework time later.

The three buttons in the Document Properties dialog allow you to manipulate the link you've created. The Update button updates your linked copy to match the original document (or just the opposite). The direction of the update depends on which way the Replace arrow is pointing in the information box. Briefcase uses a default of updating whichever document is older than the original. The Split From Original pushbutton allows you to separate the copy from the original. This comes in handy if you decide to make a new document out of the original in your briefcase. The Find Original button opens a copy of Explorer with the original document highlighted. You can use this button to quickly find a document in the Briefcase. I found it strange that this particular button doesn't appear on the context menu; you must access it using the Properties dialog.

Moving your Briefcase from work to home is just as easy as using it. Just stick a floppy in one of your drives and right-click the Briefcase icon. You should see a display similar to the one in Figure 19.11. Notice that you can update the Briefcase from here as well; you don't have to open it if you don't want to. To move the Briefcase from your machine to a floppy, just select the Send To menu option and choose a location. The Briefcase icon disappears from the desktop and reappears on the floppy. Moving it back to your desktop the next day is just as easy. Just select the floppy drive in Explorer so that you can see the Briefcase icon. Then right-click it and drag it to the desktop. When Windows displays a menu asking what you want to do, click Move. If you lose your Briefcase, you can create a new Briefcase by right-clicking the desktop and selecting New from the context menu. One of the new items you can create is the Briefcase.

Figure 19.11.
The Briefcase context
menu provides access
to some, but not all,
of Briefcase's
features.

Tip: Here's a tip for you if you have a bulging Briefcase. You can compress the floppies used to transport information from one machine to another. Use the DriveSpace utility to do this. Compressing the floppy will nearly double its carrying capacity, especially when you consider that most people carry data files, not the executable files required to edit them. Data files normally contain a lot of empty space that compression programs can squeeze out.

Synchronizing Files

Before Windows 95, the notebook user had only two choices when keeping the files in two or more machines in sync. One method was to keep all the mobile data on a floppy. All you needed to do was pass the floppy around as needed to keep the files in sync. This easy solution also had a pretty significant problem. A floppy's access speed isn't good, and its storage capacity is limited when compared to a hard drive. Suffice it to say that this wasn't the best way to go.

Another solution was to copy the files from your hard drive to a floppy and then back again. This had the advantage of using the best possible speed for opening and using the files. The big disadvantage was that it relied on the person's memory to make sure the files were kept in sync.

Using the Briefcase option in Windows 95 is a big step forward for notebook users. It has one of the characteristics of floppy-based synchronization. You just move the Briefcase around as needed. It also provides the advantage of the file copying method. Every application makes use of the hard drive's enhanced access speed when you open and edit files.

Is Briefcase the only Windows 95 solution? Probably not. I've also stored files in folders to keep one set of files on a central machine in sync. How do you use this feature if you're working on a document at home? That's where Dial-Up Networking comes into play. Instead of simply moving a Briefcase around, you can use Dial-Up Networking to call into the network and edit the files remotely. That way, even though you're working on the file from another location, your team can continue updating it as well.

Tip: Using the combination of folders and Dial-Up Networking is ideal if you're a team supervisor. It allows you to continue your work on the documentation that the team is preparing while you're on the road without resorting to the Briefcase. Even if you're currently working on the documents alone, there could be an occasion in which a team member needs them as well. Using the Briefcase means that the folks at home won't know if they're using the current documents. There's never a good reason to slow the team's progress on a project because you need to work on it while on the road. Using this combination also allows you to monitor the team's progress. Checking in each day to see the work they've accomplished will help you keep an eye on things back home while you're on the road.

Remote Dial-Up (Dial-Up Networking)

I talk about the mechanics of using Dial-Up Networking in Chapter 20, so I don't go through that process here. However, once you do get the software installed and configured, where do you go from there? If you're a notebook user, there are plenty of reasons to use this particular Windows 95 feature:

- Document access: I've already mentioned how you can use Dial-Up Networking to enable an entire group of people to work together. All you need to do is place a folder with shortcuts to the team's documents in a folder on the network. When a person calls into the network, he can open the folder and see all the pieces of the project without looking very hard. I often place this folder in the user's home directory on the network. That way, I can personalize each folder as required, and the user doesn't need to memorize yet another location on the network.

- Application access: You won't need to access applications such as word processors or spreadsheets from a remote location (at least not often). But what about the custom database that your company uses as a contact manager? Unless you plan to either print the entire database or create a copy of it on your notebook's hard drive, you need to access it remotely. In fact, this is probably the only way you could use this centralized application if it contains sales or inventory information that you need to update later.

- E-mail: Many companies depend on e-mail to keep employees apprised of events, such as getting a new access code for the security system or updating your W-2 form. Losing this communication means that you are out of touch when you return from your trip. A few minutes of online time could keep you up to date on current situations in your company and reduce that "vacation" syndrome that many people feel after a road trip.

- Emergency decisions: What if you're traveling in Europe and your company's in California? How do you find a good time to call them and make a decision that requires a 24-hour turnaround? The old way of doing things was waiting up until the wee hours of the morning and calling your company during normal business hours—either that or waking someone up at home. Using the company or an online service e-mail to leave a message, and then checking for responses later, could give you those few extra hours of sleep at night.

- Missing-file syndrome: Notebooks almost always need at least twice as much hard disk space as they really have. How often have you cleared a bunch of files off your notebook only to find that you really needed them after all? If you're on the road, it's usually too late to regain access to those files, and you have to figure out a way to do without them. Or do you? A remote connection can let you grab some files that you didn't think you'd need. Placing a copy of your desktop machine's hard drive—or at least the data—where you can access it using a remote connection will save you a lot of trouble later. Make sure you ask the network administrator's permission before you do this, however.

These are just some of the common ways you can use Dial-Up Networking with a notebook. You need to find the specialty technique that applies to your specific situation. For example, in my particular case, I find it handy to use Dial-Up Networking to grab presentations. I have room for only one or two on my notebook at a time, but I might need several during the time I'm on the road. Using this feature allows me to call in and grab the next presentation in line. The result is that each presentation is fresh and specifically designed for the group I'm talking with, yet I don't have to lug around a monster-sized hard drive or other storage.

Remote Network Users

Networking is an essential part of any business today. I've already talked about Dial-Up Networking to an extent, but now I take a look at some of the communication and other considerations you'll need to make. Using Dial-Up Networking is one thing; using it efficiently is another.

I'd like to begin by providing a little insight into one of the problems with using Dial-Up Networking. Most people know that the telephone company charges more for the first three minutes of a long distance call than for the time that follows. People try to keep their long distance calls short and to the point. The telephone company capitalizes on this by charging you more when you make several short calls instead of one long one.

Given this set of circumstances, imagine the cost differential of making one long computer call as compared to a whole bunch of short ones. It's easy to get into the habit of dialing the company every time you need a bit of information. Consolidating all your information needs into one call is better than making several short ones. You can save a lot of money by delivering all your mail during off-peak hours.

There are still times where it's impossible to take care of all your communication needs at one time. You'll still find the need to make a few short calls during the day to gather information. However, you don't have to do that for message delivery. Delivering responses to e-mail and performing other chores can always wait for off-peak hours, especially when you're overseas and the people who wrote the message won't see it until after you're in bed anyway.

The following sections describe some of the other methods you can use to reduce the cost of Dial-Up Networking. Although these techniques don't always work because your need for data exchange with another party is immediate, they work in the majority of cases.

Local Communications

There are many forms of long-distance communication, and some of them are local. Here's one scenario. You're in Detroit and your company is in Los Angeles. It's important that you send a file containing some new information about your client to an assistant for processing. You also need some additional information about another client that's stored in your company database. You have access to both Dial-Up Networking and CompuServe. Which do you use? Some people would use Dial-Up Networking because it's faster and more convenient, but the low-cost solution is CompuServe in this case. Making a local phone call to CompuServe is just as fast as transferring that file over the company e-mail, and it costs you a lot less. CompuServe requires only a local call.

However, sometimes the obvious choice isn't the one you should use. For example, suppose you need to transfer the same files and get the same information. The difference is that this time you're in another part of the state instead of another part of the country. It'll only cost about 40 cents to make the toll call to your company, so using Dial-Up Networking is the right choice. CompuServe adds a surcharge to some types of billing systems, but not to others. You should check the CompuServe rate against the toll charge to see which one is better.

> **Tip:** Once you determine a local rate, write it down for future reference. Keeping a rate sheet for the places you frequent will save you from looking up the information more than once. Most communication programs provide some method of determining your CompuServe rate. All you need to do is look at the long distance rate versus the CompuServe rate.

If your company has its own Internet address, you might be able to use it to transfer information using a local call. Of course, you need an account with a local provider to make this work. As with the other suggestions in this section, you'll want to check the cost of using an Internet solution against that of making a long-distance call.

Dynamic Networking

Despite your best efforts, you'll run into times when you need to work with the company database or other applications live. You can't solve every problem with e-mail or a file upload. There are times when working with live applications or data is the only way to get the job done. You want to keep these times to a minimum, but keeping a local database management system (DBMS) current might override other cost considerations. Fortunately, your notebook still has a few tricks up its sleeve to solve the problem. The following list provides some of the ideas I've come up with, but you can probably think of others based on your unique set of circumstances.

> **Tip:** If you're using a custom DBMS, it might be possible to add batch-updating capability to it. This allows you to use a smaller version of the application on the road, create new records, modify existing ones, and make all the changes in batch mode when you return from your trip or as part of an upload to the company database. This is a less expensive solution for inventory control or other types of sales databases than making the changes live in many cases. There are two criteria for using a batch system: You need a fairly large outside sales force to make the change cost efficient, and the company must be able to get by with daily or weekly database updates instead of real-time data. This works in most situations, but you couldn't use it for an airline ticket database, for example.

- Internet access: Using the Internet still might provide the best means of working with live data. You need to overcome two problems. The first is gaining access to a local server that allows live connections. The second is that you have to make a TCP/IP connection and use a special modem to make this work. Both problems can be solved given enough resources. In the past, this solution may have seemed more like a dream than reality. Today, intranets (the private version of the Internet) abound. Even small businesses can occasionally write off the cost of using an intranet solution because it's less expensive than anything else I've covered here. The OSR2 version of Windows 95 comes with a special feature—Personal Web Server. You can use it to at least try various intranet solutions before you invest the money in a full-sized solution. I cover Personal Web Server usage in Chapter 26, "Creating Your Own Internet Connection with Personal Web Server."

- Using a local office's PBX connection: Sometimes a local office will provide the long-distance–call solution you need. It might mean a little wrangling with the local boss and perhaps a short drive, but this solution could save your company some money.

- Keeping notes: Even if your database doesn't support batch-mode processing, you could still keep notes and make all the updates at one time. This allows you to make one phone call instead of many to record the required information. Of course, this solution still won't work with "live" data such as ticket sales and the like.

- Off-hour calling: This is probably the least likely solution. If your data needs are so time-critical that you can't afford to wait even a few minutes, off-hour calling won't work. However, you could combine this technique with batch mode or note-taking methods to work with live data on the network. You could even use this off-hour calling technique when using a local office's PBX connection. This reduces the local boss's objection to tying up the line to service your needs.

Offline Printing

Remember in Chapter 16, "Fonts and Printing," when I covered printing? I talked about two techniques that the notebook computer user will love. The first is the idea of creating a printer for every purpose. You can create printers for all the local offices you visit during a trip. That way, you can print any notes or documents you need without worrying about whether you have the proper print driver to get the job done. You can also use this technique to print at client sites that are amenable to your doing so.

However, that isn't the only way you can print. You can also print to your hard drive using offline printing technique examined in Chapter 16. All you need to do is set the printer to work offline. Everything you send to disk will wait on the hard drive until you send it to the printer.

What I didn't include in that chapter was something notebook-specific. Whenever you disconnect your notebook from the network printer or docking station, Windows 95 detects the loss of printing capability and sets the printer to work offline automatically. Unfortunately, this doesn't work all the time. I experienced a few situations in which the printer disconnection wasn't detected. Either way, detection was consistent. Check your printer the first time, and you should be able to rely on the connection being consistent from that point on.

Working with an Infrared Data Port

Infrared data ports weren't popular when Windows 95 was first released. Now the OSR2 version of Windows 95 comes with infrared data port support built in. You can also download a copy of the files required to perform an updated of an existing Windows 95 installation from the Internet.

Once you install the software for your infrared port, you see an Infrared applet in the Control Panel. Double-clicking this applet displays the Infrared Monitor dialog shown in Figure 19.12.

Figure 19.12.
The Status page of the Infrared Monitor dialog tells you if there are any other infrared ports in the area.

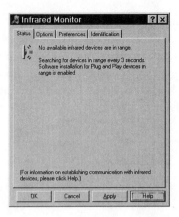

The Status page of the Infrared Monitor is where you want to look for connection information. If there aren't any ports to connect to, then you see a display similar to the one in Figure 19.12. This page also tells you the status of any existing connections. You can find out how well the connection is working. This information comes in handy when you need to transfer a large amount of data and it seems to be taking too long. Sometimes you can improve the connection by moving your machine more inline with the other infrared data port.

Figure 19.13 shows what the Options page looks like. The first check box allows you to enable infrared communication using a specific serial port. In this case, I'm using COM3. Notice that the actual communication doesn't take place on this port; I use COM4 for serial communication and LPT2 for parallel communication. It's important to keep this in mind as you set up your software to use the infrared port.

Figure 19.13.
The Options page of the Infrared Monitor dialog contains all the configuration options.

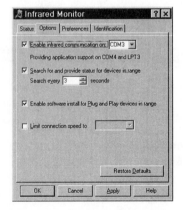

The second check box on this page enables automatic search for other infrared ports. Scanning for other ports uses processor cycles that you might want to devote to other activities. Turning off the scan feature while you're on the road won't only make your computer run faster, but it'll save some power too. Notice that there's also a field for defining how often you scan for another port. The default value of three seconds works just fine in most cases. However, you may find that a smaller value will help you fine-tune a connection faster. A longer increment could save precious processing cycles once have a connection established.

You'll find that the Enable software install for Plug and Play devices in range option of this dialog is simultaneously helpful and annoying. This option automatically configures your machine to use any Plug and Play infrared devices that happen to be in the area—making life a lot more automatic. On the other hand, I keep finding my machine getting configured for devices I really don't want. You'll probably want to keep this check box unchecked unless you're planning to visit a new location.

The fourth (and final) check box on this page allows you to limit the connection speed. That might not seem like such a good idea at first, but there are a few situations where you may find it helpful. The first is when the receiving device can't handle the full speed connection. For example, you might want to establish a connection with some type of serial device and find that it doesn't work properly. Data overruns are the first symptom of this problem. The second situation occurs when you have a good connection but keep getting data errors. For whatever reason, you're spending more time transmitting old data than new data. Slowing down the connection could reduce data errors and actually improve the data rate of the connection.

The Preferences page of the Infrared Monitor dialog allows you to set the features of your infrared port. Figure 19.14 shows what this page looks like.

Figure 19.14.
The Preferences page of the Infrared Monitor dialog allows you to place an Infrared icon on the Taskbar.

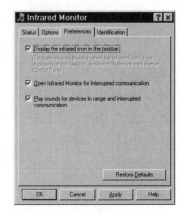

The first check box on this page allows you to display an Infrared icon on the Taskbar. As with most of the icons you'll display on the Taskbar, there are three actions you can perform: Leaving the mouse over the icon gives you the current port status, a left click performs a default action (opening the Infrared Monitor dialog), and a right click displays a context menu. The context menu contains four simple entries. The first opens the Infrared Monitor dialog. The second enables infrared communication. The third option enables automatic searches for other devices in range. The fourth option enables automatic installation for Plug and Play devices.

The next two check boxes on this page work together. The second check box on the page allows you to open the infrared port for interrupted connections. This comes in handy when the line of sight to the other port could be interrupted by someone passing by. You also want to enable it when you have a less-than-ideal connection to the other device. The third check box on the page tells Windows 95 to sound an alarm whenever it finds a device in range or if it loses a connection to another device. It would have been nice if Microsoft had used two separate sounds for these events, but at least you get some kind of an alert. Obviously, you want to turn off this option in an office where you're sharing the same space with other people. Some people find the constant noise of sounds coming from the computer more than a little distracting.

The last page in this dialog, Identification, is shown in Figure 19.15. As you can see, it contains two edit fields. The first field tells who you are. The second field provides a description of your computer. In most cases, you want to come up with something unique, yet generic, for a portable computer. There really isn't any way of knowing who will be using your computer, so a generic name is best. On the other hand, you don't want the name you chose to interfere with others on the network. Picking something unique as shown in the figure should help you meet both criteria.

Figure 19.15.
The Identification page of the Infrared Monitor dialog allows you to identify yourself to other users.

Power Management Strategies

The following list provides ideas on what you can look for on your laptop. Not every laptop provides every feature listed here and you could certainly find some that are unique to your system. The first tip is to explore the vendor documentation that comes with your laptop. You'll be amazed at the little tips you'll find there.

- Forget fancy software: Screen savers probably eat more power on a laptop than most people imagine. Because most laptop computers come with a feature for turning off the monitor automatically, there isn't any reason for you to install a fancy screen saver. In fact, because most laptops use flat screen displays, you might actually cause more harm than good by using a screen saver. A screen saver could inadvertently interfere with the automatic shutdown software and end up reducing the life of your screen, not extending it. Besides interfering with the normal way your laptop runs, some screen savers constantly access the hard disk, causing further drain on the battery. There are other culprits in this area as well. For instance, see if you can get by with a subset of your word-processing software. I installed the full version of my word processor the first time around and found that one of the features kept hard disk activity at a frantic pace. In an effort to provide me with the latest information on my files, the software was actually just eating power. I don't keep a lot of files on my laptop, so I always know exactly what I have available. Kill the fancy features of your software and you'll find that the battery that normally lasts three hours will probably last three and a half.

- Look for power-saving features: A lot of laptops come equipped with a function key (FN on my system) that's poorly understood by the majority of users. In my case, there's a faucet at the top of the screen. Pressing FN-Faucet reduces power consumption on my machine by a lot—yet I wouldn't have found this feature by simply looking at the documentation. The vendor hid it in the screen section of the text, not in the power-management section where I expected to find it. If you're in doubt about one of those buttons sitting on your laptop, keep searching the documentation until you find it. Most laptops now come with a power saving mode that you can use while on the battery. In some cases, you'll find that programs run a little slower and that the backlight doesn't seem to work as well, but you'll get a lot more life out of your battery.

- Change power-wasting habits and software configurations: I find that I occasionally develop a habit that's great in intent but short on true usefulness. For example, when I start thinking about what I want to write, I save my document. It sounds like a good habit to get into. After all, if you save during think time, then power outages and other types of hardware failure are less likely to affect you. However, consider for a second that it's fairly unlikely that you'll experience a power outage when working with a laptop unless you totally ignore the battery level. In addition, the hardware used in laptop construction is a lot less prone to failure than hardware of days gone by. Consider looking at your software configuration as well. I used to set the automatic save for my word processor to ten minutes. That was just enough time for the drive to start spinning down. As a result, I wasted a huge amount of power starting and stopping the drive. Setting the automatic save to 20 minutes proved a lot more efficient from a power perspective and I haven't lost a single bit of data as a result of the change.

- Turn off your sound: It's really nice having sound effects but sound boards consume quite a bit of power and you have to ask whether you really need to hear any sounds while working on a document at 30,000 feet. In most cases, you can turn off your sound board with a simple setting in the Control Panel. Making this small change in configuration will not only save you power, but it'll make you more popular with the person sitting in the next seat. You'll also want to avoid playing your latest music CD while on battery. A CD will keep the disk running almost continuously, greatly reducing battery life.

- Give it a break: I've seen more than a few folks eat lunch and work on their laptops at the same time. Besides the risk of spilling something in the keyboard, working and doing something else (such as eating) at the same time probably isn't the most efficient way to use laptop battery power. Simply suspend your laptop for the duration of your meal. Not only will you use battery power more efficiently, but you'll also get to enjoy your food hot for once.

Advanced Configuration and Power Interface (ACPI)

The new Advanced Configuration and Power Interface feature of Windows 98 is actually an expansion of the power-management features found in Windows 95. At a minimum, you'll be able to control when your hard drive and monitor turn themselves off after a period of non-use. What will this mean to you as a user? Theoretically, you could leave your computer up all the time. Of course, this could lead to the security problems.

You'll also find that Windows 98 supports two new features. The first is power schemes. It works just like the sound and appearance schemes you may have used in the past. A power scheme allows you to configure a method for managing the power on your machine. You select a power scheme based on your current activity. For example, you might want to use one scheme at the end of the day to shut off your machine instantly and another during the day that provides a delay so that the machine doesn't turn off every time you stop to think.

Laptop users will already be familiar with the Suspend entry on the Start menu, but it's new for desktop users. The suspend switch will allow you to electronically turn off everything on your machine without actually turning off the power. Your machine will go to sleep when you're not using it. If everything works as it should, your machine will use a minimum of power in this state—less than most night-lights do.

Remote Access Server

Some people were a little less than happy with Microsoft for not including Dial-Up Networking server support with the last release of Windows. Well, you no longer have to worry about going out and buying the Plus! pack simply because you need server support. The latest version of Windows 98 comes with the Remote Access Server (RAS) as part of the package. RAS supports both the IPX/SPX and NetBEUI protocols so you can use it in a variety of situations.

On Your Own

This chapter presents a lot of different ideas on how a notebook user can use the capabilities provided by Windows 95 to improve productivity. Of course, one of the big things I covered was the use of the PCMCIA interface. If you have a PCMCIA bus on your notebook computer, right-click My Computer and select the Properties option. Click the Performance tab to see if your system is fully optimized. Make sure you double-check the bus.

Another productivity enhancement is the combination of Briefcase and Dial-Up Networking. Split your projects into two categories: those that you're working on alone and those that you're working on with a group. Use the Briefcase method with the projects that you're working on alone. Use the folder and Dial-Up Networking combination for projects that you're working on in a group.

Make a list of the ways you can use Dial-Up Networking to improve your productivity. I mentioned the most common ways in this chapter, but your company might have special needs that I didn't cover. It's important to use a little creativity when thinking about the ways Windows 95 can help you. Keep the list handy for later and refer to it when you're looking for ways to solve a particular mobile computing problem.

Peter Norton®

V

Making
the Right
Connections

20

Hardware and Software Connections

Peter Norton®

Making your hardware and software work together is one of the more difficult parts of working with any operating system, even Windows 95. That's why this chapter focuses on getting your hardware and software working correctly with your computer. The first part explains the common hardware you may encounter such as modems, sound cards, and display adapters. The second part provides information about sharing files. The third part of the chapter covers voice communications. Voice is becoming an important feature. Not only can you use voice modems to turn your computer into an answering machine, but you can also use voice for a variety of other purposes.

Making Hardware Attachments

Finding that your printer or modem doesn't work when there's a critical deadline is a common occurrence. Fortunately, you can often identify and solve the problem if you know what to look for, as I explain in a moment.

Any Port in a Storm

The first potential problem to examine is the external ports on your machine. Unfortunately, different ports can look alike. For example, game ports and Ethernet ports often look exactly the same.

Fortunately, some types of ports are easy to identify. For example, a 25-pin port with male pins is a serial port. Nothing else on your system uses that configuration. Some external SCSI ports are also easy to identify because they contain so many pins that they fill the entire width of the expansion slot. Unfortunately, most ports require closer identification before you know what they do. For example, you can confuse a printer port (which uses a 25-pin female connector) with a Macintosh-compatible SCSI port (which uses the same connector). Plugging a printer into a Mac-SCSI port can cause physical damage to the printer or the port card or both.

The following list contains clues you can use to identify various ports:

- Ethernet: Nowadays, most Ethernet cards just have an RJ-45 connector (which looks like an oversized telephone jack). However, you may still find older Ethernet cards with a 15-pin thick Ethernet port, a coaxial-cable thin Ethernet connector, and (sometimes, but not always) an active indicator LED as well. The round coaxial connector is the same width as the slot and has two knobs on it for connecting the cable. Another version of an Ethernet card has the 15-pin connector and an RJ-45 jack.

- I/O port combo: The combination port card usually provides a 25-pin parallel port and a 9-pin serial port on the back of the adapter. The serial port is usually COM1 and the parallel port LPT1, but someone may have changed these default settings by using the jumpers on the card or software setup. An I/O port combo adapter might also include a 9- or 25-pin serial port or a 15-pin game port that attaches through the back of the machine. If your case doesn't provide the extra cable connector holes, these ports might appear in one of the expansion slot openings. Some older multifunction cards such as the Intel Above Board used this port layout as well.

- SVGA display: Some older versions of these cards provide both a 9-pin digital and a 15-pin analog port. Note that this 15-pin port is the same size as the 9-pin port. The pins are arranged in three rows of five rather than the two-row arrangement used by the game port. They're also a little smaller than the ones used by the game port. The display adapter might include a mouse port for a PS/2-style mouse. Some adapters provide only the 15-pin port (a requirement for SVGA). Other features on the back of this card might include DIP switches or three high-frequency connectors to connect to a high-resolution monitor.

- Game: This adapter usually contains two 15-pin game ports, although only one is present on some very popular models. The one nearest the top of the machine is usually the one you want to use. If you see a connector with 15 pins in two rows plus an RJ-45 connector (similar to a telephone jack), you're probably looking at an Ethernet card. If you see a connector with 15 holes in three rows, it's for (S)VGA video output.

- Sound board: You'll usually see a 15-pin game port that doubles as a MIDI port when you select the right jumper or software settings. This adapter also includes three jacks that look the same as the earphone jacks on a portable radio. The precise arrangement of these jacks varies by vendor, but they serve the following purposes: output, microphone, and line input from an external source, such as a CD-ROM drive. Some older sound boards also include a volume-level thumbwheel.

- External SCSI: You might also see a number of large connectors on the back of a machine. One type of external SCSI connector has 50 lines and looks like a larger version of the Centronics connector on your printer. Unlike the Macintosh-compatible version (which has only 25 pins and is exactly like a printer port connector), this type of external SCSI connector doesn't use the same type of pins as the more familiar serial or parallel connector. The newer SCSI-II connectors are miniaturized versions of the large 50-pin SCSI. Again, they're quite unlike anything else that you're likely to find on a PC.

- External drive: A number of older CD-ROM drives used a 37-pin plug. It looks like a huge version of the parallel port. You might see this with other types of drives as well. It's never safe to assume anything about this plug. Always check it against the vendor documentation.

- Fax/modem: A fax or modem card will usually provide two RJ-11 jacks (they look like the ones on your telephone). One jack allows you to connect the incoming cable, and the other jack is for your telephone. This adapter usually provides some DIP switches as well.

The general rule to follow is if you see a port that you don't recognize and it isn't marked, open the machine to identify it. The second rule is that you shouldn't always believe the markings on the back of your machine. If you look back there and see that all the ports you recognize are correctly marked, you can probably assume that the rest are correct, too.

Tip: After identifying the ports, mark them. Also, don't simply write down that something is a serial port. Specify COM1 or COM2 as part of the marking. Performing this little extra step can save you a lot of time later. You might want to follow this same procedure with cables, especially if the machine is connected to a workstation setup in which the cable source might become hidden. Identifying the correct cable when there are several possibilities is never a welcome task. It's easier to mark everything at the outset.

Printers

Some people think there's only one way to connect a printer—through a parallel port. However, some newer printers provide a serial port connector, a network connector (AppleTalk or Ethernet), and a standard Centronics parallel port connector.

Tip: Some printers don't provide a serial port as standard equipment; you have to buy it as a separate piece. Your vendor manual should provide details on buying the serial port option. Check whether the vendor also supports other connection options that might help in some situations. Many vendors now support a network connection as standard equipment; others support it as an optional module.

Choosing between these two connections isn't always easy. A parallel port delivers the data 8 bits at a time and at a faster rate than a serial port. Choosing the parallel port doesn't take too much thought if your machine has only one printer attached to it. What if your machine acts as a print server for many different printers? You can easily run out of parallel ports in this situation. Just about everyone resorts to an A/B switch to increase the number of available connections, but there might be a better solution. Connecting your printer to the machine through an unused serial port allows better access to it. No one will have to flip an A/B switch to use it. (Some electronic A/B switches provide an automatic switching scheme when you send certain commands through the printer cable, but this means training the user to send those commands and a lot of frustration when the user forgets to do so.) The problem is that the access is a lot slower with a serial port.

Warning: If you're thinking about using a mechanical A/B switch with a laser printer, be sure its use won't void the printer's warranty. Check with the printer's manufacturer to be sure.

Categorizing how people will use the printers attached to your machine is the next step. Placing a printer that the user is less likely to use or a printer that normally experiences a lower level of activity on a serial port shouldn't cause any problems. Just make sure that you warn people that their print jobs could take a little longer in the new configuration. I find that this allows me to connect at least four different printers to most machines. Of course, when you get to this level, you need to question whether you should dedicate a machine to act as a print server instead of trying to get by using a workstation on a peer-to-peer network.

Some printers come with a built-in NIC that attaches directly to the network without using a workstation connection. The two most popular connection types are Ethernet and AppleTalk. Of course, the appropriate selection depends on the network you're running. Whether this solution will work for you depends not on the NIC so much as on the software included with the printer. The printer actually boots as a workstation or a self-contained print server on the network. You see it just as you see any other workstation. The only difference is that this workstation is dedicated to a single task—printing. You need to find out which networks the vendor supports. This really is a great solution for a peer-to-peer network because it allows you to use the printer without overloading the workstation. Adding a printer this way also preserves precious workstation resources such as interrupts and I/O port addresses.

Printers also support some of the more exotic network connections these days, but you might be hard-pressed to find them. One solution that I see gaining in popularity is the wireless LAN. Using this type of connection, you could unwrap the printer, plug it in, and perform a few configuration steps to get it up and running without physically connecting it to a workstation or server. In the future, adding a printer to the network might be even easier than adding it to your local workstation.

Modems

The two different kinds of modems are internal and external. I prefer an external modem for several reasons including portability. I can move an external modem in a matter of minutes by disconnecting it from the current machine, moving it, and reconnecting it to the new machine. Another advantage is that even though most software displays the indicators that you normally see on the modem, an external modem has an edge when it comes to troubleshooting because the software light indicators might not always reflect reality.

Yet another advantage of the external modem is that you can turn it off without turning off your computer. This can come in handy when you must reset the modem manually and you don't want to reboot your computer. It also provides some people with added peace of mind because when the modem is turned off, no one can call into their computer. (You can keep people from calling into a computer with an internal modem simply by setting up the modem so that it doesn't answer the phone line. Seeing the modem power light off is a way to know for sure that this has been done.)

Once you get past the physical location of a modem, you need to connect the modem to the outside world. The most common types of modems are analog modems, which connect to an ordinary telephone line using an RJ-11 jack. Normally, you have to get an office wired for a modem before you can use it. Some recent phone instruments in offices and, increasingly, in hotel rooms, sport a standard RJ-11 jack labeled a "data port." Of course, home users won't run into this problem because a modem uses a standard home telephone jack. (The second RJ-11 jack on your modem is normally reserved for a telephone so that you can use the same telephone number for both.)

> **Warning:** Besides analog modems, a variety of other modem types have been appearing recently, including ISDN modems and cable modems. These newer modems need specialized connections (such as an ISDN or cable outlet), which must be installed by the telephone or cable company. For most people, ordinary analog modems are more popular and common.

Another connection for external modems is between the modem and the computer. You'll normally use a standard serial port cable (not a null modem cable) that has either a 9- or 25-wire connector at each end. (A few external modems for older portable computers differ in that they're designed to connect to your computer's parallel port.)

Modems are also rated by speed and capability. The speed at which a modem can communicate is increasing all the time. 28.8Kbps is considered a minimum speed, although most vendors have introduced 56Kbps modems. You'll soon reap the benefits of using cable modems as cable companies upgrade their transmission lines. In most cases, these lines will top out at 128Mbps. What does this mean for those of you still using 28.8Kbps modems? It's time for an upgrade, of course. A 33.6Kbps modem will be an inexpensive upgrade but consider buying a newer 56Kbps modem. Beware of buying an older 56Kbps modem because these earlier models didn't follow the latest standard for 56Kbps modems.

There are a ton of modem standards, most of which won't make a lot of difference to you as a user. However, there are some standards that you should know about. A lot of standardization has to do with the modem's speed, the way it corrects errors, or the method it uses to compress data. Knowing about these standards could mean the difference between getting a good buy on a modem or getting one that's almost useless. The following list shows the more common modem standards, but you should also be aware of any new standards that develop around higher-speed modems:

- Bell 103: The American standard for 300 baud modems. It was the rate that everyone used when PCs first arrived on the scene.

- Bell 212A: The American 1200 baud modem included both this standard and the Bell 103 standard. European standards included enough differences to require a separate modem in most cases.

- CCITT V.21: Defines the European standard for 300 baud modems. Like its counterpart, this standard is very much out of date.

- CCITT V.22: The European version of the 1200 baud modem standard. It also includes the V.21 standard.

- CCITT V.22bis: You might wonder what the "bis" in this standard number means. Just think of it as revision B. In this case, it refers to the general standard for 2400 baud modems.

- CCITT V.23: A special 1200/75bps standard for the European market that sends data at one speed and receives at another. Modems don't support it unless they're designed for overseas use.

- CCITT V.25bis: Defines an alternative command set for modems that you won't need unless your modem also supports an X.25 interface.

- CCITT V.32: Defines the 4800bps, 9600bps, 14.4Kbps, 19.2Kbps and 28.8Kbps standards.

- CCITT V.34: Defines the data-compression specifics for the 28.8Kbps standard. It also defines the 33.6Kbps standard.

- CCITT V.42: Defines a data-compression method for modems (also requires the modem to provide MNP Levels 2 through 4) that allows the modem to transfer data at apparent rates of up to 19.2Kbps.

- CCITT V.42bis: The second revision of the modem data-compression standard that allows up to a four times compression factor or an apparent transfer rate of 38.4Kbps from a 9600bps modem.

- CCITT V.FAST: This was a proprietary method of defining data compression for the 28.8Kbps standard. It has been replaced by the CCITT V.34 standard.

- CCITT X.25: Some asynchronous modems also support this synchronous data-transfer standard. You don't need it if your only goal is to communicate with online services.

- MNP 2-4, 5, 10: Microm Networking Protocol, a standard method of error-correcting for modems. The precise differences between levels aren't important from a user perspective. A higher level is generally better.

- x2 and K56Flex Protocols: These are two rival standards for defining how 56Kbps modems work. A new 56Kbps standard will combine the features of both x2 and K56Flex standards into a single universal 56Kbps standard.

The main reason to worry about modem standards is if you're planning to use a modem in another country or if you're buying a generic, no-name modem that might offer a bargain price but no promise of quality. If you stick with name-brand, popular modems, you should have no trouble getting your modem to work with other computers.

Fax Boards

The preceding section introduced you to modem connections. Fax boards characteristically appear on the same board as the modem, or perhaps on a daughter card, and usually use the same telephone connector as the modem. You should follow some general rules of thumb when selecting a fax board. The most important of these is to make sure that your modem will communicate correctly with whatever is at the other end of the line. For normal faxing to standard fax machines, support for Group 3 faxes is sufficient. Supporting various error-correction protocols can help ensure that your faxes arrive ungarbled.

Every fax/modem transfer consists of five phases. The ITU (formerly CCITT) defines these phases in several standards, which I examine later. These five phases aren't cast in concrete, and each one could repeat during any given session. It all depends on the capabilities of your fax/modem, the software you're using, and the environment conditions at the time.

- Phase 1, call establishment: Your computer calls another computer or a standard fax machine.

- Phase 2, pre-message procedure: The sending and receiving machines select parameters that allow them to transfer data at the fastest possible rate. These parameters also take into account the resolution, modulation, and other factors.

- Phase 3, message transmission: This is the phase in which the actual data transfer takes place. If the initial group of parameters set in Phase 2 end in less-than-optimal results, the fax/modem performs Phase 2 and Phase 3 again as required.

- Phase 4, post-message procedure: Some software considers each page as a separate message. In fact, that's the way your fax machine works as well. Phase 4 allows the sending and receiving machines to evaluate the results of each message and then raise or lower the transmission speed as required. This is also the phase in which the sending machine transmits a page-break marker. This is the same thing as a form feed on a printer, except that the fax might simply print a line across the page or might cut off the page at that point. Remember that faxes can be either long or short, depending on the message needs.

- Phase 5, call clear down: This is the easiest part of the conversion. The two machines hang up the phone after the sending machine transmits an end-of-transmission signal.

As with modems, there are several fax/modem specifications. You want a fax/modem that adheres to the following ITU standards. Most name brand modems follow all fax/modem standards:

- ITU T.4: Defines the image-transfer portion of the session used in Phase 3.

- ITU T.30: Defines the negotiation and interpage phases (2, 3, 4, and 5). A normal multipage transfer uses T.30 only at the beginning of the call, between pages, and after the last page.

- CCITT V.17: Defines the specifications for the 4800/1200bps speed. The slash shows that the fax receives at one speed and sends at another.

- CCITT V.27: Defines the specifications for the 9600/7200bps speed.

- CCITT V.29: Defines the specifications for the 14,400/12,000bps speed.

- ITU V.34: Defines the combined voice, fax, and data standards for 28.8Kbps and 33.6Kbps modems.

Microsoft also provides for two different classes of fax communication between fax/modems. Here's the user view of what these different classes mean. Class 1 communications send an editable fax to the other party. This means that the fax appears as actual text that the other party can edit, like sending an e-mail through the fax machine. Class 2 communications are more like the fax you usually receive. They're graphic representations of the text and graphics in the document. This is the same format as Group 3 faxes, like the one you're used to seeing in the office.

There is a real-world difference between Class 1 and Class 2 fax/modems. A Class 1 fax performs both the T.4 and T.30 protocols in software. This allows the Windows 95 drivers to perform the data translation required to create editable faxes. A Class 2 fax performs the T.4 protocol in firmware—an EEPROM in the modem that does part of the work for the processor. This is a faster solution because it removes part of the processing burden from the processor. A Class 2 fax/modem should also be able to create editable faxes. However, because the Class 2 standard isn't well defined and Microsoft didn't have dependable information on what to expect from a Class 2 fax/modem, Microsoft made the decision to restrict Class 2 faxes to the Group 3 graphics format.

Note: The Electronic Industries Association (EIA) recently approved a new Class 2 standard that stringently defines what vendors need to provide in firmware. As a result, you might see software that uses Class 2 fax/modems more efficiently in the next six months to a year. Look for software vendors to make a big deal out of the new "high-speed" fax transmission capabilities offered by their products sometime in the future. This fax/modem software uses this new Class 2 fax/modem specification.

CD-ROM and DVD Players

CD-ROM and DVD drives usually have two connections that you need to worry about. The first is the bus connector that allows data transfer between the computer and the device. Generally, this is a SCSI connector or an EIDE connection. The principle is the same; the data transfer rate might be a lot slower, depending on the method of connection. SCSI and EIDE offer comparable performance. The bus connector for a CD-ROM or DVD serves the same purpose as the equivalent connector for your hard drive. It allows you to transfer data from the CD-ROM or DVD to your machine.

Tip: The price of CD-ROM recorders has dropped significantly in recent months. There are three advantages to buying a CD-ROM recorder instead of a player. First, you can use it to make archive copies of CDs. An archive copy can make a big difference if your hard disk crashes. Second, you can use a CD-ROM recorder in place of a backup tape. A CD-ROM backup is faster than some types of tape backup, although I won't say that you can't get better performance out of some DAT tapes. One thing is certain: The random-access feature of a CD makes it a lot faster than a tape for data retrieval, plus the newer rewritable CDs let you write to it multiple times. A third advantage is that CD-ROM recordable drives can replace ordinary read-only CD-ROM drives.

Some people don't really think about the second connection. They try to use a CD-ROM with a game or another application that plays sound right off the CD—just as you do with a music CD—and discover that the game doesn't appear to work with their machine. The same could be said about playing movies off a DVD drive. The problem is that they don't have the RCA plugs in the back of the CD-ROM drive connected to anything. External drives use RCA connectors like the speaker outputs on your stereo. Internal drives usually require some type of special connector for your sound card. This is a proprietary connector in some cases; in other cases, the vendor tries to make you believe that its common cable really is proprietary. Check with your local computer store to see whether it has an inexpensive alternative to the expensive cable that the vendors normally offer.

In addition to the other connections on your CD-ROM or DVD drive, there's often a headphone connector on the front of it. Imagine my surprise when I plugged some headphones in and heard sound out of my speakers and headset at the same time. Some vendors disable the speaker output when you plug in the headset; others don't. You want to check out this feature if this is an important consideration for your application.

Making Software Attachments

Once you get your hardware up and running, you have to get some software to talk to it to do any useful work. The following sections describe several of the utilities that come with Windows 95. These utilities won't help you "surf the Net" or download the latest industry gossip, but they do help you make the necessary connections.

Peter's Principle: The Right Kind of Connection

It might be tempting to use a single type of connection to meet all your computing needs, but that isn't the most efficient way to do things. You might view a direct cable connection as the panacea for all your portable data-transfer woes, but the direct cable connection is really designed for occasional rather than daily use. A direct cable connection works fine for quick transfers from one machine to another when you have a fairly large amount of data to move. For example, it works well when you initially set up the portable.

If you use a portable on a daily basis, using such an Interlink-style connection is a waste of time. You'll want to find some other method of creating your connection to the desktop. If you have a docking station that can accept a standard network card or if you plug in a PCMCIA network card, you can use this much-faster Ethernet connection to make your data transfers. However, this works only if you have a network and a PCMCIA card. Alternatively, you can get an external Ethernet adapter that plugs into your portable's parallel port. This solution works fine, but it isn't quite as speedy as the standard network interface cards that plug into the computer's bus or the PCMCIA network adapters.

The Briefcase isn't a physical connection to your desktop machine, but it can hold a substantial amount of data if you use it correctly.

Okay, so the network and Briefcase options are out of the question because you're out of town. You can still make a connection to your desktop by using Dial-Up Networking. It isn't as fast as some of the other techniques, but it allows you to get the data you require while on the road or when working from home.

Windows 95 provides a lot of different connections. You need to use the right one for the job, and that means taking the time to learn about the various options available to you. A connection that works well in one instance could be a time killer in another. Don't succumb to the one-connection way of computing; use every tool that Windows 95 provides.

Making a Direct Cable Connection

Portable users will love the direct cable-connection feature that Windows 95 provides. You can make a direct connection using either the serial or parallel port. Of course, the parallel port is a lot faster than the serial port, but either connection will net good results. The Direct Cable Connection utility allows you to make the connection in the background, effectively freeing the host for use while the client makes the required transactions.

Windows 95 won't automatically install this utility as part of a default package. You need to load the Direct Cable Connection utility by using the Add/Remove Programs applet as described in Chapter 11, "The Windows 95 Applets."

Once you get Direct Cable Connection installed, you have to get the host set up. This means that you'll define the port that your machine will use and its mode. Take a look at this procedure first.

Tip: You can create the required data-transfer serial cable by using a standard serial cable, a null modem, and a gender changer. This provides all the components you need to make a data-transfer cable using a standard modem cable. Your local electronics or computer store can usually provide the null modem and gender changer.

1. Use a special serial or parallel cable to connect the two computers. You can normally get one of these at your local computer store. Be sure to tell them that you plan to connect two computers for the purpose of data transfer. The parallel cable uses special crossover wiring and the serial cable must be wired with the required wires cross-connected or else you need to use a null modem as well for the connection to work.

2. Share any folders or drives that you want the guest computer to see by right-clicking the folder in Explorer, choosing the Properties option from the context menu, and choosing the Sharing tab of the Properties dialog. If you don't see the Sharing tab, you need to set up file and printer sharing in the Network applet as described in Chapter 27, "Networks." You can choose between read-only and full access to the folder.

Note: Direct Cable Connection will configure itself for whatever mode you had it set up to use during the previous use after you use it for the first time. Simply click the Change button on the first dialog to get out of this mode and choose something different.

3. Open the Direct Cable Connection utility on the host computer. You should see a Direct Cable Connection dialog box.

4. Choose the Host radio button, and then click Next. The next dialog asks which port you want to use for the connection between machines. Notice that the local ports are listed automatically. You can add other ports by using the Install New Ports button.

5. Select the port you want. Be sure to use the same type of port on both machines. Click Next. Direct Cable Connection asks if you want to add password protection to your drive in addition to the protection you may have already provided through the sharing process. Checking the Use password protection option enables the Set Password button, which displays the dialog you use to enter the password.

Tip: The password option comes in handy when more than one person needs to use the direct cable connection to a machine. You could leave the host running in the background and then connect other machines as necessary—even remote machines. However, this feature is limited, especially when you consider that the Dial-Up Networking utility allows remote users to call into a machine using a better interface.

6. Check the Use password protection check box if you want to password-protect your connection. If you select this option, use the Set Password button to change the password from a blank.

7. Click Finish. Direct Cable Connection waits for the client machine to log on. If the client doesn't respond in about 30 seconds, Direct Cable Connection asks whether it's properly connected. Ignore the message until you get the other machine running.

The procedure for setting up a guest computer is exactly the same as for a host computer. The only difference is that you don't need to set a password. Once the two computers establish a connection, the client computer is able to use the resources of the host.

Creating Scripts for Dial-Up Networking

To supplement Dial-Up Networking, Windows 95 also provides a scripting capability. A script provides additional instructions for Windows 95 to use when using your dial-up connection. Adding a script means accessing the Scripting page of the Dial-Up Connection Properties dialog by right-clicking the connection and then choosing Properties from the context menu. Figure 20.1 shows the Scripting page of the Dial-Up Connection properties dialog box. As you can see, adding a script is quite easy (writing one may be a different story).

Figure 20.1.
Windows 95 provides a scripting capability that greatly enhances the flexibility of Dial-Up Networking.

This dialog box displays a File name field that contains the name of the script file you want to use. Notice the two buttons directly below this field. The first, Edit, allows you to modify your script. The second, Browse, displays a File Open dialog box that you can use to find a script file. There are also two check boxes on this page. The Step through script option walks you through your script one line at a time when you use the connection. It's useful for troubleshooting a script when you first create it, but you'll want to disable this option later. The second option, Start terminal screen minimized, is handy once you've debugged your script because it keeps screen clutter to a minimum. However, you'll want to keep this option unchecked until you're certain that the script will work as intended.

Starting a Script

Basically a script is a text file with an `.SCP` extension. Scripts use procedures, enclosing all your scripting code with a pair of statements: `proc` and `endproc`. Every script has to have a main procedure. These are the first lines of text that you'll add to your script file:

```
; This is a comment telling about the script.
proc main
endproc
```

Using Variables

You must declare all the variables you use, and these declarations have to appear at the beginning of the procedure. A declaration always contains the variable type and the variable name; you can also assign the variable a value. Variable names always begin with a letter or an underscore; you can't use reserved names for a variable. The following list shows what types of variables you can use within a script:

- Integer: Any number, either positive or negative.
- String: A collection of characters such as `"Hello World"`. You can also have strings that contain numbers.
- Boolean: Variables that are either true or false.

Here's a script with some variables:

```
; This script shows some variables.
proc main
    ; This is an integer variable.
    integer    iValue
    ; This is a string variable with an assigned value.
    string     sMyString = "Hello"
    ; This is a boolean variable.
    boolean    lAmICorrect
endproc
```

Special Considerations for Strings

A lot of servers require you to send a Ctrl+Break character before they respond. The caret translation feature takes care of this. You simply place a caret in front of one of the first 26 characters. For example, `"^M"` sends a carriage return and `"^C"` sends a Ctrl+Break. (Make sure you always use quotes when defining a string in a script, even if that string represents a control character.)

There are some text substitutions for control characters as well. For example, `"<cr>"` is a carriage return and `"<lf>"` is a line feed. Using a `"<cr>"` in your code is a lot less cryptic than `"^M"`.

Finally, you'll find that Dial-Up Networking scripts support several escape character sequences that C programmers are familiar with. For example, using `"\""` in your code produces a double quote.

You also need a way to display the caret. You do it like this: `"\^"`. Likewise, you need a way to display the backslash—`"\\"`—and the less-than sign—`"\<"`.

Using Commands

The scripting language provided with Dial-Up Networking supports certain commands right out of the box. You can also create other commands (very simple ones) using the `proc` and `endproc` keywords to create a procedure.

For a short example of a command, take a close look at the `waitfor` command. Look at a simple example first:

```
waitfor "Login:"
```

All this command says is to wait until you get a `Login:` string from the host computer. Once you get it, start executing the statement immediately following this one.

Naturally, there's a lot more to scripting than the information provided here, but you can see that scripting offers flexibility if you're willing to take the time to write a script.

Using Phone Dialer

Phone Dialer comes in handy, not for your most common calls, but for those that you make infrequently. Have you ever tried to call a government agency? I used to spend a lot of time just trying to get through, only to find that I had reached the wrong number. Phone Dialer might not fix the wrong-number part of the equation, but I've found that it works well for the first part. I can have it call in the background while I continue to work in the foreground—a handy time-saving feature.

Open Phone Dialer and you see a display similar to the one in Figure 20.2. Notice that there's a keypad on the left side of the dialog box, a list of speed dial numbers on the right, and the current number at the top.

Figure 20.2.
*The Phone Dialer
dialog box looks like a
telephone keypad with
an autodialer.*

There are several ways to dial a number. You can just cut it out of your database manager and paste it into the blank at the top. This is one of the methods I use for infrequently called numbers.

Take a quick look at the Tools menu to see what configuration options you have. This menu has three options; each one addresses a different need. If you select the Connect Using option, you see the Connect Using dialog box. This dialog box has only three fields. The first field, Line, asks which modem you want to use. Only modems that you've set up using the Modems applet in Control Panel are listed. The second field, Address, asks which telephone line you want to use to dial out. It's active only if you have more than one line available. The Use Phone Dialer check box tells Windows 95 to use Phone Dialer for all application requests. Clicking the Line Properties button brings up the Modem Properties dialog box discussed in Chapter 14, "Exploiting Your Hardware."

The Dialing Properties option of the Tools menu allows you to specify the location you're dialing from so that Phone Dialer can automatically compensate as needed for long-distance calls.

The Show Log option of the Tools menu displays the Call Log dialog box, which maintains a record of the calls you make, including the number, the person's name, and how long you were on the phone. The nicest feature of this particular dialog box is that you can double-click an entry to call it again.

There are two convenient methods for adding new numbers to your Speed Dial group. The first method is to simply click a blank spot. (The only problem with this technique is that it works only for blank buttons. Clicking a filled-in blank dials the number.) You see the Program Speed Dial dialog box. This dialog box contains only two entries: the name of the person you want to call and the number to reach him or her. The buttons on the side allow you to save, save and dial, or cancel the phone number.

You can also use the Edit | Speed Dial command to display the Edit Speed Dial dialog box. This dialog box allows you to access any of the buttons. All you need to do is click the one you want to edit. Erasing the contents of both the name and number fields blanks that button for future use.

Understanding Voice Communications

The latest rage in the world of modems is the voice modem. A voice modem allows you to exchange data and talk on the same line by using digitized voice signals. In other words, you don't need two telephone lines anymore to have an online discussion with a colleague. Having a voice/data/fax modem combination also means that you don't need a lot of messy wires hanging around the office. You can use one phone as a fax machine, network host, and answering machine. The only problem with voice modems up to this point is that each vendor has completely different drivers and command sets. What you really need are two voice modems from the same vendor to create a voice connection. At this point, bells should be going off in your mind. The Windows telephone application programming interface (TAPI) was supposed to get rid of all of the compatibility problems between modems. Fortunately, as technology changes, TAPI seems to change as well. The next few sections look at voice modems and how to use them within the Windows 95 environment.

Getting TAPI Support for Voice Modems

Windows 95 doesn't provide support for voice modems through TAPI. You need to download a special update file from the Internet at `ftp://ftp.microsoft.com/softlib/mslfiles/unimodv.exe`. This file installs Unimodem V support on your machine, which is the basis for standardized access to the voice capabilities of your modem. (In most cases, you get this update as part of any new modem purchase you make, if the vendor provides a Windows 95-specific installation program.) Chapter 14 talks about TAPI in the section "TAPI and MAPI Support." However, I do want to quickly tell you what you'll get in your Unimodem V package when you download it.

Tip: If you really want to get the developer view on what's happening with TAPI, take a look at the FTP site at `ftp://ftp.microsoft.com/developr/tapi/`. The README file in the directory will tell you about the various files and what they can do for you. Most of this information is developer-related, but there are a few sample applications that might interest users. You'll also want to download a special developer-related README file regarding Unimodem and Unimodem V from `ftp://ftp.microsoft.com/developr/drg/Modem/`.

From a user perspective, the Unimodem V package (the self-extracting `UNIMODV.EXE` file) contains four items of interest. First are the drivers that you need to use your voice modem. The package includes a new `UNIMODEM.VXD` file along with several other support drivers. Part of these driver updates includes a Telephony Service Provider (TSP). Its job is to handle program requests such as dialing and answering the phone line. The second item of interest is the Operator Agent. This is a special program that runs on your computer. It identifies whether an incoming call is voice, data, or fax and directs it to the appropriate program for handling. If the Operator Agent can't determine what kind of call you're receiving, it asks the caller for information. Finally, if the Operator Agent can't get a response from the caller, it directs the call to a default application. The third item in this package is a series of WAV file drivers that allow your telephony applications to record and play back messages. Finally, the fourth item is a series of INF files used for installation and support of the Unimodem V package.

Once you've downloaded the `UNIMODV.EXE` file and determined that you have a modem that works with Microsoft's new Voice Modem Extensions for Windows 95 drivers supplied with the package, you can install the support. The following procedure will help you get the job done:

1. Place the `UNIMODV.EXE` file in its own directory. Double-click the `UNIMODV.EXE` file to extract all the files it contains.

2. Right-click the `UNIMODV.INF` file. You see an Install option on the context menu. Select it and you see a Copying Files dialog box.

3. Once Windows 95 completes the file copying process, you need to restart your machine. At this point, the support is installed, but you still need to get your modem set up to use it.

4. Right-click the My Computer icon and select Properties from the context menu. You see the System Properties dialog box.

5. Select the Device Manager page. Click the plus sign next to the Modem entry. You should see one or more modems listed. Highlight the voice modem installed on your machine and then click Remove to remove it.

6. Click the Refresh button on the Device Manager page. Windows 95 checks for new devices and reinstalls your modem. The whole purpose behind this is to install the new drivers you need.

7. At this point, I normally restart my machine again, just to make sure that everything is installed and registered correctly. You don't absolutely have to perform this step, but it's a good step to take.

Installing the Operating Agent

Installing Unimodem V support on your machine allows one or more applications to use the voice modem support that it provides. The Unimodem V package also comes with an Operating Agent. You can choose whether to install this support, but it's usually a good idea to do so if you plan to use Microsoft products. Remember that the Operating Agent is the software that allows Windows 95 to determine whether the incoming call is fax, data, or voice. The following procedure shows how to install the Operating Agent.

Note: The following procedure assumes that you've already installed Unimodem V support by using the procedure in the preceding section. If you haven't installed this support, do so now.

1. Select the Operator icon via the Start | Programs | Accessories command. You see the Microsoft Operator wizard.

2. Click Next. You see a second page of instructions; be sure to read through them. This page tells you what you'll be doing as you use the wizard to install Operator Agent support. At this point, you need to perform three steps: Select a default message, select a default application, and select a message for those times when a particular application isn't running.

3. Click Next. You see the dialog box shown in Figure 20.3. This dialog box allows you to choose the message that a caller will hear if the Operator Agent can't determine what kind of call it's receiving. Click the Play button to hear the current message. If you want to change this message, select the Change the Greeting radio button. Otherwise, keep the second radio button selected as shown in the figure. If you choose to keep the current greeting, skip to step 6. Steps 4 and 5 help you through the process of selecting or recording a new message.

Figure 20.3.
This dialog box allows you to choose between the default message and your own custom message.

Tip: The Operator Agent comes complete with a male and a female version of the default message. The female version of the message is installed as a default. You can follow Steps 4 and 5 to choose the default male version of the message in addition to recording your own message. Make sure that you have a microphone attached to your machine, if you choose to record a new message.

4. Click Next. If you selected the Change the greeting radio button in the preceding step, you see a dialog box that allows you to save the current message by clicking the Yes radio button and then the Save button. (Because you're using the default message in this example, you select the No radio button.) After you click Save, you see a standard File Save dialog box.

5. Click Next. You see a dialog box like the one shown in Figure 20.4. This figure shows the default setup. Clicking the top radio button takes you to a recording dialog box where you can record a message, using a microphone or other media input device. This dialog box also allows you to play back the recorded message to make sure that it's correct. Clicking the second radio button in the dialog box shown in Figure 20.4 allows you to choose a prerecorded file. Theoretically, you can choose any WAV file, but you want to make sure that it tells your caller what to do. The drop-down list box shows the WAV files in your Media folder. You can use the Browse button to explore your hard drive and find WAV files located in other areas. As with the previous dialog box, the Play button allows you to hear the prerecorded WAV file that you've selected.

6. Click Next. You see a dialog box that allows you to choose the order in which the Operator Agent answers calls. In other words, if you expect to have a lot of voice messages, a few faxes, and almost no data uploads, then you want to move the Data entry to the very end.

7. Highlight any entries that you need to move, and then use the Move Up or Move Down button to change its position. If you decide that you want the default setup, click the Restore Defaults button.

Figure 20.4.
In this dialog box, you
can choose to use a
prerecorded message
or record your own.

8. Click Next. You see a dialog box that allows you to choose the message that the caller will hear if the Operator Agent can't complete a call. Setting up this dialog box is much the same as the default call-type selection message discussed in steps 3, 4, and 5, so I don't talk about it again here.

9. Click Next. You see a dialog box that tells you that you've completed the setup process. You also see some additional information concerning the Operator Agent—such as how to determine whether it's running.

10. Click Finish to complete the setup process. At this point, the dialog box simply disappears. However, if you look at the Taskbar, you see a new icon for managing the Operator Agent.

This procedure works fine the first time you set up the Operator Agent, but what if you need to change your message or another setting? As with everything else under Windows 95, you can right-click the Operator Agent icon on the Taskbar to see a context menu. There are three different options on this menu. The first opens the Microsoft Operator Agent dialog box shown in Figure 20.5. I cover the contents of this dialog box in a moment. The second option suspends the Operator Agent. The agent is still available; it just won't answer the phone. The third option, Stop Using Operator, actually removes the Operator Agent from the Taskbar. You use this option when you install a third-party product to handle your phone calls or simply don't need the capability any more.

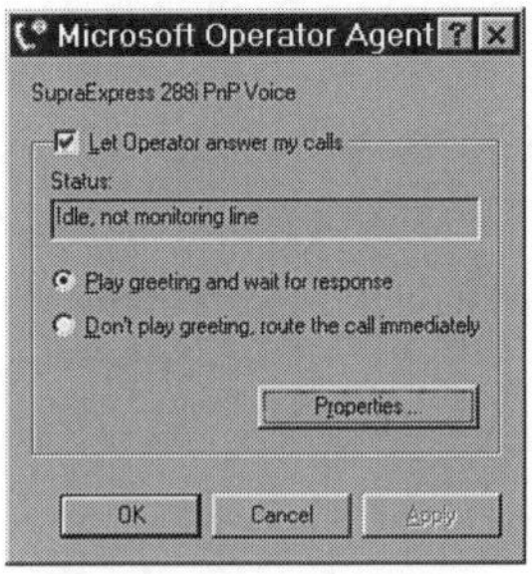

Figure 20.5.
You can change the
Operator Agent
properties by using
this dialog box.

Take a look at the dialog box shown in Figure 20.5. The first check box enables or suspends the Operator Agent. Unchecking this box is the same as selecting the Suspend Operator option on the context menu. It keeps the Operator Agent installed but prevents it from managing your phone line. Notice the edit box directly below the check box. It contains the current status of the Operator Agent. In this case, it's idle because there aren't any active applications on the test machine. An idle message doesn't necessarily mean that the Operator Agent is malfunctioning, even if you have applications installed for recording messages and so forth. An idle message also appears if none of the applications has placed the modem in answer mode. (See the documentation for the application to see how to do this.) The two radio buttons you see in this dialog box determine whether the caller hears a message. Select the first radio button if you plan on getting a lot of voice calls and want to give the caller an opportunity to choose a course of action. On the other hand, you might want to select the second radio button if you plan to get a lot of fax or data calls so that the caller doesn't think that your machine is broken. (A lot of people want an instant response from a fax or data line and hang up if they don't get it.)

Figure 20.5 also shows a Properties button. Clicking this button displays the dialog box shown in Figure 20.6. This is where you can change either of the two messages and set the order in which the Operator Agent directs calls. All you need to do is click the button corresponding to the configuration item you want to change. You actually see that part of the Microsoft Operator wizard come up and help you set the configuration.

Figure 20.6.
You can change any of the configuration settings for the Operator Agent by using the Microsoft Operator Agent Properties dialog box.

The Inner Workings of Unimodem V

Okay, so you've got Unimodem V support and the Operator Agent installed on your machine. Does that mean you're ready to go? Just having a few drivers and the right modem won't fulfill all your needs. For you to see any results, the programmer who wrote the application you're using had to use the Voice Modem Extensions for Windows 95. The application needs to know how to use the capabilities that Windows 95 provides. Most of the answering-machine–type applications on the market right now still rely on those proprietary setups that I mentioned previously.

Note: Voice modems use special command strings to activate their voice capabilities, just like any other service that they offer. If you've ever used a program like Procomm Plus, you're familiar with the Hayes command strings used to set up your modem. For example, ATA answers the phone and ATH hangs up the phone. There are other command strings to test the modem and even a few to ask it questions. Even though Hayes originated these command strings, they're now managed by groups such as ANSI (American National Standards Institute), TIA (Telecommunications Industry Association) and EIA (Electronics Industry Association). When the time came to implement voice capabilities into voice modems, there weren't any AT command strings for vendors to use, so they made up their own. Obviously, this muddies the picture greatly because Windows can't depend on using a standard command string to work with a voice modem. There's a new standard now for voice modems: ANSI/TIA/EIA standard IS-101 (Facsimile Digital Interfaces—Voice Control Interim Standard for Asynchronous DCE). This standard defines a set of AT+V commands that modems should use to enable and use voice capabilities. When buying a new voice modem, make absolutely certain that it adheres to this standard if you want to use it successfully with Windows.

How does Windows get sounds recorded as messages out to the caller? Figure 20.7 shows a block diagram of the new connections that Unimodem V creates to connect various Windows 95 subsystems together so that you can use your voice modem in a variety of ways.

The following lists the various Unimodem V subsystems:

- Windows Communication API

- Telephony API: Notice that the figure shows two different functions for TAPI. We disguise the voice data so that TAPI will work with it using the Serial Wave Driver. Even though there aren't any new TAPI files, we double the amount of work that it can do. (This particular feat is a real credit to the new modular approach that Microsoft took in designing Windows.)

- Multimedia Wave API: If you're wondering what this is doing here, you're not alone. It doesn't take long to figure out, however, that Windows has to have some way of converting the voice you hear on the phone into data that it can understand (and vice versa). Because we already have this capability built into Windows through the multimedia API, why not use it? As a result, the data you record by using a microphone or hear through a speaker goes through the multimedia API even when the source is a telephone call.

Figure 20.7.

Unimodem V creates new connections between various Windows 98 subsystems.

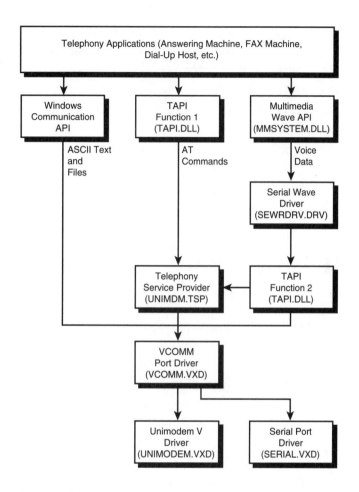

- Serial Wave Driver: This part of the picture can get a little confusing, so I'll talk about the simple version. If you've got a standard modem that adheres to all the standards, you use a serial wave driver that supports the International Multimedia Association (IMA) adaptive delta pulse code modulation (ADPCM) standard. All these fancy words mean only that the serial wave driver converts the digitized voice that it receives from the modem into something that the multimedia system can understand and vice versa. This module uses a helper DLL named VMODCTL.DLL to ease communications with the TSP. Some modems rely on a nonstandard hardware audio port to transmit digitized voice over the telephone. In this case, Microsoft adds another helper module named WRAP.DRV to coordinate voice and data transfers.

- Telephony Service Provider (TSP): This is the driver that takes care of things such as dialing the phone. It also issues all of the AT+V commands required to communicate with your modem. For example, there's one AT+V command to set the modem in voice mode and another to tell it to transfer data. (This module also supports some modems that use the AT#V command syntax, but you want to check the list I provided previously to make sure that your modem is supported.)

- VCOMM Port Driver
- Unimodem V Driver: The Unimodem V Driver now has the capacity to use the specific voice commands supported by your modem.
- Serial Port Driver

Remember that I just showed you an overview of the new additions to the communications sub-system. There's a lot more going on than I discussed, but this overview gives you enough information to better understand how Windows 95 works.

On Your Own

Look through the vendor manual that came with your printer. See whether the vendor provides any accessories for your printer that might make it more flexible to use. Especially important is the avail-ability of alternative port options. You also might want to check for third-party solutions for your printer. Some third-party vendors provide port accessories for some of the more prominent printers, such as the HP LaserJet.

If you have a fax/modem attached to your machine, identify the five phases of a fax transaction. This is especially easy when using an external model. The lights on the front of the device help you detect when the various phases occur. Tracking this type of information can help you troubleshoot a faulty connection.

If you have a notebook computer, and both a network and a direct cable connection are available for it, try both methods of transferring a file. Most people have a serial connection available, so try that first. You should find that the network connection is a lot faster, but it's interesting to see how much faster. Try the same thing with a parallel connection (if possible).

Install and set up Phone Dialer. Try it out for a few days to see whether its additional features make phone calling a little easier for your harder-to-reach numbers. Also try the log feature to see how well it meets your needs.

Create a script program for a Dial-Up Networking connection. You might want to try this with a local setup first to get a feel for the capabilities of the scripting language.

Determine whether you or your company can use a voice modem to make using the computer easier and more efficient. Be sure to check out the various criteria covered in this chapter—especially adherence to standards. You'll also want to download the Unimodem V update for your computer.

21

Network Connections with an Internet Appeal

Peter Norton®

Microsoft doesn't include much in the way of support for any online services other than Microsoft Network (MSN) in the standard copy of Windows 95. Fortunately, this is changing as Microsoft becomes more involved with the Internet. OEM Service Release 2 (OSR2) users will be surprised at the number of new communications features they find. (Chapter 20, "Hardware and Software Connections," covers the new scripting feature for Dial-Up Networking users.) There's even an Online Services folder with setups for some of the larger communications providers. Fortunately, you can download many of the new communications features. I tell you where to get them as you go through this and the next chapter.

Looking Ahead: This chapter covers standard communications; the Internet-specific communications features provided by Windows 95 are covered in Chapters 22–26. Chapter 22, "Browsing the Internet with Internet Explorer," covers new products such as Internet Explorer 4.0 and the Internet Connection wizard. Chapter 23, "Webcasting: Channel Surfing When You're Offline," shows you how to take advantage of Webcasting. If you want to get started with the Internet, look at Chapter 26, "Creating Your Own Internet Connection with Personal Web Server," for coverage of Personal Web Server (a Windows 95 version of Internet Information Server).

An Overview of the Communications Architecture

Before you get into the communications packages, take a look at the communications subsystem architecture. Actually, this chapter won't cover the total picture; Figure 21.1 reflects only the local part of the communications structure. However, if you look carefully, you see all three of the main connections discussed in Chapter 20: Dial-Up Networking, Phone Dialer, and Direct Cable Connection.

The following list provides details about all the components of the communications subsystem:

- Telephony API (TAPI): All the new modem-specific services are clustered under this API. It provides command translation for the new Windows 95 applications that use it. When an application asks about the modem setup or status, this module provides the information translation required for a seamless interface. TAPI might configure the modem from a virtual point of view, but VCOMM still manages the actual port. Modem commands flow through the port from TAPI. A good analogy of this arrangement is that VCOMM provides the pipe, but TAPI provides the water.

Figure 21.1.
An overview of the Windows 95 local communications architecture.

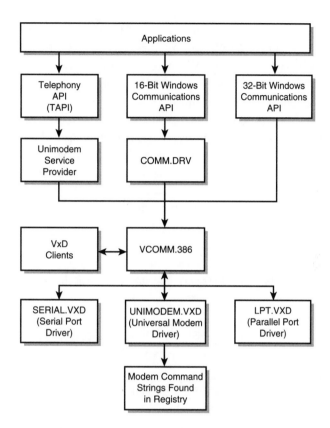

- Windows 16-bit communications API: The API is the module that accepts instructions from an application and translates them into something that Windows 95 can understand. One API instruction might actually require an entire module's worth of detailed instructions in order to perform. Windows 95 doesn't really use the 16-bit version of the Windows communications instructions. The old instructions didn't provide the robust environment that the rest of Windows 95 provides. However, instead of writing a new 16-bit module, Microsoft provides access to the new 32-bit interface through these instructions and the COMM.DRV module that I describe in a moment.

- Windows 32-bit communications API: This is the enhanced 32-bit instruction set for Windows 95. Like its 16-bit counterpart, the 32-bit API translates application requests into commands that Windows can actually implement.

- Unimodem service provider: This is the specific driver for your modem. It takes the generic commands provided by the TAPI module and translates them into something that your modem will understand.

- **COMM.DRV**: Under Windows 3.x, this module carried out the communications tasks ordered by the API. Under Windows 95, this module works with the 32-bit instructions held in the 32-bit communications API and **VCOMM.386**, increasing the speed of communications programs, even if you use an older 16-bit application.

- VxD clients: **VCOMM.386** provides services to more than just the communications subsystem. Every time any other Windows subsystem requires port access, it must go through **VCOMM.386** as well. These requests are fielded through APIs that act as clients to this module. This is an internal Windows 95 function that you'll never really notice, but you should know that there are interactions between subsystems. A port failure might not always be the result of a communications- or print-specific problem; it could be related to some interaction from another, unrelated subsystem.

- **VCOMM.386**: Calling this a part of the communications subsystem is almost inaccurate. **VCOMM.386** is a static-device VxD that Windows 95 always loads during the boot process. Part of the job that **VCOMM.386** performs is to load all the port drivers shown in Figure 21.1. Other parts of Windows also call **VCOMM.386** through their respective APIs to perform a variety of port-specific services.

- **SERIAL.VXD**: This is the serial port driver. It's the actual serial port engine. Another driver is associated with the serial port as well: **SERIALUI.DLL** provides the interface that you use while setting up the serial ports.

- **UNIMODEM.VXD**: The modem setup is a little more complex than the other port drivers supported by **VCOMM.386**. This one actually works with either a serial or parallel port to provide modem services for the rest of Windows. It's also responsible for making any modem-specific Registry changes. Every time you change the modem strings, this module records them in the Registry. As with the serial port driver, the VxD doesn't provide any interface elements. It relies on **MODEMUI.DLL** to provide these services. There's also a Control Panel element to worry about in this case. You'll find that **MODEM.CPL** manages this aspect of the interface.

- **LPT.VXD**: This is the parallel port driver. Unlike the serial port, the parallel port is usually managed by the printer subsystem. As a result, it relies on **MSPRINT.DLL** for user-interface services.

- Modem command strings found in the Registry: Many of the upper modules rely on the Registry entries to know how to interact with the modem. These strings provide those instructions. Each string defines some aspect of modem behavior. In most cases, it affects the modem's setup or the way that it communicates with another machine. You need to refer to your modem manual to get a better idea of exactly how these strings work.

The centerpiece of the communications subsystem is **VCOMM.386**. This module loads the port drivers, provides access to them during system operation, and generally manages the way Windows interacts with the outside world. It's an important role that you might take for granted until it stops working. Chapter 26 looks at some things that can go wrong with this subsystem.

Using Microsoft Exchange

You can perform almost any kind of communication that Windows 95 supports just by opening Microsoft Exchange. As time goes on, you'll see that, like Explorer, Microsoft Exchange pops up in the strangest places. Even if you think each communication module under Windows 95 is a separate entity, they aren't. They all rely on Exchange for a user interface. The details differ from service to service, but the part that the user sees remains fairly constant.

Note: OSR2 users will notice a new name for Microsoft Exchange: Windows Messaging. Microsoft Exchange and Windows Messaging are essentially the same product, but there are a few minor differences. (I cover them in this section.)

One difference I cover relates to performance. Microsoft has made Windows Messaging faster than its predecessor. For example, there's a noticeable difference in the rate that attachments get delivered. Fortunately, you can download this updated version of Microsoft Exchange from `http://www.microsoft.com/windows95/info/system-updates.htm`.

Before you begin looking at specific communication services provided by Windows 95, I want to take you on a quick tour of Microsoft Exchange. After you get acquainted with the Microsoft Exchange interface, the little differences between other components seem a lot less intimidating.

Understanding the User Interface

The following discussion assumes that Microsoft Exchange is installed. You look at how you can install individual components later; you use Microsoft Exchange for that. What you want to do now is look at the user interface itself.

Figure 21.2 shows a typical Microsoft Exchange display. Just remember that your interface will vary a little because of the settings you choose and the options you install.

By default, your Inbox is the first location that Microsoft Exchange shows. After it opens the Inbox, it updates any e-mail messages you have on the network (assuming that you're attached). You need to go online to update your other messages, but they all appear in this single Inbox (unless you change the settings I discuss later).

Figure 21.2.
The Inbox folder provides access to your messages and helps you organize them in a variety of ways.

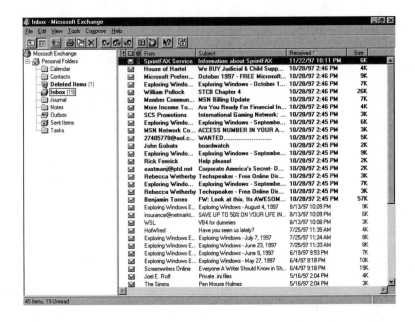

Take a quick look at how Microsoft Exchange presents your Inbox messages. I start at the very first column of the message header and work across:

- The first column can contain nothing, a red exclamation point, or a blue down arrow. Medium-priority messages receive no symbol. A red exclamation mark tells you that the accompanying message is high priority, and a blue down arrow says that the message is low priority.

- The second column tells you what type of item is stored there. In most cases, it is a message, as shown by the envelope symbol.

- The little paper clip symbol in the third column tells you that a message has attachments. You can either attach files outright or add OLE objects to your messages. I was surprised to find that you can add objects in such a way that they actually start an online session. You can also create an object that will access a file on the network.

- The fourth column houses the name of the person who sent the message or item.

- The fifth column contains the message's subject line.

- The sixth column tells you when the message was received.

- The seventh column tells you how big the file is.

Tip: It almost always pays to change this default setup. Exchange provides a wealth of column headings that old versions of Microsoft Mail didn't. You at least want to see what's available and consider how you can use it to optimize your setup.

Sorting the messages in any given folder is easy. You notice that the column headings are actually pushbuttons. Clicking a column heading sorts by that column. You can change the sort order by clicking a second time. Exchange displays an arrow in the heading by which the messages are sorted (if there's room in the heading). It uses an up arrow for ascending order and a down arrow for descending order. If you prefer a dialog interface for changing the sort order, select View | Sort to display the dialog shown in Figure 21.3. Just select a column heading (such as Subject or Size) from the list box, click the order you want to sort in, and click OK.

Figure 21.3.
The Sort dialog box allows you to select a sort order, but clicking the column headings is a lot faster.

Notice the use of bold text in Figure 21.2. Whenever you see either a folder or a message name in bold, it means that you haven't read that message or that you have not completely viewed the contents of the folder. I find that this is the fastest way to see new messages on my system. Of course, this is a little less valuable when you use the default folder setup, but it can be quite valuable as you expand your system. Along with this use of bold text are two Edit menu options. You can mark a message as read or unread using the two options on this menu.

> **Tip:** It's important to use all the Exchange features to your benefit. For example, some people might view the Edit | Read and Edit | Unread commands as superfluous, but they're really quite useful. I don't often mark a message as read, but I do mark messages as unread from time to time. This is handy when you read a message and realize you don't have time to take care of it right then; you can mark the message as unread so that you remember to look at it again later.

If you look at the default display, you can see a relationship between Exchange and Explorer. The hierarchy of folders is the same, and the messages equate to files in your post office. There are other similarities as well. For example, you can add folders to the default hierarchy to better organize your messages; simply select File | New Folder, type a name for the new folder, and click OK. Moving messages from place to place in Exchange is also as easy as in Explorer. Each entry has a context menu containing Exchange-specific functions that work the same as the Explorer equivalent. The bottom line is that if you know how to use Explorer, learning Exchange shouldn't be difficult.

> **Note:** Exchange lets you remove folders you create by using the Delete command or by pressing the Delete key, just like Explorer. However, it stops short of allowing you to delete the default folders in the hierarchy. These folders have to remain in place to support the mail structure.

When you delete a message in Exchange, the deleted message goes into the Deleted Items folder. If you delete a message in the Deleted Items folder, you remove it from the system permanently.

Using the Address Book

Microsoft Exchange provides an address book that helps you maintain a list of the people you normally contact. Before you send a message to someone, it's a good idea to add his or her name to the address book even if you intend to use the address only once. I often thought I'd use an address only once but then ended up looking all over the place for it later when I needed to send a second message.

Figure 21.4 shows the initial Address Book dialog. Exchange defaults to using the Microsoft Mail post office address book, but you can reset this default to any address book you like. It also adds all the names of people on your local network or workgroup, allowing you to send messages immediately without a lot of typing. The display normally provides, at a minimum, the person's name.

Figure 21.4.
The initial Address Book dialog shows the addresses that you select as a default.

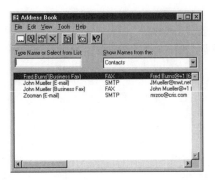

The toolbar below the menu bar provides access to the majority of the address book functions. In fact, I don't think I've ever had to use the menu itself. The following list provides an overview of each toolbar pushbutton:

- New entry: This allows you to add new names to the address book.
- Find: You can use this pushbutton to filter the names displayed in the dialog. It actually creates a new address book called Search Results.

- Properties: Use this to change the properties of the address book. Right-click a specific name to change its properties. The post office address book doesn't provide any overall properties for you to change, so Exchange displays an error message if you select this pushbutton.

Note: As of this writing, the function of the Properties pushbutton tends to change with the address book you're using. In some cases it works, but in others it doesn't. Sometimes it changes the properties of the address book itself, and other times it brings up the Properties dialog for the individual entry. The definition provided here is consistent with the current Microsoft documentation.

- Delete: This pushbutton allows you to remove an entry from the address book. Unfortunately, there's no recovery area if you accidentally erase a name you need.

- Add to personal address book: Use this button to add a name from a public or other address book to your personal address book. Exchange always creates a personal address book for you. Of course, that doesn't restrict you from creating other personal address books, but this button works only with the default set up by Exchange.

- New message: You can click one or more names in your address book and then click this button to send a message to the people you selected. The message creation dialog automatically displays the selected list of names when you open it.

- Help: As with every Windows application, you can request help using a variety of methods. Clicking this button displays the help cursor. Point to whatever you need help with and click. Windows provides context-sensitive help that will aid you in using the Address Book dialog.

Adding a New Address

Adding a new address is fairly easy. The only challenge is figuring out exactly what you need to provide. Each of the MAPI clients that Exchange supports uses a different address format because their methods of sending messages are different. However, besides a few vagaries in the way an address gets stored for a specific type of MAPI client, there are a lot of similarities.

The first step in adding a new address book entry is deciding what type of address it is (see Figure 21.5). After you decide what type of address to add and where to add it, click OK to view the format-specific address tab. Take a look at one or two of the specialty tabs in the Address Book dialog, and then I'll describe the tabs that are common to all formats.

Figure 21.5.

You need to decide what kind of address to add before you can add it.

Figure 21.6 shows a new address book entry form for Microsoft Mail. Add new entries using this tab only for users who are part of other workgroups. (All the local workgroup names are entered automatically.) This tab has four fields, each providing part of the routing information needed to send your message to its destination:

- Alias: This field should contain the person's logon name. This may or may not be the user's full name; it could be a nickname or a shortened version of his or her full name if more than one person on the network has the same name. Type whatever name he or she uses to log on to the network.

- Mailbox: This field contains the name the post office administrator used when entering the user's name in the post office. This field usually contains the same information as the Alias field.

- Postoffice: This field contains the name of the post office. This may or may not be the name of the machine that actually contains the post office.

- Network: This field contains the name of the network, workgroup, domain, or other identifying information. It's the name you see at the root of a network entry in Network Neighborhood.

Figure 21.6.

A Microsoft Mail address entry requires just a few simple pieces of information about the network routing needed to reach a recipient.

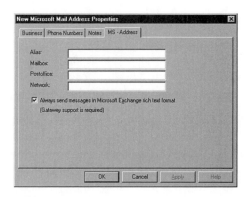

A new fax address book entry probably contains less information than you would expect. You need to supply only a name and some telephone information. I covered this dialog in Chapter 19,

"Mobile Computing: Notebooks, Telecommuting, and Remote Access," so I don't go over the specific fields again except to note the Mailbox field. It's not a functional routing entry, but it could help the person at the other end direct the message to the correct person.

You see a new Microsoft Network address entry in Figure 21.7. This is typical of most online service entries: It consists of a member name and an online identification number.

Figure 21.7.
The Microsoft Network address entry is the easiest to fill out so far. All you need is a name and identification number.

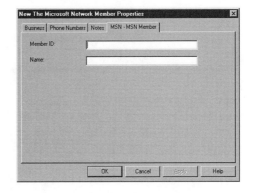

Figure 21.8 shows the last type of new address entry I cover: Internet address entry. A new Internet address entry contains three fields:

- E-mail address: This field contains the person's e-mail address. This is the same address the user would normally use if he or she were on that service.

- Domain name: This field contains the domain name, which might require a little explanation. The Internet is composed of thousands of smaller networks, each providing common access. When you see an Internet address, it usually looks similar to this one: `71570,641@compuserve.com`. The @ separates the e-mail address from the domain name. In this case, you are sending a message to someone on CompuServe. If you want to send a message to America Online, you use `aol.com` as the domain name. Every server has a unique domain name that allows it to receive messages.

- Name: This field contains the person's name.

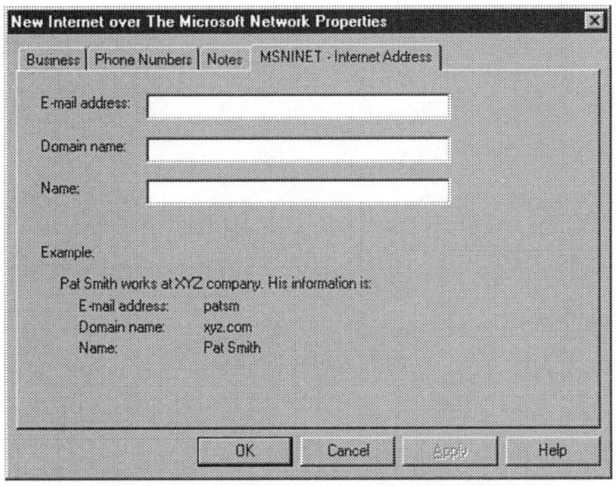

Figure 21.8.
The Internet Address tab lets you add a person's e-mail address.

Now that you've seen the format-specific tabs, look at the common tabs that the address book provides. Figure 21.9 shows the Business tab, which allows you to record all the specifics you're likely to need about contacting a person. One nice feature of this tab is the Phone number field, where you can select the location you want from the list box and then enter a number. Another nice feature is the capability to dial that phone number right from this tab using the Phone Dialer utility discussed in Chapter 19.

Figure 21.9.
The Business tab provides a fast way of recording all the pertinent contact information you need to reach someone.

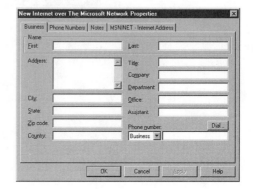

The Phone Numbers tab, shown in Figure 21.10, provides a quick list of all the phone numbers you can use to contact a person. I felt that adding the assistant's phone number was an especially nice touch. Unfortunately, you can't record any more than the eight phone numbers shown here. In most cases, this is enough unless the person you're trying to contact travels a lot or works in more than one location.

Figure 21.10.
The Phone Numbers tab allows you to enter up to eight contact numbers for each person in your address book.

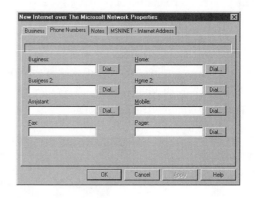

The final tab, Notes, is a big notepad. You can enter previous contact information or any other freeform information here. I often use it to track the last date I contacted someone and a brief note on what we talked about.

> **Note:** Some services might include an additional tab. For example, Figure 21.10 shows an additional tab for the Internet service. You can be certain that this tab will become prominent as third-party developers add their own MAPI drivers. Make sure you follow the vendor-supplied instructions when filling out the contents of this tab.

Finding Names in Your Address Book

Finding names in your address book is easy: Simply click the Find icon on the toolbar. Address Book displays the Find dialog, shown in Figure 21.11. All you need to do is fill in a name or even part of a name. Clicking OK displays the list of names in a new address book called Search Results. You can switch between this address book and your original one using the list box below the toolbar.

Figure 21.11.
You can use the Find dialog to whittle down a large address book into one containing just the names you need.

Changing the Address Book Properties

You can make a few configuration changes to each address book on your system except the public post office address book. Simply access the Address Book Properties dialog (see Figure 21.12) by clicking the Properties icon on the toolbar.

Figure 21.12.
The Address Book Properties dialog allows you to change the way your address book works. In this case, the properties of the personal address book are being changed.

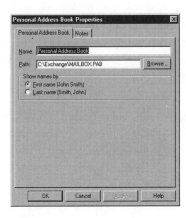

The Personal Address Book tab of this dialog contains the following:

- Name: This field allows you to change the name of the address book. In most cases, you want to retain the name of the default personal address book that Exchange sets up for you so that you can automatically add names to it.

- Path: This field contains the location of the actual address book file on disk. This, too, normally stays the same unless you move the address book to a new location.

- Show names by: The radio buttons in this section change the way the address book lists names. I find this feature quite handy when I'm looking for a specific name. For example, clicking the First Name radio button makes it easier to find an entry for someone whose last name I've forgotten.

> **Tip:** You can create new address books with specific names using the Find button. Use the Properties dialog to change the name of that address book to something else so that Windows won't overwrite it the next time you need to create a special address book.

The Notes tab of this dialog contains a miniature notebook. You can use it to track the address book and anything you do with it. It might come in handy for writing a reminder of why you started this particular address book.

Adding and Configuring Address Books

Select Tools | Options to invoke the Addressing dialog, shown in Figure 21.13. Use this dialog to perform two different functions:

- Configure Exchange to use your address books: The Show this address list first field specifies which address book Exchange shows first whenever you create a new message. If most of your messages go to company e-mail, using the default setting (Post Office Address List) makes sense. However, if you're like me, you send messages to a variety of places, including the company e-mail. In this case, you might want to select your personal address list as the first location. The Keep personal addresses in field contains the name of your personal address list. Unless you want to personalize this setting for some reason, keep the default setting. Exchange automatically creates this address list for you, so there's no real reason to change it later.

- Create new address lists and add them to your address book as needed: The list box always shows a complete index of the current address lists except for any recent searches. You can add a new address list by clicking the Add pushbutton. Simply follow the prompts to create the new address list. In most cases, you'll find that the default address books provide adequate flexibility.

Figure 21.13.
Use this dialog to configure Exchange to use your address books and to create new ones.

Finding Specific Messages

Ever find yourself buried in a mound of messages with no effective way to organize them and no quick, easy way to find the one you need? Exchange provides a handy dialog, shown in Figure 21.14, that resembles Explorer's Find dialog. Exchange's Find dialog contains quite a few mail-specific features. Of course, it won't help you find any files on your drive.

Figure 21.14.
Exchange's Find dialog looks similar to the one found in Explorer, with some important exceptions.

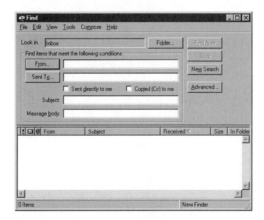

Most of the fields in this dialog are self-explanatory, but using some of this dialog's features might not be. For example, if you want to search through all your mail, you select the Personal Information Store folder. You can't search from the Exchange level. Of course, you can always go lower than this top level by looking through the folder hierarchy.

The Sent directly to me and the Copied (CC) to me check boxes aren't mutually exclusive. However, if you select the first one, you won't be able to ask for a specific person in the Sent To field even though Exchange doesn't blank it out. You can combine the Copied (CC) to me check box and a specific Sent To name, however.

Using the various fields in tandem is the key to finding precisely the message you want. Clicking the Advanced pushbutton invokes the Advanced dialog (shown in Figure 21.15), which enables you to use additional criteria to perform a more stringent search.

Figure 21.15.

You can perform a detailed search of the message base using the criteria in the Advanced dialog.

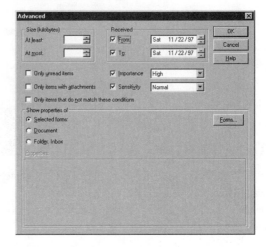

Some of these options have interesting uses. For example, if you need to make room on the server containing the post office, you can get rid of the bigger messages using the Size group. I use this option from time to time just to see how many large files I have accumulated. You'd be surprised how fast they can build up.

Getting back from vacation usually means you have a lot more work to do than time to get it done. I start by categorizing the things I need to do by placing them in separate folders. Then I use a high-priority search to find the items I need to get done right away.

You can also use the entries in this dialog to search for messages you haven't read yet or messages received during a certain time span. The time span option is nice when you know you received a message during a specific time period but you can't remember much else about it. Any attempt to look through the entire message base will likely prove frustrating.

After you select all the search criteria, click the Find Now pushbutton to display a list of matching messages in the list box at the bottom of the Find dialog. This list responds to all the usual actions, such as right-clicking and double-clicking. You can also delete messages in this list and respond to them in the normal way. The one item in this dialog that surprised me a bit was the capability to create new messages. It certainly makes life a lot easier when you remember to write an important message in the middle of or as a result of looking for something else.

Working with the Exchange Services

Windows 95 comes with a limited number of MAPI servers. (You covered MAPI in Chapter 14, "Exploiting Your Hardware." A MAPI server simply provides access to a particular online service.) Each server uses Exchange as a front end. In other words, once you learn how to use Exchange, you pretty much know how to use all the generic pieces of each MAPI server as well. The big difference between servers and the interface is the medium in which they operate. The medium determines some of the differences that you see in how the various MAPI servers operate.

Exchange might come with some or all of the servers added. The default servers are pretty much self-installing. But it's quite likely that you'll need to add new MAPI servers as third-party products arrive on the scene. For example, you might choose to use a MAPI server to access your local BBS instead of buying a full-fledged communications program. Not only would you ease the learning curve that such a product requires, but also the software vendor will be able to provide similar functionality in a much smaller package.

Select Tools | Services to display the Services dialog shown in Figure 21.16. The top of the dialog contains a list of the current servers you have installed. In most cases, you won't need to individually install the Windows 95 servers unless Microsoft comes out with an update or the original server gets contaminated in some way. The five pushbuttons below this list describe various actions that you can perform when adding, removing, or modifying a MAPI server.

Figure 21.16.
The Services dialog is where you manage the MAPI servers attached to your machine.

Adding a New Service

Adding a new service to Exchange is easy. All you need to do is click the Add pushbutton in the Services dialog (refer to Figure 21.16). Exchange displays a list of default services available for Windows 95, as shown in Figure 21.17. You can add third-party MAPI services by clicking the Have Disk pushbutton.

Figure 21.17.
The Add Service to Profile dialog allows you to add new MAPI servers to Exchange with little effort.

> **Tip:** More vendors are providing MAPI servers that you can use with Microsoft Exchange (Windows Messaging for OSR2 users) every day. In some cases, that support isn't immediately evident or you don't need to install the support as a separate item. For example, when you install Netscape Navigator, you have the option of using the mail reader that comes with the product or Microsoft Exchange. If you choose Microsoft Exchange, the Navigator installation program automatically adds the appropriate MAPI client for you. Make sure you fully understand how MAPI support gets added before you install a product; some vendors may use techniques other than the ones mentioned in this book for supporting MAPI. (Removing MAPI support almost always involves highlighting one of the services shown in the Services dialog and clicking the Remove pushbutton.)

Normally the procedure involves selecting the service you want to install and clicking OK. However, I found an interesting piece of information in this dialog: Clicking the About pushbutton displays a dialog similar to the one shown in Figure 21.18. Notice that it lists all the files required to make this service operate. You can use this dialog later if you need to know the names of the files to remove from your hard drive when a service is no longer needed. This dialog also provides helpful diagnostic information if you have problems later. For example, you can use it to determine the size of the various files, the version number of each component, and who to call for help with a particular service.

Figure 21.18.
The About Information Service dialog tells you a lot more than the usual About dialog.

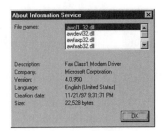

After Exchange finishes installing a new service, it usually asks whether you want to configure it. This generally involves providing routing information or perhaps some specifics about the equipment you plan to use. You don't necessarily have to configure the service right away if you don't have the required information. Clicking the Properties pushbuttonlater allows you to configure the service to meet your needs. Nonetheless, if the service requires some type of routing or equipment-specific information, you need to perform the configuration before you can use the service.

Customizing Exchange

Exchange provides a great deal of flexibility with regards to how you access information. You've already seen much of that flexibility in this chapter. As third-party vendors create more MAPI servers, that flexibility will increase. Nevertheless, Exchange's flexibility goes beyond that. You can configure just about every aspect of the interface itself. Selecting Tools | Options displays an Options dialog (see Figure 21.19) that allows you to change the way Exchange interacts with you.

Figure 21.19.
The Options dialog allows you to change the way Exchange interacts with the user.

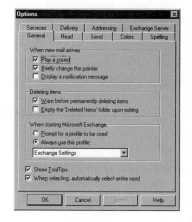

The General tab of the Options dialog contains four main sections:

- When new mail arrives: How you configure this section tells Exchange how to notify you about new mail—if you do, in fact, want to be notified. The check boxes in this group are fairly easy to figure out. You can have Exchange play a sound, change the mouse pointer, or display a message to notify you of new mail, or you can select combinations of all three.

- Deleting items: Use this section to tell Exchange what to do with deleted items. Checking the first check box tells Exchange to warn you before it permanently deletes anything, just in case you really want to keep something. You can automatically remove any deleted messages from the hard drive when you exit Exchange by checking the second check box.

- When starting Microsoft Exchange: Checking the first radio button in this section allows you to choose the profile (list of services) that you'll use each time you start Exchange. You can keep more than one profile if needed, but I usually find that centralized control of my messages is far more valuable than the flexibility of using additional profiles. The default setting is to use the standard Microsoft Exchange Settings profile.

- The final two check boxes on this tab are miscellaneous settings. The first setting affects ToolTips (the text that appears under each control if you rest your mouse cursor there long enough), which provide a quick description of that control's purpose. The second setting affects how the editor works. Checking this box means that Exchange selects an entire word at a time instead of single characters. It comes in handy for block deletes, but I find that the editor works better with this option disabled.

The Read tab of the Options dialog, shown in Figure 21.20, contains two main sections:

- After moving or deleting an open item: Use this section to tell Exchange how to move the cursor after you read and either move or delete a message. The default setting moves the cursor to the next item in the list. This is convenient when your message base is sorted by date because you waste a lot less time positioning the cursor this way. Of course, you might organize your list in reverse order to see the older messages first. In this case, the second setting works better. Whichever way you organize your messages, selecting the correct radio button can add a measure of convenience to the process of selecting and reading your messages.

- When replying to or forwarding an item: Use this section to change the tasks that Exchange automatically performs when you answer a message. The first option allows you to include the original message in your response. The second option indents the original text to make it clearer that you are including the original text. If you use the first option, always include the second for the sake of clarity. The third option closes the original item after you respond to it. This allows you to move to the next message without wasting time. Finally, clicking the Font pushbutton displays a list of fonts and font sizes in a dialog. You should normally select a typeface and font size that will help the other person see your response clearly.

Figure 21.20.
Use the Read tab of the Options dialog to change the way Exchange reacts when you read messages.

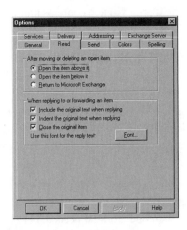

Peter's Principle: Quoting: a Waste of Money or a Friendly Gesture?

Exchange offers you the chance to include the text of the original message when you make a reply, which is called *quoting*. When you include part of the original message in your response, you're quoting the other person.

This policy generates a lot of controversy in some online services. Some people think quoting is a waste of time because the other person should know what you're talking about. Other people—those who spend a lot of time online—really like this practice because it allows them to keep individual conversations separate. They believe that the small amount of additional text is the cost of maintaining a clear dialog.

You can compromise to keep both parties happy. Simply enclose the significant part of the original text in angle brackets, like this: `<Some part of an original message>`. Make sure you place the quoted text on a separate line so that it's clear you're quoting the other person. I usually do this if I'm not sure whether the other party likes quoting or not. My responses usually include quoted questions or perhaps a comment that caught my attention. I never include more than absolutely necessary to get my point across or to clarify my response.

What about your company e-mail? Quoting is always a good idea when you're carrying on a lot of conversations with one person. I find that it helps me remember the exact nature of a particular discussion as I go from topic to topic. You may also want to use quoting when forwarding messages to another person, just so they can better understand your message. Whether you use quoting when you access an online service is a matter of personal preference. Using it with the people you work with is a matter of necessity.

The Send tab, shown in Figure 21.21, contains settings that change the way you send messages to other people. This dialog contains the following settings:

- Use this font: This setting allows you to change the font you use to create messages. Clicking the Font pushbutton displays a list of typefaces available on your machine. Always select a typeface and font size that will allow the other person to read your message with minimal squinting. Of course, the font setting will work only if the recipient also uses Microsoft Exchange to read the message.

- Request that a receipt be sent back when: This setting allows you to determine whether the other party received or read your message. I rarely use the receipt feature unless I've been having communication problems. It tends to make the other person think you don't trust him.

- Set sensitivity: This list box tells the other person how much secrecy to attach to your message. I usually include a lot more than just a sensitivity setting, however, if the information is important or if it's critical that the other person guard the contents of the message.

- Set importance: This setting allows you to adjust the standard importance associated with a particular message. Unless you're the president of the company, you'll probably want to keep it at the Normal setting.

- Save a copy of the item in the 'Sent Items' folder: Check this box to place a copy of your message in the Sent Items folder. I always use this feature because people often lose the messages I send. Most people have this problem. Keeping a copy of the message where you can grab it quickly changes a major headache into a minor nuisance.

Figure 21.21.

The Send tab of the Options dialog allows you to change the way Exchange sends messages you create.

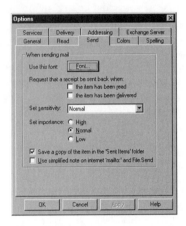

The Spelling tab of the Options dialog, shown in Figure 21.22, can save you more than time; it can save you the embarrassment of making a major spelling error on a message you planned to use to impress someone. I often wonder what the other person was thinking when he wrote a message because of the number of spelling errors. In fact, such a problem is almost inexcusable today because just about every product that works with Windows also includes a spell checker of some type.

Figure 21.22.

The Spelling tab determines when and how the spell checker will keep your messages free of spelling errors.

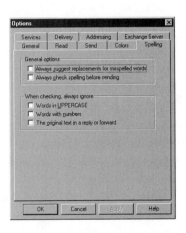

You looked at the Addressing and Services tabs in the preceding section. The Addressing tab is where you add new address lists and define the default address list to use when creating a message. The Services tab allows you to add new services to Exchange.

The Delivery tab, which appears in Figure 21.23, allows you to specify delivery information. The first two fields allow you to define a primary and secondary mail delivery location. Simply select the desired location from the list box. The third list box defines which address lists Exchange will use to process recipient addresses. You can change the order by highlighting the desired entry and using the arrows to move it up or down in the list.

Figure 21.23.
*The Delivery tab
allows you to define
the delivery location
for your mail.*

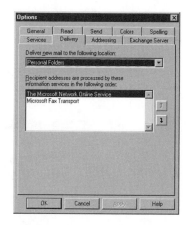

Customizing the Toolbar

I like the way the Exchange toolbar is arranged. It seems to contain everything I need without getting cluttered with things I don't normally use. However, you might need to use different Exchange features to get your work done. That's one reason I was so happy to see the customization feature.

Select Tools | Customize Toolbar to display the Customize Toolbar dialog, shown in Figure 21.24. This is where you customize the toolbar. This dialog contains two lists: The one on the left includes all the commands and other features you can include on the toolbar, and the one on the right contains all the commands and other features that are on the toolbar right now. To add a new feature to the toolbar, simply highlight the position on the right list where you want it to appear, and then highlight the item on the left list that you want to add. Click the Add pushbutton to add the new item. Likewise, if you want to remove an item from the toolbar, simply highlight it in the list on the right and click Remove.

You can also move things around on the toolbar by selecting the item you want to move and clicking the Move Up or Move Down pushbutton to make the change. If you decide that all the changes you made were in error, click the Reset pushbutton to return to the previous state. Finally, click the Close pushbutton to make your changes permanent.

Figure 21.24.
Customizing the toolbar is easy—just a few clicks in this dialog.

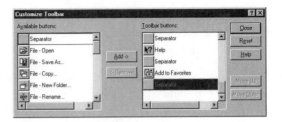

Customizing the Column Headings

Exchange allows you to modify the amount and type of data it displays. You can easily change the column widths by moving the mouse cursor between two columns, waiting for the pointer to change to a line with two arrows (one pointing each direction), and dragging the column line wherever you want it. After you get past column widths, however, you need to select View | Column to modify other column features (see Figure 21.25).

Figure 21.25.
There's no reason to keep data that you don't need. Get rid of it using the Columns dialog box.

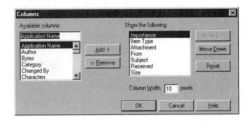

There's no reason to keep specific columns around when you no longer need them. Likewise, you might find that Exchange provides some type of information you would really like to see. I usually err in favor of too much data if I have the screen real estate to support additional columns. It's better to have too much data than to miss something important because you don't have enough.

This dialog works much like the toolbar dialog I discussed in the preceding section. To add a column to the display, simply select where you want it to appear in the list on the right, highlight in the left-hand list the data you want to appear, and click Add. Removing unneeded data is just as easy: In the right-hand column, highlight the entry you want to get rid of and click Remove.

If you find that you added or removed too many columns, click Reset to restore things to their unedited state. Moving columns around is easy too; just select the desired column in the list on the right and use the Move Up and Move Down pushbuttons to change its position.

This dialog has one additional field: width. This field allows you to set the size of the columns in pixels. I find this a little counterintuitive, and I prefer to use the mouse to change the column size using the technique I described at the beginning of this section.

Understanding the Online Services

Now that you have a better understanding of Microsoft Exchange, it's time to look at some of the things you can do with it. Exchange comes with three different MAPI servers: Mail, Fax, and Microsoft Network. Each of these servers uses Exchange as its front end to varying degrees.

The following sections explore the MAPI servers that come with Windows 95. These servers can interact with each other through Exchange. All the messages you receive appear in one place, regardless of which server you use to retrieve them. In fact, from a user perspective, you might be tempted to think that you're using a single product for all your communication needs. Of course, it's just the level of front-end integration that makes it appear that way.

Note: Microsoft Plus!, the add-on product for Windows 95, includes additional MAPI servers. One of the servers provides complete access to the Internet. If Internet access is important to you, you might want to see what Microsoft Plus! has to offer.

Microsoft Mail

Microsoft Mail is the easiest of the MAPI servers to describe. You've already looked at all the interface elements in this chapter. The only thing you'll notice as far as Mail is concerned is that any changes to your local post office automatically appear in your setup as well. I find that Mail is the most integrated of all the MAPI servers.

Sending a Mail message is easy: Simply click the New Message icon on the Exchange toolbar to display the dialog shown in Figure 21.26. Your dialog might not have all the fields that mine does; I selected all the options in the View menu so that I could show you what they look like. As with every new Windows application, this one has a toolbar that provides access to just about every feature that Mail supports.

The following list provides an overview of what the features in this dialog can do for you:

- Send: As soon as you get everything filled out in your message, click this button to send your message to the recipient.
- Save: Exchange allows you to save a copy of the message in an external file. Use this button to display the Save dialog; select File | Save As to save this message under a different filename.
- Print: Clicking this button allows you to print the current message. It uses the default print setup.

Figure 21.26.

The New Message dialog provides the basic tools for creating any kind of new message in Exchange.

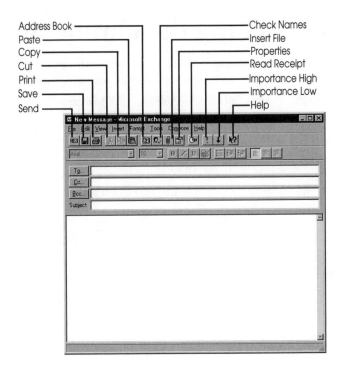

- **Cut:** Click this button to remove the selected data and place it on the clipboard.

- **Copy:** Click this button to copy the desired data to the clipboard.

- **Paste:** Click this button to place the data on the clipboard at the selected position.

- **Address book:** Click here to open the address book and find any addressees for your message. You can accomplish the same thing by clicking any of the buttons next to the address fields on the message itself.

- **Check names:** As soon as you come up with a list of people you want to send a message to, you can click this button to make sure they're all correct. If Exchange finds that a name doesn't appear in one of your address lists, it displays a dialog asking whether you want to add the name to an address list or correct it. Exchange usually supplies a list of substitutes for you. Of course, the size of this list depends on how many names in your Address Book are close matches to the one incorrect entry.

- **Insert file:** You can send someone a file as a message attachment using this button. It displays a dialog that allows you to browse your local and network hard drives. Any inserted files appear as icons within the message. Exchange doesn't actually place a copy of the file in the message; it uses an OLE link instead. You can link or embed objects in a message using the other techniques discussed in Chapter 12, "DDE, OLE, DCOM, and ActiveX," as well.

- Properties: Clicking this button invokes the Properties dialog, which tells you the basics about a message. It also allows you to select the sensitivity and importance levels. Three check boxes allow you to select receipt types and whether Exchange saves a copy of the message in the Sent Items folder.

- Read receipt: Clicking this button automatically requests a read receipt for this message. You get an acknowledgment from Exchange as soon as the recipient opens the message for reading.

- Importance high/importance low: You can select either of these buttons to send a message with a designation other than a normal importance level. Exchange displays high-importance messages with a red exclamation point and low-importance messages with a blue down arrow.

- Help: Click this button to receive context-sensitive help about any items you don't understand.

In addition to all these toolbar options, there are other configuration options on the menu. All the configuration options you saw in the Exchange section also appear here. For example, you can configure the New Message dialog toolbar to meet your needs. The service configuration option appears here as well.

Below the Mail toolbar you'll find a formatting toolbar, which includes everything you might expect. You can select a typeface, a font size, bold, italics, underline, and a font color. This toolbar also allows you to format the paragraph by adding bullets and indentation in addition to allowing you to determine whether the paragraph is right-, center-, or left-justified.

Microsoft Fax

Microsoft Fax operates essentially the same way as Microsoft Mail. You even use the same type of message editing box. However, the initial screens are somewhat different, so I cover them here. You create a new fax by selecting Compose | New Fax in Exchange. (This invokes the Fax wizard, whose initial screen is shown in Figure 21.27.)

Figure 21.27.
Use the Compose New Fax dialog to format the address portion of any fax you want to send.

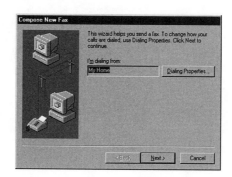

To create a new fax, do the following:

1. Describe your location in the dialog box shown in Figure 21.27, and then click Next. This issue was covered in Chapter 19 (and even looked at it again in this chapter), so I don't go though the details again.

2. Tell the Fax wizard where you want the message sent (see Figure 21.28). You can click the Address Book pushbutton to display any of your address lists and select a recipient from them. I use this method because it ensures that the address is correct and saves me time typing the required information. Clicking the Add to List pushbutton adds the current name and telephone number to the Recipient list field. Use this option when you want to send the same fax to more than one person.

Figure 21.28.
Create a recipient list using this dialog.

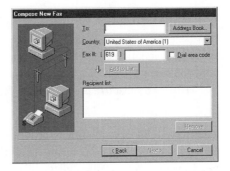

3. Click Next to display the dialog shown in Figure 21.29. This dialog allows you to select a cover page and contains an Options pushbutton that displays a configuration dialog. Optional items include the message format and when you want to send the fax.

Figure 21.29.
Use this dialog to describe some of the optional features for your fax.

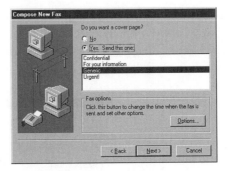

4. Click Next to display the dialog shown in Figure 21.30. This is where you define the subject and message content of this fax. It doesn't look very much like the Exchange format, but the finished fax will include all the same elements. In fact, if you had selected

the Create New Fax option from the Create New Message dialog, this display would look exactly like its Exchange counterpart. The Start note on cover page check box allows you to place the beginning of your note on the cover page. If the entire note fits there, your recipient will save paper because you only need to send a single page. Removing the check from this check box always sends the note on a separate page.

Figure 21.30.
This dialog allows you to add a subject line and message to your fax.

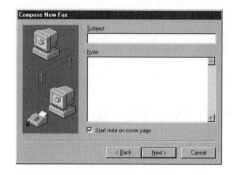

5. Click Next to display the dialog shown in Figure 21.31. This dialog allows you to attach a file to your fax. Of course, it won't appear as an OLE object this time. The attached file is sent to the recipient as a file or an attached set of pages. The list box contains a list of files that you want to send. Clicking the Add File button displays a browse dialog that you can use to select another file. Highlighting an entry in the list box and clicking Remove will remove that file from the list.

Figure 21.31.
Use this dialog to attach files to your fax.

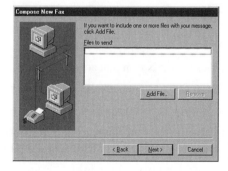

6. Click Next to display a dialog stating that your fax is ready to send. All you need to do now is click Finish to send it. If everything goes well, you should either see a new entry in the Outgoing Faxes dialog or hear the fax/modem as it whisks your message off to the recipient.

> **Note:** One of the advantages of using Microsoft Fax instead of a standard fax machine is that you can have your computer send a fax late at night when the telephone rates are low. Unlike a standard fax machine, there are no pages to jam or other mechanical problems to overcome. Of course, problems at the other end can still prevent the recipient from actually receiving your fax. If you want to get fancy, you can also use the Cover Page Editor program to design your own fax cover pages. The original version of the Cover Page Editor had a bug in it, so be sure to get the OSR2 bug fix from `http://www.microsoft.com/windows95/info/system-updates.htm`.

Microsoft Network

The Microsoft Network (MSN) is Microsoft's attempt at creating an online service. Initially, Microsoft tried to make MSN similar to CompuServe and America Online. When this proved unsuccessful, Microsoft tried redirecting MSN as an entertainment online service that provided different channels for subscribers to view. As of this writing, the Microsoft Network is still going through radical changes, so you'll probably see a lot more than I describe here after Microsoft finally decides which direction to take MSN and how to market it to the general public.

> **Note:** At the time of this writing, the latest front end for MSN was Version 2.5. If you don't have this latest version, visit `http://signup.msn.com/signup/signup.hts?`. Make sure you visit `http://www.msn.com/default.asp` as well to learn about future updates to MSN.

To access MSN, click the MSN icon that appears on the desktop or in the Start menu. This displays the dialog shown in Figure 21.32. Notice that this dialog includes the following settings:

- User name: Enter your user name here.

- Password: Enter the password for your MSN account. The Remember password check box tells Exchange to remember your MSN password between sessions.

- Settings: Click this pushbutton to invoke a centralized dialog for changing your modem and dialing properties. The only other setting that this dialog changes is your access number—a single setting that allows you to access the Microsoft Network. You change this setting by selecting the city with an access number nearest your own.

Figure 21.32.
The MSN Sign In dialog is where you enter your name and password prior to going online.

Note: Exchange remembers your MSN password between sessions only if you have some other form of Windows 95–specific password protection for your machine. If you use Windows 95 without enabling passwords, you have to enter your MSN password each time you use it. The reason for this safeguard is simple: It protects your account from misuse by other people.

After you enter your name and password and change any required settings, click Connect to proceed. You hear your modem attempt to access MSN; the dialog displays messages during this process in case your modem speaker is turned off. Figure 21.33 gives you an idea of what you might see after you connect.

Figure 21.33.
The first thing you see when you sign in to MSN is a message about any e-mail you have waiting along with lists of the different categories available on MSN.

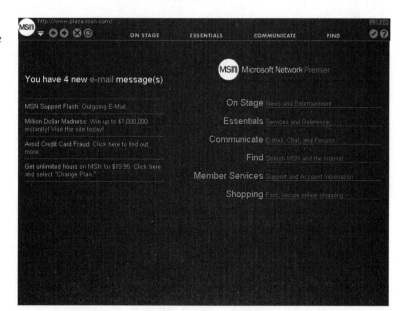

To view the other portions of MSN from this page, move the mouse pointer over any text. If the mouse pointer turns into a hand, that means you can click that text to view more information. The six sections of MSN are

- On Stage: This category provides news and entertainment channels that you can view, including MSNBC, Microsoft Slate magazine, Disney's Daily Blast, and games.

- Essentials: This category provides news and information about your local area and lists a menu of other forums and services you can explore on MSN such as Arts & Entertainment, Computers & Software, or Travel.

- Communicate: This category provides links to various areas on MSN where you can communicate with others including chat rooms, e-mail, newsgroups, and forums that cater to specific interests such as classical music, writing, or computer programming.

- Find: This category lists different Web guides to help you search the Internet. A list box at the top of the screen provides a list of search engines that you can use to find specific Web sites.

- Member Services: This category gives you the chance to change your password, change your billing plan, contact MSN's technical support, and view the MSN newsletter.

- Shopping: This category provides a list of links to various secure shopping Web sites so you can order anything from additional computer equipment to food, flowers, books, and clothes.

Tip: For a quick way to navigate MSN, click the MSN icon on the Taskbar. This displays a list of options in a pop-up menu. From here, you can click the option you want.

Take some time to explore MSN. Because MSN offers a flat-rate pricing plan ($19.95 a month for unlimited use), you can afford to spend as much time as you want browsing MSN and seeing what it has to offer.

Now that you have the basics of using MSN out of the way, I talk about a few things that you need to really use this product. The following list tells you about the language of using an online product like MSN:

- Forum: This is a gathering place for people with similar interests. Here, people leave messages, and others respond to them. You can look at the message header to determine what a particular discussion is about. In essence, think of a forum as a room in a house where people of like interests get together to talk. Finding the right forum can provide you with a wealth of information that you might not find elsewhere. It can also help you solve problems related to your software, your machine, or even your business.

- Message: A message is a single note on a particular subject. You use messages in e-mail and other places already, so the concept of a message shouldn't be new to you.

- Thread: A thread is a group of connected messages on the same topic. As each person responds to a message, he or she makes the list of messages about a given topic longer. You can read an entire list of messages (or a thread) to discover the conversation that took place on a specific topic. The fact that the messages are written rather than spoken is an advantage because you can read the messages when it's convenient. Threads are also a key way to store information for future use. Many people archive message threads about specific topics because that information can't be easily found anywhere else.

It's important to learn the rules of etiquette for forums. For example, many people frown on typing in all UPPERCASE when writing messages in a forum. Because body language is absent in written messages, people have come up with *emoticons*, which are text icons that tell the other person what you mean by a certain comment. Table 21.1 lists common emoticons that you can use to dress up any written communication.

Table 21.1. Standard emoticons.

Emoticon	Description
:-)	A happy face.
:->	An alternative happy face.
:-D	Said with a smile.
:<)	Humor for those with mustaches.
:<)=	Humor for those with beards too.
B-)	Smiling and wearing glasses or sunglasses (or a message from Batman).
8-)	Smiling and wearing glasses or sunglasses. Also used to denote a wide-eyed look.
:-1 or :-,	A smirk.
'-)	A wink.
:-(	Unhappy.
:-c	Very unhappy.
(:-(	Very unhappy.
:/)	Not funny: The receiver of a message sends this emoticon to show that a particular comment wasn't received as the sender intended.
):-&	Angry.
:-))-:	Theatrical comments: Use this for comments that are either theatrical in nature or used for emphasis.
;-)	Sardonic incredulity.
(@ @)	You're kidding!

continues

Table 21.1. continued

Emoticon	Description
: - "	Pursed lips.
: -C	Incredulous (jaw dropped).
: -<	Forlorn.
: -B	Drooling (or overbite).
: - ¦	Disgusted.
: -V	Shouting.
: -o or : -0	More versions of shouting.
: -w	Speaking with a forked tongue: You're lying to the other person in a whimsical sort of way. In other words, you're making a point sarcastically.
: -W	Shouting with a forked tongue.
: -r	Bleahhh! (Tongue sticking out.)
<: -0	Eek! You can use this for a number of purposes. You can even use it to tell the network administrator that your equipment is down and you can't do anything without it.
: -*	Oops! (Covering mouth with hand.)
: -T	Keeping a straight face (tight-lipped): Use this emoticon when you mean something in a serious way that the receiver could interpret as a humorous comment.
: -#	Censored: You'd love to use a little profanity but resisted the urge.
: -x	Kiss, kiss.
: -?	Licking your lips.
:~i	Smoking.
:~j	Smoking and smiling.
:/i	No smoking.
: -) : -) : -)	A guffaw.
: -J	A tongue-in-cheek comment.
:*)	Clowning around.
: -8	Talking out of both sides of your mouth.
<: -)	For dumb questions: Everyone knows that the only dumb question is the one you failed to ask before trashing the network. However, some people might feel that they have a dumb question they want someone to answer.

Emoticon	Description
oo	Headlights on: Use this emoticon to show someone that you want him to pay special attention to a comment.
:-o or #:-o	"Oh, nooooooo!" (A la Mr. Bill.)
¦-(	A late-night message.
(:-$	Ill.
#:-)	Matted hair.
:^)	A big nose.
:-{#}	Braces.
(:^(	A broken nose.
:-(=)	Big teeth.
&:-)	Curly hair.
@:-)	Wavy hair.
?-(	A black eye.
%-)	Broken glasses.
:	A fuzzy person.
*:**	A fuzzy person with a fuzzy mustache.
(:<)	A blabbermouth.
+<:-¦	A monk or nun.
(:-¦K-	A formal message.
¦¦*(	A handshake is offered.
¦¦*)	A handshake is accepted.
<:>==	A turkey.
@>-->----	A rose.
(-_-)	A secret smile.
<{:-)}	A message in a bottle.
<:-)<<¦	A message from a spaceship.
(:-...	A heartbreaking message.
(:>-<	A message from a thief: Hands up!
...---...	SOS.
:-I	It's something, but I don't know what...: You can't figure out what the other person is trying to say or reference.
@%&$%&	Profanity.

Each type of online services tends to attract different users. Business users tend to like CompuServe and home users flock to America Online. To find the right online service, you might have to use different ones until you find one you like.

On Your Own

Set up Microsoft Exchange to handle your faxing, online communications, and mail needs. See whether you can tell any difference between the messages you receive from the three sources. In most cases, you won't unless the sender provides some kind of clue.

Check your SYSTEM folder to see whether you can identify the various pieces of the communications subsystem. This chapter provides you with a list of the major files and many hints on how you can find the other special files that pertain to your system.

Determine whether you or your company can use a voice modem to make using the computer easier and more efficient. Be sure to check out the various criteria covered in this chapter—especially adherence to standards. You also want to download the Unimodem V update for your computer if you're not using the OSR2 version of Windows 95.

One of the fun elements of online computing is coming up with your own set of special emoticons. (Of course, this means that you have to explain them to everyone.) Create a few emoticons of your own.

22

Browsing the Internet with Internet Explorer

Peter Norton®

Microsoft Internet Explorer was not part of the original release of the Windows 95 operating system. However, it's been part of every major addition and upgrade to Windows 95 since the arrival of the Plus! package released shortly after Windows 95 itself.

Microsoft Internet Explorer is, first and foremost, a Web browser—that is, a viewer designed to request and display Web pages and other HTML documents. As such, it's a direct competitor to Web browsers such as Netscape Navigator and NSCA Mosaic. However, as Internet Explorer has evolved, it's become much more than just a Web browser. The current version, Internet Explorer 4, is designed to integrate itself into your Windows 95 operating system and add features such as the Active Desktop and interface changes such as enabling Web views of your folders. Internet Explorer 4 even comes with its own suite of companion programs for accessing e-mail and newsgroups (Outlook Express), creating Web pages (FrontPage Express), conferencing online (NetMeeting), and playing sound and video events (NetShow).

Because Internet Explorer has such diverse capabilities and varied effects on your system, I decided not to cover everything in one chapter. I introduced some of the features of Internet Explorer 4 in Chapter 1, "Opening Windows to the Internet with Internet Explorer 4," and Chapter 2, "Introducing Windows 95," and covered the Active Desktop in Chapter 4, "Working with the Active Desktop." I covered the new Web views feature in Chapter 7, "Customizing Folders with Web Views." This chapter concentrates on setting up Internet Explorer 4 to use your Internet connection, using it as a traditional Web browser, and customizing the program. I cover the new features for offline Web browsing—channels and subscriptions—in the next chapter. Outlook Express, the Internet e-mail and newsgroup program that comes with Internet Explorer 4, gets its own chapter (Chapter 24, "Outlook Express News and Mail"). I cover the remaining Internet Explorer 4 companion programs (FrontPage Express, NetMeeting, and NetShow) in Chapter 25, "FrontPage Express, NetMeeting, and NetShow."

Note: The OSR2 version of Windows 95 comes with Internet Explorer 3.0 as part of the package. The latest version is Internet Explorer 4. If you don't have the new version of Internet Explorer, you can download an update from http://www.microsoft.com/ie/. If you prefer, you can get a copy of the program on CD-ROM by purchasing it in a computer software store or ordering it from Microsoft. Even though I cover Internet Explorer 4 in this chapter, many of the same principles apply to Internet Explorer 2 and 3.

Without further ado, it's time to discover how to set up Internet Explorer for some Web browsing. I assume that you've acquired a copy of the program (purchased a CD-ROM or downloaded the necessary files) and installed the update on your system according to the instructions in Chapter 1.

Starting and Setting Up Internet Explorer

Once you get Internet Explorer installed, you want to set it up for use. There are two routes to go here, but they're both essentially the same. What you need to do is specify some type of Internet service provider (ISP). Microsoft provides full support for MSN as part of the Windows 95 package. An update to this support is available at `http://signup.msn.com/signup/signup.hts?`. You can also choose to use any other Internet service provider at this point; the only requirement is that you have the proper support (a Dial-Up Networking connection) installed for contacting them. I used PBI (Pacific Bell Internet) in this case because of its low cost and level of support.

> **Tip:** The first time you run Internet Explorer, you use the Internet Connection wizard to install support for it. You can always rerun this program using the Connection Wizard option in your Internet Explorer folder in the Start menu. Always run the wizard whenever you change Internet service providers or make some other major change to your Internet Explorer setup.

1. Double-click the Internet Explorer icon on the desktop if this is the first time you're running it. Otherwise, select the Internet Connection Wizard option from the Internet Explorer folder to start the wizard.

2. Click Next. Figure 22.1 shows the first Setup Options dialog. You need to decide how you want to connect to the Internet. As you can see, there are three ways to do so. The first option is for someone who has no Internet access arrangements in place. The Internet Connection Wizard supplies a list of ISPs that service your area and lets you select one and sign up for an account. Then it takes you through the steps to set up a connection to your new ISP. During the setup process, the wizard might prompt you for your Windows 95 CD to copy files onto your system and might require you to restart your computer. The second option walks you through the process of setting up a new Internet connection—either a LAN connection or a Dial-Up Networking connection. The difference is that it assumes that you've already got an account established with an ISP, but you may or may not have a Windows 95 connection set up. The third option is the one to use if you already have an Internet connection set up through your LAN or a Dial-Up Networking connection. It configures Internet Explorer to use your existing default connection. This particular option works best because you can set up everything with your ISP in advance.

Figure 22.1.
The Setup Options dialog allows you to choose the method of creating an Internet connection.

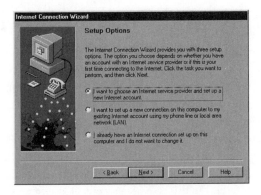

3. Click one of the three setup options. If you select the first option, proceed to step 4. If you select the middle option, proceed to step 8. If you selected the third option, then you're all done creating a connection. Just click Next, and then click Finish. The next thing you see is the standard Connect To dialog as Internet Explorer opens and begins connecting to the Internet.

4. Make sure you have the first option selected and click Next. You see a Begin Automatic Setup dialog.

5. Click Next. You see a dialog similar to the one shown in Figure 22.2. The Internet Connection wizard asks you for location information that it uses to download a list of ISPs that service your area. This list is by no means comprehensive; it usually lists several national service providers with service in your area but often omits local and regional providers that might also offer excellent service. As a result, you might not find an ISP that precisely suits your needs on the list. Still, the referral service can be a valuable resource if you're starting from scratch and want to sign up with one of the big ISPs.

Figure 22.2.
The Location Information dialog provides the information needed to get a list of ISPs in your area.

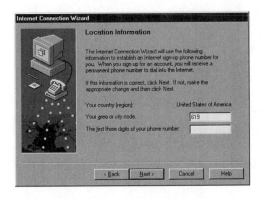

6. Enter your area code in the first field and the first three digits of your telephone number in the second field. Click Next. At this point, the Internet Connection wizard displays a

Connecting dialog, dials an 800 number, and downloads a list of ISPs that serve your area. When it finishes, you see a dialog containing a list of ISPs similar to the one shown in Figure 22.3. All you need to do to sign up for an ISP is select the one you want by clicking in the Sign Me Up column. Notice that you can get additional information about the ISP before you sign up by clicking in the More Info column.

Figure 22.3.

The Microsoft Internet Referral Service can provide you with a list of ISPs if you don't already have one.

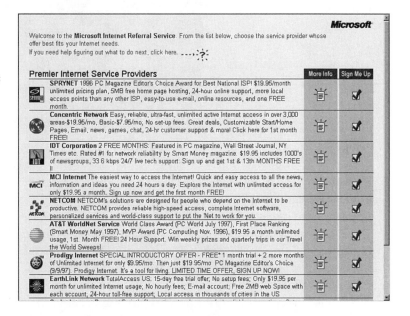

Warning: Once the Internet Connection wizard displays the ISP list, there is no way to back up to the previous dialog boxes or choose an ISP that isn't on the list. If you don't find an ISP you like on the list, scroll to the bottom of the list and click the Cancel button to exit the Internet Connection wizard. You can restart the Internet Connection wizard later and choose another setup option.

7. At this point, you need to follow the instructions for the ISP that you've selected. Once you complete the sign-up process and follow the instructions to set up your Internet connection, the next thing you see is a Connect To dialog next. Simply type your user name for the ISP, along with a password. Click the Connect pushbutton, and you are on your way to your first Internet session.

8. If you're reading this step, then you must have selected the middle option in Step 3. Select the I want to set up a new connection option and click Next at the initial dialog shown in Figure 22.1. Your first decision is how you want to connect your machine to the Internet (see Figure 22.4). There are two choices: Connect using my phone line or Connect using

my local area network. I selected the Connect using my phone line option in this case
because I wanted to use a modem connection.

Figure 22.4.
*Your first decision in
setting up Internet
Explorer is how to
make the connection.*

9. Click Next. The wizard displays a dialog box like the one shown in Figure 22.5. (If you
   choose the LAN connection instead of the phone line connection in the previous step, the
   wizard presents a couple of dialog boxes asking whether your LAN goes through a proxy
   server, and if it does, the wizard asks you to supply the proxy server names.) If you select
   the first option, Create a new dial-up connection, the wizard runs the Make New Connection wizard. I already covered how to make a new Dial-Up Networking connection in
   Chapter 1, so I don't repeat the steps here. If you choose the second option, Use an
   existing dial-up connection, you can select the connection you want to use from the list
   box under the option. That's the path I normally recommend. When you click Next, the
   wizard offers the option to change the dial-up connection settings. Selecting Yes here
   causes the wizard to present a series of dialog boxes where you can change any of the
   settings available in the Make New Connection wizard. If your connection is already
   configured properly, you can choose No and click Next.

Figure 22.5.
*From here, you can
make a new Dial-Up
Networking
connection or choose
one of your existing
connections.*

10. The next thing you see is a dialog like the one shown in Figure 22.6. You need to decide whether you want to set up your Internet mail account now. You're probably anxious to get on the Net and do some Web browsing, so you can just click No and skip the e-mail account setup for now. In Chapter 24, I show you how to set up your e-mail account in Outlook Express.

Figure 22.6.

This dialog gives you the option to set up your Internet mail handler.

11. Click Next and you see another dialog similar to the Internet Mail Account setup options. This one lets you choose to set up an account to access Internet News now or defer it until later. Click No to skip the setup for now. (You can do it later in Outlook Express. I show you how in Chapter 24.)

12. Click Next. Your next choice is whether to set up an Internet Directory Service. You probably want to click No here unless your network administrator or ISP provided you with information on how to access a directory service or LDAP account. If you choose Yes and click Next, the wizard prompts you to enter the address of the directory server, asks whether to check addresses on your outgoing e-mail against the directory address book, and asks you to supply a name for the directory account. (This is another option you can configure later in Outlook Express.)

13. Click Next and you see the Internet Connection wizard's final dialog box. You're done! Click Finish to close the Complete Configuration dialog. Unlike the other two setup options, you actually have to open Internet Explorer manually to check the connection at this point. I suggest that you do so. Remember that you can always open the Dial-Up Networking connection in the Dial-Up Networking folder and change any settings without going through the Internet Setup wizard a second time.

This procedure covered all three basic methods for setting up access to the Internet with the Internet Connection wizard. I think that the automatic setup option with its ISP referral is a good method if you just want to look at what's available before you make any permanent decisions. Most people probably want to locate an ISP that meets their needs and then follow the ISP's instructions to set up a Dial-Up Networking connection and configure Internet Explorer and Outlook Express. That's likely to entail following the middle choice offered by the Internet Connection wizard. Of course, if you already have an Internet connection that's working for you, you can just use the Internet Connection wizard to quickly configure Internet Explorer to use that same connection.

Navigating the World Wide Web

By this point, you're wondering what else you have to do to get online. Actually, the setup and configuration are all done. All you need to do now is double-click the Internet Explorer icon on your desktop. If you're connected to the Internet via your local area network, IE4 opens immediately. If you connect to the Internet via a Dial-Up Networking connection, you see a Connect To dialog. I discussed this dialog in Chapter 1. Enter your name and password (if necessary) and click Connect to get started. You see the Dialing Progress dialog shown in Figure 22.7.

Figure 22.7.
Modem users need to connect to the Internet before surfing.

At this point, a number of things could happen, depending on how you created your Internet connection. (You can also change the configuration of Internet Explorer to get a variety of results.) In most cases, you start at Microsoft's Internet Start Web page shown in Figure 22.8.

You can use Internet Explorer's scroll bars to view different portions of the Web page. From there, the details of how to navigate various Web pages and sites can vary, depending on the design of the sites you are viewing. However, the basics remain fairly consistent. Most pages are composed of a combination of graphics and text, and hyperlinks allow you to jump from the page you are viewing to another related page. Hyperlinks in text are usually highlighted in color (typically blue) and underlined. Hyperlinked graphics often look like buttons, icons, and symbols so their intended use is easy to understand. When you point to a hyperlink, the normal mouse pointer changes to a pointing hand to designate the presence of a hyperlink. Click it and Internet Explorer loads and displays the Web page referenced in the hyperlink. So it goes from page to page and site to site throughout the World Wide Web.

Figure 22.8.
You normally start your Internet session at the Internet Start home page.

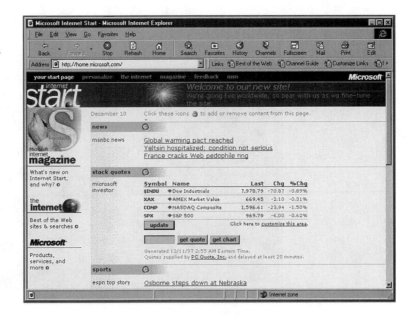

Using Internet Explorer Toolbars

Now that you're online and have viewed a Web page, start taking a look at some of Internet Explorer's controls in more detail. Everything you need is on the toolbar. I rarely use the menu system in Internet Explorer except to select a favorite site or modify Internet Explorer's configuration settings.

In addition to the toolbars that have become a standard feature of Web browsers (and other programs as well), Internet Explorer 4 introduces a new feature called Explorer bars. An Explorer bar is a panel on the left side of the browser pane that acts like an expanded toolbar. The contents of the Explorer bar remain visible while the contents of the main Web page viewing pane on the right changes as you surf. The Channel bar (shown in Figure 22.9) is just one example of an Explorer bar. There are also Explorer bars for Favorites, History, and Search.

The following list gives you a quick overview of the various controls on the toolbars. I cover some of them in more detail as the chapter progresses:

- Back/Forward: You'll find that these two buttons come in handy when you want to move quickly between several areas that you've already visited. I use the Back button most often to move from the current page back to the top level of a Web site. A new feature of Internet Explorer 4 is that each of these buttons has a small arrow button on its right side. When you click the down arrow, Internet Explorer displays a drop-down list of recently visited Web pages. You can go directly to any page on the list by selecting it from the list. This allows you to jump back or forward several pages without having to repeatedly click the Back or Forward button.

Figure 22.9.

The Channel bar is just one of Internet Explorer's new Explorer bars.

- Stop: Some Internet sites seem to provide more than the usual number of graphics. You could wait for them to all download, but I usually click this button instead. It tells the browser to stop downloading the page. The disadvantage is that you don't see all the neat graphics and buttons the Web page designer placed on the page. The advantage is that you can get back to work faster.

- Refresh: Explorer, like most browsers, uses a cache to store images. Sometimes the Internet page changes without your knowledge because your browser is looking at the cached page instead of the live page on the Internet. Use this button to reload the current page and update its contents.

- Home: Some browsers use the term "start page" for the place you always start surfing the Internet; Internet Explorer uses the term "home page." In my case, this is the Internet Start page shown in Figure 22.8. I prefer the term "home page" because it's a little more picturesque and it's the term most people use to reference this part of the Internet. Clicking this button always takes you to your home page. (You can redefine what page Internet Explorer loads when you click the Home button. I show you how later in this chapter.)

- Search: The Search button is the first of four buttons that activate Explorer bars—a new feature of Internet Explorer 4. Click it once to add the Search Explorer bar to your Internet Explorer window. The button looks "depressed" when it's active. Click the depressed button to turn off the Search Explorer bar. I cover this button (and other search-related procedures) in the section "Searching" later in this chapter. The short version is that this button opens an Internet page you can use to search for things. Normally you use some form of keyword search to accomplish the task.

- Favorites: Internet Explorer allows you to maintain a list of favorite places. You can access the Favorites list from the Favorites menu. You can also click this button to display a list of your favorite places in an Explorer bar. I cover using favorites in more detail in a separate section of this chapter.

- History: The History button is new to Internet Explorer 4. It activates the History Explorer bar, which lists the Web sites you've visited over the last couple of weeks. The sites are listed by day or week and the individual pages are sub-grouped into folders by site. To revisit a site, simply click its listing in the History Explorer bar. It's a handy way to locate and return to that cool site you remember visiting a few days ago. On the other hand, it's also a way that someone (your boss perhaps) can track what sites you've been surfing. (I show you how to adjust the length of time Internet Explorer keeps track of your browsing history and how to clear the history listing in the section "Customizing Internet Explorer" later in this chapter.)

- Channels: The Channels button activates the Channels Explorer bar (refer to Figure 22.9). Channels constitute one of the major new features ushered in by Internet Explorer 4. A channel is a Web site that is specially designed so that Internet Explorer 4 can download and display a table of contents for the site in the Channel bar. Channels can also make optimal use of Internet Explorer 4's subscription feature to download content from the site and display it later, when you're working offline. There's a lot more to say about channels and subscriptions, but I don't attempt to get into it here. I save that discussion for another chapter—Chapter 23, "Webcasting: Channel Surfing When You're Offline."

- Fullscreen: Some Web pages (and many channels) are just too full of information to fit comfortably within the confines of the normal Internet Explorer browser window. Even if you maximize the Internet Explorer window, the title bar, menus, toolbars, and other accoutrements of an application window conspire to eat up a lot of screen space, leaving a limited amount of space for viewing the Web site itself. To relieve the crowding, Internet Explorer 4 offers you the option of viewing Web pages in full-screen mode. When you click the Fullscreen button, Internet Explorer does more than just maximize its window; it also does away with the window border, menus, and nearly everything else. The entire screen is devoted to displaying the Web page. The only exception is a small toolbar at the top of the screen (as shown in Figure 22.10). To return to the normal view, click the Fullscreen button in that toolbar.

- Mail: Clicking this button displays a menu containing five options: Read Mail, New Message, Send a Link, Send Page, and Read News. The Read Mail option displays Outlook Express or another mail reader, such as Windows Messaging (depending on which you choose for your mail reader). Internet Explorer requests any new mail from your ISP's mail server and displays it in the window. The New Message option brings up a new message dialog using the capabilities of either Outlook Express or Windows Messaging. I already looked at Windows Messaging in Chapter 21, "Network Connections with an Internet

Appeal." I cover the messaging capabilities of Outlook Express further in Chapter 24. The Send a Link option works much like creating a new message. However, in this case, the message includes a link to a Web site you're currently viewing in Internet Explorer. This allows you to have a discussion with someone else concerning the particulars of an Internet site. The Send Page option is similar to Send a Link except that Internet Explorer attaches a copy of the Web page to the message instead of just sending a link to the page's URL. Finally, the Read News option brings up the Outlook Express program in its Internet News reader mode. As with the other Outlook Express features, I discuss it in Chapter 24.

Figure 22.10.
In Fullscreen view, your entire screen is devoted to displaying the Web page.

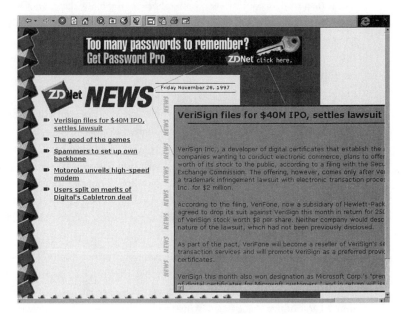

- Fonts: Generally, you'll find that Internet sites use an easy-to-read font. However, at times, you might need to see a little more or a little less of the text on a page. Use this button to change the font size. Each click cycles you through a set range of font sizes, starting at the smallest size and moving toward the largest. (By default, this button doesn't appear on the Internet Explorer 4 toolbar. If you need it, you can add it to the toolbar by checking the appropriate option in the Advanced tab of the Internet Explorer Options dialog box.)

- Print: Use this option to send the current page content to the printer.

- Edit: Clicking this button imports the current Web page into an editor. Of course, Internet Explorer defaults to sending the Web page to FrontPage Express if you have it installed.

- Address: The Address box is easy to spot; it's the big text box that occupies a toolbar of its very own. When you want to visit a Web site, you just type its URL and press Enter. Internet Explorer loads and displays the Web page (or other resource) you specified. What isn't as obvious is that the Address box is also a drop-down list box that lists the last several URLs you entered. If you want to return to any of the sites on the list, you can select the URL from the Address list and save yourself some typing.

- Links: The Links toolbar is composed of buttons, each linked to a Web page. Clicking a button takes you to that Web page. Initially, there are five Links buttons set up to link to popular pages on the Microsoft Web site. However, you can redefine the Links buttons by changing the contents of the Links folder in your Favorites list. Put shortcuts to your most-used Web pages in the Links folder and you have easy one-click access to those sites, right on the toolbar.

Automatically Complete URLs

Typing in a long URL for a Web page you want to view is seldom fun. You must take great pains to get every letter and bit of punctuation exactly right. If you make one tiny mistake, you see an error message (or the wrong page) instead of the Web page you were looking for. Fortunately, Internet Explorer does what it can to make the task of entering URLs a little less onerous.

First of all, if you enter a partial Internet address in the Address box, Internet Explorer completes the URL for you using the most common value for the missing portion of the URL. For example, if you omit the protocol at the beginning of a URL and type in something like **www.microsoft.com**, Internet Explorer automatically expands the URL to http://www.microsoft.com when you press the Enter key.

Another helpful feature is Internet Explorer's capability to automatically finish entering a URL that you entered before. As soon as you type the first few letters into the Address box, Internet Explorer tries to match them to other addresses you entered previously. If it finds a match, the program displays the full URL in the Address box. If that's the address you want to use, just press Enter. If it's not the correct address, you can continue typing and Internet Explorer continues searching for more matches. I find that entering some easily recognized URLs with this technique is even faster than selecting them from a list of favorites or recently visited sites.

Peter's Principle: From Static to Dynamic Web Pages

In the early days of the Web, almost all Web pages were static—meaning the content and formatting remained fixed until the Webmaster changed them. All the visitors to a site would see the same Web pages in much the same way. Now, Webmasters are using tools such as Java, ActiveX, cascading style sheets, and dynamic HTML to create truly dynamic Web sites—Web sites filled with pages that evolve, adapt, and change in response to input from the viewer, time of day, and many other factors. The Web page you view might be

continues

generated on-the-fly by the server just seconds before you see it. The server uses information you supply to select bits and pieces from its database to build a Web page custom-tailored to you. The result is a Web browsing experience that is more engaging.

As a Web browser user, you don't really need to be concerned about the new techniques and technologies that make dynamic HTML possible. All the hard work falls on the shoulders of the software developers and the Web site designers. They are the ones who must make the dynamic Web sites work. You just need a Web browser capable of displaying the pages they produce. Internet Explorer 3 can display some of these effects. Internet Explorer 4 supports all the latest features such as cascading style sheets and dynamic HTML. You need that capability to be able to display the latest dynamic Web sites. If you're still using Internet Explorer 3.0 or some other, older browser, the idea of missing the benefits of dynamic Web sites is probably sufficient justification for upgrading your browser software.

Favorite Sites

As I mentioned before, Internet Explorer allows you to maintain a list of favorite places—a collection of shortcuts containing the URLs of Web sites you want to revisit in the future. (Other Web browsers have a similar feature called *bookmarks*.) You might want to maintain a list of favorite Internet research sites or create a listing of sites related to a current project, for example. Internet Explorer's Favorites menu displays a list of your favorite places. There are also commands that enable you to add new Web sites to your Favorites, organize your favorite places into a hierarchy of submenus, manage Subscriptions, and update those subscriptions. As a result of the increasing integration of the Internet into the Windows 95 operating system, the Favorites menu is now a fixture in other Explorer windows, in addition to Internet Explorer. You can find the Favorites menu in windows for My Computer, Windows Explorer, and even Control Panel. You can also access the favorites list from the Start menu on the Windows 95 Taskbar.

In addition to the Favorites menu, Internet Explorer gives you another way to access your favorite sites. Click the Favorites button in the toolbar, and Internet Explorer displays the Favorites Explorer bar, as shown in Figure 22.11. Having the Favorites Explorer bar is like having a Favorites menu that stays open and available instead of disappearing after you make each selection. It's great for moving quickly through a series of favorite sites.

Figure 22.11.

Click the Favorites button in the toolbar, and Internet Explorer displays the Favorites Explorer bar.

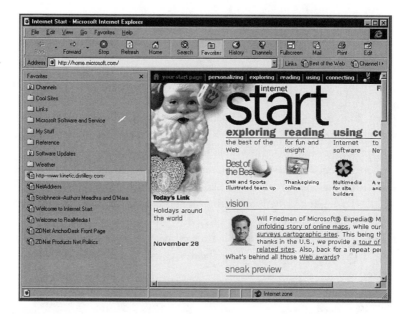

Tip: Favorites aren't restricted to Web sites. If you have documents on your local hard drive or a network drive that you need to access frequently, you can create shortcuts to them and add the shortcut in the Favorites list. Just open the Windows\Favorites folder, right-click a blank area in the folder, choose New | Shortcut from the context menu, and then enter the full filename and a display name in the Create Shortcut wizard. When you finish the wizard, you have a shortcut to your document on your Favorites list. Then you can use the Favorites list to open your document just as you use it to open Web pages.

Whether you use the Favorites menu in Internet Explorer, the Favorites menu in another Explorer window, the Favorites menu on the Start menu, or the Favorites Explorer bar in Internet Explorer, the technique for opening a Favorite site is basically the same. You open the menu or Explorer bar, click a subfolder in the list (if necessary) to display a list of sites in that folder, and then click the desired favorite site in that list. Internet Explorer loads and displays the selected Web page. If you're not already connected to the Internet, Internet Explorer initiates a connection to load the Web page. If you elect to work offline (see Chapter 23), Internet Explorer attempts to load the page from the cache on your hard drive.

Adding a Page to Your Favorites

For the Favorites list to be truly useful, it needs to contain Web sites that really are your favorites—sites that you return to time and time again. That means you need to be able to add your own Web sites to the Favorites list. Fortunately, it's easy to do just that.

First, go to the site you want to add to the Favorites. Make sure you're viewing the proper page because Internet Explorer uses the URL of the current Web page for the favorite place entry. When the page you want to add is visible in the Internet Explorer window, choose Favorites | Add to Favorites from the Internet Explorer menu. (The Add to Favorites command isn't available on the Favorites Explorer bar.) Internet Explorer opens the Add Favorite dialog box as shown in Figure 22.12. To simply add the Web page to your list of favorite places, choose the first option, (The other options have to do with subscriptions. I cover those in the next chapter.) If you want, you can edit the text in the Name box at the bottom of the dialog before you click OK. Internet Explorer adds the Web page to the Favorites list. The new entry appears immediately the next time you access the Favorites list.

Figure 22.12.
To simply add the
Web page to your list
of favorite places,
choose the first
option.

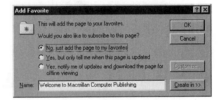

Organizing Favorites

After you begin to build a collection of favorite places, you need to organize your list or it will get too long to display conveniently. The Organize Favorites option displays a dialog you can use to move your favorite places around and create folders (submenus) in which to store them.

To begin maintenance work on your Favorites list, choose Favorites | Organize Favorites from the Internet Explorer menu. (Like the Add to Favorites command, Organize Favorites isn't available on the Favorites Explorer bar.) Internet Explorer opens the Organize Favorites dialog box as shown in Figure 22.13. Using this dialog box is pretty straightforward. You can click the Create New Folder button at the top of the dialog box to create a new subfolder that appears as a submenu in the Favorites list. You can select a favorite place item and then click one of the buttons at bottom to Move, Rename, or Delete the selected item. To move a favorite place shortcut to a subfolder the easy way, just drag and drop it onto the folder. That's all there is to it. When you're through rearranging items in the Favorites list, click Close to close the dialog box.

Figure 22.13.
You can select a Favorite place item and then click one of the buttons at the bottom of the dialog to Move, Rename, or Delete the selected item.

Tip: If you know what folder you want to place a Favorites item in when you create it, you can click the Create In button in the Add Favorite dialog to expand the dialog box to include a list of folders in your Favorites folder. Then you can simply select a folder from the list to instruct IE4 to put the favorite item there instead of just dumping it into the main Favorites folder. You don't need to open the Organize Favorites window to move the item in a separate operation.

Tip: The Favorites list is really just a collection of shortcuts stored in the Favorites subfolder of your Windows folder. (On single-user machines, it's usually `c:\Windows\Favorites\`. If you have Windows configured for multiple users, the Favorites folder is probably `C:\Windows\Profiles\username\Favorites\`.) You can use Windows Explorer to create folders and move most favorites shortcuts around in the Favorites folder just like moving objects in any other folder.

Searching

If you do a lot of research on the Internet as I do, then you realize the benefit of finding what you need quickly. Internet Explorer and its links to the Microsoft Web site provide you with some really handy tools in this regard.

Of course, there are numerous search engines and directories available on the Web. I already covered a number of the more popular search engines in Chapter 1. To use any one of them, you can simply type the search engine's URL into Internet Explorer's Address box to go to that Web site and began your search. Internet Explorer actually makes use of the same resources for its searching tools. The difference is that Internet Explorer includes some features that make the popular search engines and directories a little more accessible and easier to use.

Starting a Search from the Menu

Take a look at the most basic tool first. Just choose Go | Search the Web from Internet Explorer's menu, and you see a display similar to the one shown in Figure 22.14. (You might see a different search page if you use MSN as your ISP or if your copy of Internet Explorer was customized by your ISP or by your corporate computer support department.) This one Web page serves as a gateway to more than 30 search engines, guides, directories, and similar resources.

Figure 22.14.

You can access most of the popular search engines from this page on the Microsoft Web site.

When you arrive at the Search the Web page, one of the five most popular search engines (from the list in the upper-left corner of the page) is preselected and a data entry form for that search engine appears at the top of the page (In Figure 22.14, Lycos is the selected search engine.) If you want to conduct a search using that search engine, you can click one of the predefined search categories for that search engine (the row of round buttons near the middle of Figure 22.14) or enter a keyword in the text box and click the button that starts the search (the button is labeled Go Get It in Figure 22.14). Internet Explorer enters your search request at the selected search engine's Web site and then takes you to that Web site to display the results of your search (see Figure 22.15).

Figure 22.15.
Internet Explorer takes to the search engine's Web site to display the results of a search.

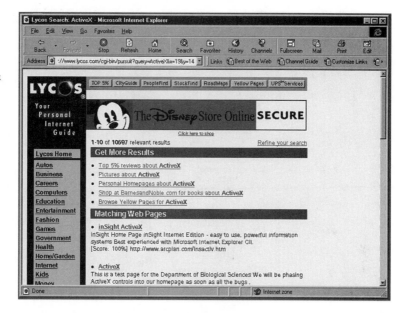

Of course, you don't have to use the search engine that's preselected when you arrive at the Search the Web page. After all, that's the point of a page like this—to give you easy access to any of several search resources. If you prefer to use one of the other search resources listed on the Search the Web page, just select it by clicking its name on the page. After a few seconds, the data entry form for that search resource replaces the default selection and you can proceed with your search.

Using the Search Explorer Bar

Previous versions of Internet Explorer included a Search button on the toolbar that served as a shortcut for the same search features available from the menu. However, Internet Explorer 4's Search button is different. Clicking the Search button opens the Search bar, one of Internet Explorer 4's four new Explorer bars that appear on the left side of the Internet Explorer window, as shown in Figure 22.16. The Search bar gives you quick access to the same top five search engines you saw in the upper-left corner of the Search the Web page on the Microsoft Web site. Like the search engine entry area at the top of the Search the Web page, the search engine that appears by default in the Search bar rotates among the five search engines. (Figure 22.16 shows the InfoSeek search engine.) You can use the search engine provider-of-the-day, or you can select one of the other search engines from the drop-down list near the top of the Search bar.

Figure 22.16.

The Search bar rotates among five of the top search engines.

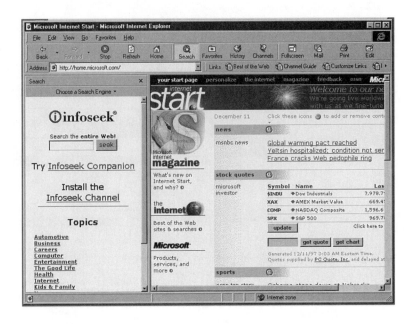

To use the Search bar, select one of the five search engines and then click one of the links to a predefined search category or enter a keyword into the text box and click the button that starts to search. Internet Explorer submits your search to the search engine, and then, instead of going to the search engine's Web page for the results, Internet Explorer displays the results of the search in the Search bar as shown in Figure 22.17. The search results are specially formatted to fit as much as possible within the Search bar.

Figure 22.17.

The results of your search appear right in the Search bar itself.

So far, the search process using the Search bar is essentially the same as the search process using the Search the Web page; it just occurs within the confines of the Search bar. The real innovation of the Search bar doesn't become apparent until you begin to follow some of the hyperlinks the search engine returned as hits.

Normally, when you click a hyperlink, Internet Explorer locates the target of that link and displays the Web page in the main viewing window, replacing the current page. That works fine on normal Web pages, but it's not always great when you're following links from a page of search engine hits. The problem is that a lot of search engine hits turn out to be dead ends, so you wind up clicking the Back button to return to the page of search results to try another hit. As a result, you spend a lot of time waiting while Internet Explorer returns to the page of search engine results again and again.

Using the search bar is different. When you click a hyperlink for a hit in the Search bar, Internet Explorer loads the target Web page and displays it in the main viewing window to the right of the Search bar as shown in Figure 22.18. Notice that the Search bar remains onscreen. If you want to check out another hit from your search, you don't have to click the Back button and wait for Internet Explorer to return to the search results page; you can just click the hyperlink for the next hit in the Search bar.

Figure 22.18.
Click a hit in the Search bar and view the target Web page in the main viewing panel to the right of the Search bar.

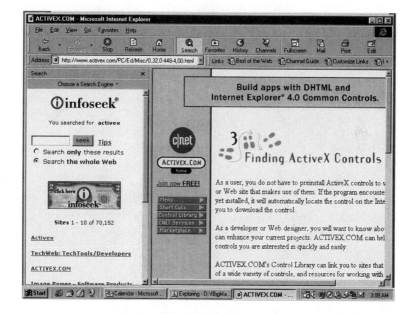

Using Autosearch

Autosearch is another handy built-in search feature of Internet Explorer 4. There are no buttons to click or commands to select when you use Autosearch; all the action takes place in the Address box. To initiate an Autosearch, you simply type a question mark followed by a space and your keyword in the Address box like so: **? *keyword*.** When you press Enter, Internet Explorer automatically submits the keyword to a default search engine (typically Yahoo!) and then displays the results of your search as shown in Figure 22.19. That's all there is to it.

Figure 22.19.
Yahoo! is the default
search engine for
Internet Explorer's
Autosearch feature.

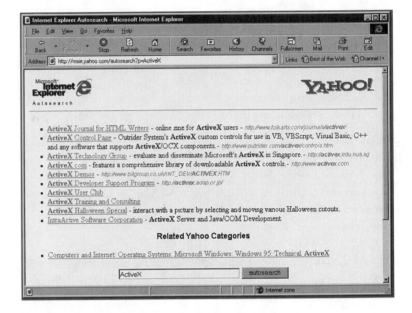

Tip: If you type a partial URL into the Address box and Internet Explorer is unable to locate a Web site at that address, the program offers to conduct an Autosearch using the domain name as the search keyword.

Tip: You can use the TweakUI Control Panel applet from the Windows 95 PowerToys collection to change what search engine Internet Explorer uses for its Autosearches. You'll find the setting on TweakUI's General tab. See Chapter 8, "Customizing with Microsoft PowerToys and KernelToys," for more details on TweakUI.

Searching for Text on a Page

Before I leave the subject of searches, there's one more kind of search to consider: finding text on a Web page. To start a search for some text, first display the Web page you want to search and then choose Edit | Find. Internet Explorer displays a Find dialog box like the one you use to find text in a word processor or similar application. Enter the text you want to search for in the Find What text box, check the appropriate options, and select whether you want to search up or down from the current cursor position. When you click the Find Next button, Internet Explorer searches the current Web page and highlights the first match it finds.

Peter's Principle: PowerToys for Internet Explorer

Internet Explorer 4 has its own set of PowerToys that add some interesting features to the program. The Internet Explorer PowerToys include a couple of especially nice search features.

Like the PowerToys and KernelToys for Windows 95 I covered in Chapter 8, the Internet Explorer PowerToys are a set of utilities and add-on enhancements released by Microsoft but officially "unsupported," which means you're on your own if you choose to install and use them. I'm not quite sure why Microsoft didn't include at least some of the PowerToys features in the official release version of Internet Explorer 4; they seem to work just fine.

Here's a quick rundown on what's available in the Internet Explorer PowerToys:

- Zoom In/Zoom Out adds commands to the context menu that allow you to right-click an image and make it larger or smaller.

- Quick Search extends the capabilities of Internet Explorer's Autosearch feature by enabling you to specify which search engine to use for a search. For example, instead of typing **? keyword** to send a search to the default search engine, you can type **ex keyword** to use the Excite search engine for your search. If you know which search engine you want to use, this is definitely the fastest way to initiate a keyword search.

- Image Toggler adds a button to the Links toolbar that toggles the Show Pictures setting on or off. This might not be as slick as a button on the main toolbar to control the display of graphics, but it sure beats scrolling through the long list of Advanced settings in the Internet Options dialog box to change the Show Pictures setting.

- Text Highlighter: With this PowerToy installed, you can select some text on a Web page and highlight it with a color. The effect is similar to the highlight feature in Microsoft Word. It's a nice idea, but I've never found much need for it when reading Web pages.

- Open Frame in New Window: I really like this PowerToy! It does just what its name implies; it allows you to view the contents of one frame from a Web page in a separate Internet Explorer window. I use this PowerToy whenever I encounter a Web page that is so crowded with frames that I can't read the main content without a lot of scrolling. I just open a new Internet Explorer window dedicated to displaying the main content frame and read away without the distraction of the other frames in the window.

continues

- Web Search: Just highlight some text on a Web page, right-click it, and choose Web Search from the context menu. Internet Explorer automatically conducts an Autosearch by sending the selected text to the default search engine. It's fast, it's easy, and I like it.

- Links List: I call this one the Dragnet PowerToy. To paraphrase Joe Friday, it gives you "Just the links, ma'am." When you right-click a Web page and choose Links List from the context menu, Internet Explorer scans the Web page looking for hyperlinks and then it opens a separate window and lists the links it found. The Links List can come to the rescue when you're searching for a particular link on a page but you're having trouble finding it because the link you're looking for is buried in a lot of text and graphics.

If you want to try out the Internet Explorer 4 PowerToys (and I recommend that you do), you can download the PowerToys installer program from `http://www.microsoft.com/ie/ie40/powertoys/`. When you run the program, the PowerToys Setup wizard allows you to select which of the PowerToys you want to install.

Customizing Internet Explorer

Internet Explorer is a highly customizable program. I already covered how you can customize your list of favorite places, display Explorer bars, and view Web pages in full-screen mode. In addition, there are a lot of options and settings that you can use to change the appearance of the Internet Explorer window and the Web pages it displays and to change many of Internet Explorer's default actions and configuration. I cover most of the Internet Explorer configuration options in this chapter, but I leave the settings related to Internet security for later. I cover those in Chapter 28, "Setting Up Security."

Rearranging Toolbars

One of the simplest changes you can make in the appearance of the Internet Explorer window is to rearrange the toolbars. Actually, there are not one, but three, toolbars. The Standard Buttons toolbar contains the navigation buttons (Back, Forward, Stop, Refresh, and Home), the Explorer bar buttons (Search, Favorites, History, and Channels), and buttons for other features such as Fullscreen and Print. The Address bar contains just one element—the Address box where you type URLs. The Links toolbar contains a series of buttons you can use to access individual Web sites.

You can choose to display or hide any, or all, of the toolbars. For example, if the Standard Buttons toolbar is visible, you can choose View | Toolbars | Standard Buttons to remove the toolbar from the Internet Explorer window. Repeat the same command to display it again. There are similar commands for the other two toolbars. Choosing View | Toolbars | Text Labels allows you to toggle the text labels that appear on the standard buttons on or off. At first, you probably need the text labels to identify the buttons on the toolbar. After you get used to using the program, however, you might find that the text labels are superfluous; the icons on each button are sufficient to identify their purpose. Without the text labels, the buttons of the Standard Buttons bar take up only about half as much space on the screen.

You can do more than just decide whether you want to see each of the toolbars. You can also change their position. Although you can't move the toolbars just anywhere in the Internet Explorer window—they must remain in a horizontal band immediately below the menu bar—you can change the horizontal size of each toolbar and their relative positions. To move or resize a toolbar, click its handle (the small vertical bar at the left end of the toolbar) and drag.

Configuring the Internet Options

The rest of the configuration options I address in this section of the chapter are all contained in the Internet Options dialog box. To open the Internet Options dialog box, choose View | Internet Options. Internet Explorer displays the dialog box shown in Figure 22.20. You can also access the same set of options by opening the Windows 95 Control Panel and double-clicking the Internet icon. The dialog box that appears has a slightly different title (Internet Properties), but all the tabs and options are identical to those found in the Internet Options dialog box.

Figure 22.20.
The General tab of the Internet Options dialog presents an assortment of options.

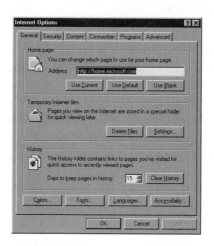

Take a look at the options available in the Internet Options dialog box, beginning with those found on the General tab (refer to Figure 22.20).

Changing Your Home Page

The first option available on the General tab of the Internet Options dialog box is to define your home page. This is the Web page that is loaded automatically when you start Internet Explorer or when you click the Home button in the standard toolbar. The address of your current home page appears in the Address box. To change your home page, you can type the URL for your new home page in the Address box, or you can click the Use Current button to insert the address of the Web page currently displayed in Internet Explorer. To return the home page setting to its default value, click the Use Default button.

If you click the Use Blank button, Internet Explorer displays a blank page when you start the program. If you use a dial-up connection to the Internet, selecting this option has the interesting side effect of preventing Internet Explorer from attempting to establish an Internet connection when you first start the program. Basically, it means that Internet Explorer automatically starts in offline mode. I use this setting on my laptop computer for just that reason.

Temporary Storage

Internet Explorer creates a lot of temporary files. Most of the Web pages and graphics that you view are downloaded and stored in a cache on your hard drive, and Internet Explorer accesses them from there. The files remain in the cache even after you move on to another Web page so that Internet Explorer can retrieve the Web pages quickly when you return to a previously viewed site. The size of the cache is limited, and the oldest temporary files are automatically removed from the cache to make room for newer files. Internet Explorer also uses the cache to store the Web pages it downloads for your channels and Web subscriptions.

The buttons in the Temporary Internet files area let you control the size and location of the folder Internet Explorer uses for its temporary files and flush out the cache when that becomes necessary. Click the Settings button to open the dialog box shown in Figure 22.21. The three options at the top of the dialog box allow you to specify how often Internet Explorer should check for the existence of a newer version of a given page before loading it from the cache. The current location of your temporary Internet files is displayed in the center of the dialog box. The slider allows you to specify the maximum amount of hard drive space Internet Explorer can use for its temporary files. Drag the slider left or right to decrease or increase the space allocation. Click the Move Folder button to open a browse box where you can select another folder to use as the cache for temporary Internet files. Because the cache files can gobble up a lot of disk space, you might want to move the folder off of your C drive and onto another drive. This can open some much needed hard drive space for Windows and your various applications. If you do decide to move the temporary Internet files folder, note that the change won't take effect until you reboot your machine. Click the View Files button to open an Explorer window where you can view the files currently in the cache. Clicking the View Objects button also opens an Explorer window, but this one shows the contents of the Downloaded Programs folder where the ActiveX Controls are stored.

When you want to clean out the cache and get rid of all the temporary files Internet Explorer has stored there, click the Delete Files button in the middle of the General tab of the Internet Options dialog box. The Delete Files dialog box appears so you can confirm your action. The dialog box has one option, a check box that allows you to delete all the subscription content stored on your local hard drive along with the rest of the temporary Internet files. Generally, you want to delete the temporary files from the cache periodically but keep the subscription content intact.

Figure 22.21.

You can control how much of your hard drive Internet Explorer can use for its temporary files.

History

As I mentioned earlier, Internet Explorer maintains a list of links to the Web sites you've visited recently. The History Explorer bar displays a list of those sites so you can locate and return to them easily. The History area of the General tab is where you can determine just how long links to the recently viewed sites should remain available. Set the appropriate number of days in the number box. If you want to flush out your history list and start over, click the Clear History button and then click Yes to confirm. Internet Explorer erases all the links in the History folder. Use this option any time the history list starts to get large and cumbersome—or any time you want to erase your tracks so no one can tell what Web sites you've been visiting.

Text, Background, and Hyperlink Colors

If you feel the need to do some redecorating, click the Colors button at the bottom of the General tab. This opens the Colors dialog box shown in Figure 22.22, where you can adjust the default colors for Web page elements. You can adjust the Text and Background colors in the Colors area on the left. Clicking either button in Colors area opens a standard Windows Color dialog box where you can click a sample color and then click OK to select that color. Although you can select the Text and Background colors individually, you'll normally want to check the Use Windows colors option to instruct Internet Explorer to use the same colors you selected for other Windows 95 applications.

In the Links area of the Colors dialog box, you can specify separate colors for hypertext links that you have visited and those that you haven't clicked yet. If you check the Use hover color option, you can specify a third color that IE4 will use to display a hypertext link when your mouse pointer moves over it.

Figure 22.22.
Redo your default color scheme for the Web pages you view in Internet Explorer.

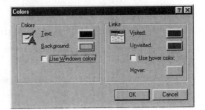

Fonts

If you want to change the fonts Internet Explorer uses when it displays Web pages, click the Fonts button at the bottom of the General tab to open the Fonts dialog box as shown in Figure 22.23. First, you select a character set from the list at the top of the dialog box. Then you can specify separate proportional and fixed-width fonts for that character set by making selections from the corresponding drop-down list boxes. You can also specify a default font size by selecting one of the five sizes in that drop-down list box. Select a character set and click the Set as Default button to change which character set Internet Explorer uses to display Web sites that do not request a different character set.

Figure 22.23.
If you're tired of the same old fonts, you can choose some new ones in this dialog box.

> **Note:** I'm skipping the settings on the Security and Content tabs of the Internet Options dialog box for now, but I'm not ignoring them. I cover those settings in Chapter 28 when I discuss security issues.

Making a Connection

Click the Connection tab of the Internet Options dialog box to display the settings shown in Figure 22.24. This is where you specify how Internet Explorer should make its connections to the Internet.

Figure 22.24.

This is where you specify how Internet Explorer should make its connections to the Internet.

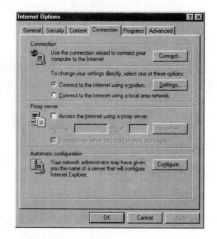

Clicking the Connect button reruns the Internet Connection wizard that you probably saw when you first started Internet Explorer. Generally, you only need to run the wizard once, but it's there if you need it.

Perhaps the most important setting on the Connection tab is the choice between connecting to the Internet using a modem or using a local area network. If you use a proxy server (a network server that controls access to and from the Internet, sometimes called a firewall) on your network, you need to check that option in the Proxy Server area and supply the appropriate Address and Port information. If, on the other hand, you connect to the Internet using a modem, be sure to click the Settings button to open the Dial-Up Settings dialog box as shown in Figure 22.25. This dialog box contains a number of important settings. The first, at the top of the dialog box, is the drop-down list box where you select the Dial-Up Networking connection Internet Explorer should use when making connections to the Internet. The Add and Properties buttons enable you to create a new Dial-Up Networking connection or edit the properties of an existing connection if necessary. Most of the other settings are self-explanatory. You can set the number of times Internet Explorer should attempt to make a connection and how long it should wait between each attempt; you can specify the user name, password, and domain to be used to log on; and you can instruct Internet Explorer to disconnect the modem if the connection isn't used for a number of minutes. If you want Internet Explorer to automatically update your subscriptions to Web sites, make sure you check the Connect automatically to update subscriptions option. According to the help files, if you check the last option, IE4 prompts you for your password before dialing your Internet connection. However, it doesn't seem to work that way.

It's possible to automatically update Internet Explorer's configuration by downloading information from a network server. If you have access to a configuration server set up by your network administrator using the IE4 Administrator's Resource Kit, click the Configure button in the Automatic Configuration area at the bottom of the Connection tab. This opens a dialog box where you can enter the URL for the configuration server and then click the Refresh button to update the Internet Explorer configuration.

Figure 22.25.

If you connect to the Internet with a modem, getting these settings correct is essential.

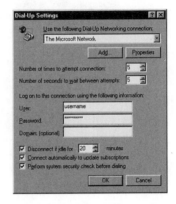

Links to Other Programs

Unlike some other browsers, Internet Explorer doesn't require a whole list of helper applications to display most Web site content. However, Internet Explorer does need to call other programs for major tasks such as handling e-mail. The Programs tab of the Internet Options dialog box (shown in Figure 22.26) is where you identify what programs you want to use to process mail, news, Internet calls, Internet calendar appointments, and your contact list. To choose a program for a category, just select it from the corresponding drop-down list box. These are the programs Internet Explorer calls when you choose commands such as Mail and News from the Go menu. You can also call the mail program by clicking the Mail button in the toolbar. Internet Explorer uses the same program to generate and send an e-mail message when you click a `mailto:` link on a Web page. If you check the option at the bottom of the page, IE4 checks whether it is the default application for viewing Web pages. If not, you see a dialog box when you start the program, giving you the opportunity to make IE4 the default Web viewer. Normally, this is a good thing because it allows you to quickly repair changes that may have been made by some program you recently installed or ran. However, if you have Netscape Navigator installed and a similar option enabled in that program, the two browsers end up trying to change the default Web page viewer setting back and forth every time you start the programs.

Multimedia and Other Advanced Settings

The Advanced tab of the Internet Options dialog box (shown in Figure 22.27) is misnamed. Despite the large number of options contained in its list box, most of the settings are not particularly advanced. In fact, it's easy to understand what most of the options do, and enabling or disabling an option is as simple as clicking a check box. If you're not sure what a particular option does, click the question mark in the title bar of the dialog box and then click the option you're wondering about and a pop-up description of the option appears.

Figure 22.26.

These are the programs Internet Explorer calls on to handle tasks such as sending e-mail messages.

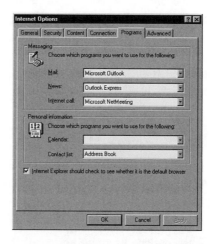

Figure 22.27.

Despite the large number of options contained in its list box, most of the settings are not particularly advanced.

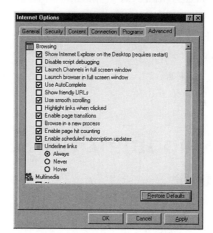

The options on the Advanced tab are grouped under several broad headings. Because most of the individual options are self-explanatory, seldom used, or both, I don't attempt to describe all of them. Instead, I just describe what kind of options you can expect to find under each heading and mention a few of the ones you're likely to want to change:

- Browsing: This is really a catch-all heading for anything remotely related to the process of Web browsing and the user interface of the Internet Explorer browser. If you prefer to view channels in a regular browser window instead of full-screen mode, you can clear the Launch Channels in full-screen window option. Be sure to check the Enable scheduled subscription updates option if you plan to schedule automatic subscription updates.

- Multimedia: The options under this heading allow you to select whether Internet Explorer displays graphics or plays animations, videos, or sounds. You want to enable all of these options to get the full Web experience, but you might need to disable some of them to speed up browsing over a slow connection.

- Security & Cookies: The default settings for the options under the security heading are appropriate for most people. The setting you want to pay attention to here is the Cookies option. You can choose Always except cookies, Disable all cookie use, or Prompt before accepting cookies. I address the cookie issue in detail in Chapter 28. For now, I just say that this is where you set the cookies option.

- Java: There are just two options under the Java heading. The first one enables Internet Explorer's built-in Java compiler. You want that option checked unless you have some special reason for shutting down Java programming. On the other hand, unless you're a Java programmer, you probably don't need the logging option enabled.

- Printing: The sole option under the Printing header determines whether Internet Explorer includes background colors and images when you print a Web page.

- Searching: These options determine how Internet Explorer handles searching for the domain name in a URL it failed to find.

- Toolbar: The two options under this heading determine whether the font button appears on the standard toolbar and the icons that appear on the buttons.

- HTTP 1.1: These settings control compatibility issues with older servers. You probably don't need to change them.

Understanding Browser Compatibility Problems

The browser wars certainly haven't done much for compatibility between the products offered by various vendors. For example, as this book goes to press, the latest version of Netscape Navigator still doesn't support ActiveX controls. You have to download a plug-in to do the job. (Most people add ActiveX support to Navigator using NCompass ScriptActive or something similar.) Using plug-ins might be an acceptable way to handle the situation from Netscape's viewpoint, but using a special plug-in for ActiveX doesn't do much for the user. Because the plug-in expects ActiveX controls to be incorporated into a Web page in a different way than IE4 does, you still can't view a Web page containing ActiveX controls with Navigator and Internet Explorer and get the same effect. The browser marketplace is constantly changing, and the next version of Netscape Navigator might add native support for ActiveX, and then again it might not. Only time will tell.

ActiveX controls are just one problem area. The browsers even differ in the way they handle certain HTML tags, which are the very foundation of Web page formatting. For example, Navigator implements plug-in support using a tag that Internet Explorer doesn't recognize. On the other hand, Internet Explorer supports specialty tags such as the background sound tag that Navigator ignores. Suffice it to say that testing every Web page using both browsers and then figuring out why one won't work with it is a major expenditure of time for Webmasters (the people who maintain Web sites). Do the problems end there? No, that's really only the beginning. There are differences in the browsers' implementation of scripting languages, such as JavaScript, and more. There are even differences between versions of the same browser for different languages or platforms.

Given the politically charged environment of software development, you can almost understand some of the differences in implementation between browsers. It's the differences in product strategy that have helped or hindered software developers from day one.

The very nature of the Internet supposes that everyone can use the information that a Web site provides—not just a fortunate few. Although it might not be possible (or even reasonable) to expect complete access to every site by every individual, it's important to make the effort. Unfortunately, browser incompatibilities make this nearly impossible.

Some Webmasters have started to handle the situation by adding alternate text to their sites. For example, if your browser doesn't support graphics for whatever reason, you might see some text that says that you'd be seeing a picture of a house if your browser could display it. This is a reasonable attempt to make the site more accessible to everyone, but let's face it: Seeing some text that tells you about the house isn't the same as actually seeing the house.

Another form of browser incompatibility repair by Webmasters is the "best when viewed by" icons that they're using. This little icon tells the person visiting a site that the site works best with a certain browser. It's kind of frustrating to view a site designed for Internet Explorer when you have Netscape Navigator (or vice versa), but at least knowing that there isn't a problem with your software is a bit of a comfort.

By now you're wondering what all this has to do with you as a user. It means that you're going to be limited by browser incompatibilities of all kinds until browser vendors start to adhere to standards. You might need to keep two or more browsers installed on your machine if you spend a lot of time on the Internet. (I certainly do.) There are times where I need the information that a site will provide, and if that means using a different browser, then that's the price to pay for the information. There's no magic bullet that will transform a single browser machine into something that can access every site on the Internet—at least not as of this writing.

Will this multiple browser situation last forever? I don't think so. Right now the Internet is in a state of growth. The various standards bodies are working to create new standards that address the needs people have expressed for content. Eventually there'll be a standard for VRML. You'll eventually see a standard for ActiveX (provided that Microsoft keeps its promise and releases ActiveX to a standards body). Netscape is planning on loosening its hold on JavaScript as well. If it does so before too many versions get released on the market, we'll probably end up with a standardized scripting language as well. Unfortunately, all this standardization takes time.

On Your Own

Install Internet Explorer 4 and then go online and look around. The default home page is usually a good place to start, but don't limit your choices.

Build a list of favorite Web sites. Don't forget to include Internet search sites such as Lycos.

Install several browsers on your machine to see how they work on various Internet sites. At a minimum, try both Netscape Navigator and Internet Explorer. You can download a free trial copy of Netscape Navigator at `http://www.netscape.com/`. Likewise, you can get a copy of Internet Explorer at `http://www.microsoft.com/ie/`. Make sure you try out some of the add-ons such as the sound-enhancing Real Audio Player (`http://www.realaudio.com/`) for both products. Although Navigator does make heavier use of plug-ins than Internet Explorer does, both products benefit from third-party add-ons.

23

Webcasting: Channel Surfing When You're Offline

Peter Norton®

Perhaps the most exciting new features of Internet Explorer 4 are the technologies that allow Web information to be "pushed" to your desktop. Until now, Web browsers have only allowed users to "pull" information to them from the Internet, displaying Web pages that have been specifically requested by the user. IE4 changes that by allowing users to have Web content sent to them automatically.

The new approach can help users take greater advantage of the Internet. In addition to familiar push applications such as stock tickers and news updates, IE4 allows anyone to take advantage of offline browsing. This approach allows users to peruse Web pages previously downloaded—say, overnight— enabling faster access of identified sites.

Understanding the Types of Webcasting

The push concept is not new. PointCast Network first introduced automated content delivery, providing news, stock quotes, and other information that gets displayed when the system screen saver kicks in during periods of inactivity. IE4 lets users subscribe to their favorite Web sites so that new content is downloaded at regular intervals.

What's more, IE4 (and later, Windows 98) introduces the concept of channels and the Active Desktop, which allows Web pages and information to display directly on the Windows desktop. Channels are services provided by a content provider that allow users to tailor information delivery. This chapter will help you make sense of these powerful new features.

Using Channels

The concept of channels might elude users who are used to clicking their way through the Internet. In a way, Microsoft's channel scheme is a bit like cable television, except that in this case, viewers must sign up for channels individually rather than in packages. To receive content from a provider, you must "subscribe" to a channel; once you subscribe, channels can regularly send updates to your PC, either at timed intervals or during periods of inactivity.

IE4 helps by presenting a Channel bar on the Windows 95 desktop for users who elect to enable the "Webified" Explorer interface. For those downloading IE4 to the Windows 95 system, the minimal browser-only installation does not include Active Desktop features. You must install either the standard or full installation versions of IE4 to work with channels that appear directly on your Windows 95 desktop.

Automatically Adding a Channel

Microsoft makes it relatively easy to access channels using IE4. Once IE4 is installed, you notice a set of small icons to the right of the Start button on the Windows 95 Taskbar. The right-most icon, which looks like a satellite dish, is the View Channels icon. To add a channel to your setup, just do the following:

1. Click the View Channels icon on the Taskbar. The Microsoft Channel Guide—essentially a customized IE4 browser window, as shown in Figure 23.1—opens.

Figure 23.1.

You find a list of available channels along the left side of the Microsoft Channel Guide, and the view pane to the right lets you browse content.

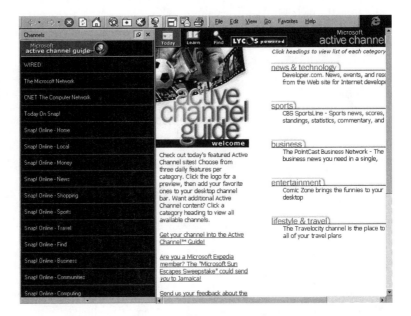

2. To view the content of one of the channels on the channel list, click the item you want. The viewing pane to the right (eventually, depending on the speed of your connection) displays text and graphics from that provider.

3. To subscribe to a service, right-click the item in the channel list and click Subscribe on the context menu.

4. In the Subscribe Channel dialog box, click the bottom radio button to have your system automatically download new content from the channel.

5. Click the Customize button. Click the top radio button if you want to download only the site home page and its links, or click the bottom radio button to download all the sub-scribed content. Click the Next button.

6. The next dialog asks if you want to receive an e-mail notice if a page is updated. For those of us who already get enough e-mail, thank you very much, click the No radio button. Otherwise, click Yes. Then click the Next button.

7. If you use Dial Up Networking to dial into an ISP, click the Dial in as needed radio button to have Windows 95 automatically dial in for updates.

8. Next, tell IE4 how often to download subscribed content using the dialog shown in Figure 23.2. By default, you are set to the Publisher's recommended schedule (which is not specified, unfortunately). You can also pick a weekly, daily, or monthly update schedule from the pick list. Automated downloads work best with always-on connections such as those on office networks, but Windows 95 can automatically dial in if you check the Dial as needed check box. You can also arrange for manual updates.

Figure 23.2.
Tell IE4 how often to
download subscribed
content.

Tip: If you use a dial-up connection, automated updates can pose a problem—particularly if you share a voice and data line for your Internet access. You might want to simply prompt channel updates yourself. Click the Manually radio button to tell IE4 to update only when prompted.

9. To customize the preset update schedule, click the Customize button.

10. In the Custom Schedule dialog box, shown in Figure 23.3, you can choose to optimize the frequency and timing of channel updates. In all cases, the check box at the bottom allows IE4 to move up or delay updates to avoid Web or intranet traffic. Click OK.

11. Click the Finish button to return to the Subscribe Channel dialog box. Click Next.

12. If the service you are subscribing to includes content tailored for the Active Desktop, the Channel Screen Saver dialog box prompts you to replace the current Windows 95 screen saver with one that displays content from the service. Click Yes to do so or No to retain your screen saver settings. You are now subscribed.

Figure 23.3.
Microsoft's preset
update settings make
a good jumping-off
point for creating
optimized schedules
of your own.

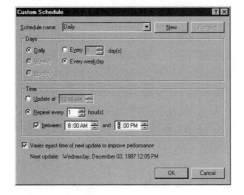

Searching for Channels

Channels are new to the Internet, so it's no surprise that they are being added all the time. For this reason, it's likely that the list in your IE4 browser will be missing the newest channel offerings from content providers. The Channel Guide makes it easy to browse the latest offerings.

1. Click the Channel icon on the left side of the Taskbar. The Channel Guide home page appears.

2. In the right-hand pane, click the topic you want to explore for channels.

3. The next page contains a list of seven available channels from which you can choose. To get a description of a channel, hover the cursor over the icon; a text description appears to the right. To see more channels, click one of the links along the left side of the view pane.

4. To preview a channel, click the appropriate icon. A page appears in the browser pane.

5. To subscribe to a previewed channel, click the Add Active Channel icon that appears in the preview. Some channels provide content for display on the Active Desktop. These channels provide an icon called Add to Active Desktop. Click the icon to add an Active Desktop channel.

6. You are presented with the standard channel subscription dialog boxes, described earlier in this chapter.

Using Channels as Your Windows 95 Screen Saver

You can also set up channels to appear as your Windows 95 screen saver. Doing this causes channel content to be displayed when your system is idle. Here's how you set up a channel to display as your screen saver:

1. Right-click the Windows 95 desktop and click Properties from the context menu.

2. In the Properties dialog box, click the Screen Saver tab.

3. In the Screen Saver list, click the Channel Screen Saver entry.

4. Click the Settings button to open the Screen Saver Properties dialog box shown in Figure 23.4.

Figure 23.4.

Assign one or more channels to display as your Windows 95 screen saver.

5. In the Channels list box, click the check box next to the services you want to appear on your screen saver display.

6. If you indicate multiple services, enter the number of seconds each should appear in the Display each channel spinner control.

7. Click the appropriate radio button to close the screen saver either on a mouse movement or with a click of the Close button. Click OK.

8. Set the standard Windows 95 controls for screen saver delay and power savings as desired. Click OK to make the new screen saver take effect.

Using the Active Desktop

The Active Desktop allows you to display Web content directly on the Windows 95 desktop. In effect, the free space on your desktop can serve as a portal into the Internet. Everything from sports scores and stock prices to breaking news can appear with your program icons, as shown in Figure 23.5. Better yet, this information can be updated automatically.

Caution: The Active Desktop feature is neat, no doubt about it. But the complexity of dynamic elements can result in problems with Windows 95 Explorer. If you notice frequent crashes or glitches when using Active Desktop, you might want to scale back on the number of active elements or turn off the Web features entirely. The easiest way to do this is to right-click the Windows 95 desktop, click Active Desktop, and then click View As Web Page.

Figure 23.5.

IE4's Active Desktop can turn your stale Windows background into a real-time news and information service.

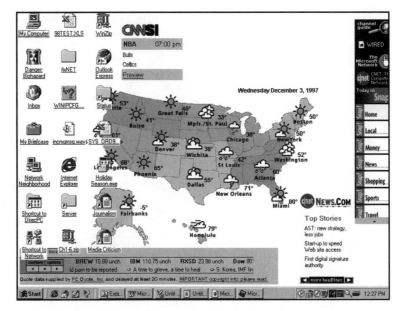

Adding Active Desktop Channels

Not all channels can exist on the Active Desktop. Providers must tailor their content for delivery on the desktop. How do you know what is available? When you are visiting a content provider's channel resources Web page, you see a standard icon called Add Desktop Channel. Clicking the icon initiates the configuration of an Active Desktop element.

To set up a channel to appear on your desktop, do the following:

1. Right-click the Windows 95 desktop.

2. In the Properties dialog box, click the Web tab.

3. Click the New button.

4. The Web sheet of the Display Properties dialog box appears, as shown in Figure 23.6. The list of subscribed Active Desktop services appears in the scrolling list box—with a check denoting those that are currently visible.

5. To add an Active Desktop channel, click the New button. You are prompted to search the Microsoft site for Active Desktop services. Click the Yes button to go to the Microsoft Active Desktop gallery, located at http://www.microsoft.com/ie/ie40/gallery/. Listed there are Active Desktop channels from a wide variety of sources.

6. Follow the instructions to browse and subscribe to Active Desktop content.

Figure 23.6.

The Web sheet of the Display Properties dialog box is your one-stop shop for adding, removing, and editing Active Desktop items.

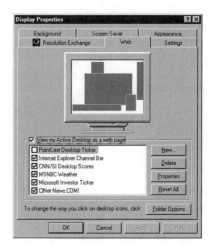

Managing Active Desktop Channels

You can tweak Active Desktop elements to suit your specific needs. However, custom tweaks are generally handled through the interface provided by the Active Desktop element or the related Web pages—not by standard Windows 95 dialog boxes.

Some things are common to all users. When you add an item to your Active Desktop, you see it on your display. To move it to a different spot onscreen, hold the cursor above the Active Desktop element. A gray border appears, including a slim header bar along the top. To move the item, click the header bar, drag it to the desired location, and release. To close an item, click the small x that appears in the right-hand corner of the header bar.

Likewise, you can hide Active Desktop elements from a dialog box interface. Follow these steps:

1. Right-click the Windows 95 desktop and click Active Desktop. Then click Customize my Desktop from the fly-out menu.

2. In the Web sheet of the Display Properties page, visible Active Desktop elements are denoted by a checked box to the left of the entry. To hide a channel, click the check box and click OK.

3. To reveal a hidden channel, click the empty box so that a check appears in it. Click OK.

4. The Windows 95 desktop reflects the changes.

You can manually update your Active Desktop elements so that they grab the latest data on command. Most useful for those with dial-up connections, manual updates are also useful if you want to grab the latest information between scheduled downloads. To update all your desktop elements, perform the following steps:

1. Right-click the Windows 95 desktop. (Make sure you don't right-click an Active Desktop element by mistake.)

2. Click Active Desktop from the context menu, and click Update Now from the fly-out menu.

3. Windows 95 pulls down fresh data for the Active Desktop elements.

Understanding Subscriptions: Browsing Offline

In addition to including various forms of channels, IE4 lets you subscribe to Web sites. Unlike channels, which represent a focused type of content delivery crafted by providers, subscribing is simply a way for your PC to automatically fetch the latest content at key Web sites. You simply have to tell IE4 which sites to download from.

Subscribing to Web Sites

Subscribing to a Web site is easy. With an Internet connection established and the IE4 browser open, perform the following steps:

1. Navigate to the desired site.

2. Click Favorites | Add to Favorites.

3. The Add Favorites dialog box shown in Figure 23.7 appears. Click the second radio button to be notified when the Web page is updated; click the bottom radio button to have the entire page downloaded to your hard disk.

4. Click the Customize button to choose how much content to download. The top radio button downloads only the selected page, whereas the lower radio button tells IE4 to download the page and any pages linked to it. Click Next.

5. If you elect to download linked pages, the next dialog prompts you to determine how deep into the links the automated downloads should go. Enter a number in the spinner control and click Next.

6. Click the No radio button to avoid being notified if a change occurs on the subscribed Web page, or click Yes to have an e-mail sent to your e-mail address. If you select Yes, you can use the Change Address button to provide a specific e-mail address. Click Next.

7. Now set your download schedule. You can use the pick list at the top to work from a daily, weekly, or monthly schedule. You can also open a dialog box for editing an existing schedule or creating a new one. The Manually radio button downloads pages only when you click Favorites | Update All Subscriptions from the IE4 menu bar.

8. If the site requires a password, click the Yes radio button, and enter your user name and password in the appropriate text boxes. Click Finish.

Figure 23.7.

You can choose to download subscribed Web pages to your PC or to simply get a warning that new information has been posted to the page.

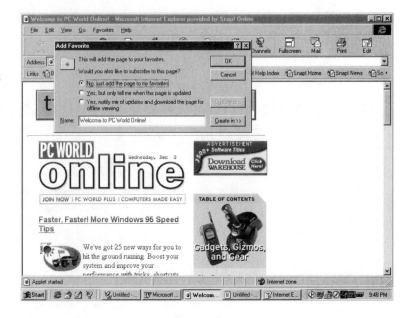

9. Upon returning to the Add Favorites folder, you can decide where to place this item. Click the Create in button to show a directory tree of favorite folders. You can create a new folder or decide to put your favorite entry in an existing one. You can also enter a custom description in the Name text box.

10. Click OK. The site is now subscribed.

Managing Subscriptions

You can change subscription settings by clicking Favorites | Manage Subscriptions from IE4. You see a list of all the subscribed Web sites, as shown in Figure 23.8. In addition to the site or content name, you see information on the last update, the frequency of automatic updates, and the date the subscription was established.

Basic Housekeeping

From the Subscriptions window, it's easy to edit, remove, and update your subscriptions. To remove a subscription, simply select the desired entry and click File | Delete. You can also right-click an entry and select Delete from the context menu.

To update a subscription from this view, click File | Update Now. You can also right-click the entry and click Update Now from the context menu. Remember, in some cases, downloads can take awhile because all the attendant graphics and binary data are downloaded along with the text-centric HTML.

Figure 23.8.

The Subscriptions window gives you a quick overview of all the subscriptions you've accumulated.

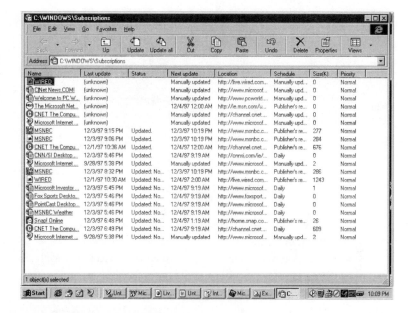

Editing Subscriptions

You find more features in the subscription Properties dialog box. To navigate this useful tool, do the following:

1. Select the subscription and click File | Properties.

2. Click the Subscription tab and you see information about your current setup. You can also unsubscribe from the page by clicking the Unsubscribe button.

3. Click the Receiving tab to set download characteristics. If you only want to be notified about changes, click the Only radio button at the top of the page; click the Notify radio button below it to download content for offline viewing. You can also get e-mail notifications of changes by checking the Send check box.

4. Click the Advanced button to reveal the Advanced Download Options dialog box shown in Figure 23.9. Here you can tell IE4 how far down to chase linked pages, using the spinner control to determine the number of links. Uncheck the Follow check box if you don't want IE4 to grab material from outside the page's Web site.

5. To prevent large files from being sent to your PC, uncheck the Images, Sound and video, and Active X Controls check boxes. You can also limit the gross size of downloads by clicking the Never download more than check box and entering a number of kilobytes in the text box. Click OK.

Figure 23.9.
You can take control of bit-bulky Web page downloads by deciding exactly what gets sent to your hard disk for offline browsing.

6. Click the Schedule tab to determine how often sites are downloaded to your PC. This sheet, shown in Figure 23.10, is nearly identical to that used to set schedules for channels, described earlier in this chapter. The exception: Checking the check box at the bottom tells IE4 to download the selected site only when the PC is not in use.

Figure 23.10.
As with channels, the Schedule sheet lets you tailor your automated downloads to suit your schedules and connections.

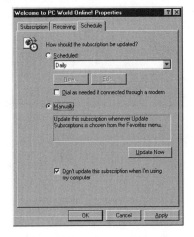

7. Click OK to save the changes and return to the Subscriptions window.

Browsing Previously Viewed Sites

Subscribing to sites can really speed up Web browsing by letting you access content that was downloaded to your hard disk earlier. To browse content offline, follow these steps:

1. Launch the IE4 browser.

2. Click File | Work Offline. A check appears next to the menu command indicating that IE4 is in offline mode.

3. Open the top page of the site you downloaded by clicking File | Open and finding the HTML file in the appropriate folder in your Favorites subdirectory.

Note: You can also browse through content in your History folder and Temporary Internet folder, both located in the Windows directory of your hard disk.

On Your Own

Go to your favorite Web sites and try subscribing to them by adding them to your Favorites folder and selecting an update schedule. Vary the specifics of the subscriptions to suit your needs for each site. Also set IE4 to notify you via e-mail when changes have occurred at sites with time-critical data.

Add Active Desktop channels content to your Windows 98 screen. Work out a roster of two or three favorite Web-based information sources that you want constantly on display. Stock and news tickers, sports scores, and weather reports are among the most popular.

Finally, get in the habit of browsing offline by having IE4 pull down data while you are asleep. Try this with a couple non-news sites because the contents of news sites may change quite frequently. Remember to click the Work Offline menu item when browsing data stored on disk.

24

Outlook Express News and Mail

Peter Norton®

Outlook Express may come as part of the Internet Explorer 4.0 bundle, but it is actually a stand-alone application for handling Internet e-mail. Designed to work much like Windows Messaging, Outlook Express provides tweaks for the Internet Environment; for example, you can choose both plain-text and HTML-based messages. Some of the file-encoding options are a bit easier to understand as well, so you can set a specific MIME type or use UUENCODE to send binary messages.

Users of Office 97 might recognize Outlook Express as the little sibling of Microsoft's full-featured messaging and scheduling application, Outlook. Although Outlook Express is a true e-mail and newsreader in its own right, it does lack many features provided by the Outlook application. For example, you won't find calendar and scheduling capabilities in Outlook Express, nor does it provide features such as task or contact management. What Outlook Express does provide is an effective set of features and a streamlined user interface for managing Internet-based e-mail and newsgroups.

Setting Up Outlook Express

You can launch Outlook Express in a number of ways:

- By clicking Start and selecting Programs | Internet Explorer | Outlook Express.
- By clicking the Outlook Express icon on the left side of the Windows 95 Taskbar. (It looks like a smaller version of the Internet Explorer "e" in front of an envelope.)
- By clicking the Mail icon on the Internet Explorer 4 toolbar.

The first time you start Outlook Express, you see a dialog box like the one shown in Figure 24.1.

Figure 24.1.
The first step in using
Outlook Express Mail
is to configure it.

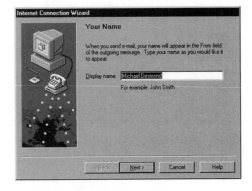

Tip: If you're a road warrior, you know one of the problems associated with using any mail reader when you have two machines: Unless you take special precautions, you never have a complete copy of all your mail in one place. Part of the mail appears on your laptop and the other part on your desktop machine.

One way to handle this problem is to configure your machines to allow you to read your messages on the road and respond to them but keep a copy of the messages on the server so you can download them to your desktop machine. Simply select Tools | Options on your laptop setup to display the Options dialog, select the Servers page, click the Advanced Settings pushbutton, and check the Leave a copy of messages on server option. Of course, the only problem with this solution is that you still don't see a copy of your responses on the desktop machine and your laptop doesn't contain a complete copy of all your messages.

There's another way to handle this problem; it's a little more complicated and isn't automatic, but it allows you to maintain a copy of all your messages and responses on both machines. Simply find the Mail subfolder under the folder with your name (or user name) in the folder where the Internet Explorer and Outlook Express data is stored. For example, the folder might be `Program Files\Microsoft Internet\Outlook Express\jdoe\Mail`. In this folder, you find a group of IDX and MDX files containing your mail messages. Copy these message files to the same location on your laptop when going on the road or to your desktop when arriving home.

To configure Outlook Express, do the following:

1. Click Next in the dialog shown in Figure 24.1 to invoke a dialog like the one shown in Figure 24.2. This is where you tell Outlook Express Mail your e-mail address. Usually, this is your Internet user name followed by the @ sign and then your ISP's domain name. For example, if your ISP is `msn.com` and your user name is Joe, you type `Joe@msn.com`. However, if your ISP has assigned you a different e-mail address, be sure to type it in exactly as it was given to you.

Figure 24.2.
The first step in configuring Outlook Express is to tell it your e-mail address.

2. Click Next, and you see the dialog shown in Figure 24.3. Here you supply the name of the outgoing SMTP and incoming POP3 server that you'll use for your Internet mail. When you sign up for your e-mail account, your ISP normally gives you a welcome kit that contains this information. Sometimes there are separate servers for incoming and outgoing mail and you must enter the appropriate name in each field. Other ISPs use a single mail server, in which case, you enter that server name in both fields.

Figure 24.3.

This dialog looks difficult, but it's simply a matter of knowing your e-mail address.

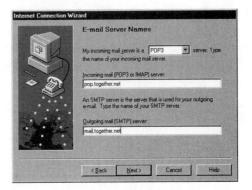

3. Click Next; this dialog (see Figure 24.4) asks for your e-mail account name and password. Usually, you can just enter the same user name and password you use to access the Internet. However, your Internet access and e-mail accounts are actually two separate accounts and the user name and password might be different. Be sure to use the e-mail account user name and password here.

Figure 24.4.

Now you need to provide your e-mail account name and password.

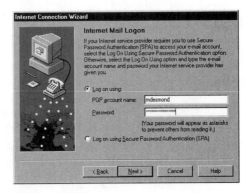

4. After you fill in your account name and password, click Next. Outlook Express prompts you to provide a friendly name for your mail account; essentially, this is a name that is easy to recognize and remember.

5. After you provide a friendly name, click Next to invoke the dialog box shown in Figure 24.5. This dialog provides three different ways to connect to your mail server. Because most of you want to create a dial-up connection, pursue that route.

Figure 24.5.
Outlook Express provides three ways to connect to your mail server.

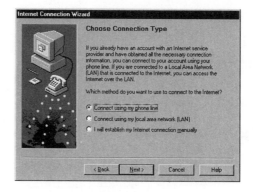

5. Select one of the three options. If you select the first option, Connect using my phone line, you also need to select a Dial-Up Networking connection. This is the same connection you used when setting up Internet Explorer to access the Internet via modem.

6. Click Next. At this point, you see a completion message. You're ready to use Outlook Express Mail.

7. Click Finish to complete the configuration process.

Figure 24.6 shows what Outlook Express looks like after you get it completely configured. You also find a few welcome messages from Microsoft in your Inbox. You'll find a lot of valuable information here, so make sure you hold on to the messages while you learn to use Outlook Express.

Figure 24.6.
By default, Outlook Express presents a splash screen that lets you jump to the program's many features.

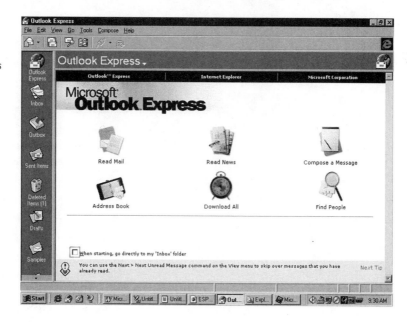

Tip: The first thing you should do is click the check box at the bottom of the Outlook Express splash screen. Doing so causes the program to launch directly into your Inbox, where you do most of your work anyway.

Using Outlook Express Mail

I begin by looking at how Outlook Express Mail works. At the top of the Inbox window shown in Figure 24.7 is a toolbar containing seven pushbuttons:

Figure 24.7.

The Inbox is the first stop for incoming e-mail in Outlook Express.

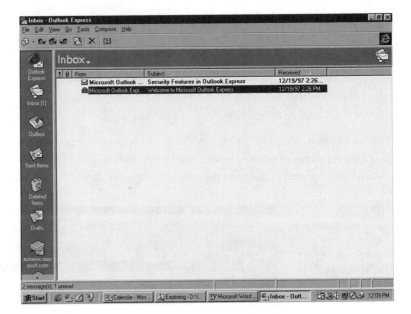

- New Message: Clicking this button allows you to create a new message. As with Windows Messaging, you can include files with your message. You can also set priorities. In fact, the message editor works much like the one found in Windows Messaging.

- Reply to Author: Clicking this button allows you to respond to an incoming e-mail message. This option sends the response only to the message author—not to anyone else listed on the message as a recipient. The author is the person who appears in the From section of the message. If there are multiple e-mail addresses listed in the From section of the message, your response is sent to all those recipients.

- Reply to All: Clicking this button allows you to send a response to everyone who received a copy of the original message as well as to the author of the message.

- Forward: Clicking this button allows you to send a copy of the current message to someone else. If you click this, you see a standard e-mail message dialog with the forwarded message at the bottom. You can add your own message to the beginning of the forwarded message. This option also allows you to provide a CC list.

- Send and Receive: Clicking this button allows you to send any messages in your Outbox folder. You also use it to receive any new messages from your ISP's mail server. New messages appear in your Inbox folder. I talk about folders later in this chapter in the section "Working with Folders."

- Delete: Clicking this button places the selected messages in the Deleted Items folder. If you're in the Deleted Items folder, this option permanently removes the selected messages from Outlook Express. This two-phase message removal system should help reduce the number of messages you delete by accident, but it's also a little more work.

- Address Book: Clicking this button opens your personal index of names and addresses. From the Address Book window, you can add new entries and edit and delete existing entries. You can also add information such as mailing addresses and phone numbers. You can send e-mail directly to an Address Book entry by right-clicking an entry and selecting Send Mail from the context menu.

Connecting to a Mail Server

All this doesn't mean a lot if you can't get online. Fortunately, connecting Outlook Express is quite easy, provided you've already mastered the intricacies of Windows 95's Dial-Up Networking or of your local area network setup. It's even easier if you are already hooked up with IE4.

Setting Up Connections

If you have a working connection configured, all you need to do is tell Outlook Express about it. Presumably, you already provided this information the first time you set up Outlook Express, but if your connection situation changes or if you want to add a second account that works through a different connection, here's how you go about getting set up. Most users use Dial-Up Networking, but Outlook Express can deal with a variety of connections, including LAN access and proprietary dialers. You can set connection properties from the Account Properties dialog box like so:

1. Select Tools | Accounts and click the Mail tab in the Internet Accounts dialog box.

2. Select the existing entry you want to edit, and click the Properties button.

3. When the Properties dialog box for that account appears, click the Connection tab to display the options shown in Figure 24.8.

Figure 24.8.
*Tell Outlook Express
how you want to
connect to your
e-mail server.*

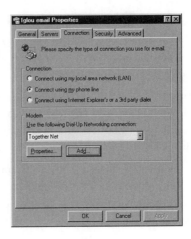

4. Select from the three radio buttons as follows:

- Connect using my local area network (LAN): Use this if your computer accesses the Internet over a LAN or another always-on connection.

- Connect using my phone line: Use this to automatically dial upon launching Outlook Express, using an existing Dial-Up Networking setup. The pick list item lets you select the dial-up setup you want to use.

- Connect using Internet Explorer's or a third-party dialer: Outlook Express assumes that you have dialed in manually before sending or receiving e-mail. Dialing can occur over Windows 95 Dial-Up Networking or via another dialer.

If you select the Connect using my phone line radio button, the controls in the Modem area are active. The pick list lets you select among Dial-Up Networking setups, whereas clicking the Add button lets you create new Dial-Up Networking sessions by launching the Windows 95 Make New Connection dialog box. Likewise, clicking the Properties button brings up the Windows 95 control that lets you edit existing connections.

Updating General Information

In addition to configuring your dial-up settings, you can also edit your mail network settings. For example, you can update general mail information like so:

1. Select Tools | Accounts, and click the Mail tab; select the mail account name you want to change and click the Properties button.

2. From the General tab shown in Figure 24.9, you can change the name of the active mail account by typing the new name in the text box at the top of the sheet.

Figure 24.9.

The General tab of the Internet Account dialog box lets you change information such as your user name and even the Reply To e-mail address that appears in your messages.

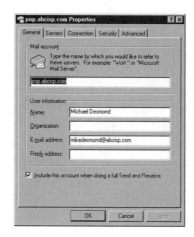

3. Update personal information by typing your name, organization, and e-mail address in the appropriate text boxes.

4. You can also specify a different return e-mail address by typing it in the Reply address text box.

Setting Up the Server

You can update the mail server from the Servers tab of the Internet Account dialog box, shown in Figure 24.10. If you find that your initial setup failed to make a connection, the Servers page can help you correct things by letting you change vital items such as your mail and pop server data, as well as your password and account name.

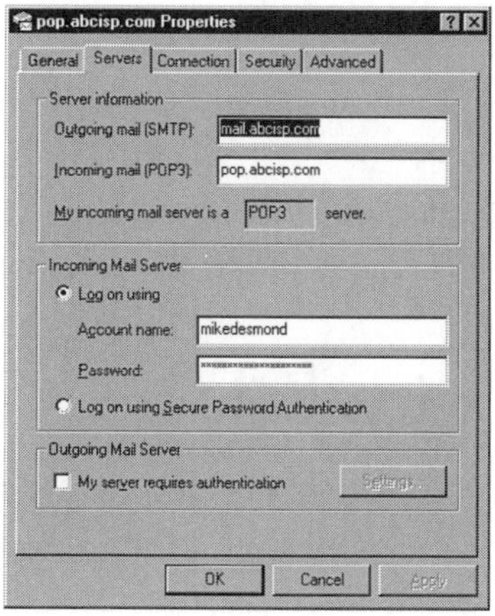

Figure 24.10.

The Servers tab can help you update important server data.

The following steps guide you through updating your server setup:

1. Select Tools | Accounts, and click the Mail tab; select the mail account name you want to change and click the Properties button.

2. Click the Servers tab.

3. To change the address of your outbound server, enter the appropriate name in the Outgoing mail (SMTP) text box. This often consists of the domain and suffix of your ISP, preceded by `smtp.` or `mail.`.

4. To change the address of the inbound server, enter the address in the Incoming mail (POP3) text box. The address is often the same as the one above it, although it may begin with `pop.` rather than `mail.`.

5. Finally, select the inbound mail server type from the pick list. In most cases, POP3 is the correct choice.

You can also change the account information for the selected server in the Incoming Mail Server area. For most users, you want to select the Log on using radio button. Below this radio button, you need to enter your e-mail account name and password in the appropriate text boxes. The password appears as a series of asterisks when you type it.

The Log on using Secure Password Authentication radio button sets up Outlook Express Mail to use a secure connection. If this option is activated, you might have to enter your account name and password when you log on with your ISP.

Finally, if your outbound mail server requires secure authentication, you need to select the check box item at the bottom of the dialog box. Then click the Settings button to open the Outgoing Mail Server dialog box. From here, you can select from the following radio buttons:

• Use the same settings as my incoming mail server: The default setting is pretty self-explanatory.

• Log on using: Enter the unique account name and password values in the corresponding text boxes, if needed.

• Log on using Secure Password Authentication: Selecting this radio button sets up Outlook Express to provide password access through a separate, secure resource.

Working with Folders

It's time to talk about folders—one of the items you use to organize your mail. Outlook Express comes with several basic folders, as shown in Figure 24.11. The purpose of each folder is as follows:

• Inbox: Receives all your new mail

• Outbox: Holds messages you want to send to someone else

- Sent Items: Holds a copy of the messages you send to other people so that you can refer to them later

- Deleted Items: Contains messages you've deleted from other folders

- Drafts: Lets you hold on to unfinished outbound messages that you intend to complete later

- Sent: Contains copies of messages already sent from the Outbox

Figure 24.11.

You get several basic folders with Outlook Express, but you can add more as needed, such as the Internet newsgroup folder that appears at the bottom.

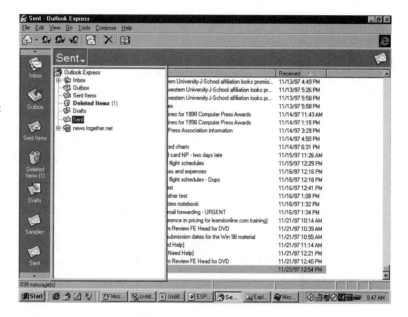

You can create new folders by selecting File | Folder | New Folder or by right-clicking a folder item along the left side of the Outlook Express window and then clicking New Folder from the context menu. In the Create Folder dialog box shown in Figure 24.12, enter the name of the new folder you want to create. Click an existing folder in the list box to tell Outlook Express where you want your new folder to appear.

Figure 24.12.

Creating a new folder is easy using the Create Folder dialog.

Creating folders lets you organize your messages by project. Better yet, when you finish a project, you can quickly clean up by simply deleting the associated folder. To do this, click the folder you created, and select File | Folder | Delete. Outlook Express doesn't let you delete its default folders. You can also rename your custom folders by right-clicking the folder and clicking Rename or by selecting File | Folder | Rename. Enter the new folder name in the Rename Folder dialog box and click OK.

> **Tip:** You can use project- or topic-related mail boxes to your advantage by creating a separate folder each time you need to separate a group of temporary messages. Outlook Express maintains two files for each folder you create in the `\Username\Mail` subfolder of the Outlook Express data folder on your hard drive. One has an `.mbx` extension and contains the actual messages; the other has an `.idx` extension and contains index information for the folder. You can simply move these two folder files to a disk or other form of archive device when you complete a project. If you need to look at the project messages later, just place a copy of the folder files in your Outlook Express folder.

By now you should be wondering how to get your messages from the Inbox folder to a specialty folder. There are a few ways to do it:

- Manual: Select Edit | Move To Folder, which displays a list of the folders on your machine. You can also select File | Copy To to leave the selected message in the current folder and copy it to the new folder.

- Drag and drop: Drag the item to the new folder and drop it there. If you hold down the Ctrl key as you drag, a plus sign by the cursor notifies you that Outlook Express will copy the message to the new location instead of moving it.

- Automatic: Select Tools | Inbox Assistant to display the Inbox Assistant dialog shown in Figure 24.13. The Inbox Assistant uses rules to determine how to arrange your folders. Whenever you get a message in your Inbox folder from the ISP's mail server, Inbox Assistant looks through its list of rules to determine whether the message meets certain criteria. As you can see, I've already defined a few rules in the dialog shown in Figure 24.13.

Figure 24.13.
The Inbox Assistant provides an auto-mated method for moving messages to the correct folder.

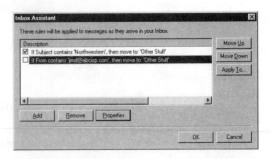

It pays to arrange the message rules in their order of importance because it can take Inbox Assistant some time to look at each rule. If a rule that you've just added will get used more often than others in the list, simply highlight it and use the Move Up button in the Inbox Assistant dialog to move it. Likewise, if a rule tends to be used infrequently, highlight it and move it using the Move Down button.

Notice the three buttons along the bottom of the Inbox Assistant dialog:

- Remove: Use this button to remove a rule you no longer need.
- Properties: This button allows you to edit an existing rule.
- Add: Click this button to display a Properties dialog like the one shown in Figure 24.14. Defining a new rule is easy: Simply tell Inbox Assistant what to look for in the message header. For example, you might want to send all messages from George to the George's Project folder. After you define what to look for, go to the Move To field and select one of the folders listed there. Click OK, and you see the new rule added to the Inbox Assistant dialog.

Figure 24.14.
Creating or editing a message rule is easy using the Properties dialog.

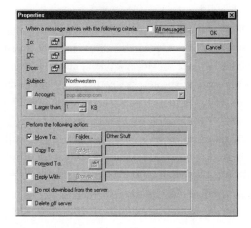

There's one more matter to cover. What happens if you want to keep a rule, but you don't need it right this second? Notice that there's a check box next to each rule listed in the Inbox Assistant dialog. If a rule is checked, Inbox Assistant uses it. Otherwise, the rule is ignored. Simply uncheck any rules you don't need to use for the current session.

Sending an E-Mail Message

After you install and configure Outlook Express, you want to use it to send messages. To do so, simply click the Compose Message pushbutton on the toolbar to open a New Message window like the one shown in Figure 24.15.

Figure 24.15.
The New Message dialog allows you to create messages for the Internet.

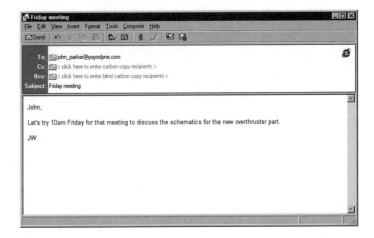

Take a look at the toolbar; it provides the features you use most often. The toolbar contains the following pushbuttons:

- Send: Clicking this button sends the message you've just created. You must define a recipient in the To field before sending a message. In addition, Outlook Express checks the Subject field to make sure it's not blank, but you can bypass this requirement by clicking Yes when Outlook Express asks whether you want to send the message without a subject. Obviously, you should make sure the message contains some kind of information, even though Outlook Express doesn't check for this.

- Undo: Outlook Express adds multiple levels of undo, allowing you to back up through many actions to the point you want. Its menu equivalent is Edit | Undo. Selecting Edit | Redo reinstates an action you previously undid.

- Cut/Copy/Paste: These buttons work much like they do with any Windows application. You can cut or copy information to the clipboard, and you can paste information on the clipboard into your message.

- Check Names: This is one of the nicer features offered by Outlook Express. Suppose you don't want to try to remember a lot of e-mail addresses when writing a message. All you need to do is type the person's name and click the Check Names button (or use the keyboard shortcut Alt+K). You see a dialog like the one shown in Figure 24.16 that lists the names Outlook Express found in your address book that match the one you typed. Highlight the recipient you want to use and then click OK; Outlook Express adds the full form to your message heading. If Outlook Express doesn't find the name in the To field, it gives you the option of adding the name to your address book.

Figure 24.16.

The Check Names feature allows you to use real names instead of e-mail addresses in the To field of your message.

• Select Recipients: Clicking this pushbutton displays a Select Recipients dialog like the one shown in Figure 24.17. All you need to do is highlight one or more of the names and then click the To, CC, or BCC pushbuttons as appropriate. Clicking OK places the names you selected in the appropriate fields of the message and closes the dialog.

Figure 24.17.

The Select Recipients dialog allows you to choose one or more people to receive your message.

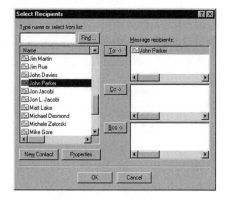

• Insert File: Click this pushbutton to insert a file into your message. Outlook Express opens a standard File Open dialog, which you use to select the file.

• Insert Signature: You can use this pushbutton only after you define a signature by selecting Tools | Stationery and clicking the Signature button.

After you've added a name or two to your recipient list, you need to type a subject for your message. The first thing you notice is that the title for the New Message dialog box changes to match the message subject. You can also define the priority level for your message, but not all browsers and mail readers support this feature. Just click the stamp in the upper-right corner of the message area. There are three priority levels to choose from, with Normal being the default. After you add some content to your message, click the Send button to send it. You see a Send Mail dialog box telling you that your message got added to your Outbox folder. It is automatically sent the next time you click the Send and Receive pushbutton in the main Outlook Express window.

Managing Your Address Book

There are several ways to gain access to your address book, but the two most common methods are to select Tools | Address Book from the main Outlook Express window or to click the Address Book pushbutton from the Outlook Express toolbar. The Address Book dialog you use to maintain your address book is shown in Figure 24.18.

Figure 24.18.
The address book helps you maintain a list of contacts on the Internet.

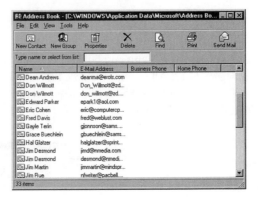

As you can see, you can create two kinds of e-mail address entries in the Address Book dialog. The first is a single entry, like those shown in the figure. Notice that this entry type uses a Rolodex page as an icon. The second is a group, signified by an icon with two people. Groups actually contain one or more of the single contacts that you create.

Creating a single contact is easy: Simply click the New Contact pushbutton on the toolbar to invoke the Contact Properties dialog. This dialog contains six tabs:

- Personal: This tab, shown in Figure 24.19, contains all the personal contact information for the new entry, such as the person's name and e-mail address. You can even add one or more e-mail addresses to the list. Notice that one e-mail address is designated as the default that you want to use; this is the address that Outlook Express uses unless you specify an alternative. You can specify a new default e-mail address by highlighting the desired address and clicking the Set as Default pushbutton. Adding a new e-mail address is easy: Simply type it into the Add new text box in the E-Mail Addresses area, and then click Add. Likewise, you can delete old e-mail addresses by highlighting them and clicking the Remove pushbutton. Highlight an e-mail address and click Properties if you need to change an existing entry.

Figure 24.19.
*The Contact
Properties dialog
allows you to add
entries to your
address book.*

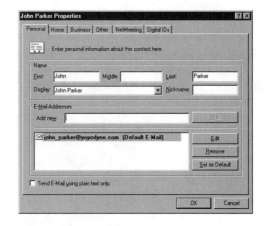

- Home: This tab contains all the personal information for your contact, including three personal contact numbers: home phone, home fax, and cellular. You can also enter the URL for a personal Web page. Clicking the Go button next to the Personal Web Page field enables you go directly to that person's personal Web page using your default browser.

- Business: This tab looks a lot like the Home tab. It contains three entries for business phone numbers: office phone, office fax, and pager. The Business Web Page field on this tab works just like the Personal Web Page field on the Home tab. Clicking the World icon on this page takes you to the business's Web page.

- Other: This tab, which contains little more than a single notepad field, houses notes about your contact. Suffice it to say that there aren't any fancy gadgets for maintaining contact information by date. You probably want to reserve this page for long-lasting notes and use a contact manager to keep track of current business information.

- NetMeeting: This tab lets you enter information needed to make Internet-based phone calls and conferences using the NetMeeting program. In the Select or Add New Text list box, you can select an existing contact or enter a new contact. This address is usually the same as the e-mail address of the user you want to contact. In the Conferencing Directory Servers area, you can enter the name of a server in the Add New text box. Here you enter the name of the server that is used by the contact identified in the pick list above.

- Digital IDs: This tab lets you verify that e-mail messages are coming from a valid source, using encrypted digital files associated with the sender's e-mail address. For more information about digital IDs, consult the section "Understanding Certificates" in Chapter 28, "Setting Up Security."

Return to the main Address Book window. You can edit a group or single contact by highlighting the desired entry and then clicking the Properties pushbutton in the toolbar. Getting rid of an unneeded entry is just as easy: Simply highlight the entries you no longer need, and then click the Delete pushbutton.

How do you create a group? Click the Group pushbutton, and you see a Group Properties dialog like the one shown in Figure 24.20. The entries for a group include a group name, a list of members, and some notes. When you send an e-mail message to a group, every member gets a copy.

Figure 24.20.
The Group Properties
dialog allows you to
create a group, which
allows you to send
one message to
multiple recipients.

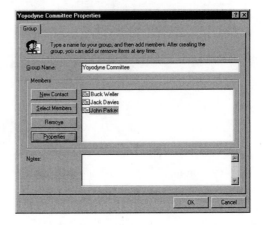

There are four buttons along the side of this dialog:

- New Contact: If you want to create a new Address Book entry and simultaneously add it to the group, click this button to open a Properties dialog box where you can define the contact.

- Select Members: Clicking this pushbutton displays a dialog box where you can select existing contacts or groups from your Address Book that you want to add to your member list for the group you are defining.

- Remove: If you want to remove a member entry, simply highlight the member name and click Remove.

- Properties: Highlighting a member name and clicking Properties displays the familiar Properties dialog box for that member where you can edit the Address Book entry.

Securing Your E-Mail Communications

E-mail can be sensitive stuff, but your messages are often open to prying eyes. Fortunately, Outlook Express Mail includes some security features that can help keep your private messages private. The most important security feature comes from certificates—also called digital IDs or digital signatures—which are used to verify the authenticity of e-mail transmissions. Obtained from a third party, the same certificate must be with both sides of an e-mail correspondence for the message to be readable.

To assign a certificate, double-click the user profile you want to update and click the Digital IDs tab; you see the dialog box shown in Figure 24.21. If a certificate for that address has been issued, you can select it in the list box and set it as the default certificate or remove it from the list. Remember: The person on the other side must first send you the digital ID to be assigned. Likewise, you need to send your digital ID to another party if you want to make use of this feature. Anyone without the digital ID file is unable to read your e-mail correspondences.

Figure 24.21.

The Digital IDs tab lets you select among digital ID files sent to you by another user. Otherwise, you can click the Import button to assign an ID file.

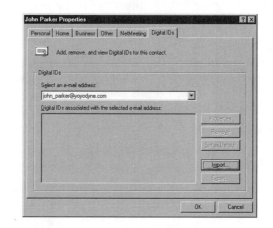

To assign a new certificate, do the following:

1. In the Digital IDs tab, click the Import button.
2. Find the digital ID file, which usually has a `.pub` extension. Click Open.
3. Select the digital ID in the text box and click the Properties button.
4. Click Trust.
5. In the Status area, change the item Not Trusted by Me to Trusted by Me.

Customizing Outlook Express Mail

Outlook Express can be tuned for your specific needs and preferences. You can alter the look of your e-mail messages, change the interface layout and elements, and even turn Outlook Express into your e-mail client for multiple accounts.

Setting Up Multiple Accounts

If you're like me, you have more than one e-mail account, forcing you to dial in to two or more e-mail accounts to retrieve your messages. Outlook Express provides relief by being able to call up multiple e-mail accounts. Assuming you've already set up your main account, here's how you add a second mailbox to Outlook Express:

1. Select Tools | Accounts, and then click the Mail tab in the Internet Accounts dialog box.

2. Click the Add button, and then click Mail in the fly-out menu.

3. Enter a name to identify the account.

4. In the next dialog box, enter the Internet e-mail address of the account you are adding in the E-mail address text box and click Next.

5. Enter the mail server name for this e-mail address. In the Incoming mail text box, you usually enter `pop.` or `mail.` followed by the domain and suffix of your ISP, such as `compuserve.com`. Similarly, in the Outgoing mail text box, you typically enter `smtp.` or `mail.` before the ISP information. Click Next.

6. Confirm that the information in the POP account name text box is correct (change it as needed), and then enter your account password in the Password text box. Click Next. If your provider uses Secure Password Authentication, you need to click the bottom radio button and follow the instructions.

7. In the Internet mail account name text box, enter an easy-to-recognize name and click Next.

8. Choose how you will connect to this account. If you usually connect using Dial-Up Networking, click the first radio button. If you are on a network, select the second radio button.

9. Click the Finish button to save the settings. You now have multiple e-mail accounts registered with Outlook Express. Click the Close button to close the Internet Accounts dialog box.

You can do the same thing with news accounts. In the Internet Accounts dialog box, click the Add button and then click News and follow the prompts to set up separate news accounts.

After you set up multiple e-mail accounts, you can check them all at once by clicking the Send and Receive button on the main toolbar of Outlook Express. The program checks the accounts one after the other, sending and receiving messages for each. If you want to access only one of your accounts, select Tools | Send and Receive, and click the desired account name from the list on the fly-out menu.

Tweaking the Outlook Express Interface

Outlook Express lets you adjust its interface to suit your tastes, which can help you save time if you tend to handle a lot of e-mail correspondence. Our first stop is the View menu item on Outlook Express' main screen. Here you see three commands:

- Toolbar: Selecting this option toggles the row of buttons on or off. If you use a laptop or have a small monitor, you might find it useful to remove the toolbar to make more space for messages.

- Status Bar: Selecting this option toggles on or off the status area that runs along the bottom of the Outlook Express window. Toggling this off saves space, but you lose useful prompts such as download status, message counts, and so on.

- Layout: Selecting this option invokes the Windows Layout Properties box, shown in Figure 24.22.

Figure 24.22.

The Windows Layout Properties box lets you optimize the Outlook Express interface to suit your needs.

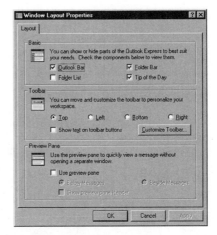

The Windows Layout Properties dialog box lets you dig a bit deeper into the layout of Outlook Express. Inside the Basic area, you can click the following check boxes:

- Outlook Bar: Toggles the vertical bar that uses graphic icons to represent folders

- Folder List: Toggles the file-tree representation of folders

- Folder Bar: Toggles the horizontal bar that displays the name of the currently selected folder

- Tip of the Day: Toggles the tips that appear at the bottom of the Outlook Express splash screen

The Toolbar area of the Windows Layout Properties dialog box lets you change the location and contents of the icon bar that, by default, appears along the top edge of the Outlook Express window. Selecting any one of the Top, Left, Bottom, or Right radio buttons moves the toolbar to the selected orientation. The Show text on toolbar buttons check box lets you display or hide descriptive text for each icon. Deselecting this check box shrinks the icons to save space.

More interesting is the Customize Toolbar button. Clicking it brings up a dialog box, shown in Figure 24.23, that lets you add, remove, and change the order of the toolbar icons. Simply select the desired items in the Available buttons scrolling list box, and click Add to have them appear in the Toolbar buttons box. (Alternatively, you can click a button and drag it over to achieve the same effect.) To change the order of toolbar icons, click the icon you want to move in the Toolbar buttons scrolling list box, and click the Move Up or Move Down button. Again, you can also click the item and drag it to the place you want.

Figure 24.23.
You can bulk up the Outlook Express toolbar with new features—or slim it down to fit in tight spaces.

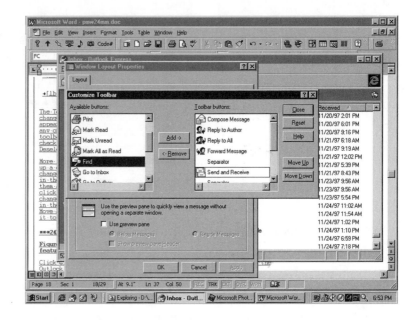

Click Close to effect the changes. If you want to restore the Outlook Express defaults, click the Reset button.

Finally, in the Preview Pane area of the Window Layout Properties dialog, you can change the layout of your message browsing window. Check the Use preview pane check box to split the main panel of the Outlook Express window into two panes—one for the list of messages and one to display the contents of the selected message. Normally, the preview pane appears below the message list, but clicking the Beside Messages radio button provides a vertical preview of the selected message item (at the cost of horizontal space for your message heading display). The Show preview pane Header check box lets you display more header information inside the preview area.

Selecting View | Columns presents a list of available and displayed column headers. To add more message header information, click the desired item in the Available columns list box and click Add (or drag and drop the item into the Displayed columns list box). You can also remove displayed columns by selecting the desired item and clicking the Remove button. You can reorder the displayed columns by selecting an item and clicking the Move Up and Move Down buttons (or by dragging them).

> **Tip:** You can reorder column headers simply by clicking a header and dragging it across to the desired position. All the related information for each message appears in the new location.

Making More of Messages

You can enhance the look and layout of incoming and outbound e-mail messages. Just be aware that others may use e-mail clients that do not recognize HTML-enhanced text, so you might want to avoid using these features extensively. Some enhancements that Outlook Express provides include the following:

- Using HTML formatting in outgoing messages
- Adding designs to outgoing messages
- Changing the font size and font type in your message browsing windows

Using HTML in E-Mail

HTML is the universal language of the Internet, and more and more e-mail clients are becoming compatible with HTML-formatted documents. You can add visual punch to your e-mail messages by sending messages in HTML format. To enable this feature in Outlook Express, do the following:

1. Select Tools | Options.
2. Click the Send tab in the Options dialog box.
3. In the Mail sending format area, click the HTML radio button.
4. Click the Settings button to change how Outlook Express uses MIME encoding of messages. You can also tell Outlook Express not to send images (such as backgrounds) with your messages to reduce messages size. You can also tell the program whether to indent existing text when you reply to messages.

When you select HTML formatting, your New Message box includes a horizontal area above the text window that includes icons for font type and size; bold, italic, and underline formatting; color; justification; bullet types; images; and links. You can use all these icons to add layout elements and items to your messages, as shown in Figure 24.24.

Figure 24.24.

Add color, fonts, formatting—even e-mail and Web links—to your correspondences via Outlook Express's HTML format support.

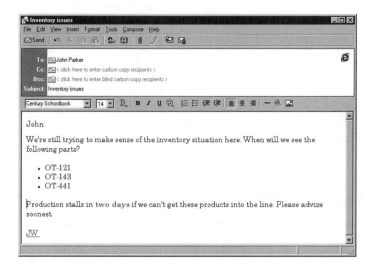

Caution: Think twice before heavily formatting your HTML e-mail messages, particularly if you are broadcasting to a large group of recipients. Not only do these enhancements boost the size of the message, but many commonly used e-mail clients still don't support HTML e-mail messages and are not able to make sense of the formatting. Those recipients end up seeing a mess of HTML tags within the text.

One neat feature of Outlook Express is its capability to create links inside your messages. Simply click the Link icon and enter the appropriate Internet address in the box. When the message arrives at an HTML-aware e-mail recipient, the user is able to click the link and go directly to the site using her default Web browser.

Using Outlook Express Stationery

Another neat feature of Outlook Express is the Stationery feature, which is a collection of pre-formatted HTML files that act as e-mail backgrounds for sending customized messages. To send a stationery-enhanced e-mail, click the arrow on the Compose Message button and select a stationery name from the list. To select from the entire list of stationery files, click the More Stationery item. The New Message window includes a graphic and text in the text area. To set a specific stationery file to appear in your message by default, do the following:

1. Select Tools | Stationery.

2. Click the This Stationery radio button and then click the Select button.

3. In the Select Stationery dialog box, select the stationery you want in the Stationery scrolling list box. A preview of the selected item appears in the Preview box to help you decide.

4. After you select a stationery, you can edit it by clicking the Edit button. Your default Web page editor launches with the HTML stationery file loaded. You can then make your changes and save the file.

5. When you have the stationery you want, click OK.

Tip: Can't get enough? Click the Get More button, and Outlook Express uses your default browser to hop onto the Internet and go to the Microsoft Web page that features a collection of additional stationery files. You can download these self-extracting files to your disk, or install them directly over the Internet. Once they are installed, you see a series of new files in the Stationery scrolling list box.

Changing Display Type

In addition to adding formatting to messages you send, you can change the way text looks when you compose and read e-mail. The easiest way to set the font characteristics is from a message window. To accomplish this, Select View | Fonts. From the fly-out menu, choose one of the following:

- Largest
- Larger
- Medium
- Smaller
- Smallest

The text in the mail message grows or shrinks to the new size. In addition, the text size in messages you compose also adjusts to the new size.

Using Outlook Express News

Outlook Express also offers a newsreader feature that remains largely unchanged from its predecessor, Internet News, except that it's now fully integrated into Outlook Express instead of appearing in a separate window as a separate application. The newsreader feature lets you read and respond to messages in a newsgroup.

A *newsgroup* is a public forum for discussing issues or for asking questions about a specific topic. One person begins the whole process by making a comment or asking a question. He uploads this information as a message. After you read the message, you can reply to it. A third person might see what you've written and respond to your message. Well…you get the idea. A series of messages forms what's known as a *message thread*. By reading the messages in a message thread in order, you can see a conversation.

Configuring Outlook Express Newsreader for Use

The first thing you need to do is configure Outlook Express for Internet newsgroups. To accomplish this, do the following:

1. Select Tools | Accounts, click the Add button, and choose News from the fly-out menu.

2. Enter the name you want displayed in your newsgroup messages in the text box. Click Next.

3. If necessary, enter your e-mail address.

4. Enter the name of your news server. This usually starts with `news.` followed by the domain and suffix of your ISP (for example, `news.compuserve.com`).

5. In the text box that appears, enter an easy-to-recognize name for this account.

6. Select the mode of connecting. Most home users need to select the top radio button to dial using their phone lines, whereas those on a network probably click the middle radio button to connect via a LAN. The third button lets you connect manually, whether through a third-party dialer program or another facility.

7. Click Finish to save the settings. The new account appears in the Internet Accounts dialog box under the News tab. You can click Properties at any time to edit these settings.

8. Outlook Express prompts you to download the newsgroup list to your PC. This can take a while because there are tens of thousands of newsgroups.

9. The Newsgroups dialog box shows a list of all the available newsgroups in the scrolling list box. To gain access to a group, simply select an entry and click the Subscribe button. Repeat as often as you want.

10. The newsgroups you subscribed to appear under a folder with the name you entered for this account. When you click a newsgroup entry, you see the list of postings for that group.

Note: Some people use false or modified addresses for newsgroups (the most common method of modification is to add an asterisk in front of your e-mail address). This tends to discourage some Internet users from sending junk mail to your e-mail address. The only problem is that it also prevents other people from privately responding to your message using e-mail. It also prevents the Webmaster from forwarding unread messages to your mailbox. The bottom line is that you must decide whether it's more of a hindrance to receive junk mail or not to get e-mail responses to your questions.

Connecting to a News Server

After you get everything configured, you're ready to connect to the news server. You could have just completed the newsgroup configuration process, which means that you have a Newsgroups dialog like the one shown in Figure 24.25. Another way to get here is to select Tools | Newsgroups to display the Newsgroups dialog. You use this dialog to change the newsgroups you frequent as your needs change.

Figure 24.25.
Subscribe to newsgroups by picking from the list that appears in the Newsgroups dialog box. The text box at the top lets you filter the thousands of available newsgroups.

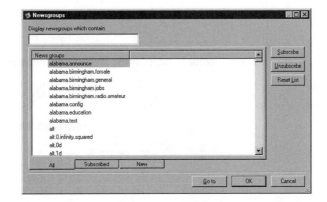

The All tab of the Newsgroups dialog shown in Figure 24.25 displays all the newsgroups that you can join. If you're a bit worried about finding a specific newsgroup in the thousands that Outlook Express downloaded, don't worry. There are a few strategies you can use to find what you need quickly. It shouldn't be too surprising to find the Microsoft-specific newsgroups in a section starting with Microsoft. In many cases, all you need is a vendor name or perhaps a good idea of what you're looking for. However, trying to find certain newsgroups can be quite a trick. For example, what happens if you want to find a special newsgroup for strategy game players? For starters, you can use the Display newsgroups which contain field to narrow your choices.

After you find a newsgroup that you think sounds interesting, click the Subscribe pushbutton to subscribe to it. After you do, you see a newspaper icon appear next to the entry. If you later decide that you don't need this newsgroup, highlight it and click the Unsubscribe pushbutton. Clicking the Reset List pushbutton downloads a new list of newsgroups from the ISP's news server.

You don't have to subscribe to a newsgroup without looking at it first. Simply highlight something that looks interesting, and then click the Go to pushbutton. Outlook Express downloads message headers from the requested newsgroup and displays them in a way that is similar to the Inbox you use to view e-mail messages. I describe how to use it in the next section.

I want to talk about the two additional tabs listed in the Newsgroup dialog: The Subscribed tab looks just like the All tab, except that it shows only the newsgroups you've subscribed to. (Subscribing to a newsgroup simply means that Outlook Express keeps the newsgroup name available for quick access; there's no fee or signup process involved in subscribing to newsgroups.) The New tab of the

Newsgroup dialog allows you to quickly find new newsgroups. It's a really handy feature; imagine digging through the thousands of available newsgroups to find the new newsgroup you need to subscribe to.

Viewing and Subscribing to Newsgroups

By now, you should have Outlook Express's newsgroup reader configured and have a few newsgroups selected. The main window looks like the one shown in Figure 24.26. Notice that I've already downloaded the headings from one of the newsgroups.

Figure 24.26.
The main window
allows you to identify
the current newsgroup
and see the headings
for messages it
contains.

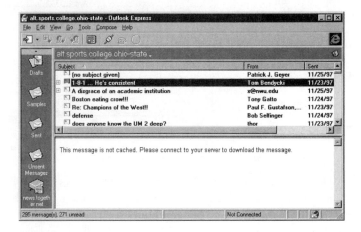

There are three sections to every Newsgroup window. The first is the Newsgroup drop-down list box, which tells you the current newsgroup name. The second section contains a list of headings for the newsgroup, which is a list of the message subjects you find in the newsgroup. If you've already read a message, the header text is unbolded and the yellow envelope icon to the left is replaced with an open letter sheet icon. The third section contains the currently highlighted message. You see the message subject and who it's from at the top of this area. The message text follows.

Like most Windows applications, this one includes a toolbar. The following list tells you what the various toolbar pushbuttons can do for you:

- Compose Message: Clicking this pushbutton allows you to upload a new message to the newsgroup. It's almost like writing a message to someone using e-mail, but in this case, you're addressing the message to a group of people in a public forum.

- Reply to Group: Click this option to send a reply for the current message to the entire group. In other words, you make a public response to a message that someone else left. You can use this option to ask for clarification of the previous sender's message, ask a similar question of your own, provide an answer to the initial message, or simply make a pertinent comment about the subject under discussion.

- Reply to Author: Sometimes a public response to a question isn't ideal. For example, the author might specifically ask you to reply using e-mail because he doesn't visit the newsgroup often. You might also want to use this option when providing personal information, answering a personal question, or providing information that the rest of the group isn't interested in hearing. I find that this method of responding is a two-edged sword. On one hand, you might spare someone embarrassment; on the other hand, you remove the rest of the group from the loop. Not only does this prevent other people from providing additional information, it's contrary to the very concept of using a newsgroup in the first place.

- Forward: You might occasionally want to make a colleague aware of some information you've found in a newsgroup that she doesn't read. Clicking this option allows you to do just that: You forward a message containing the message from the newsgroup.

- Newsgroups: Clicking this pushbutton displays the Newsgroup dialog (refer to Figure 24.25) that I described earlier.

- Connect/Disconnect: I'm not sure why Microsoft included two separate buttons, but there is one for connecting and another for disconnecting from the news server. Clicking the Connect button after you've already connected to the news server doesn't do anything. Likewise, you can disconnect only once.

- Stop: This button serves the same purpose here as it does within Internet Explorer: It allows you to stop downloading a message or message heading from the news server.

There is one additional piece of information you need to know: By default, Outlook Express Mail downloads only 300 messages at a time. To download the next 300 messages, select Tools | Get Next 300 Headers.

Writing a Newsgroup Message

Getting a message uploaded to a newsgroup is much like writing a regular e-mail message, but there are some differences. For one thing, you're addressing a public forum. You don't need to specify a recipient for your message because the entire group will look at it. I find it interesting that some people act as though they're addressing a specific person on a newsgroup, when in reality they can't. Make sure you always keep the idea of public versus private communication in mind when working on a newsgroup.

Take a look at a basic newsgroup message. Click the New Message or Reply to Group pushbuttons on the Newsgroup toolbar, and you see a dialog similar to the one for a standard e-mail message. The following lists the functions of the various toolbar pushbuttons:

- Post Message: Use this option to post your message to the news server. You probably won't see the message appear right away. Some Webmasters monitor the messages they allow to appear on the newsgroup. However, even if the news server posts messages without any

form of monitoring (as they do on most newsgroups), it still takes time for your message to
arrive at the news server.

- Undo: Clicking this button lets you undo multiple actions.

- Cut/Copy/Paste: These three buttons work much as they do with any Windows application. You can cut or copy information to the clipboard, and you can paste information from
the clipboard into your message.

- Insert File: Use this pushbutton to insert a file into your message. Outlook Express opens a
standard File Open dialog you use to select the file.

- Insert Signature: You can use this pushbutton only after you define a signature via
Tools | Options within the main Newsgroup dialog. (For some reason, there's no Options
option within the Tools menu in the New Message dialog.) You'll find the signature
options on the Signature tab of the Options dialog.

There are a few special features in your New Message dialog. Click the newspaper icon next to the
Newsgroups field, and you see a dialog like the one shown in Figure 24.27. This dialog allows you to
send your message to more than one newsgroup. I find it especially convenient when writing a new
message that could get answered by people on several newsgroups. Notice that this dialog defaults
to showing only the newsgroups to which you've subscribed. Click the newspaper at the bottom of
the dialog, and you see all the available newsgroups. Using the dialog is fairly straightforward. Just
highlight a newsgroup in the left list and click Add to add a newsgroup. You can remove a newsgroup
by clicking a newsgroup in the list on the right side and clicking the Remove pushbutton.

Figure 24.27.
*Click the newspaper
icon and you see a
Pick Newsgroups
dialog.*

Click the index card icon next to the CC field of the New Message dialog, and you see a dialog box
that enables you to select people who will receive a copy of the message through e-mail. This dialog
is identical to the Select Recipients dialog box invoked from the Outlook Express Mail toolbar. All
you need to do is highlight a user or group name and then click the Reply To or CC pushbutton.
I've already described the features of this dialog in the section "Sending an E-Mail Message" earlier
in the chapter, so I don't describe it again here.

Customizing Outlook Express News

Customizing Outlook Express News is identical to working with the Mail application. For example, column headers can be dragged to alter the order in which information appears in the heading window. Likewise, you can select View | Fonts to enlarge or shrink the type used in the message window. Selecting View | Layout launches the Windows Layout Properties box described earlier.

On Your Own

Install Outlook Express and configure the program to access your Internet e-mail account. Use it to send and receive e-mail messages. Start building address book entries for the people you correspond with.

Set up folders for each of your major projects and sort e-mail messages into those folders. Set up Inbox Assistant rules to automatically sort your messages as they arrive in your Inbox. If you're bothered by junk mail from a certain source, set up a rule to automatically move those messages to the Deleted Items folder.

If you've been using another e-mail client and decide you want to switch over to Outlook Express, check out the File | Import commands. They allow you to import e-mail messages and address book entries into Outlook Express from several of the popular e-mail client programs.

Configure Outlook Express to access the newsgroup server at your ISP and explore some of the newsgroups that interest you.

25

FrontPage Express, NetMeeting, and NetShow

Peter Norton®

So far, I've covered the Internet Explorer 4.0 Web browser and its Internet Connection wizard in Chapter 22, "Browsing the Internet with Internet Explorer." I used Chapter 23, "Webcasting: Channel Surfing When You're Offline," to cover channels, subscriptions, and Internet Explorer's new offline browsing features, and I covered Outlook Express in Chapter 24, "Outlook Express News and Mail." But I'm not through with the Internet Explorer 4.0 suite yet. In this chapter, I cover three more of the Internet Explorer 4.0 suite components: FrontPage Express, NetMeeting, and NetShow Player:

- FrontPage Express is a trimmed-down version of the Web page editor from Microsoft's popular Web site publishing tool, FrontPage. With it you can create and edit your own Web pages.

- NetMeeting is a real-time conferencing program that allows you to conduct audio and video conference calls, share applications, send files, and use whiteboard and text-chat programs over the Internet or a local intranet.

- NetShow Player is a viewer that allows you to play streaming multimedia content such as live audio and other events.

Working with FrontPage Express

You've probably heard about FrontPage, the Web site publishing program from Microsoft that's been making a stir among Webmasters. FrontPage Express is the "light" version of that same program, and it's available free of charge as part of the Internet Explorer 4.0 suite.

FrontPage Express is a WYSIWYG editor for HTML documents that gives you most of the standard features of its more powerful sibling, FrontPage Editor. It enables you to create Web pages quickly and easily, without getting involved with programming details. Of course, FrontPage Express does not include the site management capabilities of the FrontPage Explorer component of FrontPage 97, nor does it include advanced editing features such as the capability to create frames and GIF animations. Even with its limitations, FrontPage Express is a reasonably capable HTML editor.

HTML documents are used for many things these days, but their main use is as Web pages. FrontPage Express is included in the Internet Explorer suite to give you a tool for creating and editing Web pages. However, before I look at how to use FrontPage Express to create an edit Web pages, it's worth taking a moment to consider why you want to create a Web page in the first place.

Note: In addition to editing Web pages intended for viewing on the World Wide Web or a local intranet, you can use FrontPage Express to edit HTML documents that create the Web view for your folders. See Chapter 7, "Customizing Folders with Web Views," for details on customizing folders with Web views.

Creating Your Own Web Page

In Chapter 22, I looked at the Internet from a surfing point of view. I answered the question of how to get the most information with the least amount of effort. You'd be wrong to think that the Internet ends there. The Internet isn't simply about grabbing information. It's also about exchanging information and presenting your own point of view about issues that affect you most.

A lot of Web sites talk about everyday events and interests. For example, I occasionally visit a Web site for cat owners and another for one of my favorite television show—"Babylon 5."

Suffice it to say that creating a Web page doesn't have to involve a commercial enterprise; you might simply want to talk with someone about a topic of special interest to you. That's what this section is all about. I look at why you should even bother to put a Web site together and then take a brief look at how to do it with FrontPage Express.

> **Tip:** Building a Web page isn't the same thing as building an Internet site or even an intranet site. Some Internet service providers (ISPs) allow you to upload your own Web page to their server. The only requirement in this case is that you maintain the content of your Web site. The ISP takes care of the server and everything else needed to create the actual Internet site. Obviously, there are some limitations when you take this route, and you might have to pay for the privilege of displaying your own Web site, but most non-commercial users will find the costs low and the constraints minimal.

Why Bother?

Most people are fairly excited at the thought of creating their own Web site until reality sets in. After all, maintaining a Web site is a lot of work and the benefits (at least at the outset) are of dubious value at best. In addition to a lot of work, some Web sites are so poorly thought out that other people won't even visit them. The typical response at this point is: "Why bother?" Creating a Web site that no one wants to visit wastes the creator's time and doesn't do a lot to make the Web a nice place to visit. Some people never begin their own Web site because they feel anything they create is going to be a waste of time. If you're approaching your Web site with this kind of attitude, I have to admit that there isn't any reason for you to go forward.

You don't have to doom yourself to failure though. Creating a good Web site is as easy as thinking about it first. Ask yourself what you want to get out of the Web site you design and what you're willing to do to get it. A well designed Web site normally begins with some really great ideas. If you can't come up with your own ideas, talk to other people with Web surfing experience. Better yet, visit other Web sites that appear to contain elements that you want to include with your site. Seeing what other people do can help you figure out what you want to include relatively fast.

There's another good reason to visit Web sites: You can quickly learn what works and what doesn't. If you find that you get annoyed waiting for a Web page to download, other people probably do as well. How does the Web page look from an aesthetic point of view? Is it inviting; do you want to come back? How hard is the Web site to look at; does it include glaring color combinations? Is the text easy to read? (Hard-to-read text ranks high on many people's lists of places not to visit.) Asking yourself these questions as you visit other Web sites is about the best way to figure out what you want on your own.

> **Tip:** Remember that you can't assume anything about the computer that visits your site. Just because a gimmick or method of formatting content looks great on your machine doesn't mean it'll look great on a Macintosh. Some people get around this issue partially by saying something like, "This page looks best when viewed by Internet Explorer." A simple statement of the requirements for viewing a Web site might not win you any friends, but it'll reduce the number of hostile comments you get from people who can't use your site for whatever reason.

The bottom line is that you need to figure out what you want to do before you figure out whether a site is worth the effort. You may find that you have a lot more to offer someone than you originally thought and that building a site is a good idea. As the Internet gets ever bigger, it's important to offer as much as possible to the people visiting your site. The question of "Why bother?" should be a little easier to understand now. Most people take the time to set up and manage an Internet site because they expect to get something out of it. Whether that gain is in the form of new friends, contacts for a venture, information, or even monetary in nature is little consequence. All that matters is that you see the value behind the site you set up and convey that value to people who visit it.

Determining Whether Your ISP Provides a Free Home Page

Simply creating a Web page doesn't make it available for others to see. For that, you must post your page on a Web server. Setting up a Web server is a major undertaking, but you don't need to do it on your own. Normally, you rent space on an existing Web server that belongs to an ISP or Web hosting service. In fact, many ISPs include a small Web site as part of the package when you sign up for an Internet access account. These free Web sites usually carry some restrictions, such as limitations on the amount of disk space your files can occupy and the amount of traffic your site generates, but they are usually adequate for most personal needs. You may already have a Web site and all you need to do is post your page on that site. If you don't know whether your Internet account includes a free Web page, the best way to find out is to call or e-mail your ISP's customer service department and ask. The customer service representative can also supply instructions on how to access your site—the folder where your Web site files are stored on the Web server and the ID and password you need to use to access that location.

If you don't have access to a free Web site as part of your Internet access account, your ISP will probably be able to provide Web hosting service for a small fee. Another option is to check out one of the services that provide free Web sites in online communities in order to draw advertising. A couple of examples are GeoCities (`http://www.geocities.com`) and Metro City (`http://www.metrocity.net`).

Using FrontPage Express

After you do some preliminary planning for your Web page, you'll have a good idea of what you're trying to accomplish, what the page will look like, and where you're going post it when it's done. Then you can open FrontPage Express and use it to create your Web page. To start the program from the Start menu, choose Start | Programs | Internet Explorer | FrontPage Express. When the FrontPage Express window first appears (see Figure 25.1), it looks rather like a word processor with a blank document in the work area. In fact, it behaves like a word processor in many respects. To enter text into the blank HTML document you're editing in FrontPage Express, you simply type in the work area just as you do to enter text into a blank word-processing document.

Figure 25.1.
The FrontPage Express window looks a lot like a word processor.

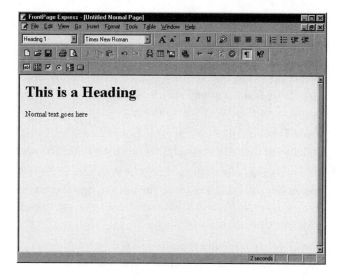

Tip: If you want to edit an existing Web page instead of starting from scratch creating a new page, you can start by viewing the page you want to edit in Internet Explorer. With the page displayed in the browser window, click the Edit button on Internet Explorer's toolbar. Doing so automatically launches FrontPage Express and loads the Web page you were viewing. Then you can use FrontPage Express to edit the page.

Tip: Nowadays, many word processors and other programs can save documents in HTML format. That makes it a relatively simple task to open existing documents and convert them to documents that you can use as Web pages. You'll usually want to open and edit those documents in FrontPage Express, but you won't have to re-create them from scratch.

FrontPage Express may not have all the bells and whistles of the full-blown FrontPage Editor, but it still has plenty of features for creating and editing Web pages. I can't possibly cover them all in detail in the space of the next few pages, but I can give you a get-acquainted tour of FrontPage Express that will give you a head start on your own explorations of the program. I start with the toolbars.

No doubt, many of the buttons on the FrontPage Express toolbars will look familiar; you've probably seen them before in a word processor or similar application. For example, the first ten buttons on the standard toolbar (the middle row of buttons in Figure 25.1) are New, Open, Save, Print, Preview, Cut, Copy, Paste, Undo, and Redo. These buttons represent standard commands that are common to many different applications, and each one does exactly what you expect it to do. On the other hand, the next four buttons of the standard toolbar are more specialized. They pertain directly to FrontPage Express's role as a Web page editor:

- Insert WebBot Component: Inserts a special FrontPage programming component into the Web page at the cursor location. You can choose from WebBots that allow you to include another Web page, provide a Search feature, or timestamp your Web page. For the WebBots to work, they require support software on the server. (You need to check with your ISP to find out whether the Web server supports the FrontPage Extensions that are necessary for these WebBots to work.)

- Insert Table: Inserts a table at the cursor location. You can specify the number of columns and rows in the table by simply dragging the pointer across a pop-up grid.

- Insert Image: Inserts an image into your Web page at the cursor location. Clicking this button opens a dialog box where you can specify a filename or a URL for the image you want to insert, or you can choose one among the selection of clip art images that came with FrontPage Express.

- Create or Edit Hyperlink: Select some text or an image and then click the Hyperlink button to open a dialog box where you can define the target of the hyperlink. You can choose from any available bookmark on an available page, specify an Internet URL, or type the name of a new page that you then create with FrontPage Express. After you complete the hyperlink definition and return to the Web page, the selected text is a functional hyperlink.

The next four buttons of the FrontPage Express standard toolbar are borrowed straight from a Web browser. They are Back, Forward, Refresh, and Stop. It should come as no surprise that clicking these buttons in FrontPage Express has the same effect as clicking their counterparts in a Web browser. The last two buttons on the standard toolbar allow you to show or hide formatting marks and to access the FrontPage Express help document.

The format toolbar (the top toolbar in Figure 25.1) also contains an assortment of buttons that look like they were taken straight from a word processor. However, in this case, looks can be deceiving. When you click a button from the format toolbar, the effect on the document you're editing will probably be similar to the effect the you get by clicking that button's counterpart in a word processor. However, be prepared for some subtle differences due to the characteristics of the HTML document standard and HTML formatting tags. When you make formatting changes in a word processing document, you are usually directly manipulating the appearance of the selected text to achieve the look you want, but you can't exercise the same degree of control over an HTML document. For example, when you format a Web document with a paragraph style, it's like giving generic instructions such as "make this a heading" and leaving it up to the Web browser to determine the exact text attributes to apply to a heading. Another example is text size. Instead of specifying a certain point size for text, you choose one of seven arbitrary sizes, such as "normal," "+3," or "-1." The user's Web browser determines what size text to use for "normal" and each of the six standard variations. FrontPage Express displays your Web page using typical implementations of your formatting commands, but you must remember that the page may look different when it's eventually displayed in a Web browser. Here's a rundown of the buttons on the format toolbar and what they do:

- Change Style: Assign one of the standard HTML paragraph styles, such as Heading 1, to the selected paragraph. Select a paragraph and then select the style from this drop-down list box.

- Change Font: Select some text on the page and then select a font from this drop-down list box. FrontPage Express displays the text in the chosen font. However, other viewers don't see the same font when they view your Web page in their browsers unless they have exactly the same font installed on their system. Theoretically, you can choose any font for the text on your Web page, but as a practical matter, your choices are limited to a few common fonts (such as Times Roman, Arial, and New Courier) that are installed on nearly every computer.

Tip: Microsoft is promoting an expanded list of standard Web fonts by supplying those fonts with Internet Explorer and by making the fonts available for free download from the Microsoft Web site. The list of Web fonts includes the traditional standards plus Impact, Comic Sans, Georgia, Trebuchet MS, and Veranda. You can download the fonts by going to `http://www.microsoft.com/truetype/` and following the links to the Web fonts.

- Increase Text Size: Clicking this button bumps the selected text up one size. Remember that text sizes on a Web page are defined as normal or as one of six variations from that normal and that the normal size in the viewer's Web browser might be different from what you see in FrontPage Express.

- Decrease Text Size: Clicking this button reduces the size of the selected text by one size.

- Bold: Select some text and then click this button to make it **bold**.

- Italic: Select some text and then click this button to make it *italic*.

- <u>Underline</u>: Select some text and then click this button to <u>underline</u> it.

- Text Color: Clicking this button opens a color selector dialog box where you can click a color sample to apply that color to the selected text. Note that this color selection doesn't apply to the color of hyperlinks. Hyperlink colors are controlled from the Page Properties dialog box (I explain the Page Properties options in a moment.)

- Left Align: Aligns the selected text with the left margin. Note that this applies to the entire paragraph.

- Center Align: Aligns the selected text with the center of the browser's viewing window (or with the center of the table cell). Note that I didn't say the text is aligned to the center of the page because the page size of a Web page varies to fit within the browser's viewing window.

- Right Align: Aligns the selected text with the right margin.

- Numbered List: To use this formatting option, you normally select several paragraphs and then click the button to transform them into a numbered list. The browser automatically indents the paragraphs and adds sequential numbers.

- Bulleted List: To create a bulleted list, select several paragraphs of normal text and then click this button. Like a numbered list, the browser automatically indents the paragraphs and adds a bullet in front of each one.

- Decrease Indent: Move an indented paragraph one notch back to the left toward the left margin.

- Increase Indent: Click this button to indent a paragraph one notch from the left margin. Click again to increase the indent distance. You can adjust how far a paragraph is indented by indenting it a number of steps, but you can't control the size of those steps.

The forms toolbar (the short, bottom toolbar in Figure 25.1) gives you the tools you need to create onscreen forms for collecting information from visitors to your Web site. Clicking one of these buttons places a box containing the corresponding form element on your Web page at the cursor position. Then you can type a text label beside the form element. After you place a form element on the page, you need to right-click it and choose Form Properties, Form Field Validation, or Form Field Properties to open dialog boxes where you can specify form handling instructions and define such things as default values for a field. (If you're not familiar with HTML forms, you need to refer to a good HTML book, such as *Teach Yourself HTML 3.2 in 24 Hours* written by Dick Oliver and published by Sams Publishing. The topic is beyond the scope of this book and the FrontPage Express help documents don't shed much light on the matter.)

- One-Line Text Box: As its name implies, this button inserts a one-line text entry box into the form. You can stretch or shrink the text box horizontally.

- Scrolling Text Box: If you need a larger text entry area on your form, this is the button to use.

- Checkbox: Inserts a simple check box that users can check or clear to indicate yes and no answers.

- Radio Button: Inserts a single radio button into the form. Normally you add two or more buttons in a column to give the user a choice of one of several options. FrontPage Express automatically groups adjacent radio button objects together.

- Drop-Down Menu: Inserts a drop-down list box into your form. You definitely have to edit the properties of this form element to define the menu items that appear on the drop-down list.

- Push Button: Inserts a button into your form that users can click to perform a task such as submitting the data on the form or resetting form fields to their default values.

Note: Although FrontPage Express can easily create Web pages that include HTML forms, you might not be able to use those forms on your Web site unless the Web server provides the necessary support services to collect and process the data that Web visitors enter into your forms. Be sure to check with your Web posting service to find out if you can use forms on your Web site before you invest the time and effort in developing forms.

FrontPage Express toolbar buttons give you ready access to almost all the commands you need to create a Web page. However, one notable exception is the important ability to define such characteristics of the page as the background color, background image, left margin, and so on. For that, you need to choose File | Page Properties from the menu to open the Page Properties dialog box shown in Figure 25.2. As you can see in the figure, the General tab is where you define the page title and other details such as base location, HTML encoding, and background sound. The Background tab allows you to define a background or watermark image and colors for the background, text, and hyperlinks. The Margins tab allows you to specify the top and left margins for the page. The Custom tab is where you can specify system variables and user variables for the page.

Figure 25.2.
The tabs of this dialog box enable you to define background effects and other characteristics of the page.

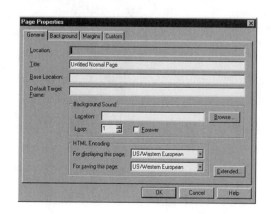

Warning: The Background Sound setting only works when you view the pages you create in Internet Explorer. Netscape navigator doesn't recognize the <BGSOUND> tag that FrontPage Express uses to define the background sound.

After you create a Web page in FrontPage Express, you'll want to save it and share with others. Naturally, you click the Save button or choose File | Save As from the menu. FrontPage Express responds by beginning the process of saving your Web page—but that process might include a few surprises. I know it surprised me the first time I used it. If you're like me, you probably expect the Save command to have the effect of saving the current document on your hard drive. However, FrontPage Express seems to operate on the premise that the HTML documents you create with the program are destined to become Web pages on a Web server. The default action for the Save command is to first open the Save As dialog box shown in Figure 25.3, and then, when you enter the Page Title and the Page Location and click the OK button, FrontPage Express initiates an Internet connection and launches the Web Publishing wizard. As you step through the pages of the Web Publishing wizard (see Figure 25.4), the wizard gathers the information it needs to log on to your Web server and post your Web page and all its accompanying images and other files to your Web site.

Figure 25.3.
Supplying an appropriate title is an essential part of saving a Web page.

Figure 25.4.
The Web Publishing wizard prompts you for the information it needs to automatically post your Web page on the server.

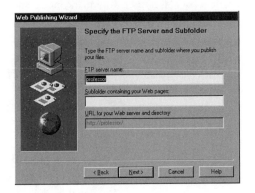

When the Web Publishing wizard works, it's great. However, not all ISP Web servers are compatible with the Web Publishing wizard, so the wizard isn't always a reliable way to publish your Web pages. If the Web Publishing wizard doesn't work, you can save your Web pages as HTML files on the hard drive and then manually copy those files to the Web server. Fortunately, it's easy (but not very obvious) to save your FrontPage Express document as a file instead of posting it directly to the Web server. All you have to do is click the As File button in the Save As dialog box (refer to Figure 25.3) to open a more traditional Save As File dialog box where you can select a folder, specify a filename, and click the Save button to save your work as an HTML document.

Working with Microsoft NetMeeting

Online conferencing is becoming more than just a convenience. Many companies are looking to this solution to reduce their business travel costs. I look at the Microsoft solution to this problem, NetMeeting, in this section of the chapter.

Tip: There isn't any need to limit the use of NetMeeting to the Internet. You can also use it to hold meetings over the intranet in a company setting; no longer will people feel left out as they strain to see what's going on from the last row of the meeting room. You can also use NetMeeting for training purposes. A company training specialist can hold company-wide training where anyone can join in. This is a lot better than limiting the number of people trained to the size of a meeting room. Another use of NetMeeting is as a device for brainstorming sessions. Rather than wait until you can get everyone together for a formal meeting, you can discuss an idea with a few colleagues while the idea is fresh in your mind. In essence, you can use NetMeeting anywhere you can use a standard meeting room. The only difference is that it's more convenient for everyone concerned.

Like most software in this category, NetMeeting is still more fluff than substance. The technology is not yet robust enough to replace personal face-to-face contact in many cases. However, I find that NetMeeting is an outstanding tool in some situations. For example, if you have a meeting where everyone needs to provide some form of input, NetMeeting may actually be a better solution than a face-to-face meeting. Consider the possibilities for a moment. No one will feel inhibited because of the public nature of the meeting, and you'll find that people participate better when they can actually see what's happening. Whether online meeting software will serve your company's needs is not the issue here. You need to decide that issue for yourself. What I look at are some basic usage techniques for reducing the NetMeeting learning curve.

Getting Set Up

NetMeeting is part of the suite of programs Microsoft distributes with Internet Explorer 4.0. The program is also available for free download from the Microsoft Web site at `http://www.microsoft.com/netmeeting/`. Even if you obtained and installed a copy of NetMeeting with Internet Explorer or Windows 95, you should check out the Web site to see if a newer version is available. (As of this writing, the current version is already up to 2.1, which is a minor upgrade from the 2.0 version that shipped with Internet Explorer 4.0.) Installing the program (or upgrade) is easy; you just download the setup program from the Microsoft Web site and then double-click its icon to run it. The installation wizard takes care of the rest.

To start NetMeeting, choose Start | Programs | Microsoft NetMeeting. The first time you use NetMeeting, you'll need to provide some configuration information to get the program set up and operating properly. The Microsoft NetMeeting wizard (see Figure 25.5) starts automatically and, as you step through its various pages, the wizard prompts you for all the information and choices you need to provide.

Figure 25.5.
NetMeeting
automatically starts
the configuration
wizard the first time
you start it.

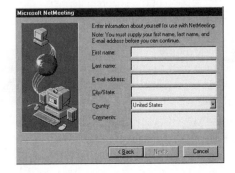

Here's a summary of the information you need to supply during the setup process:

- Select a user locator service directory server. The wizard gives you the option of automatically logging on to a directory server when you start NetMeeting and asks you to select the directory server you want to use. You need to decide if you want to be part of a user location service—an online directory of NetMeeting users who are available for conferences. If you're only using NetMeeting for conferencing with coworkers within your local network, then it might not be important to join a user location service (ULS) because you'll probably know the addresses of the folks you need to call. On the other hand, if you're using NetMeeting as a company approach to meeting with individuals from a variety of places (including other companies), it makes sense to use this service. Your system administrators may have set up a ULS for NetMeeting users on your network. If so, they can provide you with the address. Otherwise, you can select one of the public ULS providers listed in the wizard.

- Enter identifying information about yourself. You supply the information NetMeeting and the user locator service directory use to identify you to other NetMeeting users so that you can establish connections and converse with other people. As a minimum, you have to provide your first name, last name, and e-mail address. I suggest filling out all the entries (City, State, Country, and Comments) so you don't have to do it during long distance meetings in the future. You can elect to have your personal information listed in a personal, business, or adults-only category.

Tip: You can use the Comments field in your personal information for a variety of purposes. Two of the more important items you can include are your position within the company and the department you work for. Coming up with a standard approach to using this field companywide will make it even more useful.

Tip: When you install NetMeeting is a good time to check the status of your audio drivers. NetMeeting uses full-duplex audio. (Both parties can talk simultaneously.) However, some vendors such as Creative Labs didn't have duplex audio capabilities built into their drivers at the time Windows 95 OSR2 was released. This means that you'll experience problems using the NetMeeting voice call capability with some sound boards such as Sound Blaster. Fortunately, you can download updated drivers for most sound boards from the vendor. For example, Creative Labs makes updated, full-duplex drivers available at `http://www.creativelabs.com`.

- Select the modem or connection speed. The speed of your modem or network connection affects the amount of data it can transfer. Even though audio compression algorithms have improved, the speed of your modem still affects the quality of the sound that you hear. (It also affects the quality of the sound you send to the other party and the speed of the connection as a whole.) The lowest speed modem you can use with NetMeeting is 14.4Kbps. The program works best over a local area network.

- Run the Audio Tuning wizard. The NetMeeting setup wizard automatically runs the Audio Tuning wizard. (It's also available within NetMeeting so you can retune your audio settings as needed.) The Audio Tuning wizard allows you to set your speaker volume, and then it asks you to read into your microphone as it adjusts the record volume to an optimum setting. (See Figure 25.6.)

Figure 25.6.
The Audio Tuning wizard automatically adjusts your microphone volume as you read a sample sentence.

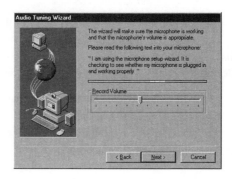

After you complete the initial setup, the wizard runs NetMeeting and you are ready to begin conferencing. The next time you start NetMeeting, you don't have to repeat the setup with the configuration wizard; instead, NetMeeting starts immediately. If you elected to log on to a directory server when you start NetMeeting, the program automatically connects to the Internet, adds your listing to the directory server, and begins downloading information about other users listed on the server.

Using NetMeeting with the Company Intranet

I don't see the Internet as the first place you'll use NetMeeting; the speed at which we communicate right now is just a little too slow to get the high-quality connection that people expect. (This isn't to say that at least some people will use NetMeeting on the Internet occasionally.) The first place I see this tool used is on an intranet or LAN. It doesn't actually matter where you use NetMeeting; the usage details are the same.

Begin by creating a simple conversation. Several people in the same company need to discuss a project, but there aren't any meeting rooms available at the moment. Each person has his or her copy of NetMeeting running, so calling someone over the company LAN isn't a problem. All you need to do is click the Call button (telephone icon) in NetMeeting's toolbar and enter the name of the machine you want to call in the dialog box that appears. When you receive a call, you see a dialog like the one shown in Figure 25.7.

Figure 25.7.
Receiving or making a call is the first step in establishing contact with another person.

At this point, you decide whether to accept the call. If you do accept the call, the NetMeeting display shows who is involved in the meeting as shown in Figure 25.8. The initial connection is usually audio, although a video connection is possible as well if the participants have digital video cameras installed. (Notice the video box beside the list of participants.)

If there are just two people connected in a NetMeeting call, you are able to talk to each other freely. However, audio connections are possible only between two conference participants. Additional people can join the call and participate in other conferencing features, but you can maintain an audio (and video) connection to only one other participant at a time.

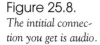

Figure 25.8.

The intitial connection you get is audio.

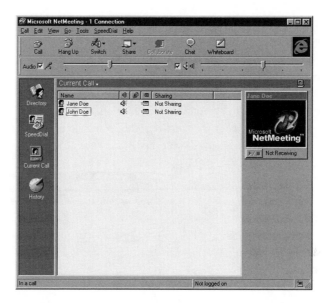

Talking with someone on an audio link through your computer can be interesting at first, but you'll soon realize that a telephone call is more convenient and you'll definitely get better sound quality from a telephone connection as well. That's where some of the other features of NetMeeting come into play. Before I go much further, I want to introduce you to the toolbar buttons and other features of the NetMeeting window:

- Call: Click this button to initiate a NetMeeting call with another user.
- Hang Up: Use this option to stop your participation in the current meeting.
- Switch: This button allows you to switch your audio and video connection to another conference participant.
- Share: I show you how this feature works in a few seconds. Essentially, it allows you to share an application running on your computer with other conference participants. That doesn't necessarily mean though that other people get to actually use the application, but they can see it on their own screens. I really like this feature because it makes it a snap for a company training expert to put on a live demonstration of how to perform a task—and simultaneously share it with trainees throughout the company.
- Collaborate: This button works with the Share Application option. It allows you to open your shared applications so that other conference participants can take over and use your shared applications by remote control. You can also use the button to stop collaboration.

- Chat: The Chat feature allows you to communicate with other conference participants via typed messages. When you click the Chat button, it opens a Chat window like the one shown in Figure 25.9. You type in the text box at the bottom of the window and when you press Enter, your message appears in the Chat window on the other conference participant's screens. Sure, it's not as handy as talking, but everyone can participate instead of being limited to one-on-one conversations as with the audio feature. Also, Chat uses a lot less bandwidth, so you can keep Chat going along with shared applications and other features without slowing down everything to a snail's pace.

Figure 25.9.
The Chat dialog allows you to type conversations to each other.

Tip: One way that the Chat feature actually works better than voice communication is when it comes time to create minutes for a meeting. If you use the Chat feature, the meeting notes are already typed. I can guarantee they are more accurate and in depth than meeting notes that rely on voice communication as well.

- Whiteboard: Every meeting needs some place for people to draw out their ideas. That's what the whiteboard is for. Clicking this button displays a whiteboard similar to the one shown in Figure 25.10. Notice that you get a full set of drawing tools, including the normal circle and square drawing tools. Just so you don't get this confused with a regular drawing program, it also includes things such as a highlighter. One of the features I really like is the remote pointer. It looks like a great big pointing hand. You can use it to point at things on the whiteboard in a way that everyone can see.
- Audio: This toolbar contains controls for your microphone and speakers. You can use the check boxes to turn off and on the microphone or speakers. The sliders let you adjust the volume.

In addition to the toolbar controls, there's a navigation bar located along the left side of the NetMeeting window. The icons in the navigation bar let you select what you want NetMeeting to display in the main window:

Figure 25.10.
The whiteboard is one of the handier tools included with NetMeeting.

- Directory: During the setup process, you were given the option of publishing your name on a ULS server. Clicking this icon takes you to the ULS server that you chose during the setup process and provides you with a list of people who have registered there. If you see someone you want to call, just highlight his or her name on the list and then click the Call button.

- SpeedDial: As you use NetMeeting, you can develop a list of people you've called and save them in a SpeedDial list, not unlike the speed dial numbers you can program into many phones. Clicking the SpeedDial icon opens your SpeedDial list, where you can select a person to call.

- Current Call: Clicking this icon displays the list of participants in the current call. To learn more about a conference participant, right-click his or her name and choose Properties. NetMeeting displays the personal information.

- History: When you want to see a list of all the NetMeeting calls you've received, click the History icon. You can select a name from the list and call by clicking the Call button or see the personal information by right-clicking and choosing Properties.

Take a look now at sharing an application. I see this as one of the more important uses for the current version of NetMeeting because there are so many ways you can use this feature.

How do you share an application? Begin by opening the application. You might want to also open any files you intend to use because the application can get a bit sluggish once you establish the NetMeeting setup. After you get the application open, you need to click the Share button in NetMeeting and select one of the running applications from the list that NetMeeting presents.

At this point, you're sharing the application, but you're not collaborating. Other conference participants can see the application window on their screens, but they can't work in the shared application. It's strictly look but don't touch. The other party can tell by a message that NetMeeting displays when he places the cursor over the application title. Figure 25.11 shows the message you receive. Notice also that this figure shows that the application displays the initiating user's name over the top. This way you can tell who "owns" the application.

Figure 25.11.
NetMeeting tells you when you can't actually manipulate the application. It also indicates who owns it.

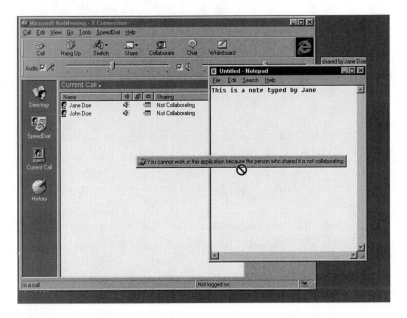

Click the NetMeeting Collaborate button, and everyone involved in the meeting can change the contents of the application. (They need to click their Collaborate buttons as well.) You can always tell who is collaborating and who owns the target application by monitoring the NetMeeting window. Figure 25.12 shows what the NetMeeting window looks like when one person has control over an application and another is collaborating. Only one person can take control of the application at one time. Everyone else has a pointer that tells them to click to take control. Although it doesn't show in the figure, the pointer also contains the initials of the person who has control so that you don't have to constantly monitor the NetMeeting window.

Another interesting feature of NetMeeting is the capability to send a file to the other conference participants. Choosing Tools | File Transfer | Send File opens a standard File Open dialog box. Select the file you want to send and then click OK. Everyone in the meeting sees a dialog like the one shown in Figure 25.13. They can choose to accept or reject the file. Once the file is completely sent, you see a completion dialog.

Figure 25.12.
NetMeeting allows several people to share an application and collaborate on the contents of a file, but only one person has control at a time.

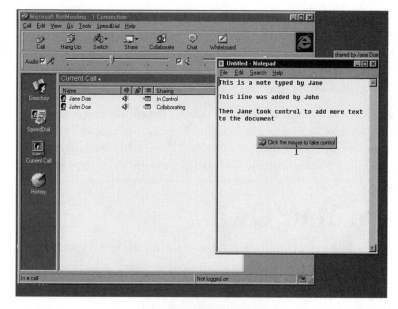

Figure 25.13.
You see a dialog like this one if someone sends you a file using NetMeeting.

Working with NetShow

Microsoft NetShow gives Web site developers the ability to deliver multimedia content over the Internet. NetShow can stream multimedia content so that sounds, video, and animation start playing after only a few seconds delay and proceed to play, even as your system continues to download the data files for the multimedia content.

The main NetShow software resides on the server that provides multimedia content. You use the NetShow Player to listen to audio content and to view videos and animations. The combination of the NetShow server and the NetShow Player make it possible to deliver live audio feeds such as music events and radio shows across the Internet.

Although the NetShow Player is part of the Internet Explorer suite, the player software might not have been loaded automatically when you installed Internet Explorer. You might need to return to your Internet Explorer CD to locate and install the player software. You can also download the player software free of charge from the Microsoft Web site at `http://www.microsoft.com/netshow/`. After you download the software, just double-click its icon to install NetShow Player.

After NetShow Player is installed, you hardly need to think about it again. Although it is possible to run NetShow Player as a standalone program, it normally runs automatically after you click a hyperlink on a Web page that leads to some NetShow content. In some cases, the NetShow content is embedded in the Web page and the NetShow Player doesn't even appear as a separate window.

On Your Own

Plan a Web page of your own and then create it using FrontPage Express.

Test your new Web page using Personal Web Server (see Chapter 22) and then post it on your ISP's server if your account includes a Web site. After you post your Web site, view it using Internet Explorer and other Web browsers to see how the different browsers render your page.

Download an updated copy of NetMeeting from the Internet at `http://www.microsoft.com/netmeeting/`. Install it at several workstations on a LAN or on a single workstation that has an Internet connection. Once you get NetMeeting installed, establish contact with one or more people so that you can see how the product works. You'll find that a LAN connection works surprisingly well, but that the Internet connection is marginal at best in most cases. Make sure you try the various features such as the whiteboard and Chat.

Download and install the Microsoft NetShow Player software and then go exploring for live multimedia content. You can start at the Microsoft NetShow Web page at `http://www.microsoft.com/netshow/`.

26

Creating Your Own Internet Connection with Personal Web Server

Peter Norton®

You've created a Web page and now you want to post it on a server so that others can view your handiwork. But your Web page isn't intended for the whole world to see; you just want to make it available to your colleagues on your local intranet. Perhaps you do want to make your Web site available to the world, but first you want to test it to make sure everything works the way it's supposed to. When you need to set up a simple, small-scale Web site, whether it's for use on an intranet or for testing your Web design work before you post it on the Internet, Personal Web Server is just the tool for the job.

Personal Web Server is the smallest and newest version of Internet Information Server (IIS) provided by Microsoft. It's not designed for running an Internet site; you'd use it for testing purposes or perhaps a small in-house intranet Web site. I use it to test my Web pages before uploading them to a live site. This is a new feature for the OSR2 version of Windows 95, but you can use it with older versions as well. All you need to do is download the Personal Web Server files from Microsoft's Web site at `http://www.microsoft.com/ie/download/`.

Peter's Principle: What Is an Intranet?

Some people confuse the idea of the Internet with an intranet. It's true that there are some similarities between the two, but they're used for entirely different purposes. In some cases, they're configured differently as well.

Let me clear up the major difference between the two first. An intranet is normally private; I don't think I've ever seen a public one. The Internet, on the other hand, is always public. Private versus public access makes a great deal of difference in the way that you configure the two setups.

Another difference is size. The Internet invites literally thousands of people to view your site. The private nature of an intranet precludes inviting thousands of people; you might be inviting hundreds instead. This consideration affects the amount and type of equipment you buy. You'll find yourself spending more on security and less on hardware when setting up an intranet.

Compatibility considerations are another area where the Internet is different from an intranet. If you set up an Internet site, you want to make it as compatible as possible with a broad range of browsers. Intranet sites concentrate on flexibility and power instead. Because you control the browser used for the site, you also get to use all the capabilities and features it provides.

Finally, an Internet is always available through a worldwide connection. You can keep an intranet company based and not make it available to anyone but the few people in one location. For that matter, an intranet can simply become an extension of your LAN and nothing more.

This chapter is going to look at what you need to do to install Personal Web Server. I also look at some configuration issues. The one thing I don't look at is designing Web pages; check the section on FrontPage Express in Chapter 25, "FrontPage Express, NetMeeting, and NetShow," for that information. I also don't spend any time on Internet-server–specific issues because Personal Web Server isn't designed for that purpose. (You'll be disappointed by the results if you even attempt to use it in this way.)

Installation

Installation of this product couldn't be easier. There are two techniques you can use. The first is for OSR2 users. All you need to do is right-click the Network Neighborhood icon and select Properties from the context menu. When you see the Network properties dialog, click the Add pushbutton. Select Service in the Select Network Component Type dialog and then click Add. You see a Select Network Service dialog. Highlight the Personal Web Server entry in the Microsoft section as shown in Figure 26.1. Click OK. Windows 95 prompts you to insert your Windows 95 disk, copies some files, and then asks you to restart the machine.

Figure 26.1.
Personal Web Server
installs much like any
other service under
the OSR2 version of
Windows 95.

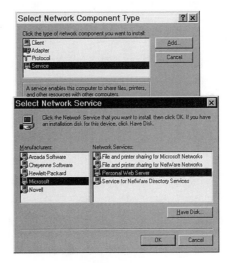

The second method for installing Personal Web Server is even more automatic. Download the `PWS10A.EXE` file from the Internet site I mentioned earlier in this chapter. After you download the file, double-click its icon. You see the program copy some files. Once it completes this task, it asks you to restart your machine.

Note: Personal Web Server is now available as part of the Windows NT 4 Option Pack, which is a huge (27MB) file to download and a more complicated installation. If you want only the Personal Web Server, choose Personal Web Server 1.0 for Windows 95 from the list of versions available for download from the Microsoft Web site.

Immediately after you restart your machine, you notice a new Personal Web Server icon in the Settings Area on the Taskbar. Right-clicking this icon displays a context menu with three entries: Administer, Home Page, and Properties. The section "Configuration," later in the chapter, shows how to use these options.

Testing Your Setup

Personal Web Server normally runs right out of the box. You don't have to do anything more at this point if you don't want to. People with access to your machine over your local intranet can display any Web pages you create and place in Personal Web Server's Web folder. Every link will work as expected. In short, Personal Web Server's default configuration is more than enough to set up a help desk or perform other tasks that you can do using HTML pages. I find it helpful to test my setup right after installation to see if it works at all.

You need a browser to test your setup. The first thing you need to know is how to access the Web site. It's easy. Just type `http://Name of Machine` when asked for an URL. For example, I have two machines named `PROFESSOR` and `MINNOW` on a test network. Personal Web Server is installed on `PROFESSOR`, so I use `http://PROFESSOR/` as an URL. Make sure you perform this initial test from every computer that needs to access the Web site. That way, you can fix any communication problems before you perform a lot of setup.

Tip: If you have Internet Explorer configured for Internet access via a Dial-Up Networking connection, Internet Explorer might insist on making a dial-up connection before loading a page from your Personal Web Server. If you want to follow links to resources on the Internet, you might need that connection. However, if you just want to work on your local machine or intranet using Personal Web Server, you can temporarily reconfigure Internet Explorer to use your local network instead of a dial-up connection. To do so, select View | Internet Options, click the Connections tab of the Internet Options dialog box, select the Connect to the Internet using a local area network option, and then click OK to apply the setting.

At this point, you want to turn on your FTP server if you intend to use it. (Microsoft installs Personal Web Server with the FTP server shut off.) Double-click the Personal Web Server icon on the Taskbar and you see a Personal Web Server Properties dialog. Select the Services page as shown in Figure 26.2. This is where you decide which services are on and off. For example, you might simply want to provide a central download point for everyone in the company. All you need to do to start the FTP service is highlight the FTP entry in the Services list box and then click the Start pushbutton. The Status column entry changes from Stopped to Running.

Figure 26.2.

Starting a service is relatively easy; simply select the service you want and click Start.

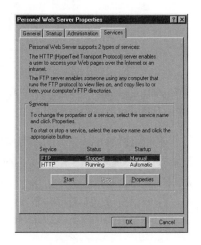

Notice that this dialog shows that the FTP service starts manually. (Look in the Startup column.) If you want to use the FTP service every time you start Personal Web Server, highlight the FTP entry and click the Properties pushbutton. You see an FTP Properties dialog like the one shown in Figure 26.3. Change the Startup Options setting from Manual to Automatic. Notice that you can also use this dialog to change the home directory for the FTP server. I talk about this setting in the section "Configuration" later in the chapter. Once you make any needed changes on this page, click OK to make the changes permanent. You'll want to verify that Personal Web Server accepted the change by looking at the Startup column in the Services list box. The FTP entry should now say Automatic instead of Manual. Click OK to close the Personal Web Server Properties dialog. (You don't have to restart Windows 95 for the changes to take place; in fact, you don't want to if you didn't set the FTP server to start automatically.)

Even though there aren't any files in the FTP directory, you can still see if the site works. In this case, type `ftp://`**`Name of Machine`** when entering the URL in your browser. Figure 26.4 shows what the FTP site on my test machine looks like. Notice that the directory contains a single file placed there during installation. It's a simple text file that contains a single statement saying, "Microsoft Personal Web Server FTP Service." (You'll see this string in the browser if you click the entry.)

Figure 26.3.

If you plan to use the FTP server every time you start Personal Web Server, make sure you change the Startup Options entry on the FTP Properties dialog.

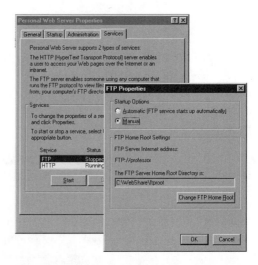

Figure 26.4.

The FTP directory contains a single default file.

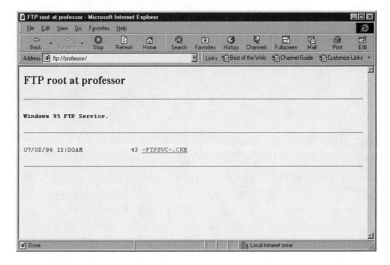

Remember that this initial test isn't the end of the process. You'll want to continue testing your Web site as you develop it. Make sure you maintain private areas for testing new pages if you plan to actually use this as a small intranet for your office. Otherwise, you can treat the site as you do your production site. You'll be able to test new pages using the same links that a visitor to your site would.

Configuration

There are a lot of configuration options in Personal Web Server, although not nearly as many as you'd find with other versions of IIS such as the one that comes with Windows NT Server. In fact, I was able to run Personal Web Server using HTTP without changing any configuration items at all.

As soon as you want to do anything other than display HTML pages, however, you need to change the default configuration. You'll likely want to at least tune your setup once you get it going—even if your only goal is displaying HTML pages.

I'm going to look at how you perform the three most common tasks using Personal Web Server in the following sections. Make certain you have Personal Web Server installed and working before you attempt to display any of the pages shown. You need to start the FTP server using the procedure described in the section "Testing Your Setup" if you want to view the FTP-specific configuration page. If you want to maintain local security over the Web site, then you need to disable file and print sharing; for this reason, you probably want to keep your intranet site on a different workstation from the directories you normally use to share information. (To disable file and print sharing, right-click Network Neighborhood, select Properties from the context menu, click the File and Print sharing pushbutton in the Network Properties dialog, and uncheck all the boxes. You need to click OK twice to close the two dialogs and then restart your machine.)

You can view all the Personal Web Server configuration features from the Internet Services Administrator Web page installed as part of the initial setup. To view the administration page, right-click the Personal Web Server icon on the Taskbar and then select Administer from the context menu. Figure 26.5 shows the initial Web page that you see. Note that using a Web page to administer your site allows you to make changes from any workstation on the network that has access to the Personal Web Server site.

Figure 26.5.
The main administration Web page allows you to configure your Personal Web Server setup.

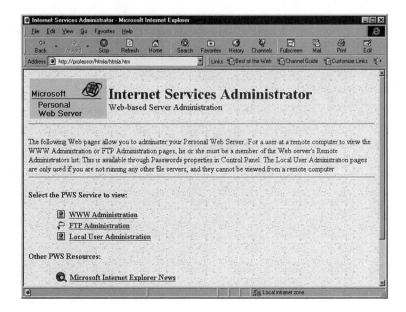

Note: Even though there's an applet in the Control Panel for Personal Web Server and a properties page accessible from the Taskbar icon, all the configuration options are on the Internet Services Administrator Web page. Any time you access a configuration item from the Personal Web Server Properties page, you start a copy of your default browser. For this reason, you must have a browser installed on the Web server if you intend to maintain the site from that location. I covered all the unique Personal Web Server Properties dialog settings in the section "Testing Your Setup" earlier in the chapter.

HTTP (WWW) Administration

Personal Web Server usually works fine right out of the box if all you want to do is test Web pages you've created before posting them on a live Internet server. However, you need to spend a little time optimizing your HTTP site before it's ready to use in an intranet environment where it will be accessed by others. You access the configuration for this part of Personal Web Server by clicking the WWW Administration link shown in Figure 26.5. Figure 26.6 shows the page you use to perform the configuration. I scrolled the image so that you can see all of the controls; the page normally contains a header. Notice that this Web page contains several tabs. Each tab relates to a different part of the configuration process.

Figure 26.6.

The Internet Services Administrator WWW page allows you to configure the HTTP settings.

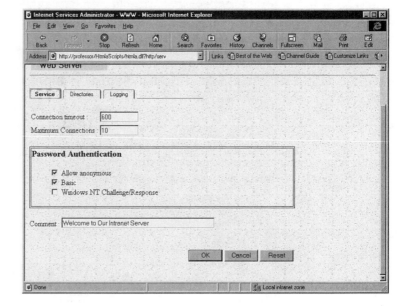

Tip: Notice that you actually access a DLL to display Internet Services Administrator—WWW page. You'll also figure out that this page doesn't appear in your WEBSHARE folder. It appears in the \Program Files\WEBSVR\HTMLASCR folder or the \Program Files\Personal Web Server\HTMLASCR folder. Besides the DLL, a wealth of files with the .HTR extension appear in this folder. These files use standard HTML code that you can modify if needed. For example, you might want to add a quick link between the HTTP configuration page and the FTP configuration page. Make sure you take the time to make a copy of the HTR files before you modify them.

The Connection timeout field defines how long the Personal Web Server waits before terminating a connection that hasn't had any activity on it. I find that the default value of 600 seconds (10 minutes) works fine in most cases.

You use the Maximum Connections field to limit the number of people using the Web server. The astronomical value of 300 that Microsoft uses as a default probably won't work very well because the server will bog down. I set a limit of 10 in the figure, which is probably a little low. You need to experiment with this setting to see how many users you can add without bogging down the server.

The next section relates to security. Even though the figure shows that you can use anonymous connections, I usually disable this feature to maintain strict control over access by forcing everyone to use their names. You get better log files because they'll contain actual names instead of anonymous entries. Checking the Basic option in this group tells Personal Web Server that you want to use passwords using standard base 64 encoding. This isn't secure because someone can easily break into your system by decrypting passing messages and using stolen passwords. Using the Windows NT Challenge/Response option enhances security through the use of fully encrypted passwords. You can also choose both options, although this doesn't provide much added security.

You also find a Comment field on this page. You can use this for just about anything that you want other administrators to see; no one else will see it. I usually put a last-modified date here.

Once you configure this page, you need to send the information to the Personal Web Server. To send the information on this page, click OK. Otherwise, click Reset. This returns any values to their original settings. Click Cancel to leave the Web page without making any changes.

Personal Web Server also requires you to set aside a number of directories to store content and specialty pages such as the administration pages you see. Figure 26.7 shows the Directories tab and the default entries for it. You must maintain these directories or some of the links for Personal Web Server itself will break.

Figure 26.7.

The default directory setup used by Personal Web Server should meet all your needs.

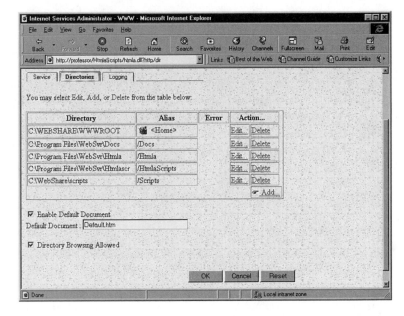

Normally, you'll find that these directories work just fine. However, what happens if you move a directory to another drive? Click the Edit entry next to the affected directory and you see a dialog like the one shown in Figure 26.8. At the top of this page is the Directory field. It contains the actual directory location on your hard drive. The Home Directory option allows you to choose which directory a visitor to your site will see first. Below it, you see the Virtual Directory section. This is how someone refers to the directory if he accesses the Web site. The virtual directory setting doesn't necessarily have anything to do with the actual directory location; it's a way to refer to the directory in reference to the root Web page. For example, I may have a \Stuff\Good folder on my machine that has a virtual setting of \GoodStuf. You'd access this directory as http://professor/GoodStuf/ if you were using a browser on my test Web site. (My Web site is http://professor/ in this case.) Finally, you see an Access section. This defines what kinds of things someone can do in the directory. You notice that this directory is marked as Read. If you place applications in the directory, you'll also want to mark the Execute option.

Adding a new directory to the mix follows essentially the same course as editing. However, you click the Add link instead of an Edit link in this case. You see the same form shown in Figure 26.8. You can click the Browse button if you want to select an existing site on the hard drive without typing it. The Select Directory page also contains an option for creating a new directory. Interestingly enough, you can select a location on any hard drive that the Personal Web Server workstation can access.

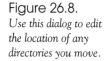

Figure 26.8.
*Use this dialog to edit
the location of any
directories you move.*

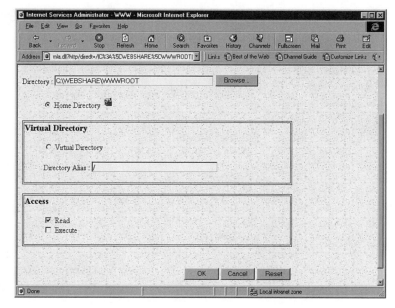

Deleting a directory is almost too simple. All you need to do is click the Delete link next to the directory you want to get rid of. Use this feature with extreme caution, however, because you won't get any kind of a warning about deleting essential directory entries. In other words, you could delete your link to the administration directory and find it difficult to regain access later.

There are two more entries on the Directories tab shown in Figure 26.7. The first is the Enable Default Document option and associated Default Document text box. You use this entry to define a default document that will appear automatically when a visitor enters your site. In most cases, the default setting works just fine. All you need to do is edit the existing document to meet your needs. The final option, Directory Browsing Allowed, allows the visitor to move from one directory to another. This is a fairly dangerous option to enable on a Windows 95 machine because your ability to truly control access is somewhat limited. A better choice is to offer more virtual locations for the visitor to view.

The final tab on the Internet Services Administrator WWW page is Logging. Figure 26.9 shows what it looks like. The first option, Enable Logging, tells Personal Web Server to maintain a record of special events such as someone logging on. Once you enable logging, you need to determine how often Personal Web Server creates a new log and select a location for the log. Personal Web Server defaults to your Windows directory, but you can choose any other option you like. (I usually change this setting to a special log directory to keep my Windows directory from getting any more crammed than it already is.)

Figure 26.9.

You'll find that maintaining a log of special events can help you locate problem areas such as security breaches.

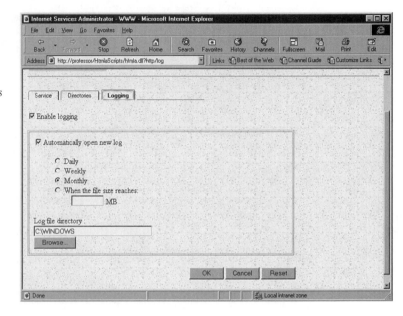

FTP Administration

Once you work with HTTP (WWW) administration for a while, the FTP administration should come fairly easy. Figure 26.10 shows the initial page that you see. As with the Internet Services Administrator WWW page, this one uses tabs. You'll find that the Directories and Logging tabs work just like the ones I discussed in the HTTP (WWW) Administration section, so I don't discuss them here again.

The Connection timeout and Maximum Connections fields work just like they do on the Internet Services Administrator WWW page. However, you have to tune these pages differently. Notice that I'm using the default value here. You don't want people to try multiple downloads from your FTP server, so watch the number of connections closely. You'll also find that you need a longer timeout value because a download could get delayed. (Just watch how hostile users get if you don't set this value for a long enough interval.) Unlike the HTTP connections, it's less likely that someone will leave a lot of connections open when using the FTP portion of your intranet site.

It's not uncommon for people to log on using an anonymous connection to an FTP site. However, as before, you may want to disable this option on your intranet to improve security. Notice that this page also contains an Allow only anonymous connections option. This feature is designed more for Internet pages. If you allow only anonymous connections, it's a lot harder for hackers to get in using the supervisor account.

Figure 26.10.
The Internet Services Administrator FTP page works much like its WWW counterpart.

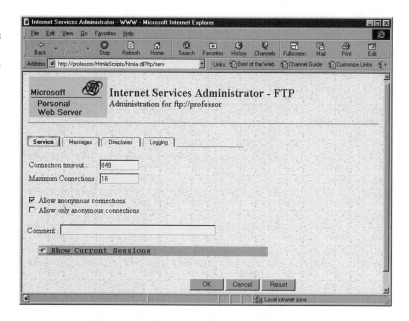

The last entry on this first page is Show Current Sessions. Clicking this link displays a page like the one shown in Figure 26.11. The center portion of this page contains a table with user names, IP addresses, and the time they logged on to the FTP site. You also see a Disconnect link next to each entry in the last column of the table. Clicking this link terminates that user's connection. You can also choose to disconnect everyone using the Disconnect All link near the bottom of the page. The Close link closes the page without making any changes.

Figure 26.11.
You can use this page to monitor FTP site status or to disconnect an errant connection.

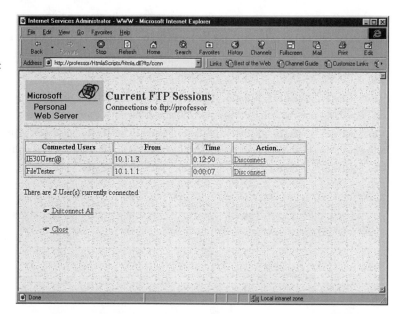

The next tab you examine is Messages. Figure 26.12 shows what this page looks like. There are only three messages you need to worry about when using an FTP site. The first welcomes the user to your site. The second tells them goodbye when they complete their file downloads. The final message tells them that the number of connections has been exceeded and they need to try again later.

Figure 26.12.
The FTP Administrator Messages page contains the three messages you need to send to visitors of your site.

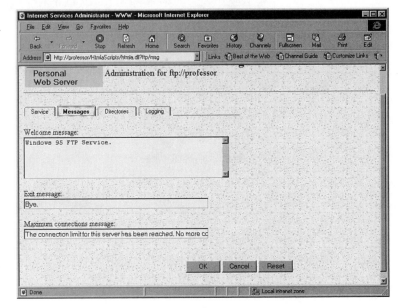

Working with User Accounts

Maintaining security is a major concern on the Internet and an even bigger concern on local intranets. Personal Web Server provides a simple security mechanism modeled after the one you already use under Windows 95. Figure 26.13 shows the main page for this feature. Notice that you have three tabs to examine in this case.

Notice that Figure 26.13 shows two users in the User List field. Add another user to the list. Click the New User pushbutton and you see another page where you can type a user name in the User Name field and then type the password for that user twice (once in the User Password field and again in the Confirm Password field). Click Add to complete the process. You return to the Internet Local User Administrator page and see the new user added to the User List field.

Warning: The current version of Personal Web Server doesn't support null passwords. You must assign a password to every user.

Figure 26.13.
You can work with both users and groups when using Personal Web Server.

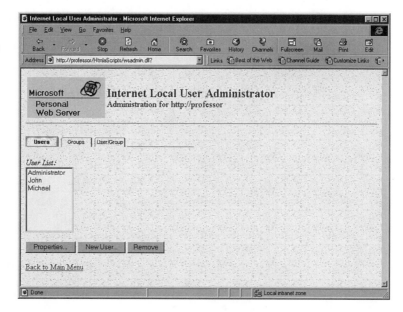

The Properties button displays a page similar to the one you used to define the user you select. There is only one major difference: You might also see a list of groups that the user belongs to at the bottom of the page. You can use the Properties pushbutton to change the user's name or password as needed. Using the Remove pushbutton is fairly simple. Just highlight the user you want to remove and then click the Remove pushbutton. There aren't any safety messages, so make sure you really want to remove a user before doing so.

Look at the Groups tab. It appears in Figure 26.14. I've already entered a group into this page. As before, there are three buttons: one that allows you add new groups, another for viewing the properties of existing groups, and a third for removing groups that you no longer need. The dialog you see when adding or modifying groups consists of a single field for adding the group name.

The last security related task that you perform using the Internet Local User Administrator appears on the User/Group tab shown in Figure 26.15. To assign a user to a group, select a user from the User List field and a group from the Group List field. Click the Add user to group pushbutton to complete the process. Likewise, to remove a user from a group, click the Remove user from group pushbutton.

There is one last task you need to perform to make security work. You need to give these users and groups access to specific areas of your Web site. Suppose that you want to share the WWWROOT folder so that people can access the content of your Web site. Open the appropriate folder in My Computer. Right-click the folder you want to share and select Sharing from the context menu.

Figure 26.14.
The Groups tab allows you to add new groups to your setup.

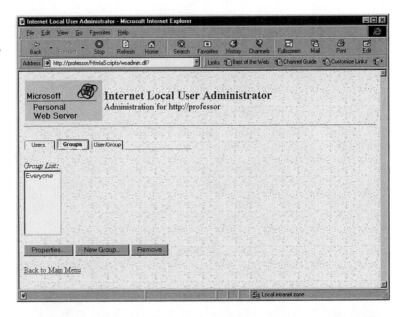

Figure 26.15.
Assigning a user to a group consists of selecting one of each and clicking the appropriate pushbutton.

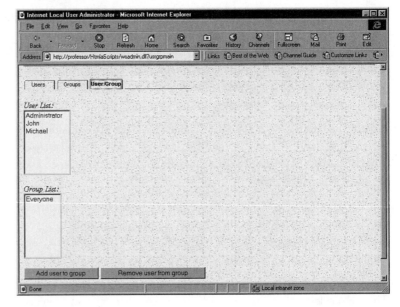

When the dialog box appears, click the Shared As radio button and you see that the Web Sharing button at the bottom of the page becomes active. Click this button and you see a dialog like the one shown in Figure 26.16. This is where you decide what level of intranet sharing you'll provide. As you can see, there are levels for both HTTP and FTP access. I cover the advantages and disadvantages of specific levels of access in the section "Internet Security" in Chapter 28, "Setting Up Security." Once you make a decision on the level of Web access, click OK.

Figure 26.16.
Deciding on what level of intranet access to provide is an important security decision.

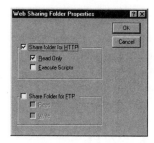

Now you need to decide who should have access to your directory. Click the Add pushbutton in the folder Properties dialog. You see a dialog like the one shown in Figure 26.17. This is where you add users or groups to the access list. All you need to do is highlight a user or group name and then click the level of access you want to grant. Notice that all the users you created in the Internet Local User Administrator appear in this dialog. Once you select a group of users, click OK twice and you're done.

Figure 26.17.
This dialog allows you to decide who gets access to your Web site.

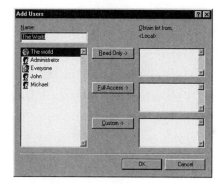

Limitations

Personal Web Server doesn't include many of the supplementary features that you'll find in other versions of IIS. For example, it doesn't include some of the less-used protocols such as Gopher. However, I consider this particular shortcoming to be of minimal importance for Personal Web Server's intended purpose.

One of the more important differences between Personal Web Server and a full-fledged Web server is that you can't manage several Web servers from one site using Personal Web Server. In addition, this server doesn't appear in the Microsoft Internet Service Manager utility provided for Windows NT. As I mentioned earlier, this product is designed for small intranets. You wouldn't want to use it in places where you needed several Web servers.

You'll also want to limit the number of users attached to Personal Web Server. Setting up a Personal Web Server generates more traffic on the network and results in more work for the host. A machine that could normally support 20 network connections will probably support 10 to 15 Personal Web Server connections. In other words, use this option with care. Installing your local intranet on a machine other than the one you use for file and print sharing is always a good idea.

On Your Own

Download and install Personal Web Server so that you can learn some of the ins and outs of managing your own Web site. It's very helpful when it comes time to working on a Web site within your company. You'll also find that Personal Web Server comes in handy when it's time to design and test your own Web pages.

To publish your own Web site using Personal Web Server, simply copy the Web pages, graphics files, and other elements that make up your Web site to the root directory for Personal Web Server (usually `C:\webshare\wwwroot`). Alternatively, you could redefine the Web server home root setting in the HTTP Properties dialog box to point to the folder containing your Web site files.

VI

Networking and Security with Windows 95

27

Networks

Peter Norton®

This chapter discusses the networking capabilities provided by Windows 95. For the most part, I avoid discussing networks in general or comparing your various options for one simple reason: A single chapter can't possibly contain everything you'll ever need to know about networking. There are literally volumes of information about this topic—and some people think that those volumes are just barely adequate.

Looking Ahead: I look at some networking issues such as differences between Novell's Client 32 and Microsoft's NDS client for Windows 95. If you still can't find what you need, check out the `microsoft.public.win95.networking` newsgroup.

The discussion in this chapter assumes a certain level of knowledge on your part. I strongly suggest that you also spend some time learning about networks in general before you actually install one. You don't need to be a networking guru to understand this chapter, but you need to know what logging on is about, and you need to be familiar with some of the easier terms, such as network interface card (NIC).

The Client Module

This section examines the *how* of network support under Windows 95. What can you expect? Why do things work the way they do? These are just some of the questions I answer here. Before you become embroiled in the details of using Windows 95's network capabilities, I'd like to spend a little time looking at its architecture. Figure 27.1 shows the Windows 95 network architecture. Notice that a request can follow two discrete paths. Windows 95 provides a 32-bit, protected-mode path for networks it directly supports and uses a real-mode path for drivers it doesn't support. Both paths end up at the NIC driver.

The following list describes the individual components of the Windows 95 network architecture:

- 16-bit thunk API—Windows 95 provides full network support using 32-bit code. However, many 16-bit applications must be supported as well. This module replaces the standard 16-bit API with calls to the 32-bit API. To do this, it must provide thunk support.

- 32-bit API—All application requests start at this module. I don't go into details about the API, but Microsoft has gone to great lengths to reorganize and simplify it. A user won't notice these details—except in the way they affect network performance—but they make a definite impact on the effort required to program. The API translates one application request into one or more standardized network requests. Quite a few files are involved in creating the network API under Windows 95. The two most prominent are `NETAPI.DLL` and `NETAPI32.DLL`. Loading `NETAPI32.DLL` also loads `NETBIOS.DLL`, which provides most of the low-level functionality the API requires.

Figure 27.1.

An overview of the Windows 95 network architecture.

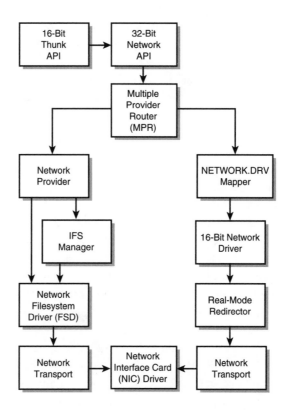

• Multiple provider router (MPR)—You can use more than one protocol with Windows 95. Theoretically, you should be able to mix and match protected-mode and real-mode drivers on the same network. Realistically, you can't always do so.

All network protocols require a network provider. The function of the MPR is to accept network requests from the API and send them to the appropriate network provider (NP). (Each request states which NP to use.) However, some requests, such as a request for the status of the entire network, are generic. In that case, the MPR calls each NP in turn to fulfill the application request. In other cases, a request might not include enough information for the MPR to know which NP to use. In this case, the MPR polls the NPs to determine whether one of them can fulfill the request. If none of the installed NPs can, the MPR returns an error message. The MPR functions appear in the SYSTEM folder in MPR.DLL. This DLL gets loaded when Windows 95 executes MPREXE.EXE during startup. An intermediate file, MPRSERV.DLL, performs the actual loading process. Loading this set of DLLs also loads ADVAPI32.DLL; the MPR uses the functions in this DLL to view the contents of the Registry to determine which NPs and other network resources are available.

The MPR also loads MSPWL.DLL, which checks for your password and performs other security-related activities. There is also a path from the MPR to NETWORK.DRV; this path becomes active when you use a real-mode driver in place of a Windows 95–specific NP. The MPR can't poll the real-mode driver or perform any of the other NP-specific tasks I described earlier. NETWORK.DRV provides the NP services that Windows 95 requires. I describe this part of the network a little later in this chapter.

- Network provider (NP)—The network provider performs all the protocol-specific functions that an application requires. It makes or breaks connections, returns network status information, and provides a consistent interface for the MPR to use. An application never calls the NP; only the MPR performs this function. Even though the internal structure of NPs varies, the interface they provide does not. This mechanism allows Windows 95 to provide support for more than a single protocol. The code used by the MPR can remain small and fast because none of the NPs require special calls. If an NP can't fulfill a request because of a limitation in the network protocol, it simply tells the MPR that the required service is unavailable. The NP also keeps the IFS Manager up to date on the current connection status. This is how Explorer knows when you've made a new drive connection.

- IFS Manager—When the IFS Manager obtains new status information from the NP, it calls the Network File System Driver (Network FSD) to update file and other resource information. For example, when the NP tells the IFS Manager that it has made a new drive connection, the IFS Manager calls the Network FSD to provide a directory listing. The same holds true for other resource types, such as printers.

The IFS Manager also performs its normal duties of opening files and making other file system requests. The MPR doesn't know what to do with pathnames, so it passes such requests through the NP to the IFS Manager to fulfill. Of course, applications also access the IFS Manager in other ways. The only time the MPR becomes involved is if a network-specific request also requires its intervention.

- Network File System Driver (FSD)—Each server on the network can use a unique file system. For example, if you make a connection to an OS/2 server, you could require access to an HPFS drive. NetWare and other client-server networks all use special file systems that the vendor feels will enhance performance, security, reliability, and storage capacity. Because Windows 95 understands nothing about HPFS or any other special storage system, it needs a translator; the Network FSD performs this task. It translates the intricacies of a foreign file system into something that Windows 95 can understand.

A Network FSD is usually composed of a file-system–specific driver and VREDIR.VXD, which provides the Windows 95 interpretation of the file system specifics. Although there's normally only one Network FSD for each NP, there is nothing to enforce this limit. An NP might require access to both a FAT and an NTFS Network FSD for a Windows NT server. If so, both drivers get installed when you install network support. The IFS Manager also calls the Network FSD for support. Although the NP usually makes requests for network status or connection information, the IFS Manager takes care of application needs such as opening files and reading their contents. These two modules—NP and IFS Manager—work in tandem, each fulfilling completely different roles.

- Network transport (NT)—Figure 27.1 shows a network transport (NT) as a single module. In reality, this module consists of many smaller modules and drivers. The number of pieces in an NT is determined by the complexity of your setup and the requirements of the protocol. The smallest NT could consist of a mere four drivers. For example, you could create an NT for the NetBEUI protocol using the following files:

  - `VNETBIOS.VXD`—This file virtualizes access to the protocol. This is why more than one virtual machine running on your system can access the network drives at the same time.

  - `NETBEUI.VXD`—This file talks with the NDIS (network driver interface specification) module. It takes protocol-specific requests and translates them into smaller, standardized network requests.

  - `NDIS.VXD`—This file translates each Windows 95–specific request into a call that the NIC driver can understand, and the NIC driver talks to the NIC itself. The driver can take into account such things as port addresses and interrupts—everything needed to talk to the NIC. Of course, the NIC converts your request into an electrical signal that appears on the network.

NT requires other files as well. For example, `NDIS30.DLL` provides the actual API support for `NDIS.VXD`, and `NETBIOS.DLL` performs the same function for `VNETBIOS.VXD`. In essence, it takes several different modules to create one transport. If you want to use a different NIC, you just need to change the NIC driver, not any of the protocol-specific files. If you want to use two different levels of NDIS support, you add an additional driver and its support files.

Tip: The OSR2 version of Windows 95 provides support for the NDIS 4.0 NIC drivers. Unfortunately, you can't download this support as a separate package. You'll also find support for the 32-bit DLC (data link control) protocol for SNA (simple network architecture) host connectivity (mainly IBM) in OSR2. Users of older Windows 95 versions can download this support from `http://www.microsoft.com/windows/windows95/info/system-updates.htm`. You can also obtain the updated ISDN (Integrated Services Digital Network) support found in OSR2 at `http://www.microsoft.com/windows/getisdn/dload.htm`. Finally, you can download the NDS (NetWare Directory Services) support I mentioned earlier at `http://www.microsoft.com/windows/software/msnds.htm`. Make sure you read any update instructions before you attempt to install this support. You also need to make certain that your hardware and drivers are capable of supporting the features provided by these updates.

- Network interface card (NIC) driver—I mention this part of the NT because this driver is hardware-specific. It has to communicate with the NIC on a level it can understand. That's the first problem—finding a driver that provides a standard Windows 95 interface yet talks with the NIC installed in your machine. The second problem is that there can be only one driver. I mentioned earlier that there was a chance that a real-mode and a protected-mode network could coexist but that it wouldn't happen in a lot of cases. Here's why: If you can't load a Windows 95–specific NIC driver because it interferes with a driver that the real-mode product requires, you must decide which network to use.

Tip: Even if you've invested in a real-mode networking product such as LANtastic, the performance and reliability increase you get from running a Microsoft network under Windows 95 might make it worth the effort to switch. Of course, you have to consider the trade-offs: Windows 95 might not provide many of the features of other networking products.

- NETWORK.DRV—This file provides the interface to your real-mode network that Windows 95 requires in order to use the network. In this case, the NP also acts as a mapper—a module that maps the Windows 95–specific calls to something that the 16-bit driver will understand. It also provides a thunk layer to translate the 32-bit requests into their 16-bit equivalents. Remember that you still need to install the old 16-bit Windows version of the network drivers. In the case of LANtastic, you need the LANTASTI.386 and LANTNET.DRV files from your distribution disks.

- 16-bit network driver—As I mentioned in the preceding paragraph, you still need a Windows driver for your real-mode network. Otherwise, there's no magical way that Windows 95 is able to talk to it. There must be a framework for discussion before a discussion can take place. The 16-bit network drivers typically translate any requests into something that the real-mode redirector can understand. They then ask Windows 95 to make the transition to real mode so that the redirector can do its job.

Tip: In some cases, it's nearly impossible to get a good real-mode network installation under Windows 95. Some of the problems include the real-mode network setup program overwriting Windows 95–specific files, and the use of undocumented Windows 3.x features. A few setup programs also require Program Manager to complete their installation, so you might want to start a copy of Program Manager before you begin. I've found that the best way to get a good real-mode network installation under Windows 95 is to install a copy of Windows 3.x first, install the real-mode network there, and then install the copy of Windows 95 over the Windows 3.x installation. It seems like a roundabout way of doing things, but it ensures that you have a minimum of problems.

- Real-mode redirector—This network component translates your requests into network calls. It works with the real-mode network transport to create an interface with the NIC. Essentially, it performs about the same function in real mode that the IFS Manager and Network FSD do in protected mode.

This might seem like a lot of work just to create a workstation, but that's only half the picture on many peer-to-peer installations. Once you get past being a workstation, you have to take care of network requests as well. The next section shows you how Windows 95 provides peer-to-peer network services. You'll look at Windows 95's peer-to-peer support from a server level, and you'll look at a lot of the implementation details.

Peer-to-Peer Support

Peer-to-peer networks represent the easiest and least expensive way to get started in networking. In the past, the standard method for sharing resources was to buy additional machines (called *servers*) and place the common components there. The investment in hardware and software for a full-fledged network can run into tens of thousands of dollars—prohibitively expensive for many companies. Peer-to-peer networks take a different route. One or more workstations also act as servers. In fact, if you work things right and the network is small enough, everyone will probably have access to everyone else's machine in some form. This means that except for the NICs and cabling you need, a peer-to-peer solution under Windows 95 is essentially free.

Windows 95 provides peer-to-peer networking capabilities right out of the package. All you need to do is install a NIC in each machine, run some cable, and add a few drivers to your setup. Of course, once you get everyone set up, you want to install a few extra utilities, such as a centralized calendar and e-mail.

I was actually a little disappointed with the network utility feature set that Microsoft decided to provide for Windows 95. Exchange is a wonderful e-mail system, but past versions of WFW (Windows for Workgroups) came with Schedule+. Windows 95 doesn't provide this feature, and almost everyone will notice. With IE4, Microsoft has introduced a program similar to Schedule+, called Outlook Express. Of course, this brings up another problem—that of incompatibility between Schedule+ and Outlook Express. No matter which way you look at it, Schedule+ will become a thing of the past unless you're willing to perform a major upgrade of all your PCs at the same time—something I doubt most businesses could do even if they wanted to and had the required resources.

Peter's Principle: Grabbing a Piece of the Past

You don't have to do without Schedule+ in your new Windows 95 installation if you still have the files from your old version of WFW lying around. Even though that version of Schedule+ won't work with Exchange, you can still share information with other people on the network by copying the required files to your drive. Here are the files you should copy to your Windows folder:

```
*.CAL
DEMILAYR.DLL
MSCHED.DLL
MSMAIL.INI
MSREMIND.EXE
SCHDPLUS.EXE
SCHDPLUS.HLP
SCHDPLUS.INI
TRNSCHED.DLL
```

You'll also need to copy the following files to your SYSTEM folder:

```
AB.DLL
FRAMEWRK.DLL
MAILMGR.DLL
MAILSPL.EXE
MSSFS.DLL
STORE.DLL
```

If the new version of Microsoft Mail doesn't exactly meet your specifications, you can still use the old version under Windows 95. Simply copy these files to your Windows folder:

```
MSMAIL.EXE
MSMAIL.HLP
MSMAIL.PRG
```

You also need to copy VFORMS.DLL to your SYSTEM folder.

After you copy all these files, make any required changes to the INI files. For example, you want to change the directory names so that they match the new location. The only problem I've detected with this arrangement is that Schedule+ won't remember your password. This is a small price to pay for using an old and familiar utility program.

A Look at the Architecture

You've already examined what it takes to provide workstation support under Windows 95, but what happens if you also want to act as a server? Providing server support means your machine must accept and process requests from other workstations and return the requested information. Figure 27.2 shows the Windows 95 peer-to-peer network server support.

Figure 27.2.
An overview of the Windows 95 server architecture.

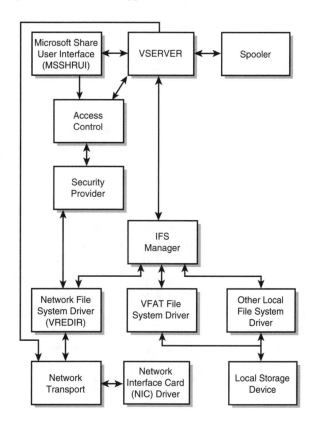

The following list describes each component in detail:

- Microsoft Share User Interface (MSSHRUI)—This module responds to external requests from the user for network resource configuration. Every time you right-click a resource and tell Windows 95 you want to share it, this module fields that request. It works with the access control module to set password protection. An interface to the MPR and `ADVAPI32.DLL` allows the MSSHRUI to set the proper entries in the Registry. You'll find it in the `MSSHRUI.DLL` file in your SYSTEM folder.

- VSERVER—The central point of all activity for the server is the virtual server driver, `VSERVER.VXD`. As with all the other drivers in this chapter, you'll find it in your SYSTEM folder. This component provides direct access of all local resources to network requesters through the NT. It works with the IFS Manager and access control modules to limit access to shared resources and to ensure that any access is performed properly. Each access to shared system resources is maintained in a separate thread. This means that access by one requester need not interfere with any other request. In addition, a single requester can make multiple requests. Of course, the number of actual requests is usually limited by the protocol settings you provide.

- Spooler—If you grant someone access to your printer, VSERVER will send any requests for print services to the spooler module. This module works just as it would for a local print request. As far as it's concerned, the request originated locally. There are three spooler-specific files in your SYSTEM folder: SPOOLSS.DLL, SPOOL32.EXE, and WINSPOOL.DRV.

- Access control—Windows 95 uses this module for a variety of purposes, not just network access control. For example, Windows calls on this module to verify your initial logon password, even if you don't request access to a network afterward. Unlike the other modules discussed so far, the access control module makes use of PWL files on your drive as well as Registry entries to verify and set security. You'll find access control in the SVRAPI.DLL file in the SYSTEM folder.

Tip: You can get around a potential security problem by removing user access to all the PWL files on your drive. If a user erases one of these files, it becomes a lot easier for him to override any security you provided. In addition, you can erase a user's PWL file to give him access to Windows 95 if he forgets his password. Unfortunately, this means you'll also have to perform the setup required to re-create that PWL file. If security is a major concern, make sure you install Service Pack 1 as well. It contains several fixes to the Windows 95 password system. One of the most dangerous problems this patch addresses is the ability of others to decrypt your encrypted PWL files (especially because the algorithm for doing so was posted on the Internet). The new algorithm used by the patch is 2^{96} times more difficult to decrypt. (The OSR2 version of Windows 95 includes these fixes as a default.)

- Security provider—There are a number of sources for this module. In fact, even if you choose to install a Microsoft network, you can still choose between the Microsoft network client and the Windows 95 logon module as a security provider. The Microsoft network client is a network-specific security provider that might include features that the Windows 95 logon module (a generic dialog box) might not provide. You can always access the Windows 95 logon module, even if the network isn't running. The advantage of using it is that the logon module is always available, even if you change the network setup or remove it altogether.

The security provider performs two tasks. First, it's the module that asks you for a password. Second, it combines the user's logon name and the password she provides to verify any network requests.

- VFAT file system driver (FSD) and other local file system driver—I covered both these modules in detail in Chapter 10, "The Windows 95 File System."
- IFS Manager, Network FSD, Network Transport, and NIC driver—I discussed these modules at the beginning of this chapter.

Sharing Files and Printers

Sharing is the main reason to install a network. The very concept of networks came from the need to share expensive peripheral devices and files. Windows 95 provides an easy-to-use interface that allows you to share just about everything on your network with a few clicks of the mouse. Take a look at what you need to do to share files and other resources located on your machine.

The first thing you need to do is install support for file and printer sharing:

1. Right-click the Network Neighborhood icon.
2. Select Properties.
3. If you have a peer-to-peer network installed, the File and Print Sharing button is enabled. Click it to display the dialog shown in Figure 27.3.

Figure 27.3.
The File and Print Sharing dialog allows you to determine what level of sharing support Windows 95 will install.

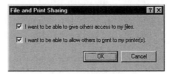

Notice that you can select file and printer sharing individually. Of course, installing support doesn't give everyone access to your system. You still have to select the specific items you plan to share.

Tip: The NETCPL.CPL file in your SYSTEM folder provides the interface you use to configure the network. Some real-mode or older 16-bit Windows network installation programs will insist on changing this file. If you ever lose your Network icon (as I once did), check to make sure this file didn't get overwritten or otherwise corrupted. In fact, you might want to make a copy of this file before you install any real-mode network on your machine.

After Windows 95 enables file and print sharing, you need to select the items to share. Right-clicking any of your drive or printer icons and clicking Properties (depending on what support you installed) displays an additional Sharing tab like the one shown in Figure 27.4. (The context menu also includes a Sharing option, which takes you directly to this tab.)

Figure 27.4.

The Sharing tab of the
Print or Drive
Properties dialog lets
you define the level
and type of sharing
for that device.

The first two radio buttons on this tab allow you to determine whether the resource is shared. Selecting Not Shared means that no one can see the resource, even if they have other access to your machine. If you select shared access, some additional blanks become available.

You need to provide a resource name in the Share Name field. This is how Windows 95 presents the resource in dialog boxes, such as with the Drives field of the File Open dialog. The optional Comment field allows you to provide more information to someone who wants to share the resource. I normally include the precise resource name and my name as part of the comment. This reduces the chance that someone will accidentally try to use a resource on my system.

Use the Access Type group to define the level of access to a particular resource. You can provide two actual levels of access: read-only and full. The third option allows you to assign two different access passwords. This gives one person full access, whereas another can read only the contents of the drive or other resource. The two password fields allow you to define the password required to access that resource.

Windows 95 doesn't limit you to providing access to an entire drive or printer. You can define access to an individual directory as well. I find it convenient to set aside a temporary directory on my machine for file sharing. People can upload their files to a specific directory and avoid changing the contents of the rest of my drive. You can use the same principle for other resources. The key is to maintain control of your system.

Peter's Principle: Maintaining Control of Your System

Sharing doesn't always mean that you allow everyone to access every resource on your machine. It's easier to simply provide access to an entire drive than it is to set the required level of security folder by folder, but providing access to an entire hard drive might not be feasible.

For example, many of us work with confidential information that we must keep safe, but we also work with other people who need to see some of the things we work with. Someone working in the accounting department might need to share analysis files with a workgroup. However, can you imagine what would happen if she also shared access to the payroll files? What about the new plans that your company might be working on? Even though you need to share access to the current project, you want to keep that new project a secret. A little bit of discretion can save you a lot of headaches later.

It's important that you provide the right level of access to everyone in your workgroup. Allow others to use the resources you have available, but don't allow misuse of those resources. It's up to you to do your part to maintain the proper level of network security.

Logon Scripts

Windows 95 provides several support mechanisms for logon scripts. The best support is for most versions of Novell's NetWare, but the same principles hold true (for the most part) with any other NOS (network operating system) that Windows 95 supports. This support doesn't extend to real-mode networks such as LANtastic. You need to perform any logon script requirements as a call from AUTOEXEC.BAT before you enter Windows 95. In most cases, this means running STARTNET.BAT for LANtastic. Check the vendor documentation for any requirements for using a logon script with your real-mode network. You follow the same procedure that you did prior to installing Windows 95.

Now that you have the real-mode networks out of the way, look at the kind of support you can expect for supported networks such as NetWare. The first thing you need to do is disable any AUTOEXEC.BAT or other batch files that you used to use under Windows 3.x. You don't need to log on to the network before entering Windows 95. Any workstations that use NetWare must have an account on the server before you install Client for NetWare.

Note: I was surprised to find that the protected-mode Client for NetWare networks isn't under the Novell entry of the clients listing. You'll find it in the Microsoft list of clients. Novell didn't supply the protected-mode client for NetWare with Windows 95; Microsoft did.

If you install either of the entries from the Novell listing, you'll be using real-mode drivers. Not only does this reduce performance and cause some level of system instability, it also removes many of the benefits of using an integrated approach to networking. For example, you won't be able to use a single logon screen for both NetWare and Microsoft; you'll have to enter them separately. Always try the protected-mode drivers first, just to see whether they'll work with your system setup.

continues

Fortunately, you can download the Novell version of the NetWare client at `http://support.novell.com/Ftp/Updates/nwos/nc32w952/Date0.html`. This site includes other Novell-supplied Windows 95 fixes and patches as well. Be sure to read any update files associated with the drivers before you install them.

After you get Client for NetWare installed, select it in the Primary Network Logon field of the Network Properties dialog. You access this dialog by right-clicking the Network Neighborhood icon and selecting the Properties option. The first time you run Client for NetWare, you see two logon dialogs. The first dialog logs you on to a preferred server, and the second takes care of the Windows 95 security requirement. As long as the user name and password for NetWare and Windows 95 are the same, you see this dual logon dialog only once. The next time you log on, you see only one dialog, which takes care of both logon needs.

To enable logon script processing on the NetWare server, you need to check the Client for NetWare Networks Properties dialog, shown in Figure 27.5. This dialog has three fields. The one you're interested in is a check box that will enable logon script processing. You also see fields for the preferred server and the first network drive.

Figure 27.5.
*The Client for
NetWare Networks
Properties dialog allows
you to enable logon
script processing.*

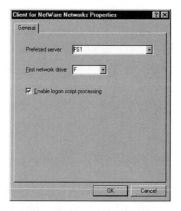

Enabling logon script processing allows an administrator to maintain the pre–Windows 95 security policy on the server. It also provides a means for creating automatic drive mapping and other NOS-specific features. You need to check the documentation that came with your network to see exactly what types of script file processing you can perform.

Warning: The Windows 95 protected-mode script processor can't run TSRs. The TSR starts in a separate virtual machine, which terminates with an error when the script file processing completes. This lack of TSR processing in your script files means you have to come up with a different way to install backup agents and other files that you normally install using the logon script. In most cases, you need to install such files as part of the AUTOEXEC.BAT or within a DOS session after you start Windows 95.

TCP/IP and PPP: It's in There!

Windows 95 provides a fairly complex and complete set of Transmission Control Protocol/Internet Protocol (TCP/IP) features. A protocol establishes rules that allow two nodes—workstations, mainframes, minicomputers, or other network elements such as printers—to talk to each other. TCP/IP is one of the more popular sets of network communication rules. Point-to-Point Protocol (PPP) is a set of communication rules that provides a method for connecting to a UNIX host or the Internet.

Before you can use TCP/IP, you have to install it. Let's quickly go through a few of the things you need to do to install TCP/IP support:

1. Right-click the Network Neighborhood icon and select Properties.
2. On the Configuration tab, click the Add button. You see the dialog shown in Figure 27.6.

Figure 27.6.
The Select Network Component Type dialog allows you to choose the type of network component to install.

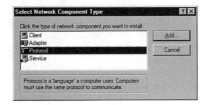

3. Select Protocol and click Add. Scroll through the list of manufacturers and select Microsoft.
4. Select TCP/IP in the listing on the right side of the dialog shown in Figure 27.7.

Figure 27.7.
Use the Select Network Protocol dialog to select TCP/IP as the protocol you want to install.

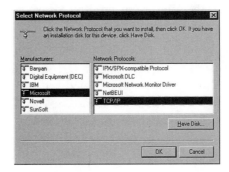

5. Click OK to complete the selection. Click OK again to close the Network Properties dialog. Windows 95 prompts you for installation floppies or the CD-ROM as needed. After it installs the required files, it asks if you want to restart the system. Click OK to complete the installation process.

Tip: Installing TCP/IP support before you install Dial-Up Networking will save some extra steps later. The Dial-Up Networking installation routine automatically installs the required protocols for you if you install TCP/IP support first.

Configuring the TCP/IP support once you get it installed is easy:

1. Select the TCP/IP entry in the Network Properties dialog.

2. Click the Properties button. You see a dialog similar to the one shown in Figure 27.8.

Figure 27.8.
The TCP/IP Properties dialog allows you to configure TCP/IP support under Windows 95.

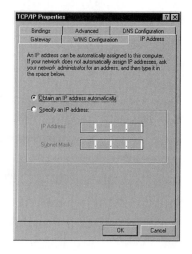

Essentially, all the tabs in this dialog allow you to set the addresses and other TCP/IP properties for your machine. All the setup options available for automatic setup are present when you use this manual technique.

After you complete this initial installation process, you need to perform other installations to provide specific levels of support. For example, you need to install Dial-Up Networking, and then the TCP/IP support that Windows provides, before you can access that support for a remote connection. The following sections show you how to configure Windows 95 to use both TCP/IP and PPP. I also cover a few of the usage issues you need to know.

SNMP Support

Windows 95 provides remote monitoring agent support for agents that use the Simple Network Management Protocol (SNMP). SNMP was originally designed for the Internet. It allows an application to remotely manage devices from a variety of vendors, even if that device doesn't normally work with the managing device. For example, a mainframe can use SNMP to send updated sales statistics to a group of satellite offices in a large company. You can use an SNMP console to monitor a Windows 95 workstation once this support is installed. SNMP support under Windows 95 conforms to the Version 1 specification. Microsoft implements SNMP support for both TCP/IP and IPX/SPX using WinSock (which I describe later). The following procedure allows you to install SNMP support under Windows 95:

1. Right-click the Network Neighborhood icon and select the Properties option.

2. From the Network Properties dialog, click Add and then double-click Services. You should see the dialog shown in Figure 27.9.

Figure 27.9.
You'll find a list of the common network services in the Select Network Service dialog.

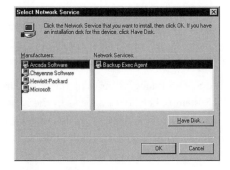

3. Click Have Disk and then click Browse. Search for the `\ADMIN\NETTOOLS\SNMP` folder, shown in Figure 27.10. Notice that the dialog automatically finds the INF file required to install this service.

Figure 27.10.
Browsing is the easy way to find the network component you need to install.

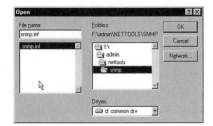

4. Click OK twice. You should see the dialog shown in Figure 27.11, which allows you to select from the list of network components that the INF file will install. In this case, there's only one on the list—SNMP support.

Figure 27.11.
This Select Network Service dialog presents a list of services supported by the INF file you selected.

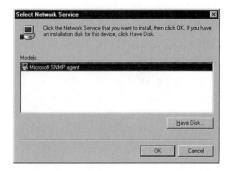

5. Select the new service and click OK. You see that SNMP support is part of the installed component list of the Network Properties dialog.

6. Click OK to close the dialog. Windows 95 installs the required files from the CD. When it completes this task, Windows 95 asks whether you want to shut down and restart the operating system. You need to do this before SNMP support will take effect.

Unlike just about every other feature in Windows 95, there is no Properties dialog for SNMP support. You need to edit the various properties using the System Policy Editor. Simply open the System Policy Editor and select File | Registry to open the Registry.

You can install the System Policy Editor using the procedure found in Chapter 11, "The Windows 95 Applets." The System Policy Editor appears in the `\ADMIN\APPTOOLS\POLEDIT` folder of the CD-ROM. Double-click the Local Computer icon and select the SNMP option of the Network policy, as shown in Figure 27.12. There you can change all the SNMP policies for your machine.

Figure 27.12.
The System Policy Editor provides the only method for changing your SNMP configuration.

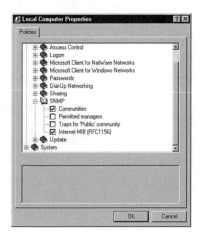

As you can see from the figure, you can change four different settings:

- Communities—This setting defines the hosts your computer can connect to for administration purposes. You must belong to a community before you can use SNMP services on it. Even though they aren't exactly the same, you could look at a community as a NetWare group or a Windows NT domain.

- Permitted managers—This setting defines a list of IP or IPX addresses that can query the SNMP agent installed on your machine. If you don't provide a value here, any IP or IPX address can query the agent.

- Traps for 'Public' community—Use this setting to define a list of host IP or IPX address to which you want to send SNMP traps. A *trap* is essentially an automatic monitoring method that updates the host when specific events occur on your machine.

- Internet MIB (RFC1156)—This setting determines a point of contact and location if you're using the Internet MIB.

The System Policy Editor configuration procedure comes in handy for more than just SNMP installation and configuration. I refer to it several times in this chapter. You can also use the System Policy Editor to affect the condition of other network settings. However, I normally find that the Properties dialog that comes with this feature usually provides an easier-to-use interface.

Using the Telnet Utility

The Telnet utility lets you create a remote session on another computer. This is another utility program that Windows 95 installs automatically when you install TCP/IP support. The strange thing is that Windows 95 doesn't automatically install it in your Start menu. You need to add it manually. The Telnet utility always appears in your Windows folder.

When you open the Telnet utility, you see a dialog similar to the one shown in Figure 27.13. It's fairly simple to operate this application. The four menus provide a basic set of features for logging on to a host and keeping track of your session.

Figure 27.13.
Telnet provides a basic terminal-like front end for a host connection.

The Connect | Remote System command displays the Connect dialog, shown in Figure 27.14. This dialog has three fields: The first contains the name or address of the host you want to connect to, the second contains the host type, and the third specifies a terminal type. In most cases, you won't have much of a choice about terminal types, but I find that the ANSI terminal is a bit easier to use if you can gain access to a host that supports it. Disconnecting from the host is very easy. Just select Connect | Disconnect.

Figure 27.14.
The Connect dialog is
where you tell Telnet
how and where to
make a connection.

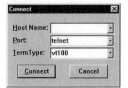

Figure 27.15 shows the dialog that appears when you select Terminal | Preferences. The Terminal Options and Emulation groups are pretty self-explanatory: They configure the way the host machine interacts with the terminal emulation program. The Fonts button allows you to select a font other than the default Fixedsys. You can also add a little color to the display by clicking the Background Color button. I normally keep it as is because you can't change the foreground color. The Buffer Size field allows you to change the number of lines of text you see in the terminal window. Telnet uses a default setting of 25, which seems to work well with most hosts.

Figure 27.15.
Use the Terminal
Preferences dialog to
configure Telnet to
the host that you plan
to connect with.

Desktop Management Interface (DMI) Support

Desktop Management Interface (DMI) is part of Systems Management Server that works as the hardware auditing component of this utility and follows the standards set by the Desktop Management Task Force (DMTF).

Note: The OSR2 version of Windows 95 provides support for the 1.1 version of DMI. This new version of DMI will give network administrators a better look into the hardware by examining dependencies. For example, a fan failure might cause a hard drive to fail. It's also designed to work with servers, even if they aren't running Windows 95. (Of course, the server hardware has to be DMI-compliant.) Although a download site wasn't available at the time of this writing, Microsoft plans to make the update available to users of older versions of Windows 95. You can contact the DMTF—Desktop Management Task Force Web site at `http://www.dmtf.org/` for further details on this update.

A vendor writes a management information file (MIF) that contains all the particulars about a piece of equipment. When the System Management Server looks at a workstation and finds this file, it adds its contents to a SQL database that you can open with any number of products. Besides the hardware information, System Management Server adds to the database the software auditing information that it finds. The combined software and hardware information will give you the data required to know whether a particular workstation can run a piece of software without an upgrade.

Unfortunate as it might seem, none of this is fully implemented in Windows 95 as of this writing. DMI client support is present, but you won't find System Management Server anywhere on your CD. (The client support level for the original and Service Pack 1 versions of Windows 95 is 1.0; OSR2 provides Version 1.1 support.) Adding server support is an upgrade that Microsoft might make to Windows 95 in the future. Although it might not help you right this second, it's good to know that help is on the way. However, if you have the following equipment, you can implement System Management Server today:

- Windows NT Server Version 3.5 or later.
- Microsoft SQL Server Version 4.21 or later.
- A 486/66 or better processor.
- 32MB of memory (recommended).
- A hard disk with at least 100MB available.
- A network-accessible CD-ROM drive.
- A network adapter.
- A Microsoft mouse or compatible pointing device. (A mouse is recommended but optional.)

Remote Procedure Calls (RPC) Support

Remote procedure calls (RPCs) are a somewhat new concept for Windows 95. They're implemented as a network transport mechanism using named pipes, NetBIOS, or WinSock to create a connection between a client and a server. RPC is compatible with the Open Software Foundation (OSF) Data Communication Exchange (DCE) specification.

What does RPC do for you? OLE uses it, for one. (Actually, OLE uses a subset of RPC called light RPC, or *LRPC*, to allow you to make connections that you couldn't normally make.) I discussed this issue in detail in Chapter 12, "DDE, OLE, DCOM, and ActiveX," so I don't talk about it again here. However, OLE is only the tip of the iceberg. There are other ways in which RPC can help you as a user.

Think about it this way. You're using an application that requires any number of resources in the form of DLLs, VxDs, and other executable code. Right now, all that code has to appear on your machine or in a place where Windows is certain to find it. That means every time a network administrator wants to update software, he has to search every machine on the network to make sure the job gets done. What if you could borrow the DLL from someone else's machine? That's what RPCs are all about. An RPC lets your application grab what it needs in the form of executable code from wherever it happens to be.

You won't find a lot of RPC support in Windows 95 right now, but there's one way to see how it works. If you're running a Windows NT network, Microsoft provides a remote print provider utility in the \ADMIN\APPTOOLS\RPCPP folder. Installing this utility allows a Windows 95 client to administer printer queues on Windows NT servers. Using this print provider, a Windows 95 client can obtain complete accounting and job status information from the Windows NT server.

Windows Sockets (WinSock) Support

Windows sockets (WinSock) started out as an effort by a group of vendors to make sense of the conglomeration of TCP/IP protocol-based socket interfaces. Various vendors had originally ported their implementation of this protocol to Windows. The result was that nothing worked with anything else. The socket interface was originally implemented as a networked interprocess communication mechanism for version 4.2 of the Berkeley UNIX system. Windows 95 requires all non-NetBIOS applications to use WinSock if they need to access any TCP/IP services. Vendors may optionally write IPX/SPX applications to this standard as well. Microsoft includes three WinSock applications with Windows 95: SNMP, Telnet, and FTP.

Think of a socket as one of the tube holders found in old televisions and radios. An application can plug a request (a tube) for some type of service into a socket and send it to a host of some kind. That host could be a file server, a minicomputer, a mainframe, or even another PC. An application can also use a socket to query a database server. For example, it could ask for last year's sales statistics. If every host uses a different-sized socket, every application will require a different set of tubes to fit those sockets. WinSock resolves this by standardizing the socket used to request services and make queries.

WinSock provides another advantage. An application must normally add a NetBIOS header to every packet that leaves the workstation. The workstation at the other end doesn't really need the header, but it's there anyway. This additional processing overhead reduces network efficiency. Using WinSock eliminates the need for the header, and the user sees better performance as a result.

Sockets are an age-old principle (at least in the computer world), but they are far from out of date. The WinSock project proved so successful that Microsoft began to move it to other transports. For example, Windows 95 includes a WinSock module for both the IPX/SPX and NetBEUI transports.

Of course, WinSock is really a stop-gap measure for today. In the long term, companies will want to move from the client-server model for some applications and use a distributed approach. This will require the use of a remote procedure call (RPC) interface instead of WinSock.

What does it take to implement WinSock on your system? Five files in your SYSTEM folder are used to implement WinSock:

- WINSOCK.DLL—This 16-bit application provides backward compatibility for older applications that need it. For example, an application such as Ping uses this DLL.

- WSOCK32.DLL—32-bit applications use this DLL to access the WinSock API. It provides support for newer socket applications such as Telnet.

- VSOCK.VXD—Windows uses this driver to provide both 16-bit and 32-bit TCP/IP and IPX/SPX WinSock support. It provides virtualized support for each virtual machine, enabling Windows to perform more than one WinSock operation at a time. This is the general driver used for both protocols. If Microsoft added more WinSock interfaces later, they would all require this file for interface purposes.

- WSTCP.VXD—TCP/IP requires a protocol-specific driver. This file provides that support.

- WSIPX.VXD—IPX/SPX requires a protocol-specific driver. This file provides that support.

Configuring TCP/IP—the Short Form

The same flexibility that makes Windows 95 so easy to use with TCP/IP makes it nearly impossible for an inexperienced user to configure it. With this in mind, I decided to provide a fast and easy method for you to configure TCP/IP for a local intranet. I assume that you're going to use Personal Web Server on a LAN in this section, but the principles apply equally well to other kinds of setups. To configure TCP/IP, do the following:

1. Install TCP/IP. (Refer to the section "TCP/IP and PPP: It's in There!" earlier in this chapter.)

2. Modify its properties so that other computers can see you. Simply right-click the Network Neighborhood icon, choose Properties from the context menu, and then select the TCP/IP protocol on the Configuration tab of the Network Properties dialog box. (You might have more than one entry here; select the TCP/IP entry for your NIC, not for dial-up connections.)

3. Click the Properties button, and you see the TCP/IP Properties dialog.

4. Select the IP Address tab, and you see a dialog like the one shown in Figure 27.16.

Figure 27.16.

Use the TCP/IP Properties dialog box to set up TCP/IP on your machine for local intranet use.

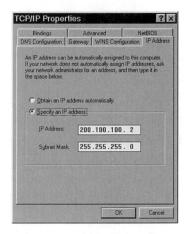

5. Note how I've configured the IP Address tab in my dialog box. You need to worry about only two fields, which work together:

   • IP Address—An IP address is composed of two parts: The first part defines your organization, and the second part defines your individual computer. The IP address is composed of four numbers separated by periods. You can choose up to three of those numbers to represent your organization. The remaining numbers represent your computer. A single entry can contain any value from 0 to 255. All four entries combined make up the IP address. If you were on the Internet, you'd have to apply to InterNIC to get an IP address. On a local intranet, however, you're not really talking to anyone but your own organization. You just have to make sure that each machine has a unique IP address and uses the same subnet address.

Peter's Principle: Selecting Your IP Address (Intranet)

I normally select three, easy-to-remember numbers for my organization and then use the remaining IP address entry to sequentially number the computers on my network. In this case, I've chosen 200.100.100 to represent my organization and 2 to represent the workstation.

   • Subnet Mask—The subnet mask contains four numbers separated by periods, where each number ranges from 0 to 255. As you can see from the figure, I used a value of 255 for the first three numbers because those numbers represent my organization. I placed a 0 in the last position because it represents my workstation.

6. Finally, you must enable one computer to talk to another. Every computer on your network must use the same organization number or it won't be able to hear the other computers. In addition, every computer must have a unique node number. Because 1 is already in use, I

use 2 for the next node. You must configure all the computers on your network before they can talk to the intranet server on your workstation.

Note: Checking these connections is relatively easy. Windows 95 provides a DOS utility called Ping (Packet Internet Groper), which checks your capability to communicate with other TCP/IP workstations. All you need to do is type PING *workstation IP address*. To make sure your own workstation is configured properly, use the PING command, such as typing **PING 200.100.100.1**, where 200.100.100.1 identifies your own workstation. Ping transmits three packets and listens for a response. If you see three responses from a particular workstation, you'll know you've configured it properly.

Using Microsoft NDS Client

Beta
Release

NetWare Directory Services (NDS) support in Windows 95 was less than adequate for most users. Problems ranged from an inability to use some NetWare features to not being able to log on at all. Even though the Microsoft client was small and efficient, it just wouldn't do the job for some people. Novell came out with a 32-bit NDS client, which works a lot better and contains more features than the one provided by Microsoft. The only problem with this client is that it consumes huge amounts of memory.

Using Novell Client 32

When Microsoft introduced Windows 95, there were no 32-bit NDS clients for Novell NetWare, and it didn't take long for users to get irate about this. After all, one of the benefits of using NetWare 4.*x* was NDS—the idea that you could manage a large network from one location using one utility.

Microsoft's client arrived on the scene a short time after Windows 95 appeared on the market. Unfortunately, the client was buggy and had limited capabilities. The first version of the Microsoft client barely allowed you to log on to an NDS-enabled NetWare server.

After the Microsoft client appeared on the market, the Novell version appeared. This client was just as buggy but offered all the features a user might need to manage NetWare server.

Both clients are getting better, although neither is bug free even to this day. Microsoft and Novell are working on patches to fix various problems. Suffice it to say that you're going to need an update or two no matter which client you select.

What are the differences between the two NDS clients? Microsoft's client is lean. It consumes few system resources when compared to Novell's, but it doesn't offer many of the features you need. For example, you'll see in the section "Using Explorer with Client 32" later in this chapter that the Novell client modifies how Explorer works. It allows you to view and assign user rights to directories and files (provided you have the proper rights). As you'll see in the section "Differences in Network Neighborhood" later in this chapter, the Network Neighborhood display is enhanced. You'll also see that the Novell offering provides extensive configuration flexibility—something you really need if you want to get the most out of your network. The added flexibility also comes in handy when you start experiencing compatibility problems or other network-related configuration problems. Finally, you absolutely have to have the Novell client if you want to use the NWAdmin utility. Microsoft's latest client is supposed to provide support for this essential utility program, but the level of that support is minimal at best.

Obviously, all these added features come with a price. Although the Novell client will help you find things more quickly and does provide a generally faster interface, you're going to pay a heavy penalty in memory usage. Don't even attempt to use this client with a minimal machine configuration. In fact, you want to make sure that every machine using the Novell client has at least 32MB of RAM installed. You'll also give up some hard disk space. The current version of the Novell client (including patches) consumes 3MB of hard disk space, not including all the files it places in your SYSTEM folder. Finally, even though I find that the Novell client is a little more reliable than Microsoft's, you'll find that all the features this client offers can get confusing. At minimum, you'll find that users have more questions when it comes to Network Neighborhood. Be prepared to spend a little more time holding the user's hand after you install the Novell client.

> **Tip:** There's no rule that says you have to use one client on your network. In most cases, I use the Microsoft client on the majority of machines. It's small and easy to use, so users feel more comfortable using it. I install the Novell client if a machine has problems accessing the network or needs added flexibility. Every network administrator machine also gets the Novell client, as do manager machines where the manager needs access to NDS.

Installing the Client

Getting Client 32 installed on your machine is about as easy as software installation gets:

1. Download the required software from http://support.novell.com/Ftp/Updates/nwos/ nc32w952/Date0.html or from CompuServe.

2. After you download and unpack the software, double-click the Setup icon. You see a dialog similar to the one shown in Figure 27.17.

3. Click Yes if you agree to the license terms. You see a dialog like the one in Figure 27.18. Simply click Start, and the Setup program takes care of all the details for you.

Figure 27.17.
The license agreement is the first thing you see when you start the Client 32 installation.

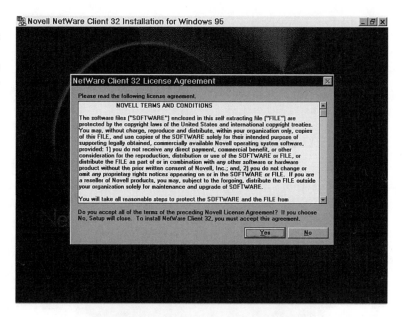

Figure 27.18.
Simply click Start at this dialog, and Setup takes care of the rest.

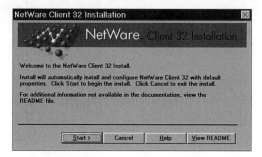

The first thing Setup does is remove your old client. I mention this because you might want to run the installation from a local drive instead of from the network. Although Setup doesn't actually disconnect you from the server, a failure requiring reboot at this point could leave you with no client at all (making the file server inaccessible).

After the old client is removed, Setup installs a few new files in the Windows INF folder. At this point, it forces Windows 95 to rebuild its drivers list based on the contents of the new INF file. Setup automatically selects and installs the new client. You see another rebuild of the driver list after the new client is installed.

After all the files are copied and Setup performs a basic setup, you are asked to reboot your machine. After you do so, you'll be using the new client. Getting started couldn't be much easier than that.

Tip: Make sure you know your current context and NDS tree. You need this information the first time you restart your machine with the Novell client installed. The preferred tree and context information gets recorded so you don't have to enter it again.

Configuration Options

Configuring Novell's Client 32 is much like configuring any other network-related driver: Open the Network properties dialog (right-click Network Neighborhood and select Properties from the context menu). Select the Novell NetWare Client 32 entry in the components list shown on the Configuration tab. Click the Properties button. You see a Novell NetWare Client 32 Properties dialog similar to the one shown in Figure 27.19, which displays the Client 32 tab.

Figure 27.19.

The Novell NetWare Client 32 Properties dialog enables you to configure the client.

The Client 32 tab contains the following fields:

- Preferred server—Leave this field blank unless you want a bindery connection in place of an NDS connection.

- Preferred tree—Enter the name of the tree that you want the client to search for your name in this field.

- Name context—This field should contain the name of your organization and workgroup. (The figure shows only the organization name.)

- First network drive—Enter the first network drive in this field. Unlike with the Microsoft client, you can select a drive below F if you want to. For example, you might have only a hard drive and CD-ROM installed on your machine. Selecting E as the first network connection will save you one drive letter.

When you log on to the network, you see a single-page logon dialog similar to the one used by the Microsoft client. This works well if only one user uses the same network configuration on a single machine each day, but if you have a user with special needs, you want to modify one or more of the sections in the Login tab of the Novell NetWare Client 32 Properties dialog (see Figure 27.20):

- Display connection page—Use the settings in this section to tell Client 32 that you want to see the page that enables you to select a preferred server or tree each time you log on. This allows you to change the default server you use each day, providing added flexibility for those times you have to log on as the network administrator instead of as a regular user. This tab contains the following options:

  - Clear current connections—Select this check box to clear all the connection information each time you log on. I normally disable this check box because I use the same server every day unless I need to perform administrative duties. However, if several users use a single machine, you probably want to keep it checked for security. Using this feature enables you to keep a hidden server hidden.

  - Bindery connection—This check box, which forces a bindery connection to the server instead of an NDS connection, isn't highlighted in this case. Selecting the Log in to server option highlights this check box.

- Display script page—The administrator typically assigns a default set of scripts to each user on the network. These scripts set up any drive mappings or other essential network configurations. Client 32 allows you to select one of the NDS scripts using a script page during logon, which is what the Display script page section is all about.

  Notice that this section contains two separate fields for script names: Login Script and Profile Script. You can choose NDS script objects or a simple batch file on your machine; Client 32 will work with either one. Two check boxes affect the way the scripts are run. Selecting the Close script results automatically option closes the script window when it is complete. In most cases, you want to keep this checked; unchecking it allows you to observe results of a script during debugging. The Run scripts check box tells Client 32 to run the scripts you've selected. You can uncheck this box if you don't want to run any scripts during the logon process.

- Display variables page—This section also relates to scripts. Selecting the Display variables page check box displays a third additional page during the logon process. You can use the fields on this page to pass variable information to your scripts. This is especially handy if you want to build one script file to serve a number of purposes.

Figure 27.20.
The Login tab allows
you to modify the
appearance of your
logon dialog.

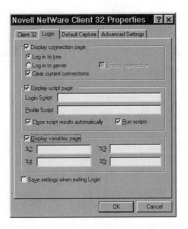

The Default Capture tab of the Novell NetWare Client 32 Properties dialog, shown in Figure 27.21, allows you to get around certain printing problems. If you have worked with printers before, you should recognize this page as a generic form of the one I discussed in the section "Installing a Printer" in Chapter 16, "Fonts and Printing." Because these settings perform the same purpose, I don't discuss them here. Just remember that these settings affect the network printers as a whole, the settings of printers you have already installed. Windows 95 overrides any settings you make on this page.

Figure 27.21.
The Default Capture
tab allows you to
change the default
settings for new
network printers.

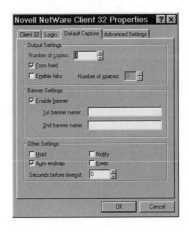

The final tab on the Novell NetWare Client 32 Properties dialog, Advanced Settings, is shown in Figure 27.22. Although you might never need to adjust these settings, some of them can help you fine-tune the way Client 32 works. For example, the Delay Writes setting can help in situations where an application repeatedly opens and closes files on the server (such as overlays). The client holds the file write for a given number of clock ticks to ensure that the application actually wants to write the information. In essence, this setting works as a disk cache. One of the handier troubleshooting aids is the Log File setting. You can tell Client 32 to log any errors it encounters. The Log File Size setting allows you to keep the file size under control.

Figure 27.22.
*The Advanced
Settings tab allows
you to fine-tune your
Client 32 settings.*

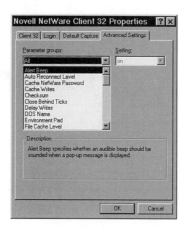

Differences in Network Neighborhood

Novell's Client 32 does things a bit differently from Microsoft's client when it comes to Network Neighborhood. The first thing you want to look at is the NetWare Connections option on the Network Neighborhood context menu. Selecting this option displays a Current NetWare Resources dialog like the one shown in Figure 27.23.

Figure 27.23.
*The Current
NetWare Resources
dialog provides more
information than its
Microsoft counter-
part.*

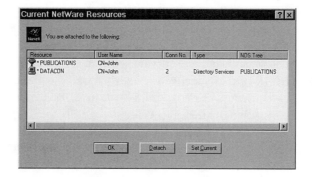

Not only does this dialog tell you what server you're connected to and the type of connection, it tells you all about your context, including the tree you're logged on to. This dialog provides a lot more information than its Microsoft counterpart. The only problem is that novice users think they're using two connections. Although it might appear that you're using two connections, you're actually using one, even if the Conn No. column of the dialog displays the number 2.

Double-clicking Network Neighborhood presents a few surprises as well. Figure 27.24 shows a typical setup; notice that there are three NetWare-specific entries instead of the one. The first looks like a standard computer and shows the file server (DataCon). The second looks like a tree; it's the NDS tree you're logged on to (Publications). Finally, you see the default context you're logged on to (which looks like a white square in the figure). Each of these icons serves a different purpose, but the one you use most is the server icon.

Figure 27.24.
Network Neighbor-hood takes on a slightly different appearance when you use Client 32.

If you double-click a server icon, you see something similar to the display shown in Figure 27.25. As you can see, this typical Explorer display resembles the ones you've seen. However, I have one bit of advice: Get all your drive mappings from this view of your server. Don't use the Resource view that you get by double-clicking the content icon. You get friendlier names in Explorer if you use this view. For example, if you map the SYS volume shown in Figure 27.26, the name you see in Explorer is \\DataCon\SYS. Map the same drive from the context view of the server resources and you get something like \\PUBLICATIONS\.DATACON_SYS.DATACON_SVCS. It's still readable, but less so than the standard UNC name you get in the server view.

Figure 27.25.
Double-clicking the server icon displays a standard Explorer view of resource like the one shown here.

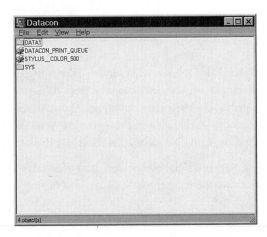

Figure 27.26.
The context view of your server resources provides more information than the server view.

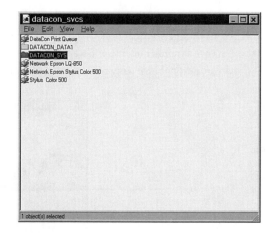

The context view provides information you won't find using the server view. Figure 27.26 shows what you'll probably get if you double-click the context icon. You should notice two things:

- This view of server resources uses long names. I find that it's more readable when I need to search for a system resource.

- You get to see all of the resources. The standard server view in Figure 27.25 shows only the print queues, whereas the context view in Figure 27.26 shows both the print queues and the printers.

Each of the three icons provide some different context menu entries as well. Figure 27.27 shows the context menu for the server icon. Notice that you can use this context menu to log on, log off, display a dialog showing who you are on the network, and authenticate your server connection. (Authentication ensures that you're connected to the server you think and that you're connected in the proper context.)

Figure 27.27
The server icon context menu helps you maintain your server contact.

Like the context menu for the server icon, the NDS Tree context menu, shown in Figure 27.28, allows you to log on and log off as before, but this time it's to the tree rather than to the server. You can also display a dialog showing who you are and authenticate your connection as before. Another entry here allows you to change your context. Select it to invoke a dialog that asks you to change your context. You can type a number of entries here, but use ROOT as an example. Using this context takes you from the organizational level (my normal logon level) to the root of the NDS tree.

Figure 27.28.
The NDS tree context menu contains a special entry for changing your current NDS context.

The final context menu you'll examine, which is shown in Figure 27.29, belongs to the context icon. About the only thing this context menu will do for you is set the context to the default you provided in the Novell NetWare Client 32 Properties dialog (refer to Figure 27.19).

Figure 27.29.
The context icon context menu allows you to reset your NDS tree context to its default value.

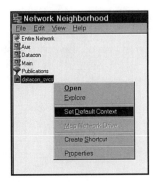

Using Explorer with Client 32

Client 32 affects the way Windows Explorer displays the Properties dialog for a network drive. Figure 27.30 show a typical example. Notice that you have several new tabs to use, including the NetWare Volume Information tab shown here. As you can see, this tab provides statistics on current disk usage and the amount of resources left.

Figure 27.30.
Client 32 adds three new tabs to the standard Explorer display.

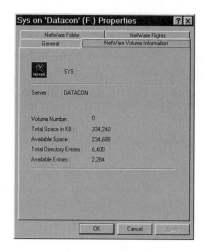

The NetWare Folder tab (Figure 27.31) gives you access to the volume attributes. (Files provide a similar tab with file-specific rights such as Transactional, so I don't discuss it in this section.) Notice that you can change NetWare-specific attributes such as Don't Compress and Compress Immediately. Normally you'd have to open the NWAdmin utility to change these settings. Other important pieces of information are shown on this tab: The first tells who owns the folder (or file). In this case, it's Supervisor. Notice that the tab also includes a Name Space field. You can use this information to determine which directories would be affected if you decided to remove the OS2 name space support required for long filenames from a volume. Finally, you get to see the folder's creation date, last update, and the date it was last archived. Unfortunately, you have to perform your backups from the server to keep this information current.

Figure 27.31.
The NetWare Folder tab allows you to control the folder attributes and presents statistical information.

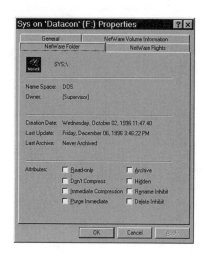

The NetWare Rights tab shown in Figure 27.32 allows you to view and assign the trustee rights for users of a folder or file. Notice that this dialog shows two trustees and the rights they have to the folder in the Trustees list. To change the rights for a particular individual or group, simply check or uncheck one or more of the rights check boxes. Removing a trustee is equally easy: Simply highlight the trustee you want to remove and click the Remove button.

Figure 27.32.
The NetWare Rights tab provides the most capability when it comes to administering a network.

The second section of the NetWare Rights tab provides a list of groups and users in the current context. (You need to change your context if you want to see users and groups in other parts of the NDS tree.) To add a user to the Trustee list, simply highlight the name, and then click the Add button. The user automatically gets a default set of rights assigned, but you can just as easily change them. You need to click Apply or OK to make the changes permanent.

The final section of the dialog shows effective rights. At first, it's easy to think that it shows the effective rights of the highlighted trustee. The fact is that it shows your effective rights to the folder or file. Even if users can't change trustee rights, they can use this tab of the dialog to see what their rights are to the folder.

32-Bit Data Link Control (DLC)

If you need to access a mainframe computer, you probably need to use the Data Link Control (DLC) protocol. Windows 95 originally provided only 16-bit support for this protocol (although Windows 95 with OSR2 provides 32-bit support as well), so mainframe access was a tad slower and more prone to crashes than access to other parts of the network. Windows 98 fixes both problems with a new 32-bit DLC protocol.

On Your Own

Use the information in this chapter to determine which of your system resources are shared and which are not. You might want to create a written list of who has access and where for future reference. This allows you to plug any security leaks whenever someone leaves the company.

After you determine who has access to your machine, look for any security leaks. Make sure you change passwords on a regular basis, especially after someone leaves the company. Check to see how the use of your system resources by others affects system performance and overall usability.

I discussed the network subsystem architecture in this chapter. Go through your SYSTEM folder to see whether you can identify the components that compose it. See if your network needs any special components because it uses an unusual protocol normal. You might also want to look for real-mode drivers still lurking around your hard drive.

28

Setting Up Security

Peter Norton®

Network security is a major thorn in the side of most network administrators. Even a small network requires some level of planning, and many managers fail to see the value of implementing the type of security they really need. Of course, I've seen the opposite side of the coin as well. Some administrators wrap the people who use the network in a tight cocoon of regulations and passwords. The choke hold these people create inhibits any kind of creative resource management and often impedes work.

It's difficult to create a bullet-proof network setup that offers the level of flexibility that most users require. Adding a bit of flexibility normally means that you also open a security hole. I find that a network administrator must reach an important balance. The first thing you need to realize is that there's no such thing as a bullet-proof security system. Any security system you design can be breached by someone else.

What do you do? Just leave the network open to whoever might want to access it? That's not the way to go either. The real goal is to put reasonable security restraints in place. You need to assess your security risks and do whatever it takes to reduce your risk to an acceptable level.

More important than physical security and password protection is the cooperation of those around you. I recently went into a client's office to check his network setup. He let me use one of his employee's desks to get the work done. Right in front of me was one of those yellow reminder pads. It contained not only the employee's password, but the superior's password as well. User names were all over the desk. Anyone could have walked into the office and gained access to the network because of this security breach. This incident reminded me of the importance of the human factor in any security plan. To implement a good security system, you need to consider the following elements:

- Physical security: Place your file server in a locked room. I can easily break the security for a NetWare setup (or most other networks, for that matter) if I have access to a running file server. If you lock up the file server, I can't access it unless I have a key.

- Software protection: Using passwords and other forms of software protection is your next line of defense. Make sure that all the right kinds of security measures are in place. I cover this topic in greater detail later in this chapter, but this is one area where Windows 95 can really help. It contains all the right features; all you need to do is implement them.

- Cooperative security: You can't secure the network by yourself. The larger your network, the more you need every user's cooperation. If you expect the users to cooperate with you, you need to talk to them to find out what's reasonable. No one will use an unreasonable security plan. This cooperative strategy also extends to management. If you don't tell management what your security problems are, they won't be able to help. You also need to make sure that management knows what kinds of security risks are present in the current setup. This reduces the chance of someone getting surprised later.

- Training: It's never a good idea to assume that users know how to use the security features that Windows 95 provides. You can implement a lot of the physical security, but it's the users who will use the software part of the equation. An untrained user might not use a particular security feature correctly or might not even know that it exists.

- A written security plan: I don't find this step necessary on small networks. However, as your network becomes larger, it becomes vitally important to get the rules put down in writing. Otherwise, how will a user know what's expected or how to react in a crisis? Writing everything down also makes management aware of the security you have in place.

This might seem like a lot of work to implement security, but it isn't when you consider the loss that a single security breach can cause. A pirate isn't going to steal last week's letter to the general public; he's going to steal something valuable. The more secret something is, the better the pirate likes it. Just think about what a competitor could do with your new marketing plan or the design for that new widget you plan to produce. Even if pirates don't take anything, they could leave something behind. What would a virus do to your network? Imagine your entire setup crumbling as a virus infects it.

In this chapter, I show you the features that Windows 95 provides to help you implement a companywide security plan. You've looked at many of these features already, so I don't go into a lot of detail in some areas. (I tell you where the detailed information does appear in this book, however.)

Local Security

Presumably, you've evaluated your security needs and designed a plan for setting up appropriate security measures. Now take a look at what Windows 95 can do to help. I was pleasantly surprised by some features but a bit dismayed by others. For example, the ability to assign two levels of password protection to every resource is nice and will probably work fine for a peer-to-peer network. The inability to assign a password to a specific file didn't sit well with me. Sometimes you need to protect one file in a directory but not another. Some older applications really need to have their configuration files in the same directory as the rest of the executables. I usually like to make my executable files read-only so that the user doesn't erase them.

However, putting these inconveniences aside, you can still implement a significant security strategy using Windows 95's built-in capabilities. The following sections describe these features. In most cases, I describe how to use and implement these features in other chapters, so I don't cover that aspect again here. I show you how to use the features that Windows 95 provides to implement a security plan.

Peter's Principle: When Will a Hacker Break Into Your Machine?

For me, the first sign of trouble when I visit a site to offer advice on security is the level of confidence that I find. If the system administrators are confident that a hacker can't break into their system, I'm almost positive a hacker will find a way to do so. The only sure thing

continues

about security software of any kind is that it keeps an honest person from going down the wrong road. If someone really wants to break into your system, he'll find a way to do it.

Think about the very concept of security software for a second. That software is designed by a programmer who wants to provide you with the best protection he can think of. Any software designed by a programmer can be overcome by an equally competent hacker thinking along the same lines. All the hacker really needs to do is figure out what line of reasoning the programmer followed when creating the security software and then think of a way around it. The idea that anyone can overcome your security precautions is important to remember. In other words, the very idea of a secure system is an illusion and a dangerous one at that.

If you can't count on your security software to prevent a break-in, what good is it? There are three ways security software can help. First, it acts as a direct deterrent to people who are basically honest and don't want to cause problems. Second, it can slow down even good hackers, which gives you time to react and prevent any major problems. Finally, good security software admits that it didn't stop the hackers, alerting you to the problem at hand. The one way in which security software won't help is to deter hackers from breaking in. The better your security, the more a hacker a will want to break it. In most cases, the hackers are after the thrill of killing your security; they don't even care what they find on your system.

The number-one way to stop hackers in their tracks is to start by assuming they're going to get past your security software. After you get that idea in mind, you can start looking for breaches in your security. A good piece of security software works with you to help you locate holes or unauthorized entry (which could be as simple as a break in someone's normal pattern of system access or an unusual number of password retries). Unfortunately, looking for holes is the only way you'll prevent someone from damaging your system.

Logon

The best way to prevent a security breach is to prevent someone from getting onto the network in the first place. The dialog you see when you start Windows 95 is your first line of defense against someone who tries to break into your system. I talked about the logon feature of Windows 95 in several places; you looked at it as part of the Control Panel applets in Chapter 11, "The Windows 95 Applets," and again in Chapter 27, "Networks." You also looked at how you can change the source of the network logon using the Network Properties dialog in Chapter 26, "Creating Your Own Internet Connection with Personal Web Server." Look at how you can actually use the Logon dialog to help implement a security strategy.

You can initiate the logon password in several ways. The most automatic method is to install a Microsoft (or any other) network. You also see a password screen if you allow users to configure their own desktops. No matter which way you install password protection, you need to manage it from time to time, and that's the purpose of this section.

The Passwords Properties dialog box displays when you open Control Panel and double-click the Password applet. You use the Change Windows Password option to change the password you see when you initially log onto the system. The same password is in effect whether you enable passwords through multiple user configurations or by using a Microsoft network.

> **Tip:** Windows 95 maintains an encrypted password file for each user. The filename corresponds to the user name and has an extension of .PWL. Windows 95 stores the PWL file either in the main Windows folder or in the user's profile folder. Erasing this file effectively erases the passwords stored for that particular person. Anyone who gets access to your system could erase all the stored passwords you use to access networks and dial-up networking connections by erasing that one file. The positive side of this is that if a user forgets his password, you can always regain access for him by erasing his password file.

The second option of the Change Passwords page allows you to change passwords you might have for other resources or networks. If you have access to another network in addition to a Windows peer-to-peer network, for example, you can use this option to change the password Windows uses to log you onto that network.

The actual process of changing your password doesn't vary much. Select the password you want to change and Windows displays a dialog box containing three fields. (Clicking the option to change your Windows password bypasses the password selection dialog box.) The first field contains your original password. This ensures that someone else won't come along and change your password without your permission. Type the new password into the second field and then again into the third field so Windows can verify it.

The Remote Administration page allows someone else to manage the Registry on your machine from a remote location. With this option, a network administrator can make changes to every machine on a peer-to-peer network without ever leaving his desk. I covered exactly how this works in Chapter 27. Fortunately, you can also password-protect remote administration. Type the access password into the first password field and again in the second field for verification purposes.

Windows 95 allows you to select from two different desktop configuration methods. You can either force every user of a single machine to use the same desktop, or you can allow multiple desktops by selecting the correct option on the User Profiles page. I covered implementing user profiles to enable customized desktops for each user in Chapter 4, "Working with the Active Desktop."

Standalone Security

It always amazes me when someone asks why it's important to take the time to protect a standalone workstation. Does the fact that a workstation doesn't connect to the network reduce the quality of the data it contains? The only part of the security picture that changes is that a standalone workstation at least keeps someone from accessing your data on the network. The fact that many standalone workstations contain valuable data is still important. In fact, I think you'll find that most standalone machines at your company are either relics that no one wants to use or engineering workstations that no one wants to expose to the security risks of network use. Either way, if your standalone machine has Windows 95 on it, it's pretty certain that the data it contains is valuable. The initial strategy to follow for a standalone workstation is to enable password protection using the Password Properties dialog, shown in Figure 28.1. Simply open Control Panel and double-click the Password applet.

Figure 28.1.

Protecting a stand-alone machine might require you to enable the multiple desktops feature, which requires each user to log in.

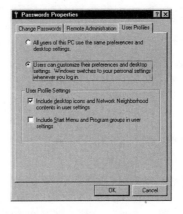

Tip: If security for a specific workstation is so important that software alone won't take care of the problem, consider one of several alternative solutions. For example, you can add a locking bolt to the back of the machine to prevent people from opening it and use the BIOS password feature to prevent access by any means until the user provides the correct password. Physical locking mechanisms are also available. One of them goes over the floppy disk drive to prevent the user from accessing it. You can also add a lock to a standard PC On/Off switch. Unfortunately, most of these solutions are expensive, inconvenient, or both. It's almost always worth your while to seek other solutions to the problem.

Note: You need to install the System Policy Editor using the Special Utility Installation procedure in Chapter 11. The required INF file appears in the \ADMIN\APPTOOLS\POLEDIT folder. After you install the System Policy Editor, you can access it by selecting Start | Programs | Accessories | System Tools.

Of course, just enabling passwords doesn't help you very much. What would prevent someone from coming along and turning the settings off? I always back up my configuration changes with a policy change to go with the password setting. This means opening the System Policy Editor and turning off various types of access. For example, you can turn off the Control Panel settings using the options shown in Figure 28.2. Notice that one of the settings in this list is the Passwords applet. Select File | Registry to load the current settings from the local Registry. The File | Save command saves any changes you make in the Registry before you exit the System Policy Editor. You see two icons after loading the Registry—one for the user and one for the machine. You want to modify the user settings. You need an administrator account to use the System Policy Editor this way. The following list explains each Control Panel restriction in detail.

Figure 28.2.
The System Policy Editor can help you protect Control Panel.

- Restrict Display Control Panel: You can choose to disable the entire Display applet, or you can select which pages in the Display Properties dialog get disabled. The first option in the list disables the entire applet. Every other option disables a single page at a time. This particular setting comes in handy for setting a screen saver password and then shutting off the page so that the user can't disable it.

- Restrict Network Control Panel: As with the Display applet, you can choose to disable the entire applet or individual pages. The Access Control page is the one to check here, but it really applies only when you have a network set up on the machine.

- Restrict Passwords Control Panel: This is one of the few applets I suggest disabling completely. Every page on this applet can produce potentially harmful effects for your setup. Of course, the big ones in a standalone setting are the User Profiles and Password pages.

- Restrict Printers Settings: The only good reason to implement this policy is if you're afraid the user will add a nonexistent printer or delete one installed on the machine. This policy affects only the General and Details pages.

- Restrict System Control Panel: This policy affects the Device Manager and Hardware Profiles pages. It also removes the Virtual Memory and File System buttons. Whether you disable these settings depends largely on the user's expertise. In most cases, you probably gain more than you lose by leaving these settings alone because the user will be able to help you troubleshoot many system problems if he can access the information these pages provide.

Note: If all this policy editing seems a little cumbersome or intimidating, you might want to check out Protect It!—a small utility that puts a simple face on basic access control for a standalone machine. It's designed for families and allows the owner (parent) to set restrictions on what resources other family members can use. Protect It! doesn't do anything you can't do with some judicious policy editing, but it's a bit easier to use. With a couple of mouse clicks, you can enable or block access to the modem, system settings, and programs that aren't on the Start menu or desktop. If necessary, you can restrict access to a list of approved programs. Protect It! also gives you access to the parental controls in Internet Explorer, so all the security controls you're likely to need are located in one convenient place.

Access to the program itself is password controlled. With Protect It! installed, your system won't be able to withstand an attack by a determined hacker, but it can be reasonably protected from accidental damage by novice users—whether they're kids or inexperienced new employees.

Protect It! is part of the Microsoft Plus! for Kids package. The other components of Plus! for Kids include Talk It! (type a word or phrase and listen to Talk It! say what you typed), Play It! (a kid-friendly onscreen keyboard), Paint It! (an updated version of the Paint drawing applet with special effects), and several desktop themes that appeal to kids in the target range for the program (ages 3–12). Because Plus! for Kids costs about $25, you might consider buying it just to get Protect It!.

I mentioned in Chapter 27 that a user can circumvent the password by erasing the PWL file. You can prevent this from happening by taking another preventative measure. Figure 28.3 shows the System Restrictions policy. Checking all four of these items prevents the user from accessing the hard drive in any manner other than the one you allow. You can restrict access to applications to only those required to complete the user's work. Disabling the DOS prompt also prevents the user from erasing the PWL files that way. Of course, the user who has to live with these restrictions might see them as constricting. Even though this strategy gives the network administrator the tools needed to prevent user meddling, it can backfire somewhere along the way.

Figure 28.3.

*The System
Restrictions policy
allows you to control
user access to
potentially harmful
applications.*

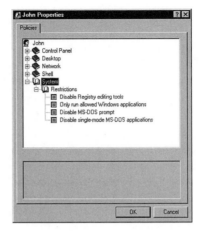

Tip: Disabling users' access to the hard drive after they start Windows 95 doesn't prevent other forms of access. For example, someone can boot a system using a floppy and remove the PWL and POL files. (The System Policy Editor stores its data in the POL file, and the system passwords appear in the PWL file.) This effectively disables any restrictions you placed on the user. Removing the floppy disables this form of access but makes it difficult to troubleshoot the machine or add new applications. You also need to set specific MSDOS.SYS settings to prevent users from exiting the boot sequence.

Using a combination of these settings allows you to restrict user access to most of the harmful features that Windows 95 provides. It is a lot better, however, if you can participate in a cooperative form of security rather than resort to these harsh measures that will likely cause a lot of user unhappiness.

You can impose a final level of restrictions on the user of a standalone machine. Figure 28.4 shows the Shell Restrictions policy options. As you can see, most of these options effectively prevent a user from exercising any form of control over the shell itself. Notice that these policies also provide some network settings. I refer to them again in the next section.

Of all the policies presented here, disabling the Run command is probably the most reasonable. It allows you to restrict the user from starting applications on the hard drive. This is especially important if you maintain a set of diagnostic tools on each local machine. For example, it's fairly likely that you wouldn't want the user to access the Registry Editor or the System Policy Editor.

Most of these settings are pretty self-explanatory, but the one that really caught my attention was the Hide all items on Desktop policy. About the only use I can think of for this setting is when you create the general system policy. You can disable access to everything, including the desktop. That way, if attackers manage to bypass the Logon dialog, they don't see much of value when Windows 95 starts.

Figure 28.4.

The Shell Restrictions policy allows you to control user access to the shell itself.

Peer-to-Peer Security

All the policies I covered in the "Standalone Security" section apply here as well, but there are several important differences. First, you'll probably load the system policies from a POL file instead of directly from the Registry. Second, you'll probably see more than just one user; this dialog includes groups as well. I covered the details of creating a policy file for a peer-to-peer network in Chapter 3, "Installing Windows 95: A Setup Primer."

Whether you set policies by groups or by the individual (or even a combination of both), the settings that I cover in the preceding section are the same. You can restrict the user from doing just about anything by implementing the right set of policies. The problem is that the more you restrict users, the harder it is for them to get anything done. As I mention at the beginning of this chapter, creating a security plan is often more a matter of considering an acceptable risk rather than trying to seal all the holes.

I'd like to again direct your attention to the Shell Restrictions policy shown in Figure 28.4. I want to talk about quite a few network restrictions in this section because they don't really apply to standalone machines. There are three Network-Neighborhood–specific settings here. The problem with implementing these policies is that they restrict users from exploring the network. This could be a good policy if you're working with a computer novice who has managed to damage network files by accident in the past. However, restricting users from exploring their computers only removes any reason for them to really learn about it. Training users is almost always a matter of sparking their interest in what the computer can do. Inhibiting that interest is about the most counterproductive thing you can do. That said, you'll probably want to think twice about implementing these policies for most users.

There's one set of policies you should probably consider implementing on a structured network, especially if you manage a lot of machines. Figure 28.5 shows the Network Sharing policies. There are two of them—one for printers and one for drives. Disabling users' ability to share (or not share) resources on their machines could save you a lot of trouble in the long run. Users might not always understand why you granted someone else access to their hard drives. Unless you want to explain each and every setting on every machine on the network to every user, you'll probably want to disable these settings.

Figure 28.5.
The network administrator, not the user, should set the policy regarding drive and printer sharing.

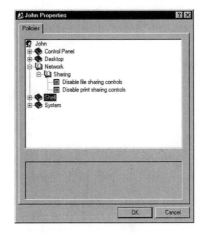

Peer-to-peer networks also need to consider the machine settings for each computer in the System Policy Editor. For example, how do you want the various machines to talk to each other, and which protocols will they use? I covered many of these issues in Chapter 27. Other settings are discussed in the following sections. The important thing to see right now is the overall picture. Figure 28.6 shows the overall settings picture for the machine-network settings.

Figure 28.6.
Machine-specific settings become important in a peer-to-peer networking environment.

The Access Control setting performs the same function as that page in the Network Properties dialog. It's included here so that you can set that policy using a remote terminal. (In fact, every important setting that you can change with a Properties dialog also appears somewhere in the System Policy Editor so that you can change it remotely.)

The System policies for a machine can provide some additional security as well. Figure 28.7 shows the various settings you can change. One of the settings I use quite a bit is Network path for Windows Setup. This policy allows you to place a copy of Windows 95 on a file server and then prevent the user from accessing it. The network administrator can update a system with ease, but the user is restricted from adding new Windows 95 features.

Figure 28.7.
Although it's not immediately apparent, the System policy can help you implement a security strategy.

The three Run policies provide an opportunity to load network monitors and other applications. A monitor can help you keep track of how the user interacts with the network as well as the current status of the workstation itself. Of course, you can also use this policy to add default applications to the user's setup. For example, company policy might dictate that everyone use a specific contact manager or e-mail program. You could add either program to the Run policy in order to load them automatically for the user.

Client/Server Security

As I mentioned earlier, you can use the same settings I described in the "Standalone Security" section with a client/server security setup for a NOS such as NetWare or Windows NT. You can also add the peer-to-peer networking security that I described in the preceding section. Windows 95 provides some additional capabilities for client/server setups that I didn't describe earlier. Some of these settings appear in Chapter 27. For example, you can implement a remote monitor using SNMP.

The major addition to security that Windows 95 provides for client/server networks is the capability to download system policies from the file server. You must install the Group Policy features using the same procedure you use for installing the System Policy Editor. Placing the GROUPPOL.DLL file in your SYSTEM folder enables Windows 95 to download group policies included in your POL file to the local workstation.

You need to know some things about group policies. First, Windows 95 doesn't override an individual user policy with a group policy. If you want to use groups, don't define any individual policies for that particular user. Second, Windows 95 processes the groups in the order of precedence that you set using the Options | Group Priority command. The Group Priority dialog, shown in Figure 28.8, allows you to change the way Windows 95 views each group policy. A policy in a high-priority group always overrides a policy in a low-priority group. This means that you have to set the priorities to reflect the security requirements of the network. Otherwise, you could accidentally give a user access to something he would normally not require access to.

Figure 28.8.

*Use the Group
Priority dialog to
change the order in
which Windows 95
interprets each group
policy.*

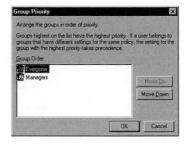

The Password Cache

Windows 95 implements something called a *password cache*. The PWL or password list file in either the main Windows 95 or your individual profile folder contains more than just the password for your system. This file also remembers the password for Microsoft Network (MSN) or any of the resources that you need to access. Your password unlocks this file, which in turn contains the passwords that unlock all the other resources you can access.

Setup normally provides password caching as a default. (This means that Windows 95 remembers your password when you use programs such as Microsoft Network.) In fact, there isn't any place to turn it off in a Properties dialog. However, if you open the Network Passwords property of the Local Computer Properties dialog (see Figure 28.9) using the System Policy Editor, you see an option for disabling password caching.

The other three policies here are pretty self-explanatory. Notice the Minimum Windows password length policy: It can help you make it more difficult for a hacker to break into the network. Some people use a single-character password—or none at all. Setting a minimum password length of five characters greatly reduces the chance that a hacker will guess a user's password and break into the system. In fact, the longer the password, the harder it is to break in. Of course, there's a point where you'll spend a lot of time bailing the user out because he forgot his password. Setting a reasonable length between five and ten characters is usually sufficient. You should also set a policy of using a combination of letters and numbers that don't form birth dates or other combinations that a hacker who knows the user could easily guess.

Figure 28.9.

Normally you want to keep password caching on to make life a little easier for the user.

What happens if the PWL file becomes corrupted? Windows 95 also provides a Password List Editor, shown in Figure 28.10, to remove corrupted passwords from the file. As you can see, there's no way for the administrator to know the user's password, but he can remove a specific password from the list. In this case, the PWL file contains two Microsoft Mail passwords and one for MSN. You find the Password List Editor in the `\ADMIN\APPTOOLS\PWLEDIT` folder.

Figure 28.10.

The Password List Editor is a simple utility for removing old or corrupted passwords from the user's PWL file.

Warning: There are a few caveats about using the PWL editor. First, the user needs to log on to unlock the file. This means you can't edit a PWL file remotely; you must do it at the user's machine. Second, the Password List Editor might corrupt a PWL file if an application adds a password in an unknown format. Make sure you create a backup of the PWL file before you edit it.

Network Security

Get back to peer-to-peer networking for a while. Windows 95 provides several levels of security that fit different kinds of networking needs. You can select only one level at a time, so it's important to select the correct one. Changing your policy later is a time-consuming chore if it becomes necessary.

The following sections provide you with the details of Windows 95 security. This information is very peer-to-peer-network–oriented, but I threw in a few bits of information that you can use with client/server networks as well.

Tip: Under DOS, you could use the hidden and read-only file attributes to marginally hide files and directories from a user. Windows 95 exposes these files through Explorer, making it easier for a novice user to delete much-needed files without much thought. Win-Secure-It is a product that helps you get past this new set of problems. It allows you to hide and optionally protect files as needed. You can get all the details and download a shareware version of this product from Shetef Solutions at `http://www.shetef.com/`. This vendor makes a variety of other useful Windows 95 utility programs, including the Security Programmable Interface for Windows 95, which is a special set of libraries for programmers who want full control over file security on Windows 95 machines.

Share-Level Versus User-Level Security

The first level of security that Windows 95 provides is share-level access control. You get to this setting using the Access Control page of the Network dialog, shown in Figure 28.11. The other security level is user-level access control. Each of these security levels provides a different set of features, and each has different qualities that make it useful in a given situation.

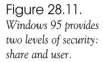

Figure 28.11.
*Windows 95 provides
two levels of security:
share and user.*

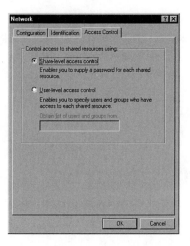

Share-level access control allows you to assign a password to each resource on the network. You can use the same password for each resource or a variety of passwords. Share-level access control also allows you to determine whether a user gets read-only or full access based on a password. This is my favorite form of access on a small network. I normally use three different levels of security:

- No password: Because users must log in to the network in the first place, you can assume that they already have a certain level of security clearance. I don't assign an additional password to low-priority resources. Those users have already proven that they're supposed to be on the network, so why ask them to prove it again?

- Read-only: When I do assign a password to a resource, I give it both a read-only and a full-access password. The read-only password allows me to give people quick access to documents that they can either copy to their hard drive or simply read online. This works well with applications that don't provide a revision marks feature because I can see who made what comments. Of course, I still have to go to the trouble of consolidating the comments later.

- Full: Anyone who is working on a sensitive project with me usually gets full access to the resource. This allows us to work together on a single document. I normally use Word for Windows for group projects. (Of course, if you're working on a financial projection, you'll probably use something such as Excel or Lotus 1-2-3 instead.) Turning on the revision marks feature allows me to see who made what changes. It also allows all of us to interact without actually setting up a meeting.

User-level access control allows you to set resource access by user name or group. This is the same type of access that client/server products such as NetWare use. I use this form of access control when the user will also interact with a larger network. The advantage is obvious: I don't have to spend a lot of time retraining users to use the peer-to-peer setup. They already know how to use it based on their previous experience with NetWare.

There is a more important reason to employ user-level access control: This is the method that makes it practical for you to use a policy file created using the System Policy Editor. However, you can't implement user-level security on a Windows 95 peer-to-peer network; you need access to a security provider such as a Windows NT or Novell NetWare server for user-level security to work.

Internet Security

The issue of Internet security has received a lot of press lately, and I imagine it'll get a lot more before anything gets resolved. In a lot of respects, the issue is not really a matter of security; it's a matter of access. *Security* implies that you're locking up something; that's clearly in opposition to how people actually use the Internet. Shared information, but shared with only the people you want, is what Internet security is really about.

There are a number of ways to look at information exchange. You can either exchange information willingly, or someone can steal it from you. Just consider one form of information exchange that people consider stealing: You register your software electronically instead of using the mail-in card. Getting online is easy, but it seems to take a long time. Only after you actually look at what got transferred do you realize that the vendor not only received the information you provided (such as your name and address), but also conducted a complete survey of the contents of your machine. The mail-in card didn't request any of this information and the vendor didn't bother to tell you that you would have to supply this information when registering online. That's one form of stealing that is widespread. Knowing exactly what kind of hardware you use and the type of software on your machine is a big advantage to the vendor that knows it.

There are other forms of unintentional access as well. For example, you might decide to visit an Internet site. During the process of downloading the Web page, you also download a destructive ActiveX control that wipes out your hard drive. An investigation by authorities shows that there wasn't any malicious intent on the part of the control's author; the control simply conflicted with a disk utility running in the background. Who's to blame? What could you have done to prevent the unauthorized access of your hard drive by a foreign ActiveX control? Damage to both hardware and software becomes a real issue when you start running those cute-looking controls springing up on Web pages worldwide.

The effect of unrestricted access on your machine's hardware and software isn't the only consideration. Many people are beginning to shop online; I'm one of them. How do you know that the vendor is using your credit card information correctly? For that matter, how do you know that someone isn't monitoring your conversation with the vendor and copying that number? You could end up paying for someone's new car or clothing with your credit card. The most insidious part of this whole plot is that your credit card is still in your pocket. At least if someone steals it outright, you have a chance of canceling it before the thief uses it. If someone steals your credit card number through an insecure Internet connection, the first sign of trouble is the end-of-the-month statement or your inability to use the card at a store.

The need to restrict access doesn't affect only the user. What happens to companies that lose their competitive edge when someone snoops through their "secret" files? It happens. Just look at all the news in the trade presses regarding updated firewalls and other security items. A lot of the security software that people depended on the most ends up having some flaw that rendered the security features useless. (Fortunately, firewall and other security software is becoming a lot more secure due to the hard work of both vendors and users.)

It doesn't take too long to realize that creating a secure environment on the Internet might be more difficult than you first thought. I'm not going to spend a lot of time telling you horror stories of companies that lost millions of dollars due to seemingly petty crimes committed by hackers. Nor do I explore the test cases of home users who let their guard down for a few moments only to discover that those were the most important few moments of their computer's history. You can find such stories in any number of books on the market, not to mention the stories that appear in the trade presses you read on a weekly basis. Instead, I concentrate on the security measures you can take to protect yourself when using a standard browser under Windows 95. After all, preventing a break in is at least as important as recovering once one occurs.

Assigning Zones in Internet Explorer 4.0

There are a lot of available Web sites and resources that you can view with your Web browser, ranging from shared documents available on your local intranet to major Internet Web sites maintained by high-profile international corporations and even personal Web pages from who knows where. The security risks associated with accessing those sites can vary almost as much as their content. To address the variation in security risks presented by different Web sites, Internet Explorer 4.0 institutes a new security feature called *security zones*. Recent versions of the popular Web browsers have made available an assortment of security options. The problem is that when you configure the browser's security settings for the level of security you need when browsing unknown or potentially dangerous sites (for example, by preventing the downloading and running of ActiveX controls), you disabled features that you would want to use when browsing friendlier, trusted sites. As a result, many users were constantly stopping to reconfigure security settings in their browsers as they traveled from one portion of the Web to another. To address this problem, Internet Explorer 4.0 divides its world into four zones and allows you to define separate security settings for each zone. As you move from zone to zone, Internet Explorer 4.0 automatically applies the appropriate security settings:

- Local Intranet—Internet Explorer assumes that your local intranet is separated from the larger Internet by a proxy server and any Web address that does not go through the proxy server is part of the local intranet. Because intranets are normally private networks under the control of a system administrator, local intranet sites probably present a relatively low security risk.

- Trusted Sites—This zone consists of a list of Web sites you believe you can trust. The sites themselves might be on your local intranet or on the Internet, but regardless of their location, they are the sites where you can confidently download and run files without fearing damage to your system. The Trusted Sites zone starts out empty; you create the zone over time by adding to the list URLs for specific trusted sites.

- Restricted Sites—This zone is the opposite of the Trusted Sites zone. This is a list of sites that you do *not* trust, no matter where they are located. Like the Trusted Sites zone, you build the Restricted Sites zone by adding URLs to the list. When you visit sites in the Restricted Sites zone, you want your security settings dialed up to maximum.

- Internet—This zone encompasses the rest of the world. If a Web site isn't located on your local computer or assigned to one of the other zones, it is, by default, part of the Internet zone.

- Your Local Computer—This isn't actually a zone, but it functions as an implicitly trusted zone. Internet Explorer assumes that files on your local hard drive are safe and loads and executes those files without notifying you or waiting for your permission.

You can build the lists of trusted sites and restricted sites yourself. (I show you how in just a moment.) Your intranet system administrator can define what addresses belong in the Local Intranet zone using the Internet Explorer Administrator's Kit. You can't change the contents of the Internet zone because it is, by definition, everything else.

Internet Explorer comes with preconfigured sets of security settings for three security levels: High, Medium, and Low. By default, the Trusted Sites zone is assigned the Low security level and the Restricted Sites zone is assigned the High security level. The intranet and Internet zones both start with the Medium security level. You can reassign the security settings for any of the four zones using any of the three preconfigured security levels, or you can create custom settings of your own choosing. For example, I usually change the Local Intranet zone to the Low security level. Here's a brief overview of what the security levels do:

- High leaves some scripting capabilities enabled but automatically rejects most downloads that could potentially harm your system.

- Medium enables most forms of scripting and ActiveX controls but prompts you before downloading potentially dangerous content.

- Low automatically downloads and runs ActiveX controls and Java scripts and applets without prompting you.

To adjust the Internet Explorer security settings, select View | Internet Options, and then click the Security tab to open the Security page of the Internet Options dialog box, shown in Figure 28.12.

Figure 28.12.
You can configure
different security
settings in each of
four different zones.

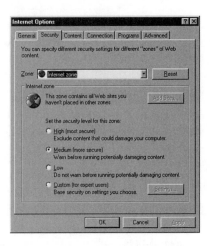

To change the security settings for a zone, select the zone from the drop-down list box near the top of the Security page to display the current settings for that zone, and then select the desired security level for that zone from the four options on the lower half of the page. You can choose from one of the three standard security levels (High, Medium, Low) or choose Custom and create your own customized security settings for the zone.

If you elect to go with a Custom security setting, click the Settings button to open the Security Settings dialog box, shown in Figure 28.13. This dialog gives you access to a long list of detailed security settings, and you can adjust each one individually to get just the mix of security and convenience you desire. There are a lot of options and the list may look intimidating at first, but it's really not too bad. Most of the settings are self-explanatory, and if you need more of a description, you can click the question mark button and then click the setting. For most security settings, you have three options: Enable, Prompt, and Disable.

Figure 28.13.
You can tailor the
security settings for
any of the four zones.

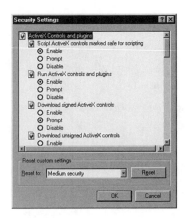

Because the list of security settings is long, it can take some time to change them all from one security level to another. Fortunately, you can speed up the process somewhat by starting with the security settings list configured to match one of the three standard security levels. Just select the security level you want to use as a starting point from the drop-down list box at the bottom of the dialog and then click the Reset button. This automatically adjusts the security settings to match the selected security level. Then, you can scroll through the list, changing just a few settings instead of changing nearly all of them.

In addition to setting the security level for the Trusted Sites and Restricted Sites zones, you also need to define the lists of Web sites that define those zones. Select the zone you want to define from the drop-down list box on the Security Page and then click the Add Sites button to open a dialog box for that zone. Figure 28.14 shows the Trusted Sites Zone dialog box.

Figure 28.14.
Build your own zone by adding and removing sites on this list.

The Restricted Sites Zone dialog is essentially the same as the Trusted Sites Zone dialog. To add a site to the zone, type its URL in the Add this Web site to the zone text box and click the Add button. To remove an existing site from the zone, select its URL from the Web sites list and click the Remove button. One option that appears in the Trusted Sites Zone dialog box but not in the Restricted Sites Zone dialog is the Require Server Verification option. Check this option if you want Internet Explorer to verify that each site is operating in secure mode before accessing the site. This is an all-or-nothing option; it's useful only if all the sites in the zone are located on secure servers.

Parental Controls

One of the biggest Internet topics in the press is the issue of protecting children from exposure to inappropriate content. There's a lot of wonderful information available on the Internet that can be a great benefit to kids who have access to it; there's also some content that's inappropriate for children. The problem is how to provide and even encourage free access to the good stuff while preventing kids from stumbling across the inappropriate material as they surf the Web. The Content Advisor in Internet Explorer is an attempt to do just that. It uses a rating system, not unlike the rating system for films, to rate Web site content by the level of offensive language, nudity, sex, and violence the sites contain. The Content Advisor acts as a filter to allow certain levels of questionable content to pass through, but no more.

By default, the Content Advisor is not activated. If you have children who will be using your computer and you want to use the Content Advisor to filter the content of Web sites viewed with Internet Explorer, you need to enable the feature and then configure the filter settings as you please.

To enable Content Advisor, select View | Internet Options, click the Content tab, and then click the Enable button in the Content Advisor area. The first time you activate the feature, you need to define a supervisor password by entering the password twice. Make sure you remember the password; you need it to make any changes to the Content Advisor settings.

After you enable the Content Advisor, you'll want to adjust the filter settings. Start by clicking the Settings button on the Content page. After prompting you to enter your supervisor password, Internet Explorer displays the Content Advisor dialog box (shown in Figure 28.15). On the Ratings page, you can select a category from the list and adjust the Rating slider to determine what level of content is allowed to pass.

Figure 28.15.
Adjust the slider to determine what material viewers are allowed to see.

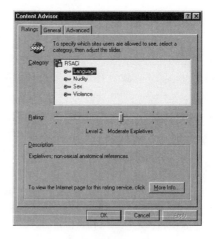

Click the General tab to display the options shown in Figure 28.16. If you're serious about not wanting users to see potentially inappropriate material, you need to disable the Users can see sites that have no rating check box. This prevents Internet Explorer from displaying any Web site that doesn't carry a rating below your threshold levels. The trouble is that most sites do not participate in the rating program, and the vast majority of them contain no offensive content. You'll be locking out a lot of good material to prevent something bad from slipping through. Checking the second option offsets the restrictive nature of the first option somewhat by allowing the supervisor (you) to enter your password to temporarily override the Content Advisor filter and display a Web site that triggered the restrictions. (Of course, you need to be available to enter the password—and if you're going to be sitting there as your kids surf the Web, you can monitor their activities yourself and you don't really need to rely on the Content Advisor.) Click the Change Password button to define a new supervisor password.

Figure 28.16.
The User options section of the General tab controls how Internet Explorer handles unrated Web sites.

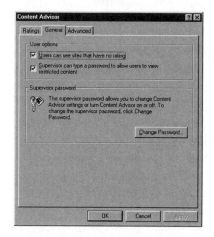

The settings on the Advanced page of the Content Advisor dialog box allow you to import a ratings file from a rating system. You can also select a ratings bureau that Internet Explorer uses to check out Web sites before displaying them.

Understanding Certificates

The beginning of this section noted some very distinct problems with the current Internet setup when it comes to secure downloads. How do you know that an ActiveX control won't destroy your hard drive while you're using it? Currently, there are efforts underway to make downloading ActiveX controls, Java applets, or anything else from the Internet just a little safer. Some of the trade press calls this new technology a *certificate*, although other people use the term *digital signature*.

Figuring out the precise technology behind certificates or digital signatures is a little like nailing Jell-O to the wall; you might be able to do it, but who would want to try? Suffice it to say that the precise details are changing on an almost daily basis. However, there's a simple way to look at a digital signature from a user perspective. Think of it as resembling an identification card because it has the same function. A digital signature identifies an Internet object such as a Java applet or an ActiveX control, specifies who created it and when, and could potentially provide a wealth of other information. For example, if the object happens to be a client or server, a digital signature shows the current owner. In other words, you'd know the true identity of the person or company you're dealing with.

Giving someone a digital signature for the life of an object leaves a few things in doubt. For example, what if a company sells the rights to an ActiveX control to another company? To alleviate this problem, the digital signature, like a driver's license, expires—forcing vendors to keep proving they are who they say they are. The expiration date also gives hackers a lot less time to figure out how to steal the certificate. (Because each certificate is a separate item, learning to steal one won't necessarily buy the hacker anything.) Using a digital signature helps keep everyone honest because it forces everyone to go through a central verification point. A digital signature avoids the one big problem with the honor system used by the Internet to date: It doesn't rely on one person to maintain the security of your machine. Now you have direct input into who gets access and when. (This implies some level of user training to ensure that people actually know how to use this feature.)

Looking for Digital Signatures

How do you identify someone who has a digital signature versus someone who doesn't? You always see some kind of warning dialog when accessing an insecure site. In the case of the dialog shown in Figure 28.17, the site doesn't have a digital signature for the ActiveX control on its page. Likewise, accessing a site with a digital signature always looks the same. You see a dialog like the one shown in Figure 28.18. Make absolutely certain that the date is current and that the digital signature belongs to the person or company that you thought it would belong to.

Figure 28.17.
You get a warning dialog if you try to download an ActiveX control or other object that doesn't have a digital signature.

Figure 28.18.
The first time you visit a site that has a digital signature, your browser should display a dialog showing it to you.

Warning: If the digital signature you see doesn't look like the one shown in Figure 28.18, it isn't a real digital signature. The capability to display these certificates isn't part of the browser itself; it's part of a lower-level Windows API. The browser calls this API to test the certificate to determine whether it's real. As a result, you get the same certificate dialog no matter which browser you use.

Notice that the Authenticode Security Technology dialog gives you a few options for optimizing your system. First, you want to check the certificate to make sure it's valid. For example, make sure that the vendor listed is the one you expected. Also check the date to make sure that the certificate hasn't expired. Second, you have the ability to bypass the verification stage for this vendor if you want to. The first check box below the certificate allows you to add a particular company to the list checked by WinVerifyTrust; this is a special API function designed to check the security of the certificate. If you check this box, you won't get asked each time you request a download from that particular vendor. This is a good risk with some vendors but might not be such a smart thing to do with others. You have to determine how far you trust the vendor. The second check box allows you to accept all access from any vendor certified by a specific authority, such as VeriSign (the vendor shown in this case). Unless you're very comfortable with the certification process, you probably want to leave this box unchecked.

The Authenticode Security Technology dialog also has an Advanced pushbutton; Figure 28.19 shows what you see when you click it. This is a list of the trusted companies in your Registry. Every time you check one of the two options on the first dialog, you get another entry in this one. Notice that I don't have any entries here. I prefer to take the time to view each certificate. You might not feel the need to take this extra precaution, but it never hurts to do so. The dialog shown in Figure 28.19 also contains a Remove pushbutton; you should remove any vendors that you don't trust or whose certificates you haven't used in a while. Never take chances when it comes to security on the Internet.

Figure 28.19.
The Advanced pushbutton shows a list of vendors that you trust.

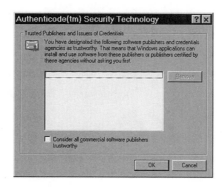

Obtaining a Digital Signature

Just as you want to know whom you're dealing with, people are going to want to know who you are. For that reason, VeriSign (and any other digital signature providers that might be around when you read this) provides a way for you to get a digital signature as well. All you need to do is visit VeriSign's Web site at `http://digitalid.verisign.com/`. When you load the initial VeriSign Web page, or one of the first pages of the application for a digital signature, you see a Security Information dialog saying that you're about to request a secure document when you visit the site. Don't worry about clicking Yes. The secure document helps to ensure that the information you send to VeriSign remains secret. I started my application for a digital signature by clicking the Enroll button at the top of the Web page.

Tip: You can always tell when you're making a secure transmission by looking for special icons provided by your browser. Internet Explorer shows a lock near the center of the status bar. Navigator shows a key on the left side of the status bar. The more teeth in the key, the higher the security level (one and two teeth are all you see).

I won't attempt to show you the step-by-step procedure of applying for a digital signature; VeriSign has changed some of the forms and details in the past and will probably do so in the future. Instead, I give you an overview of the process, tell you what information you need to supply, and what choices you need to make to get a digital signature. Note that this information applies to getting a *personal* digital signature; getting digital signatures for Web sites and software developers is a little more involved and the fees are significantly higher.

When you apply for your digital signature, you need to do so using the machine and browser version you plan to use with the digital signature. One of the first choices you need to make in the application process is what browser you use. (There are different versions of the digital signatures for Netscape Navigator and for Internet Explorer.) You also need to specify whether you're applying for an individual digital signature for yourself or your business to use as simple identification, for your Web server, for your software programs, or for other content you will make available to others.

Tip: The digital signature you obtain for your browser will work for S/MIME-enabled e-mail in the associated e-mail program. For example, an Internet Explorer digital signature will also work in Outlook Express.

Next, select the class of digital signature you want. You have two options:

- Class 1—Provides you with a unique name and e-mail address within a repository. VeriSign (or whatever certificate vendor you choose) can verify that the name and the e-mail address go together. A mail-back process is the only verification that VeriSign uses in this case. You have to own an e-mail address in order to receive the certificate. Tying each certificate to a verifiable e-mail address makes it hard for a hacker to obtain a fake certificate. This class of digital signature normally costs $9.95 per year to maintain, but a 90-day free trial version is available.

- Class 2—To obtain a Class 2 certificate, you must provide third-party evidence of your identity. (This limits access to a Class 2 certificate to people in the United States at the moment.) The big difference between a Class 2 certificate and a Class 1 certificate is that VeriSign actually checks information you provide against a consumer database maintained by EquiFax (a credit reporting agency). This class of digital signature costs $19.95 per year to maintain.

Notice that the trial version of the Class 1 certificate is free at the moment to promote the use of digital signatures. That's going to change in the future, but VeriSign hasn't told anyone when. However, you can't really argue with a free digital signature and the security it can provide.

After you choose which class of digital signature you want, you need to fill out an onscreen form to supply VeriSign with some information. The form isn't all that difficult to figure out. For a Class 1 certificate, simply type a first and last name (you can even use an alias for a Class 1 certificate). For a Class 2 certificate, you need to supply more information, such as your real name, your street address, phone number, and Social Security number. For both digital signature classes, you must supply an e-mail address; that's how your certificate gets issued. After you enter this information, you need to decide whether to include your e-mail address or street address as part of the certificate. For the most part, you don't have a choice when it comes to the e-mail address. In many cases, people simply won't accept your certificate if it doesn't include the e-mail address as part of the package. Because a Class 1 certificate counts on e-mail address verification, it's not too difficult to figure out why this is such a big issue. On the other hand, you don't have to include the street address if you don't want to, and for privacy and security reasons, you probably won't. You also need to enter a challenge phrase. I prefer to look at this as a password. You definitely want to choose something out of the ordinary because VeriSign uses the challenge phrase when you need assistance with your certificate. If you're applying for the free trial certificate, you don't need to enter any more information. However, you need to supply payment information (credit card numbers and so on) if you apply for the full Class 1 or the Class 2 certificates. (You're connected to a secure Web server, so all the information you submit, including credit card numbers, is encrypted to keep it safe during transmission on the Internet.)

One required step in the application process is to accept VeriSign's license agreement. You need to read the agreement online and click a button to accept its terms. In the course of filling in the onscreen forms, you may also need to click one or more buttons to submit information for your application.

After you fill in and submit the enrollment information for a digital signature, the VeriSign Web site processes the information and then displays a page confirming your enrollment. For a Class 1 certificate, this generally takes only a few seconds. Class 2 certificates take much longer (up to three minutes or so) because of the verification process. If VeriSign has trouble verifying your information for a Class 2 certificate, you need to fill out the application again and resubmit it. Common causes of a failure are using variations of your name instead of your formal legal name, mismatched addresses (have you moved recently?), typos on the application, and spaces or punctuation in your credit card number.

After your information is verified, you receive a confirmation e-mail from VeriSign. This usually happens quickly. The e-mail will probably be in your mailbox by the time you can read the instructions on the Web page. The e-mail from VeriSign contains a link to a Web site where you can download your digital signature. It also contains a special PIN (personal identification number) that you have to use at the download site. After the e-mail arrives, follow the link to the Web page and enter the PIN in the blank provided. The PIN is a long, complicated string of numbers and letters, so I suggest that you copy it from the e-mail message and paste it into the VeriSign Web page. This will greatly reduce your chances of mistyping the PIN.

When you submit your PIN, VeriSign generates your digital signature. Again, the process is almost instantaneous for a Class 1 certificate but might take a few minutes for a Class 2 certificate. After VeriSign generates the digital signature, you see the pertinent information from the certificate and get instructions for installing the digital signature in your browser. For example, to install a digital signature in Internet Explorer, all I had to do was click the Install button on the Web page and then click OK in a dialog box. When the installation is complete, you'll probably see some sort of confirmation screen.

Viewing Digital Signatures on File

Internet Explorer 4.0 makes it easy for you to keep track of the digital signatures you have kept on file. You can access the dialog boxes that allow you to view digital signatures from the Content tab of the Internet Options dialog box (select View | Internet Options and then click the Content tab). As you can see in Figure 28.20, the Certificates area is located in the middle of the tab.

Figure 28.20.
Access digital signature certificates from the Content tab of the Internet Options dialog box.

To view your own digital signatures, click the Personal button. This opens the Client Authentication dialog box shown in Figure 28.21. If you have any digital signatures installed, they are listed in this dialog box. To view the contents of a digital signature, select it from the list and click the View Certificate button to open the Properties dialog box shown in Figure 28.22. You can also export a signature to a file by selecting a certificate from the list and clicking the Export button. (For example, you might want to make a copy of the certificate so you can move it to another machine.) To import a certificate from a file, click the Import button.

Figure 28.21.
This dialog box lists your personal digital signatures.

Figure 28.22.
Check out the exact contents of a digital signature.

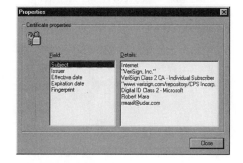

Internet Explorer checks the certificate of any site with which you attempt to create a secure connection. If the site has an unexpired certificate from a trusted certifying authority, Internet Explorer accepts the secure connection. Otherwise, the program alerts you to a possible security breach. Clicking the Authorities button on the Content Page of the Internet Options dialog box opens the Certificate Authorities dialog box shown in Figure 28.23. Make a selection from the Issuer Type drop-down list box to view the list of certificate authorities of that type. A check mark beside a certificate authority indicates that its digital signatures are trusted. If you want to revoke the trusted status for an authority, clear the check mark. You can also select an authority from the list and click the View Certificate button to see the contents of its certificate. Select an authority and click the Delete button to remove that authority from the list.

Figure 28.23.
This dialog shows a list of certificate authorities that Internet Explorer considers trustworthy.

Earlier, I mentioned a kind of certificate called Authenticode. When you view an Authenticode certificate, you have the option of instructing Internet Explorer to automatically accept software with Authenticode certificates from that publisher in the future. To see a list of the software publishers you designated as trustworthy, click the Publishers button on the Content page of the Internet Options dialog box. This opens the Authenticode Security Technology dialog box shown in Figure 28.24. If you decide that you want to remove a publisher from the list, select the publisher and click Remove.

Figure 28.24.
This dialog lists software publishers you designated as trustworthy.

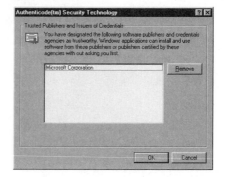

Microsoft Wallet

Microsoft Wallet is new software designed to facilitate shopping on the Internet by making it easier to enter information when you make a purchase. Basically, Microsoft Wallet lets you enter your name, billing and shipping addresses, and credit card information for several credit cards and stores that information on your hard drive in an encrypted, password-protected file. When you make a purchase from a Web site, you can use Wallet to supply your billing information instead of typing it each time. Because the Microsoft Wallet feature is password-protected, you're the only one who can authorize its use.

Microsoft Wallet also ensures that your payment information is protected when you make an online purchase. Internet Explorer and Microsoft Wallet support the industry-standard SSL (Secure Socket Layer) security protocol to encrypt data being transmitted to a Web site. Microsoft Wallet also supports the new SET (Secure Electronic Transactions) system for added security.

Microsoft Wallet is built in to Internet Explorer 4.0. In addition, the software is available as an optional add-on for Internet Explorer 3.0 and for Netscape Navigator.

Although Microsoft Wallet looks like a good idea that holds a lot of promise, that promise has yet to be fulfilled. The problem is that it's not enough to have Microsoft Wallet installed on your system and set up with your payment information. For the process to work, the Web site where you're making a purchase must be specially configured to exchange payment data with Wallet. Microsoft Wallet is new and, so far, sites where you can use it are scarce. Only time will tell whether Microsoft Wallet achieves the widespread acceptance that it needs to become truly successful.

If you want to enter your personal information into Microsoft Wallet so you are ready in case you encounter a Wallet-enabled site, select View | Internet Options and then click the Content tab. In the Personal Information area at the bottom of the Content tab, click the Addresses button to open the Address Options dialog box (shown in Figure 28.25). This is where you maintain the list of addresses that you can send over the Internet.

Figure 28.25.
This dialog lets you manage the list of addresses in Microsoft Wallet.

Note: The system can keep track of several different addresses for shipping and billing information at your home and business. The buttons along the side allow you to add, edit, and delete addresses. At the bottom of the dialog box is an option that instructs Internet Explorer to issue a warning before sending addresses over the Internet. It's hard for me to imagine why you would want to disable this feature, so make sure the option is checked.

To set up credit card numbers in Microsoft Wallet, click the Payments button on the Contents tab of the Internet Options dialog box. This opens the Payment Options dialog box shown in Figure 28.26.

Figure 28.26.
Keep track of the
credit card numbers
in Microsoft Wallet
from this dialog box.

To add a credit card number to the list, click the Add button, choose a credit card type, and then follow the instructions of the Add a New Credit Card wizard to enter the credit card information, select or enter the billing address for the card, and create a password for the card. (You need to use the password each time you access the credit card record.) The other buttons in the Payment Options dialog allow you to select a credit card from the list and Edit or Delete it. The Methods button allows you to select which credit card types (Visa, MasterCard, Discover, or American Express) you want to have available in Microsoft Wallet.

The Cookie Monster

If you spend much time in some of the browser-oriented newsgroups on the Internet, you'll find some amount of talk about cookies. A cookie is a small file with configuration information that a Web site can write to. Normally you find this file in a special directory that you can monitor, and the Web site uses it for things such as your name and site preferences. When cookies are used for their intended purpose, they pose no threat to your system.

Some people, however, are concerned about the ability of Webmasters to use cookies to track your movements into, through, and out of their Web sites and don't like the idea of anyone compiling demographic data based on their Web surfing habits. This is a privacy issue, not a security concern. However, there aren't any real limitations on what kind of information a Web site can write to the cookie, and that can create problems. For example, what would prevent a Web site from writing executable code to the cookie and then fooling the operating system into actually executing it? This problem actually occurred, but fortunately, the results were more along the lines of a bad joke than actual damage to the system. It could have been different, however, and that's why people are concerned about cookies.

There are two approaches regarding the storage of cookies. The Netscape Navigator approach is to place all the cookies in one file named COOKIES.TXT in the Navigator folder. You can examine this file, but make sure you don't change anything it contains. The disadvantage of the Navigator approach to cookies is that you have to erase the entire file to get rid of an offending site. On the other hand, this approach is space efficient, and it's easy to locate the file you want.

Internet Explorer stores the cookies in separate files in the Cookies or Temporary Internet Files folder within your main Windows folder. Each cookie is represented by a user name, followed by an @, followed by the site name. For example, if a person named Ted visited `http://www.msn.com`, there would be a cookie file named `Ted@MSN` in the cookies folder. The main advantage to this approach is that every user can have her own configuration settings for the same site, even though more than one user visits a single site with the same machine. In addition, getting rid of the settings for a site you no longer use is as easy as erasing a single cookie file. The disadvantages include inefficient disk use and the fact that some users find it difficult to figure out which cookies to get rid of (if they even know the cookies folder exists). Obviously, neither the Internet Explorer nor the Navigator approach is perfect.

The point is that you know where the cookies are stored and how to reject them if so desired. Both Internet Explorer and Navigator provide the means to reject cookies you don't want. In Internet Explorer, you can change the way the browser handles cookies by following these steps:

1. Select View | Internet Options to display the Internet Options dialog.

2. Select the Advanced page and scroll down to the Security heading. You'll find three options under Cookies:

    - Always Accept Cookies—Select this to accept all cookies automatically.

    - Disable All Cookie Use—Select this to automatically reject cookies.

    - Prompt Before Accepting Cookies—Select this to make Internet Explorer open a notification box each time it receives a request from a Web site to place a cookie on your system. You have the option to accept or reject each cookie as it arrives. Normally, this check box isn't checked because cookies are a normal part of life on the Internet and having to manually accept or reject each one can be a hassle.

Getting to the appropriate option when using Navigator is just as easy:

1. Select Options | Network Preferences to display the Preferences dialog.

2. Select the Protocols page. You find an Accepting a Cookie check box here that tells Navigator to display a message before accepting a cookie. This box is normally unchecked.

If accepting cookies is a normal part of surfing the Internet, yet accepting them could be dangerous, how do you work with cookies on a daily basis? I normally keep cookies enabled because I'm generally visiting sites that are business oriented and known to be trustworthy. I switch on the prompt so that I can choose to accept or reject cookies when I expect to be visiting a small site that I'm unsure of or a nonbusiness site that I haven't looked at before. For the most part, however, cookies are pretty safe.

Because the cookie file is the only file that a standard Web page can write to, you'll find that most cookies do just what they're supposed to do: store configuration settings. Because ActiveX controls and Java applets give more power to hackers who really want to harm your system, I'd spend more time worrying about these potential breaches in your security.

Sandbox Approach Versus Open Access

Security is more complex than it needs to be right now because the Internet is going through a lot of changes with regards to capability and flexibility. Two main players in all this are ActiveX controls and Java applets. (Scripting languages also play a role, but they normally interact with ActiveX controls or Java applets.)

Java applets take what's known as the "sandbox" approach to security; they don't do anything outside the purview of the applet. For example, accessing the hard drive isn't allowed because the applet would have to use the operating system to do so. Some developers complain that the sandbox approach hinders them from writing fully functional applications and, to a certain degree, they're right. If an applet can't access system resources, it can't do much more for you from a system level than standard HTML can. On the other hand, many users feel safer knowing that the Java applet they just downloaded won't erase the contents of their hard drive or do something equally devious.

There's another good reason to use the sandbox approach: It allows a developer to write a single applet that works on a lot of platforms. Because the applet doesn't rely on system services, all it needs is provided by the Java engine. In other words, a Java applet is self-contained and doesn't really rely on anyone else. (The Java engine is obviously platform specific.)

Microsoft has taken a different approach with ActiveX. It's actually an extension of OLE technology. Unlike a Java applet, ActiveX controls can interact with applications on your machine, access the hard drive, and look into the Registry. This makes ActiveX controls a lot more flexible from the developer perspective and makes them more useful from the user perspective as well. The problem lies in the level of access that they obtain. An ActiveX control has the same level of access as any other application on your machine, which means that an ill-behaved control could cause more than a little damage. In addition, it means that the user can't simply download a control without first thinking about its origins.

At first glance, it would seem that the distinctions between ActiveX controls and Java applets are pretty clear. You'd accept Java applets if security was foremost on your mind. ActiveX controls would provide added capability, but only if you were willing to accept the consequences of a reduced security net. Take a look at that dividing line though; it's not as clear as you might think. People have had Java applets use back doors to access the system. There have been a few documented cases where they've actually caused damage. Supporters of Java have stated that these security holes are all sealed up, but how can you be certain?

ActiveX supporters further muddy the waters by stating that an ActiveX control falls under the same guidelines as any OLE control. In addition, the author has to sign the control to show the user who is downloading it who created it. (You can still download the control if the author doesn't sign it, but both Internet Explorer and Navigator display warnings against this practice.) The use of digital signatures means that you always know who created an ActiveX control and make a reasonable decision about downloading and using it. (Java controls get downloaded automatically; you don't get a chance to review a digital signature for them in advance and you often don't know who created them.)

The only thing I can say about the sandbox approach versus the open approach is that neither one is clear cut. About the only thing you can do is watch whom you download controls from. If you're uncertain about a site, don't take the risk of using it. Security is a user matter right now. Look before you leap. Make sure you know who created that Java applet or ActiveX control before letting it run on your machine.

> **Tip:** You can avoid the whole question of downloading Java applets you don't want by disabling them. Navigator provides this capability on the Languages page of the Preferences dialog. You access it via Options | Network Preferences. (If you don't want to use ActiveX controls in Navigator, don't install a plug-in such as NCompass's ScriptActive.) Likewise, you can disable both ActiveX and Java on the Advanced page of the Internet Options dialog for Internet Explorer. You access this dialog via View | Internet Options.

On Your Own

Take this opportunity to design your own security plan. Work with network users and management to design a plan that is both fair and reasonably secure.

Spend some time training users on your network about security. It's important that you also take the time to explain what types of passwords are acceptable. Spend a little time with each user who has problems understanding the security plan.

If you're a home user, set a variety of security options on your machine. For example, you might want to create a security profile for young users that gives them access to programs they can use but removes access to programs that could damage your machine. Use the System Policy Editor and the other tools I described in this chapter to make the process of creating a home security plan easy.

Anyone who uses the Internet for more than just casual browsing should have their own digital signature. Use the procedure in the "Obtaining a Digital Signature" section of the chapter to get your own digital signature. Make sure you reread the rest of the section as well. It's always good to know when you can trust the party at the other end of the connection.

29

Software
Problems

Peter Norton®

Microsoft designed Windows 95 with two goals in mind: compatibility and stability. Compatibility is important so Windows 95 can continue running MS-DOS and Windows 3.x applications along with the newer Windows 95 applications. Stability means that Windows 95 can run multiple MS-DOS, Windows 3.x, and Windows 95 applications without crashing.

Unfortunately, remaining compatible with older applications while offering stability is an elusive goal, which means Windows 95 is likely to crash, freeze, or act erratically occasionally. Because you're likely to run into problems with Windows 95 eventually, this chapter provides some guidelines and clues for troubleshooting any problems that may appear.

Startup and Configuration Errors

Configuration problems normally manifest themselves in several ways. The most devastating is during system startup when Windows 95 simply stops running.

The other types of configuration problems are a lot more devious. One such problem that I found was with my sound board: The MIDI Balance setting kept getting out of whack. I checked to make sure I had the correct device driver, the proper hardware settings, and the correct CD software to use the sound board. After several days of searching, I found that the problem occurred only when I ran a specific version of After Dark. Problems such as these can really make you want to pull your hair out.

Tip: Sometimes, one program will overwrite or delete files needed by another program. To help solve this problem, I've made every effort in this chapter to tell you which files affect what functions.

If you have plenty of disk space, copy all the files in your Windows directories. (To save space, you might also compress them using a utility such as WinZip.) If anything goes wrong, compare the files in those directories to see what might have changed.

Startup Problems

Startup problems are the worst kind of configuration problem to fix because you can't easily use the tools provided by Windows 95 to find them. Usually, the settings for one or more devices conflict, get lost, or are somehow incompatible with the device you're using.

Tip: You might get Windows 95 to start only to find out that your Registry is corrupt. For example, suppose you find out that an important driver is no longer registered, so Windows 95 can't find it. If you see a Registry corruption message, don't panic. You can download a special Registry cleaning program that might fix the problem at `http://www.microsoft.com/kb/softlib/mslfiles/regcln.exe`.

You want to use this program only as a last resort because changes you make to the Registry when Windows 95 is unstable are fairly permanent. You also want to note any messages that the utility displays. The information could come in handy as you complete the restoration process.

One thing to remember: Some of your applications could be affected by the Registry cleaning utility. If an application won't run properly, don't risk further Registry corruption. Uninstall the program if possible and then reinstall it from scratch. This will ensure that you have the proper Registry entries in place.

If you have trouble starting Windows 95, you can often start the machine in Safe mode. This mode starts your machine with only the display adapter and the hard drive. It's extremely unlikely that these two devices will have conflicts. Windows also uses a generic VGA display driver. This will get rid of the rest of your problems. Even if your display driver is somehow corrupted or you've used the wrong settings, the generic VGA display driver will work.

Figure 29.1 shows a machine in Safe mode. Notice that you'll always know when you're in this mode because "Safe mode" appears in all four corners of the screen.

There are two ways to get into this mode: automatically and manually. When Windows 95 detects a booting problem, it automatically sets up the machine to reboot in Safe mode. Of course, this depends on Windows 95 actually detecting the problem; sometimes it doesn't. For example, if you make it most of the way through the boot process, Windows 95 might not detect a startup problem.

One of the most difficult problems to detect is a sound board problem. Suppose the system is most or all of the way through the boot sequence before a sound board problem occurs; if Windows fails to detect the startup problem, use the manual startup method. You can force a manual Safe mode boot by pressing the F8 key when you boot your machine. Normally, pressing F8 displays a menu. This menu has one or more entries for Safe mode. Here is a complete list of the items you can expect to find on the boot menu:

- Normal—This option allows you to normally boot the machine. The only reason you need to use this entry is if you accidentally press F8 during the boot process.

Figure 29.1.
*It's easy to see when
you're in Safe mode.*

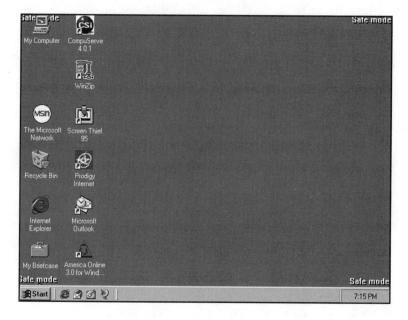

- Logged (\BOOTLOG.TXT)—The contents of BOOTLOG.TXT can help you determine precisely where the boot sequence is failing. Of course, it takes a bit of time to analyze the contents of the files. The advantage of this method is that it gives you the best picture of exactly what's going on during the boot process.

- Safe Mode—This is the entry you normally select to find boot problems. It starts your machine with the minimum number of devices enabled. Windows 95 doesn't process the contents of CONFIG.SYS or AUTOEXEC.BAT, and none of your Startup folder entries are processed.

- Safe Mode with Network Support—Use this entry if Safe mode startup doesn't tell you where the problem is and you suspect that the problem relates to your network card. Always use this startup after you try Safe mode; otherwise, you can't be certain that the failure isn't hidden by something else. For example, I had a conflict with my COM port. The fault showed up as a mouse not responding; the COM port showed no errors at all. If I hadn't taken the time to look at what was going on, I could have missed the conflict and replaced my mouse, thinking it had finally bitten the dust.

- Step-by-Step Confirmation—If you must use real-mode drivers, this option allows you to find a real-mode driver conflict. You can restart your machine several times and tell Windows 95 which device driver to use or exclude from your AUTOEXEC.BAT or CONFIG.SYS files. By doing this multiple times, you can find the one device driver that's causing problems with your Windows setup. Of course, the best way to get rid of these types of conflicts is to get rid of the real-mode drivers so that Windows can help configure your machine.

- Command Prompt Only—Use this option if you need to get to the command prompt to check something out. It does process your CONFIG.SYS and AUTOEXEC.BAT entries, so any real-mode drivers you need get loaded. This is a great setting to use if you need to install an older MS-DOS application that insists on not having anything else loaded. I also found it handy when installing the NetWare client software.

- Safe Mode Command Prompt Only—I find this setting handy if I need to get to the MS-DOS 7.0 prompt. For example, if a CONFIG.SYS or AUTOEXEC.BAT entry is causing problems, I can get to the MS-DOS prompt, make any required modifications, and reboot the machine. Windows 95 boots to a MS-DOS prompt without processing either CONFIG.SYS or AUTOEXEC.BAT when you select this option.

- Previous Version of MS-DOS—You see this option only if you include the BootMulti=1 setting in MSDOS.SYS. It allows you to boot the previous version of MS-DOS (assuming, of course, that your previous version of MS-DOS is still available). Removing the previous version should disable this feature. Also remember that some types of installations remove your capability to boot your old version of MS-DOS.

Note: Some MSDOS.SYS settings disable the capability to use the F8 key. A network administrator could use this setting to prevent users from circumventing network security. If this happens, you need to use your startup disk to start the machine from a floppy.

After you get your machine booted in Safe mode, start looking for hardware or software conflicts. You might want to begin by removing all the applications and data files from your Startup folder. Also check WIN.INI to ensure that it contains no LOAD= or RUN= lines. Comment out any lines you find so that the application doesn't run the next time you start Windows. After you make sure all the conflicts are resolved, start your machine again.

Hardware Configuration Problems

Hardware-specific configuration problems are fairly easy to find because Windows makes most of them pretty obvious. All you need to do is right-click the My Computer icon. Look at the Device Manager page of the System Properties dialog to see whether there are any conflicts. I covered the ways of using this dialog in Chapter 13, "Exploiting Your Software: DOS, 16-Bit, and 32-Bit Windows Applications." You need to look for conflicting devices and change their settings as required. Windows 95 displays the conflicting device, as shown in Figure 29.2.

In most cases, you can figure out the cause of the conflict by looking at the Resources page, shown in Figure 29.3. Notice that this page lists two conflicts, but there could just as easily be three or even four. You need to clear the ones that Windows 95 detected the first time around to see whether there are others.

Figure 29.2.
Hardware conflicts that Windows 95 can detect are pretty easy to find.

Figure 29.3.
IRQ conflicts are the most common hardware configuration problem.

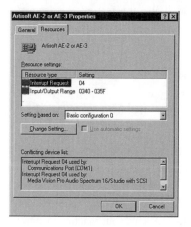

The problem with some hardware conflicts is that you might not see them immediately. For example, if Windows 95 doesn't manage a particular device, it might not know that a conflict exists. Any device that requires a real-mode device driver to operate generally falls into this category. This means you need to find the configuration problem by scanning the documentation that came with all the pieces of hardware in your system, looking for what DMA channels, IRQ lines, and port addresses they use. Then you have to manually set them to non-conflicting values.

Another problem could occur if Windows 95 provides a generic driver for a specific device and the vendor introduces a version of that device that conflicts with the driver. For example, there's only one driver for the Pro Audio Spectrum 16 Plus sound card, but there are four revisions of that board and even more of that driver. Which revision you use could make a difference in how compatible the device driver and board really are.

Even more problematic is if you think you disabled a device feature but really didn't. Take another look at that Pro Audio Spectrum sound board. It includes a game port that doesn't work well on high-speed machines. You might disable the game port and use those same settings for an adjustable game port. What happens, however, if the driver fails to do its job? I ran into this problem. The only solution was to reinstall the driver, but I was probably lucky in this case. Even if Windows thinks it has disabled a feature, you might want to view it as a potential area of conflict.

Windows Software Configuration Problems

There are many ways a Windows application configuration can go wrong. For example, have you ever noticed that many applications want to modify your path statement in AUTOEXEC.BAT? If you let every application have its way, you'd have a mile-long path. Many applications run just fine without out a path statement. However, there are two different ways in which an application can fail.

I ran across the first problem area by accident. I added the file association required for a new application I installed. Whenever I double-clicked a data file, however, I got a message that the application couldn't find that data file. The application started fine, but it wouldn't load the data file. After a few hours of troubleshooting, I found that I could get rid of the problem by adding the application's location to my path.

Some applications, including CA-Visual Objects and other large applications, fail in a big way if you don't add them to the path statement. They usually provide some nebulous error message and quit before you can get them going, or the application loads and then refuses to load add-ons because it can't find them. You might see symptoms of this problem when an application refuses to maintain the settings you save from session to session. When in doubt, add the application to your path statement and see if the problem goes away.

DLL or other shared-file corruption is another problem area. The DLL might not actually contain bad data; it might work fine with several other applications. However, one application might require an older version of the DLL because it uses an undocumented feature of that DLL or uses some bug to its advantage. Sometimes you need to keep the old version of a DLL on disk to satisfy the needs of a particular application.

What happens if one application needs the new version of the DLL and another application needs the old version? Unless one or both applications keep their own version of the shared DLL in their own directory (which is a regrettably uncommon practice), you must make a decision about which application to keep. In most cases, I use this situation as an excuse to upgrade my software. There usually isn't any reason to keep an old application if it refuses to work with all your newer applications. In fact, incompatibility of this type usually indicates that it is time to retire the old application and get the newer version.

Memory-Related Problems

You could have quite a few memory-related problems under Windows 95; they fall into several categories, as shown in the following list. It's important to know which one you're dealing with before you attempt to fix it. Go through the list to see if you can find the symptoms that match your particular problem:

- Real-mode memory manager conflict—Some memory managers, such as 386MAX and QEMM, could cause problems when you use Windows 95. The benefit of using them is that they provide a few additional kilobytes of conventional memory when using real-mode drivers. Although they do a better job than Windows 95 does, you now have two different memory managers fighting for control of the machine, and the user is always the loser. Some symptoms of this type of problem include the following:

  - Windows 95 fails to boot.

  - The machine suddenly freezes.

  - Abnormal device problems, such as errors in displaying data, occur.

  If you experience this problem and your application really needs the additional conventional memory, consider creating an MS-DOS–mode setup for using the memory manager with that particular application.

- Memory leaks—A few Windows applications don't manage memory properly. They grab a lot of memory from Windows but don't release all of it when they terminate. The result is a gradual loss of memory capacity that you can actually track using the Memory field of the application's Help About dialog box. You'll also notice that your other applications start to slow down as the system starts using a larger swap file to make up for the memory loss. If you have an application that shows a gradual loss of memory, you can start it once and leave it open the entire time you need it. As another alternative, try exiting and reloading the application. When you exit the application, it frees up memory.

- Too many frills—Some types of memory problems are created when you have too many frills on your machine. For example, suppose you find that your machine runs very slowly or displays GPFs errors (General Protection Faults) after you add a screen saver to the system. Most people associate utilities with small memory requirements, but this isn't necessarily true. You'll find that many MS-DOS applications had to stay small to keep their conventional memory requirements to a minimum. Windows utilities have no such limitation; designers have fewer reasons to keep applications small because Windows is designed to allow for better memory management. I have one screen saver that grabs an entire megabyte on my system and more than a few percentage points of system resources as well.

- Windows system space corruption—I find it incredible that some vendors put so little effort into testing their products that this type of problem could actually go unnoticed. What usually happens is that an errant pointer in an application starts overwriting the Windows system area. Windows 95 usually detects this problem and displays an appropriate dialog. It recovers by terminating the application. On a few occasions, Windows 95 doesn't detect the problem and simply freezes. In most cases, you want to contact the vendor to see whether a work-around or fix is available.

- Disk thrashing—If you try to use an application that your system can't support, you might experience something called disk thrashing. This happens more often under Windows 95 than it did under Windows 3.x. You know your system is thrashing if the hard disk light stays on for abnormally long periods of time and the application runs really slowly. The only way to fix this problem is to add more memory. Of course, you can also look at some of the memory-saving techniques I discussed in Chapter 5, "Performance Primer."

- Display memory corruption—Some older Windows applications might experience problems when writing to the display. One of these situations is when one application changes the palette (the display colors) without regard for any other applications running on the system. The application window will probably look fine, but everything around it will use really strange color combinations that might produce unreadable text. The big problem occurs when an application leaves the display in this state, even after it exits. You might see other forms of display corruption as well. For example, it's possible for an application to corrupt the icon cache. You might see icons that no longer match the function associated with them, or your icons might disappear altogether. The fix is to exit the application and reboot the system, but sometimes that doesn't work. You can also fix any icon problems by running TweakUI, as explained in Chapter 8. If the problem persists, you might have to erase the ShellIconCache file in your main Windows 95 folder and reboot the machine again. The ShellIconCache file contains an archive of the most recently used icons. Windows 95 loads this file when it starts to reduce the time it spends reading the icons from disk. Some types of corruption become embedded in this file when Windows exits with a corrupted icon cache in memory.

There are probably other ways to corrupt memory as well. For example, Windows 95 uses other cache files, any of which could become corrupt and cause problems for your system. You need to spend some time looking for the particular cache files on your system. Besides the ShellIconCache, I also had a ttfCache and a frmCache.dat file on my system. ttfCache affects the fonts listed in the Fonts folder. You might find that the fonts listed no longer match the fonts actually in the directory if certain types of memory corruption occur. The same holds true for the frmCache.dat file. Any type of cache corruption is easily cured by erasing the corrupted file and allowing Windows 95 to rebuild it during the next boot cycle.

After you identify and clean up a memory corruption problem, it's usually a good idea to find the application responsible. Most memory corruption problems don't simply go away. You'll find that the corruption occurs over and over again at the worst possible moment. After you identify the culprit, you usually have to contact the vendor to find out whether a fix is available. If one isn't, you need to decide whether to live with the corruption problem or get a new application—hopefully one that doesn't exhibit the memory corruption problem you're trying to get rid of.

How do you find the culprit? You can't simply assume that the culprit is the foreground application; it could be a background application. For that matter, it doesn't have to be an application at all. A device driver could be causing the memory corruption as you use a specific device, or the problem could result from the interaction between two applications or an application and a device driver. Nonetheless, you have to start somewhere, and looking at the running applications is a good place. You can follow this simple procedure to find many, but not all, of the memory corruption problems on your system:

1. Start a list of potential problem applications. I usually note all the applications I had running when a memory corruption problem occurred. It's also important to note any devices you had running. Of course, some devices are always running. It doesn't pay to list those.

2. Run the suspect applications, one at a time, to see if you can get the problem to repeat. Make sure you start Windows with a clean Startup folder and no applications loaded using WIN.INI. It's also important to reboot after each test to make sure you're starting with a clean memory environment.

3. If you don't find the culprit, go back to your normal setup and try various combinations of applications. You could be seeing some type of interaction problem.

4. Test the devices on your machine one at a time to eliminate any device drivers.

5. Keep a running list of active applications each time the memory problem appears. Eventually, you'll see a pattern of one or more applications that are always present when the problem occurs. Load just this group of applications to see whether you can get the problem to happen again. Keep whittling the list down until you end up with one or two applications that won't work together. The solution is to avoid running them at the same time.

6. If you don't see an application pattern emerge, the problem is definitely device-driver–oriented. Disable one peripheral device at a time to see whether you can find the problem. Don't discount the effects of real-mode drivers on Windows; make sure you check those first.

This kind of testing is time-consuming, but if you do it right, you can usually track down a stubborn problem in a matter of days. Unfortunately, memory problems are incredibly difficult to locate in an environment such as Windows 95 because so many things are happening at once. Each application and device driver interact. You'll discover that the hardest problems to find are those that result from three or four applications or device drivers working against each other. It always pays to take your time and do a thorough job of testing each potential problem area.

Of course, after you come to a conclusion, finding a permanent fix could prove to be the most difficult part of the journey. You've probably gone through this before—the waiting on the phone as each vendor points the finger at someone else. The reality of the situation is that there might not be an easy fix for some types of memory problems. You might just have to avoid the situations that cause them in the first place, get a newer version of the same application, or even go so far as to update your hardware.

New Windows 98 Problem Resolution Utilities

Beta Release

Microsoft hasn't completely changed everything in Windows 98. You'll still see a lot of old friends from previous versions of Windows, and for the most part, they work the same as before. Fortunately, Microsoft has been busy fixing up some of these utilities and enhancing others. They're not older, just better. The following sections give you an overview of the changes you'll find in your old friends.

System File Checker Utility

Have you ever installed a new program only to discover that it overwrote some DLL you really needed? What happens more often than not is that all or part of the operating system fails to work the next time you start it. The System File Checker utility helps you get around this problem. It checks a variety of important system files, including DLL, COM, VXD, DRV, OCX, INF, and HLP, to make sure you have the right version.

Not only does this utility help you figure out which files have been overwritten, but it also gives you an easy way to correct the problem. A few button clicks are all you need to restore the original files required to keep Windows 98 running.

Windows Tune-Up Wizard

Maintenance seems to be the bane of most users. Just try to remember the last time that you actually did something good for your machine. If you can't think of the last time you performed maintenance, you're not alone. Fortunately, Windows 98 comes with a tool specially designed to make maintenance less of a chore: the Windows Tune-Up wizard. You can use the Windows Tune-Up wizard to schedule maintenance tasks for times when you're not using the machine. For example, you could schedule a disk defragmentation during your lunch hour or scan the disk for errors during a weekly meeting. Scheduling these events one time means that you only have to think about it once; the job gets done automatically.

System Troubleshooter

Getting someone to tell you the precise source of trouble with an ailing operating system can be difficult, especially when you have to wait a long time before talking to them. A lot of us don't have time to wait for someone to get around to helping us resolve a problem. It's especially frustrating when that problem turns out to be something relatively simple that we could have fixed ourselves.

The System Troubleshooter is Microsoft's answer to this problem. It helps you diagnose many simple system problems using the same techniques the human counterpart over the phone would use. Is this solution perfect? I found that it works well on simple problems but gets progressively more difficult to use as the problem becomes more complex. However, considering the number of simple problems I've seen, I bet you'll find that this utility saves you some time over the phone.

Microsoft System Information Utility

The Microsoft System Information Utility performs a complete survey of your machine. In essence, this utility takes the pain out of gathering information for the user as well as for any technical support people who might be trying to help you. Even if you don't know what kind of widget you have installed (or even what task that widget performs), the technical support person can guide you to the right place to look for it.

The Dr. Watson Utility

The Dr. Watson utility of old was a good idea but didn't really go far enough. Sure, it logged the fact that your system froze, but in some cases, it didn't tell you much more than that. Because you already knew your system had frozen, Dr. Watson ended up telling you not much at all. The new version of Dr. Watson gathers a lot more information about the cause of a disaster on your machine. I won't say it's perfect yet, but I am finding that Dr. Watson now provides useful information more often than not.

Windows System Update

Let's face it: Few pieces of software go out the door without a few bugs. In fact, with an operating system as complicated as Windows 98, you can bet that there are a few bugs in the final product. Even if your software was bug free when you got it, you can't be sure you have the most up-to-date drivers unless you check on a continuous basis. Updated drivers might have additional features that you need to get work done quickly or to use every capability provided by your hardware or software.

Windows Update Manager is Microsoft's solution to the problem of outdated drivers and buggy software. It uses a connection to the Internet to determine whether you have the latest available drivers. All you need to do is select Windows Update Manager; this starts a process whereby Windows checks with Microsoft's server on the Internet to verify that you have the latest software installed on your machine.

Obviously, Windows Update Manager needs to dial your ISP. Once Windows Update Manager creates a connection to the Microsoft server, you see a connection screen. All you need to do to check the current status of your software is click the Update button.

The first thing Windows Update Manager needs to do is download an ActiveX control to your system. You'll probably see a request to download the control; this is a safety feature used by Internet Explorer to ensure that you always know what's going to your hard drive. After the download is complete, you see Windows Update Manager search your system for old components. If your system contains old software components, you see one or more entries in the Updates Available column of the Update Manager screen. Select the updates you want to install and then click the Install button. (Some updates might be README files that help you understand new Windows 98 features or warn you of pending changes.) That's all there is to updating your system under Windows 98; just follow any prompts that the update installation program provides.

On Your Own

Reboot your machine and press F8. See which of the menu settings discussed in this chapter are present. If you don't see all eight options, find out why. Check your MSDOS.SYS file to make sure you can access this important feature when needed if the F8 key doesn't work. You might want to check with your network administrator regarding company policy for this particular setting.

Look at the Device Manager page of the System Properties dialog box to familiarize yourself with its contents. I discussed this feature in Chapter 13, but it's a good idea to know what this display can do for you. It's one of Windows 95's major troubleshooting aids.

If you have an application that you currently run in MS-DOS mode, find out whether you can make it run under Windows. You might find that the sound board or other device settings you're using don't match those used by Windows. If there's a conflict, change the DOS application settings to those used by Windows to see whether that will allow you to run the application normally. Also check for environment settings that could affect your ability to use the application within Windows.

30 Hardware Problems

Peter Norton®

Although hardware problems are generally less of an issue than software problems under Windows 95 (or any operating system, for that matter), they do exist. These problems usually fall into two easily recognized categories:

- Catastrophic—You can quickly determine that a catastrophic failure has occurred because the device in question no longer works. For example, you try to turn on your monitor and nothing happens, or your computer refuses to recognize your internal modem. Figuring out the sources of these problems is easy; fixing them is even easier (albeit expensive).

- Compatibility—A common symptom of compatibility problems is that the device appears to have failed, but later testing shows that it hasn't. You've seen some fixes for this type of problem in Chapter 14, "Exploiting Your Hardware"; you'll find that these problems are easy to trace and fix under Windows 95.

A Quick Look at Catastrophic Failures

Determining that a catastrophic error has occurred is easy; it's a bit more difficult to determine the exact nature of the problem. Here's a typical scenario: You start your machine in the morning and Windows 95 comes up fine, but you can't use the mouse. You look around but find no conflicts, and you haven't installed anything new recently. The cause of this problem is probably some type of hardware failure. (At least, that's a good place to start searching for a problem that doesn't appear on the Device Manager tab of the System Properties dialog box.)

All kinds of problems fall into the catastrophic category. For example, severely crimping a cable (putting an obvious dent in it) normally causes some type of hardware failure. It might be as simple as a device that won't respond or a network connection that seems to work intermittently. Port failures don't happen often, but they do happen. You'll also find that NICs fail from time to time. Of course, everyone knows that hard drives fail.

Part of the problem for a network administrator or a home user is confirming that the suspected problem is indeed the problem. You can replace one component at a time until you locate the problem, but a simpler solution is to use diagnostic aids and other troubleshooting tools.

Tip: Most sound board and display adapter vendors include a complete diagnostic for their products as part of the package, and some hardware vendors include this feature as well. I found one motherboard vendor—Hauppauge—that provides a diagnostic disk with its products. The diagnostic disk tests basic motherboard functionality and any installed memory.

The following sections aren't designed to include every tool you'll ever need, but you might find that they provide just enough help that you can get through a repair with minimal effort.

Peter's Principle: Using an MS-DOS–Based Versus a Windows-Based Diagnostic Program

You can rely on most Windows diagnostics to provide useful and easy-to-read information, and these diagnostics also detect a majority of the hardware problems you could experience. Nonetheless, there is no reliable way to completely test your hardware within Windows. The multitasking nature of the operating system makes this impossible. Some diagnostic programs require total access to the hardware as well, which Windows won't allow. Many diagnostic tools don't require Windows at all, whereas others just run from the MS-DOS prompt, where they have better control over the hardware.

There's another problem with Windows diagnostic programs: What happens if a hardware conflict or failure prevents Windows from starting? I've encountered this problem more than a few times. Using an MS-DOS diagnostic means that if the system will boot at all, you can at least figure out what's going on.

Here's the bottom line: If you're going to rely on only one diagnostic program, choose an MS-DOS–based one rather than an Windows-based one. Use the latter only if it's a supplement to the MS-DOS–based one.

Note: Although you could probably run MS-DOS diagnostic products within Windows, the results you get are inaccurate at best. Always run your diagnostic programs in MS-DOS mode, preferably from the MS-DOS prompt before Windows 95 starts. You can access the Windows 95 MS-DOS prompt by pressing the F8 key and selecting the Safe Mode Command Prompt Only option. Chapter 29, "Software Problems," covers this topic in greater detail.

TouchStone CheckIt

To fully examine and troubleshoot your computer, you should get a third-party diagnostic tool. The diagnostic tool that I like using is CheckIt.

CheckIt is essentially a total workstation diagnostic on a disk. In fact, you can place both of the MS-DOS version CheckIt Pro 3.x 360KB floppies on one 1.2MB or 1.44MB disk and have plenty of room left over for the MS-DOS boot file and your network drivers. For the latest information about

CheckIt, contact TouchStone at http://www.checkit.com or 714-374-2801. CheckIt costs roughly $45 for either the MS-DOS or Windows version. It's much more than a hardware inventory program because it includes the following:

- A variety of diagnostics
- A virus scanner
- A hard disk formatter
- A floppy disk alignment checker

Using CheckIt

CheckIt (shown in Figure 30.1) shows four basic tasks that you can perform:

- Collect data about your machine
- Load an existing configuration file
- Skip the data collection process
- Exit the diagnostic program

Figure 30.1.
CheckIt uses a straightforward front end that makes it easy to figure out what you want to do.

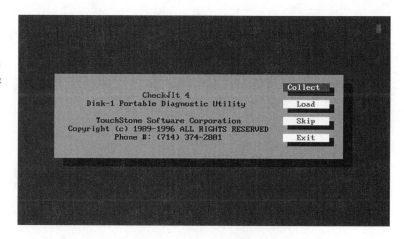

In most cases, you want to select either the Collect or Load option because there isn't a lot you can do without knowing the configuration of the machine. (The Collect, Load, and Skip options all end up at the testing screen shown in Figure 30.3.)

Selecting the Skip option takes you directly to the testing screen. Fortunately, you can use the options on the File menu to either load or collect data later. Selecting the Load option displays a standard File Open–type dialog box that you can use to choose an existing configuration file. You must collect data and save it to disk before this option will work.

Selecting the Collect option displays a dialog box like the one shown in Figure 30.2, where you specify what to collect and how in-depth to look. There are two or three columns of options for each device on your machine (some devices don't include the Advanced option):

- X (Exclude)—Checking this option specifies that CheckIt should skip the selected piece of hardware.

- S (Standard)—Checking this option specifies that CheckIt should provide only an overview of statistics relating to the selected piece of hardware; CheckIt looks exclusively in the system CMOS for this information. Use this option if you have problems when CheckIt examines a specific piece of hardware or when an in-depth look at the hardware isn't required.

- A (Advanced)—Checking this option specifies that CheckIt should provide in-depth information about the selected piece of hardware. When this option is selected, CheckIt tests the hardware to see what it can do. You get information such as the IRQ that the hardware actually uses (versus the setting that Windows thinks it uses).

  Getting this information can take quite a bit of time, so use the Advanced setting with care. In addition, because the Advanced option actually tests the hardware, you might find conflicts with other software you have loaded.

Figure 30.2.
CheckIt allows you to determine how much time you want it to spend collecting data.

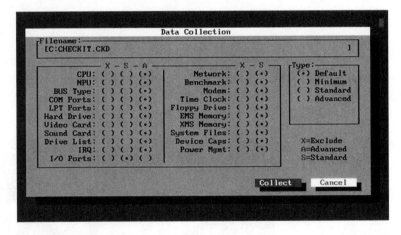

You'll also notice some preset defaults in the Type group. I find that the Standard option provides me with just about everything I need to know on a regular basis, without requiring a lot of time to get it. I use the Advanced option if I need to troubleshoot a specific hardware-related problem. In such a case, getting all the information you can is a good idea if you don't want to overlook the obvious. The Default setting in the Type group selects a combination of Standard and Advanced options that TouchStone assumes most people need. The Minimum setting obtains the level of information that you absolutely must have to use CheckIt to its potential.

After you choose the level of information you need, click the Collect button. CheckIt displays a series of screens as it checks your hardware and then shows the testing screen I mentioned earlier. Figure 30.3 shows a typical testing screen, although the information in your screen will differ from the information in mine. At this point, you're ready to use CheckIt for a variety of purposes, such as single-component testing or verifying your hardware settings.

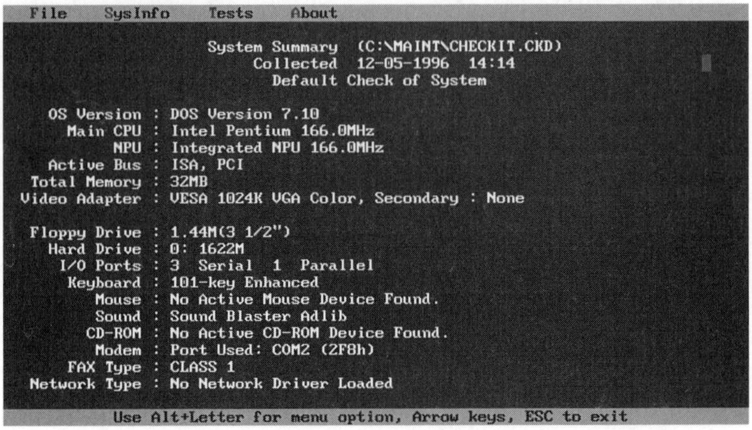

Figure 30.3.

CheckIt provides an overview of the information it collected in the initial testing screen.

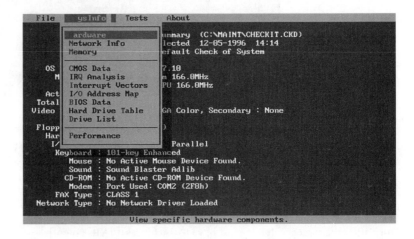

The two menus you're most interested in are SysInfo and Tests. The SysInfo menu, shown in Figure 30.4, allows you to obtain concise details about the facts CheckIt collected about your machine. Figure 30.5 shows an example of what you might see for the modem. Notice that the check not only determines the address of the modem port, but it also tells you whether buffers are available (an important consideration in a multitasking environment such as Windows 95). This screen also shows the results of various AT information commands.

Figure 30.4.

You can get information about any part of your system by using the SysInfo menu options.

Figure 30.5.
A typical information display provides every piece of information you need about the device in question.

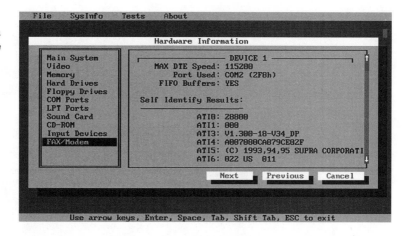

The Tests menu provides a list of tests that you can run by using CheckIt. Figure 30.6 shows a list of the tests that CheckIt currently supports. Notice that along with standard tests such as those you'd run on the system board or ports, there are tests you can run on your CD-ROM or modem.

Figure 30.6.
The Tests menu provides a complete list of the kinds of tests you can run with CheckIt.

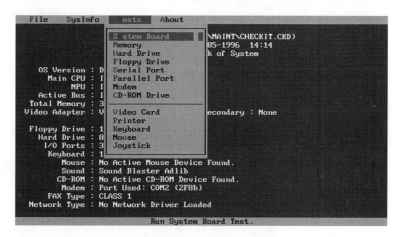

Every test on this list is fully configurable; Figure 30.7 shows a typical example. In this case, you're looking at the Memory Test configuration dialog box. Notice that you can choose the area of memory to test along with the level of test you want to perform. Unlike the previous version of CheckIt, you can't choose a precise memory range to test. This is one of the few areas where the new version of CheckIt doesn't quite perform as well as its older sibling, but the loss in functionality is minimal.

Figure 30.7.
You need to decide how to run the various diagnostic tests.

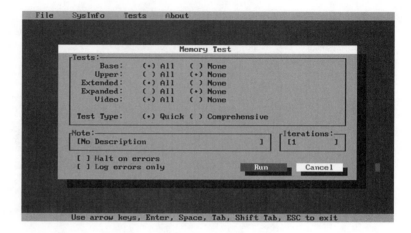

Burn-In and Batch Testing Using SysTest

CheckIt includes a separate burn-in and batch testing utility named SysTest. (Figure 30.8 shows the initial display for this program.) The main reason for using SysTest instead of CheckIt is for burn-in or certification testing. You can also use it to find intermittent problems with hardware. For example, you might have a memory problem that shows up only in certain conditions, or you might have a partially failed part that gives you problems. Batch testing can help find it. You might even want to use batch testing to verify that you've completely fixed a problem. There have been a few cases where two bad components caused a system failure, and finding the second component after the first one was fixed proved problematic.

Figure 30.8.
SysTest allows you to perform burn-in, certification, and other forms of batch testing.

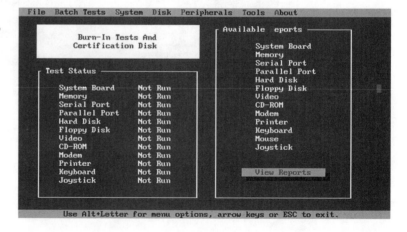

The menu system for this utility looks a bit more complicated than the one used for CheckIt, but you can break it down into four areas:

- The File menu allows you to look at reports. It's also where you select a custom batch file that you want to run or change the location of program output. (You might want to use a printer rather than the screen for batch testing because the printer can provide a history of each test.)

- The Batch Tests menu allows you to run and create various kinds of batch and burn-in tests. I discuss this menu in more detail later in this chapter. Suffice it to say that this is the heart of the SysTest utility.

- The System, Disk, and Peripherals menus operate in much the same way as the Tests menu does for CheckIt. In fact, you'll find that SysTest uses the same configuration menus for the various tests. The only difference is how the tests are arranged on the menu. Use these menu selections if you want to test one hardware item multiple times.

- The Tools menu allows you to save the contents of your CMOS to disk—a handy feature if you think you might run out of battery backup power sometime in the future (and who doesn't?). You can use this same tool to restore a CMOS configuration file that you've saved to disk. Figure 30.9 shows the Save/Restore CMOS dialog box that you see after selecting Tools | Save CMOS. The Tools menu also contains entries for RAM Exam (an advanced memory-testing program) and Rescue Disk (a utility that creates a boot disk you can use in case of emergency).

Figure 30.9.
The Save/Restore CMOS dialog box allows you to save or restore your hardware configuration settings.

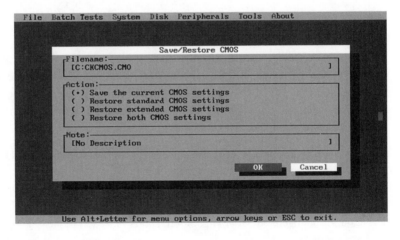

Now it's time to look at the meat and potatoes of this program: the batch-creation utility. Select Batch Tests | Custom to display the Custom Batch Tests dialog box (see Figure 30.10), where you specify which tests to run and how to run them. This dialog box contains two option groups: Select Test, where you select what basic type of test should be run, and Configure Test, where you select to configure tests chosen in the Select Test group. If you select to configure a test, you see a dialog box much like the one shown in Figure 30.7.

Figure 30.10.
Creating a custom
batch testing job
results in a BAT file
that you can run from
the MS-DOS prompt.

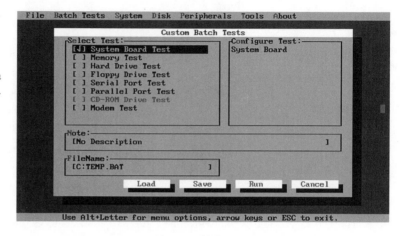

Notice the FileName field in Figure 30.10. The output of this custom batch-testing process is a BAT file. After you create it, you don't even have to enter SysTest or CheckIt to perform a standard test of your system. Simply type the name of the batch file at the DOS prompt, and you're ready to go. You lose the capacity to view reports within the CheckIt environment, but you can still use a standard text editor to view the test results file.

TouchStone WINCheckIt

Nothing beats a Windows diagnostic program for ease of use. At $50, WINCheckIt is only slightly more expensive than its MS-DOS counterpart, and you gain the convenience of the Windows interface. In addition, WINCheckIt provides full, 32-bit support and some special Windows 95 features. What you lose in the exchange is some of the detailed diagnostics that the MS-DOS version of the product provides.

When you start WINCheckIt for the first time, it inventories your machine. I found that the inventory was fairly complete, but it missed some of my hardware the first time around. (A second run of the check found the missing hardware.) The program also misinterpreted my network, informing me that I had NetWare installed when I was using a Microsoft Network for the purposes of the test. WINCheckIt did figure out what kind of serial ports I had and properly noted that I had one bidirectional parallel port. (You can rerun the inventory any time by clicking the Collect button.)

After WINCheckIt collects this information, it displays a main screen like the one shown in Figure 30.11. This screen includes a resource monitor, whose dials tell you about your current resource status, including swap file and CPU usage, free memory, and disk space used. A system summary is also included; this information is on par with the MS-DOS version of CheckIt Pro. (WINCheckIt doesn't even begin to touch the thoroughness of the MS-DOS CheckIt version.) Essentially, it tells you what you have installed on your machine in the barest possible terms.

Figure 30.11.
WINCheckIt
provides quick access
to its features and
gives you a summary
of your system's
resources.

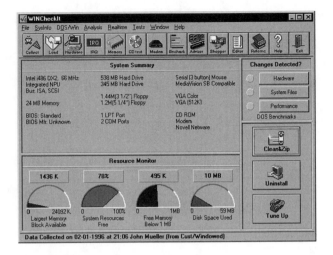

Note: I find that the System Summary display comes in handy for a quick check of the system, but I've been able to fool WINCheckIt in several ways in the past. Using some types of communications programs before I run the collection utility, for example, causes WINCheckIt to tell me that I don't have a modem installed. As I mentioned, WINCheckIt never did figure out what kind of network I had installed.

The main screen of WINCheckIt also contains several toolbar buttons across the top of the display. I don't want to discuss each one, but a few deserve special mention:

- CD Test—Clicking this button displays the dialog box shown in Figure 30.12. Notice that this isn't just a CD-ROM drive test; it's an actual check of your machine's capability to run multimedia programs. As shown in the figure, you can check three levels of compliance. My test machine failed the second two Multimedia PC Marketing Council (MPC) compliance tests because of the way that WINCheckIt performed the check. (It looked only at my first hard drive partition.) Even though the test machine had more than 850MB of drive space available, WINCheckIt reported a mere 60MB—the amount on the first drive partition.

- Modem—Clicking this button launches a test that far exceeds anything I've found in an MS-DOS utility, except in CheckIt. Not only does it test local modems, but it tests remote connections as well. After you click the Modem button, WINCheckIt displays a dialog box that asks whether you want to run a local or a remote test. If you elect to run a remote test, you must provide a telephone number to access the remote modem. When WINCheckIt completes the test, you see a dialog box like the one shown in Figure 30.13. I found that the report provided by WINCheckIt is superior to the one you can get from Windows 95; the tests are also a little more thorough. (Obviously, Windows 3.*x* doesn't even provide modem diagnostics.)

Figure 30.12.
*You can use
WINCheckIt to
determine the
multimedia status of a
workstation.*

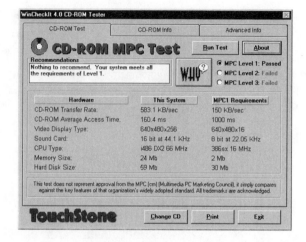

Figure 30.13.
*The capability to
check the status of
your modem is one of
the better features of
WINCheckIt.*

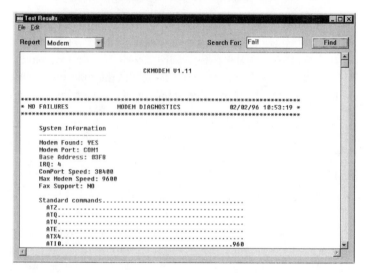

Now I get to the feature you really want to hear about: the capability to test your hardware. Unlike with most other features in WINCheckIt, you must use the Tests menu to check a piece of hardware. This menu has a Test Everything option, along with the capability to test separate subsystems. WINCheckIt examines everything you ask it to and then displays a test results window. You can scroll through the entire report or simply select specific subsystems by using the drop-down menu.

In addition to the things I've shown you, WINCheckIt provides a wealth of user-related features that have little to do with diagnosing hardware problems. The Software Shopper utility is a database of more than 2,000 products; use WINCheckIt to compare the needs of your system with the capability of a product. WINCheckIt provides a list of any upgrades you need to make to your system before you can use the software product. Clicking the Benchmark button takes you to a display that allows you to extensively test your system. It also includes the capacity to compare your system to a variety of test systems. This is nice to have, but it's not really essential.

Of the features WINCheckIt provides, the Tune-Up button seems the most useless. It's supposed to defragment system memory and enhance performance. Although the monitor did display a slight improvement on my test systems, I couldn't see it in any concrete way. Although your results might vary from mine, this feature of other programs has received a lot of bad press lately.

What's missing from this program? In case you didn't notice, I didn't say a word about burn-in tests or any of the other things you'd normally associate with a heavy-duty diagnostic program. You won't find these features in WINCheckIt. Overall, it's a lightweight diagnostic aid at best. You'd be better off looking at TouchStone's DOS product if you need something substantial.

Serial and Parallel Port Loopback Plugs

You can't fully test the serial and parallel ports in a workstation without loopback plugs. These plugs pass the signal from the port's output back to its input. To create a loopback plug, use a blank connector without wires and then connect wires between specific pins. Most of the high-end diagnostic programs you buy (such as PC-Technician, AMI Diags, or the Norton Utilities) provide these plugs. Others, such as CheckIt, don't provide them. However, Touchstone tells you how to build them and will sell them to you as a separate product.

Tip: Although the list of modems supported by Windows 95 grows with every release, you won't find a NULL modem driver for Windows 95 in the standard list of hardware options. This makes it impossible to create a dial-up networking connection that requires a NULL modem setup. Don't worry, however; you can download a NULL modem driver that operates at up to 115Kbps from `http://www.vt.edu:10021/K/kewells/net/index.html`.

Table 30.1 provides the pin connections for a parallel port. Every parallel port uses a 25-pin male connector. (Another designation for this type of connector is DB25P.) You need to create two connectors to test serial ports. There are 9-pin (DB9S) and 25-pin serial ports (DB25S), and every serial port uses a female connector. Table 30.2 lists the pin connections for a 9-pin serial port, and Table 30.3 gives the pin connections for a 25-pin serial port. You can find the blank connectors and wire you need at most electronics stores.

Table 30.1. Parallel port (DB25P) loopback plug connections.

First Pin	Connected to Second Pin
11 (Busy +)	17 (Select Input –)
10 (Acknowledge –)	16 (Initialize Printer –)

continues

Table 30.1. continued

First Pin	Connected to Second Pin
12 (Paper Out +)	14 (Autofeed −)
13 (Select +)	01 (Strobe −)
02 (Data 0 +)	15 (Error −)

Table 30.2. Nine-pin serial port (DB9S) loopback plug connections.

First Pin	Connected to Second Pin
02 (RD: Received Data)	03 (TD: Transmitted Data)
07 (RTS: Request to Send)	08 (CTS: Clear to Send)
06 (DSR: Data Set Ready)	01 (CD: Carrier Direct)
01 (CD: Carrier Detect)	04 (DTR: Data Terminal Ready)
04 (DTR: Data Terminal Ready)	09 (RI: Ring Indicator)

Table 30.3. Twenty-five-pin serial port (DB25S) loopback plug connections.

First Pin	Connected to Second Pin
03 (RD: Received Data)	02 (TD: Transmitted Data)
04 (RTS: Request to Send)	05 (CTS: Clear to Send)
06 (DSR: Data Set Ready)	08 (CD: Carrier Direct)
08 (CD: Carrier Detect)	20 (DTR: Data Terminal Ready)
20 (DTR: Data Terminal Ready)	22 (RI: Ring Indicator)

As you can see, the pin connections are relatively easy to make. Whether you buy premade loopback plugs or make your own, this is an essential tool for your toolkit. Without loopback plugs, you never know whether the serial or parallel port you tested really works.

Cable Scanner

Network administrators, especially those managing large networks, can spend a lot of time tracing cables. An average cable scanner costs about $1,000, but you can usually find them a little cheaper. Alternatively, you can build your own cable scanner for about $200 using plans in some electronics magazines. For example, *Circuit Cellar INK*'s October/November 1992 issue contains a set of plans on page 22.

One of the better cable scanners on the market is the Cable Scanner from Microtest. (Microtest provides many other cable scanners with more features, but the Cable Scanner model provides the minimum feature set you need to maintain a network.) This product tests for opens, shorts, and improper terminations. It tells you the distance from your current location to the cable fault. In most cases, all you need to do is track the cable for the required distance and you'll find the problem. To help you trace the signal, the main unit outputs a signal that you can pick up on a remote unit. Instead of taking down every ceiling tile in your office, you simply use the remote unit to trace the cable.

You can send the data collected by Cable Scanner to a serial printer. The unit collects the data, stores it, and allows you to output it later. Cable Scanner provides both text and graphic output. This is a handy feature for maintaining records on your system. All you need to do is print the results of the cable check and add it to the network documentation.

Cable Scanner provides a few other unique functions that you might not use very often. For example, it can detect the noise level of the cable on your system. This means you can reduce the number of packet errors by reducing the noise that the packet signal must overcome. You can also interface the Cable Scanner with an oscilloscope. This allows you to actually monitor the signal that flows across the network. An experienced network administrator can use this information to troubleshoot problem installations.

Incompatible Hardware

For the most part, any hardware that runs under the MS-DOS and Windows 3.x environment will also run under Windows 95. Even if you have to use a real-mode driver (which I talk about in the next section), you should be able to use that old device if you really want to. The problems start when you mix that old hardware with new hardware or when the old device uses some of the undocumented features provided by previous versions of MS-DOS.

Windows 95 really does try its best to figure out which interrupts and port addresses are in use, but it doesn't always succeed if you have an eclectic mix of old and new. Older devices often require real-mode device drivers to work at all; that's not a problem. Unfortunately, some of these devices don't register themselves properly. A device driver is supposed to register itself in a device chain and provide certain types of information as part of that registration process. If the device doesn't provide the right level of information, Windows 95 can't detect it. What happens next is inevitable, given such circumstances. If Windows 95 doesn't see the device driver, it might assume that the interrupts and port addresses it uses are free. The result is that you might find two devices trying to share the same interrupt or port address.

Of course, one of the best ways to eliminate some of the problems is to make a checklist of all your hardware and the settings that each device uses. You need to include port addresses, interrupts, and DMA addresses. Physically check the settings on cards that use jumpers. You might want to take this opportunity to physically check your card's BIOS revision. An undocumented update can make a big difference in the settings you need to use with Windows 95. Make sure that you double-check any settings included in CONFIG.SYS or AUTOEXEC.BAT. A software-configurable device always includes the current settings as part of the command line. All you really need to do is get out the vendor manual and determine what the settings mean. Because some device drivers provide a default setting, you need to check for the default if the entry in CONFIG.SYS or AUTOEXEC.BAT doesn't contain a complete list of settings.

After you write down all the settings, check your list for potential conflicts. Windows 95 might tell you that there aren't any, but it's possible that you'll find some anyway. For example, someone I know recently tried to install Windows 95 but found that he couldn't. The machine he was using included two SCSI adapters. Windows 95 recognized one adapter but not the other. As a result, Windows 95 didn't recognize the CD-ROM drive attached to the second adapter and therefore couldn't install itself properly. Removing the second SCSI adapter and connecting the CD-ROM drive to the first one cleared up part of the problem. At least Windows 95 would install. However, performance on the network was very slow, and the user still experienced some problems. A check of Windows didn't show any device conflicts. However, a physical check of the remaining SCSI adapter showed that it was using the same interrupt as the NIC. (Windows 95 had claimed that the NIC was using interrupt 5 and that the SCSI adapter was using interrupt 3.) Physically changing the SCSI adapter's interrupt setting cleared up the remaining problem.

Sometimes you might not be sure that you got all the settings right during the first check. You can determine the equipment settings by viewing the port and interrupt addresses that a device uses with MSD (Microsoft Diagnostic program) or a separate diagnostic program such as CheckIt. In fact, using this technique coupled with physical inspection of your CONFIG.SYS and AUTOEXEC.BAT ensures that you have all the settings for each device. Even if there aren't any conflicts, you still want to maintain a complete record of your hardware and any real-mode drivers you need to use. Avoiding problems with real-mode drivers starts with the detective work you perform during this phase of the installation. Record real-mode driver settings and then avoid using the address and interrupt, even though Windows 95 says it's free. This also means that you have to manually configure your setup rather than rely on the Windows 95 automatic configuration features.

Tip: Watch out for older plug-in cards and some of the cheaper "no-name" ones. In the early days of PCs, no one used any port addresses above 3FFh, and most cards decoded only the low-order ten bits of a port address to find out whether a command was intended for that card. Now many cards use higher addresses (all the way up to FFFFh). If you have one of these newer cards and an older one in the same PC, you can run into a subtle sort of problem. If the addresses used by the newer card are the same in the low-order ten bits as those used by the older card, the older card will think that commands meant for the newer card were meant for it. There's no telling what will happen in this case, but it might not be pretty!

Real-mode device drivers often cause problems too. A well-behaved device driver makes direct access only to the hardware it controls by calling on the ROM BIOS routines for other types of service. An older device might use direct hardware access to other devices as well as to the device it controls in order to make the driver faster. Windows 95 normally ignores the device if you try to use a device driver of this type. Sometimes a device driver of this type can actually cause the system to freeze when Windows switches to running a real-mode interrupt service routine. Previous chapters covered many of the architectural aspects of this problem.

Unfortunate as it might seem, an ill-behaved device driver normally looks like a malfunctioning device rather than a piece of software that Windows 95 won't work with. I was surprised when I found myself in this position with an old CD-ROM drive. Fortunately, I was able to get from the vendor a newer driver that did work. This is the solution you should try as well. Many vendors will even allow you to download the upgrade directly from their Web sites. They also might make the upgrade available through a commercial information service such as CompuServe or America Online.

Some older devices include their own BIOS. Sometimes the BIOS routines conflict with Windows 95 and cause various types of system failures. Most vendors upgrade their BIOSes as time goes on. They fix bugs and perform some types of optimizations. If you have an older piece of hardware with a BIOS that's causing problems with Windows 95, check whether the vendor has some type of BIOS upgrade that might fix the problem. Installing a new chip is usually cheaper than buying a new peripheral.

By now it should be apparent that hardware incompatibility can cover a lot of ground. Everything from misinterpreted settings to a poorly designed device driver can make it appear that your hardware is incompatible with Windows 95. Take a look at the hardware compatibility problem from a procedural point of view:

1. Get into MS-DOS mode and test the hardware to ensure that there's no problem with the device itself. It's important to test the hardware with the same device driver that you plan to use with Windows 95 if you intend to use a real-mode driver for it under Windows 95.

2. Check the device settings to see whether there's a conflict with any of the devices that Windows supports directly. This is especially important when you mix older hardware with new Plug and Play–compatible hardware. If Windows insists on using a specific setting for a Plug and Play–compatible board, see whether your old board can use a different set of unused settings.

3. After you determine that the hardware is working and that it doesn't conflict with anything, see whether the vendor documentation provides any insights as to the requirements for using the device driver. For example, you'll probably find that device drivers written to work with versions of MS-DOS prior to 3.3 will have some problem with Windows 95. These older device drivers often wrote directly to the hardware and definitely didn't use all the features that newer versions of MS-DOS provide to support device drivers. Check whether the vendor can provide a new set of drivers.

4. Check your BIOS revision level. Many adapter cards that have a BIOS extension ROM on them display a version number onscreen during the boot process. With other pieces of add-in or connected hardware, you have to determine the revision level in some other way. Vendors provide a variety of ways to detect this information, so you have to check your documentation for details about your particular device. My modem uses a Hayes-compatible AT command to display the BIOS revision number. A display adapter that I own has an actual program that I run to display the BIOS and setup information. Check with the vendor to see whether a newer version of the BIOS is available. You might have to send the device to the vendor's repair facility to get the BIOS replaced. It depends on the vendor's policy concerning sending BIOS updates to customers. If your machine supports Plug and Play, your system BIOS might offer an option to block out certain addresses or interrupts so that you do not configure the Plug and Play cards that use those settings. Block different addresses or interrupts to see if an address or interrupt conflict might be causing the problem.

5. If all else fails, see whether replacing the board with a similar board from another vendor helps. In this way, you might find that a software or other conflict is disguising itself as a hardware problem. For instance, the mouse incident I described at the beginning of this chapter was an example of a problem with a serial port that disguised itself as a faulty mouse. You might find that other types of problems disguise themselves.

Tip: There's an easy way to distinguish a serial mouse problem from a serial port problem. To do so, first run a diagnostic on the serial port with a loopback plug installed. If the port passes the test, test the mouse.

Incompatible hardware rarely is incompatible. There's usually some problem that you can define, given enough time and resources. The question that you have to ask yourself is whether that old hardware is really worth the effort. In my case, I replaced the hardware that was giving me problems, which probably saved me time and frustration. Some types of expensive hardware might be worth the effort involved in looking for the cause of incompatibility, but make sure you get some type of payback.

When All Else Fails—A Look at HelpDesk

Part of the problem with providing help on fixing Windows-related hardware problems in the past was that hardware evolves at a fairly fast rate. By the time Microsoft developed help files and sent out a new version of Windows, at least part of the information was already out of date. That isn't going to be the case nearly as often with Windows 98.

Windows 98 will provide a special feature called HelpDesk, which uses the Internet to connect you to the latest information for solving various problems with Windows 98.

On Your Own

Buy a diagnostic program and completely test your system, especially the hard drives. Be sure to get a diagnostic that's easy to use and that tests everything your machine has to offer. Use the loopback plugs provided with the diagnostic program to test your ports, or create your own loopback plugs by using the procedure in this chapter.

Check any real-mode device drivers installed on your system. Make sure they're the most current drivers that the vendor has to offer. Do the same with any peripherals that provide their own BIOS, including modems and display adapters. You'll also find a BIOS on most hard-disk controllers and many other devices installed on your machine. Using the most current BIOS not only ensures that you have the least number of bugs to contend with, but it could also mean a slight speed boost because of optimizations that the vendor made to it.

Don't wait until you have a problem to make this detailed checklist of all the device drivers in your system. This can be much easier to do when your PC is working normally. Then, when it fails in some way, you are already a good way down the path toward a solution to the problem.

A

Glossary

Peter Norton®

Note: Although this glossary contains all the acronyms you'll see in this book, it doesn't contain acronyms you'll see in other places. If you don't see an acronym you need here, check out the site at http://syrup.hill.com/acronyms/. It contains more computer-related acronyms than the average person will ever need.

Active Desktop   A new feature of Windows 95 in combination with Internet Explorer 4, the Active Desktop enables Windows to display on your desktop Web pages and other objects that have live connections to the Internet or to an intranet.

aggregate   A collection of facts or figures used to create a graph. Some presentation graphics programs use these numbers to create a graph showing both the component parts and their sum. For example, the individual wedges in a pie chart represent the components; the entire pie represents their sum.

American Standard Code for Information Interchange   See ASCII.

API (application programming interface)   A method of defining a standard set of function calls and other interface elements. It usually defines the interface between a high-level language and the lower-level elements used by a device driver or operating system. The ultimate goal is to provide some type of service to an application that requires access to the operating system or device feature set.

application independence   A method of writing applications so that they don't depend on the specific features of an operating system or hardware interface. It normally requires the use of a high-level language and an API. The programmer also needs to write the application in such a way as to avoid specific hardware or operating system references. All user and device interface elements must use the generic functions provided by the API.

application programming interface   See API.

ASCII (American Standard Code for Information Interchange)   A standard method of equating the numeric representations available in a computer to human-readable form. For example, the number 32 represents a space. There are 128 characters (7 bits) in the standard ASCII code. The extended ASCII code uses 8 bits for 256 characters. Display adapters from the same machine type usually use the same upper 128 characters. Printers, however, might reserve these upper 128 characters for nonstandard characters. For example, many Epson printers use them for the italic representations of the lower 128 characters.

B-step processor   An older 80386 processor type that incorporated elements that are incompatible with Windows 95. The normal reason for using this processor type was to provide additional system functionality or improved speed characteristics.

bidirectional support Defines a printer's capability to transfer information both ways on a printer cable. Input usually contains data or printer control codes. Output usually contains printer status information or error codes.

binary value Refers to a base 2 data representation, as in on/off settings for some items in the Windows Registry. Normally used to hold status flags or other information that lends itself to a binary format.

bitmap font See raster font.

BMP files Windows standard bitmap graphics data format. This is a raster graphic data format that doesn't include any form of compression. OS/2 can also use this data format to hold graphics of various types.

cascading style sheets See CSS.

CDF (channel definition format) A proposed standard for a special Web page that Web developers can use to define a sort of table of contents for a site that IE4 can refer to when setting up a subscription. The CDF transforms a regular Web site into a "channel" from which users can select certain branches they want to subscribe to. The CDF also allows the site developer to define recommended subscription update schedules.

CDFS (compact disc file system) The portion of the file subsystem specifically designed to interact with compact disc drives. It also provides the user interface elements required to tune this part of the subsystem. The CDFS takes the place of an FSD for CD-ROM drives.

channel A special Web site set up to take advantage of the IE4 subscription feature to deliver targeted information in an efficient manner. Channels are set up to allow you to identify and download specific portions of a site instead of subscribing to the entire site.

channel definition format See CDF.

class ID See CLSID.

client The recipient of data, services, or resources from a file or other server. This term can refer to a workstation or an application. The server can be another PC or an application.

CLSID (class ID) A method of assigning a unique identifier to each object in the Registry. Also refers to various high-level language constructs.

CMOS (Complementary Metal Oxide Semiconductor) Normally refers to a construction method for low-power, battery-backed memory. When used in the context of a PC, this term usually refers to the memory used to store system-configuration information and the real-time clock status. The configuration information normally includes the amount of system memory, the type and size of floppy drives, the hard drive parameters, and the video display type. Some vendors include other configuration information as part of this chip as well.

compact disc file system   See CDFS.

Complementary Metal Oxide Semiconductor   See CMOS.

compound document   An OLE document that contains two or more embedded or linked documents. For example, a word-processing document could contain graphics and spreadsheets in their original formats.

Compressed Serial Line Interface Protocol   See CSLIP.

container   Part of the object-oriented terminology that has become part of OLE. A container is a drive, file, or other resource used to hold objects. The container is normally referenced as an object itself.

CSLIP (Compressed Serial Line Interface Protocol)   An IETF-approved method for transferring data by using a serial port. This particular data transmission method uses compression to improve performance.

CSS (cascading style sheets)   A method for defining a standard Web page template. This might include headings, standard icons, backgrounds, and other features that tend to give each page at a particular Web site the same appearance. The reason for using CSS includes the speed of creating a Web site (it takes less time if you don't have to create an overall design for each page) and consistency. Changing the overall appearance of a Web site also becomes as easy as changing the style sheet instead of changing each page separately.

DAT (digital audio tape) drive   A tape drive that uses a cassette to store data. The cassette and the drive use the same technology as the audio version of the DAT drive. However, the internal circuitry of the drive formats the tape for use with a computer system. The vendor must also design the interface circuitry with computer needs in mind. DAT tapes allow you to store large amounts of information in a relatively small amount of space.

Data Link Control   See DLC.

datacentric   The method used by modern operating systems to view the user interface from a data perspective rather than from the perspective of the applications used to create the data. Using this view allows users to worry more about manipulating the data on their machines than about the applications required to perform a specific task.

DCOM (Distributed Component Object Model)   The advanced form of the component object model (COM) used by the Internet. This particular format enables data transfers across the Internet or other nonlocal sources. It adds the capability to perform asynchronous as well as synchronous data transfers—which prevents the client application from becoming blocked as it waits for the server to respond.

DDE (dynamic data exchange)   The capability to cut data from one application and paste it into another application. For example, you could cut a graphic image created with a paint program and paste it into a word-processing document. Once pasted, the data doesn't reflect changes made to it by the originating application. DDE also provides a method of communicating with an application that supports DDE and requesting data. For example, you could use an Excel macro to call Microsoft Word and request the contents of a document file. Some applications also use DDE to implement file-association strategies. For example, Microsoft Word uses DDE in place of command-line switches to gain added flexibility when a user needs to open or print a file.

device-independent bitmap   See DIB.

DIB (device-independent bitmap)   A method of representing graphic information that doesn't reflect a particular device's requirements. This has the advantage of allowing the same graphic to appear on any device in precisely the same way, despite differences in resolution or other factors that normally change the graphic's appearance.

digital audio tape drive   See DAT drive.

direct memory access   See DMA.

disk defragmenter   An application used to reorder the data on a long-term storage device such as a hard disk or floppy disk drive. Reordering the data so that it appears in sequential order—file by file—reduces the time required to access and read the data. Sequential order allows you to read an entire file without moving the disk head at all in some cases and only a little in others. This reduction in access time normally improves overall system throughput and therefore enhances system efficiency.

Distributed Component Object Model   See DCOM.

DLC (Data Link Control)   Normally, a protocol used to establish communications with a remote server. For example, the Microsoft DLC provides connections to mainframes and network printers.

DLL (dynamic link library)   A special form of application code loaded into memory by request. It isn't executable by itself. A DLL does contain one or more discrete routines that an application can use to provide specific features. For example, a DLL could provide a common set of file dialog boxes used to access information on the hard drive. More than one application can use the functions provided by a DLL, reducing overall memory requirements when more than one application is running.

DMA (direct memory access)   A memory-addressing technique in which the processor doesn't perform the actual data transfer. This method of memory access is faster than any other technique.

DOS protected-mode interface   See DPMI.

DPMI (DOS protected-mode interface)   A method of accessing extended memory from a DOS application, using the Windows extended-memory manager.

drag and drop   A technique used in object-oriented operating systems to access data without actually opening the file by using conventional methods. For example, this system allows the user to pick up a document file, drag it to the printer object, and drop it. The printer prints the document using the printer's default settings.

dual-ported video RAM   See VRAM.

DVORAK layout   An alternative method of laying out the keyboard so that stress is reduced and typing speed is increased. It's different from the more familiar QWERTY layout used by most keyboards and typewriters.

dynamic data exchange   See DDE.

dynamic link library   See DLL.

EIA (Electronics Industry Association)   The standards body responsible for creating many hardware-related PC standards. For example, the EIA was responsible for the serial port interface used on most PCs. The EIA also participates in other standards efforts.

Electronics Industry Association   See EIA.

embedded systems   A combination of processor, operating system, and device-specific applications used in concert with a special-purpose device. For example, the control used to set the time and temperature on a microwave oven is an embedded system. Another form of embedded system is the computer that controls engine efficiency in a car.

EMF (enhanced metafile)   Used as an alternative storage format by some graphics applications. This is a vector graphic format, so it provides a certain level of device independence and other features that a vector graphic normally provides.

EMM (expanded memory manager)   A device driver such as `EMM386.EXE` that provides expanded memory services on 80386 and above machines. (Special drivers work with 80286 and a few 8088/8086 machines.) An application accesses expanded memory by using a page frame or other memory-mapping techniques within the conventional or upper memory area (0 to 124KB). The EMM usually emulates expanded memory by using extended memory (XMS) managed by an extended-memory manager such as `HIMEM.SYS`. An application must change the processor's mode to protected mode in order to use XMS. Some products, such as `386MAX.SYS` and `QEMM.SYS`, provide both expanded and extended memory services in one driver.

EMS (expanded memory specification)   Several versions of this specification are in current use. The most popular version is 3.2, even though a newer 4.0 specification is available. This specification defines one method of extending the amount of memory that a processor can address from the conventional memory area. It uses an area outside of system memory to store information. An EMM provides a window view into this larger data area. The old 3.2 specification requires a 64KB window in the UMB. The newer 4.0 specification can create this window anywhere in conventional or UMB memory.

enhanced metafile   See EMF.

expanded memory manager   See EMM.

expanded memory specification   See EMS.

FAT (file allocation table) disk format   The method of formatting a hard disk drive used by DOS and other operating systems. This technique is one of the oldest formatting methods available.

FAT32 disk format   A newer, high-efficiency method for formatting a hard disk drive. This format was introduced as an option in the OSR2 version of Windows 95.

file allocation table disk format   See FAT.

file system driver   See FSD.

file transfer protocol   See FTP.

floptical   A specialized form of floppy disk drive that relies on optical media to extend its data storage capacity. The most common size floptical currently in use stores 20MB of data. One thing that differentiates a floptical from other optical media drives is that a floptical can normally read standard floppy disks as well.

FSD (file system driver)   A file subsystem component responsible for defining the interface between Windows and long-term storage. The FSD also defines features such as long filenames and what types of interaction the device supports. For example, the CD-ROM FSD wouldn't support file writes unless you provided a device that could perform that sort of task.

FTP (file transfer protocol)   One of several standard data transfer protocols originated by the IETF. This protocol is designed for efficient file transfer.

GDI (graphics device interface)   One of the main Windows root components. It controls the way that graphic elements are presented onscreen. Every application must use the API provided by this component to draw or perform other graphics-related tasks.

GDT (global descriptor table)   A memory construct that contains the information required to control all the extended memory in an 80386 or above processor. The GDT normally passes control of smaller memory segments to the LDTs used by an individual application.

general protection fault   See GPF.

GIF (Graphics Interchange Format) file   A raster graphic file format originally developed by CompuServe that has good compression, accommodates various color depths, and includes features such as simple animation. The GIF file format has become the de facto standard for images on the Web, and most Web browsers (including Internet Explorer) can display GIF images without the aid of helper applications.

global descriptor table   See GDT.

global positioning satellite   See GPS.

GPF (general protection fault)   A processor or memory error that occurs when an application makes a request that the system can't honor. This type of error results in some type of severe action on the part of the operating system. Normally, the operating system terminates the offending application.

GPS (global positioning satellite)   A special satellite that sends positioning data to a location on Earth. Using satellite tracking allows for precise position updates to a device such as a PC. The PC must include special software and hardware that allows it to display the positioning data on a map overlay.

graphical user interface   See GUI.

graphics device interface   See GDI.

Graphics Interchange Format   See GIF file.

GUI (graphical user interface)   A system of icons and graphic images that replaces the character-mode menu system used by many machines. The GUI can ride on top of another operating system (such as DOS or UNIX) or reside as part of the operating system itself (such as Windows or OS/2). Advantages of a GUI are ease of use and high-resolution graphics. Disadvantages are higher work-station hardware requirements and lower performance over a similar system using a character-mode interface.

handheld PC   See HPC.

high memory area   See HMA.

high-performance file system   See HPFS.

HMA (high memory area)   The 64KB area of memory beyond the 1MB boundary that the pro-cessor can access in real mode on an 80286 or above processor.

HPC (handheld PC)   A special little PC designed to replace small notebooks or calendars. Many HPCs run a limited version of the Windows operating system (called Windows CE). Most don't offer features such as handwriting analysis that plagued earlier versions of the pocket-sized PC.

HPFS (high-performance file system)   The method of formatting a hard disk drive used by OS/2. Although it provides significant speed advantages over other formatting techniques, only the OS/2 version of Windows 95 (and Windows NT 3.1 and higher) and applications designed to work with those operating systems can access a drive formatted using this technique.

HTM file   See HTML file.

HTML (Hypertext Markup Language)   A special language that relies on a series of tag words to define character and paragraph formatting. In some cases, HTML has been extended to provide graphic information as well as access to ActiveX controls and Java applets. In essence, HTML de-fines all the characteristics of a Web page.

HTML file   A Web page document file—actually a plain-text file containing text and HTML tags describing a document to be displayed by a Web browser or similar viewer. Systems (such as Win-dows 95) that support long filenames typically use .HTML as the extension for files containing HTML data, whereas systems that must conform to the DOS 8.3 filenaming convention typically use .HTM.

HTTP (Hypertext Transfer Protocol)   The IETF-supported protocol used to transfer an HTML-formatted document from a Web server to the client browser.

hub   A device used to connect two or more nodes on a network. A hub normally provides other features such as automatic detection of connection loss.

Hypertext Markup Language   See HTML.

Hypertext Transfer Protocol   See HTTP.

ICM (image color matcher)   A special component of the graphics subsystem that allows Windows to match the colors produced by one device with those available on another device. The result is that the output of both devices doesn't show the normal variations in color that Windows applications currently produce.

icon   A symbol used to graphically represent the purpose or function of an application or file. For example, a text file might appear as a sheet of paper with the filename below the icon. Applications designed for the environment or operating system usually appear with a special icon depicting the vendor's or product's logo. Icons are normally part of a GUI environment or operating system such as Windows or OS/2.

IETF (Internet Engineering Task Force)   One of the main committees charged with developing and administering the standards that make the Internet possible.

IFS (installable file system) manager   The API component of the file system. It provides a consistent interface that applications can use to access a variety of devices, local and remote. This component also provides a standard interface that device drivers can use to provide services such as file opening and drive status.

IFSHLP (installable file system helper)   A special real-mode component of the IFS manager used to permit access of Windows drive functions by DOS applications. It uses the same DOS interface as before, but all processing is performed by the protected-mode manager.

image color matcher   See ICM.

IMA (International Multimedia Association)   A standards body responsible for defining multimedia standards on the Internet. One of the more important efforts of this standards body is the adaptive delta pulse code modulation (ADPCM) standard, which is used for the serial wave driver in Windows 95.

INF file   A special form of device or application configuration file. It contains all the parameters that Windows requires to install or configure the device or application. For example, an application INF file might contain the location of data files and the interdependencies of DLLs. Both application and device INF files contain the Registry and INI file entries required to make Windows recognize the application or device.

Infrared Data Association   See IrDA.

installable file system helper   See IFSHLP.

installable file system manager   See IFS manager.

International Multimedia Association   See IMA.

Internet service provider   See ISP.

interrupt request   See IRQ.

IrDA (Infrared Data Association)   The standards association responsible for creating infrared data port standards. These ports are normally used to create a connection between a laptop and a device or network. Devices include printers, PCs, modems, and mice.

IRQ (interrupt request)   The set of special address lines that connect a peripheral to the processor. Think of an IRQ as an office telephone with multiple incoming lines. Every time a device calls, its entry lights up on the front of the phone. The processor selects the desired line and picks up the receiver to find out what the device wants. Everything works fine as long as there's one line for each device that needs to call the processor. If more than one device tried to call on the same line, the processor wouldn't know who was at the other end. This is the source of IRQ conflicts that you hear about from various sources. Older PC-class machines provided eight interrupt lines. The newer AT-class machines provide 16. However, only 15 of those are usable because one line is used for internal purposes.

ISP (Internet service provider)   A vendor that provides one or more Internet-related services through a dial-up, ISDN, or other outside connection. Normal services include e-mail, newsgroup access, and full Internet Web site access.

Joint Photographic Experts Group   See JPEG.

JPEG (Joint Photographic Experts Group)   A standards group responsible for developing a file format for raster graphics containing photographic images.

JPEG file   A raster graphics file format developed by JPEG for storing photographic images. The format excels at handling images with a lot of subtle colors and provides for a wide range of file compression. The JPEG file format allows the file creator to compromise image detail to achieve higher compression, which can result in small file sizes for some images. The .JPEG extension identifies this file format on systems that support long filenames; .JPG is the three-character counterpart for DOS-compatible systems.

JPG file   See JPEG file.

LAN (local area network)   A combination of hardware and software used to connect a group of PCs to each other or to a minicomputer or mainframe computer. There are two main networking models in use: peer-to-peer and client/server. The peer-to-peer model doesn't require a dedicated server. In addition, all the workstations in the group can share resources. The client/server model uses a central server for resource sharing, but some special methods are provided for using local resources in a limited fashion.

LDT (local descriptor table) A memory construct that controls access to the memory used by a single application or a group of applications that share the same memory. The LDT is subservient to the GDT that manages system memory overall.

list box A windowing construct that contains a list of items. Normally, the user selects one or more of these items in order to respond to an application or operating system query.

local area network See LAN.

local descriptor table See LDT.

macro One of several methods for performing automated tasks on a computer. Macros normally include a simple programming language that's executed by an interpreter within an application. In some cases, the application automatically records a macro, based on user keystrokes. The user can later modify this file as needed to complete a task.

management information file See MIF.

MAPI (messaging API) The set of functions and other resources that Windows provides to communications programs. It allows the application to access a variety of communications channels using a single set of calls and without regard to media. This is the component of Windows 95 that allows Microsoft Exchange to process information from e-mail and online services by using the same interface.

MCA (microchannel architecture) A specialized bus introduced by IBM. It's faster than the old ISA bus and gives the operating system information about the peripheral devices connected to the bus. It also provides the means for devices to become self-configuring. However, it never really caught on and is now obsolete.

messaging API See MAPI.

microchannel architecture See MCA.

MIF (management information file) A vendor-supplied file that contains all the particulars about a piece of equipment. When the System Management Server on a Windows NT Server looks at a workstation and finds this file, it adds its contents to a SQL database that you can open with any number of products.

miniport driver A specialized Windows component that provides access to a resource, normally a peripheral device of some type. It's also used to access pseudo-devices and network resources.

MMX (multimedia extension) processor The latest edition of the central processor chips from the major manufacturers include multimedia-specific commands within the chip. Instead of issuing multiple commands to perform a multimedia-related task, one command will do. This version of the chip should boost overall system performance. It should also allow vendors to produce less expensive PCs by using less-complex parts in construction.

Motion Picture Experts Group   See MPEG.

MPEG (Motion Picture Experts Group)   A standards group that provides file formats and other specifications in regard to full-motion video and other types of graphic displays.

MPG file   A file format defined by MPEG for full-motion video.

multimedia extension processor   See MMX processor.

multiple-boot configuration   A method of creating a configurable environment that was introduced with DOS 5.0. The user simply selects the operating environment from a list of environments presented prior to the boot sequence. This technique provides an additional layer of flexibility and allows the user to optimize the operating environment to perform specific tasks.

multitasking   The capability of some processor and environment/system combinations to perform more than one task at a time. The applications appear to run simultaneously. For example, you can download messages from an online service, print from a word processor, and recalculate a spreadsheet, all at the same time. Each application receives a slice of time before the processor moves to the next application. Because the time slices are fairly small, it appears to the user that these actions are occurring simultaneously.

multithreading   The capability of an application to perform more than one task at once. For example, a word-processing application could print in the background while you type in the foreground. Using multithreading techniques allows an application to make maximum use of processor cycles. In most cases, it does this by processing data in the background while the foreground task waits for user input.

national language support   See NLS.

nested objects   Two or more objects that are coupled in some fashion. The objects normally appear within the confines of a container object. Object nesting allows multiple objects to define the properties of a higher-level object. It also allows the user to associate different types of objects with each other.

network interface card   See NIC.

network provider   See NP.

NIC (network interface card)   The device responsible for allowing a workstation to communicate with the file server and other workstations. It provides the physical means of creating the connection. The card plugs into an expansion slot in the computer. A cable that attaches to the back of the card completes the communication path.

NLS (national language support)   A method of reconfiguring the keyboard and other system components to support more than one language through the use of code pages. Each code page defines a different language configuration. Unfortunately, this technique doesn't change the language used for display purposes. In other words, NLS won't cause your English-language version of Windows to suddenly display prompts and other text in German.

NP (network provider)   The software responsible for performing all the network protocol-specific functions that an application requires. It makes or breaks connections, returns network status information, and provides a consistent interface for the multiple provider router (MPR) to use. An application never calls the NP; only the MPR performs this function.

NTFS (Windows NT file system)   The method of formatting a hard disk drive used by Windows NT. Although it provides significant advantages over other formatting techniques, only the Windows NT operating system and applications designed to work with that operating system can access a drive formatted using this technique.

object conversion   A method of changing the format and properties of an object created by one application to the format and properties used by another. Conversion moves the data from one application to another, usually without a loss in formatting, but always without a loss of content.

object linking and embedding   See OLE.

OCX (OLE custom extension)   A special form of VBX designed to make adding OLE capabilities to an application easier for the programmer. Essentially, an OCX is a DLL with an added programmer and OLE interface.

ODBC (open database connectivity)   A Microsoft-supported standard method for accessing databases. In most cases, this involves three steps: installing an appropriate driver, adding a source to the ODBC applet in the Control Panel, and using SQL statements to access the database.

OEM (original equipment manufacturer)   One term used to identify hardware vendors that produce some type of PC hardware. For example, a vendor that designs and builds display adapters is considered an OEM. An OEM is normally responsible for writing drivers and other software required to use the hardware it sells.

OLE (object linking and embedding)   The process of packaging a filename and any required parameters into an object and then pasting this object into a file created by another application. For example, you could place a graphic object within a word-processing document or spreadsheet. When you look at the object, it appears as if you simply pasted the data from the originating application into the current application (similar to DDE). When linked, the data provided by the object automatically changes as you change the data in the original object. When embedded, the data doesn't change unless you specifically edit it, but the data still retains its original format and you still use the original application to edit the data. Often you can start the originating application and automatically load the required data by double-clicking the object. The newer OLE 2 specification allows for in-place data editing as well as editing in a separate application window.

OLE custom extension   See OCX.

open database connectivity   See ODBC.

original equipment manufacturer   See OEM.

packet Internet groper   See PING.

password caching   A method of saving the passwords for resources that a user might need to access. The user still needs to enter the main password required to access Windows, but Windows remembers the passwords required to access other resources, such as a network or an online service that directly supports the Windows password-caching capability.

PCMCIA (Personal Computer Memory Card International Association)   A standards group responsible for the creation of credit-card–sized devices originally used in laptop PCs. A PCMCIA card (also called a "PC card") could contain devices such as a modem or network card. Some of the more esoteric uses for this card include solid-state hard drives and added system memory.

PCX file   A raster graphic data format originally used by ZSoft Paintbrush. This format has gone through many nonstandard transitions and occasionally presents problems when accessed by applications other than the original. It provides for various levels of color and includes data compression.

PD (port driver)   Performs the task of communicating with the device through an adapter. It's the last stage before a message leaves Windows and the first stage when a message arrives from the device. The PD is usually adapter-specific. For example, you would have one VxD for each hard drive and one PD for each hard drive adapter.

PDA (personal digital assistant)   A small PC normally used for personal tasks such as taking notes and maintaining an itinerary during business trips. PDAs normally rely on special operating systems and lack any standard application support.

Personal Computer Memory Card International Association   See PCMCIA.

personal digital assistant   See PDA.

PIF (program information file)   A special configuration file that Windows and OS/2 use to define the environment for a DOS application. The PIF usually includes various memory settings along with the application's command path and working directory.

PING (packet Internet groper)   A special utility program used to determine whether a TCP/IP connection exists between a workstation and a server. This utility is normally used in conjunction with the Internet, but it can be used to test any TCP/IP connection.

Plug and Play   The combination of BIOS, operating system, and peripheral device components that provides a self-configuring environment. This self-configuring feature allows the operating system to avoid potential hardware conflicts by polling the peripheral devices, assessing their requirements, and determining and implementing optimal settings for each device.

PNG (Portable Network Graphics) file   A raster graphic file format developed as an alternative to GIF files for use as images on Web pages and similar applications. PNG files feature good compression for small file sizes and have capabilities similar to GIF files. Most newer browsers can display PNG files without add-ons or helper applications. Because CompuServe has not pressed for application of widespread license fees for using its GIF file format, PNG files have been slow to replace GIF files as the standard format for Web graphics.

port driver   See PD.

Portable Network Graphics   See PNG file.

POST (power-on self test)   The set of diagnostic and configuration routines that the BIOS runs during system initialization. For example, the memory counter you see during the boot sequence is part of this process.

power-on self test   See POST.

program information file   See PIF.

protected mode   The processor mode in which the processor can access all of extended memory. This mode also provides a better level of application error detection than real mode as part of the processing cycle.

protected-mode mapper   A special application that converts real-mode device driver calls into those used by a protected-mode counterpart. It enables you to use your DOS drivers under Windows. Without the support of this VxD, Windows couldn't support legacy devices that lack Windows-specific drivers.

quoting   The practice of including all or part of an original message within a response. Quoting allows the viewer to see what the original question was without looking up the original message.

raster font   A font in which each character is stored as a bitmapped image. Unlike vector fonts, raster fonts can't be resized or manipulated by the computer or printer. On the other hand, raster fonts print quickly because they are already bitmaps and require no processing by the printer. Raster fonts aren't used much anymore because it's inconvenient and inefficient to maintain separate raster fonts for each type size you need when you can use just one vector font and resize it as needed.

real mode   A Windows operating mode that supports the capabilities of the 8088/8086 processor. This essentially limits you to loading one application within the confines of conventional memory. Windows versions after 3.0 don't support this mode. You must use these versions with workstations containing an 80286 or higher processor.

REG file   A special file used by the Windows Registry to hold a text version of the keys and values it contains. Some applications provide REG files that you can use to incorporate their file associations and OLE capabilities into Windows.

Registry key   This is a Registry heading. It provides the structure required to hold configuration values and other information required by both Windows and the applications it runs.

Registry value   Each value provides some type of Windows configuration information. There are three types of Registry values: string, DWORD, and binary. Of the three, the only human-readable form is string.

remote access   The capability to use a remote resource as you do a local resource. In some cases, this also means downloading the remote resource to use as a local resource.

remote procedure call   See RPC.

RPC (remote procedure call)   The capacity to use code or data on a remote machine as if it were local. This is an advanced capability that will eventually pave the way for decentralized applications.

SCSI manager   Windows NT introduced something called the miniport driver. With Windows 95, you can use the Windows NT miniport binaries. However, before you can actually do this, Windows 95 must translate its commands to a format that the miniport driver will understand. The SCSI manager performs this service.

SCSIzer   This is a file subsystem component that deals with the SCSI command language. Think of the command language as the method that the computer uses to tell a SCSI device to perform a task. The command language isn't the data the SCSI device handles; rather, it's the act that the SCSI device will perform. There's one SCSIzer for each SCSI device.

serial line interface protocol   See SLIP.

server   An application or workstation that provides services, resources, or data to a client application or workstation. The client usually makes requests in the form of OLE, DDE, or other command formats.

shell extension   A special application that gives some type of added value to the operating system interface. In most cases, the application must register itself with the Registry before the operating system will recognize it.

simple network architecture   See SNA.

simple network management protocol   See SNMP.

SLIP (serial line interface protocol)   An IETF-approved method for transferring data by using a serial port. One of the problems with this method is that it doesn't compress the data and therefore suffers from poor performance. CSLIP is a newer form of this protocol that provides improved performance.

SNA (simple network architecture)   A standard IBM mainframe networking protocol. A PC user would normally use this protocol to access the mainframe using a dial-up connection.

SNMP (simple network management protocol)   A network protocol originally designed for the Internet to manage devices from different vendors.

subscription   Instructions for Windows and Internet Explorer 4 to automatically check the status of a Web site and then notify you of any changes or download pages from that site to your hard drive for later offline viewing.

system resource   Data, peripheral devices, or other system components used to create, delete, or manipulate documents and produce output.

system VM (virtual machine)   The component of the Windows operating system tasked to create virtual machines and manage DOS applications.

TAPI (Telephony API)   An interface used by applications to interface with various types of communication equipment. This currently includes both modems and fax devices.

task-switching   The capacity of an operating system to support more than one application or thread of execution at a time. The foreground application or task is the only one that executes. All other threads of execution are suspended in the background. Contrast this with multitasking, in which all threads—background and foreground—execute.

Telephony API   See TAPI.

Telephony service provider   See TSP.

terminate-and-stay-resident program   See TSR.

thunk   The programming interface that translates 32-bit data and system calls to their 16-bit counterparts. The opposite translation takes place, going from a 16-bit application to its 32-bit counterpart.

TrueType   A special form of vector font originally provided with Windows but used with other operating systems as well. This vector font provides hinting (instructions for intercharacter spacing adjustments) and other features that give it a smoother appearance onscreen.

TSD (type-specific driver)   Part of the file subsystem, this layer deals with logical device types rather than specific devices. For example, one TSD handles all the hard drives on your system, and another TSD handles all the floppy drives. A third TSD would handle all network drives.

TSP (Telephony service provider)   A special Windows 95 driver that handles program requests such as dialing and answering the phone line. It's normally associated with voice modems.

TSR (terminate-and-stay-resident) program   An application that loads itself into memory and stays there after you execute it. The program usually returns you directly to the DOS prompt after loading. Pressing a hot-key combination activates the application, allowing you to use it. In most cases, TSRs provide some type of utility, print spooling, or other short-term function.

type-specific driver   See TSD.

UAE (unrecoverable application error)   A processor or memory error that occurs when an application makes a request that the system can't honor. The operating system normally doesn't detect an error of this type. The result is that the system freezes or becomes unstable to the point of being unusable. See also GPF.

UART (universal asynchronous receiver transmission)   The chip that allows a serial port to communicate with the outside world. Serial-type devices such as internal modems also rely on this chip for communications purposes. Newer versions of this chip include special features such as a buffer that stores incoming and outgoing characters until the CPU can process them.

UMB (upper memory block)   The area of memory between 640KB and the 1MB boundary. IBM originally set aside this area of memory for device ROMs and special device memory areas. Use of various memory managers allows you to load applications and device drivers in this area.

universal asynchronous receiver transmission   See UART.

universal serial bus   See USB.

unrecoverable application error   See UAE.

upper memory block   See UMB.

USB (universal serial bus)   A new form of serial bus that allows multiple external devices to share a single port. This technique reduces the number of interrupts and port addresses required to service the needs of devices such as mice and modems.

VBA (Visual Basic for Applications)   A true subset of the Visual Basic language. This form of Visual Basic is normally used within applications in place of a standard macro language. Normally, you can't create standalone applications using this language in its native environment; however, you can move a VBA program to Visual Basic and compile it there.

VCPI (virtual control program interface)   A method of accessing extended memory from a DOS application by using a third-party XMM. See also DPMI.

VDD (virtual display driver)   Windows 3.x used this module as its sole source of communications with the display adapter. Windows 95 provides it for compatibility purposes and for DOS applications. It translates application requests into graphics commands and draws the result in video memory.

vector font   A type of font that uses mathematical expressions instead of a bitmap to define its characteristics.

vector table   The place in lower memory where ROM and DOS store pointers to operating-system–specific routines. Most of these routines allow an application to access a device or perform some specific task, such as opening a file.

VESA (Video Electronics Standards Association)   A standards group responsible for creating display adapter and monitor specifications. This group has also worked on other standards, such as the VL bus used in some PCs.

VFAT (virtual file allocation table)   An enhanced method of disk formatting based on the FAT system. It allows for additional functionality, such as long filenames.

Video Electronics Standards Association   See VESA.

virtual anything driver See VxD.

virtual control program interface See VCPI.

virtual display driver See VDD.

virtual file allocation table See VFAT.

virtual memory management See VMM.

Visual Basic for Applications See VBA.

VMM (virtual memory management) The device driver responsible for managing extended (and in some cases expanded) memory. VMMs first appeared in the DOS environment. In the Windows 95 environment, this device driver is also responsible for managing the swap file on disk.

volume tracking driver See VTD.

VRAM (dual-ported video RAM) A special form of memory that allows simultaneous reads and writes. It provides a serial read interface and a parallel write interface. The advantage of using VRAM is that it's much faster and doesn't require as much detection code on the part of the application or device driver.

VTD (volume tracking driver) This file subsystem component handles any removable devices attached to your system.

VxD (virtual anything driver) A special form of DLL that provides low-level system support.

WAN (wide area network) An extension of the LAN, a WAN connects two or more LANs together using a variety of methods. A WAN usually encompasses more than one physical site, such as a building. Most WANs rely on microwave communications, fiber-optic connections, or leased telephone lines to provide the internetwork connections required to keep all nodes in the network talking with each other.

wide area network See WAN.

Windows NT file system See NTFS.

wizard A specialized application that reduces the complexity of using or configuring your system. For example, the Printer wizard makes it easier to install a new printer.

Index

W

MACMILLAN COMPUTER PUBLISHING USA

A VIACOM COMPANY

Technical ---- Support:

If you need assistance with the information in this book or with a CD/Disk accompanying the book, please access the Knowledge Base on our Web site at **http://www.superlibrary.com/general/support**. Our most Frequently Asked Questions are answered there. If you do not find the answer to your questions on our Web site, you may contact Macmillan Technical Support **(317) 581-3833** or e-mail us at **support@mcp.com**.